THE ART OF
SEAMANSHIP

THE ART OF
SEAMANSHIP

EVOLVING SKILLS, EXPLORING OCEANS, AND HANDLING WIND, WAVES, AND WEATHER

RALPH NARANJO

INTERNATIONAL MARINE / McGRAW-HILL EDUCATION

Camden, Maine ◆ New York ◆ Chicago ◆ San Francisco ◆ Lisbon ◆ London ◆ Madrid ◆ Mexico City
Milan ◆ New Delhi ◆ San Juan ◆ Seoul ◆ Singapore ◆ Sydney ◆ Toronto

1 2 3 4 5 6 7 8 9 10 11 12 13 14 15 QVS/QVS 1 9 8 7 6 5 4

ISBN 978-0-07-149342-0
MHID 0-07-149342-5
E ISBN 0-07-179158-2

Library of Congress Cataloging-in-Publication Data is
available from the Library of Congress.

McGraw-Hill Education books are available at special
quantity discounts to use as premiums and sales pro-
motions or for use in corporate training programs. To
contact a representative, please e-mail us at bulksales@
mheducation.com.

Questions regarding the content of this book should be
addressed to www.internationalmarine.com

Questions regarding the ordering of this book should be
addressed to

McGraw-Hill Education
Customer Service Department
P.O. Box 547
Blacklick, OH 43004
Retail customers: 1-800-262-4729
Bookstores: 1-800-722-4726

All photos by the author unless indicated otherwise.

To family, friends, and shipmates
who appreciate the sea
and the encounters it affords;

To those who've helped me turn
a book concept into reality;

Finally, a toast to a sailor's son
who's gone from dinghy racing
to aircraft carrier driving and knows
the value of good seamanship.

CONTENTS

INTRODUCTION

The science of seamanship surrounds us—new sailboats flaunt tank-tested designs, extensively field-tested electronics, and flashy technology—making sailing safer, faster, easier, and more comfortable than ever before. And yet, all too often we hear of crews being helicopter lifted to safety—abandoning races and giving up on voyages gone awry. Some of these incidents filter back from far away oceans, but others unfold within view of more familiar landfalls. SeaTow and its sequels are doing banner business, so perhaps good seamanship calls for more than what science and technology have to offer. It's this very thought that prompted me to write a book about skill acquisition, vessel preparation, and crew training—key themes in *The Art of Seamanship*.

Just as my publisher and I approach the launch phase of this worthy effort, print, television, and social media sources have coalesced around the misadventures of a California cruising couple who set to sea with an infant, young child, and dreams of a voyage around the world. Only weeks after their departure, the dream turned into a nightmare as boat problems and a sick one-year-old caused parents to call for help. The U.S. Coast Guard's Rescue Coordination Center (RCC) shunted U.S. Navy and California's Air National Guard assets their way. Parachuting guardsmen heroically delivered medical assistance to the vessel drifting 900 miles off the coast of Mexico. Before departure the family had lived aboard their 36-foot cutter in San Diego, but had to scuttle the boat as part of the abandon-ship rescue procedure, a harsh death to a long-time dream. A multi-phase effort by rescue crew ensured that no lives were lost. Other sailors have not been so fortunate.

In the wake of this ill-fated voyage, questions have arisen about one's freedom to pursue adventure, what constitutes child endangerment, how vessel readiness should be determined, and why risk assessment—a multifaceted process involving not just boats and gear, but also crew and all the atmospherics of weather, sea, etc.—is so essential. The "Today Show" will mainstream the atypical sailing story, regulatory bodies are already shaking their heads, and sailors will try to leverage important lessons learned. I'm more caught up in this event than most, partially because of its seamanship implications and partially because several decades ago my wife Lenore and I, and our 4- and 6-year-old children, departed on what would turn into a 5-year voyage around the world. We sailed a boat about the same displacement as the one abandoned in the Pacific, and our firsthand experience with the challenges of such a voyage (chronicled in *Wind Shadow West*) evolved into the themes of seamanship outlined in the pages that follow—an approach that will stack the deck in favor of the successful outcome of all your voyages.

Throughout this book, I've emphasized a common-sense approach to ocean voyaging, one that merges traditional seamanship skills with insights into the most modern and time-tested gear afloat in order to provide a recreational sailor with enough information—and, more importantly, with a mindframe—to hone and develop backup-plans as a natural course for all voyages. The objective is to lower the risk and maximize the reward in your sailing. I don't attempt to gauge your perspective toward adventure, but I do emphasize the importance of a crew realizing the hazards ahead while simultaneously mitigating their influence.

Lastly, most of us cherish the time we spend aboard our boats. Somehow even the prospect of bottom painting and spring outfitting rises well above the drudgery it portends. The really good times are exemplary, and shaping a cruise or race into an optimum experience is well worth the effort.

Seamanship revolves around an understanding of the variables involved, especially the implications defined by the interaction of the ocean and the atmosphere. When we sailors have a better knowledge of the sea, weather, and sailboat design, plus the skill sets required when casting off, we can shape an even more enjoyable sailing experience. Chapters in *The Art of Seamanship* are like a skilled shipwright's best friend—a useful array of sharp-edged tools to help accomplish the job at hand.

THE ART OF SEAMANSHIP

Whether you're holding course in a tight, current-scoured channel or anchored securely in a South Seas lagoon, your seamanship abilities underpin a safe and enjoyable voyage. Specifically, seamanship refers to the manner in which you carry out the vital tasks that define good performance and safe passagemaking. As such, seamanship is not a commodity found on chandlery shelves but is a capacity best developed by those who get underway regularly. I see it as more akin to a tightly tucked reef than a verbatim recital of the Beaufort Scale.

During the time I spent racing offshore with Rod Stephens, I got to see a talent that could engage the entire crew with insights into the technical side of sailboats—a subject he understood from the tip of the keel to the top of the masthead.

Good seamanship, like good citizenship, has widespread support. Who would claim to be against either? However, as a concept, each is difficult to define fully. So instead of providing a "one size fits all" approach to acquiring seafaring skills, this book builds a case for seamanship's component parts, broken out in separate chapters. In addition, we'll lobby for the value of self-reliance and then leave it up to sailors to pick and choose which skills and approaches to implement aboard their own boats.

Freedom is one of the fringe benefits of boat ownership, along with the autonomy that a skipper and crew assume once they've cast the docklines free. But this freedom comes with an inherent price tag that can be paid for with personal responsibility and crew competency. We view seamanship as the currency to cover the transaction; for those who sail local and coastal waters, the invoice is usually more modest than the one presented to the bluewater voyager. The inshore sailor can get away with a smaller reserve in their seamanship fund, but open ocean passagemakers often are called upon to dig deep into their stockpile of skills. However, seamanship abilities developed before departure and during a lengthy voyage will prove to be an annuity of significant value.

To use another analogy, we can liken acquiring seamanship abilities to creating a good stew: both tasks rely on the quality and quantity of key ingredients, which, when combined correctly, result in a whole that's greater than the sum of its parts. As with all acquired talents, whether culinary or seafaring, the best measure of success involves evaluating the outcome.

For those aboard sailboats, the feedback loop includes how efficiently we execute sail changes, how easily a docking maneuver plays out, how quickly and safely we can reef a sail, and how well an anchor is set. The nuances of good seamanship are not always easy to notice because they so often involve preventing the undesirable from happening. Seamanship may show itself in a deft hand on the wheel that avoids a broach, or when a facile navigator keeps the skipper from sailing into the wrong side of a developing weather system.

Some sailors prefer to distinguish between the cerebral side of a mariner's skill set (navigation, rules of the road, weather assessment, and so forth) and the physical side of seamanship (boat handling, sail trim, and other skills linked to dexterity). But I find that the cerebral and physical sides to seamanship are inextricably linked, and together they form a foundation of essential components that define the art of seamanship. I prefer the Collins English Dictionary definition of seamanship: *"skill in and knowledge of the work of navigating, maintaining, and operating a vessel."*

THE SAFETY TRIANGLE

We can think of a crew's seamanship, the vessel's seaworthiness, and the safety-enhancing features of the boat's equipment as the three legs of a 30-, 60-, 90-degree right triangle, with each leg's length proportional to its relative importance to safety. The longest leg—the hypotenuse—represents seamanship, the absence of which can sink even the most seaworthy and well-outfitted vessel. Most tragedies at sea, like most highway accidents, involve operator error.

The next longest leg represents the vessel's seaworthiness. In many well-documented cases, ill-prepared crews have been saved by the strength and stability of the vessel they were sailing. Time and again we hear of a vessel and crew that lay ahull through a storm as a last resort. The waves breaking on deck did not stove in a port or hatch, nor did the conditions accelerate the boat's roll moment to the point where a knockdown turned into a capsize. (Looking ahead to Chapter 12, you'll see how to match a spe-

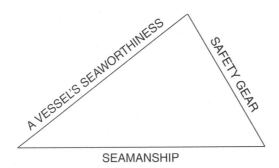

The safety-at-sea triangle shows the significance of seamanship. Comprised of physical talents, tactical awareness, teamwork, and effective decision making, seamanship is the bedrock of successful cruising and racing, and key to bringing the boat home safely.

SEAMANSHIP CHARACTERISTICS

Physical Abilities
- Balance and agility attuned to vessel motion
- Strength enough for a firm grasp on handholds and the dexterity to handle the tasks at hand
- Adequate vision for chart work and keeping watch

Vessel Awareness
- Knowledge of every nook and cranny
- Experience with the boat's motion in varied wind and sea states
- Perception of actions and areas of elevated risk

Core Competencies
- Hand, reef, and steer
- Boat handling under power and sail, in a range of conditions
- Anchoring
- Navigation, weather tracking and predicting, communications
- Specialty skills such as rescuing crew overboard, jury-rigging, and troubleshooting failed equipment and systems
- The waterman's arts: going aloft, dinghy operation, swimming, and diving

Psychological Factors
- Crew compatibility and teamwork
- Ability to assimilate a shipboard routine
- Ready adaptation to changing dynamics underway
- Willingness to put up with spells of rough weather

cific cruise or ocean passage with a boat of appropriate scantlings and stability.)

The shortest of the three legs represents portable gear, electronic equipment, and other elements of the "kit" that aren't part of the hull, decks, rig, or essential systems. This third-place standing by no means suggests that communications equipment, navigation electronics, life rafts, harnesses, jacklines, and the like are unimportant. However, when it comes to staying out of trouble in the first place, crew skill and vessel seaworthiness trump safety equipment.

The Risk of Human Error

Human error is the leading cause of accidents afloat. Recently, an entire crew of four perished shortly after they had begun motoring (allowable in the cruising division) in the Ensenada (California) Race. On a clear night with calm seas the crew powered right into the steep cliffs and rocky shoals of the northern Coronado Island. The vessel was equipped with modern electronic navigation equipment, a tracker that pinpointed and broadcast its position every 10 minutes, and all the safety gear required by the race organizers. Only a few weeks earlier, the crew aboard another race boat cut the corner of one of the Farallones Islands off San Francisco too closely and was heaved onto a surf-swept ledge by breaking seas. Five of the eight crew perished in that incident.

Crew knowledge and expertise are no less critical when it comes to successfully making decisions and responding to problems that do occur. For example, we can look at the lessons learned from the 1979 Fast-net Race disaster off the coast of United Kingdom. A Force 10 storm pinned down the fleet, causing many panicked sailors to abandon ship prematurely and perish as life rafts flipped pitching crews into the sea. The day after the storm, the boats of many of the dead sailors were still afloat.

Consequently, the lopsided safety triangle I offer emphasizes the human side of the equation, backs it up with the importance of the boats in which we sail, and ranks equipment behind seamanship and seaworthiness while still designating it a key safety ingredient. We cover all three sides of the safety triangle in this book, because no seamanship decision, maneuver, or operation is independent of the other two sides.

SEAMANSHIP BY THE BOAT

Offshore voyaging is a graduation of sorts for inshore sailors who turn from the coastline and head to sea. It's also a test of self-reliance, resourcefulness, and the other talents lumped under the rubric of sea-

When a loud bang draws the crew's attention to the rigging and a noticeable sag appears in a V-2 (upper vertical) shroud, the helmsperson immediately tacks the boat, and a crew volunteers to go aloft to discern what's wrong.

Rough weather on Lake Michigan—the result of a fast-moving cold front—is a reminder that large inland bodies of water can develop ocean-like conditions very quickly.

manship, but it isn't the only such test. The call for above-and-beyond seamanship depends more often on the tempo of weather systems than one's distance from land. Close-to-shore sailors also are accountable to rough weather, and along with it, the hazards that many assume only stalk the bluewater sailor.

I've been hemmed in by gale-force winds and threatened by lee shores on the Great Lakes, and I've turned around and run for shelter on the Albemarle Sound on the coast of North Carolina. I've also experienced 70-knot gusts in the well-traveled 26-mile span between Catalina Island and Los Angeles off the coast of California. All of these encounters were made worse, not better, by shallow water or a lack of sea room. From ancient times, mariners have always shared a respect for the deep and a fear of a lee shore.

Coastal cruising can put you squarely in the crosshairs of a storm system just as surely as if you were a passagemaker in midocean. Yes, the option of seeking and perhaps gaining safe shelter is a big plus, and the waves may not be as mountainous when the fetch is limited; however, the *(continued next page)*

WHAT IS SEAMANSHIP?
Sheila McCurdy

What should go through your mind if, suddenly, turning the ship's wheel no longer turns the boat? This happened on our 38-foot sloop halfway to Bermuda. The helmsman immediately took the emergency tiller from its bracket and set it in place, and the boat was back under control in seconds. Seeking the source of the problem, I visualized the entire steering system and shimmied my way under the cockpit. Under the steering pedestal I found a pile of sprocket chain and slack wire cables leading to the quadrant. I had the tools to repair the broken chain and the knowledge to re-lead the chain and steering cables while underway. Meanwhile, the rest of the crew steered, navigated, and attended to the daily routine aboard. This was not an emergency. It was a demonstration of seamanship.

Seamanship encompasses boat handling, navigation, maintenance, and crew work. The term has a quaint, old-time quality to it, and for some it might conjure the smell of tarred marline or skills like boxing a compass. But seamanship remains as relevant today as it always has been. Canvas has given way to Kevlar and satellites have in many cases replaced stars for navigation, but seamanship still determines the odds of leaving and returning to port in good order.

The sea is an alluring but hostile environment. Humans need vessels to cross it. At its most basic, a boat is the floating cocoon we need to survive for longer than minutes or hours at sea. For any sailor, crossing an ocean in a small boat is an accomplishment. Some sailors are lucky, some are prepared. It is better to be prepared.

Seamanship manifests as the constant state of vigilance and care at the meeting of wind and wave. It is an attitude and a practice; it is boat preparation and crew training. It also is equipment selection and proper use, as well as daily maintenance and ability to perform once-in-a-lifetime jury-rigging. Seamanship leads to the critical questions: "What now?" and "What if?" It's catching a minor problem early, and it's slowing down a developing emergency. It is at once forethought and instinctive reaction, redundancy and double-checking. Seamanship puts the crew's safety before all else. Ultimately, it is the risk management you practice each time you slip on a life jacket or assess a weather window. Those who get into trouble usually are overly optimistic about their abilities and underestimate the risks ahead.

A cruising skipper with seamanship in mind chooses a passage within the capabilities of both the boat and the crew. The objective is to incur the least wear and tear to equipment and keep the experience pleasant for all involved. Along with this, the guideline that "timing and intermediate stops are determined by conditions" applies.

A racing skipper faces a scheduled start and the uncertain challenges of a known course. Boat speed and efficient crew work are paramount. The crew and equipment must be prepared for the full range of possible weather and sea conditions. *(continued next page)*

Sheila McCurdy has competed in more than a dozen Newport Bermuda Races, including winning her class. Her regular crew—including her brother Ian, John Rousmaniere, and others—know how to work together and use experience to their favor. Sheila passes along her leadership skills in the US Sailing training programs she helped to shape.

WHAT IS SEAMANSHIP?, CONTINUED

The objective is to reach the finish before anything breaks—or at least before anything that affects speed breaks. Crew experience and skills redraw the acceptable limits of risk management on a racing sailboat. That said, even on a race boat, seamanship plays a crucial role in preparation and safe practices aboard.

Sheila McCurdy has sailed 90,000 miles offshore, including 15 Newport-Bermuda Races, two Marion-Bermuda Races, nine transatlantic passages, and a Bay- *view Mackinac Race. As skipper and navigator in the 1994 and 2008 Newport-Bermuda Races, she and her crew finished second overall in divisions of over 120 boats. She also sailed in her family boat, Selkie, a 38-foot cutter designed by her late father, Jim McCurdy. Sheila runs US Sailing's National Faculty for Training and is a moderator for Safety at Sea Seminars. She's also past Commodore of the Cruising Club of America (CCA) and a longstanding member of the U.S. Naval Academy's Fales Committee.*

▶ *Over the years I've had the pleasure of watching our son Eric evolve from a boat-agile cruising kid to a dingy racer of some skill and on to the role of a naval officer. Again a civilian, he currently stands his watches on the bridge of ships as the navigator, and more recently as Chief Mate, in an era of electronic positioning. He still lays fixes on paper charts but also consults with the nearby electronic chart display and information system (ECDIS) display. We get to sail together on occasion, and from what I can see, what he learned at the Naval Academy and in later International Standards of Training, Certification & Watchkeeping for Seafarers (STCW) professional mariner training was all beneficial. What makes him an especially skillful mariner, however, is the time he's spent at sea piloting craft ranging from an 8-foot Optimist dinghy to a 1,000-foot aircraft carrier. When it comes to seamanship, time underway is the currency that counts the most.*

obstacles in your way are more numerous, and the navigation and collision-avoidance challenges more significant. Therefore, pursuit of more-than-ordinary seamanship is just as valuable inshore as it is to an ocean passagemaker.

Take a look at a classic midsummer line squall in the Chesapeake Bay or western Long Island Sound, or even a solitary supercell thunderstorm towering up to elevations as high as 50,000 feet. These short-lived torrents of wind and sea can turn a flat-calm afternoon into chaos. Whether you're anchored in a quiet cove or transiting under power in the hope of an afternoon sea breeze, the abrupt violence that's driven home by a fully developed thunderstorm can test the seamanship skills of any crew.

All things considered, sailing in crowded or current-driven waters, through unpredictable inlets, in crowded shipping lanes, or more than a few hours from your own dock or mooring gives you good reason to improve your seamanship skills, not ignore them. You could be caught out and find yourself in a strengthening gale, with night approaching, cold seas building, shoals to leeward, and a passage that will take your measure.

For some reason, too many boatowners are reluctant to amble down to the local sailing school and sign up for a course designed to take them to the next skill level. But once they take this initiative, they're usually quick to agree that the effort is well worth the time and expense. Those who do things backward and improvise a self-taught seamanship course by prematurely heading to sea usually have a few ordeals to talk about later. If their hard knocks convince them to take some training rather than head for shore quickly and permanently, they generally admit that "learning the hard way" is just another phrase for "learning without guidance."

Having been both a seat-of-the-pants learner and a participant in more formal learning, I've come to see the merits in each. Messing around in small boats was ingrained in me in childhood. I was fortunate to have parents and a Sea Scout skipper who saw value in boating experiences and what could be learned on the waterfront. And growing up in the Long Island Sound community of Cold Spring Harbor, New York, I had plenty of chances to develop an affinity for the sea. I learned early the value of a bowline, bronze oarlocks, and a good anchor—and I still stand by those childhood discoveries today.

In the following sections of this chapter, we'll look at seamanship through the lens of what I've learned and practiced aboard a series of vessels I know well. This cross section of my seamanship career takes us from small boats to large, from inshore to offshore, and from low-tech to high-tech—a progression familiar to many sailors. Some of the boats I've sailed are yachts of exceptional character, while others are modest production boats able to deliver experiences far beyond their humble lineage. We'll visit boats built of wood, aluminum, and fiberglass, and by considering each as a seamanship laboratory, we'll sum up ideas about going to sea. We'll also invite in some other voices to add in their own wisdom and experience.

While describing this range of boats and specific experiences that demonstrate the value of seamanship—and the consequences of its absence—I'll touch on numerous topics involving the components of the safety triangle described above. In coming chapters, as you make your passage through this book, you'll find these areas of seamanship skills discussed in greater detail. Whether you need information about sail plans, electronics, handling heavy weather, or navigation, you'll find answers to some of the most common questions and dilemmas all mariners encounter. You'll also find detailed, concrete examples to illustrate principles that might otherwise seem abstract—perhaps even intimidating. In other words, if you find yourself here in unfamiliar waters, rest assured that by the time you absorb what's presented in coming chapters, you'll gain the familiarity you've been looking for.

What better way to test the rules that guide all mariners on all vessels than to board these boats and head "out there"?

A Fitting First or Last Boat

The Cape Dory Typhoon is one of Carl Alberg's most successful designs. This 19-foot daysailer blends a traditional long keel and graceful low sheer line with the scaled-down features of his larger cruisers. At the head of the list of handling attributes are good directional stability and a moderate approach to draft,

The Cape Dory Typhoon is harmony afloat, a little sloop that's nice to look at and even nicer to sail. She's well-mannered but not underpowered, and the long run of full keel adds good directional stability. She's also very responsive to the helm.

ballast, and sail area. This evenly proportioned blend of aesthetics and performance has earned the boat a long-lived following. In fact, down-at-the-heels Typhoons are a popular choice for do-it-yourselfers looking for a worthwhile project. Typhoons never stay on the used-boat market for long.

The Typhoon is always ready to go for a sail, especially if tethered to a mooring that's friendly to departures and returns under sail. As soon as the mainsail cover is off and the jib hanked on, the main can be hoisted, making sure that the boom vang is slack and the downhaul (cunningham) is free. Halyard and outhaul tension are set according to wind velocity: the fresher the breeze, the more tension in each. As in most fractionally rigged boats, the main is the major power source, and it's a good habit to look at the leech, reefing line, and draft as the sail is set. Releasing the boom from its backstay pendant with the mainsheet slackened keeps the mainsail from drawing as you prepare to sail.

As the jib is hoisted, the helmsperson picks the favored tack on which to head away from the mooring—or, if it's a day for singlehanding (easy and delightful on this boat), you can use a pair of bungee cords to position the tiller while completing other jobs. This bit of multitasking can turn into a fire drill, however, if you set too much sail resulting in a boat-handling snafu. The best prevention is simply to take a little more time and work out a step-by-step plan for sailing off the mooring.

The Cape Dory has an easy-to-fit cast bronze outboard motor bracket and a convenient cockpit locker for a 2- or 3-horsepower motor. Despite the ease of transitioning from sail to power, I've found the boat able enough in light air, so the engine seldom comes out of the locker. In light air, easing the main halyard and outhaul a bit adds more draft to the mainsail, increasing lift and power. (See Chapter 7, Sails and Sail Handling.)

Even with its relatively long keel and attached rudder, the small Cape Dory is surprisingly responsive, allowing a crew to short tack in tight confines and maneuver into estuaries that provide limited space in which to gather way. In a light air with leftover chop, the best bet is to ease the sheets a little and confront the chop with the added power of a close reach rather that attempt to pinch and hobbyhorse over the waves.

One of the most valuable lessons learned when sailing a small boat like the Typhoon in a protected estuary is how significant left and right repetitive wind oscillations can be. Early on it becomes clear that staying "in phase" with wind shifts can significantly enhance progress. In essence, by repeatedly tacking on the headers, you turn them into lifts—and it's much easier to tack a Typhoon than a larger, less nimble boat with more powerful sails. Such wind oscillations vary in degree and duration, and by getting a feel for how often they reverse, you can make gains on both sides of an oscillation. All it takes is a compass and watch, and you can get a feel for the way a wind oscillation or a steady shift affects you.

The first bit of data crunching to do in your head involves determining the average wind direction. An easy approach to this challenge is to keep track of the compass heading just as you tack through the eye of the wind and the mainsail passes by the centerline. Making a couple of such tacks when a lift or header is most extreme and timing a couple full cycles of the oscillation provide the range and time of a complete cycle. With this information, you can switch tacks to stay lifted on either side of a regular oscillation. Many smaller bodies of water see such pendulum-like swings in wind direction, and from the cockpit of a Typhoon these are easy to read and harness.

A shifting breeze can also be a friend, and in some areas the shifts come with predictable regularity. On the Chesapeake Bay, where *Merlot*, our Cape Dory Typhoon is moored on long-term loan from our son-in-law and daughter, an occasional fall phenomenon gives us a northerly breeze on which to broad-reach out of our South River estuary, shifting to a southerly for a broad-reach return to port. Downhill both out and back! This happens as a nearly exhausted post-cold-front offshore breeze gives way to a building sea breeze. We don't often see this type of abrupt shift, however. We usually encounter the more common veering or backing breeze. The way to make use of such situations is to understand the weather conditions in which they occur and, when beating to weather, follow a racer's rule of thumb by sailing to the new breeze, as described above. (The term "sail to the new breeze" means to head the boat in the direction of where the shifting wind is trending, a key to success in a persistent shift [continuously veering or backing breeze]. This "tack when you're headed" strategy puts you in a better position to leverage the new wind direction, lessens the negative effect of being headed, and uses the favored side of a wind shift to sail to weather more efficiently. See Chapter 10, Reading the Sea and Sky.)

A great aspect of small-boat daysailing is the opportunity to use race-course tactics in a performance-cruising context. For example, at the same time you're attempting to use the geometry of wind direction and near-term variations in your favor, you have a continuous opportunity to trim sails more efficiently. The Typhoon's large mainsail-dominated sail plan should be powered up (given more draft) in a wind under 10 knots and flattened and eventually reefed as true wind approaches 15 knots. The depowering process in a building wind starts with extra halyard and outhaul tension; when the breeze builds over 12 knots, allow the top of the sail to twist by easing the vang. Telltales on the leech of the mainsail and a Windex at the masthead provide vital information. Part of the fun of daysailing lies in harnessing as much efficiency as the sail plan will deliver.

Tiller feedback helps resolve questions about balance and sail trim. Ideally, when you're sailing to

Just the right size for a quick getaway and a couple of hours of sailing, the Typhoon sits at a mooring awaiting a breeze. The self-draining cockpit and foredeck setup with cleats and chocks enable this scaled-down pocket cruiser to handle an overnight adventure with a crew ready to rough it.

weather, the tiller has only a few degrees of weather helm and never exerts a wrenching feel. The Typhoon responds to an overtrimmed main with increased tiller load (i.e., weather helm). Even the slight nuance of setting up the rig with just a tad too little or too much rake can alter the feel of the helm. The optimum test is being able to steer with two fingers even when the little Cape Dory is marching to weather near hull speed.

So far, we haven't ventured very far "out there," but we've singlehanded off a mooring, sailed reefed-down in winds over 15 knots, and explored how a boat responds to the wind. We've also seen that a boat as small as the Typhoon can be amply seaworthy when used as its designer intended. The Typhoon has a deserved reputation for seaworthiness while sailing inshore waters. But the boat isn't designed to take us offshore.

Referring again to the safety triangle, the accepted practice is to scale two of the legs—the seaworthiness of the boat and the quantity of safety gear carried aboard—to the kind of sailing you're planning and the conditions you could encounter. Only the third leg, seamanship, is independent of context. The seamanship experience you can acquire in encounters with gales at sea in all manner of boats will serve you well if your little Typhoon is ever overtaken by a fast-moving line squall on a summer afternoon on the Chesapeake Bay. Seaworthiness and safety gear are relative, but seamanship is absolute—one more reason for its primacy in the safety triangle.

Sea Legs in the Excalibur 26

Those of us who develop our sailing skills in a protected area like the Chesapeake Bay, Long Island Sound, or Puget Sound tend to master sail trim and boat handling tasks a bit differently from those who learn at sea, where ocean swells are dominant. For example, during spring and fall on the upper Chesapeake, 20-knot nor'westerlies are fairly run-of-the-mill after a cold front passes. The stronger breeze grabs our attention but doesn't intimidate us by the third or fourth encounter. However, it's a beast of a different nature when the 10-foot swells of the Santa Barbara Channel change the cadence. In such conditions, ordinary considerations, such as when to reef and whether to tow a dinghy or get it up on deck prior to departure, take on greater meaning. Honing your seamanship skills on the ocean rather than the bay really pays off if your cruising or racing agenda includes going to sea. For those conditions, the Excalibur 26 is capable of going offshore. Bill Crealock designed this boat in 1966 as a fin-keel, spade-rudder cruiser/racer, and this hearty little sloop rapidly grew

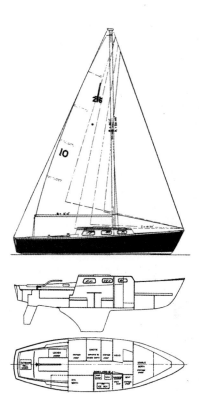

Designed with a low center of gravity, high displacement-to-ballast ratio, low-profile trunk cabin, and enough lateral plane for good directional stability, our Excalibur 26 morphed from an inshore racer to coastal cruiser—finally becoming a pocket-sized passagemaker.

popular. Eventually the Excalibur 26 became a West Coast regular in early Midget Ocean Racing Club (MORC) events and a key player in club racing from San Diego to Seattle.

The flip side of the boat's racing personality is its pocket-cruiser capability. Those willing to forego the amenities of a bigger boat find the nice-to-sail Excalibur makes an ideal weekender. Because of its above- and below-the-waterline configuration, some call the boat a 26-foot version of the Cal 40. For my wife, Lenore, and me, *Intuition*, which we owned from 1970 through 1974, was a key to ocean cruising and the chance to explore the coves of California's rugged Channel Islands with our 1- and 3-year-old in the crew. *Intuition* proved a capable vest-pocket cruiser. Plus, its unpredictable outboard motor made us better sailors.

The Excalibur 26 is only 7 feet longer than the Cape Dory Typhoon, but its offshore sailing features make it better suited to cope with conditions in a seaway and prepare a crew for what's ahead. The boat also handles differently. The deeper keel, masthead rig, and higher beam-to-length ratio make for a markedly different performer, especially in a stiffening breeze. (See Chapter 12, The Boats We Sail, for more on understanding boat design.) The sail plan, like the Cape Dory's, is an ultrasimple main-and-multiple-headsail configuration, but the emphasis in the masthead-rigged Excalibur is on the headsail inventory, not the main.

The often-used 150% genoa is much larger than the mainsail, and we took care to avoid the fire drill caused by waiting a little too long to downsize from the big genoa to the midsize headsail or the even smaller working jib. The piston hanks on our headsails were the ultimate in reliability, but the foredeck wrestling match could become quite a spectacle. One shortcut I often used involved detaching the bottom hank of a jib or genoa from the forestay while the sail was still flying, and attaching all of the hanks of the new sail I planned to hoist. I had two snap shackles permanently affixed to the stemhead fitting, which allowed me also to attach the tack of the sail we were preparing to hoist. I also led a second set of jib sheets through the large genoa cars. With the new sail thus secured, I would then douse the sail that had been flying—usually the big genoa—and gather it quickly and tie it to the rail with a couple of sail ties. Next I swapped the halyard to the replacement sail, unhanked the big genoa, switched sheets, and checked the new headsail to be sure it was ready to hoist. No one who has changed a sail on a pitching foredeck will deem my approach overly fussy.

While I was on the foredeck, using one hand for the boat and the other to keep myself on board, my wife steered a deep reach to minimize the wind across the deck and lessen the pitching moment, making the change and hoist much easier. Don't let the deep reach become a run, however, because then you risk a flying jibe, never a welcome event in a strong wind anywhere, but especially at sea. These were days when the value of a preventer became apparent, a lesson I've put to good use on every boat I've cruised aboard. (See Chapters 5 and 11 for more on preventers.)

In the days before reliable roller-furling headsails, foredeck agility was part of the job description for all crewmembers. Another fact of life for boats with short booms and masthead rigs was a very real need for off-the-wind sails that could stay filled and keep a boat moving in light air. One solution was the venerable drifter or reacher that had half as many piston hanks as a general-purpose headsail and could easily be set on the forestay and flown when sailing off the wind in light air. A spinnaker pole or whisker pole increased the angle off the wind at which this light Dacron or nylon sail could be set efficiently. A set of light-air sheets added even further to its versatility.

The Excalibur 26 had a built-in outboard motor well that seemed best for deploying an outboard motor aboard a sailboat. Unfortunately, exhaust fumes often found their way into the engine's air intake, and chronic fuel-air mix problems shortened spark plug life and hurt engine performance. The upside of this problem was the many opportunities to practice sailing in close quarters. In the end this made us

Carrying the mainsail into a harbor is a contingency plan in case the engine or drive train acts up. It's also easier to douse and flake the sail in the harbor's calmer water and abated wind. Note American Promise's *high-cut jib, or Yankee, is a good choice for a strong breeze offshore.*

better sailors, more willing to tackle harbor entries and docking maneuvers under sail rather than power. Today a cantankerous outboard well makes a perfect slot for an electric outboard, confirming a good design idea but one ahead of its time.

Over time, I developed considerable mistrust for propulsion by engine on a sailboat, a byproduct of my Excalibur experience that proved valuable. No doubt I overreacted, but nevertheless that flawed outboard provided an incentive to maintain a backup plan. To this day I keep the mainsail up until well into a harbor and never navigate through a tight pass without sails set—just in case.

Later in this chapter I'll describe lessons I learned aboard the powerful 60-foot sloop *American Promise*, a purpose-built, round-the-world voyager. Completing an Annapolis-to-Bermuda run, a crew of midshipmen and I were headed through the narrow pass into St. Georges when the diesel quit. Still carrying the mainsail, we unfurled the jib and short-tacked our way out of a situation that could easily have turned ugly. Having a contingency plan at the ready is always good insurance, and part of the practice of good seamanship.

Because of its modest size, but with a complete set of offshore sailboat paraphernalia, our Excalibur 26 was an unusually well-suited training boat, always providing opportunities to learn. One important lesson arrived with a loud bang some 30 miles offshore when a piece of rigging exploded and the deck-stepped mast fell into the sea. With a bit of wrestling, my wife and I were able to haul the rig alongside, strip the sails, retrieve all the running rigging, and hoist it on deck. We were able to do so thanks to the lee of Santa Rosa Island and a reasonably tranquil sea state. With only three gallons of gas left for the outboard, and the forecast calling for a building breeze, we decided on a VHF radio call that brought a 41-foot U.S. Coast Guard cutter to our aid.

The tow back to Channel Island Harbor, off the California coast, gave us time to ponder how things might have played out had we been well off the beaten path or the falling mast injured one of us. After reaching our home port, we carefully inspected our rig and found that a stainless steel upper shroud toggle had suffered what an engineer would call a brittle metal failure, meaning it ruptured because of the cyclical tension loads associated with sailing-induced fatigue. The 7-year-old sloop had been raced hard by her previous owners, and the original rigging had been on the shy side when it came to its designed safety margin.

Any good seamanship regimen includes taking steps to prevent such minor fitting failures and subsequent major problems. In this case, my approach

Heading for Hawaii in July 1974, Intuition, *our Excalibur 26, taught me that several days of foggy dampness was a toll to be paid in order to reach much more sailor-friendly easterly trade winds. (Courtesy Jerry Schudda)*

resulted in increasing the size of the toggles and turnbuckles and switching to silicon bronze, a more malleable metal than stainless steel and one that shows signs of elongation in clevis-pin holes well before it fails. (See The One-Size-Larger Rule later in this chapter.) I also added a forward lower shroud to assist the rear lower shroud and formed the habit of regularly checking turnbuckle engagement and clevis pin security.

Most sailors give little thought to how well their boat's rig, rudder, and keel are attached to the hull, but nothing should ever be taken for granted, especially with rigging that relies upon so many interconnecting potential points of failure. If you and your crew lack the time or desire to become completely familiar with all components of your boat's rig, you should regularly make use of a professional rigger. It's essential to keep track of the age of wire or rod standing rigging and the hardware that connects the rigging to the spar(s) and chainplates. Many riggers use 10 years or a voyage around the world as the lifespan of standing rigging. But rig geometry, the designed safety margin, and metallurgy also play a big role. New high-modulus fiber rigging comes with an even bigger question mark when it comes to lifespan.

Cruising *Intuition* with my family showed me that ocean swells typically impose loads on a sailboat much more aggressively than protected inshore waters. The always-changing angles of heel affected by moving wave faces exert righting-moment changes. The hull's buoyancy and the secondary righting moment from the lead ballast send loads through the hull. Pressure on the rudder foil and keel also add to these "global" loads, creating stress and strain pat-

Intuition*'s light weight and light-air efficiency let us nudge the edge of the Pacific high and still make good progress toward Hawaii. A lightweight drifter and a spinnaker added versatility to the sail inventory. Learning to cope with single-digit true wind speeds was as crucial as learning to handle enhanced trade winds and large rolling seas.*

terns that constantly bombard a hull and deck made of fiberglass (fiberglass-reinforced plastic, or FRP).

Learning how such energy transfers take place taught me why it is so important also to check the bulkhead tabbing that secures the bulkhead beneath a deck-stepped mast, as well as to inspect the chain-plate attachment points. When the Excalibur 26 was hauled for bottom painting, it was just as critical to closely inspect the rudder blade and garboard area adjacent to the keel attachment. In short, the small sloop had to be treated in the same manner as a 40- or 60-footer, the major difference being a lack of secondary systems that might draw my attention away from the essential characteristics of an offshore-capable sailboat. That was yet another thing that made *Intuition* a good training platform.

After a couple years of sailing *Intuition* in coastal waters, I taught myself the rudiments of celestial navigation and talked two adventurous friends, Jerry and John, into joining me for a voyage to Hawaii. The first few days were a demoralizing chilly, fogbound passage south and west through the prevailing downcoast westerly winds, which felt cold compared to the desert-like climate of Southern California. These winds are part of a circulation pattern that rotates around a large mid-latitude high-pressure system, cooled by upwelling and the currents moving down from the Arctic. Advection fog (formed when warm, moist air settles over a cooler surface, usually in light winds and under clear skies) added a damp, dank quality to the offshore waters. For the first several days we could only dream of sunny trade-wind sailing.

At last our course delivered us to the friendly easterly trade winds and a complete change of mood and clothing. Before leaving California, I'd had a second row of reef points sewn into *Intuition*'s mainsail just below the second batten from the top. When deeply reefed, the mainsail area was just right for the enhanced trade winds we were about to encounter.

The coming days tested our resolve in other ways, however. Our small crew and lack of self-steering led to a sleep-and-steer schedule it took a strong will to appreciate. Lesson learned: a self-steering vane and/or autopilot may introduce another complexity, but there's usually no higher priority for the offshore sailor than relief from helm duty. Given a choice between refrigeration, digital charting, a watermaker, or a reliable self-steering system, passagemakers almost always opt for the last.

It wasn't only the need for constant steering that besieged this passage. I'd hoped that the dismasting my wife and I had experienced earlier would be the last full-blown emergency at sea I'd ever have with *Intuition*. Halfway to Hawaii, on a breezy trade-wind, moonless night, it became clear how wrong I was. The event taught me once again that all mariners must consider their responses to damage-control scenarios.

With two of us below in our berths and one at the helm, we were surfing down the faces of the steeper waves making knots toward our destination. I was awakened from a deep-REM sleep by one of the most dreaded of shipboard alarms coming from the crew on watch: "We're sinking!"

Bolting out of my berth, I splashed in water well above the cabin sole. Reflexively I threw back the sole boards and went to each through-hull fitting, feeling in the darkness for a leak. One of the cockpit drain hoses had separated from a seacock, not from inadequate hose clamps but because a wave impact had caused a heavy toolbox to levitate out of its bin and impact the hose barb/hose junction, shearing the bronze fitting. A quick throw of the now partially damaged seacock stemmed, but did not stop, the leak. I jammed a conical shaped soft wood plug into the hole to fully stop the water ingress. But the danger was far from over.

Each new wave face brought a change in trim, with the water inside the boat rushing forward, causing the forward portion of the hull to submerge to a greater extent—much like doubling the weight at one end of a seesaw. This resulted in a pivoting broach just as we reached the trough of a large wave. My two shipmates and I began bucket bailing, a process that when fueled by adrenaline lifts water far faster than most built-in manual bilge pumps. After about an hour, dawn began to illuminate the eastern sky, and we could start dealing with a bilge and cabin invaded by a slurry of powdered milk, oatmeal, paper products, and other bilge-stowed dry goods.

Lesson learned: beware the "free-surface effect," which is naval architecture speak for the downhill surge of uncontained water in response to the slightest incline. Inside a modern canoe-body hull, this proclivity can have profound consequences, especially as the vessel heels or changes its angle of trim. With a weight of about 8 pounds per gallon, a few hundred unwanted gallons of water sloshing about in your cockpit or cabin becomes a ton or more of mass acting to exacerbate any plunge, heel, or squat your boat is subject to. Free-surface effect dramatically changes the stability of a boat, and always for the worse. As the vessel heels and water runs toward the low side, the righting moment decreases. Trim also changes as water rushes forward or aft, causing the problems we faced aboard *Intuition*. This is why water tanks are baffled, and it's also one reason why cockpit drains need to be big enough to empty a filled cockpit fast.

Prevention of flooding and downflooding is equally important. Had the toolbox not smacked into the hose barb, the flooding would never have occurred. Setting up the boat for the dynamics of a seaway includes lashing down and locking in place all the heavy equipment. (This incident is reexamined in Chapter 13, in the sidebar "We're Sinking"— Lessons Learned.)

Other, less dramatic learn-by-doing experiences on this passage included my first foray into offshore navigation in the era before GPS or any other reliable electronic navigation system. I claimed only fledgling celestial navigation skills at best; my capabilities were limited to noon sights from which to generate a daily latitude and a very rough idea of longitude. The routine worked acceptably well until the sun's declination and our latitude became nearly the same, when the great orb rose to our zenith at local noon, dancing about *Intuition*'s masthead. This is the very worst condition in which to attempt a noon sight, and a simple shift to a midmorning line of position (LOP) and an early afternoon LOP would have made more sense. A fix could then have been generated by advancing the morning line of position to the time of the one shot in the afternoon—but what did I know? (See Chapter 8, Navigation.)

Fortunately, a few powerful AM broadcast radio stations in Hilo, Hawaii, and a radio direction finder (RDF) beacon confirmed to our satisfaction that the odd jet passing overhead was indeed headed to Hawaii. After 21 days at sea, tiller-steering all the way, we made landfall on Hawaii's Big Island. With our sometimes serene and sometimes shaky rite-of-passage behind us, we'd earned our valuable experience.

The wind and sea had been stern taskmasters, but the seakeeping quality of my sloop and the crew's resourcefulness helped us pull off a learn-the-hard-way approach to passagemaking. After landfall, Jerry and John headed home in one of the jets we'd been watching, and Lenore and the kids soon took their places. We then enjoyed a summer of cruising among the Sandwich Islands, so named by Captain Cook in honor of the Fourth Earl of Sandwich, who had helped to finance Cook's 1770 voyage of discovery. Some two hundred years later we were following in Cook's wake, as we would do on future voyages.

Around the World in the Ericson 41 *Wind Shadow*

Two years after our Hawaiian adventure, Lenore and I sold our house and bought *Wind Shadow*, an able 41-footer with a masthead double-headsail sloop rig and 750 square feet of working sail. *Wind Shadow* needed some TLC, but doing the work ourselves left us intimately familiar with the boat. After a year of living aboard and coastal cruising, we headed west from California on what we planned as a voyage to the South Seas. Before we were done, however, our traditional keep-systems-simple approach and a spirit of adventure turned our South Pacific cruise into a five-year westward voyage around the world. Tara and Eric were 4 and 6 when we set sail aboard *Wind Shadow*.

Fitness and reasonable decision-making skills helped make up for our limited voyaging experience. By the time we departed Cape Town, South Africa, to cross our third ocean, we had indeed developed competency through a trial-and-error approach. During the decades of cruises that followed we made a point of learning more and more about how others approached the same challenges.

From the start we could "hand, reef, and steer" (a phrase originally used for the designation of Able Seaman, in practical terms meaning "able to do it

The light-air efficiency and ability to handle a blow of our Ericson 41, Wind Shadow, *helped get us where we wanted to go. Almost all sailboats will do just fine with 15- to 20-knot trade winds, but an offshore boat needs to be able to handle both extremes as well. Dinghy towing during inshore sails was fine, offshore, even during coastal passages, the dinghy was stowed on deck.*

all")—skills critical to early mariners and just as important today. I learned to row an anchor to windward in a blow, to dive to clear a line or release a snagged anchor fluke, and to repair whatever broke. Epoxy, fiberglass tape, hose clamps, and a variety of well-chosen hand tools were my familiar friends. My celestial navigation routine expanded to include sun, moon, and planet sights as well as a three-star fix at dawn and dusk. We also learned that our old-fashioned DC refrigeration system was too power-hungry to put up with. While in New Zealand we traded our wind instruments for an all-chain anchor rode and a manual Nilsson windlass. Priorities change with experience!

Adding a radial-clewed 2-ounce lightweight drifter and a bulletproof storm trysail on a separate mainmast track addressed both ends of the wind spectrum and better equipped us for the passage from New Zealand to Africa. We kept our priorities straight, and sails and ground tackle played heavily in the equation. In short, we adopted the philosophy and developed the skills of earlier mariners—a hand, reef, and steer curriculum. In retrospect, we might have experienced less drama if we'd learned some of our lessons under more controlled circumstances. I wish I'd had a firmer grasp on the way weather systems develop and the differences between trade wind and Roaring Forties sailing. On the other hand, we're unlikely to forget what we learned the hard way.

A Custom Wooden Yawl

Puffin is a custom 47-foot yawl designed by Olin Stephens as an ocean racer/cruiser for the late Ed Greeff, an experienced offshore sailor from Long Island, New York. Built in 1969, the vessel typifies a concept pioneered by the designers Sparkman and Stephens (S&S), in which a deep draft, moderate displacement, ample sail area, and a skeg-hung rudder combine to create an able offshore sailboat. Similar S&S designs such as the Swan 48 and 65 were good performers at sea but really proved their worth in heavy weather, thanks to their conservative scantlings and seakindliness. Though later eclipsed on inshore race courses by wide, canoe-bodied hull shapes, these S&S legends have remained favorites among cruisers looking for performance on all points of sail and accommodations that remain viable at sea.

I came to know *Puffin* in the 1980s as a crewmember racing to Bermuda and on overnight distance races up and down Long Island Sound. I also skippered the boat on a delivery to the Caribbean and got to know the yawl inside and out at a boatyard I managed. With this familiarity I appreciated the blend of traditional yacht styling with a very functional sea boat. It was built by the Danish boatbuilder Wolstead, known for cold-molded wooden hulls with bronze castings for the floor frames to carry chainplate loads and reinforce other high-stress areas such as the cabin

The classic lines of Ed Greeff's Sparkman & Stephens yawl Puffin *hid the structure and stability of a capable passagemaking racer/cruiser. The cold-molded mahogany skins and cast-bronze floor frames added to a strong and stiff structure. Beating to weather in a lumpy seaway created neither squeak nor groan.*

corner posts. The focus on structural integrity came from an experience Ed Greeff had had aboard a previous *Puffin,* when he and his wife and a few friends were caught in a vicious Mediterranean mistral and knocked down by a steep breaking sea. The vessel recovered from the capsize, but the cabinhouse/coachroof was torn from the deck. With frantic bailing and careful steering the crew kept the boat afloat. The event was chronicled in an early edition of K. Adlard Coles's seafaring classic *Heavy Weather Sailing.* Interestingly, S&S had also designed that *Puffin,* and the construction plans included drawings and callouts describing bronze drift bolts to anchor the coachroof to the deck carlins. However, the Far East builder had disregarded that engineering requirement, fastening the coachroof with wood screws instead. This sort of deviation from "as designed" to "as built" is one of boatbuilding's never-ending problems.

The Wolstead-built *Puffin* is one of the best-built boats I've ever sailed. We never had to worry that something might come adrift when caught overcanvassed or when pounding into a steep seaway. Currently owned by the boatbuilder Cabot Lyman, *Puffin* is still going strong from its new base on the coast of Maine.

For me, *Puffin* became the standard by which to measure other wooden boat construction. You could drive hard through Gulf Stream squalls and know

With a full mizzen, reef in the main, and a high-cut furling jib and forestaysail set, Puffin's *classic double-headsail rig powered us on a close reach to the Antilles.* Puffin *had a kind motion in a seaway, and with a good dodger and large dorade vents, the cabin was comfortable. Not a drop of water got below.*

that the rigging and the engineering that held chainplates securely to the hull would not let you down. With each spate of heavy weather, I'd watch fellow crewmember Rod Stephens do his magic with minor trim adjustments and sheet-lead changes. Though a cruising sailor at heart and not prone to getting excited about intentionally doing battle with the sea and competitors, I found the race time I spent aboard *Puffin* to be a graduate course in seamanship. Specifically, what I learned from sharing boat-handling tasks with an experienced crew proved easily transferable to a cruising mindset.

Puffin delivered a few negative lessons, including a realization that the yawl rig made little sense. The rig had come into vogue because of a race-handicapping rule that failed to penalize the boat for the sail area of the mizzen or the mizzen staysail flown when sailing off the wind. All that non-penalized sail area was just too good for racers to do without.

According to some sailors, the jib-and-jigger configuration—a tiny storm jib on the headstay balanced by a small scrap of mizzen (known as a "jigger") sail aft—seemed the ultimate way to handle heavy weather. However, this myth ended when enough sailors saw breaking seas carry away poorly stayed mizzenmasts and their reefed mizzens. A conventional storm trysail and storm jib make a much better option for yawls and sloops alike, and *Puffin's* double-headed rig was more sloop than yawl.

The One-Size-Larger Rule

Another byproduct of my time aboard *Puffin* was an appreciation for what I call the "one-size-larger rule" for hardware and fittings. In many ways it's the reverse of what's seen on many boats today. Lighter may be faster, but that also conjures up the saying "The flame that burns twice as bright burns half as long." Long-term, long-range cruising relies upon the strength and durability of gear, and the fatigue caused by cyclical loading is a bitter enemy. The more closely a working load approaches the breaking strength of a part, the shorter its lifespan, and breaking strength also plunges closer to the outer limit of the lifespan. Going one size larger increases the safety margin and usually also extends the equipment's life. This added safety margin in essential rigging and high-usage blocks and leads provides greater durability that is usually well worth the extra cost and additional weight.

A Dark Time for a Great Boat

Ted Hood designed the 60-foot sloop *American Promise* for Dodge Morgan, who was looking for a vessel to sail singlehandedly nonstop around the world. Later, after completing his quest, he donated the sloop to the U.S. Naval Academy (USNA). In 1990, during the boat's initial tenure as a platform for midshipman sail and leadership training, the sloop sailed down the Chesapeake Bay on a breezy, overcast, rainy night in March. A lazy jibsheet without a figure-eight stopper knot in its end pulled through one of the genoa cars and wrapped itself around the working sheet. The next time the crew tacked away from the western shore, the headsail backwinded but refused to cross the foredeck, leaving the sloop hove-to.

Stuck with the jib backed, the crew's attention focused on the running rigging snafu at the expense of the bigger picture of what was happening around them. They turned on a bright set of spreader lights to illuminate the foredeck problem, which greatly hampered their night vision. This is when the dominos began to topple.

In an attempt to gain control of the vessel by motorsailing, the crew failed to notice a line trailing in the water, which then fouled the prop and stalled the engine. The radar was not being operated effectively, and the VHF was tuned to Channel 82A rather than scanning Channels 16 and 13. The midshipman on the helm thought she saw a red and a green light to windward and reported it, but her report did not gain the attention of the duty officers in charge of the training cruise.

More often than not, such problems get sorted out and a crew learns not to make the same mistakes again. This time, however, the crew had placed themselves in an unintentional hove-to situation in overcast conditions and had used neither the radar nor the VHF appropriately. By the time the officers in charge saw the barge pushed by a tugboat bearing down on them from windward, they had no control of their sailboat. The barge hit the sloop directly amidships, dismasting *American Promise* and pinning it broadside under the sloping stem of the barge. The crew scrambled up the clutter of rigging onto the barge. However, it took some time for the officer in charge to realize that one crewmember was missing.

The cold March water added the threat of hypothermia to the night's other calamities, and a desperate search began immediately. Using his powerful searchlight, the tug captain quickly spotted the person in the water; fortunately she wore an inflatable PFD with reflective tape that stood out in the bright beam of the searchlight. Despite the 60-foot sloop impaled on the stem of his barge, the tug's skipper maneuvered the combined mass close enough to the midshipman to get a line to her and hoist her from the 50-degree Fahrenheit water. It's fair to say both her life jacket and the tug's skilled crew saved her life.

When the U.S. Coast Guard arrived on the scene, they decided the tug, barge, and pinioned yacht constituted a hazard to navigation and directed the tug skipper to maneuver to the west, out of the channel. The skipper's effort to comply smashed a 30-foot hole in *American Promise*'s starboard side, and the boat sank quickly in 60 feet of water.

After a full review of the incident, The National Transportation Safety Review Board issued a scalding rebuke of the chaos aboard the USNA sail training vessel at the time of the loss. They pointed out a series of seamanship shortfalls that caused the crew of *American Promise* to put themselves in harm's way. The report underscored how relatively minor omissions and distractions led to a loss of effective watchkeeping and set the stage for the calamity that followed.

Since Monday-morning quarterbacking is always free from the chaos of the moment, we can too easily assign blame for something that was or wasn't done. The constraints of the marine environment and the evolving and intensifying heat of the moment are always missing in reviews conducted in a dry office. The lessons learned from this event are worth passing on, however, and the follow-up observations are worth airing.

The command structure aboard the *American Promise* fell apart, a major reason it collided with the tug and barge. The highest-ranking officer aboard was one of the least experienced sailors, and a lower-ranking officer in charge (OIC) failed to make and implement several pivotal decisions. No one capable of using the VHF or radar correctly was assigned to the task, and the radar lookout failed to keep track of the contact noticed well before the collision. The inadequate boat-handling skills that disabled the vessel also prevented the crew from removing the boat from the situation.

The crew had had options. Among them, they could have jibed the vessel and run off in order to more easily roller-furl the headsail and then deal with the sheet issue. Instead the crew continued to try to turn the vessel into the wind, even though the jib was backed and the turn impossible to make.

In addition, the crew could have run a new sheet, cut away the old one, and dealt with the fouled line once the load was on the new sheet. Of course, before using the engine, the crew should have checked for lines in the water and hauled them aboard and out of the way. The OIC should have assigned a radar operator who knew how to handle the tune, gain, and range-selection functions; that person also could have broadcast a VHF security message announcing the vessel's problem and location. We can see many

Like a phoenix rising from its own ashes—a tale even more compelling than the sinking—American Promise *returned to action in the mid-1990s and for a dozen years was the flagship of Naval Academy Sail Training. The vessel was cutter rigged, and every crew who sailed aboard the boat learned the tradition of hand, reef, and steer. Learning to reef and handle sail changes first in light-to-moderate breezes and then in more demanding conditions is key to developing good big-boat seamanship. Note that the blade-cut staysail nicely balances the deeply reefed main.*

chances along the way to resolve this scenario harmlessly rather than allowing it to escalate and go so wrong. (See Chapter 14, Communications.)

We also recognize that responses to often-ignored safety issues can cause a minor breakdown or failure to cascade into a major problem. But by removing one of the links in the accident chain, we can often halt the toppling dominos. This ability to get a handle on what's unfolding before it becomes too late is at the heart of crisis management. It requires the dual capacity to see the big picture and respond to its individual parts—to be deep in the trees yet still aware of the surrounding forest. Or think of it as pulling out the fuse rather than preparing for the aftermath of an explosion.

For example, let's look at a vessel being driven down repeatedly by wind gusts in a squall. Some crewmembers simply scramble to the windward rail to contribute to the righting moment of the vessel rather than dealing with the cause. Instead, we'd have more control if we leaped to leeward and stood ready to ease the sheets; this action would respond to the problem rather than the symptoms. Lessening the heeling moment caused by the sail plan would cope with the issue at hand and allow for more options if the next spiral band in the squall packs even more punch. In other words, while responding to symptoms might keep problems from escalating, it's equally or more important to attend to the causes behind a problem. This type of "sailboat triage" involves ongoing risk assessment, crew management, and decision making. This triage ability becomes a preeminent seamanship skill in extreme situations, such as avoiding collision or coping with a fire or flooding.

Because both sail and power cruisers spend more time aboard than racing sailors, they're more likely to encounter boat-handling or breakdown incidents. Therefore, an important aspect of good seamanship involves learning to be ready at all times to respond to a propulsion failure with the ground tackle—or with a quick set of the sails. This is analogous to a doctor having a plan ready to respond to unexpected trauma or unforeseen errors.

To its credit, the U.S. Navy soon sent a salvage crew to the site of the *American Promise*'s sinking. They raised the vessel, placed it on a barge, and subsequently returned it to the Naval Academy's small-craft repair division facility (SCRD) in Annapolis, Maryland. Despite the massive hole in the side and the devastation caused by the flooding, the remainder of the hull was intact. An out-of-court settlement with the tug and barge company provided funds for a rebuild, and the SCRD craftsmen took on the challenge of cutting away the damaged area. They made templates of the hull curves from the other side of the vessel and fabricated a mold surface to duplicate the original hull shape.

After slow but steady progress, *American Promise* rose from a watery grave back to a floating, fit status. The new rig donated by the owner of the ocean racer *Kodiak* stood 9 feet taller than the original rig Dodge Morgan had sailed around the world. A rebuilt diesel and new systems (quite simple by yacht standards) rounded out the refit.

Over the next decade, *American Promise* answered the question of whether an FRP vessel could be repaired to oceangoing status. Not only have midshipmen annually pushed the boat hard and claimed trophies in ocean races to Newport, Marblehead, Halifax, and Bermuda, but the sloop has successfully tallied four more transatlantic crossings.

During one particularly nasty eastbound crossing, I had a chance to spend plenty of off-watch time checking the chainplates and the old-to-new skin scarfs as gale- and even storm-force winds drove the powerful sloop across the Atlantic. The rebuild had indeed proven that an FRP scarf, if well overlapped and reinforced with enough hanging knees and other transverse and longitudinal structures, can be at least as strong as the structure had been originally.

One of *American Promise*'s best attributes is the long, deep keel that all but negates the woes of leeway. The massive FRP spade rudder and titanium rudderstock refute claims about spade rudders being inappropriate for oceangoing vessels. The big sloop rig with a removable inner forestay proved to be a great performer in a seaway with a breeze of 12 knots or more. With roller furling only for the jib, sail handling, especially mainsail reefing, was a labor-intensive effort, more than sufficient to occupy a crew of young midshipmen.

Passagemaking with Navigation Electronics

Thomas Watson, that captain of industry whose steady hand steered IBM, decided he wanted a ketch built for long-legged voyaging, and his desire resulted in *Palawan VI*. At 60 feet, the same length as *American Promise*, *Palawan VI* is another example of a consummate sea boat. Conceived as a comfortable long-range cruiser, able to press south of the 60-degree latitude line and explore the Antarctic Peninsula, this very special S&S design was built in Germany by Abeking & Rasmussen. The high-strength alloy structure and modest ketch rig embody the parameters dictated by the high winds and breaking seas of the great Southern Ocean.

After completing a trek to Antarctica in exemplary fashion, *Palawan VI* was (continued page 20)

During a post transatlantic run from the Caribbean to the mainland, owner David Webb enjoys some time at the helm. Palawan VI's center cockpit allows enough room to stow the rigid inflatable boat (RIB) on the aft deck instead of compromising seaworthiness and aesthetics with davits.

Rod and Olin Stephens conspired to create a sea boat, not just a set of lines. Palawan VI is at its best when the chips are down and has earned the right to be deemed structurally impressive and a seakindly passagemaker. A four-cylinder Caterpillar diesel turns calms into an 8.5-knot march.

Form and function dominate a finely finished interior on Palawan VI. In true S&S fashion, there are sea berths in two side-by-side cabins as well as a handsome owner's stateroom aft.

eventually sold, and a larger Hood design became as iteration VII in the Palawan line. *Palawan VI* languished in the Mediterranean until David Webb, a friend of the Watsons who had sailed aboard the vessel in his youth, took on the challenge of restoring the boat and making some voyaging plans of his own. For a refit most owners can only dream about, David engaged the crew at Zimmerman Marine in Cardinal, Virginia. *Palawan VI* was completely disassembled, was sand-blasted, and had some plating replaced. Weeks turned into months, and finally more than a year later, *Palawan VI* emerged from her shed in better-than-new condition. Staying faithful to the vessel's original build but adding a few upgrades in navigation equipment and systems, the effort produced a boat that's at its best when shorthanded passagemaking is the rule of the day.

The Hood in-mast furling system on *Palawan VI* has stood the test of time, as have the power headsail furlers. The pushbutton setting, reefing, and furling option allows a one- or two-person watch to handle all that usually needs to be done. And when you're not sailing with eight or ten eager, fit midshipmen at the ready, a power-furling split rig makes a lot of sense on a boat this size.

Palawan VI allows those on watch to carry out the boat-handling routine from the all-weather protection of an alloy-and-Plexiglas dodger enclosing the forward portion of the cockpit. Equipped with two multifunction displays, watchkeepers have radar and a separate digital chart at their fingertips. The crew can quite literally steer, trim, and navigate through the worst of a three-day low without getting soaked in the process. Dual autopilots provide backup just in case one goes down during a long passage.

The passages I've made aboard *Palawan VI* have been lessons in sailing with automation. In addition to pushbutton winching and furling I had a chance to put a well-setup digital charting system to the test. Being a dyed-in-the-wool traditionalist and firm believer in Murphy's Law, I kept a printed ChartKit on deck next to the double-screen digital display. The two stand-alone units nestled under the permanent dodger allowed concurrent display of radar and chart information, but without the squeezed view of too much data on one screen.

The first big decision was whether to use a north-up or heading-up display format. The latter orients the digital chart so that the vessel's bow always points to the top of the screen, and the chart rotates accordingly. In the north-up format the vessel's heading changes on the screen while keeping true north (or in some cases magnetic north) up, as in a printed chart held upright. Each orientation takes a little getting used to, just as it's a bit disorienting at first when you learn to steer according to an unfamiliar magnetic compass. (If the magnetic compass's lubber line is at the forward end of the dome, the card appears to spin one way, but if the lubber line sits on the after, closer side of the card, it appears to move the opposite way.) In addition to getting used to how the ship-shaped cursor moves, we also must become familiar with differences in how a raster or vector chart looks on the screen. In addition, we needed to learn how to zoom in and zoom out to compensate for the screen limited size, which provides a substantially smaller image area than a paper chart. (See Chapter 8, Navigation.)

LESSONS LEARNED ON A BERMUDA RETURN

Sailing is a lifelong learning experience and every voyage is different. Over the years, I've had the good fortune of curing many of my own bad habits and misperceptions by cruising and racing with others. The following account is an example how even a milk-run return from Bermuda can set the stage for valuable lessons learned.

Passagemaking on a Swan 48 MKII with Weather Data

Dragon, a well outfitted and carefully maintained Swan 48 MKII, had held its own in a rough Marion Bermuda Race in June 2009. Three of the crew for the return passage had weathered that lumpy race crossing, and my son-in-law and I had just arrived in Bermuda, along with two others, raising the big sloop's total crew to seven.

The big news greeting sailors arriving in this favored British outpost was that the usual Bermuda High was AWOL and would remain missing for a good portion of the summer. Without that stationary summertime high-pressure area parked overhead, upper-level troughs paraded from west to east, bringing with them unsettled weather and often near-gale-force squalls. The identified culprit was a recurring cut-off midlevel low over or near the Great Lakes. This weather scenario gave the U.S. Northeast wet and chilly days and weeks—a nonexistent summer. The onset of a strong El Nino event had come as no surprise, bringing with it a southerly shift of the main axis of the jet stream and more volatile weather in the middle latitudes. All this meteorological excitement added up to atypical passages for sailors heading to and from New England. (For more on weather, see Chapter 10, Reading the Sea and Sky.)

Two days before my son-in-law and I joined the *Dragon* crew, the National Hurricane Center had stuck a yellow circle on an easterly wave nearing Cuba and noted a 30% likelihood that it would become a tropical storm. Even more significant, the forecast track of the disturbance intersected our return route, seemingly placing us right in its proverbial crosshairs. The day before we left for Bermuda, the forecast kicked up the probability of a tropical storm forming to 50%.

After considering these increasingly dire forecasts, I had called a friend, Joe Sienkiewicz, the science officer at the Ocean Prediction Center (OPC) of the National Weather Service, a very important branch of the National Oceanic and Atmospheric Association (NOAA). He thought the westerly shear that had tamped down tropical development all season would likely do the same to this new package of tropical energy. According to Joe, a bigger concern stemmed from the extratropical weather linked to the troughs moving off the New England coast.

Our flight to Bermuda had confirmed the forecast. Not only did we never once see the ocean after leaving Long Island, but atmospheric potholes kept the seat belt sign glowing. Once there, we found Bermuda lush and green thanks to unrelenting rain (unlike the usual sun-parched foliage we typically see during a Bermuda summer). Wind gusts in the an-

On the flight from New York to Bermuda we stared out at building cumulonimbus cloud tops, and by the time we reached Bermuda the turbulence was all too noticeable. We all knew what lay ahead.

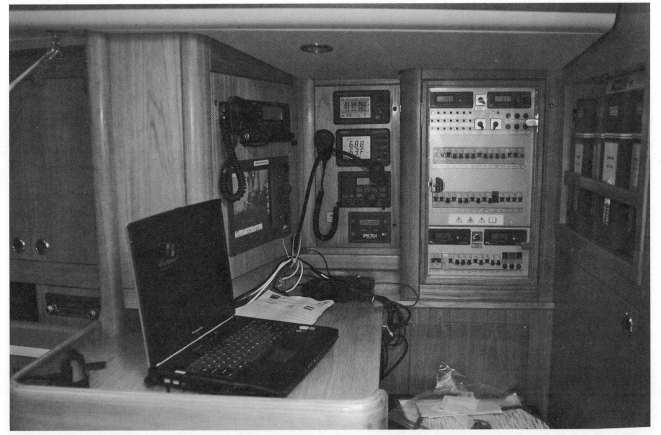

It was handy to have software and a satellite phone link aboard Dragon, *a Swan 48, to download forecasts as well as raw GRIB data. These data were predicting a lumpy passage but with less than gale-force conditions.*

chorage were 30 knots, and had we not had a solid means of keeping track of weather data, we likely would have postponed departure.

Download the GRIBs or Favor the Forecasts?

NOAA's OPC forecasts (at http://www.opc.ncep. noaa.gov/) gave us a clear picture of the near-gale-force conditions facing us upon departure. They showed how a series of low centers would develop on a trough that was approaching Bermuda. These forecasts incorporate GFS (Global Forecast System) and other model data. As good as they are, some sailors like to augment them with *gridded information in binary form* (GRIBs), and recently the Ocean Prediction Center has set up the OPC Gridded Marine

A FIRST OCEAN PASSAGE

As it happened, our return passage from Bermuda aboard *Dragon* was my son-in-law Scott Mitchell's first long-distance ocean passage. Shortly after our return I asked him for candid responses to a few questions. Our conversation follows.

Q. What did you hope to derive from the offshore passage? I hoped to have fun, confirm I wanted to spend more time on my own boat, and learn some specifics about sail setting, trim, steering, and navigation. Of those, I spent less time on navigation than the other areas. But I saw how GPS and radar take much of the guesswork out of it. The celestial navigation information was valuable, and I learned that although the tech information is a great luxury, dead reckoning, paper charts, and standing watch are probably more reliable in the long run.

Q. What skills did you find were most in demand and enhanced by your experience? It's always important to have crew who can work the deck safely and properly. More than ever, I realized how important it is to think and communicate about what you plan to do *long before* you do it. This leads to safer decisions. "Safety first" was also a big lesson. With no land in sight, quick-stopping [a maneuver used to retrieve crew overboard] a 50-foot vessel in the night would not have been fun.

Working in a small crew underscored the balance between following and challenging authority. Although a chain of command is critical, we shouldn't forego the possibility of a better decision simply because the boss issued an order. It's tricky to challenge authority, but if done correctly and well, it can lead to greater respect between supervisor and subordinates.

Having a plan b is always important, so I learned not to be afraid to try something different. Also, no matter what happens, like losing a shackle, getting sick, or a jammed sheet, you have to go with the flow. That's where open communication can solve a potential problem before it becomes an emergency.

Q. In hindsight, was your anticipation about ocean passagemaking accurate? What sailing skills did you hope to learn more about after the passage? My advance thinking was pretty much dead on with the reality–except for getting sick. We had ev-ery type of weather short of storm-force winds. We worked as a team, accepted each other's weaknesses, and harnessed our strengths. I would have provisioned the boat *much* differently, with more fruit and vegetables and, overall, simply better food. Water is key, but better drinks would likely have helped us stayed hydrated more easily.

Aware of my limitations, I knew when I needed to ask for help. I was also aware that I was new at this and that it was okay to ask for help or double-check my actions. I said this to everyone on board before we left the dock. I want to cruise more often on my own boat now—it's fun work and a great experience for the kids and me. In addition, I was super-excited about the passage and wanted to give it my all. I also appreciated the need to psych myself up for "anything goes" during an ocean passage, making the best of every situation and making a difference where I could. Since the skipper took care of the navigation, I took that for granted, which means I need to make a trip where I'm more involved in wind direction, forecasts, currents, and so forth.

Q. What do you see as the positive and negative attributes of the Swan 48? How did it function as an offshore passagemaker? She's a great boat to steer and behaved well in heavy wind. She also has a great foredeck setup with the double-headsail rig. As for a less advantageous feature, the standing rigging is too far inboard and hard to get past without jumping up onto a *big* coachroof. It was difficult to pass outboard too. The forward pit seems awkward, but with plenty of crew it was not a problem. The aft cabin needs more ventilation; I'd get rid of the lockers outboard of the bunks and make the bunks wider. The heads are great, and so is the galley—you can lean against something on either tack, even at tremendous angles of heel, and still be comfortable preparing food. A better location for the reefer [fridge] would be where the garbage bin is now, and it should be top-opening—it's stupid to have it open outward. The hatches need to open forward for more ventilation, and the dorade boxes leak and need attention. On the other hand, the watermaker is an awesome piece of equipment.

Forecasts on the website (http://www.opc.ncep.noaa.gov). GRIBs provide a detailed picture of raw wind speeds and directions calculated with algorithms—in other words, an informed, computer-generated guesstimate. I prefer OPC forecasts with a professional meteorologist's knowledge added to the mix. The OPC website offers a useful introduction and will help you merge raw GRIB data files with meteorologist-evaluated forecasts.

On this passage, the OPC forecasts and raw GRIB data agreed far more often than not, and though we found GRIB wind velocity predictions occasionally slightly off, we experienced OPC's predicted locations of troughs, frontal boundaries, and sea states as nearly spot on. As we sat in our Bermuda anchorage, the long-range forecast showed little advantage in postponing departure. As it happened, Joe, my OPC science officer friend, had hit the nail on the head—the westerly shear had torn apart the easterly wave, and no tropical development was in the picture.

Leaving a Breadcrumb Trail/ Electronic Tracking

Low-orbit satellites also make possible another handy technology, basically a digital version of the fabled breadcrumb trail. *Dragon* and other sailboats competing in the 2009 Marion Bermuda Race carried an iTrack position-reporting system that automatically sent GPS fixes to a downlink station and then on to race headquarters. This "track the fleet" feature provided a nearly real-time view of progress and highlighted the capability of low earth orbit (LEO) satellite communications. This feature allowed regular updated position reports to be displayed on the race's website.

I had also tucked into my seabag a SPOT handheld tracking device, which uses the Globalstar constellation of satellites. Each time I pushed the "fix" button, a position report went to a SPOT downlink; from there, all contacts on my preselected list received the report through email. It functioned flawlessly as a position-relay device. In addition, the unit's portability, water-resistant sealed structure, and low power consumption add to its value. However, the device is not part of the Cospas/Sarsat system (the network of satellite systems used internationally by search-and-rescue agencies); SPOT therefore is not a replacement for a 406 MHz EPIRB (emergency position-indicating radio beacon) or PLB (personal locator beacon). Pressing the SPOT beacon's emergency button sends a distress signal to company headquarters, from which it

Jenifer Clark's Gulf Stream consulting service provides routing information to many Bermuda Race competitors. One of her current charts showing the stream axis and eddies was taped to the bulkhead of Dragon, a Swan 48. Also note the padding for the table and cabin sole, an effort to race-proof the joinery.

is relayed to a rescue coordinator in the region nearest the signal's source. This feature, used as a secondary distress confirmation to corroborate a mayday from a 406 MHz EPIRB, constitutes a belt-and-suspenders approach to distress signaling that seems to make sense (and SPOT reports can be delayed, so only consider it as a backup, never as a prime means of distress signaling). (These electronic safety enhancements are described more fully in Chapter 14.)

Watchkeeping, Collision Avoidance, and a Weather Eye

Dragon's skipper and I divvied up responsibilities: he handled navigation, weather forecast updating, communications, and some forays into gourmet cuisine, while I ran the three-watch system. With six crewmembers (not including the skipper), we had two per watch, with the next team in the rotation designated as the on-call backup in case more hands were needed on deck. Making a delivery with a good-size crew is a real luxury, and in this case, even though seasickness had half of the team feeling more than a little queasy, the efficient watchkeeping routine carried on. To minimize fatigue, we shortened night watches by implementing a 4-4-4-3-3-3-3 schedule that automatically rotated crew through the night watches because of the uneven number of watches:

Time:	(0800-1200)	(1200-1600)	(1600-2000)	(2000-2300)	(2300-0200)	(0200-0500)	(0500-0800)
Watch:	I	II	III	I	II	III	I

In low-visibility sailing such as in this passage, more attentive watchkeeping is needed, and shortened watches provide that payoff. The radar, AIS (automatic identification system, showing positions of nearby ships), and cockpit-mounted VHF certainly enhanced our ability to avoid collision. During our passage, however, we observed that only a small percentage of contacts were transmitting an AIS signal (see Chapter 14, Communications), and radar proved a much more useful collision-avoidance tool.

This was another paperless passage using digital charts. We had a digital display at the helm and another at the nav station, and our position reports were automatically logged. We had paper charts for

backup if needed, however. Having a fulltime navigator provides a tactical advantage you can leverage as you compete with the elements. We demonstrated this on the return passage from Bermuda to the U.S. East Coast. We tracked weather systems and ocean currents and optimized our performance by playing the angles. The vessel's polar plots (see Chapter 12, The Boats We Sail) were factored into the equation as well, and we sought to maximize our boat speed (through the water) as well as current lift (over ground) when choosing our headings.

Before the race, Jenifer Clark provided the Gulf Stream and eddy forecast, which we displayed prominently on the bulkhead. (Leonard Walstad—working with Ken Campbell—and Frank Bohlen provide similar services.) Though the race was over, significant features of the Gulf Stream were likely largely unchanged and offered us a slingshot effect if we could approach the gyres from the right angle. Our navigator weighted each influence and balanced a throttled-back, delivery-level performance with the best lift from wind angles and current set. Each new forecast led to refining the track. We encountered light air during our Gulf Stream crossing, a welcome break from the lumps and bumps of the first few days. Once past the current's north wall, we picked up what would prove to be a 2-knot lift thanks to the accuracy of GPS-based navigation, the accuracy of Clark's eddy forecast, our navigator's tenacity, and the *Dragon* crew's willingness and ability to steer a straight course.

Sail Handling on the Swan 48

The Swan 48's triple-spreader rig is large enough to make a conventional masthead spinnaker more than a handful in the lumpy seas left in the wake of a weak frontal boundary, so I was glad to see the big sloop converted to an asymmetric spinnaker system. The sock-doused kite was easily hoisted aloft before hauling up the funnel shaped "snuffer" that unleashed all its might. We tacked the asymmetric kite to a small mini-sprit stem projection that kept its leading edge away from the turbulence around the furled genoa.

This arrangement worked well until the apparent breeze swung abaft the beam, at which point our solution was to set the conventional spinnaker pole to windward with the kite still tacked to the mini-sprit. Once the pole gear was in place, we simply clipped the afterguy to the tack of the kite and, under complete control, transferred the load to the pole. Moving the kite's tack to windward helped eliminate the stall induced by the mainsail and let us sail a deeper angle. The position of the outboard end of the pole was kept a bit higher than the sprit, allowing the shoulders of the kite to lift, project forward, and fill in clean air.

Hanking on a staysail halyard is a two-hand challenge while the Dragon *crew needs to maintain a grip on the forestay or be tethered to a jackline—doing both is a good idea.*

We could have tacked downwind, but the optimum point of sail with a sprit-tacked reaching spinnaker was not deep enough to make that the best choice. The leftover sloppy sea was not aligned with the new wind direction, and the favored tack kept the apparent breeze just aft of the beam and the seas almost dead astern. Unfortunately, we overlooked one important detail. After swapping the tack from the mini-sprit to the pole, we failed to recognize that the mini-sprit could snag the foot of the spinnaker whenever wave-induced pitch and yaw caused the kite to momentarily dip and fill. During one such oscillation the foot tape overlapped the small sprit, and as the chute refilled, a tear radiated out from the point load of the sprit to an adjacent seam. We "rip stop" repaired the sail and recognized that we should have removed the mini-sprit once the load transfer to the pole had been made.

One other sail-handling observation worth mentioning is the value of an efficient headsail roller-furling system when wind velocity changes are abrupt and significant. To cope with this phenomenon, we used a high-cut number-three genoa like the throttle on a motorboat, dialing back sail area as each pulse of wind rolled through. This let us keep the mainsail reefed and inner forestaysail set even when the breeze momentarily dropped below 20 knots.

The secret to our success was a well-installed headsail furler with an efficient bearing system and lead blocks that added as little friction as possible to the process. Because this vessel has electric cockpit winches, we were especially careful when furling the headsail to avoid any damage from the Herculean tension concealed by a simple button push. Much of the time we could haul in the furling line hand over hand—the sign of a very efficient roller furler.

Less than 70 miles from Newport the warm, moist tropical air gave way to New England's chilly gray fog. This abrupt shift signaled the end of an efficient transit, one in which blue skies and a prevailing reach proved the exception rather than the rule. But during our passage of not quite four days, we tangled with the elements a bit, got to know the traits of an efficient passagemaker, and shared a few sea stories along the way.

THE ARC OF CHANGE: THE SAFETY TRIANGLE IN THE ERA OF OFFSHORE RALLIES

Over three decades I've transitioned from sextant to satellite navigation, swapped long walks carrying heavy water jugs for a high-pressure watermaker, and finally given in to the convenience and common sense of roller-furling headsails. Over the same period I've remained a strong advocate of large anchors and small storm sails, and I continue to marvel at how a well-trimmed sail plan and servopendulum self-steering gear can handle the helm without tormenting the battery bank.

In short, depending on the circumstances, I've both embraced and resisted change. When it comes to welcoming new technology aboard, I liken the process to inviting a friend to join the crew: it's best to know what you're in for ahead of time.

Today, too many boats fitted for *in*shore cruising are headed *off*shore. One look at the growing popularity of rallies such as the Salty Dawg and the Caribbean 1500 tells the tale of how cruising has changed over the past couple of decades. Both of these are organized sailing rallies that leave from Virginia and end in Tortola, British Virgin Islands. Another popular rally leaves from Newport, Rhode Island, for the Caribbean, while still another crosses the Atlantic. We can see the impact of rallies on sailing offshore, and it is a phenomenon with multiple overtones.

The Lure of the Rally

The predecessors of today's passagemakers read the books of pioneering voyagers of their time: Eric Hiscock, Donald Street, Bernard Moitessier, and many others. Their readers and followers viewed their vintage sailing wit and tales of privation as a primer to traditional voyaging. Fast forward to the new century: today, rally sailors take a fast track to the fun and fraternity of passagemaking en masse. We see a Pied Piper appeal in this event, and it draws crews with the promise of a great escape and a common bond. To attract a cruising crowd, nothing is quite like the thought of leaving winter astern and fetching up at a landfall surrounded by blue water and palm trees.

In addition, with a rally like the Caribbean 1500, the organizers' pitch is compelling, and the package experience promises much more than token handholding and a little help with getting your boat from here to there. For example, the 1500's predeparture shoreside support includes inspecting your vessel for readiness, formal training in safety and seamanship, and an expert's weather wisdom. But the passage itself holds a "safety in numbers" appeal for many first-timers anxious about ocean voyaging.

The 1500's founder, Steve Black, always reminded participants that once the docklines are hauled aboard and the fenders stowed, you're on your own. That means you must already have the requisite skills: steering, reefing, navigation, and watchkeeping—and all the basic elements of *seamanship*. Black also en-

🚩 *Veteran rally sailors like Keith Walton, shown here at the nav station on a NAJAD 490, carry less gear lashed to the decks of their boats and have a sail plan with some light-air capability.*

couraged greener crews to recruit more experienced sailors for their first passage to the tropics.

In short, this rally offers a sensible pitch: *why learn the hard way when the rally can make it much easier and a great deal more fun?* True, it's not the answer for every cruiser with dreams of sailing to the tropics, especially those who see an offshore voyage in terms of solitude and independence. But the Caribbean 1500's endgame is not a written test at the end of a course; it's finding yourself anchored safely in a lovely landfall.

In recent years, if we look at the fleet as a whole, we see a couple of important trends. The typical boatowners are a retired or semiretired couple who have focused on careers and their families and have put off going to sea until the time is right for some adventure. Another undeniable trend: this new generation of passagemakers isn't leaving much at home.

The individuals involved in this kind of adventure typically choose boats substantially larger than those who sailed in the wake of Susan and Eric Hiscock. These modern boats brim with antennas and sensors that hint at the technology below. Generator sets, washer/dryers, entertainment centers, air conditioning, and diesel heat have become *de rigueur*. Take a look in the engine room and bilge and you'll see complex systems and rich, fertile ground for Murphy's Law to find a foothold. The old wisdom

of knowing how to maintain all the gear on your boat or being ready to do without it still prevails. But the savvy rally organizers have developed a network of mechanics, riggers, electronics technicians, and others stateside and in the islands to help crews ready their boats for the passage and handle problems once they arrive.

Lugging the comforts of home comes with a downside on a sailboat—and it can play out as a naval architect's nightmare, quantified as an assault on stability and measured as a big increase in the payload/displacement ratio. It begins when the crew stow twice the amount of gear, provisions, and cruising accoutrements as the designer had intended as payload. In addition, a smaller, "cruising-friendly" sail plan and easy-to-handle furling sails that sacrifice shape for furling efficiency provide less power. This means performance is impeded under sail.

Booms are creeping higher and higher to stay clear of the Conestoga wagon–like dodgers, biminis, and side-curtain combinations, which often sit even higher atop an already-high center cockpit. All this adds up to a significant rise in the mainsail's center of effort (CE) with reduced sail area. Meanwhile the waterline is rising too under the weight of gear and possessions, increasing the wetted surface area and its drag.

Modern canoe-body hull shapes have less room below the cabin sole than traditional boats with deeper bilges; this means a large genset, 1200 amp-hours of batteries, a scuba compressor, and other heavy gear are installed higher in the boat. The result is even less sailing ability in a vessel that was a mediocre performer to start with. There is nothing wrong with this when the owner, designer, and builder recognize it as a motorsailer and have engineered it accordingly. Too often, however, despite a larger engine, fuel capacity is not correspondingly increased. (Don't get me wrong: I'm fond of solidly built motorsailers, which are a practical solution to a lack of light-air efficiency.) If many coastal cruisers seriously considered how they use their boats all summer long, they wouldn't be surprised by the quantity of fuel needed to head south in a hurry. After all, the aim of most Caribbean rally boats is to quickly head south and east.

The November weather north of Cape Hatteras is nothing if not fickle. It's a picture of extremes—calms and gales. The only sure thing is that light conditions won't last very long. It's advantageous to depart on the heels of a cold front with a high-pressure system hopefully hanging around for a while. During these precious few days of good weather, the fleet sprints south. And no dillydallying in light air. Most in the rally crank the diesel and push on toward lower latitudes anytime the progress under sail drops below their normal cruising speed.

A secondary challenge complicates this plan: the need to make as much eastward progress as possible before reaching 30 degrees north latitude. At that point you'll likely encounter easterly trade winds pushing waves that can turn a rhumb-line passage into an unwelcome hobbyhorse ordeal.

For the first part of this escape, fuel is the limiting variable. You need enough to power through light conditions and help get across the Gulf Stream, around Cape Hatteras, and east to Route 66—the preferred longitude before turning south. The rally fleet may be involved in a friendly race, but the real race is against the next November gale that will churn the temperate portion of the Atlantic into a fury. The fuel required is correlated with the boat's sailing inefficiency in light air. Unfortunately, too many participants fail to do the math soon enough.

For many, the solution to inefficient light-air sailing involves lashing jerry jugs full of diesel to the lifelines, thus making two mistakes at once. First, the on-deck storage of liquids raises the center of gravity of a vessel, and many modern production cruisers have a rather modest limit of positive stability (LPS) to start with. This number expresses in degrees how deep a capsize a vessel is expected to recover from. (See Chapter 12, The Boats We Sail, for more on stability.)

Some of the vessels in recent rallies to the Caribbean have had an LPS too low to qualify for the Newport Bermuda Race. Many of the boats derive significant form stability from a wide beam and have less lead ballast than traditional boats. Many cruising boats weigh in with about a 30% ballast ratio. Combined with a shoal-draft keel, lighter ballast produces less secondary righting moment and reduces the boat's ability to recover from a deep knockdown. Stacking the decks with fuel jugs and heavy gear further decreases stability.

Yacht designers and boatbuilders consider lashing jugs to the lifelines a serious mistake, pointing out that all it takes is a big breaking sea or a moderate knockdown to rip stanchions from the deck and turn this secondary fuel supply into a big oil slick. (A cruising boat needs fuel tanks capable of meeting its mission; unfortunately designers often underestimate how much motorsailing many cruisers customarily do.) Lashing kayaks, fenderboards, fenders, and fuel tanks to the lifelines might be an acceptable practice on the Intracoastal Waterway (ICW), but if you're headed offshore, it's simply an invitation for big trouble.

Another disturbing trend is the prevalence of derrick-like stern davits carrying large inflatable dinghies on ocean passages. Many owners seem to believe that if the davits are high enough, that will keep the dinghy, radar, solar panels, and communications equipment out of harm's way. The resulting influence—the weight aloft negatively influences the LPS and trim—and windage is substantial, to say nothing of the repercussions of encountering a serious gale at sea. These risks appear to be underestimated.

At a minimum, any sailor who encumbers the decks with gear should have an emergency plan for coping with torn stanchions and/or a damaged transom and how to jettison the carnage in the midst of a serious storm. A naval architect I asked about the practice had this to say: "Imagine a vessel being shoved to leeward by a large wave, and the jerry jugs compressed by the hydraulic force of green water and acceleration. The jug tops will burst open and a plume of fuel will cover the deck just as the stanchions are ripped away."

Self-Reliance in the Blend of Old and New

Self-reliance is the bottom line for offshore voyaging, and the old adage, "You're on your own out there," still holds true—or at least it almost does. Contemporary communications options, such as single-sideband radio and a variety of satellite systems, provide an alternative to complete isolation. In particular, rally advocates tout the upside of staying connected. In essence, you add a network of consultants to your crew list. There's mechanical, electrical, meteorological, and medical advice available on the other end of a communication link, and as long as a crew doesn't see this as a guarantee that someone else is there to get them out of trouble, that's well and good.

It makes sense to use the rally as a high-seas network for technical assistance, but don't count on it to make up for a shortfall in crew competency. True, the twice-a-day position reports, weather briefings, and situation updates are a good safety practice. In bad weather it's a big help to know what conditions others are encountering. However, knowing that when the coastline disappears astern, you really are on your own is part of the original appeal of sailing offshore.

To return where this chapter began, safety at sea involves three legs of a triangle: the seamanship of skipper and crew, the seaworthiness of the boat, and the safety gear aboard. Of these, good seamanship underway is primary. The vessel itself places second in importance, with safety gear coming third but useful in response to a shortfall of boat or seamanship. Nonetheless, the current trend toward overreliance on safety gear—or advice of rally officials—can result in the misleading assumption that we can install the "right" equipment—or advice—to ensure a safe cruise or race, an obviously dangerous belief. This is especially true when we stow the gear and leave it, never using it in a meaningful training context.

Incorrect actions, or inaction when action is called for, upstage vessel failure as the primary cause of most boating mishaps. It stands to reason that for boating safety, developing good seamanship skills should be front and center.

In the words of ocean voyager Dave Martin, *"Adventure is what you make of it and what it makes of you."*

PLANNING IS SEAMANSHIP

Planning and responding are the flip sides of seamanship. These two distinct types of decision making include planning well ahead of time and on-the-fly calls made in the thick of an unfolding situation. Cruising and racing offer abundant opportunities for a skipper to demonstrate both talents, but decisions on the fly are a greater challenge. Take, for example, collision avoidance and close-quarters boat handling. A skipper may have laid a course, read the *Coast Pilot*, and scrutinized the charts well ahead of time, but when he or she encounters a vessel whose bearing remains constant as its range decreases, all that planning takes a backseat and the challenge of the next maneuver becomes paramount. This two-track management style is by no means unique to boating, but it is always amazing how many varied situations can arise on boats that require nearly instantaneous responses. The bottom line? The need to react to what's unfolding around you regularly reshuffles the longer-range plans.

Many sailors upgrading their skippering skills find the decisions required for fitting out and predeparture planning easier than the snap judgments needed when a piece of rigging goes slack with a bang. In the long run you need some facility with both. However, the mariner who recognizes the value of a standing-rigging upgrade before a big cruise is less likely to have to respond to the sound of a cold head fitting exploding or a wire terminal letting go at 0300 in a gale-swept sea.

Much of this book is intended to help you prepare for making decisions on the fly, as may be required on any waterway from the Mississippi River to the Malacca Strait. In this chapter, however, we look at predeparture planning for safe seamanship, the practice of which is most critical for offshore passages that take you far beyond sheltered waters and safe anchorages.

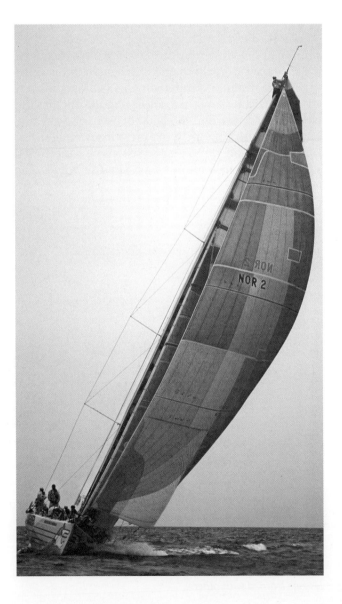

Around-the-world racers daily immerse themselves in "Don't try this at home" feats of sailing and seamanship. Nonetheless, they have a pretty good safety record, a testimony to crew agility, careful training, and advances in naval architecture. This Volvo Ocean Race crew agreed that the leg around Cape Horn was nowhere near as rough as the rounding of Cape Hatteras had been. When planning your own passages, anticipate weather extremes and consider ways to avoid them along with how you would handle being caught out there.

ARE YOU PREPARED?

A sailor's skill level is correlated with the seaworthiness of their vessel, on the one hand, and how well they fare in difficult situations, on the other. It's the safety triangle again: safety gear is wonderful, but it's the shortest leg of the triangle. If your seamanship is good and your boat sound, you're unlikely ever to need that safety gear.

In the same week in June 2010, safety-at-sea advocate John Bonds died quietly in his sleep aboard his treasured J/35, *Alliance*, and 16-year-old adventure sailor Abby Sunderland narrowly escaped death while battling a winter gale in the Southern Ocean. She was rescued thanks to two EPIRB signals, an Australian aircraft search-and-rescue effort, and a French fishing vessel that plucked her from her foundering 40-footer *Wild Eyes*. Like bookends for the range of ways to approach ocean sailing, these two sailors give us a look at very different perspectives on handling risk.

For decades, Captain John Bonds, U.S. Navy (ret.), combined his sense of organization with an academic's keen reasoning. Both qualities figured in his belief in effective training. Underlying his sailing ethos was a fundamental view that sailors should understand what they are getting into and have a realistic awareness of how to cope with the most likely challenges. He spearheaded US Sailing's nationally sanctioned Safety at Sea Seminar programs, often serving as the

John Bonds—heading to sea on his last ocean passage in June 2009—epitomized the modern sailor: a racer/cruiser ready to embrace technology, savor time at sea, and share lessons learned with others.

voice of reason in balancing the real risks of going to sea against the unwarranted worries of the overly risk-averse who never go to sea at all.

Abby Sunderland's quest had only a small safety margin for the unexpected. Her solo voyage had to ignore the requirement for constant watchkeeping in the International Navigation Rules. In addition, her attempt to cross the infamous Southern Ocean coincided with winter in the southern hemisphere, a time when storm-bred winds and seas are at their worst, temperatures plunge, and hypothermia and fatigue saps the crew's energy. Summiting Everest without oxygen would have made more sense than Abby's voyage plan.

Bonds would have been the first to defend the right of an individual to choose when and how to go to sea, but he'd also question the wisdom of a 16-year-old setting off on such a hazardous quest. Abby's parents had earlier been praised by the media for the success of their son's risky singlehanded voyage around the world; now they were criticized for their daughter's mishap. Some believe that teenage solo sailing is no more inherently dangerous than teen driving, arguing youth have the right to drive or set sail to attain a personal victory for the record book. Others think it's a stretch to equate driving and solo voyaging, pointing out that most parents don't give a kid with a shiny new driver's license the keys to a Corvette and encourage a cross-country drive. As it turned out, Abby Sunderland's voyage was more like a NASCAR race than a transition from a learner's permit to driving her mother's car to school.

Whether you're for or against the right of adolescents to strive to set a record, it's worth wondering how John Bonds might have influenced Abby Sunderland. He'd probably have invited her to sail as crew in a Bermuda Race, and if all went well he might have encouraged her to join a doublehanded Bermuda run or sprint to Hawaii the following summer. In the meantime, he would have shared with her his fascination with weather and what it means to tackle the Southern Ocean.

The summer before John died, I sailed from Bermuda to the U.S. with him and an able crew aboard a well-outfitted Swan 48 (described in Chapter 1). We faced a potentially volatile weather pattern but had multiple sources of forecast data and meteorological advice. We also had our crew's experience to fall back on. John's own considerable weather acumen greatly influenced our decision when to leave Bermuda. His prediction of a rough but less than gale-force northeasterly harmonized with Ocean Prediction Center (OPC) data, and that was the weather we had in our passage back to the States.

What's the larger point? An important part of

🚩 *Ice and gales stalk Southern Ocean sailors year-round. During the winter months, temperatures hover just above freezing.*

planning a passage involves understanding all conditions you might encounter in an area in a given season. Bad weather between Bermuda and the U.S. can make for tough going, but it's nothing compared with a winter Roaring Forties/Furious Fifties passage across the South Pacific. There, daylight is short and the risk of hypothermia pervasive, and these two constraints make simple reefing efforts much more demanding. Cold front passages are brutal, and pre-front squalls can double the wind velocity in mere seconds. The Southern Ocean is an area that sailors try to avoid during the winter months. It therefore seems misguided to try to justify a lengthy passage through these latitudes at the worst time of year just to break a record.

By no means averse to risk, John Bonds had held command in the U.S. Navy and understood mission-first logic. But he was a cerebral sailor who leveraged technology to obtain weather data and oceanography information. A consummate passage planner, Bonds worked with pilot charts, *Sailing Directions*, and Gulf Stream data to better understand the conditions ahead. Although summer usually brought the best weather for a transit between Bermuda and the States, Bonds knew that by early July the risk of tropical storm formation began to rise. With a crew of seven and a three-watch rotation, our wet, lumpy passage on the Swan 48 caused no undue fatigue, and mild air temperatures brought no risk of hypothermia.

Abby Sunderland wasn't as fortunate. As a singlehander she faced short days, many hours of darkness, and pervasive cold, damp, overcast weather interspersed with occasional sunny gales. In addition, a knockdown or capsize was likely when low-pressure systems and angry frontal boundaries rolled through. Fortunately, Abby survived her ordeal. Unfortunately, this young woman never had a chance to sail with a

🚩 *The fetch (or area over which a wind blows) in the Roaring Forties and Furious Fifties turbocharges the waves circling the Southern Ocean. The average seas appear more benign from the bridge of a 500-foot ship than from the deck of a 40-footer.*

mariner like John Bonds, which might have widened her perspective and shaped her judgment.

Adventure or Ordeal?

Precruise preparation provides the best chance to prevent a great adventure from turning into an ordeal. This is when to put the crews' cumulative skills to good use to stack the odds in your favor. We'll look now at the three key components of preparation: outfitting the boat, training the crew, and developing a sensible itinerary. Keep in mind the following guidelines during the frantic rush to get underway:

- A brand-new boat is by no means a boat that's ready to go to sea.
- Offshore experience is best acquired by degrees.
- Have a contingency shorter-duration itinerary to fall back on in case the primary itinerary becomes too hectic.
- Avoid gambling with winter gales or the height of hurricane season.
- Early spring and late fall low-pressure systems can also usher in storms or gales as malevolent as hurricanes.

IS THE BOAT PREPARED?

When it comes to fitting out their boats, many experienced voyagers have to balance priorities against a realistic budget. Before deciding exactly what to add to your checklist, however, do you understand the material condition of your boat? That puts you in a better position to decide what parts of the refit are essential and those that are secondary projects.

Obviously, the primary projects involve the vessel's ability to stay afloat—its structure and stability—and the boat's ability to get from point A to point B safely and efficiently, which includes the condition of the rig, sail plan, and engine. This means your to-do list begins with a question: "Is the boat I own or plan to buy up to the challenge of the voyage I'm planning?"

A "no" or "maybe" answer leads to two possible conclusions. You may plan to upgrade the shortcomings of the vessel or significantly downgrade your sailing/cruising plans.

The foremost concern must be the boat's stability and structural strength—no sidetracking into refrigeration systems, a bow thruster, or furling mainsail. In addition, it's dangerous to base your judgment of a vessel's suitability solely on the boat's design and original construction because without intervention a boat's structural integrity never improves over time. When voyaging in an older vessel, wise captains have a capable marine surveyor or boatbuilder evaluate the material condition of the boat.

Deciding whether a given boat is fit for a given voyage often involves a gray area rather than a black-or-white choice. Still, there are a few signposts in this otherwise nuanced realm. For example, consider the inshore-appropriate sailboats seen at boat shows around the world. In this growing armada, we see high-volume, low-ballast-to-displacement-ratio (B/D) sailboats featuring a shoal draft and a plethora of big hatches and large windows in a relatively flimsy trunk cabin. Although comfortable for coastal cruis-

ing in sheltered waters, these boats are vulnerable to damage from a deep knockdown or large breaking seas, either of which can deliver a lethal blow to any underbuilt boat. Realistically, a refit won't address such deficiencies.

Chapter 12 covers boat design and construction, but for now, suffice it to say that it's difficult to retrofit a lightly ballasted sailboat with a poorly reinforced deckhouse and large windows. It's the wrong choice for ocean crossing. Owners of such a boat are better off selling it or trading it in and replacing it with a more modest but better-built boat designed for offshore voyaging—or limiting the cruise plan to more protected, near-coastal waters. The third alternative is to play the odds and gamble that the weather remains in your favor. You hope to get from point A to point B before the bottom falls out of the barometer—a risky gamble at best.

I've seen such a gamble play out too many times, such as every fall when East Coast sailors head for the Caribbean. They get ready to dive through the fickle weather window separating hurricane season from the season of brutal North Atlantic fall gales. The goal is to begin the offshore passage south and east on the heels of a cold front with a high-pressure system in the works and no tropical weather stirring up the Atlantic, as discussed in Chapter 1. However, this is like the search for the ideal stock investment—elusive! Many sailors discover this weather window isn't as prevalent, easy to recognize, or guaranteed as they'd hoped. Nevertheless, many cruisers latch on to this "get out of Dodge" strategy and dive in at the first likely looking forecast window to cross the Gulf Stream en route to the Caribbean. Their boats are usually overloaded with jerry cans of diesel, dinghy davits, and derrick-like deck protrusions. To some degree, their success hinges on stability in the midlatitude autumn weather patterns.

The assumption that you can always avoid bad weather is a myth, and the downside can have dire consequences. A closer look at this "sprint south" approach will help explain the challenges potentially encountered.

First, a beamy, shoal-draft, lightly ballasted, high-volume sailboat has a fairly low limit of positive stability (LPS), defined as the heel angle at which the righting moment becomes zero and the boat is as likely to turn upside down as it is to return to an upright position. The consensus among naval architects and ocean voyagers is that oceangoing sailboats less than 50 feet long should have a LPS of no less than 120 degrees.

Many modern production sailboats, especially those designed predominantly as coastal cruisers, have an LPS of 110 or a little less in normal trim.

Before heading offshore, their crews overload them with gear and supplies stowed above the center of gravity. The result is a further elevation of the center of gravity, peeling another 5 degrees or more off the LPS. If the boat you currently own or are considering purchasing combines wide beam, shoal draft, and a very low ballast ratio (B/D less than 33%), it's LPS will likely be less than 110 degrees. If the designer's calculations are not available, the boat can be inclined by a local measurer who does this service regularly as a part of the US Sailing handicapping system. In this measurement process, the boat is heeled a few degrees and its righting moment is calculated; these data are compared with hull shape geometry, and an accurate measure of the vessel's limit of positive stability is attained. This is not the only measure of seaworthiness, but it is one of the most important.

On the other hand, loading up your sailboat like a Conestoga wagon works for an inshore or coastal itinerary, such as the Intracoastal Waterway (ICW), where you won't encounter rogue waves. You can find plenty of places in Long Island Sound, the Chesapeake Bay, or the ICW to hide from the regular autumn nor'easters that challenge those caught offshore. You don't need a vessel capable of rounding Cape Horn if you've defined your goal as meandering up and down the estuaries of the East and Gulf coasts. Indeed, for this sort of cruising, your shoal draft boat is ideal.

■ *Preparations to head south from the U.S. East Coast—or to head to sea from anywhere—always entail a battle against the list of last-minute little jobs and loose ends that need squaring away. Painting marks on the all-chain rode, as this crew is in the midst of, is about the last item remaining on this crew's list, and their moderately proportioned, seakindly sloop is a good choice for the passage ahead.*

■ *Good weather routing at the start of a fall Caribbean transit may give you a couple of decent days to get across the Gulf Stream from the U.S., but heading offshore with your decks brimming with obstacles to a breaking sea is asking for trouble. It's a game of chance, and the deck is stacked in the ocean's favor.*

Again, your first job is to see how the vessel you own or intend to build or buy stacks up against your intended cruise. If you lack the technical skills, have a good marine surveyor go over the boat, and ask point blank if the vessel is strong enough for offshore or transoceanic use. Some surveyors don't like to be pinned down, but most will offer an opinion.

Sail inventory is another key consideration. In addition to good working sails for 10- to 20-knot breezes, an offshore-bound skipper should have sails to handle the extremes: heavy-weather or storm canvas for gales, and lightweight, deep-draft sails for 6- to 9-knot breezes that would otherwise require using the engine. Standing and running rigging, winches, deck hardware, and furling gear are of primary concern. In addition, you must assess the operational ability of all the components. (Chapter 7 looks at sails and sail-handling systems.)

Assessing the Boat

European authorities on seamanship have categorized small craft according to the conditions they are designed and built to handle. These authorities' efforts resulted in a four-tier rating system based on a stability index that considers a boat's resistance to capsize, recovery from a knockdown, flooding potential, and other factors. The European system also mandates certain strength-of-build characteristics, or scantlings, based on the pressure loads imposed by specific sea states.

Chapter 12 covers these International Standards Organization (ISO) design and construction standards and their considerable influence on modern vessel design. For now, the important point is to recognize that sailboats are designed with specific uses, and since most boat buyers aren't packing up and heading across oceans, boats designed for inshore waters are most common.

Likewise, racing sailors refer to guidelines set up by the International Sailing Federation (ISAF), augmented by US Sailing standards. Like the ISO recreational-craft directive, the ISAF categorizes recommendations and requirements according to the wind and seas a vessel is likely to experience. Category 0 is the most extreme ISAF race designation, including around-the-world racing and high-latitude transoceanic events. At the other extreme, Categories 4 through 6 involve close-to-shore, short-duration, daylight races. Unlike the ISO standards, which address design and construction, the ISAF rules and recommendations are weighted more toward how ves-

---

CONSIDERATIONS WHEN MATCHING VOYAGE AND VESSEL (SEE CHAPTER 12 FOR MORE DETAIL)

Voyage Classifications and Examples

Expeditionary: High-latitude, transoceanic voyaging—adverse conditions likely; ISAF Category 0. Cape Horn rounding, Atlantic to Pacific via the Northwest Passage.

Offshore: Trade-wind and temperate transoceanic voyaging; ISAF Category 1. Trade-wind circumnavigation, Bermuda and Hawaii races, etc.

Coastal: Summer ocean conditions, safe havens nearby; ISAF Category 2. Nearshore cruise from New England to Florida, Florida to the Bahamas, San Francisco to San Diego, cruising and racing on the Great Lakes, etc.

Inshore: Open water with protective shorelines; ISAF Category 3. Cruising the Intracoastal Waterway, Long Island Sound, the Chesapeake Bay, Puget Sound, inland lakes, etc.

Expeditionary Voyage Vessel Priorities
- High limit of positive stability (LPS), hull and deck structural strength
- Strong keel attachment, rig, and rudder scantlings
- Long-term remote operability, extreme durability to minimize repairs in remote waters, extra

tankage, permanent dodger, redundant systems, capable of carrying greater payload
- Uniform upgrade in quality and capacity of all systems (see "The One-Size Larger Rule" in Chapter 1, gear with top-quality fabrication, engineered for longer run times, etc.)

Offshore Voyage Vessel Priorities
- Stability and strength tempered with performance under sail
- Efficiency in a wide range of sailing conditions
- Accommodations underway and at anchor

Coastal Voyage Vessel Priorities
- Shoal draft, high volume, emphasis on form stability
- Lighter scantlings
- Optimized for zero-heel accommodations
- Easy handling sail plan

Inshore Voyage Vessel Priorities
- Lighter scantlings, lower limit of positive stability
- Optimized for lighter winds and smaller seas
- Assumption that seeking safe shelter is the heavy-weather strategy

 In addition to setting standards for boat preparation, the ISAF Special Regulations define what onboard training a skipper and crew must have annually. Sharing knowledge and offshore experience helps new crew evolve into seasoned sailors. Here Butch Ulmer aboard the J/130 Dragonfly *trains Safety at Sea Seminar participants how to properly reef a mainsail (see photo on page 164 for the completed reef).*

sels and crews should be equipped. For example, the safety-gear requirement for Cat 0 and Cat 1 events is much more extensive than for Cat 4, 5, or 6 racing, since offshore events are more challenging for the vessel and crew. (Recent changes in ISAF structure and stability requirements have shifted toward using the ISO four-tier system mentioned above.)

Clearly there is a big advantage to starting with a clean slate and buying the right boat for the job at hand. Shoppers must be able to discern boat-show spin from fact and grasp why the right boat for one person may be the wrong boat for another. The accompanying sidebars on matching voyages to vessels, and boat buying tips offer many factors to consider.

PREPARING THE CREW

Crew skills can save the day, but more importantly, a skilled crew can prevent a problem from developing in the first place. This also shows us the value of *proactive seamanship* at all times. We could unknowingly be running into shoal water just when a large ground swell is in play. We could be getting knocked down by a gust in a vigorous frontal passage. Or, we find ourselves watching the mast go over the side because we failed to perform a simple cotter pin check. In such cases a lack of crew preparedness can cause

BOAT BUYING RULES OF THUMB

- ◆ Match vessel attributes with the physical challenges of the voyage.
- ◆ For ocean passagemaking, a smaller, better-built boat trumps a larger, less structurally sound, less stable vessel.
- ◆ An inshore cruise does not require an offshore-capable vessel.
- ◆ Too large a vessel can hamper any cruising experience.
- ◆ Set aside 20% of your boat-buying budget for fitting out.
- ◆ Understand the costs of complexity (maintenance, energy demand, reliance).

even a well-designed, well-built, well-outfitted vessel to come to grief. Remember, seamanship is the longest leg of the safety triangle.

Seamanship involves preparation but it can be tested abruptly. When a boarding sea or a foredeck snafu intrudes on the job at hand, seconds count, and it's often a sailor's first reaction that sets up a pathway to either success or a chain-reaction disaster.

Sometimes warning bells sound first. An intuitive question may arise in the back of your mind,

Don't avoid breezy days. Rather, set a smaller headsail and make sure reefing lines are run before getting underway. By sailing in progressively more challenging conditions, a crew becomes better able to handle heavy weather. It looks like this boat's anchor rode has been left to dry on the foredeck—but it had best be stowed before the boat reaches open water and starts to pitch and roll, or it might wind up over the side. The BBQ hanging on the stern might also benefit by being stowed if the crew is headed out of San Francisco Bay.

A good shipmate is capable on deck, is willing to share galley chores, and above all possesses the good humor to bridge good days and bad.

caused by a new sound such as a halyard running over a sheave with a bad bearing or an exhaust system receiving a little less water. If such signals are ignored, problems are bound to occur. But it takes time and experience to build the skills to be attuned to the warning signs and precursor symptoms that demand the skipper and crew to make fast, competent decisions in response to the need of the moment.

Conditions at sea are always changing, and an action of sound seamanship under one set of circumstances can be pure folly in another. Take the challenge of crossing a shallow bar or skirting a shoaling coastline. Boaters often see ocean swells and wind-driven waves as the same thing; they equate light winds with flat seas, especially if most of their time under sail has been inshore. They might fail to account for a ground swell spawned by a storm hundreds of miles away that sends long-period rollers of pure energy through water whose surface is not ruffled by wind. As these swells reach shallow water, however, they change from benign undulations to tumultuous plunging seas that threaten to capsize and dismast anything in their way. This is why seasoned sailors have deep respect for areas such as San Francisco's Potato Patch, the Santa Clara River mouth off Ventura, California, and the infamous stretch of coastline between Diamond and Frying Pan Shoals off North Carolina. Merging seafaring knowledge with boat-handling skill is at the heart of crew preparation.

This type of crew awareness is best developed through a combination of experience underway and formal training. The "school of the sea" makes demands just like any shoreside curriculum. In fact, we can think of inshore sailing and cruising in protected bodies of water as primary and secondary education, while crossing large expanses of open ocean is the equivalent of a higher education. Few would try to progress directly from eighth-grade algebra to college-level differential calculus, and it's just as unrealistic and challenging to attempt a crossing of the North Atlantic as your first bluewater exposure. The skipper's role includes controlling the steepness of the learning curve. Such decisions call for an understanding of the capabilities of all on board.

Some cruising sailors make the mistake of stopping sailing when they are preparing for an extended voyage, but this sacrifices important crew training underway. Some spend a year or more tethered to a boatyard or marina, rebuilding the boat and gearing up for the impending cruise. This is okay if the upcoming voyage starts with small steps, such as a prolonged shakedown cruise before an ocean crossing, or if the crew has plenty of bluewater experience. But if the crew is green when the deadline draws near for a midautumn escape from the clutches of approaching nor'easters, the big question should be not whether the watermaker, bow thruster, and entertainment system will work but whether the crew has the skills to handle the challenges ahead.

A too-steep learning curve can significantly dampen the dream of the great escape. Skippers with less experience are better off with a seasoned crew during the initial passage; even better, before making the jump to ocean passagemaking, the less experienced benefit from a season living aboard and coastal cruising. Classroom and sailing school training can help, too; Chapter 3 describes training options. Those who train with experts serve an apprenticeship of sorts, and that helps them avoid mistakes caused primarily by inexperience.

All cruisers overtly or inadvertently set the redline on their "precaution meter." Folks meandering up and down the Intracoastal Waterway may find their meter pegged by a brisk northerly gusting down the Albemarle Sound. On the other hand, adventure sailors Dave and Jaja Martin circumnavigated in a beefed-up 25-footer, had kids along the way, and went on to sail a 34-footer across the North Atlantic and into the Arctic, savoring the gale-swept waters of Iceland, Spitsbergen, and Greenland. Those willing to endure more trying conditions certainly get to the more remote outposts of globe, but that doesn't mean they enjoy their adventures any more than a coastal cruiser exploring a tranquil estuary.

The key lies in aligning your precaution meter with your "skill scale." The inshore sailor may see

OUTFITTING PRIORITIES FOR PASSAGEMAKING

- ◆ Structural issues prioritized according to the survey
- ◆ Rigging and sail inventory upgrades
- ◆ Mechanical propulsion reliability (enhanced with preventive maintenance)
- ◆ Added gear (must have vs. nice to have, budget permitting)
- ◆ Match onboard energy system with power requirements of equipment to be added

gale-force gusts of 45 knots in thunderstorms, but it's a different benchmark of experience to wrestle with a full-blown gale offshore, with several days' worth of sustained 45-knot wind speeds and a thousand miles of fetch which builds a mountainous wave train. We're always called on to reset our skill scale to match conditions.

If all your boat-handling experience comes from inshore sailing, it's difficult to know what to expect from offshore conditions. A key difference between 1,200 miles of bays and estuaries and 1,200 miles of uninterrupted ocean is the presence or absence of an unfettered fetch and the effect of wind on an open expanse of sea. Many West Coast sailors acquire offshore experience while coastal cruising, gaining an

Flatwater meandering through coastal waters can be very rewarding. Big seas seldom threaten, and it is usually possible to find shelter from high winds. But good navigation and watchkeeping are a must, with close attention to shoal-water risks and collision avoidance.

advantage over East Coast sailors. Regardless of location, however, regular extended cruising helps prepare sailors for seagoing challenges they're bound to face eventually. For example, those who usually sail in sheltered waters but plan to head offshore would do well to race or cruise with others in ocean conditions. Ideally, they could crew for a capable skipper with a well-designed and well-fitted vessel, thereby serving an old fashioned apprenticeship. No amount of additional gear or sheltered-water training makes up for a lack of even incremental exposure to the sea.

POSSIBLE VESSEL AND CREW EMERGENCY SCENARIOS —BE PREPARED

Crew Overboard
(See Chapter 13 for specifics on how to deal with these.)

- Assign a spotter; provide buoyancy, a marker, and a light to the person in the water (PIW).
- Mark the PIW position electronically.
- Begin a recovery maneuver.
- If the PIW is not seen immediately, issue a MAYDAY call.

Collision or Allision
This is with another boat or with a bridge, pier, or other fixed object, or floating object such as a container.

- Check for flooding.
- Treat injuries.
- Communicate the situation.
- Evaluate the vessel's seaworthiness.
- Amend the voyage plan if necessary.

Grounding

- Attempt to turn toward deeper water.
- Check for flooding.
- Heel the vessel with crew on the boom (hauled out with a forward guy) and power to deeper water.
- Set an anchor to windward and a second one toward deeper water, and power, heel, and kedge the vessel toward deeper water.
- In some situations, try reverse gear.

Dismasting

- Check the crew for injury.
- Recover what can be saved.
- Unpin or cut rigging and jettison the remainder.
- Implement jury-rigging.
- Set up emergency antenna.

Daysails can lead to overnight cruising and experience with sail handling at sea and watchkeeping.

Once at sea, skippers should try to avoid a "clipboard mindset." The challenge is not only to develop an optimal onboard routine and garner the crew's respect but also to respond to all manner of minor and major unexpected intrusions. A vicious squall, grounding, or even flooding can quickly change the priorities, and skippers must be ready to respond.

To develop these important skills, we recommend developing a less formal version of the ship's bills used by professional mariners and the navies of the world. These guidelines help orchestrate the response to any emergency situation. For example, personal qualification skills (PQS) are enumerated, and each crewmember is trained and signed off on according to specific qualifications. For example, just as damage control is a big deal on a warship, sailors must learn to deal with fire, flooding, and other disasters along with their myriad associated problems and their solutions. Recreational sailors don't carry clipboards and aren't seeking sign-offs in their PQS booklet, but they too need to "learn the boat," and skippers need to know each crewmember's extent of knowledge and skill.

Most of us are unlikely to write a formal "yacht bill." Still, the open-ocean, long-range sailor needs to develop a game plan for unlikely but potentially devastating scenarios, such as those given in the accompanying sidebar, Possible Vessel and Crew Damage Scenarios—Be Prepared.

In addition to the scenarios listed in the accompanying sidebar, plan for responding to rudder or keel loss, fire, flooding, and for abandoning ship (see Chapter 13 for more specifics on dealing with these situations). Developing these procedures as part of your cruise planning helps ensure you have the gear and spare parts you'll need. With this planning you and your crew will also have reviewed the steps to take in these emergencies. Whether it's replacing a raw-water pump or going aloft to clear a fouled halyard, some member of the crew needs to be ready to tackle the job.

Skippers must decide how much training to provide to those aboard. For the average daysail, briefly review potential hazards such as the boom, slippery areas on deck, the location of the PFDs, and instructions for donning them. Agile crew may roam the boat, but direct passengers unaccustomed to a boat's motion to more confined, better-protected areas such as the cockpit. It's a good habit also to review navigation basics, including an update on where the vessel is headed, anticipated weather, and what sights, obstacles, and experiences are likely to unfold. Those sailing the vessel need to know how to respond to a crew-overboard situation and what gear is used in the rescue. All on board should be told how the rescue procedure for a PIW would be carried out and should examine the rescue gear used. With longer, farther cruises, crew knowledge should grow accordingly. Practice crew-overboard recovery drills regularly to test and fine-tune the crew's skills.

With the doublehanded crews that are common today, the skills described above are more challenging. One-person watches provide less capacity to cope with something going awry when there is so much on board to keep track of. The best plan is to prevent incidents rather than respond to them. Skippers need to focus more, for example, on reducing the risk of a squall-induced knockdown or crew being washed over the side by a breaking sea.

Preventive measures such as reefing before a front hits, using a sturdy anchor rather than a "lunch hook," and wearing a harness clipped to a jackline on the foredeck at night help preclude an incident demanding an "all hands" response. The smaller the crew, the more careful a skipper must be when carrying out major sail changes and other labor-intensive acts. Power furling and winches can help a shorthanded crew handle sail area, but with added complexity comes more concern about maintenance and what happens when things go wrong.

Ideally, the fitting-out process is completed about the same time the skipper is confident the crew is ready to go. The right season for the passage is nearing, and weather systems have been scrutinized. Safety drills have been carried out, and every crewmember knows what to do at the helm if a shipmate falls overboard or a piece of standing rigging lets go with a resounding bang.

The ideal voyage begins in fair weather and incrementally exposes the crew to more and more rigorous conditions. But in reality, as soon as any small craft heads to sea, the crew needs to be ready for whatever occurs. The accompanying sidebar provides a checklist of prevoyage preparedness.

Chapter 3 discusses the desirable capabilities of skipper and crew in greater detail. For our purposes here, we now look at the third major planning component: making sure your itinerary is a good match for your boat and crew.

PREPARING THE ITINERARY

Obviously it's more difficult to prepare for a three-month Caribbean adventure than a three-week summer cruise down the bay. All cruises begin with an initial vision of time and distance, but this undergoes a nautical version of "reality therapy" as events unfold. What's needed is a practicality litmus test that sorts

---

PREVOYAGE PREPAREDNESS

Communications
- Mutually develop and agree on the voyage plan.
- Determine the core expertise of crewmembers.
- Have regular "how are we doing" discussions.

Crew Skill Acquisition
- Don't underestimate the satisfaction and value of developing core competencies.
- Build crew skills or recruit other talent.
- Set a timeline for the crew to develop skills.
- Encourage and acquire a blend of fitness, agility, and cerebral learning.
- Go sailing to sea-trial the lessons learned.

Evolving the Game Plan
- Iron out any early misassumptions and recalibrate the departure date.
- If necessary, amend the cruise itinerary.
- Keep asking yourself whether you want to survive an ordeal or enjoy a meaningful cruise.

Trial Runs and Dress Rehearsals
- Get the boat launched and commissioned as soon as possible.
- Sea-trial new skills and gear and turn weekend cruises into fun training opportunities.
- Determine who excels at specific tasks.
- Don't shy away from bad weather; gradually increase exposure to heavy weather sailing.

Train for the Change
- Sail to new landfalls close to home.
- Acclimate to overnight sailing—flat water first.
- Make reefing, anchoring, and dinghy handling second nature.
- Sample the challenges of 24/7 watchkeeping and navigation.

---

the feasible plan from the pipe dreams. Experienced mariners do their own voyage sanity check, while less experienced sailors preparing for their first major cruise often seek a second opinion. But in all cases good seamanship begins with our choice of itinerary.

Planning a passage around climate variations and weather patterns is a skill worth developing. It involves collecting weather data from several key sources. Seasonal climate changes have a pronounced effect on weather. And those crossing oceans need to understand when and where the calms and gales move with these changes in season. Climate is a long period variation in what's going on in the lower atmosphere, and weather is a short period sequel.

Planning a cruise includes looking over both large- and small-scale charts and developing a feel for what lies ahead. One of the biggest challenges is matching available passage time with the distances to be covered. Many veteran passagemakers say that after you first plan your route, cut that distance in half and you'll have a much happier cruise.

During the pre-departure planning process a savvy skipper takes a keen interest in how near-term and long-range forecasts evolve. This is a chance to become familiar with a continuously morphing data stream. You'll constantly check the information, and depending upon the evolving scenario, you may find it necessary to modify your itinerary or planned departure date.

The best preparation is to build enough time in your schedule to be able to inch your way into the voyage rather than plunging in with a dangerous late-season departure with a risk of punishing weather systems. Only the foolhardy ignore climate and seasonal weather changes. Planning too aggressive a schedule and an inflexible itinerary practically guarantees you'll ruin a potentially wonderful cruising experience. Chapter 10 discusses weather planning in much more detail.

Finally, when planning your itinerary, time is always the limiting variable. Avoid overcommitment. If you're always in a big hurry and prefer time at sea to exploring new landfalls, go racing rather than cruising. But if you're cruising, don't make it a perpetual sprint. Those who plan too much too fast will inevitably have bad weather or other factors that put

them behind schedule, and falling further and further behind schedule only induces stress while increasing the risks.

Building an Itinerary: A U.S. East Coast Example

When it comes to putting together a cruising itinerary, the old saying about understanding what you're getting into resonates loudly. I've adopted a procedure in which I tally up the individual legs, giving each a carefully considered difficulty rating, much as alpine ski trails are rated. Skiers understand how conditions affect each trail beyond its rating, however. Perfectly groomed packed powder can make a "black diamond" trail friendly to an intermediate skier, but an ice glaze under a thin dusting of snow can turn a less steep "blue intermediate" trail into a miserable experience for the same skier. The same goes for weather conditions affecting stretches of water. In the accompanying table I use the same rating colors for the legs of a hypothetical passage from Maine to the Florida Keys or the Bahamas as green (easy), blue (moderate), black (difficult), and double diamond (hazardous), keeping in mind that bad weather always ups the difficulty level. This itinerary spans 20 degrees of longitude and offers a special nautical experience to sailors and powerboaters eager for treasures of a bountiful coastline, perhaps over a 12-month voyage. Each leg has its own nuances that raise or lower the reading on our difficulty scale.

Starting in June, the great escape can be kicked off with a leisurely run Down East with a respite

RATING OF PASSAGES ON HYPOTHETICAL EAST COAST CRUISE

Maine to Boston: ocean swells and a granite coastline	blue–black
Boston to Long Island Sound: the Cape Cod Canal, currents and bays	green–blue
New York and the Jersey shoreline: the East River and sand shoals	green–blue
Delaware and Chesapeake Bays	green–blue
To Beaufort, NC via the Intracoastal Waterway or	green–blue
Heading south outside via Cape Hatteras	black–double diamond
Beaufort, NC to Beaufort, SC via the ICW	green–blue
In and out of ICW inlets	blue–black
Florida on the ICW	green–blue
Crossing the Gulf Stream to the Bahamas	blue–black

from the heat of summer. The cruise might include a leisurely gunkholing trek in Long Island Sound or around Martha's Vineyard or Maine. Summer ends early in the Northeast, however. As August turns to September, those who have pressed on to Nova Scotia or Newfoundland experience shortening days and more frequent spells of bad weather. Summer southwesterlies afford an easy run east, but when it's time to turn around, they become a headwind pushing up short, lumpy seas—and the demeanor on board can change. Making the transit south on the backs of post-cold front northerlies can be a good game plan if you have enough time banked to make waiting for a favorable breeze feasible.

Although late-season hurricanes are a possibility, October is a good time to be in the Chesapeake Bay, a great cruising ground known for A+ anchorages. But be careful not to overstay your visit. Dwindling daylight and November gales will soon shut the weather window and lessen the appeal of either a coastal or offshore passage south.

The climate in the part of the world you cruise sets the stage for how you handle your boat, the priority you place on safe havens, and the attention you pay to long-range forecasts.

TURNING A PLAN INTO A GOOD PLAN: PLANNING RESOURCES

A key part of preparing for a voyage is imagining challenges you've yet to experience, landfalls yet to be viewed, and parts of the ocean and coasts you have yet to reach. To help build a picture of what lies ahead, use the following resources. (See Chapter 8, Navigation, for more details.)

◆ Pilot charts—small-scale, month-by-month, ocean-sector-by-ocean-sector graphic compilations of meteorological and oceanographic data including wind speed and direction probabilities, sea states, and ocean currents—yield valuable insights for seasonal passagemaking. Remember the wind speeds and directions shown are averages; squall-spawned gusts can be much higher.

◆ Sailing Directions and Coast Pilots provide written descriptions of currents, tidal ranges, confluences and influences of land, and locations and hazards of shoal ground.

◆ The National Data Buoy Center's website and other NOAA locations provide cumulative wind data by region. When the Internet is available, I use three crucial websites. The first is the Ocean Prediction Center at www.opc.ncep.noaa.gov, a vital source of weather analysis and forecast information for U.S. coastal and North Atlantic and Pacific waters. The National Data Buoy Center (NDBC) at www.ndbc.noaa.gov offers near-real-time wind speeds, sea states, and oceanographic data for coastal and offshore regions. During hurricane season the National Hurricane Center (NHC)

is a critically important asset for detailed descriptive and graphic profiles of developing and mature tropical waves, depressions, tropical storms, and hurricanes, at www.nhc.noaa.gov.

◆ Cruising guides, bulletins, and articles are informative but not as well vetted as government publications. Be careful using some of these nongovernmental resources. You're asking for trouble if you just blindly plug waypoints from a guidebook into your chartplotter and check off the "done" box on your navigation effort. Cruising guides are much more reliable than bar talk, but don't rely on them for stand-alone answers in a thorough navigator's voyage planning process.

◆ Navigation charts are the sine qua non of voyage planning, but not all charts are equally accurate. In the days of celestial navigation, when fixes were vaguely accurate, mariners knew to be cautious about possible cartographic flaws. But your GPS-determined fix may be a lot more accurate than the charted locations of the hazards around you. U.S. and Western Europe charts are impressively accurate, but this isn't necessarily the case elsewhere. You're rolling the dice more than you may realize if you simply follow an image on your display screen as your sole guide through a tight pass or around a wave-swept headland. Passage planners, like navigators, benefit from a skeptical streak and double-checking all route plans.

PASSAGES TO BERMUDA AND HAWAII

Bermuda and Hawaii are iconic landfalls, oases in a saltwater desert, and key in the sailing dreams of many North American coastal voyagers pondering an offshore passage. Hawaii is three times farther from the coast than Bermuda, but much of the transit can be made in friendly easterly trade winds. Bermuda-bound sailors must cross the fickle Gulf Stream and cope with changeable weather patterns of the middle latitudes. Both are fitting challenges for those prepared to go to sea, and the reward of arrival leads many sailors to become repeat customers.

Both passages are best made in June, allowing sailors to avoid volatile early spring weather and the mid-summer hurricane season. For the West Coaster, the priority is heading south and out of the fog-bound, damp, cold weather of the California Current. Reaching the trade-wind latitudes always puts a smile on sailors' faces with a quartering breeze and porpoises surfing the bow wave. East Coasters have a warm current to cope with, and knowing where the Gulf Stream's axis and warm and cold eddies lie can be a big strategic help. Gulf Stream information is available from private services such as Jenifer Clark's (see Chapter 1) and NOAA's Ocean Prediction Center, now featuring a composite NAVY and Real Time Ocean Forecast System current axis track. (www.opc.ncep.noaa.gov/sst/GulfStream_compare.shtml)

Both offshore venues require a readiness to cope with calms as well as the odd gale. The boat should meet the safety standards required of an ISAF Category 1 racer and ISO Category A structural and stability standards (see Chapter 12). Probably the two most significant differences between the Hawaii and Bermuda passages involve the 2,200 mile run to Hawaii's predictable trade wind reach and the challenge of getting back home. Those leaving Bermuda normally have 650 miles of summer variable winds to cope with in the return passage to the East Coast, though an occasionally volatile weather bout may intrude; generally the challenge is usually no greater than the outbound passage. In contrast, the West Coast sailor leaving Hawaii needs to head farther north to get around the calm conditions in the omnipresent Pacific High and reach the temperate-zone westerlies. Thanks to the cold-water currents in the eastern Pacific, fog and overcast punctuate the return voyage; cold, damp conditions plunge much farther south than on the East Coast, ushering in a regular progression of late-summer gales. Because of the lengthy exposure to such weather and the greater distance, a return from Hawaii usually involves tougher sailing than the return from Bermuda.

Regular crew discussions about the cruising plan and landfalls help keep everyone informed and invested. The late Bill Buckley—an avid sailor as well as journalist, shown here—turned "chart talk" into onboard oratory. The response to a squall or a dragging anchor may not lend itself to democratic processes, but decisions on where to go and what to see certainly do.

Fortunately, the Intracoastal Waterway (ICW) offers a third option. The ICW is an inshore, protected waterway for boats that draw around six feet or less and have mast heights (including masthead lights and instruments) less than 65 feet. A fascinating, boater-friendly confluence of cuts, canals, rivers, bays, and estuaries, the ICW wends its way from New Jersey to Texas. Those who traverse long stretches of this unique waterway learn to be attentive to the marks and gain a new appreciation for the nation's nautical heritage and diverse coastal and estuarine flora and fauna.

For those lucky enough to escape winter and linger in Florida, the Dry Tortugas may be the end of the road and the point from which many cruisers begin their return north. For others, the next step may be a passage to the Bahamas, Bermuda, the Caribbean, or farther into the Atlantic. See the accompanying itinerary for a one-year East Coast adventure.

In a passage down the U.S. East Coast, New York Harbor is the gateway between the fog, waves, and rocks of a Down East summer from the sand shoals and river mouths of the Middle Atlantic States. Transiting the metropolis by boat for the first time is a good test of your chart-reading skills and awareness of currents. The merchant traffic in New York Har-

One of cruising's many rewards is the special places you experience. In the outer islands of the Bahamas there are fewer footprints in the sand, and the water is clean, warm, and inviting.

bor ranges from high-speed ferries to massive freighters and tankers. The tight, bridge-laced channels on the east side of Manhattan's skyscrapers give way to the open upper and lower bays. Avoiding collisions and staying clear of the numerous shoals that await the unaware can be trying, especially at night. Vessels running with the current have the right of way, and ships constrained by draft have right of way over vessels under sail. Cruisers making their first run through these waters are better off in broad daylight with a favorable current.

Transits through New York City, the Cape Cod Canal, the Chesapeake and Delaware Canal, and numerous current-bound areas of the ICW drive home the importance of keeping track of the phases of the moon and the times of ebb, flood, and slack tidal currents at various points along the route. Sailors unaccustomed to large tidal ranges and fast currents are often surprised by lags between tide changes and tidal current changes; even local mariners are sometimes tricked by the fact that the tide can be rising while the current is still ebbing, or vice versa. Each body of water presents its own constraints, and a prime factor in one may be insignificant in another. Sailors develop an ingrained response to the nuances of their home waters, but they need to be able to switch gears quickly when cruising from one water body to the next.

A dramatic example of this transition occurs in a cruise down the Chesapeake Bay followed by a passage around Cape Hatteras. Any skipper trading the gunkholing ICW meander through tidewater Virginia and North Carolina for a passage around Hatteras needs to be wary of how quickly a low-pressure system can

SAMPLE ITINERARY FOR A ONE-YEAR EAST COAST ADVENTURE

- ◆ A Down East summer, perhaps to Maine or Nova Scotia.
- ◆ The fall migration south. Once south of the Chesapeake Bay, either keep to the sheltered ICW or very cautiously make hops outside around Cape Hatteras, Cape Lookout, and the Frying Pan Shoals.
- ◆ Explore the Georgia islands and the mid-Florida coast en route to south Florida.
- ◆ Explore the Florida Keys.
- ◆ Cross the Gulf Stream to reach the Bahamas and winter in the Exumas.
- ◆ In May or June, ride the Gulf Stream back home.

develop. Sailors also must realize there is no safe shelter between the mouth of the Chesapeake Bay and the entrance to Beaufort, NC. In heavy weather, the extensive sand shoals off Cape Hatteras cause waves to steepen and break, and the Gulf Stream nearby adds more storm-building energy to the equation. Many experienced sailors rue the day they decided to take the offshore route rather than ducking into the ICW to avoid Cape Hatteras altogether.

We can think of no better way than cruising the ICW to see America's backyard while avoiding the worst of spring and fall weather. For sure, shoaling cuts and channels and closed bridges teach patience. In addition, if you're not used to following a trail-like line of buoys marking a waterway, you'll have a clean keel by the time you finish the transit.

In the Carolinas, the ICW squeezes down into a series of cuts, canals, and river courses just inshore of the ocean dunes. A series of sounds inside islands make up the Georgia transit, where large tides and strong currents once again come into play. The Florida transit is a long water highway between mainland development and barrier beach communities. Altogether, there is much of interest on the ICW. In recent decades, many low bridges that required bridge tenders have been replaced with fixed structures offering 65 feet of vertical clearance. This makes for easier transit and much less time spent waiting for bridges to open. If you duck out into the ocean for coastal runs in good weather, you must be careful with currents in the inlets. Make sure, when approaching a low, closed bridge with a fair current that you factor in the increased distance needed for a 180-degree turn.

When sailors hear the siren song of the Bahamas, seamanship priorities shift once again. The transit from the East Coast involves crossing the Gulf Stream, but the passage from Florida is short enough that picking a good weather window can avoid most of the dreaded lumps and bumps. Once on the Bahamian banks, however, you must find water deep enough to prevent grounding. You need to keep a decent anchorage in mind to be able to ride out the next cold front.

You'll find many ways to gather information to help prepare for what lies ahead, but it's hard to completely grasp the unfamiliar. While it helps to read the cruising accounts of those who have crossed oceans and traversed the waters you plan to explore, don't be surprised if you encounter diverging accounts and advice. As in all research, track the consensus view as well as outlying remarks. Weigh skill preparation with risk taking. All crew need to understand how far out on a limb they're willing to go and how much faith they have in the skipper's plan. Skill is a developable commodity, but luck is not. You can increase your willingness to take risks by improving your skills, but pay attention also to how much of a gambler you really want to be.

CASTING OFF WISELY: AVOIDING HARM'S WAY

In much of the U.S., summer sailing breezes are usually light and light-air sails get more worn out while heavy-air canvas languishes in the bag. This is why coastal cruisers with plenty of safe havens nearby often don't bother with smaller sails. They simply rely on an easily reefed mainsail, an easily roller-furled

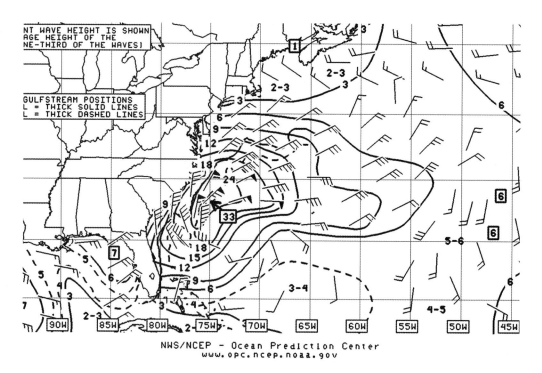

NWS/NCEP - Ocean Prediction Center
www.opc.ncep.noaa.gov

Sixty-five-knot winds and 33-foot seas create an anomalous but by no means unheard-of weather event off Cape Hatteras. Four sailors and four sailboats were lost in this 2007 storm (see Chapter 10). Those caught in this tragic encounter failed to monitor or chose to disregard Ocean Prediction Center (OPC) weather warnings issued two days in advance. Instead of encountering average conditions they encountered March-like weather in May. (Courtesy OPC) headsail, and a sprint for safe shelter when heavy weather brews. Although this may seem sensible, it can be a risky gamble. You can be caught out and forced to contend with gale-force conditions only a few miles from safe shelter.

In such situations, a Solent stay with a hanked-on heavy-weather staysail can be the right answer. The Solent stay is a secondary, removable headstay located just aft of the permanent headstay; it does not transform a sloop into a cutter rig and does not need to be balanced with running backstays. Gearing up for what lies ahead is a major theme in being prepared for heavy weather (see Chapter 11). Even if the pilot chart shows only a 3% frequency of gale-force winds, that means one thing for a two-hour open-water passage between islands but quite another for a two-week open-ocean transit. Longer exposure means much greater risk.

The importance of weather cannot be overstated. Again, using pilot charts and NOAA climatological data helps one plan the itinerary. But the frequency of calms and gales and the average wind velocities do not tell the whole story. Many areas may experience rapid changes in wind direction, speed, and sea state. Never assume the weather of the moment will last indefinitely, an assumption that often results in foolish departure decisions. Leaving port on a sunny day may lift the spirits of the crew, but it's more important to know what's in store for the next three days and where weather systems are likely to come from further down the road.

The fate of a Cal 34, *Morning Dew,* and its inexperienced crew show us the tragedy that may result if preparation delays cause the departure dates to slip as the midlatitude autumn advances and turns toward winter. The crew finally headed south in the Intracoastal Waterway, not in the usual fall migration but in the short, cold, windy days of late December. Most likely as a navigation mistake, the skipper, who was committed to a coastal run, exited an inlet and turned the flatwater cruise into an offshore run. The passage from Winyah Bay, South Carolina, to Charleston occurred during a windy, rainy night, and the approach to the Charleston breakwater was a disastrous mistake.

At 0217 hours, the U.S. Coast Guard radio watch in Charleston decided to disregard what would later be determined to have been a short, garbled Mayday call. As dawn approached, the bosun on a commercial ship entering Charleston heard cries for help in the dark, and the pilot on board relayed this to the pilot office. The pilot office contacted the Coast Guard and also directed the crew of the pilot boat to the location to look and listen for a person in the water. The pilot boat found nothing.

Passagemaking during the hurricane, cyclone, or winter storm season is a gamble with poor odds. If unforeseeable circumstances delay your departure, either amend the itinerary to avoid offshore vulnerability or lay over and wait for the storm season to abate.

The subsequent investigation revealed that although at least two broken-up VHF radio calls had been received and the merchant crew had reported shouts for help near the Charleston entrance jetty, the Coast Guard did not launch a search-and-rescue effort until near midday, when marine police contacted them to report bodies on the beach. In early afternoon it was confirmed that the sloop *Morning Dew* had run into the outer jetty and had been holed and sunk. The crew—a father, two sons, and a nephew—had all drowned.

The National Transportation Safety Board assigned blame to both the skipper of the *Morning Dew* and the U.S. Coast Guard, as is clear in their summary:

> The major safety issues identified in this investigation are the adequacy of the reasoning and decision-making of the operator; the fatigue and hypothermia suffered by the operator; the adequacy of the reasoning and decision-making of U.S. Coast Guard Group Charleston's watch standers; the adequacy of Coast Guard Group Charleston's personnel, equipment, and procedures for responding to an emergency; and the role of the Coast Guard in providing factual information for safety investigations.

Admiral Loy, the Commandant of the Coast Guard, cited the incident to underscore the Coast Guard's need for a better communications system. Family members sued the Coast Guard and settled for $9 million in compensation. Responsibility for the tragedy, however, belonged even more to the skipper, who had poorly prepared for the voyage, set off too

🚩 *Regardless of the forecast, GRIB file analysis, or weather consultant's advice, the skipper and crew need to make regular visual observations of the conditions and dress for the weather at hand. Visually track thunderstorm cells and be ready for a quick reef or sail change. Keep a lookout for the telltale clouds, monitor their movement on radar, and note the behavior of any sailboats in the path of the storm. Anticipate the timing of the storm and its impact—when squalls roll through reefing and sail dousing become more hazardous.*

late in the season, and made a fatal decision to enter conditions he was incapable of handling—in this case, 25 knots of wind and rainy, overcast conditions.

The lesson for all sailors is not that the Charleston Coast Guard station failed to respond appropriately to a distress call. It's this: with the freedom to voyage comes the responsibility to be self-reliant. When skippers decide to depart on a passage, they take on the responsibility for the crew and vessel. Three factors must be in place:

- The skipper must have a clear picture of the passage that lies ahead and an understanding of the navigation constraints.
- The crew must have the skill to cope with boat handling in conditions lying ahead.
- The vessel needs the safety gear that can save lives, and those on board need to know how to use them in extremis (PFDs, flares, EPIRBS, handheld VHF radios, life rafts, etc.).

In the *Morning Dew* tragedy, the skipper mishandled all three factors.

Another Cal 34—a venerable old Bill Lapworth design that has earned a good reputation as a versatile coastal cruiser/racer—was involved in a tragic case of being caught short at sea. A southern California married couple had sailed westward across the Pacific in their sloop, *Drambuie*. Like all sailors heading toward Africa, they were racing to arrive in Durban, South Africa, before the onset of the cyclone season in the southwestern Indian Ocean. After their late start leaving Australia, the small sloop fell further behind schedule as they made their way from island to island in their trade-wind march across the tropical Indian Ocean. Nearly all of the vessels making the same transit had already been in Durban for a month when *Drambuie* made its last mid-December radio call, describing mountainous seas and howling winds as cyclone Claudette lined up with and eventually intersected their track.

This crew had made a two-part gamble, starting with a December approach to Africa on a passage that should have been completed in the narrow October-November window. In December the volatile cyclone season ramps up. In addition, the western portion of every ocean basin tends to receive the brunt of the worst tropical weather. This occurs because tropical storms travel east to west, developing in intensity as they go.

Their second gamble was relying on a boat designed and built as a coastal cruiser/racer to carry them around the world. Until they encountered the cyclone, the small, light-displacement sloop had proven adequate for milder conditions. Her relatively short waterline length limited her hull speed, however, and prevented them from making up for delays in the Indian Ocean.

No wreckage was ever found, and despite much speculation, no one knows exactly what happened to the crew of this Cal 34. We do know that the track of cyclone Claudette, with winds over 120 knots, intersected the course that *Drambuie* was sailing. The crew broadcast their last ham radio message and position update when encountering the outer rain bands of the powerful storm. A well-built 40- or 50-footer could have suffered a similar fate in those Force 12 conditions. The tragedy of *Drambuie* underscores why it is so important to stack the deck in your favor. It's essential to commit to careful planning, matching your boat to the cruising/voyaging plan, and making passages in the right season.

In the next chapter, we'll delve into ways seamanship skills can continue to develop and evolve over time.

EVOLVING AS SKIPPER OR CREW

"A good sailor isn't fearful of high winds and big seas—he's petrified of the deep!"
—a favorite saying of Ernest Shackleton, commander of the 1914–16 *Endurance* expedition, and Frank Worsley, captain of the *Endurance*

At some time or another, all offshore veterans settle in their berth and ponder the hull skin that separates their tiny seagoing habitat from the great abyss beneath. Since the human mind is imbued with both a strong sense of survival and inductive reasoning, it's not surprising that most crews step up and care for their vessels. Nor is it surprising that we continue to see naval architecture and engineering advance and evolve. Sea sense coaxes a skipper to commission a refit, develop survival strategies (including a rational damage-control plan), replace tired rigging, upgrade firefighting gear, and take steps to avoid capsize.

This same sea sense leads skippers to develop an onboard routine that allows the crew a safe and enjoyable passage from point A to point B. Few land-based activities allow such complete control over day-to-day operations. However, this control also brings profound responsibility for both what skippers do on board and what they fail to do. Therefore, prudent skippers learn to match their decisions to the boat's strength, the conditions at hand, and the crew's abilities.

Skippers and crew find themselves continuously tested. Whether arriving, departing, or sailing in between, the never-ending changes in wind and sea reset the stage, even on familiar, often-repeated passages. Veterans of twenty-plus Bermuda runs will tell you that no two passages are ever quite the same.

Skills are typically acquired in incremental steps, and as discussed in the previous chapters, if your goals include long-range cruising, we recommend developing those skills closer to home. Even simple things should be part of the skipper's set of skills, such as knowing how to use an aft spring line when coming alongside a dock or to back against a forward

During a summer sail-training cruise, U.S. Naval Academy midshipmen and an active duty officer work out the time-honored skills of watchkeeping.

spring line to outwit an offsetting current. We know that some voyagers learned to navigate on their way to Tahiti and lived to tell about it, but we also know such impulse voyaging more likely ends with less-than-ideal memories.

A seafaring New Zealander and good friend, Ross Norgrove always expressed his insights into cruising with a quizzically impish grin. Here's one of Ross's favorite observations: *More great voyages have been made despite rather than because of the vessel in which they were sailed.* This characteristically backhanded Kiwi compliment underscores the importance of a competent crew, the most valuable component in any voyage and the first line of defense when the going gets rough. True, a seaworthy boat is surely a safer boat, which is why we've included Chapter 12 to consider the attributes of seaworthiness. But the seamanship of the skipper and crew matter *(continued page 49)*

TRAINING OPPORTUNITIES

Local Learn-to-Sail Programs

Many boatowners never experience the value of a local sail-training program. While the quality of such programs can vary greatly, depending in part on the instructor's sailing and communications skills, many programs now have a stronger curriculum and better training process. US Sailing and the American Sailing Association are two primary overseers of sail training across the country, training instructors, developing standards, and publishing instructional materials. US

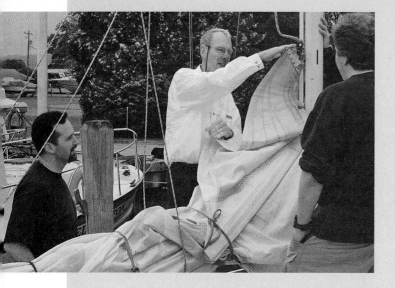

Sailing uses sea trials to gauge their instructors' competence. For decades, Timothea Larr and Sheila Mc-Curdy have helped guide US Sailing's National Faculty and Training Committee. The group annually gathers together professional and amateur sailors to develop training materials for sailors ranging from youthful beginners to experienced ocean passagemakers.

Sailing schools have put great effort into improving the instructional process. Like the U.S. Power Squadrons and the U.S. Coast Guard Auxiliary, they are committed to improving safe boating with engaging training opportunities.

Offshore Sailing School

Programs pioneered by Steve and Doris Colgate offer a fast track for entry-level sailors to gain boat-handling and sail-trimming skills. Much of the US Sailing curriculum came from Steve and other master trainers. Graduates of entry-level programs can often continue to higher-level courses within the same school and progress from basic boat handling to cruising skills that prepare them for chartering in remote locations or heading off on their own boats.

■ *Small sailing schools across the country, such as Bay Breeze on Little Traverse Bay, Michigan, fine-tune their training with local conditions in mind. Every coastal or lake region has a unique set of weather patterns and challenges in the local waters—another reason why local training counts.*

■ *J/World Annapolis owner Jahn Tihansky, also the head sailing coach at the U.S. Naval Academy, checks over the running rigging on a new Navy 44 MKII. He stresses to midshipmen and civilian students that whether you are cruising or racing, vessel preparation can make the difference between a good and bad day on the water.*

TRAINING OPPORTUNITIES, CONTINUED

Colgate's Offshore Sailing School, like many other sanctioned programs, uses textbooks jointly developed with US Sailing. The Colgates have sailing schools around the country.

J/World
Another sailing school, J/World, also offers great learning opportunities, with a greater emphasis on boat speed and competitive tactics—what racing sailors call performance sailing. Participants at the Key West, Annapolis, and other J/World bases spend a week learning the tricks with which the pros cross the finish line ahead of the rest of the fleet. At Key West winter weather conditions provide good sailing breezes to help ensure that onboard action is fast paced and full of learning experiences. Having a professional sailor guide you as you practice spinnaker sets and takedowns can clean up bad habits and add the nuances that translate into extra seconds saved in a mark rounding.

The Annapolis School of Seamanship
Without question, some skills are better learned on deck than in the classroom, but the reverse is also sometimes true. The Annapolis School of Seamanship provides one of the most effective shoreside training programs, and its founder/owner, John Martino, built a reputation for teaching cruisers and commercial mariners exactly what they need to know. His navigation programs merge theory with practical, hands-on piloting skills. Then he segues to the latest 3-D digital electronic charting simulations and blends both techniques. Simulator training is part of the classroom experience, as close to learning underway as a shoreside experience can be. His hands-on diesel lab and systems training prepare cruisers for the problems that always seem to crop up along the way. In addition to these lessons for those cruising under sail or power, the

The Annapolis School of Seamanship runs both recreational and Coast Guard–approved licensing courses at a variety of locations nationwide. A growing trend among boaters is to seek specific information on topics ranging from electronic navigation to diesel repair, and these professional training programs are a good source for such learning.

school offers U.S. Coast Guard licensing training and special underway learning experiences.

Hands-on Safety Seminars
The Hands-on Safety Training Opportunities sidebar later in this chapter describes several training sessions aimed specifically at emergency situations.

For more on organized learn-by-doing training opportunities, see The Lure of the Rally in Chapter 1.

more than the seaworthiness of the boat. In the safety triangle discussed in Chapter 1, seamanship is the longest leg.

We can see Norgrove's salty wisdom in many legendary stories. The heroic and legendary seamanship of Frank Worsley is one of the best examples of all time. Worsley, Sir Ernest Shackleton's stoic sea captain and master mariner aboard ships as well as small craft, brilliantly displayed his skills piloting the *Endurance*'s 22-foot lifeboat, the *James Caird*. Worsley successfully maneuvered the lifeboat in an escape mission from the ice-choked waters of Elephant Island in the Antarctic Convergence to the relative safety of South Georgia Island. Against the odds, this incredible voyage resulted in the eventual rescue of the *Endurance*'s crew. These men had spent more than

18 months shipwrecked in the unforgiving Antarctic —living on an ice floe and enduring unimaginable hardships and deprivation.

The *Caird*'s 26-day voyage crossed 700 miles of the roughest ocean in the world and remains a standard for measuring great seamanship skill (along with an ample dose of good luck). It's a case study for those interested in how far the human will and spirit can be stretched. Nearly shipwrecked before making landfall at the cliffs on the southwest side of South Georgia, Shackleton, Worsley, and four shipmates were anything but home free after stumbling ashore. Their final challenge was to traverse an uncharted mountain range to reach help at the Stromness whaling station. Met initially by disbelief, their arrival led to an all-hands effort to recover Shackle-

I recall the first time I shot a round of star sights with a GPS unit to grade my work. I would like to think the Selective Availability scramble put the GPS fix off, rather than my fix being a mile off. But in truth, a celestial fix that's only a mile off gets a nod of approval from most navigators. (Courtesy Lenore Naranjo)

ton's crew, and Sir Ernest once again arrived on Elephant Island, more than a welcome sight for the rest of his stranded crew.

True, Shackleton's can-do attitude contributed to getting his crew into trouble in the first place. Some attribute this advertisement for the voyage to Shackleton himself: "MEN WANTED: FOR HAZARDOUS JOURNEY. SMALL WAGES, BITTER COLD, LONG MONTHS OF COMPLETE DARKNESS, CONSTANT DANGER, SAFE RETURN DOUBTFUL. HONOUR AND RECOGNITION IN CASE OF SUCCESS. SIR ERNEST SHACKLETON." That attitude, together with his leadership in the face of adversity, made possible the crew's rescue. However, the crew themselves played a vital role in their own survival. Working as a team, Shackleton's crew possessed a rare tenacity. They showed their ability to rise to any occasion, dealing with unforeseen circumstances and using their carefully honed skills and talents to cope with what fate dealt them. Competence and toughness allowed them to persevere while stranded on the ice floe. The crew on the *James Caird* endured the Drake's Passage crossing in a proverbial cockle shell.

Shackleton's benevolent leadership skills and Worsley's consummate seamanship held the crew together throughout their ordeal. In his book, *Shackleton's Boat Journey,* Worsley recalls conditions en route to South Georgia Island:

"We rolled and plunged along in the dark. . . . Dark hills of water reared suddenly . . . ahead and astern capped by gleams of breaking seas. A hiss of water at the bows as she ran heeling down a long sea. Dark shapes of sails overhead and forward bellied to leeward. Drenched through again and again there was yet a certain satisfaction in holding her to her course."

The days of adventure-seeking gentlemen enduring such ordeals appear to be mostly behind us. For better or worse, today's average boater likely spends more time dealing with refrigeration system malfunctions than worrying about running into slabs of ice. But the challenges confronting today's sailors should be met as the crew of the *James Caird* met theirs. Weigh your options, use well-tested seamanship skills, and anticipate the vessel and crew's attributes and limitations.

Many of the most competent sailors I've met developed their seamanship skills both learning by doing and under the guidance of others. Some launched their first boat and sailed, rowed, or steered a tiny outboard about the same time they were learning to ride a bicycle. Others started with junior programs, family cruises, or community sailing and then carried their sailing interest farther afield. Getting a start in sailing before adolescence has set the hook for many competitive racers and serious cruisers, but plenty of highly competent recreational mariners didn't begin until adulthood.

Two key factors affect the best approach to learning: the type of boating skills you hope to acquire, and whether you need more theoretical knowledge or boat-handling experience. For both, training options are available to help reach your goal. We've listed some in the accompanying sidebar.

In my own case, I acquired skills in a number of ways. Messing around in boats as a child led to a meaningful Sea Scout experience, dinghy racing in Southern California segued into MORC (Midget Ocean Racing Club) racing, and a young family nudged us toward cruising. Between my family's voyage around the world and our next cruising stint, I ran a full-service boatyard, occasionally spending time racing with clients and delivering boats to and from the Caribbean and other destinations. It was a good time to become more familiar with the seafaring syllabus, so I taught myself what was needed to acquire a U.S. Coast Guard 100-ton license. Operating commercial small craft helped me gain a feel for the nuances of the International Regulations for

Preventing Collisions at Sea (COLREGS) Rules of the Road—the lights and shapes and the stand-on and give-way requirements.

I also took a course on astronomy and the spherical geometry implications of celestial navigation. Until then I had been a plug-and-chug worksheet devotee, eventually moving to a programmable calculator to solve the celestial triangle. Finally learning the theory behind what I had been doing with the sextant and time calculations was rewarding, albeit a little anticlimactic. After all, despite my less-than-stellar grasp of the principles behind solutions to the celestial triangle, my practical, cookbook approach had gotten us around the world. Today, at the Annapolis School of Seamanship I teach the arcane science and history of John Harrison and his chronometer, including explaining why solving the celestial triangle to derive latitude and longitude still makes sense in the age of GPS. But I don't lose sight of the most important job at hand: coming up with an accurate and reliable fix every time the need arises.

Learning a task in a classroom and performing it at sea can prove to be quite different. For example, in one of my navigation classes the brightest students grasped what it took to reduce sights using trigonometric equations and a handheld calculator. In the final exam the class went to sea and had to find an offshore tower. Soon after setting off on a lumpy sea with big swells, the skipper and two thirds of the crew—including the most gifted students—became

Join others on offshore passages and races. Time at sea with a good crew and capable vessel is time well spent.

Most training cruises are not quite as expeditionary as those aboard Australis, which regularly sails between Cape Horn and Antarctica, and recently accompanied filmmakers and adventure sailors on the 100-year anniversary recreation of Shackleton's escape from Antarctica.

so violently seasick that they could take few sights and no one could sit at the chart table long enough to plot a line of position (LOP). One of the underachievers in the class popped up with an RDF and efficiently took a series of bearings on a weak beacon signal, crossed it with his sun LOP, and navigated the crew toward success.

You can acquire learn-by-doing skills through sailors in a local marina, an active yacht club, or a good sailing school. This is the modern recreational sailor's equivalent of the traditional mariner's before-the-mast training to hand, reef, and steer. Skills for setting sail, reefing, line handling, and general boat handling comprise a good portion of seamanship. Even when you're excited about turning your attention to outfitting and preparing a vessel for a specific cruise, there's good reason to continue building your skills.

ATTRIBUTES OF A GOOD CREWMEMBER

Capable crewmembers are attuned to the vessel they're aboard and the mission it serves. Daysailors, ocean racers, and long-distance voyagers each face a particular combination of challenges, and their skills evolve to meet those demands. For example, foredeck crew on a race boat must be especially physically fit

Agility and fitness are one side of the crew competency coin, and the flip side is more cerebral and involves effective decision making. Those who cultivate both usually fare best.

and agile and possess sail-handling skills they can also use aboard cruising boats. When it comes to handling ground tackle in bad weather, however, racing sailors often come up short. Racing crews might deal with a gale at sea or while tethered to a dock or club mooring, but they seldom face peril on an anchor rode. As a result they tend to see an anchor as clutter on the forepeak and therefore may prefer a light-weight aluminum anchor that can be disassembled and hidden away.

Cruisers, on the other hand, spend more time on board with a lower percentage of time underway, so they're more likely to encounter bad weather in anchorages. They stake the well-being of vessel and crew on the anchorages and ground tackle they choose. Of course, cruisers also need the skills to cope with heavy weather at sea.

The goal here focuses on acquiring the versatile seamanship needed by capable cruisers, defined as an array of skills equal to almost all occasions, except perhaps the extremes encountered by adventurers as fearless and imprudent as Ernest Shackleton. Five key attributes form the foundation: mental acuity, physical agility, vessel-handling skills, ingenuity, and forehandedness. By no means are these the only attributes shared by proficient mariners, but to some degree they're common to all competent sailors.

Mental Acuity

Of all the seafaring attributes I've admired, I consider mental acuity most notable among capable long-distance voyagers. Perhaps the word *savvy* best describes this reflexive wisdom that emerges from a combination of experience and decision-making ability and is tested and augmented in every new encounter. More than versatility, this acuity involves a hair-trigger action for the correct solution sooner rather than later.

Not long ago I read an account of an encounter with Ambrose Light. *Axel Spirit*, an 819-foot merchant ship, had been anchored in the open roadstead off Long Island. It got underway at night, in good visibility, to make the short transit into New York Harbor. The master gave the second officer the course to steer. Then the bridge watch noticed that the ship's track was directing it toward a potential allision (collision with a fixed object) with the tower.

The master approved a 5-degree course alteration to port, but a side-setting 1-knot current negated the effect of the small correction and the tanker's starboard side struck the light tower and tore away most of its structure above water. A subsequent National Transportation Safety Board (NTSB) investigation found that the master "failed to use all available means to determine the vessel's position."

Given all the formal training and certification required to operate a tanker carrying 441,000 barrels of crude oil, how could such an incident occur? In truth, even with years of class time, required formal training, and corporate oversight, we can't always prevent operator error, especially when communications break down. In this case the lowest-ranking member of the bridge team, the lookout, saw the developing problem unfold and knew a larger course correction was needed, but the mate and master failed to perceive the strength of the side-setting current. We also need to consider having one's "mind in the game." Standing watch requires absolute vigilance and situational awareness, and when attention wavers, bad things can happen. In this case, Ambrose Light came to a sad end when its remains had to be dismantled. As sailors and ship captains had in the past approached the busy harbor, Ambrose Light had served as a welcoming beacon that validated their piloting.

Physical Agility

Crewmembers who are to contribute fully to the operational routine of the vessel must be boat-agile as well as physically fit. Mobility aboard a docked sloop is one thing, but if you've ever patrolled the foredeck of that same vessel while beating to weather in a steep seaway at 0100 you know that the bow can pitch down faster than your body can follow. In those conditions your strength and agility, along with knowing the location of every handhold along the way, can be what keeps you upright.

The maxim "one hand for your ship, one for yourself" has likely been part of seamanship since the ancient Dorians explored the coast of Greece. Today, it's still unfailingly passed along from old salts to young apprentices. It's simple common sense but remains effective advice regardless of the latest technology. This simple guideline helps prevent crewmembers from falling overboard. Today, the U.S. Coast Guard—and other coast guards around the world—continuously remind boaters of the value of wearing a life jacket. US Sailing, the national governing body for sailboat racing, continues to fine-tune its guidelines for harness, tether, and jackline use. Agility may get short shrift in some of these discussions, but it's as important as purchasing safety gear from the local chandlery. It's a given that you need the necessary safety gear on board and in good working order, but you must also be proficient in its use—a proficiency developed at sea.

Onboard agility goes beyond being able to cross a swaying deck and remain aboard. Agility is needed to go aloft to re-reeve a halyard or repair a fitting. It may

A fit, agile bowman is always a big plus. Even aboard the most sedate cruiser, situations arise that require someone fit enough to go aloft or over the side to clear a fouled prop.

include skills such as donning a mask and flippers and going over the side to free the prop or rudder from a line. Even in a gentle seaway, when working in cold water you'll be amazed how vulnerable you feel under that pitching stern, how quickly exhaustion overtakes you, and how difficult it is to direct your energy to the task at hand—being fit and agile will help.

A crewmember may have to turn an inflatable dinghy into an impromptu pushboat or haul a storm anchor to windward. A shorthanded crew needs to be as versatile as possible, and agility and overall physical fitness make it much easier to learn new techniques and implement them in rough conditions.

Early mariners needed much more physical strength than we do today, thanks to improved design and engineering. Even so, at times a strong, agile crewmember is the most valuable hand on board. A "tug-yourself" trip to the masthead or a hand-over-hand descent down the anchor rode to inspect the anchor's set can quickly convince someone that sailing or cruising is indeed a physical activity and that a reasonable level of fitness can pay big dividends.

To be able to perform efficient work on deck, the crew must adapt to the motion of the boat underfoot. Seakindly racer/cruisers like the venerable Navy 44 MKI offer wide side decks and an evenly cadenced pitch and roll.

The smaller the crew, the more manageable the sail plan should be. Adding lazyjacks and a sail-catching cover and running all lines aft to the cockpit makes it possible for a shorthanded crew to handle trimming and reefing requirements.

Vessel-Handling Skills

In the era of iron men and wooden ships, an entry-level able-bodied seaman was expected to "hand, reef, and steer"—meaning that he could haul up sails, tuck in reefs, and hold a steady course during his jig at the helm. When Richard Dana, lawyer, politician, and author, published *Two Years before the Mast* in 1840, few sailed simply for the fun of it. Today the tide has turned, and commercial sail is nearly extinct. However, that three-part job description remains the backbone of coastal and ocean sailing and a good basis for judging the competence of any new crewmember. By enumerating what skills are needed, skippers can share responsibilities with their regular crew in a logical and equitable fashion. The larger the crew, the more specialized individual roles tend to become, but for safety's sake and crew morale and engagement, we should always welcome overlap.

The verb "hand," originally describing the act of hauling on a halyard or climbing the rigging hand over hand, now refers to most sail and line handling. Able crew have additional skills under the "hand" banner that go beyond hoisting sail and hauling ground tackle. These include tasks such as handling a tender, stepping a spar, repairing rigging, or unpinning a rudder. We can use the term to refer to most actions that require lifting, hoisting, and operating running rigging. We cover boat handling in Chapter 4 and line handling in Chapter 5.

Whether you've known the boat you're sailing for a decade or you've just stepped aboard, you should become as familiar as possible with every line, valve, and electrical cable. Unfamiliarity is one of the biggest dangers during an offshore passage, and a bewildering deck layout or through-hull array, for example, can compound a difficult situation.

Experienced sailors aboard a new boat spend time determining what lines lead where, and especially for a delivery, they may bring along some 3M long-life silver masking tape and a waterproof marker to add temporary labels to rope clutches, halyard leads, manifold valves, and electrical panel breakers. This simple effort can prevent mistakes such as releasing the wrong line or selecting the wrong fuel valve. For example, when a crewmember attempts to release a down guy held in a rope clutch and inadvertently blows the spinnaker pole topping lift, the result can be more than just a big surprise to the bowman.

The versatility of a sail plan is as important as its ability to deliver high-end performance in average wind strengths. A capable crew knows how to harness lift and mitigate drag in a variety of wind and sea conditions, and they recognize that a roller-furling jib and roller-furling mainsail do not cover the whole range of weather possibilities. Many cruisers discover that the only way to avoid having to run the diesel auxiliary frequently (and installing a larger fuel tank) is to carry and know how to use specialized sails for light air and heavy weather. A storm jib and storm trysail make sense for the latter, but light-air sails for single-digit wind velocities require some forethought. We'll look in detail at sail handling in Chapter 7. For now, it's enough to say that having a storm jib, storm trysail, and light-air sails aboard does little good unless the crew knows how to fly them. Light-air sails can be tested when light air arrives, but you'd better know how to set the storm sails before they're needed.

The ability to reef is the second of the three vessel-handling attributes of the able seaman. The fact that it isn't lumped in with other "hand" tasks highlights its importance. Even in a world of electrical relays and a ballast load of batteries, reefing still requires significant crew interaction. Modern light-displacement, mainsail-dominated, agile sailboats keep their crews in sync with minor changes in wind velocity and the reefing actions required.

Capable cruisers tend to reef before a reef is needed and are much happier to shake out a premature reef than face the task with 10 knots more breeze than can be reasonably handled with the present spread of sail. In contrast, race crews hold off as long as possible, flattening and thus depowering the mainsail by means of sheet, vang, traveler, and outhaul adjustments and tucking in a reef only when significantly overcanvassed, but this approach requires multiple skilled hands and careful boat handling. (The ins and outs of efficient reefing are detailed in Chapter 7.)

The ability to steer a steady course is the third trait in the able seaman's vessel-handling repertoire. This too is still a good test of the modern recreational mariner. In addition to maneuvering in tight confines

or being among the first tier of competitors charging a starting line, steering is a talent that makes you comfortable as a boat handler. The learning process begins with discovering how a vessel reacts to rudder angle and how doggedly it *carries way,* or maintains motion through the water once the sails are completely luffing or the engine is in neutral. So that all crew gain the feel of "coming alongside," we recommend practicing the skills of arriving and departing a dock or mooring. The cardinal rule is to arrive with as little way on as possible; the heavier the vessel, the more significant this becomes.

Today's sailboats and motorsailers with a low ratio of sail area to displacement depend more on the diesel engine, although too many sailors try to ignore it. But this trusty but often maligned fuel-burning source of propulsion is a true work of genius. We should recognize our reliance on the "iron genoa" for propulsion and to generate energy. The diesel engine has grown ever more efficient and more compact over the years and is the engine of choice for sailing

Modern reefing is far less dramatic than reefing from a yardarm, but the midshipmen on this transatlantic voyage nevertheless had many occasions to master the skill of tucking in and shaking out reefs.

Midshipmen at the U.S. Naval Academy undergo a fast-track training program using sailboats for seamanship training and as a leadership laboratory. Sailboat racing and cruise training are both available. Volunteers like the late Rear Admiral Henry Morgan teach midshipmen about sailboat racing and commanding a nuclear submarine. These experiences on the water align with course work in navigation and other seamanship training.

Many sailors can steer, trim, and track a course on a chart, but few can find a fuel line leak on the suction side of the fuel pump. If you can, you'll prove your value over and over again.

auxiliaries. But too much reliance on its thrust turns sailing into powerboating.

Every crewmember on a sailing vessel equipped with a diesel auxiliary needs to know when and how to start and engage the engine. Statistics show that sailing crews tend to call on the engine in times of emergency, such as performing crew-overboard rescues. Since there's always a chance that you can't use the engine because of a line around the prop or a victim vulnerable to injury from spinning blades, however, the crew should practice overboard rescues under sail as well as under power.

Hand, reef, and steer. In coming chapters we'll expand the list of attributes essential to passagemaking in small craft and suggest how to avoid the seven deadly sins of seamanship.

Ingenuity

The classic TV series *MacGyver* elevated the handyman to rock-star status and drove home the value of an individual who can jury-rig a solution to almost any problem. Such skills are never more appreciated than on an ocean-crossing sailboat, where sailors, like the crew of a space station, are truly on their own. An ability to diagnose problems and come up with viable solutions even when the right parts aren't readily available will always be worth its weight in gold.

To be truly ready to head to sea, a crew needs to be able either to cope with mechanical/electrical breakdowns or do without the convenience provided by the malfunctioning system. Fixing breakdowns requires membership in the tinkerer's guild, a cult of do-it-yourselfers who can step in and turn the lights back on or fix an autopilot that has gone on strike. They know how to substitute a string of light bulbs for a 12-volt DC voltage regulator, use hose clamps to help splint a broken reaching strut, or mix a batch of epoxy to rebuild a broken fuel filter housing. Mac-Gyver is always welcome on a boat.

Ingenuity comes not from clairvoyance but from technical knowledge. Sailors who understand Ohm's Law, Peukert's equation, and other basics of DC circuitry are more likely to figure out how to get the power back on. Solutions to problems arising offshore stem from the collective knowledge of the crew.

Forehandedness

Every capable mariner thinks ahead and stays mindful of the changing conditions likely to influence what's happening aboard a small craft. The concept of forehandedness applies to implementing changes demanded by a new landfall or the influence of a new weather system. Experienced cruisers get so accustomed to sifting data on charts and in the *Sailing Directions* and cruising guides about the waters ahead that they can experience a déjà-vu feeling on reaching landfall. This anticipatory awareness helps temper the unexpected and often leads a crew to note an adverse change well before it can cause a problem.

Planning ahead entails developing a detailed approach to a passage or a boat project, but it also requires remaining flexible enough to handle the unexpected. There's always more shoal water ahead than we expected, figuratively as well as literally. That's why it's important to cultivate the mental agility to cope with new situations and arising challenges, a skill perhaps even more important than planning ahead. As an insightful flag-rank military officer once said, "The best of battle plans seldom withstands the first volley." What separates success from failure is often how well the skipper and crew respond to changing circumstances.

MY EVOLUTION AS CREW
Lenore Naranjo

Ralph and I, together with our children, were sailing along the Coromandel Peninsula in the Hauraki Gulf of New Zealand, having left Auckland to head for Great Barrier Island. The weather had turned black and nasty. We had tucked in a reef, sent the kids below, and put in the hatchboards as we watched a wall of black clouds roll our way. A half mile to windward, a 100-foot fishing trawler was hit by a gust and heeled to its rail. Ralph was on the helm, concentrating on the wind line and already easing the sheet. I realized that the weather would be upon us in a matter of seconds and it was time to drop the mainsail rather than add a deeper reef. As I headed to the mast, *Wind Shadow* was knocked down so far that at one point the mainsail and spreader tips were in the water. Holding onto the gooseneck with one hand, I released the halyard brake with the other and clawed down the stubborn mainsail. Gusts of about 50 knots momentarily turned the surface of the sea white, but with the mainsail down and only the small staysail set, we recovered.

Onboard agility played a key role in my ability to respond to the squall. Time underway in tropical trade-wind conditions had familiarized me with the boat's motion and rigging, so I was able to accomplish that task without much forethought. I think it's vital to develop a strong sense of "boat" and all things affecting its motion. Fortunately, this incident was an exception rather than the rule, but long-term shorthanded cruisers can't afford a habit of waiting with sails up for a downburst to hit.

Toward the end of a long passage, we always felt joy when we saw flocks of seabirds heading home for the night and we knew landfall was not far off. We'd always compete to see who could be first to shout out, "Land Ho." It was glorious to see that little bit of green on the horizon and to know that all our sextant sights and plots on the chart had led us to our destination.

Our little hard-bottomed dinghy took us on some amazing rowing and fishing expeditions, too. We became accustomed to donning snorkeling gear, leaping over the side after a cursory look to see who, or what, was about, and spending an hour looking at beautiful fish and reefs.

It took time for me to evolve into a skilled, productive, and beneficial part of our shorthanded crew, but my strong desire to see new places and share them with the children bolstered my ability to put up with occasional hard times. Along with this sense of adventure, however, came the responsibility of lessening the risks. At times this meant reefing early, and at other times it meant knowing the political and security atmosphere of our destinations. In addition, I learned to feel pending weather changes and heed the portents of a rolling shelf cloud. (continued next page)

MY EVOLUTION AS CREW, CONTINUED

So many things helped me meet the challenges of open-ocean sailing and the cruising life, from becoming a boat-agile sailor, discovering and honing my sense of adventure, to enjoying the small pleasures along the way. The following thoughts underscore what Ralph has written in this book:

Sailing skills go way beyond sail hoisting, trimming, and tacking. This book points out the importance of close-quarters boat-handling skills, handyman abilities, and above all the need to quickly reach the right decision in varied situations. This ability to decide on the fly is one of the most important skills to develop in the transition from crew to watch captain and to skipper.

Handling a fully crewed race boat is different from handling a midsize cruising boat. Doublehanders have more in common with singlehanders than with eight or ten crew aboard a 44-foot race boat.

Although many new vessels are designed for less agile, less knowledgeable sailors, that doesn't negate the importance of traditional boat-handling and seamanship skills. This know-how will come in handy when the power quits or the bow thruster sucks up a spring line.

GPS, chartplotters, AIS, satellite phones, power winches, and so forth can create a false sense of empowerment. Learning to sail without the gadgets is like putting a little extra cash in your savings account. A rally to the Caribbean has its place, but crews must realize that once they set sail, they're on their own.

Spending time at sea and living aboard often begins with the pure pleasure of regular weekend getaways.

Practicing crew-overboard drills, firefighting, damage control, and other emergency procedures will drive home their step-by-step procedures and help you recall what to do when it really becomes a necessity. But it's even more important to practice the methods and behaviors that prevent the need for such interventions.

Aboard a shorthanded cruising boat, skipper and crew become sailing master, navigator, bosun, carpenter, cook, and doctor. The roles are blurred, so willingly learn them all.

More than one person in the crew should be familiar with vital equipment and procedures, especially setting/dousing sails, operating the engine, controlling the self-steering, and using radios and emergency signaling equipment, as well as being able to navigate as needed.

Good leadership begins with a crew's and skipper's respect for each other.

Early on, Lenore Naranjo kindled a prudent sense of adventure, first on small voyages and inland explorations and later with more distant horizons. As a teacher, she homeschooled our children aboard and turned each landfall into a social studies lesson. Somehow life aboard was as cohesive as the life our family experienced ashore. Without such a partnership, we can't call any cruise truly complete.

Going Along, Getting Along

The modern recreational vessel might get a nod of approval from B.F. Skinner, the father of operant conditioning, which refers to how a stimulus produces a response. The renowned Skinner likely would have loved watching the crew of a sailboat handle heavy weather. Nautical stimulus-response reactions to the passage of a cold front, though more complex than a lab rat pushing a lever to get a food pellet, certainly involve conditioning. Viewed through Skinner's lens, the act of shortening sail to lessen heel, decrease the violent motion of the vessel, and improve crew morale becomes a predictable response.

In addition to being an effective teaching tool, a boat underway also acts as a social platform. With exquisite Shakespearean detail, human interactions play out on a close-quarters stage. We can't ignore this human dynamic, because it's a critical piece of the seamanship equation; how a crew gets along with one another can be as important as how they handle

sail changes. Close proximity, the potential for adverse weather, and the need for a cohesive crew make ocean passagemaking a splendid test of human dynamics.

To gain as much as possible from the experience and to contribute to shipboard harmony, every crewmember must adapt as well as possible to onboard routines. The zen of being at peace on board starts with finding value in how you handle the routine.

The experience you gain from day sails or ocean crossings alike reinforces the value of routine, and you'll soon merge your individual identity with the act of being underway. This is quite different from a feeling like "I'd like to own that boat." Ownership and its material status are only a small part of the equation, but the desire to be aboard a vessel and underway is a much more durable impulse.

The experience of being under sail—flinging the water aside in purposeful forward motion—sets the hook for some, while others are drawn to the broader dimensions of cruising. Many are content with simply arriving at the boat and enjoying a weekend away from daily land routines. Time on the water always offers a sense of autonomy, a brief or prolonged break from the mainstream. Whatever the prize, we need to value the component parts of the experience: a sense of exploration, the opportunities of friendship, an appreciation of nature, and a love of tinkering with all the boat gear. Crewmembers soon recognize what makes their small-craft experience so important.

Those who have spent decades sailing with a wide variety of crew tend to remember most fondly those shipmates who showed up for their watches 5 minutes early, who volunteered for any miserable job, and perhaps most of all, who had a sense of humor that could turn a mean, gray day at sea into something to laugh about. The title "good shipmate" is the *cum laude* of crew distinction, and it's a title earned one watch at a time.

Frank Worsley acknowledged the kind of crew shipmates remember fondly. In the midst of a spume-blowing gale in the icy Southern Ocean, a sailor named McCarthy turned the helm of the 22-foot longboat *James Caird* over to skipper Frank Worsley, exclaiming, "It's a fine day, sir."

One of the key roles of the crew on watch involves making sure the off-watch crew are able to get some sleep. Poor course keeping and sail handling can work against that goal, as can a loud, raucous crew yakking it up in the cockpit at 0300. The loud clack of a harness tether hook being dropped and dragged along the deck is another sign of seafaring thoughtlessness, often completely missed by the crew on watch.

Small gestures are appreciated by shipmates, and considerate behavior can become contagious. Questions like "Can I get you something from the galley while I'm below?" or "Shall I bring up your foul weather jacket?" are a shipboard courtesy that lifts morale. The able seaman of old abided by the hand, reef, and steer code, but today's nonindentured, non-shanghaied crews appreciate some fun and reward in a small-vessel passage.

ATTRIBUTES OF A GOOD SKIPPER

Most well-run sailboats function in an egalitarian fashion, but despite the first-name familiarity of a friendly crew, only one person fills the undisputed role of skipper, even though on most boats the skipper also doubles as one of the crew. Skippers have the added responsibility of making tough calls when challenges arise. If a skipper acts too much like a crewmember, there is a risk of vacillation in the face of adversity, resulting in a collective deer-in-the-

The importance of who's in command isn't a vestige left over from Admiral Nelson's quarterdeck. It's a paramount issue, as the captain's role is as important aboard a 40-foot sailboat as any naval warship. Competence and decision-making capacity trump gender, age, and shoreside acclaim.

headlights response that immobilizes and may endanger the crew.

Daysailors can enjoy an afternoon sail with no command structure whatsoever, and some cruising couples prefer co-skippering. However, in an extreme situation, this laissez-faire command tends to break down at exactly the time when leadership is paramount and quick, effective decision making is the difference between safety and danger. Nothing is surprising about the value of good leadership; the challenge lies in developing the capacity and improving our ability to perform under stressful conditions.

Competent skippers, like crew, need an able seaman's keen ability to hand, reef, and steer. They also cultivate an ability to fathom what lies ahead, a trait even more valued in skippers; forehandedness makes a good skipper even better. Since a sailing vessel transiting a large body of water always runs the risk of being caught at sea by heavy weather, anticipating what's ahead and knowing how to handle it remain key traits of skilled skippers.

Some sailors of tall ships have described their lives before the mast as "long spans of monotony punctuated by moments of chaos." Those moments of chaos proved the worth of captains, but they had to demonstrate their abilities in routine times too, keeping their crew, if not happy, at least engaged in the job at hand. The same principle holds true today, but instead of the goal of getting grain to market ahead of other ships, the recreational sailor tries to savor the experience of being at sea, so the skipper's role includes enhancing conditions for all on board. Skippers who fail to engage the crew, regardless of their seamanship competence, are soon polishing their skills as singlehanders.

A common interest is the best mortar to cement the commitment of a crew. We've seen performance-oriented skippers pointed toward Bermuda leaping over two waves and then diving under the third; these skippers benefit from a boatful of type A personalities eager to finish first. A cruiser with less penchant for blunt trauma and more interest in enjoying the port visit at the end of the passage appreciates a little less drama and a lot less pounding. A family that enjoys playing in the water and gunkholing from one cove to the next may have much fonder memories of a summer cruise than those who sail five times as far in the same time. Some cruisers won't leave port without fishing gear, and others carry along a sailboard or small kayak, and these peripheral interests can make life aboard more enjoyable.

The Skipper as Comprehensivist

On several occasions in this book I refer to R. Buckminster Fuller, "the poet of technology." Known as Bucky to those who followed his work and thinking, this designer, architect, mathematician, and author is best known for his enduring concern for the future of humankind. But to sailors around the world, his headstone inscription, "Call me trim tab," summarizes his ideas in words sailors can appreciate: a little nudge in just the right place can steer a large rudder to change the course of the *Queen Mary*. Metaphorically speaking, the skipper's role, like a trim tab's, is pivotal for leveraging the most positive attributes of a vessel.

In 1968, Bucky and yacht designer Charlie Morgan decided that the new Morgan 30 Fuller had commissioned should be sold to someone else. Instead, Bucky would commit to one of the new keel/centerboard 41-footers that Morgan had just started to build. He named the vessel *Intuition,* and scattered throughout Bucky's written work we see allusions to voyaging and to sailing's influence on humanity.

One of Bucky's unwavering themes was an ongoing condemnation of superspecialization in graduate-level education and life. He believed an overly narrow focus turns the best and brightest into myopic, detail-oriented experts who know much about little. He remedied this educational/occupational dilemma with a system in which the pinnacle of education and life experience lies in becoming a "comprehensivist"—a scholar/implementer who knows a lot about many different subjects. One can argue about the practicality of this thinking applied to life gener-

ally, but when it comes to the seafaring word, Bucky's approach is an ideal roadmap to crew competence in general and skipper competence in particular. Fuller's own love of sailing may have influenced his outlook.

A proficient skipper must be as multifaceted as possible, not just in breadth of knowledge but also in the kind of wisdom that's acted out on the pitching deck of a vessel at sea. Those who spend significant time at sea come to know its ways, developing a feel for the portents of wind, sea, cloud cover, barometric changes, and vessel dynamics. Such "tells" help validate weather forecasts and hint at the changes that may lie ahead.

Chief Cook and Bottle Washer

Onboard routine includes myriad tasks. The U.S. Navy breaks the mariner's skill set into its most basic components, labeling each task a personal qualification skill (PQS). The objective of detailing specific skills is being able to move sailors and officers from ship to ship without disruption. At least in theory, any officer or enlisted crew can fill a job slot carrying the same rating. In wartime, when casualties are a factor, it is vital to replace the fallen and essential to clearly understand a crewmember's capability. Likewise, the U.S. Coast Guard and merchant marine follow a highly prescriptive curriculum for training personnel. This results in a good fit between a crewmember's or officer's rating and his or her capacity to fill a specific billet.

The less structured world of a cruising boat requires a less fine-grained division of responsibilities, and for that we can look to the Royal Navy that ruled the oceans two centuries ago. The British saw four key roles as essential aboard their ships: master, bosun, carpenter, and cook. Those job responsibilities are still relevant today. Fortunate skippers can delegate them, but with fewer crew skippers must carry out the tasks themselves. On a shorthanded boat the skipper may fill two, three, or even all four roles.

Traditionally, the bosun and carpenter managed vessel upkeep and maintenance. The bosun was the epicenter of marlinspike seamanship and rigging, while the carpenter dealt with the ship's hull, decks, spars, and ancillary small boats. On smaller vessels today, all crewmembers are part bosun and have talents ranging from that of rigger to painter and plastics expert. Commonly, though, the owner/skipper has the role of chief bosun, capable of do-it-yourself efforts that can keep the vessel in good operational and cosmetic order.

Today's practiced bosuns know how paints and plastic resins behave. They can stitch a sail or execute a fiberglass repair away from a full-service shipyard. And when it comes to jury-rigging a replacement for a broken part, the bosun's input into creative design and fabrication can prove quite insightful.

You're on your own when home waters fade astern, and the most memorable cruising often occurs away from the yachting infrastructure of boatyards, marinas, and anchorages. The more self-sufficient the crew, the more likely you'll ably cope with whatever situation arises. As one Viking voice advised in an early saga, "Tar the seams well, bring sturdy gear, and make your ship pleasant for the crew." This wisdom is as useful today as it was over a thousand years ago.

In the Age of Sail, the bosun and carpenter kept the ship afloat and moving, while the cook kept the crew going. Cookie was essential, despite the less-than-appealing fare he might serve up. Cooks are as essential today as they ever were. Since the crew were not hijacked aboard by a press gang and are probably accustomed to good food ashore, cooks are now judged by higher standards. Even if crew rotate through the cook's role, never lose sight of its significance.

Voyagers cherish routines including food, conversation, and a ritual toast at landfall. Crew morale can wax and wane in direct proportion to what happens in the galley, and the sensory appeal of good soup and baking bread can't be overstated. In all but the worst conditions, sailors value mealtime, and the art of sea cuisine includes matching sea state with what the cook can reasonably prepare and the crew can reasonably keep in their stomachs.

Medical Officers. In the past, Cookie might also serve as steward, responsible not only for preparing meals but for distributing them to the crew. In extreme situations, cooks might also fill in as medical officers—let's give silent thanks that we're not shipping under those conditions! While serious medical problems are an exception rather than the rule on board today, shorthanded sailors need a game plan to deal with the unlikely. One of the crew needs first aid skills, along with adequate supplies in the medical kit to cover possible though unlikely scenarios; that same crew should also monitor the inventory in the medical kit. The farther from medical care a voyage plan takes you, the more intensive should be the medical training and the larger the inventory of supplies. Also have plans for emergency communications and possible medical evacuation. Skippers are responsible for making sure this medical role is covered and the medical kit well stocked, even if they don't fill the role themselves.

Ship's Master. The ship's master, the most visible role, is the last of the four vital traditional shipboard roles. In addition to running the show and being accountable for the ups and downs of whatever happens on board, the master served as the final decision maker in all matters of navigation and vessel safety. He commanded the deck crew and, along with the mates who assisted on larger vessels, guided the seamen who sailed the ship.

Aboard racing sailboats today, the afterguard comprises the decision-making portion of the crew. The larger the vessel, the more players are involved; consensus building becomes an art form when the owner and skipper (not always the same person) are joined in the afterguard by a sailing master, a watch captain, and a navigator/tactician. On doublehanded cruising boats this administrative overlay is replaced with a streamlined hierarchy—a breath of fresh air. With the skipper as owner, master, and navigator, consensus becomes easier even if multitasking gets harder.

Navigator

The navigator (or multitasking skipper-navigator-cook-deckhand) shoulders the responsibility for safe navigation, using the latest electronic navigational equipment plus traditional piloting. We must fix our position, but we also must ponder our projected course options, considering weather data and surface current set and drift along with the future position of the vessel. Part astronomer, part meteorologist, and part oracle, the navigator second-guesses the future. While the digital era has freed navigators from pencil calculations and walking dividers across a paper chart, it has also replaced stubborn sextant shots with hunting for web downloads and weather fax broadcasts, which often are as hard to acquire as an accurate reading of the lower limb of the moon on an overcast evening. (See Chapter 8 for a full discussion of Navigation.)

Knowing your position is necessary for staying out of trouble, and "knowing" requires more than a circle-surrounded dot plotted on a paper chart or a blinking symbol on the screen. The navigator bridges the simulated position on paper or digital display with the actual surroundings. What counts is the real world of water depths, clearances above the masthead, proximity to a lee shore, and the constraints of fixed and moving objects; thus, a navigator's true job involves using both equipment and the senses when attending to the surroundings.

In addition, navigators maintain an active dialogue with each watch, placing a high priority on avoiding collision. A good working knowledge of the International Rules of the Road is a vital qualification for a navigator—and for any experienced mariner. (Chapter 9 covers the Rules of the Road.)

Today's communication options link the navigator to a wider array of assets than ever before. The VHF, MF, and HF radio frequency bands, as well as higher-frequency satellite linking systems, offer data

A good navigator regularly shoots bearings and plots a traditional fix even though a digital display pinpoints the vessel's location. It's easy to compare a bearing-compass reading with an electronic bearing readout on a multi-function display; setting the reading format to "magnetic" simplifies the process.

downlinks that can deliver weather information, engine failure analysis, or even specific medical advice. It's vital to understand what each system offers in terms of your specific cruise plans, safety requirements, and general communication. This knowledge helps you pick the best option for a given cruise and budget. While it's important to have reliable communication equipment, it's even more important that more than one crewmember is familiar with and able to operate the equipment. (See Chapter 14, Communications.)

Engineer

The need for an engineer aboard keeps growing as the systems on an average 40-footer grow increasingly complex. The marine industry strives for reliable turnkey operations, but installing complex systems in hot, damp, confined spaces keeps that goal elusive. An engineer can prevent a system catastrophe from dampening the cruising experience, and when such a catastrophe happens anyway, the engineer may be able to fix it. All amateur engineers need a familiarity

with the most important hardware on board, starting with the engine(s). The engineer must be able to at least troubleshoot the peripheral equipment that engine operation relies upon: water pump, fuel filters, starter, alternator(s), heat exchanger, exhaust system, and other peripherals.

Engineers should know Ohm's law and how a DC electrical system functions. As sail and powerboats have grown more and more mechanically and electrically dominated, so have the electrical systems that energize these components. Troubleshooting a high-voltage AC electrical system, in contrast, may be beyond the skill level of the skipper or crew. In addition, the uninformed shouldn't poke around in the AC system, which, more easily than the DC system, can kill you.

Of course, it's paramount to understand the fundamentals of how DC current gets to navigation instruments, running lights, the fuel lift pump, and other essential equipment. You can probably do without a microwave oven. But if the batteries are not charging and you have backed yourself into a corner, by going 100% digital, the charts you need exist only when electrons energize an MFD screen. This is why you'd better be able to replace an ailing alternator or voltage regulator and it makes sense to carry a backup portfolio of paper charts.

More often than not on shorthanded boats, the skipper serves as the engineer. In any case, a serious cruiser needs someone on board who either already is familiar with mechanical/electrical systems or can quickly learn them. These systems include the engine, drive train, control systems, generator, DC system, and an array of subsystems such as the refrigeration, watermaker, autopilot, and digital charting equipment.

Knowledge Is Safety

The word "autonomy" best describes a key trait the skipper attempts to develop. Autonomy means an internalized state of operational independence not reliant on shoreside consultants to tell you what turn the weather will take, for example. You or a crewmember knows how to download a weather fax, track barometric readings, and note changes in wind and cloud cover. In short, you've spent enough time observing weather systems and have studied forecast interpretation enough to understand the implications of fronts and moving air masses. Knowledge is power, and self-reliance is at the heart of skipper competence—and knowledge helps you develop confidence in your autonomy.

Unlike many other nations, the U.S. doesn't burden small-craft skippers with excessive regulatory

Paul and Dawn Miller race and cruise a well-tended classic wooden Herreshoff Rosinante, appreciating the feel of tradition. Paul is a professor of naval architecture and a materials specialist with a fondness for a neatly spiled plank.

mandates. Formal training and licensing remain options, not requirements. In contrast to flying or driving, recreational boaters in the U.S. can educate themselves, train their crew, and be tested by the operational demands of the waters sailed.

Whatever its downside, linking freedom and personal responsibility fosters an ethos of self-sufficiency. This pays off when conditions deteriorate when you are alone at sea. Having consultants to guide you through tough decision-making situations might make sense in a boardroom, but it's not the best option for those headed offshore. If the vessel is too complex for those aboard to thoroughly understand, it's better to postpone your departure, hire a professional skipper or engineer, or trade down for a vessel you can understand, handle, and maintain.

In the last couple of decades we've seen a trend in two-person crews purchasing oversized vessels. Yacht brokers are telling green sailors—with straight-faced assurance—that a bow thruster, pod drive, and a call ahead to the dockmaster will enable a neophyte crew to handle a 55-footer. Part of developing competence, however, involves knowing our limitations. Letting a salesman with minimal experience at sea define our ability is as problematic as assuming that a towing service will always be on hand to clear up the shortfalls.

When the crew is prepared for what lies ahead, the right sails are on board, and the navigator looks at the horizon as well as at equipment, the voyage is more likely to be safe and successful. Many of the recent sailing accidents resulting in loss of life have involved flawed navigation decisions and inattentive watchkeeping.

The Skipper as Leader

The cerebral side of being a good skipper goes beyond the need to navigate and understand the implications of a weather map filled with stacked isobars. It even transcends being a MacGyveresque mechanical, electrical, and plumbing guru and troubleshooter extraordinaire. The final challenge for any skipper is the transition involved in becoming a leader.

Effective leadership begins with the crew's respect for the captain's competence. Crews of all sizes must have faith in their captain's ability to make sensible decisions. While all crewmembers want the skipper to consider thoughts and interests, the overall well-being of the vessel and crew is even more important than individual interests. Regardless of differences in preferences or interests, all is forgiven if the crew trusts the captain to choose the best options for the current and near-term situations.

Communication

The contribution of an effective crew is greater than the sum of what the individuals offer, and good leadership elicits the most desirable outcome. Two-way communication is a primary aspect of leadership. In an urgent situation, the right decision needs to be made, and it must be passed along to all crew as succinctly as possible. This is not the time to hold court on the efficacy of the decision, because prompt implementation is often critical. This is why a good leader knows when to be a consensus builder and when a dictatorial approach is necessary. Really great skippers have a knack for making the right snap decisions, but they can also dialog with shipmates and genuinely take their input to heart. Few captains of larger crews have more expertise than the sum total of others on board, but they know how to leverage the knowledge of others to collectively solve or prevent problems. They also understand that some crew members need to be encouraged to speak out while others don't.

Communication when the wind is howling and everyone is engaged in efforts to keep things under control is most effective based on these principles:

- Eliminate distracting (nonessential) side conversations.
- If assigned a task, repeat it for confirmation.
- If you observe something astray or a pending problem, tell the watch captain or skipper and make sure they acknowledge they understand what you're saying.
- When reefing or going through a heavy weather sail change, a quick description in advance of "who does what" is often worth the time.

Good communication also gives the skipper a feel for the crew's well-being, as enjoyment of being at sea should be a major part of the cruising experience. The first few days at sea is often an adjustment: some are feeling seasick, others miss those left astern, and the skipper is managing the transition to an engaging onboard routine. Adding new crew to the mix can raise some challenges, and a skipper who can resolve issues early is more likely to maintain harmony. Getting along with crew while exerting leadership when handling heavy weather can be challenging, but preventing a mutiny is just as important as keeping the mainsail in one piece.

The Skipper's Briefing

Have a safety briefing each time you prepare to leave the dock or anchorage, ideally when the whole crew is on board but before easing the docklines. This predeparture summary can be as short or as detailed as conditions warrant. For an afternoon sail, it may include only the location of PFDs and fire extinguishers, a quick mention of crew-overboard recovery procedures, and comments on the route or destination, the weather conditions expected, and any concerns. The briefing begins an operational dialogue among all on board and encourages the crew to engage in the planning process.

Longer passages naturally warrant greater detail. The skipper can kick things off by checking PFDs and stating the boat policy for when to wear them, including how and when watchstanders should be clipped in with a harness. Skippers make the call about when crew must wear PFDs, but they also encourage crewmembers to wear a PFD whenever they choose. This is a good time to remind shipmates about checking the gas cylinders and auto-inflation bobbins in their inflatable PFDs.

Skippers should point out the location of all COB rescue equipment and familiarize each crew with engine starting procedures, VHF and other communications equipment, and emergency signaling beacons. It's also wise to go over the gear inventory and show where you stow flares and other distress signals. If appropriate do a step-by-step abandon-ship drill that includes how the life raft would be deployed. In short, part of the skipper's role is to maintain an ongoing training routine that the crew enjoys and from which they derive useful knowledge. This process allows skippers to share their specialized knowledge with others in the crew.

The Skipper's Routines

On any boat, it's handy to adhere to a single approach for making up cleats, coiling lines, stowing gear in lockers, and organizing the toolbox. This isn't an obsession with uniformity but a shipboard routine that prepares everyone on board for an efficient response to a reefing challenge, mechanical repair, or any situation in which a line or specific screwdriver is needed in a hurry. For example, consider a violent squall that blows through at 0300 on a moonless night. The first gusts lay the boat over, and the crew's reefing efficiency gets its best test. Whether you're slab reefing or rolling the sail into the mast or boom, the process works best if everyone knows exactly how the lines were coiled and where to reach for the right winch handle. Doing things the same way each time is the best way to garner such familiarity.

You can explain to crewmembers that their own approaches may be just as good as yours—perhaps even better—but you have adopted your set routines to make it easier for the crew to work together. Of course, if a better solution is offered, the skipper shouldn't disregard it just to stay with the familiar way. Test out the new and better approach, and if all goes well, then adapt it to fit your preferred routine.

Skippers can best familiarize crew with their routines and preferences during a time of calm sailing, to develop a mutually embraced approach to key tasks. This might include details such as your method of coiling a halyard tail, for example. Conventional coil-

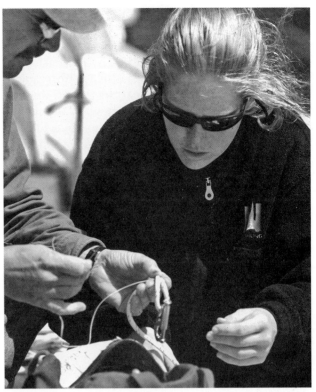

One of the best ways to learn any nautical skill is to be taught by an experienced sailor on a passage in which the skill could really count. Lashing and hand sewing skills may be a vestige of the 1800s, but they still come in handy today.

Good teamwork is all about knowing how your shipmates will respond in specific sailing situations and making sure you're holding up your end of the bargain. Competent skippers ensure that information flows in both directions, and they make sure the entire crew is attuned to their roles as well as the bigger picture. Crossing shipping lanes at dusk is a time for extra awareness.

ing of a long, two-part mainsail halyard can introduce hockles because each loop requires placing a twist in the line. An alternative is to fake the line in a figure eight rather than circular coil. In this approach each twist lies the opposing direction, and each turn cancels the line-snarling effect of its partner. When the halyard is released, the line is far more likely to run free rather than snarl in a ball and end up 10 feet above the deck with the mainsail flogging like a wet terrier.

This one task demonstrates the value of using a single, crew-wide approach for handling lines—whether running rigging or docklines—and makes a drama-free response to a midnight emergency more likely.

The Skipper's Human-Resource Responsibilities

When the basics of staying afloat and heading in the right direction are under control, the skipper can

SEASICKNESS

Seasickness is a big challenge for many sailors, and inevitably conditions occur in which most sailors may become susceptible. Ideally, everyone aboard recognizes their susceptibility to motion sickness and can find ways to lessen the impact. One of the most widely accepted ways to lessen the effect is to take the helm and watch the horizon, with just enough cursory glances to the compass or digital readout to hold a good course. This combination of fresh air and sustained focus on the horizon often has a calming effect. An alert skipper can use this remedy for queasy crew.

Seasickness begins in the semicircular canals of the inner ear, a biological accelerometer that registers the roll, pitch, yaw, heave, and surge of the vessel as relative motion and inclination. Meanwhile, if the eyes are looking around the cabin and seeing fewer signs of motion than the inner ear is registering, confused signals are sent to the brain, triggering a stimulus to the vagas nerve that causes the stomach to react. A drug that elicited the same feeling might be the optimum diet pill, but the patient would quickly begin to suffer from dehydration, and that's exactly what those who succumb to seasickness must be concerned about.

Many sufferers find water less than palatable, especially if it tastes of the tank and is not charcoal filtered. Those who have suffered past bouts of seasickness often have preferred treatments, and many claim that ginger ale is more likely than water to stay in their stomach. Others prefer cabin biscuits, saltines, and ginger snaps as staple foods for the first couple of days at sea.

Some medications may prevent seasickness altogether. For example, meclizine tablets (in brand names such as Bonine and Dramamine) have for decades been readily available in virtually all drugstores. Some individuals become drowsy, however, and others experience no effect at all. Overall, the side effects are less bothersome than those produced by most other prescription products.

Prescription scopolamine patches are a wonder drug for many seasickness-prone sailors. However, a few unlucky souls suffer challenging side effects, including hallucinations and psychotic symptoms.

Therefore, before using this patch therapy on board, it's common sense to try it when you're able to handle the side effects—and if you experience them, never use the drug again.

Some sailors try products like Stugeron (an antihistamine) that are not FDA approved, to battle the effects of seasickness; it acts to relieve nausea, vomiting, headaches, and so forth, rather than to prevent seasickness. The availability of the drug varies from country to country; in Mexico, for example, a person can purchase Stugeron over the counter in 25, 75, or 150 mg tablets, although serious problems can occur when taken in 75 and 150 mg doses. In larger doses, prescription Stugeron is FDA approved to treat the side effects of other diseases, generally those that that produce symptoms of imbalance and vertigo. The list of unintended consequences shows us exactly why sailors should be cautious in using the drug. The side effects include jaundice, gastro-intestinal issues, impaired judgment, dry mouth, and relaxed arteries. People with Parkinson's disease, liver problems, and a host of other health problems should not take this drug.

Regardless of these difficulties, the drug has been around since the 1970s, and the FDA has approved the primary ingredient, cinnarizine, for uses other than seasickness. The FAA prohibits airline pilots from taking the drug because of its potential to impair decision making. For the same reason, sailors should also be cautious.

If you decide you need to medicate seasickness, do so in conjunction with your physician, and make sure you consider any preexisting condition that precludes using any of the aforementioned drugs. On a passage I made from Bermuda to the U.S., the skipper had purchased Stugeron over the counter and told the crew that the only reason the FDA had yet to approve the drug was that "the drug company did not want to bother paying for the testing." He encouraged the crew of seven to take the pills, and six did; of those six, three became seasick. The best practice is to encourage each crew to develop a means of preventing or coping with *mal de mer* during shorter passages before letting it become a problem on a longer voyage.

turn to crew health, welfare, and morale. A long-term group of shipmates is advantageous because it allows team building to evolve over time. Every crew, regardless of size, has wide-ranging sets of skills, both physical and cerebral. By getting to know each person on board, a skipper has a better chance to match jobs with skills and proclivities. We've already discussed the job descriptions. Fortunate is the skipper who has these crew to whom to delegate tasks:

- An agile, fit foredeck crewmember ready to go up the mast.
- A sailing master to lead in reefing, setting, and dousing sail.
- A navigator to track progress, lay out routes, and monitor the weather.
- An engineer to fix what breaks.
- A chef who enjoys feeding the crew.
- A bosun who maintains the boat in port and jury-rigs it offshore.

Whether you're sailing with a full crew complement or doublehanding with your spouse, part of the skipper's leadership role involves setting up opportunities for each crewmember to excel.

Conditions at sea vary, and mood changes in those aboard often mirror the pendulum-like swings between calms and gales. Therefore, skippers should be alert for both weather and mood shifts and do their best to draw out those affected or to lighten the general mood. Baked bread, baked potatoes, and tasty soups and stews can be a morale booster, as are cookies from a special box or tin. Cold night watches can be especially debilitating, and in addition to assigning shorter night watches, capable skippers keep a close eye out for signs of hypothermia.

Sometimes what looks like moodiness is in fact incipient seasickness. Little tricks like tucking in a reef to reduce speed and motion before meals often result in a crew that feels more like eating and might help them keep their meals where they belong. During predeparture provisioning, good skippers should ask about crewmembers' food preferences and use this to establish palatable menus and make life easier for the cook(s). Responding to seasickness with ginger ale, saltines, and ginger snaps plus quick deck-to-rack (berth) transitions can help the stricken (see the Seasickness sidebar).

Even this culinary impaired author has a chance to gain compliments at sea. Feeding a hungry crew has a reward all its own. Keeping the crew well fed enhances readiness. (Courtesy Lenore Naranjo)

WHAT CRUISERS CAN LEARN FROM RACERS

Competitive offshore sailors have earned a reputation as die-hards and are often stereotyped as type A personalities, ready to test their skills against each other as well as the sea itself. Many nonracers wonder what the lure of the sport is all about. One answer is the desire to achieve and elevate performance by challenging others with similar skills. It's all a part of human nature.

It's often said that when two sailboats are near each other, it's a race. Even in more passive souls, we see a competitive spirit alive and well. At sea, we can shape this competitive trait into a 24/7 expression of teamwork and seamanship. Offshore racing is a logical extension of inshore racing, and for those not prone to seasickness, the sport has much to offer.

Offshore racing merges a sailboat and the crew in a manner that's hard to duplicate ashore. A 24-hour motor race is viewed as an ordeal, but a five-day jaunt to Bermuda ranks as another run-of-the-mill offshore race. Transoceanic sailors sprint for days on end, and Volvo Ocean Race crews endure a mountaineer's privation with a race car driver's need for focused attention. In short, whether you sail a coastal overnight race or in an ocean-crossing event, the commitment to team building and vessel readi-

ness is in many ways unmatched by other forms of sailing.

When it comes to developing seamanship, we acquire skills at all levels of sailboat racing, from the smallest of one-design dinghies through the most esoteric of monohull and multihull classes. The International Sailing Federation (ISAF) is the controlling body of the competitive sport worldwide, and the national organization in the United States is US Sailing. Run by sailors, this grassroots organization dovetails the global big picture with specific domestic needs of the sport. Self-regulation and safety training are part of the mix, and membership in US Sailing requires only a modest annual fee.

From a seamanship perspective, one-design racing is analogous to working out in a gym with a wide array of fitness equipment and a bevy of personal trainers. Dinghy and one-design racing generates a noticeable uptick in sail-handling skills, an important benefit. This boot camp for boat agility is hard to beat, and ocean racers and cruisers with some one-design racing in their sailing resumes usually benefit significantly.

Differences exist between the seamanship honed sailing around the buoys in short-course racing and

Inshore big-boat racing hones skills that benefit racers and cruisers alike. As John Bonds once put it, "Sailboat racing is like war without the guns." Agility on deck, quick sail changes, and acclimation to the boat's motion pay off whether you're racing or cruising.

Around-the-world racers are a breed unto themselves, learning early that if you don't finish you can't win; these boats (a Volvo 60 is shown here) are well engineered and versatile in a variety of weather conditions.

the kind called for during a lengthy offshore race. For starters, an ocean race more closely resembles a marathon than a sprint, and the crew has to finish the race in order to win. In countless cases, driving a vessel too hard in heavy conditions has caused gear failure that turned an in-the-money performance into a did-not-finish (DNF) outcome.

The decision-making part of seamanship involves knowing both when to dial back and when to add more sail. The full-sail-all-the-time character of dinghy sailing is tough to replicate offshore. An ocean racer quickly realizes that reducing sail area can often actually result in better boat speed. When a cruising sailor goes racing, the lessons include a better feel for the fine line separating speed from calamity and an improved ability to coax more speed from a given sail area. Experiencing the all-hands fire drill of a nasty knockdown helps a normally shorthanded cruiser understand what to avoid.

We also see a distinct value in developing a feel for how much energy you need to harness to attain the final half knot of hull speed. Acquiring on-the-edge performance feedback builds your sea sense to the point where you can *feel* when it's time to reduce sail ahead of a broach rather than after it has occurred. Racing also teaches you how to better handle light-air conditions, thus reducing the hours spent running the diesel.

For racers and cruisers alike, one of the big fringe benefits involves how the most skilled crewmembers handle their specialty jobs. For example, a highly skilled bowman has an intuitive feel for vessel roll and uses the induced moment of inertia to unload a pole just before switching spinnaker guys or clipping in or out of a dip-pole jibe. This kinesthetic awareness of boat motion and energy flow is akin to how a figure skater harnesses the energy of his partner's movement to help lift her into the air.

Momentary increases and decreases in the kinetic energy transferred through a genoa sheet cycles in cadence with the roll of the vessel, and by staying in phase with decreasing loads, a savvy trimmer can adjust the car position much more easily. Similarly you can put to good use the peaks and valleys associated with roll and spinnaker-induced energy. This type of on-off cycling of loading occurs in all sails and can be used to advantage to slide sheet leads on tracks, to take up on a loose halyard, or simply as an aid to hoist a sail hand over hand. (continued page 73)

The Melges 24 puts crew agility and stamina to the test; crew weight adds to the righting moment whenever maneuvers or sail changes aren't in play. When it comes to developing boat agility, sport-boat racing is even better than going to the gym. In the racing community, as with the entire sailing community, there is quite a bit of debate over the need to wear a PFD—a really good idea in colder water.

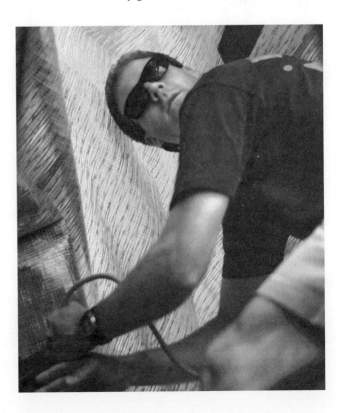

Sail changes on a race boat are never savored. The pace of the race carries through during a headsail change, and the better the crew learn their jobs, the faster sail swapping becomes. Repetition is the best teacher, and new crew need to learn the new boat's layout and idiosyncrasies.

HANDS-ON SAFETY TRAINING OPPORTUNITIES

In recent years sailors talked so much about hands-on safety-at-sea training that the waterfront pros at the U.S. Merchant Marine Academy at Kings Point, New York, and the U.S. Naval Academy now provide such training. SUNY Maritime and the Storm Trysail Club have also been leaders in on-the-water training.

Both service academies have harnessed a new rendition of safety training to benefit their midshipmen as well as the boating public at large. Their efforts to network with local sailing communities and enlist the help of experts from the marine trades have created what US Sailing refers to as a "best-of-both-worlds training experience."

These two-day events provide auditorium lectures and small-group hands-on learning experiences. They include on-the-water crew-overboard rescue drills, damage control, firefighting, in-water life raft and PFD training, safety gear testing, and flare deployment. Kings Point hosted the first of these ISAF-approved, US Sailing–sanctioned events over 35 years ago. (See Chapter 13 for more detailed coverage of these topics.)

Crew-Overboard Recovery

The underway crew-overboard (COB) recovery exercise aboard Farr 39s and J/105s was perhaps the most daunting portion of that first training event. Each boat had a skilled Kings Point Sailing Team skipper, a training coordinator, and an eager crew of seminar participants facing an early spring easterly. Most crew stepping aboard were strangers to one another and to the skipper/instructor. Many had never before sailed either a Farr 40 or a J/105, and some definitely stretched the limits of their skills in the gusty 20-knot conditions that typify Long Island Sound's fickle early April weather. The water was a hypothermia-provoking 52°F.

Safety boats followed the fleet, and the caliber of the Kings Point staff assigned to each group and boat allowed for vigorous training in real-world, "live-fire" conditions. The drills began under full sail and spinnaker, and participants got to see that the harder a vessel is driven, the more threatening and potentially hazardous a crew-overboard incident becomes. Fast boats quickly separate from victims, and if a quickstop maneuver is not executed immediately, a real need arises for an effective, reliable position-marking method such as the electronic MOB button on a VHF or GPS receiver. The recorded coordinates should also be written in the log just in case the electronic function is accidentally erased.

Adjusting to the changing weather and crew skills provided a lesson in itself. The Kings Point organizers understood the significance of cold water, gusty

Participants in an ISAF-approved safety-at-sea seminar held at the Merchant Marine Academy, Kings Point, receive hands-on training in setting storm sails, crew overboard recovery techniques, and numerous other emergency drills.

HANDS-ON SAFETY TRAINING OPPORTUNITIES, CONTINUED

pre-cold front conditions, and crews who had never sailed together. They effectively exercised their plans to ratchet back sail area as wind velocity warranted, going from full to reefed sails and eventually to storm sails as conditions deteriorated. This type of hands-on training with capable sailors is immensely valuable, but it's also a serious challenge for event organizers, who are responsible for setting up learning situations with an acceptable risk but not excess hazard. A by-product of this session was a clear understanding of the essential role of training to prevent COB incidents.

Those practicing COB recoveries also learned how important communication can be among crewmembers. Their new-to-the-boat, new-to-each-other status reinforced the value of developing crew cohesiveness and keeping a nucleus of regulars together so that you can effectively mentor new crew. The importance of leadership and the skipper's role also played out as each recovery maneuver was implemented. Most crews greatly improved their performance after only a small amount of practice; attendees then returned home with the idea that the same would hold true aboard their own boats.

Firefighting

The facial expressions on program attendees as they faced down and extinguished a small fire in a metal bucket drove home a fear of flames. Each person had a chance to put out a small blaze with a short-lived dry chemical extinguisher, and by the end of that experience each understood why it's essential to get the fire out quickly. They likely also understood the importance of making sure that fuel, electrical ignition sources, and even oxygen are removed from the conflagration. Once a fire gets out of hand, confronting it with a small dry chemical extinguisher is like hunting big game with a single-shot .22 caliber rifle.

Abandon-Ship Drill

Jumping into a swimming pool fully clothed and wearing a PFD doesn't produce the same anxiety as abandoning your boat in the middle of the night in a storm-tossed sea, but you can simulate reality enough at least to gain a good idea about how the gear works. All boaters should have the chance to test their PFD in benign conditions and discover firsthand what it takes to transition from a sinking or burning vessel to a cramped but floating life raft. For example, those jumping in with inflatable PFDs discovered that manually pulling the inflation tab causes the PFD to fill instantaneously. This eliminates the need to wait for automatic inflation, which can often take 10 seconds or more.

Because climbing into a life raft while wearing clothes and a PFD can be challenging, new raft regulations mandate a boarding assist to help get tired, sick, or injured crew into the raft more easily. Kings Point program participants also had a chance to use the line and webbing on the bottom of a raft to help right it when capsized. They had time to get a feel for the cramped conditions in *(continued next page)*

🚩 *The proper use of a dry chemical fire extinguisher includes pointing the nozzle at the base of the flames and sweeping the discharge across the base of the flames. Due to limited volume, the extinguisher operation is measured in seconds, so it's vital to deploy this tool early and use it accurately.*

🚩 *It's more difficult to board a life raft wearing a PFD, but the value of wearing a life jacket outweighs its impact on mobility. Boarding ladders, small boarding ramps built into the raft, and a strong crew already in the raft can assist others. Note the value of high-reflectance SOLAS-grade tape on the raft, foul-weather gear, and inflatable life jackets.*

HANDS-ON SAFETY TRAINING OPPORTUNITIES, CONTINUED

a filled-to-capacity raft, allowing them to see why long-distance sailors often opt for a raft with more capacity than their crew size.

Troubleshooting and Damage Control

With three of the nation's top technical experts on hand to describe and demonstrate what to do in emergencies, participants were guaranteed a special learning experience. America's Cup boatbuilder Eric Goetz, mechanical and electrical expert Steve D'Antonio, and ocean racer/boatyard manager Mike Keyworth were all on hand at this training event. These individuals collectively brought more nautical savvy to the forefront than I've seen at any other safety-at-sea presentation.

Each expert detailed and demonstrated how to cope with damage resulting from hull penetration, elaborated on jury rigging after a dismasting, and delved into specifics about handling the loss of a rudder. For example, Steve focused on downflooding associated with through-hull and valve failures and problems caused by electrical malfunctions, including fires stemming from incorrectly wired high-current, low-voltage electrical systems.

Distress Signaling

Henry Marx of Landfall Navigation was on hand with a full load of safety gear. Each group viewing his display had a chance to inspect and evaluate the latest technology in safety and signaling equipment. Discussion topics included personal EPIRBs (emergency position-indicating radio beacons), laser illuminators, hand-powered watermakers, waterproof lights, and VHF radios. Each attendee went home with a clear understanding of what should be kept in a well-stocked abandon-ship bag.

For over a century, pyrotechnics have been a mainstay of distress signaling, and despite the huge strides made in electronic communications flares remain a mandatory part of a vessel's safety gear. Because they believed watching a flare's deployment is nowhere near as effective as learning to deploy a signal yourself, the training team set up a hands-on flare-firing station at the downwind end of a pier. They manned it with a group of safety experts who talked each participant though the nuances of a safe launch.

In the overcast conditions the daylight-visible

Damage control training includes learning to patch holes in the hull with both internal and external coverings, as shown on the stern of this sailboat. Attendees at this seminar also learned how to jury-rig after a dismasting, using smaller sails, a spinnaker pole, and the mast stub to effect a viable solution.

HANDS-ON SAFETY TRAINING OPPORTUNITIES, CONTINUED

pyrotechnics appeared even brighter, and during each launch the participants became aware of the heat and slag expelled from the burning pyrotechnic. They also saw that a SOLAS-grade (i.e., approved by the International Convention for the Safety of Life at Sea) parachute rocket flew higher, burned brighter, and lasted longer than other USCG-approved versions of the same signaling device. The event built a keen awareness of the hazards associated with flares and the need to handle these devices with special care.

Underway Safety Training: Risks and Rewards

"Operational risk management" is a buzz phrase among safety types. It's usually associated with how close to the edge a training program should venture before the possible downside eclipses the gains made on the upside. For example, Navy SEAL training includes live rounds and near-drowning experiences, but recreational sailors need less reality and more security in their learn-by-doing experiences. The Kings Point crew kicked off their first-of-its-kind underway safety-at-sea training session at a level of challenge they were ready to modify if needed. Overall, only one minor injury occurred—not perfect, but pretty good.

Only a few days after that event, a UK hands-on training session resulted in a tragic injury. When a trainee was deploying a white handheld pyrotechnic signal, the entire flare exploded at once, seriously injuring the trainee's hand in the blast. Even worse, the flare tube itself penetrated the trainee's abdomen.

Some say we can cover more information with a traditional lecture, and that may be true in some situations. However, if we want to develop physical abilities, then we're far more likely to accomplish that if we include a physical training component in the process. Educators have long understood the value of combining lecture with laboratory experiences, and when it comes to safety at sea and how best to train sailors, there's definitely good reason to blend physics with physical education.

Handheld flares are always held downwind in a life raft. Burning hot slag dripping onto an inflated raft tube will melt through the fabric and create an even more desperate situation. Bright SOLAS flares will gain the attention of those in the area, but the burn of all flares is relatively short, so their use needs to be well timed.

Another learning experience offered by sea time on a race boat involves fine-tuning how to get around a three-dimensionally gyrating deck and cabin. By the time they join a race boat crew, many cruisers already have well-seasoned sea legs. But the true test of boat agility comes when the vessel is pounding to windward, heeled 20 degrees, and climbing over and crashing through an unending parade of waves. Forethought and forehandedness come into play then, as do jacklines and harnesses. As one sailing friend said, "Any fool can strap on a harness and clip to a jackline, but it's a skilled crew that can still carry on the work at the mast and on the foredeck while dragging a tail."

Experiencing rough going aboard a sound race boat handled by a skilled crew is one of the best ways to learn by doing. No matter how many times you go through training in contrived, hands-on, flatwater learning sessions, it lacks the real-world challenges of coping with heavy weather at sea. It's hard to tell someone how to ride a bike, for example, and it's just as hard to describe reefing. Yes, we can outline the basic steps and students can memorize them, but going through the process in a light wind on a flat sea is the right way to introduce the concept. To develop true proficiency, however, there's nothing like getting a chance to use those skills on a wet, windswept deck in a rolling seaway at 0300 while the boat's motion and the energy traveling from sails to sheets complicate each step in the process.

Offshore Race Training

The offshore racing interests guided by ISAF have set in place a set of rules that range from equipment specifications to safety training mandates. These self-imposed requirements and feedback from disasters like the 1979 Fastnet Race and the 1998 Sydney to Hobart Race have led to a combination of lectures and hands-on training designed to prepare sailors to cope with emergencies at sea as well as preventing them in the first place.

US SAILING SAFETY AT SEA CURRICULUM

Classroom Training

Care and maintenance of safety equipment
Storm sails
Damage control and repair
Heavy-weather crew routines, boat handling, drogues
Crew-overboard prevention and recovery
Rendering assistance to other craft
Hypothermia prevention and treatment
Search-and-rescue organization and methods
Weather forecasting

Hands-on Training

Life rafts and life jackets
Fire precautions and use of fire extinguishers
Communications equipment (VHF, GMDSS, satellite
    communications, etc.)
Pyrotechnics and EPIRBs

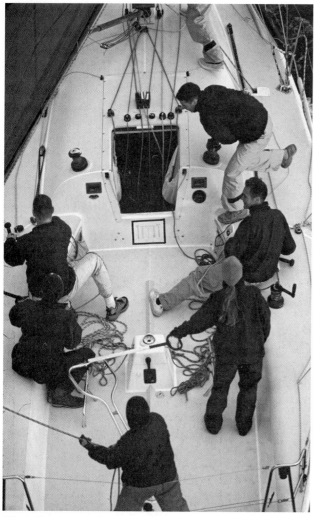

Agile crewmembers move like cats, neither tripping over lines nor wasting steps when moving from here to there. Fore-and-aft trim is a big deal on light, fine-bowed race boats with a well-trained crew. The crew know what changes should be made as the breeze builds or drops and where weight should be distributed on every point of sail.

The US Sailing-sponsored Safety at Sea Seminar Program, linked to the ISAF-endorsed curriculum, focuses on the needs of various categories of racing aboard fully crewed sailboats. The curriculum is comprehensive, as shown at left, including both classroom and hands-on experiences.

The sidebar (Hands-on Safety Training Opportunities) offers more detail on safety training opportunities. If you can't attend one of these formal trainings, make sure you and your crew are trained on all these topics informally if you are planning on sailing offshore.

From a racer's perspective, as rigorous and compelling as the ISAF curriculum is, it's not the last word for a shorthanded cruiser. The operational routine aboard a cruising vessel is anything but a sprint from A to B followed by an airline ride back home. Cruisers, who tend to be much longer-term residents of their vessels and the sea, increase their exposure to the elements over time. Cruisers also seldom push their vessels to the extent that racing sailors do, and they usually spend far more time at anchor than under sail. Thus, it's no surprise that one size of sail training doesn't fit all sailors.

Among the topics missing in the ISAF training are handling heavy weather with an in-mast furling sail plan (see Chapter 7), anchoring in gale-force conditions (see Chapter 6), dinghy handling and stowage, and singlehanded crew-overboard recoveries. For example, when compared to its usefulness for a full racing crew, the quick-stop crew-overboard recovery maneuver (see Chapter 13) is much less valuable to a doublehander who instantaneously becomes a singlehander.

We also need to consider issues involving emergency maneuvering under power, safety and system awareness, and the implications of long-term weather patterns for planning passages (see Chapter 10). The ISAF curriculum also doesn't address watchkeeping (see Chapter 1), the Navigation Rules (see Chapter 9), and other important safety topics.

In short, cruisers need to rethink the issue of safety at sea and arrive at a set of training priorities suitable to the type of sailing they're most involved with. Racing compared to cruising is in some ways analogous to differences between sprinters and distance runners: their workout routines may have some similarities, but their needs are quite different.

Whether racing or cruising, a skipper and crew learn to interface with their boat through evolving seamanship. Boat handling is an ongoing field test that validates skills, helps hone new ones, and informs which areas require more practice. The next chapter highlights key boat-handling skills and charts a course that will help you acquire what is necessary.

BOAT HANDLING

oat handling involves the implementation of sea sense—a seamless blend of knowledge and kinesthetic ability. Nothing measures your skill as a mariner quite as visibly as performing the various maneuvers involved in handling your boat in a range of situations, including docking, picking up a mooring, pre-start maneuvering on a race course, or attempting to tack up a narrow channel. What occurs in these settings will affirm your basic boat-handling skills or reveal the lack, for at such times there's no room for posturing and the circumstances at hand take center stage.

Like numerous other activities that involve both mental and physical skill, sailing critiques your competency. Taken together, these boat-handling talents represent opportunities to self-evaluate and implement changes. In reality, if we look closely at the components of boat handling, we see the essential outline of the curriculum all boaters begin studying the first time they step aboard. These lessons apply regardless of whether your dream or plan is to cross oceans or stay in the bay.

Tom Reardon, Ticonderoga's professional captain for over 20 years, believes in using only basic technology that a resourceful mariner can fix or work around. He likes hand-cranked winches and piston hanks on headsails, and he trains his crew to be aware of what surrounds them and have a contingency plan in mind should plan A go astray.

CONTINGENCY THINKING

Aviators say that there are "old pilots and bold pilots, but very few old, bold pilots." The dividing line perhaps isn't quite as dramatic for mariners. Still, we can look at similarities between flying and boating, particularly the reality that both activities prove safer when we mentally update our contingency plan. In Chapter 3, we called it forehandedness, but we could just as accurately call it "thinking ahead of your boat."

Start by asking yourself questions such as these:

"If the engine quits suddenly off that lee shore, will I have time to get the sails up in a favorable breeze or the anchor down so I can keep the boat off the beach?" (If you're not sure, you're too close to shore.)

"If the wind shifts 180 degrees during the night, will this anchorage be safe?" (If the answer is no, you'd better be confident in your forecast.)

"If a gust causes me to round up while I'm sailing under the stern of this anchored boat, will I have room to avoid him?" (If in doubt, give the boat a wider berth, and if you can't do that because of other boats to leeward, look for a safer path through the anchorage; if you can't see one, you probably shouldn't be carrying sail through this moored or anchored crowd.)

Equipment and Hardware Failures

Part of contingency planning involves staying aware of what can fail. Do you understand how your essential hardware works? Do you know what to do if your engine fails in the midst of a maneuver? Consider the possibility of gear failure before the gear in question becomes critical. Awareness of risk doesn't mean precautionary paralysis, but it does mean understanding potential pitfalls and preparing for contingencies. (Later, in Chapter 13, we look at some of the ways around-the-world voyagers abide by aviators' and sailors' beliefs in backup plans.)

Most veteran passagemakers recognize that safe boating requires much more than a boatload of orange and yellow safety gear. They see boat handling as a primary means to avoid accidents; they live by the principle that *steering clear of a problem is much better than overcoming it.*

Expecting the Unexpected

Your final approach to a slip, for example, is another excellent time for contingency planning. Many boaters charge rapidly toward their slot at the seawall, girded by blind faith in their engines and running gear. The hard charge is bold, dramatic, and decisive, and it minimizes the effects of wind and current. And it works—as long as slamming the shift lever into reverse results in a big pulse of boat-stopping back-down thrust. But the day this faith in the cables, linkages, reverse gear, and drive train goes unanswered will be the day that the hard charge proves truly dramatic.

A few years ago I watched the crew of a large sloop attempt this type of high-speed docking maneuver. Unbeknownst to the helmsperson, a crucial pin holding the cable linkage of the single-lever control had slipped off the reverse-gear shift lever, and what started as a casual quest for reverse progressed instantly into sheer panic. Not only did the drive train refuse to shift out of forward, but the single-lever control continued, perversely, to act as a fully functional throttle. Finding himself in extremis, the helmsperson's final, desperate act was to yank the single-lever control to the full-speed-astern position. Unfortunately, only half his wish was granted. Full speed was indeed engaged, but the gear remained in forward! To put it gently, the vessel's bow and the concrete seawall shared an unambiguous "transfer of kinetic energy," teaching all on board an important lesson: *Never put absolute trust in a boat's ability to deliver reverse on demand.*

By testing back-down power a little ahead of time and keeping boat speed to a bare minimum, this skipper could have avoided damaging his boat, the seawall, and his reputation. He was fortunate that no serious injuries resulted.

THE ELEMENTS OF BOAT-HANDLING CONTROL: SAILS, ENGINES, GROUND TACKLE

An auxiliary sailboat has essentially three levels of control: sails, engine, and ground tackle. Except in a motorsailer, the sail plan is foremost. A skilled crew on a vessel that's agile under sail relegates the diesel engine to junior-partner status. Even so, the engine's turnkey thrust can play a critical role in both safety

and convenience. For example, engine power has prevented many fine sailboats from blowing ashore when a fouled anchor started to drag. Likewise, an engine has brought many a vessel quickly and directly back to the spot where a crewmember went over the side.

Whether considered a secondary means of control or not, engine power demands a set of nuanced handling techniques. It's helpful to have an understanding of the details, which in normal conditions may have only marginal importance. However, in certain situations, this secondary means of control becomes the primary means of maneuvering. This is why we recommend you understand the influence of prop rotation direction, for example, as well as the responsiveness of the rudder in forward and reverse gears—and these differ in every boat.

Ground tackle is an all too often ignored third component of boat control. Stowed securely in a bow roller at the stem of the vessel, ground tackle should be prepped and ready to go. Most long-term, long-distance cruisers can tell a tale or two about encounters in a windless narrow pass or current-ridden channel when the diesel sputtered into silence, leaving only a scant few minutes—or less—to deploy and set the anchor. The ability to anchor quickly can keep a vessel free of fringing reefs, breakwaters, and other potentially perilous encounters. (See Chapter 6 on Anchors and Anchoring.)

The ability to skillfully handle ground tackle illustrates another take on the philosophy of contingency planning: *If you can't keep going in the direction you want, the next best thing is staying right where you are.*

BOAT-HANDLING FACTORS

You develop an awareness—a feel—for boat handling from two different realms:

- The behavior of your boat;
- The influence of surrounding natural forces.

All mariners build their boat-handling abilities based on the vessel's rudder response, turning radius, and seakeeping abilities. (We'll discuss specific seakeeping abilities later on in this chapter.) Since these each contribute to a boat's responsiveness, understanding your boat forms a baseline, and you can build your boat-handling skills from there.

The forces of wind and water cause a vessel to move downwind or downcurrent and more often than not to assume a beam-on attitude. Whether the challenge at hand is surviving storm-force conditions or maneuvering through a crowded marina, coping with natural forces is key to successfully handling the situation.

Rudder Response

We start with rudder response. Other things being equal, larger and (especially) deeper rudders deliver more turning moment, but there's more to a boat's maneuverability than its rudder size. For example, as the length-to-beam ratio of a boat increases or the length of its keel increases, so does its directional stability, that is, its tendency to stay on course. When you want to stay on course, it's advantageous to have a boat that can hold a course even when your hands are off the wheel or tiller. However, there's a downside, which is the corresponding inability to make a sharp turn.

Simply put, a long, lean sailboat or one with a long run of keel has a larger turning radius than a short, wide sailboat of similar underwater volume. The helmsperson of the long, lean boat will find it easier to eat a sandwich while steering a straight, undeviating course, but when it comes time for a pronounced turn, he or she will have to start the maneuver earlier, assist the turn (if in tight quarters) with the engine's reverse gear, or perhaps even anchor to avoid getting caught in an overly difficult docking situation.

Some years ago I was evaluating crew-overboard (COB) rescue techniques and various types of recovery equipment. Part of the testing protocol involved using a half dozen differently designed vessels. At one extreme, we had a J/105, a light-displacement 35-footer with flat bilges, minimal underwater surface, and a high-aspect fin keel with bulb. The other extreme included an Island Packet 37, a full-keeled boat that is 2 feet longer on deck than the J/105 but weighs four times as much.

We executed the US Sailing–endorsed quick-stop rescue maneuver on each boat, and this proved to be a far more useful technique aboard the ultramaneuverable J/105. The Island Packet's directional stability made the quick-stop technique less satisfactory; in that case, a better choice was a figure-eight or reach-and-return COB rescue. This example shows us that boat handling, whether in a critical rescue situation or for day-to-day docking, should work with rather than against a vessel's inherent design and steering characteristics.

Boat Maneuverability Factors

To better understand boat maneuverability, we need to look at the hull underbody shape, steering appendages, drive train, and other features that influence a boat's ability to turn. Boats like the Island Packet 37 with a long run of keel want to keep going in the direction they are pointing; the more *lateral plane* (underwater profile) in play, the more energy is needed to make a turn.

Fortunately, when the rudder alone is not enough to spin a boat on a dime, we have other ways to help. For example, most outboard-powered boats are highly maneuverable with or without a rudder. You're likely familiar how the thrust of an outboard motor directed to starboard pushes the stern to port, and vice versa. This makes outboard-powered boats more responsive and, broadly speaking, easier to dock.

Many vessels today ranging from cruise-ships to small craft have rotational thrust pods that function like an outboard's prop wash, vastly improving their ability to maneuver. For example, a Chouest tugboat moving directly sideways at 3 knots and turning 360 degrees in its own length is a great advertisement for a state-of-the-art rotating diesel-electric drive system.

Trawlers with Zeus drives and bow thrusters can all but parallel-park on a crowded wharf, and more and more sailboats are being built with bow thrusters. Beneteau has introduced a Dock & Go rotating-thrust saildrive engine that combines with a bow thruster to make sailboat handling a joystick exercise. In contrast, a traditional saildrive delivers thrust to the propeller through two right-angle thrust changes; the first leads to a vertical leg down through the hull skin, and the second turns the horizontal prop shaft. Time will tell whether Beneteau's innovation represents a maneuvering breakthrough or an unnecessary complication.

When a sailboat's prop is mounted just forward of the rudder or in an aperture, the rudder blade deflects the prop wash to aid tight turns—but only when the engine is in forward gear. We must become accustomed to the reduced ability to steer in reverse, and that's one factor to consider when handling a sailboat under power. The degree of reduced ability to maneuver in reverse varies greatly from boat to boat.

Lacking prop wash, a rudder must rely on the area of its blade and a combination of water-flow deflection and the hydrodynamic lift generated by its cross-sectional foil shape. When the boat is just beginning to gain way, little water flows over the foil and therefore little steering ability is present.

The term *steerageway* refers to the boat speed at which a vessel responds to a turn of the wheel or a tug on the tiller with an answering change of course. Like all lifting surfaces, the modern sailboat rudder develops low pressure on one side, producing a net force known as lift. When the boat is moving forward, this lift component is always directed away from the side toward which the rudder is turned. If the rudder is turned to port, the stern is lifted to starboard and a left-hand turn results.

Turning Radius

A racing sailboat with a deep fin keel and a high-aspect (deep and narrow) rudder mounted at the very stern of the boat represents the ultimate in sailboat maneuverability. An abrupt turn of the wheel or tug on the tiller stalls the deep keel foil and turns it into a pivot point. As rudder lift rotates the stern one way and turns the bow in the opposite direction, the crew hangs on, feeling the G-force of the directional change. Such agility can be either friend or foe. In the tight confines of a starting area or a dogleg entry into a slip, it's a helmsperson's best friend. On the other hand, while at sea, the helm needs constant attention from a person, self-steering vane, or autopilot.

The modern cruising sailboat has a fin keel with greater fore-and-aft length relative to its depth (a lower aspect ratio) than a racing keel; it also has a shallower rudder. It has more directional stability than an out-and-out racer, but it also has a corresponding increase in the radius of turn when not assisted by a bow thruster. Since it also gives a cruiser

less draft and keeps the rudder tucked out of harm's way, we view this as a fair trade-off.

The biggest challenge in handling large monohulls and multihulls in close quarters is learning how responsive a particular vessel is to *rudder deflection*, that is, the degree of change of direction relative to the degree of water deflection that results from moving the tiller or wheel and thus the rudder. This influences the movement of the boat in any direction, including a turn. However, sailors need to assess all the elements involved in steering and controlling movement. For example, gauging the best time to start a turn is as important as gauging how much rudder deflection to use. Both calculations are affected by water flow over the foil when going into the turn, a factor that's crucial to the lift generated by the rudder and thus to the turning moment itself.

We also add wind and current into the equation. Fortunately, the human mind is rather good at analyzing variables. In particular, after accounting for the variables of wind and current, experienced sailors learn to estimate the response time of actions involved with turning. Ideally, we end up exactly where we planned at the moment movement stops. If you're headed upstream in a current, for example, this means that you're still making way through the water and have steering control even though you are at a dead stop alongside the dock. This is the reason, by the way, that we prefer upstream maneuvering when coming alongside a fixed or floating dock. (See the section on downwind landings later in this chapter.)

DOCKING

Docking issues should be considered well before any piers and pilings come into sight. It all begins with a close look at a large-scale paper chart or zoomed-in digital display. The goal is to line up the approach while noting depths and any obstacles. This is also the time to discern what tidal depth coincides with your approach to the dock and whether a current will affect your approach. This predocking bit of research can make a new harbor feel more like an old friend. Not only do you have a chance to preview how a pier, floating dock, or slip will be influenced by wind and current, but you'll have a chance to see what other anchoring and tie-up options are available.

The Effects of Turning Radius and Prop Walk on Docking

Motorsailers and their engine-only trawler yacht cousins often handle the issue of turning radius in a slightly different fashion from auxiliary sailboats. Many en-

A modern, beamy, high-volume cruiser with a long run of keel may not tack on a dime, but its inherent directional stability is a positive attribute at sea, appreciated by the crew as well as the autopilot.

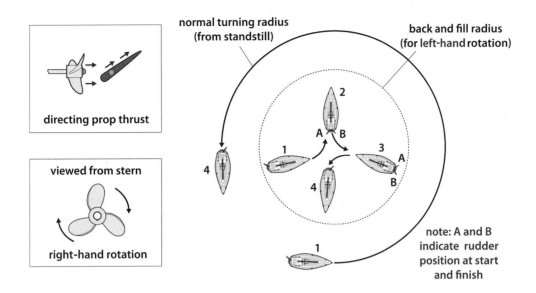

normal turning radius
(from standstill)

back and fill radius
(for left-hand rotation)

directing prop thrust

viewed from stern

right-hand rotation

note: A and B
indicate rudder
position at start
and finish

▰ *This modified "back and fill" technique is a means or rotating the boat when there's not enough room to carry out a simple turn, and/or the vessel has either too much prop-to-rudder separation or too much lateral plane to simply pivot in place by repeatedly shifting from forward to reverse, momentarily spiking the RMPs after each shift. The technique incorporates the use of prop wash and, in cases where prop shafts are not parallel with the surface, prop walk. These sources of thrust cause a sailboat to rotate much more efficiently in one direction over the other. Left-hand rotating props, when running in reverse, rotate the boat's stern to starboard. The converse is true for right-hand rotation drive trains. This effect is greatly reduced with sail drives and V-drives that impart thrust much farther forward.*

The outer ring represents the normal turning radius of this single-screw sailboat. The inner ring represents the reducing turning radius possible when backing and filling. The steps involved are these: 1. Go forward rudder hard to port. 2. Reverse, with rudder still to port. 3. Put the boat in reverse, with rudder to starboard. 4. Motor forward with rudder to port. (Joe Comeau)

gine-dependent vessels have a long run of keel, so at low speeds their turning radius can become problematic—even unacceptable. The standard solution for many single-screw vessels (one stern propeller) is to "back and fill," torquing (turning or rotating on an axis) the vessel around in more or less the same spot. This is best accomplished with a large three-, four-, or five-blade prop set well aft near the rudder blade.

A single-screw vessel will back to port or starboard, depending upon the prop's direction of rotation. A right-handed prop (common in a single-screw boat) swings the stern to port when backing with the rudder centered; the opposite occurs with a left-handed prop. So, to make a right-hand turn with a right-handed prop, swing the rudder hard to starboard for a brief burst of forward power, and then apply reverse power with the rudder centered. Alternate back and forth to ensure the boat stays more or less in place while spinning. This works well when the wind is light and there's little or no current to deal with.

When you begin to back into a slip and no wind or current is pushing on the starboard bow, the boat will want to back to port if your boat's prop is right-handed. This tendency holds until the motion through the water generates enough water flow and resulting hydrodynamic lift over the rudder blade to overcome the prop walk (in this case, the asymmetric effect of reverse motion).

Gaining sternway makes maneuvering into a slip more doable, especially in a breeze or current. The skill involves learning to accelerate astern in open water, gain steerage, and then gauge deceleration, with its resulting loss of helm control, to coincide with the vessel nudging into the slip. As long as you anticipate the pivoting effects, it's fine to use a few power thrusts in forward to tamp down excess sternway and to counter a swinging of the stern one way or the other.

However, let's say that too much sternway is carried into the final approach. In this case, the helmsperson can place the stern toward the port-hand side of the slip. Using forward thrust, with its inherent tendency to walk the stern to starboard, will stop the sternward movement and swing the stern toward the center of the slip.

As you can see, this type of maneuver involves blending rudder steering with thrust pivoting. However, the actions and responses vary from boat to boat. Understanding how your boat behaves is at its heart the way you develop a feel for your boat, in this case when maneuvering using engine power.

Backing a single-screw vessel into a slip is a lesson in relative motion, especially when a side-on current complicates the picture. One hint is to stand forward of the wheel, face aft, and steer as if the stern were the bow. When you're backing, some motion through the water must occur before rudder movement generates a response.

Docking Aids

Aids to help you dock include the use of spring lines or a bow thruster.

Spring Lines

An aft-leading spring line to the dock is another useful docking tool. If the fairlead (a cleat, chock, or genoa car to make off the line on) is located amidships, or more precisely near the center of the lateral plane, which is the point around which the hull pivots, the vessel's slight forward motion at the end of a docking maneuver will cause it to be pulled laterally toward the dock. When using this spring line technique, you aim your boat to keep the hull a foot or so off the dock and allow the tensioned spring line to breast it gently in. This removes the last of your headway—and saves your topside finish in the process. This is also a good way to cope with a head-on current: once the boat is alongside, the thrust of the engine idling in forward will keep the boat pulling against the aft-leading spring line and nestled against the dock while you deploy a bow line, stern line, and forward spring line. When you shut down the engine, little or no readjustment is needed.

Bow Thrusters

An internally installed bow thruster can compensate for circumstances that are less than ideal, such as having too few crew, less experienced or skilled crew, or poor docking conditions. This is true for both sailboats and motorboats. Bow thrusters maximize turning power, giving boats spin-on-a-dime dexterity that removes much of the anxiety of docking. All it takes is a push of the port or starboard toggle switch to make the bow pivot in one direction or the other.

Regardless of the switch's labeling, we recommend doing a quick predocking check to make sure the unit is wired to pivot the bow to starboard when the toggle is moved in that direction. While it may seem counterintuitive, on some boats the switch toggles in the direction of the thrust rather than in the direction of the pivot. The important point is to determine the function ahead of time, not at the last moment when a tight turn is essential. Like all mechanical devices, at some point the bow thruster will quit, so a backup plan must be ready to go.

A test for the bow thruster. Most bow thrusters are effective in calm conditions, but what happens when the thruster must overcome wind or a contrary current? This is the real test. No matter how much power a thruster provides, its ability to pivot the boat can be seriously affected by a strong wind pushing on the expanse of topsides and superstructure forward.

Current doesn't affect a boat's turn relative to the water, but it does influence the radius of a turn relative to the harbor bottom or a fixed structure such as a pier being approached. Even if your vessel is equipped with a bow thruster, you must factor wind and current into your docking maneuvers.

Protecting dock lines from the bow thruster. When docking, you always have a plethora of dock lines arranged near the rail, and keeping them out of the bow thruster is as important as keeping them out of the prop. The suction side of the athwartship tube that houses the thruster is a ravenous line swallower, and contact with a line can destroy the fast-turning thruster blades.

Knowing Your Boat: Sensing Speed and Steering When Docking

A headwind and water friction will quickly slow a light boat once propulsion energy stops, but large ships can coast—carry way—as much as a mile before coming to a complete stop. This is one of the first concerns to confront when you're handling an unfamiliar boat. Every boating pro knows this and tries to sense how much way the vessel carries. For example, a hefty, lean traditional cruiser headed toward a dock at a few tenths of a knot may glide twice as far as a light one-design sailboat.

Considering a wide range of boat speeds, how much distance do you need to stop your boat? Knowing the answer and having a good sense of your boat under these conditions are as important as the ability of a boat to spin on a dime. It's equally important to understand your ability to control steering during the deceleration process.

Docking Success

The ideal outcome begins with an ideal approach to a dock, slip, or pier. That means skippers make a good call on how the wind and current conditions affect

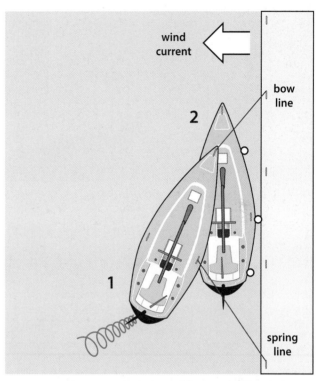

A spring line is particularly useful when docking with an offsetting wind and current. 1. As you approach the dock get your spring line over to the dock, then power against it, turning the rudder to port. 2. When alongside the dock, secure the boat with bow and stern lines, in addition to the already set spring line. (Joe Comeau)

Outboard tie-ups on floating docks make coming alongside a straightforward procedure. They are less available than in the past, however, and many larger cruising boats are being built or retrofitted with bow thrusters.

A light-air, no-current approach to a dock.

Agile crew may like the "bridge the gap" feel of a leap to the dock, while others simply nudge up against the float and step off with dignity.

their boats in the present circumstances. At what point can these skippers shift to neutral for the final, gliding approach?

A perfect landing is one in which a boat loses all way just inches before touching the dock, allowing easy securing of lines and fenders. Too little momentum is usually better than too much. With too little way, nudging the shift lever adds more thrust and closes the gap. Sadly, too much way can lead to "dock buster" status, a situation that can ruin more than a reputation.

Common Docking Challenges

Sooner or later, you'll face the challenge of wind and/ or current shoving your boat onto the dock. First, ask yourself in advance if you have other alternatives. In a "box canyon" situation you have only one way into the slip and you need to fully understand that conditions can get ugly fast. If things go wrong, you might not be able to bail out and come around for another run—no second chance. For example, when the wind is blowing 25 knots or more or a strong ebb or flood current harasses the slip entrance, the alternative might be to anchor instead—if you can.

If you're determined to come alongside or you have no alternative, then be prepared for what lies ahead. First, have extra lines and fenders ready, and look for a friendly-looking piling that's free of spikes and cleats. That way, if you flub the maneuver, you can lay against the piling while you get lines in play to salvage the situation.

Downwind Docking

A downwind approach into a narrow slip on a windy day is one of the classic boat-handling challenges.

A DOWNCURRENT DOCKING STORY

Schaefer's Canal House Restaurant, once a familiar landmark to anyone transiting the Chesapeake & Delaware Canal, was one of the best arenas on the East Coast for watching good and not-so-good docking. This day's show was put on by the crew of a sloop returning from a good showing in the Newport Bermuda Race. Transiting the canal on their last leg of the passage back to the Chesapeake Bay, they were moving an impressive 9 knots over the ground, thanks to a favorable 3-knot current and a willing diesel.

Approaching the fabled Schaefer's restaurant, the crew decided to have a well-earned celebration. Eager for shore leave, they saw an open slot on the dock between the stern of one powerboat and the bow of another, and without considering the whopping current boost, the skipper turned on a downstream approach into the open space. The bowman leaped ashore and dropped a bow line over a stout dock cleat. Restaurant spectators watched in dismay as the boat fetched up hard against the line, spun through a whiplash-inducing 180-degree pirouette, and came to rest beam-to-beam against the downstream powerboat. Such ignominious landings and apologies made great dinner theater for those dining on the Schaefer's deck. We hope the crew learned the lesson that despite how well they might do in ocean races, they still had some seamanship techniques to learn, including always approaching a dock against the current.

🚩 *Snubbing a line prior to making it fast is a good habit to develop. In windy conditions or with larger vessels you may need a full turn around a cleat base to create enough friction for braking.*

🚩 *With ideal docking conditions, these crewmembers have elected to make fast the bow and stern lines first, then add spring lines as necessary. Current and wind can turn this leisurely process into a more urgent pursuit, however! When that happens, an aft-leading spring line can be used to arrest any leftover forward movement before making bow and stern lines fast. Powering against the spring line will hold the vessel in place while bow and stern lines are set (see illustration on page 81). Many experienced cruisers prefer not to have spliced eyes in their docklines so that they can make adjustments at either end.*

Some sailboat owners prefer to back into a slip, which makes for an easy exit. However, don't attempt a stern-first entry in adverse conditions. Simply tie up bow first, then back out and pivot when you depart in calmer weather.

Stern-First Docking: Not for All Boats

When approaching a dock at slow speed, some sailboats maneuver more efficiently stern first. In a stern-first approach, a boat with a large rudder and prop placed well aft is analogous to having front-wheel drive. Even though water is flowing over the prop blades and rudder from the wrong direction when a boat is backing, the steering moment of the rudder is enough, at the right speed, to provide a responsive helm. The lower the speed at which the helm is responsive, the better suited the boat is for stern-first maneuvering. Since a right-handed prop tends to walk the stern to port in reverse, a port-side-to approach is likely optimal.

Stern-first approaches are especially effective when backing into the wind. Since a sailboat's natural tendency is to point downwind, backing into the wind capitalizes on this tendency rather than fighting it. If help is needed to stop sternward momentum, a quick shift into forward provides much more thrust

than you can get from reverse in a bow-first approach. However, be careful of the pivot effect inherent with the change in prop rotation. This can be quite noticeable aboard boats with modern underbodies and short, deep keels. When you are operating in reverse, the stern behaves like the bow and heads in the direction in which you turn the wheel. Visibility is ideal when the helmsperson faces aft in an aft cockpit steering in reverse. This is why so many able boat handlers like to do their close-quarters maneuvering stern first.

Stern-first docking works best when the prop is placed well aft at the end of a straight shaft. A sail-drive or V-drive shaft often places the prop too far forward, which means the torque it generates causes the vessel to pivot rather than gain sternway. In addition, modern underbodies with high-aspect fin keels depend on motion through the water to combat leeway and provide directional stability. Boats with such a design have too little low-speed directional stability to cope with crosswinds, and leeway becomes just as big a problem as it is in a bow-first approach.

UNDERSTANDING LEEWAY AND CURRENT—VISUALIZING RELATIVE MOTION

Although navigators think of a vessel's motion in terms of direction and speed *over ground*, those at the helm, when steering by compass and knotmeter, tend to reference speed and direction *through the water*. When the boat is maneuvering in tight confines, however, the helmsperson is also oriented "over ground."

The lurking presence of unyielding terra firma or structures requires gauging progress against stationary geography, not a water column that may itself be moving. But it is the moving water that makes boat handling either much easier or a nightmare.

At such times the helmsperson must visualize the boat's relative motion. The current's set and drift—and its conveyor-belt effect on boats—must be factored in along with wind-induced leeway. A 0.5-knot side-setting current becomes significant when approaching a dock at 1 knot; we may have to point our bow 30 to 40 degrees toward or away from the dock to compensate and land effectively. Add a gusty breeze trying to blow the bow off course and we may wind up with more nuances than can be solved with a bow thruster alone. (See illustrations on pages 86 and 87.)

Leeway

Simply put, *leeway* is the sometimes imperceptible sideways motion—slippage—of a boat caused by current and/or wind. Leeway is relevant both when underway and when anchoring or docking. Understanding and compensating for leeway is a difficult element in the curriculum for many apprentice boat handlers. However, with experience, skippers learn to perceive, project, and compensate for the crab-like track of a leeway-influenced course. A boat's underbody profile and foil shapes also affect leeway, visualized as slippage resulting from insufficient keel and rudder area and the lift that they provide.

Modern beamy, shoal-draft cruising sailboats are notorious for sliding sideways when heeled under sail because their big, round bilges cause a shift in the heeled center of buoyancy and further reduce the vessel's already-minimal lateral plane. The design trend of increased freeboard (the distance between the waterline and the deck) and reduced keel area increase leeway.

Many factors influence leeway, including windage, the surface area blown by wind. For example, the trend toward large canvas cockpit enclosures greatly increase windage—some are the size of wedding tents! So do large-radius spars for in-mast furling and roller-furled headsails, or a large dinghy hanging from davits 8 feet above the water. All these features add windage, which ups the skill ante when it comes to approaching or leaving a dock in boisterous conditions. The importance of this windage-induced leeway is obvious in power cruisers with cabins on top of cabins on top of high topsides, but may be less apparent in a sailboat. In any case, if you must handle a high-windage boat, a few tricks exist to lessen the problems. Start a dock approach by first finding the "equilibrium" heading—a course where side-setting influences balance out and speed over the ground can be slowed to a minimum. Try to approach the dock, pier, or mooring on this heading and recognize how the natural forces will move the boat as the final maneuver is made. Vessels with excessive freeboard and windage may have to carry more headway to remain maneuverable during docking. Such boats are good candidates for bow thrusters.

The modest 1.5 knot current in the East River running along Manhattan Island, New York, (left) and a 4.5 knot current at the height of a spring tide ebb (right). Speed over the ground is impressive when running with such a current, but with such a "lift" there is no room for errors in navigation—and the helmsperson must be able to hold the required course. Running aground at such a rate of drift can instantaneously turn into a downflooding situation, swamping a vessel that's already aground.

Currents

Every coastal mariner should develop the habit of gauging currents. Any fixed buoy, navigation mark, or seabed protrusion will do as a reference point. The up-current side of the object shows a slight pileup of tiny waves; the current splits around the buoy, stake, or other object, meeting again downstream in a series of eddies. As a reference for set and drift at any given time, these simple direct observations are better than a current table. The latter fails to calculate the effect of strong winds that can significantly affect an inshore current. A networked knotmeter or GPS/plotter with current calculating software gives a fairly accurate measure of the actual current at any given time. The variable that remains is leeway and that may be soon resolved with magnetic pulse-sensing knotmeters that provide velocity in a 360 degree reference—a big deal for racing sailors.

Local navigators learn that it takes 2 knots of current to heel a particular mark to 45 degrees and 3 knots of current to begin to drag another familiar channel mark beneath the surface. You can use the current to your advantage. The first step is to increase your awareness of what the current is doing in any given location and time.

Heading into the Current

A boat is easier to control when headed into the current. You can slow your speed over ground to a near standstill yet still maintain steerageway by virtue of the current and the prop wash (if under power) running over the rudder blade. In a strong current you can even throttle back and move astern relative to the fixed geography while still moving bow-first through the water.

As an illustration of this advantage of moving against the current, a sailor I know used this technique to make a mid-tide passage beneath the fixed bridge over Moosabec Reach in Jonesport, Maine. Unsure if he had sufficient clearance for his mast, he turned his bow away from the approaching bridge and into the current, and then inched under the bridge stern-first, maintaining steerageway in forward gear. If the mast touched the bridge, a burst of forward throttle would power him out of danger. As it happened, he had just enough clearance, although his masthead VHF antenna had to bend to pass beneath.

Running with the Current

Conversely, running *with* the current reduces your control and is akin to driving a vehicle downhill on a slippery road. The speed might be exhilarating, but you pray no obstacle appears ahead. The current doesn't help at all, for example, when you initiate a simple 180-degree turn while running with a 4-knot current under your stern. Only your speed through the water and the prop wash on your rudder blade (if under power) helps you turn. Since you are being swept downcurrent as you maneuver, the turn becomes a highly elongated inverted J. You might think to throttle back to shorten the radius of the turn, but this has the opposite result because the turning force from the rudder is greatly diminished while the speed of the current remains the same.

At no time is this phenomenon more apparent and immediately relevant than when approaching a closed bridge; if the opening is slow, you'll be forced to turn rapidly to keep from being swept into the bridge.

The Challenge of Side-Setting Currents

Side-setting currents are less dramatic but more complex. Calculating the effect of such a current is a classic problem in vector addition. Unfortunately, this art has been all but lost in the age of GPS navigation. However, in order to proceed crabwise along your intended course, steering may require heading many degrees to port or starboard of the rhumb line.

In a tight channel or on the approach to a dock, a side-setting current can get exciting. A current pushing you *away* from a shoal or dock is easier to work with than one that's determined to shove you *onto* the obstacle. Therefore, when possible, pick a berth at which the current pushes you away from the dock or pier for both approaching and departing. When a side-setting current has pinned your boat in, leaving a dock is a tough test for a shorthanded crew.

Accommodating the Current

Rather than challenging a current that's faster than your boat, consider anchoring or docking—even if the current is going the same way you are. Maneuvering in tight confines becomes extremely tricky in such a strong current, and you can't count on avoiding such situations altogether. We recommend waiting for slacker water.

For example, when I was transiting the Dundas Straits in Australia, I'd move out of the channel and anchor when a foul 9-knot tidal current made forward progress impossible. In another South Pacific islands adventure I tried to motorsail *Wind Shadow* into the pass of Mopelia atoll. Because of waves breaking on the windward reef and forcing water into the quiet lagoon, the current was ebbing even though the tide was flooding. Like a sauce pan being overfilled, the pass on the leeward side of the atoll kept ebbing at all tides, and when the wind was up and the seas large, the current in the pass exceeded 5 knots. As we approached the narrow entrance, we reached a point where we could make no further progress. Rather

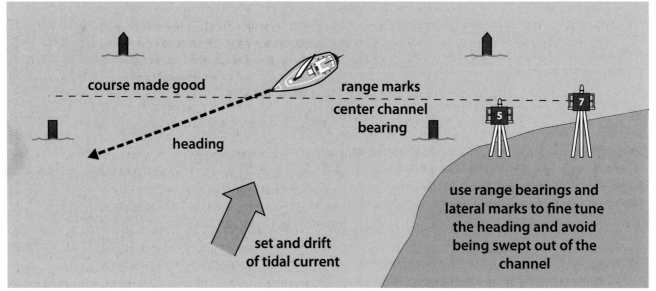

🚩 *When you encounter a side-setting current in a narrow channel, range marks can help ensure you remain in the channel. In this case, use the range marks as back bearings to judge your progress (lining up two features on shore, e.g., a dock and tree, will provide the same kind of relative bearing). When no range marks are available, the navigator and helmsperson should use bow and stern lateral marks as reference points to determine leeway, i.e., how much the current is setting the vessel off its intended course. When wind and current approach from the same side of the vessel their combined effect is greater. (Joe Comeau)*

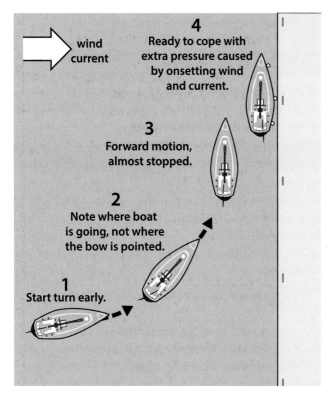

🚩 *Approaching a dock with a side-setting current causes a boat to defy its heading. To artfully come alongside, steer to compensate for the set and drift of the current. When approaching a dock with an on-setting wind and current, decrease speed (you'll get plenty of force from the wind and current), turn to place boat parallel to the dock—with fenders deployed—half a boat length from the dock. Have bow and spring lines ready to toss over to the dock, and you may want a couple of extra fenders at the ready. (Joe Comeau)*

than attempting a turn in the narrow inlet, I simply eased off on the throttle, and, still making about 3 knots forward through the water, *Wind Shadow* backed away from the hungry coral heads ahead.

The streamlined hull of a sailboat behaves quite benignly when streaming with a current. However, if a stern anchor is also being used or if the boat is tied to a dock or float in a manner that puts the beam to the current, the current's effect on the underbody's lateral plane can be devastating.

SPECIAL MANEUVERING SITUATIONS

Eventually, most sailors encounter special situations that require boat-handling skills in challenging close quarters. These might include downcurrent landings, a Mediterranean mooring, or locks. The first step is to accurately assess the magnitude of the challenge *while you still have time to change your mind*. In other words, survey the site to evaluate wind, wave, currents, maneuvering room, traffic, and lurking hazards. Stack up these factors against your own experience and your boat's and crew's abilities. You don't want to be in the middle of the maneuver, past the point of no return, when you realize you're not in Kansas anymore.

An alarm should trigger in your forebrain in the presence of telltale indicators, such as a strong breeze, a scouring current, or a congested anchorage. Two questions should immediately arise: do you really want to commit to the challenge, and what are your other options?

To answer the first question, I always flip through recollections of similar situations, comparing the challenge at hand with previous efforts and outcomes. "What if" situations move center stage, including the potential for hazard to the crew and boat if things go south. In essence, I ask myself if my bail-out plan involves a second chance or whether this is a situation in which, once I commit, there will be no turning back. If the latter is my answer, then my ability to predict the likelihood of success is crucial. Delusional optimism can be as debilitating as a deer-in-the-headlights reaction.

Before even thinking about pointing the boat toward the seawall, dock, or pier, make sure you've digested all the available data. Scrutinize the largest-scale chart you have of the area and know where the shallow spots are hiding. Peruse a cruising guide or *Coast Pilot* for further details, and do a drive-by, noting the soundings, wind direction, current set and drift, and any obstacles that will impede your approach. Decide which side of the boat will contact the wharf and what lines and fenders will be needed; deploy them all ahead of time, with all lines free to run.

A Downwind or Downcurrent Landing

As pointed out earlier, it's best not to be backed into a corner, either figuratively or literally. For example, a pier, wharf, or seawall that is buffeted by an onshore wind, an on-setting current, or both, deserves the same respect that square-rig sailors once accorded a lee shore. In both cases a conveyor-belt force sets you in a direction different from the one the bow points to. In such a situation those who cruise alone or with a small crew might be better off relying on ground tackle rather than stumbling into tight confines or relying upon strangers on a seawall to handle lines and fend off the boat.

That said, if you sail long enough and far enough, sooner or later customs officials will require you to come alongside the windward face of a steep commercial wharf or circumstances will force you to lie alongside a fuel dock that runs squarely across the current.

When that day comes, your equipment becomes critical. The side of the vessel lying against the berth should be well protected with cylindrical fenders and fenderboards (if docked against pilings) or with large spherical fenders (if docked against a seawall or other solid vertical surface). In addition, secure your dinghy and make sure it stays out of the way. Nothing adds drama to a downwind landing like the dinghy

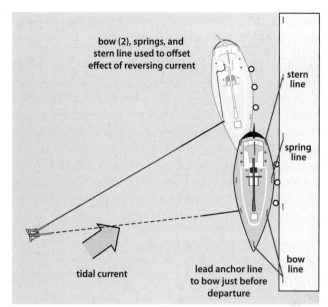

When you face a situation in which the wind and current will be setting you onto a pier or dock, it may make sense to drop an anchor during the approach and use it to breast off while docking, as well as once you're tied alongside. This anchor to windward insurance will also simplify getting off the dock if at departure you again face a foul breeze and current. The real art in this process lies in pre-running the rope rode so it feeds from a fairlead amidship just after you deploy the anchor from the bow. The correct geometry includes deploying the anchor far enough from the dock so it sets and leaves you with enough scope to hold, and angling it so the rode is close to being in line with the wind and current. (Joe Comeau)

getting between the boat and the dock. If possible, identify any rig-snagging wharf projections or overhangs ahead of time.

Using the Anchor

If the seawall is dead downwind, it might make sense to set an anchor well to windward and snub your way toward the wall. However, you may not need the anchor if there are pilings or a dolphin on which to set a windward *warping line*. The goal in either case is to secure a line to windward that you can use as a brake during your approach and to keep the vessel breasted off the wall, pilings, or wharf timbers while you're alongside. A taut tether to windward will also expedite the process of getting away from the quay when that time comes.

This line to windward can be a high-stakes gamble. If it's attached to an anchor, the anchor must be large enough not to drag. Whether you use an all-chain anchor rode or a secondary rope rode attached to a kedging anchor, this is no time for using undersized gear. In essence, placing ground tackle to windward is akin to the first step in a Mediterranean mooring (see below). It's critical to pick the right distance from the seawall at which to deploy the anchor.

If you deploy the anchor too far from shore, you may run out of rode before you reach the wall or you may end up with a rode angle so shallow it risks being snagged by passing deep-draft boats. On the other hand, if you deploy the anchor too close, the scope may be too short for the anchor to set and hold. With a good-sized anchor, the snubbing process can begin at a scope of about 3:1 (ratio of the length of rode to the vertical drop from bow chock to bottom); the anchor should set well before you fetch up against the seawall and any other boats that are berthed there. The line to windward acts as a safety valve, a means to delay contact with the structure to leeward.

In the last phase of the approach, you transition from a stern-first to a beam-on attitude. Plan ahead how you'll transfer rode tension from the bow roller to a location more amidships. I often use a snatch block or chain claw (hook) on an old genoa sheet and lead it through a block on the rail to shift the line tension, increasing its breasting effect and holding the boat off the seawall. A rope rode can even be run to a point on the beam—outside all stays, shrouds, and lifelines—before it's uncleated at the bow. The transition from bow-on to beam-on attitude increases the pressure exerted by a brisk wind on broad topside expanses or by a strong current on the underbody profile. Without this line the boat would be pinned against the seawall like a wrestler pinned to the mat. This is when the holding power of the anchor set upcurrent or upwind is really tested.

Beam-on downwind or downcurrent docking should be done as infrequently as possible, and only for a short time as well. You'll need to regularly adjust the lines with the tidal rise and fall and changes in wind and current. When it comes time to depart, the line to windward will prove worth its weight in gold. If you carefully return the direction of the pull to the bow, ideally with a reliable rope drum or chain gypsy doing the work, you avoid being pinned to the dock by the on-setting wind or current.

Mediterranean Mooring

Mediterranean mooring is a variation on the approach described above, but without transitioning to a side-on docking configuration. A stern-to berth perpendicular to the seawall is more common, although some shorthanded cruisers prefer to use a stern an-

These boats are Med moored on the quay in Porto Cervo, Sardinia. The Med mooring ritual is a developed skill and a test of composure. You have one chance to be a hero, a second chance to get it right, and after that you are the afternoon spectacle. Good gear is a must. The anchor needs to be sized correctly and reliable, and the chain must be able to freewheel smoothly off the windlass (see Chapter 6) yet be stopped and snubbed regularly as the helmsperson backs and fetches up against the rode while inching stern-first toward the quay. The crew operating the windlass is as important as the person on the helm. Late in the afternoon, the wind may be up and all the good spots taken. Make sure you know how to control your boat in reverse with the wind on the beam, and bring along plenty of fenders.

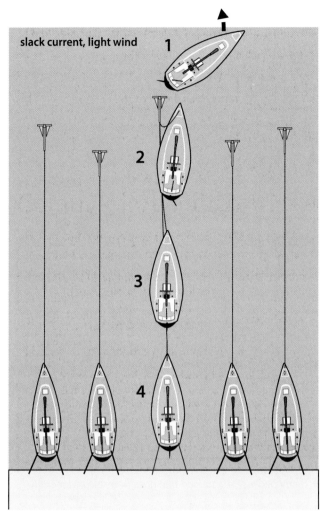

slack current, light wind

1

2

3

4

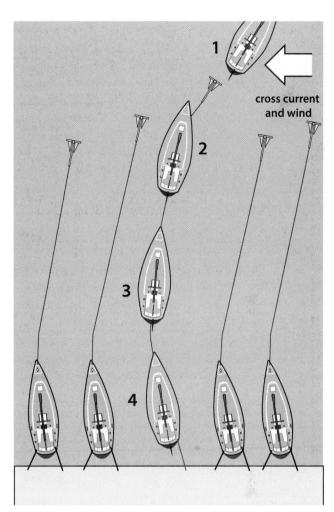

cross current and wind

1

2

3

4

🏴 *Med mooring is a skill worth practicing. In a slack current and light wind, turn your stern to the pier, drop the anchor 4 to 5 boat-lengths from the pier, and back in as shown. 1. Turn. 2. Drop anchor. 3. Back toward quay. 4. Snub anchor, center boat, deploy stern lines. (Joe Comeau)*

🏴 *Med mooring in a cross current and wind requires more attention to how the wind and current set your vessel, and the location of the other anchor rodes. 1. Turn your vessel up-current and up-wind. 2. Backdown, favoring up-current side of the slot. 3. Drop anchor to weather perpendicular to your slot on the quay. 4. Favor the up-current side of the slot. Center your boat in the slot. (Joe Comeau)*

chor and approach the seawall bow-to, thus reducing the risk of hitting the wall. In either approach a bow thruster helps significantly, especially when the wind is blowing beam-on to the approach.

Once you've taken care of lines on the quay or seawall and you've run fenders galore down both sides of the boat, it's time to set up your *passerelle*, or gangplank, to bridge the gap between land and boat. Whether it protrudes from the bow or the stern, the gangplank needs to be long enough that the bow or stern can be kept far enough off to avoid being hammered by the quay. Tidal range is small in most of the Mediterranean, and space alongside wharves or in a slip is limited, so this cheek-by-jowl nestling of boats has become standard operating procedure. Some harbors have underwater cables intended to hook bow anchors and provide additional security. Others have mooring ball attachments for bow lines.

None of these alternatives is as secure or pleasant as the mooring, anchoring, and marina options found in U.S. waters, but cultural experiences usually make up for any docking tribulations. Some shorthanded cruisers set up their boats with a substantial stern anchor and roller, and after anchoring from the stern they maneuver bow-in toward the quay. A bow-deployed gang plank completes this alternative.

Lock Logistics

Ever since the Egyptians and Romans started fiddling with ways to navigate through land, locks have been the canal builder's solution to changes in elevation. Whether in a transit from the Atlantic to the Pacific across Panama or moving a barge along the C&O Canal, all locks have upstream and downstream gates and

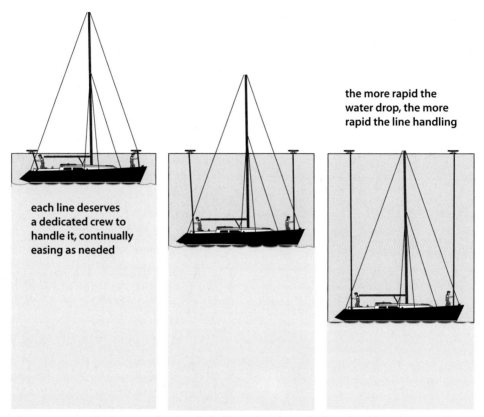

the more rapid the
water drop, the more
rapid the line handling

each line deserves
a dedicated crew to
handle it, continually
easing as needed

Locking down from one water body to another is a little like a time-lapse look at the tide going out. (Anyone who has left their boat tied to pier and not anticipated the tidal range will not forget a bar tight bow line, or if they are not so lucky, what the deck looks like where the cleat once was affixed.) Continuously handling and slackening lines as a vessel locks down is a paramount part of canal seamanship. If possible, have one crewmember per line. If you are shorthanded ask for help from those ashore—this is no place to be a hero. A sharp knife should be at the ready because a snagged line goes from inconvenient to calamitous in mere seconds. (Joe Comeau)

fill and empty with water. To raise the water level in a lock, the downstream gate is closed, water is allowed to flow in from upstream, and then the upstream gate is opened. To lower the level, the process is reversed. As the lock is either filled or emptied, docking lines must be lengthened or shortened to cope with the changing water level. The ride up is generally easier than the ride down; the larger and faster the rise or drop, the more attentive the line handlers need to be. Because the ride down is usually more turbulent, a line with light tension can quickly become overloaded and hard to release—if poorly attended.

You must be alert to the rapidly changing geometry of a line that is more vertical than horizontal. Anyone who has experienced what happens when a dropping tide tightens a bow line understands how quickly gravity can influence the load on a line. Tension spikes when a boat is partially suspended by a bow line with too little slack, and if the line is made fast with a yachtsman's cleat hitch, it will cinch so tightly that it becomes impossible to release. That can happen too when "locking down." When securing a tending line to a horn cleat, use a full turn around

the cleat base followed by three figure-eight turns, but do not finish with the usual locking half hitch. This will prevent the need for a knife or axe to release a loaded line. With constant attention you can prevent such overloading. In addition, pay special attention to your lines in fast-draining locks, especially when a small crew must handle multiple lines.

In some cases it's possible to tie alongside a larger commercial vessel and ride up or down a lock without any special line handling. This sounds fine, as long as the other vessel's line handling is competently managed and your boat doesn't become an impromptu fender if the large vessel surges toward the lock wall on your side. If you're lucky enough to ride up or down in a center-tie position, you avoid the fender drama experienced by a side-tied vessel as it slides up or down the lock walls. In addition, watch for the prop wash of large commercial vessels exiting a crowded lock, and keep fenders ready for both sides of your boat.

The lock at Great Bridge, Virginia, on the Intracoastal Waterway is an example of a relatively tame experience. This lock provides a sample locking experience in the bucolic Virginia countryside and has all the earmarks of big-league encounters, but there is less rise and fall in water level within the lock.

All lock passages involve maneuvering, line handling, fendering, and communications with the lockmaster. Most cruisers loop a line over the bollard and control both ends from the boat. One end is cleated, and the other is hauled or eased depending upon whether the boat is locking up or down. Those transiting the Erie Canal, with its water level changes of about 30 feet, or cruising through locks of the Saint Lawrence Seaway and Great Lakes get a taste of what sailors experience transiting the Panama Canal. There, you may be required to rent lines and use line handlers, but the ritual is much the same as in any other lock although with significantly greater elevation changes.

GETTING UNDERWAY

So far, we've been discussing boat handling in close quarters and special situations. For most cruisers, however, boat-handling skills come into play with the moment of first getting underway. After a quick engine check and crew briefing, the dock lines are

Approaching the locks on the Erie Barge Canal. (Top) The downstream lock gates are open, inviting in the "locking up" vessels. (Above) Once both sets of gates are closed and the valves are closed at the lower end and opened at the upper end, the lock begins to fill. When the lock is filled, the upper gates open, allowing the "locking up" vessels to exit and those vessels desiring to "lock down" to enter. (Left) As the water level drops, the downstream-headed boaters ease their lines. Shortly the downstream gates will open and these boats will exit.

When leaving a mooring, placing the mooring pendant's eye over the stem of the pick-up buoy allows both to be retrieved together next time. When leaving the mooring under sail, set the main, cast off the mooring pendant, allow the bow to fall off, and then hoist or unfurl the jib.

If this line is loaded by an increase in wind or current, it would take a sharp knife to free it from the cleat. Yes, it could be released at its shoreside end, but the ability to control a line from the boat can pay big dividends when unanticipated events occur. A better way to make off a bow line is to cut off the eye splice, melt/whip the end of the line, take a turn on the cleat, and top it off with a figure eight.

"singled up"—reduced to the minimum required to hold the vessel in place just before getting underway. Many daysailors who plan to return to the same slip leave the lines on the dock.

If you're not planning to return to the same slip, the best strategy for retrieving a dock line is to loop it around a piling or dock cleat; when the time comes to cast off, simply release one end and haul in the other. Be careful not to let the line drop in the water near the spinning prop, and make sure nothing can snag the line after its end has been released. To prevent that potential hazard, many experienced cruisers do not use dock lines with a loop spliced in the end. Snagging an obstruction can add a bad ending to a good plan.

During the few moments of casting off, skippers multitask: they handle the helm while overseeing the line handling and watching for a forgotten spring line, a still-connected shore-power cord, or a nearby piling festooned with hungry nails. At this moment it's easy to be so consumed by what's happening around your boat that you fail to see the tour boat passing your slip or the kayaker about to cross your track. Commercial vessels sound one prolonged blast before leaving their slip for this very reason.

Once you're clear of the slip or mooring, the fenders are brought aboard. Lines are coiled, and unneeded gear stowed. Every vessel and crew has a routine for getting underway that differs slightly from that of the sister ship moored nearby. The key steps remain the same, however, and for sailors the process begins with setting sail. Roller-furling sail plans have grown more and more popular, with headsail furling found on over 90% of cruising boats these days. Mainsail furling is also becoming much more popular. (See Chapter 7 for discussion of the sails you need.)

DEVELOPING BOAT-HANDLING ROUTINES

Racers, cruisers, and daysailors develop an onboard routine according to the waters they navigate, and they develop boat-handling skills to coax their boats to perform in the conditions they encounter. For example, a commuter who leaves work early to unwind under sail may rendezvous with the club launch for a ride to the mooring, and in a matter of minutes the mooring pendant splashes and the roller-furled genoa unwinds. Perhaps this sailor is tired from an arduous day at work and leaves the mainsail cover in place to enjoy an hour or two of peaceful light-wind reaching under just the genoa. This is reward enough for that day.

Meanwhile, while our commuter drifts around the harbor, a couple of friends have left a nearby mooring and are now three weeks into a transatlantic passage. They've grown accustomed to the routine of setting up the inner forestay and running backstays, hanking on the storm jib, and putting the slugs of the storm trysail into its separate track on the mainmast. With storm sails at the ready, they're prepared for the gale the forecast promises. And not for the first time. They've prepared just as thoroughly for two other gales over the previous weeks. For 20 days they have stood back-to-back watches and faced up to headwinds and other challenges of the Atlantic. Soon they'll reach the south coast of England and sail into Nelson's Solent, a goal they have dreamed of for years.

What distinguishes the daysailor's routine from the voyager's is more depth than dimension. The typical, capable daysailor knows something about the influence of natural forces and probably has felt the tempest of an afternoon thunderstorm. Voyagers, however, need to understand the extent of the offshore commitment they are making. The big challenge for voyaging sailors lies in the potential escalating difficulty of conditions they may experience.

Acclimating to Motion

The rougher the conditions, the more three-dimensional the sea surface becomes. When the flat liquid plane becomes a conglomeration of peaks and troughs with only a rough semblance of predictable patterns, a boat's behavior is determined by more than the sea's surface. Hull shape and the longitudinal distribution of its weight and volume are factors, along with what the crew does to mitigate the wild carnival ride.

Engineers use accelerometers to measure the six motions a boat undergoes in a seaway:

- Up-and-down *heaving*
- Forward and sternward *surging*
- Linear lateral side-to-side *swaying*
- *Pitching* (rotation about an athwartship axis, like a hobbyhorse)
- *Rolling* (rotation about a fore-and-aft axis, like a skewered pig over a barbeque pit)
- *Yawing* (rotation about a vertical axis, like a weathervane)

As you might imagine—or already know—these gyrations have a marked effect on the crew. At the

very least, lessening one or more of these motions can go a long way toward preventing or easing seasickness. Equally important is preventing the sleep deprivation crew can develop when violent boat motion keeps the off-watch crew from sleeping.

Wind and Swells

It's also important to assess the direction of the dominant swell and how that relates to your course, along with existing and future wind angles. Don't expect the crests of the ocean swell always to be perpendicular to the prevailing wind direction. Waves travel faster than weather systems and tend to be signs of a nearby new breeze. Short-period waves (those closer together) are often perpendicular to local winds, but

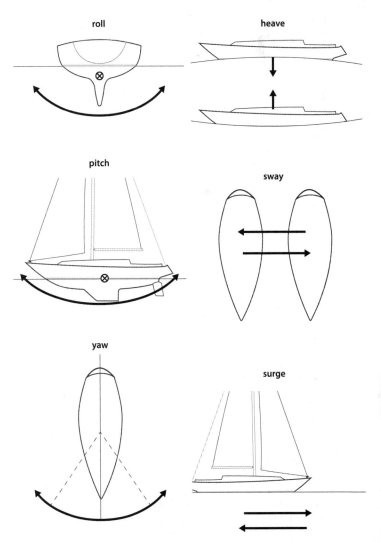

Sailboats gyrate through six specific motions. The left three—roll, pitch, and yaw—are more familiar. Each of these involves the boat rotating about a specific axis. The right three—heave, sway, and surge—are less familiar concepts. Each involves an actual change in position and is independent from course and speed. (Joe Comeau)

When the forecast promises a building nor'easter off the East Coast of North America, experienced sailors either head for a safe haven or scramble for sea room. Vessels designed and built to handle heavy weather give a crew more options and a greater likelihood of weathering a blow unscathed.

don't ignore larger, longer-period waves. They are often the advance guard of an approaching storm and can influence your course.

Later, in Chapter 12, we'll look at fore-and-aft versus athwartship stability and explore the reasons that vessels tend to be far more stable along their centerline axis than across their beam. Briefly, we see more dimensional stability along the longitudinal axis of the waterline plane. Consequently, waves arriving on the beam of a vessel cause much more rolling than occurs when the same wave train arrives from the quarter.

Rough weather sometimes means it makes sense to divert from the original rhumb line. (See Chapter 11 for storm strategies.) For example, let's say a boat is riding the north-setting Gulf Stream north to New England from the Caribbean but is caught by an approaching and rapidly deepening nor'easter. The impending gale is creating large swells that grow even steeper as the waves encounter the Stream's northward flow. (Some have estimated that a 1-knot contrary current doubles the height of a wind wave, and stronger currents increase wave heights and steepness even further.) In this situation, the crew has several options. When they hear that conditions are forecast to worsen, it makes no sense to stay in the Gulf Stream. One alternative, for example, is to beam-reach toward the shelter of Morehead City, North Carolina, which has a good inlet into the Intracoastal Waterway. It is also closer to New England than to Charleston, South Carolina, which lies about the same distance away but is farther south. However, deciding which bailout plan to act on involves considering the state of the sea and the point of sail. A

beam reach headed west would put the largest breaking seas on the beam in the most precarious position, whereas heading southwest to Charleston would put those waves on the quarter and offer a better sailing angle if conditions worsen. In addition, gales north of or in the vicinity of Cape Hatteras tend to create worse weather around Cape Lookout and the region around Morehead City than in the approach to Charleston. The point here is that boat-handling decisions in heavy weather include determining which angle of sail favors stability and coincides with the optimal course for a safe haven—a win-win decision.

Reducing Weight and Windage

Weight and windage contribute to boat motion and are especially detrimental to performance. We recommend starting the season with some spring cleaning to lighten the load, lessen hull skin drag, and gain performance on all points of sail. Whatever doesn't need to be on board can be taken ashore. Deep in the bilge and in the back of every locker lurk storm anchors ready for hurricane season, an extra shot of chain, a spare alternator and starter, scuba tanks, dive weights, and other gear ready for that dreamed-of big cruise but not necessary if adventure is not on your short immediate agenda.

In addition to lightening the load, smart skippers also attempt to keep the movable payload weight as near amidships and as low in the boat as possible, as opposed to near the ends of the boat. This helps lessen the boat's pitching moment, which is one of the most uncomfortable and performance-robbing motions a sailboat goes through. Think of two hefty adults balanced on a seesaw: when one pushes off, inertia—the body put in motion—drives the other person toward the ground. Substitute two light children on the seesaw and the inertial force is greatly diminished. This explains why excess weight in the ends of a sailboat is so detrimental.

If you're a cruiser who enjoys an occasional race, it makes sense to remove a heavy plow or claw anchor from the bow roller before the race. Secure it amidships, deep in the bilge, or store it and its chain rode ashore. Naturally, keep aboard a lightweight flat-fluked anchor (such as a Danforth) and a rope anchor rode of sufficient size for emergencies.

Modern boats tend to have high-volume, light-displacement hulls, but the skin drag associated with wide beam and relatively flat sections can be significant. Some designs have a finer waterline footprint that depends on not overloading the vessel. The displacement-to-payload ratio must remain high on such a boat; overloading it will prove highly detrimental to performance, just as it is with a multihull.

Cruisers consider full water tanks money in the bank, but water weighs more than 8 pounds per gallon, and 150 gallons in tanks can increase the "full trim" displacement by more than 1,200 pounds. Given the effect of water and fuel weight, it doesn't make sense to fill or fuel tanks before an overnight race. Take only what is necessary.

Reducing Windage

Windage is another insidious performance thief. A dodger, bimini, and stern arch davits holding a big RIB (rigid inflatable boat) lashed athwartships rob upwind performance as surely as trailing a bucket off the stern. Sailboats that look like Conestoga wagons—the present trend—often have jerry jugs of diesel fuel lashed to the rail in order to feed the motorsailer unintentionally created.

When you consider purchasing new gear, we advise factoring in weight and windage to assess the potential adverse effects on performance. A roll-up inflatable stowed in a locker may not be quite as versatile as a heavy RIB hung in davits from a stern arch, but the weight will be positioned lower within the boat and the windage is much less. If you're caught in a gale at sea you won't have to worry about a breaking wave tearing away the RIB along with a good part of the stern.

Performance Tweaks

The speed of a sailboat may be a relative thing, but one thing is certain: even a slight increase shown on the knotmeter raises the crew's spirits. A performance upgrade doesn't necessarily mean the price tag of a new carbon spar or involve the monumental undertaking of fairing the underwater foils (keel and rudder) and the entire bottom. True, a new mast, new sails, and a speed-shop bottom job will certainly jolt the knotmeter, but less dramatic makeovers also allow you to coax a welcome increase in boat speed. (See Chapter 7 for full discussions of sail area, trim, the use of a vang for sail shaping, and more.)

Reducing Drag

You can gain the performance advantage of a smooth, fair bottom from some fairly straightforward (if tedious) DIY efforts. For example, start by eliminating marine growth during the season with a regular wipe-down—in or out of the water—using a sponge, cloth, or light abrasive pad. When the boat is hauled out, repair any flaking paint and evenly sand the surface before recoating.

Note: *It's essential to use gloves, goggles, and coveralls to protect yourself from the antifouling chemicals in* *bottom paint.* In terms of performance it's worthwhile to purchase bottom paint with an excellent antifouling reputation as well as having a smooth surface. For the average cruiser/racer, a copolymer or ablative paint makes sense.

Carefully rolling and tipping the paint (a time-consuming process) won't produce the slick surface of a sprayed finish, but it will certainly be smoother than a slapdash job. You can smooth out brush strokes and surface imperfections with subsequent wipe-downs. Top-tier racing competitors often prefer harder spray-applied coatings, which you burnish into a very slick surface. However, as the late Steve Moore, a savvy sailmaker, once put it, "If you want to win, spend 50 hours sailing your boat for every hour you spend wet-sanding the bottom."

BOAT HANDLING AT SEA

Boat handling at sea involves much more than sail selection and trim (see Chapter 7 on Sails). Rather, it's a comprehensive process that includes using navigation and weather inputs to shape the course and the routine on board. If you're not racing, there is no need to make the crew miserably uncomfortable to squeeze out every last tenth of a knot of boat speed, especially in rough conditions. In fact, the difference between racing and cruising is best described in terms of sail area. The racer needs to set enough sail to cope with the holes or light spots that oscillate through on a regular basis. When the puffs hit or the breeze fills in, the crew doesn't want to reef for fear of being undercanvassed in the next lull of an oscillating breeze.

The traditional remedy is to twist off power, that is, "open" the upper portion of the leech to spill wind by easing the vang, easing the sheet a bit and trimming with the traveler. Depowering the mainsail in this fashion helps; however, the wave-jumping slams that may occur when going fast may not be reduced. One-design sailors often depower the main by adding tension to the halyard, outhaul, cunningham, and vang in order to flatten the mainsail, and then use the sheet and traveler to spill the breeze evenly from top to bottom. Cruises are better off taking a more conservative stance and tucking a reef in early.

Whether viewed as the ultimate exhilaration or as torment under sail, we can say for sure that ocean racing ranks as a legitimate test of boat and crew. If you're less interested in testing the boat and crew than enjoying the serenity of an offshore voyage, you can tuck in a reef when the wind pipes up. So maybe you wait a little too long to shake it out once the wind begins to lighten, but that's no big deal. Shorthanded crews typically sail larger boats with 20% to 30% less sail set than the same vessel would be carrying with a full crew.

Just as a piston-hanked headsail of a certain size is appropriate for a certain range of wind velocities, a furling jib or mainsail can be enlarged or reduced to match the wind. Furling mains are trickier than headsails. In-mast furling complicates matters, and little nuances such as the boom angle and outhaul tension greatly influence the outcome of a furling effort.

During a long ocean passage, conditions may dictate reefing at night. In that case, one of the biggest challenges is preserving night vision while still being able to see what's going on with the sails. Some crews use spreader lights on a dimmer switch, while others get by with a flashlight or two. Reliable slab reefing requires less gadgetry and you don't need to worry about the way the luff tape is leading from the mast track to a furling boom or whether vertical battens hang up as they are fed into a slotted furling spar. Crew using the latest furling gear need to recognize its operational requirements and be ready to respond to them day or night.

A servopendulum vane with a horizontal pivoting windvane linked to an articulated paddle that actuates two opposing levers linked to the wheel drum. The process is hard to envision but easy to use. Windvanes respond to deck-level apparent wind, which is affected by vessel motion and vortices off the leech of the mainsail.

Self-Steering Ability

At sea we must carry out certain tasks regardless of the weather. Like controlling the sail area, steering ranks near the top of the list. A racing boat with plenty of crew always has people ready for the helm along with great incentive for precise hand steering. When cruising shorthanded, however, we face a different challenge.

On day sails everyone wants a chance at the helm, but the appeal diminishes by the second or third day of a lengthy passage. Only stoic souls look forward to staring at the compass for 3 or 4 hours at a time. That's why self-steering technology is a vital ally of shorthanded crews on long cruises.

Windvane Self-Steering

Only a few decades ago, we viewed autopilots as useful for motor vessels with power to spare. Sailors, on the other hand, depended on quirky gizmos that, once bolted to the transom, used wind energy and vessel motion to control the helm. Crude at first, these home-brewed fabrications became better engineered over time. Eventually, a sailboat yawing along toward Timbuktu under windvane self-steering began to look more purposeful and less like a drunken sailor reeling from tavern to dock.

Nick Franklin mainstreamed the self-steering appendage conceived by Blondie Hasler. He shrank Hasler's miniature oil rig into the functional Aries servopendulum self-steering vane. Others followed, and windvanes by many names were fabricated: Hydrovane, RVG, Cape Horn, Sailomat, and Monitor were only a few that hit the market. Innovation continued, resulting in increased reliability of these units.

Like solar panels, these devices convert natural energy into usable power, in this case a reliable steering force for a sailing vessel. Boats with a balanced sail plan and easily actuated rudders take kindly to self-steering, but even the best vane–boat marriages can't completely eliminate the two-step yaw to port and starboard as the boat rolls and surges in a seaway. A jibe potential always exists during a deep reach. Coaxing the best behavior out of the gear starts with trimming the sails for the optimum course.

Self-steering gear eventually fell into two design categories: the auxiliary rudder and the servopendulum style vane. Both systems use a vertical or horizontal pivoting windvane in the upper portion that tilts or pivots in response to the apparent wind blowing more directly on one side than the other. A series of pushrods and levers or a cable-and-pulley assembly telegraphs the movement of the windvane to the immersed blade to affect steering.

With auxiliary-rudder self-steering, the submerged portion of the gear is either a secondary rudder equipped with a trailing trim tab or a highly balanced secondary spade rudder. In either case, the blade is set up to be turned on its vertical axis by the rather light force from the windvane sensor; this results in a steering moment like that generated by the boat's primary rudder. The challenge has always been to set things up so that a smaller rudder can do the job of the large one, and a balanced sail plan is essential.

An auxiliary-rudder system involves coping with the galvanic corrosion that develops because of the metals used in the system. These skippers must also live with an immersed appendage hanging from the transom, often cursing their choice during stern-first maneuvers. On the other hand, if the main rudder fails, a backup is already in place.

The servopendulum approach is a little more complicated. The portion of the unit submerged in the water is not a rudder but an athwartship-swinging paddle that uses the vessel's motion through the water to generate steering energy. That energy is then routed to the vessel's main rudder through two lines and a series of blocks. Initially the windvane is aligned with the apparent wind; as a heading change causes the vane blade to tilt or rotate, the linkage twists the vertical axis of the immersed paddle. Rather than causing a steering moment, the immersed paddle, supported at a single point, swings toward one side of the vessel or the other, pulling on a line that leads to the tiller or to the drum of the wheel. This approach has an advantage, because the faster the vessel moves, the more the paddle arm develops energy and the more powerful the helm response becomes.

Boats with a long keel and unbalanced attached rudder fare better with auxiliary-rudder steering gears. Such boats have inherent directional stability and respond to the nudging effect of a less powerful auxiliary-rudder vane. On the other hand, fin-keelers with a semibalanced spade or skeg-hung rudder are quicker to yaw, thus needing a more powerful steering response, which usually means using a servopendulum steering vane.

The Monitor self-steering system is today's best example of servopendulum self-steering. Hans Bernwall developed an interest in self-steering gear when he and his good friend Carl Seipel sailed a classic 40-foot Alden cutter around the world. This six-year voyage took place in the 1970s, and they spent time tinkering with a homemade Hasler vane and entertaining the locals wherever they went. Their successful circumnavigation was a firsthand lesson in how vital a mechanical self-steering system can be for small to medium-sized cruisers.

Bernwall and Seipel subsequently took over the manufacture of the Monitor vane, and their refinements of the concept led to many technical and structural improvements. The Monitor vane remains a system of choice for those headed to sea.

If seas were always flat and wind didn't shift and oscillate, the job of self-steering gear would be much easier. But we see an inherent problem in the simple fact that the desired course is linked to apparent wind direction. The apparent wind is altered by gusts and lulls and by the boat's rolling, any of which can cause the boat to wander off course. Fortunately, these deviations to either side of the desired course tend to even out over time.

Autopilot Self-Steering

With no landmarks to watch, an offshore cruiser using windvane self-steering wanders along a course that by no means is held with perfection. For those willing to spend the dollars and amperes, an electronic autopilot offers more precise course keeping. The harder it blows, however, the more electrical energy an autopilot consumes, and a failure in the battery charging system can shut down the whole show.

An autopilot steers a boat on a selected compass course using electrical, or hydraulic, steering actuators. Autopilots can also be programmed to adjust and steer a course based on a wind direction indicator. This can be tricky if a persistent or an abrupt windshift occurs. Autopilots are both a cruiser's curse and a dream come true.

Thanks to digital circuitry and efficient DC motors, the power and accuracy of autopilot steering have both increased. Gone are the days of hand steering using a slowly spinning compass card with a dim light sensor. In current autopilots, nearly instantaneous heading data are digitally crunched by an algorithm, and the "smart pilot" can sense and react to vessel yaw characteristics. The rudder is controlled with an electric hydraulic ram. This capacity to hold a course is generally more accurate than a helmsperson. With a high-quality, properly installed autopilot, you'll get good results.

Yet there are two downsides. Even the best, most reliable systems have hefty dollar and ampere price tags, the latter most evident when sailing off the wind in heavy weather. In such cases, the system can easily consume 100 amp-hours or more in a period of 24 hours.

Like many plug-and-play modern electronics, autopilot systems are easy to wire, although mounting is more difficult. The installation must be strong enough to transmit the hundreds or thousands of pounds of force delivered by a hydraulic ram. The ruggedness of the ram hardware shows the potential

The world has a nearly inexhaustible inventory of welcoming anchorages, reached by passages just waiting to be sailed.

Making Landfall

There's an old saying among mariners that safety is found at sea, away from the shoals, dense traffic, and other intrusions we associate with land. In deep water, ocean swells even out and the expanse of water has a more even cadence. Yes, storms come and go out there. Still, there is more to the old adage about the value of sea room than the lack of risk of being blown ashore. When waves pile up on a shoreline and the friction of the continental shelf aggravates sea conditions, we wish for open sea. This is but one reason sailors approaching land must be at the top of their game, and the phrase "safe harbor" says nothing about what it takes to approach that harbor. Regardless of what coastline you sail, you need to understand all-weather safe havens that afford not only protection but a tenable approach in a gale.

A quick look at a large-scale chart reveals water depths in the vicinity of the harbor entrance and any potential dangers. Safe navigation demands knowing the locations of rocky outcrops, granite ledges, coral heads, and sandbars. Some harbors, especially those adjacent to prominent points, submarine canyons, and river mouths, notoriously attract large swells. When you're unsure whether a particular entrance is safe in all weather, then it's best to rely on standard references, such as the *U.S. Coast Pilot*, a nine-volume publication from NOAA (the National Oceanic and Atmospheric Administration Office). These volumes offer details about the coastal landscape and conditions, information that can't be shown on nautical charts. The information can be downloaded from NOAA's website and other online resources. The information is useful for commercial shipping as well as for fishing and pleasure boats. These volumes are updated yearly.

In addition, *Sailing Directions* is a multivolume publication from the NGA (National Geospatial-Intelligence Agency). These publications also include details of the coastline useful for all mariners and are available from many retail marine vendors such as Landfall Navigation.

In heavy weather the largest waves break on outer reefs and sandbars. Even if there is a deep channel across a bar, you must be careful not to be swept off course into shallower water. Using range marks, buoys, back bearings, and GPS fixes makes it easier to stay on course. Even with a good sailing breeze it makes sense to have the engine running in neutral at such times, ready to help in an instant if staying on course requires a bit of extra thrust. Getting over a bar as quickly as possible is always good, and a motorsailing dash is often the best way to do this.

When waves pile up on shore in heavy weather, a current is often present up or down the coast. In

forces generated, and the rudderstock bracket and hull connection need to be similarly strong. Simply tabbing a small support base to the inside skin of a cored hull is asking for trouble.

To get a feel for the loads involved, consider the pull on a 6-foot tiller when steering on a reach in an ordinary gusty afternoon breeze. Now shorten the tiller from 6 feet to 6 inches and multiply the peak load you felt by a factor of 12. Factor in the influence of big breaking seas attempting to broach your vessel and you get a sense of what the autopilot's electromechanical drive or hydraulic ram must regularly overcome. Its attachment to the hull must also endure such on-and-off compression and tension loading. The bottom line is that a heavy-duty autopilot deserves a heavy-duty installation.

addition, a tidal current can rage through an inlet, causing waves to stand on end. A vessel transiting such confines should be closed up, with hatches dogged and the crew ready to take breaking waves aboard. Concluding a voyage in heavy weather requires knowledge of what you're racing toward, which is why it then makes sense to approach only a deep-water harbor and to do so in daylight. Fortunately, most customs and immigration offices are in deep-water commercial ports, and these usually have safe, straightforward entrances.

A new landfall, reached across an ocean or across the bay, involves transitioning from the routine underway to a different rhythm. A race crew might scramble for airports and hotels, but cruisers generally revel in the tranquility of a vessel at rest. Cruisers often switch to coastal exploration mode and get to know the place they've come to. The rewards of time in port act as a counterpoint to the days or weeks at sea. Shifting from boat handling to being at anchor is a change usually as welcome as your initial departure.

In this chapter we've looked at many aspects of boat handling, from docking to steering to landfall. Now we'll turn our attention to another specific aspect of controlling the boat: handling lines and the rigging.

5

LINES, LINE HANDLING, AND RIGGING

A rope in the hands of a skilled sailor is like a sharp chisel wielded by an able craftsman. Such tools measure the practitioner's expertise. Simple tests like tossing a loop over a piling, heaving a rope to someone on the pier, or leading lines fairly through chocks to cleats say much about the sailor. Lines and line handling are actually another form of boat handling, including knowledge of knots, skills for splicing different kinds of rope, and the ability to make tight lashings stay put. The line-handling techniques used today have evolved over centuries, a reminder of the era of hand, reef, and steer.

The skills you need today to make a vessel fast to a dock or pier include using an array of dock lines that will be tossed, passed, or simply made fast to a cleat. Your choice of appropriate leads must match the conditions. How you make up a cleat or coil the tail of a halyard speaks loudly about your seamanship. As discussed in the previous chapter, you'll encounter occasions to warp a boat in to a dock against the pressure of an aft or forward spring line, or you may use engine power against a restraining spring line to hold a boat against a dock while passengers board or disembark. Despite bow thrusters, directional drives, and electric winches, it's highly unlikely that any automated docking system will ever make line handling obsolete.

Sailors learn to handle running rigging with similar skill. Docking or underway, you'll not just trim and ease lines but also check, snub, or surge them, and you may also need to overhaul a line or sway a halyard. Preparing an anchor rode for storage or coiling it proves just as important as putting it to use. Some lines hockle (form an unwanted twist or kink) easily and others tend to snag, but if you understand what's demanded in any given line-handling task, you're more likely to use the right technique for the job.

🚩 *Over time, sailors develop their own ways of coiling halyard tails, topping lifts, and other cordage. There are differences of opinion whether it's better to wrap a few turns around a concentrically coiled line or fake the rope in a figure eight and position it on the deck ready to run. But we do know that the entire crew, whether that's two or ten, should handle lines the same way. You'll know why when a squall hits at 0300 and a line snarls during a sail douse.*

LINE SELECTION

Cordage has been used for at least 28,000 years, as evidenced by carbon-dated twine imprints in clay shards found in Europe. Some 6,500 years ago the Egyptians may have been the first to use tools to make rope. For millennia the materials of choice for laid or twisted rope were hemp, manila, sisal, jute, cotton, and other natural fibers.

Most sailors today started messing around in boats well after natural-fiber rope was put on display in marine museums. The aroma of tarred marlin and huge reels of manila anchor rode may linger in the memories of old salts, but today the word *rope* usually refers to nylon and Dacron (polyester) cordage. (Note: In traditional usage, rope is what a manufacturer produces in the factory, and a line is a length of rope put to a specific nautical use. For example, a halyard is a line made of a specific type of rope.)

Rope Materials

In 1935, DuPont's young research director Wallace Carothers and his team came up with the synthetic polymer dubbed nylon, a fiber that soon found its way into stockings, toothbrushes, and rope around the world. In the 1940s, polyethylene terephthalate (PET), another long-chain polymer, was developed in England. PET has many uses, including plastic bottles, but boaters know it as the polyester resin polymer in fiberglass boats. Mariners also know it as the polyester fiber manufactured under the trade names Terylene in England and Dacron in the U.S., where it joined the DuPont lineup in 1951. Polyester fiber soon joined nylon as a staple for sailmakers and cordage manufacturers around the world. It proved much less stretchy than nylon, 90% as strong, and less affected by ultraviolet rays.

Together, nylon and Dacron dominated nautical cordage for a half century. These miracle polymers have better mechanical properties than natural fibers, and they are free of the ancient problem we know as rot. They are made from filaments thinner than a human hair and bundled in much the same way we handle plant fibers. The resulting line rope is stronger, tougher, and suppler. Nylon has been the standard choice for anchor rodes or any other line where stretchiness is a virtue, while Dacron became preferred for sheets, halyards, and other lines where stretchiness is a fault.

The old DuPont slogan "Better living through chemistry" is nowhere more apt than in the rope revolution. While Dacron and nylon were the prototypical synthetics, the search for stronger, lighter, less stretchy high-tech ropes continues. Spectra, Vectran,

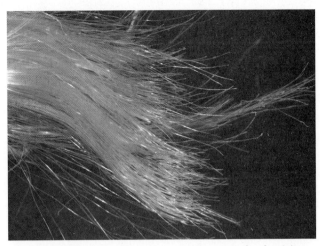

Nylon filaments offer greater tensile strength, elasticity, and abrasion resistance than natural fibers and also resist rot and chemical degradation. Nylon filaments can be spun into yarns, which are twisted into strands that are then laid into ropes, in a process similar to how rope makers used natural fibers for hundreds of years.

In the final stage of rope making, the new three-strand nylon is put on a spool maintaining a tight, even run the entire way.

PBO, Technora, Dyneema, and a host of other tongue twisters are the newest big things in fiber technology. Stronger than steel and ten times lighter, these new fibers have much less stretch and double or triple the tensile strength of nylon and Dacron. In addition, they can be used in a wide variety of constructions: they can be stranded, braided, or plaited, and tucked inside familiar polyester or polypropylene line covers for protection from sun, salt, and abrasion.

Rope manufacturers purchase yarns from chemical companies that produce a wide range of filaments along with coatings that enhance their performance. Cordage manufacturers often blend fibers in braided lines to reach specific strength and price targets.

High-modulus fibers with limited stretch and more than 1.5 times the strength of polyester or nylon are available for sheets and guys. Higher modulus lines for halyards have even less stretch and higher strength. There are specialized fibers (PBO and carbon) with so little stretch and such high strength that they are used for standing rigging. When considering a rigging upgrade, also evaluate other properties of these fibers, such as UV stability, creep, ease of handling, turning radius, and cost.

Similar in diameter but vastly different in strength, stretch resistance, and ease of handling, these braided lines give different options for fine-tuning your running rigging. Double-braid Dacron remains the status quo for sheets, while a higher-modulus line such as Spectra or Dyneema has significantly less halyard stretch. In addition to high strength and low stretch, running rigging should have good handling characteristics.

Some skeptics assume this proliferation of new rope materials and constructions is just so much marketing spin. But specs such as tensile strength have clear differences among different lines that may look similar on chandlery shelves. At the low-tech end of the spectrum, independent testing has shown that 7⁄16-inch three-strand nylon has a 5,900-pound breaking strength, while a high-quality Dacron (polyester) braid of the same diameter has a 6,600-pound tensile strength. At the high-tech end, New England Ropes' Endura 12 and Pro PBO, Samson's Progen II, and Yale's PoBOn have an astounding tensile strength rating of 24,000 pounds in 7⁄16-inch line—four times stronger!

Elongation, the elastic phase of stretch that occurs with repetitive loading, is another important factor when choosing line, and here too high-tech fibers really earn their keep. Take, for example, lines of the same diameter, each loaded to 30% of breaking strength. A 100-foot length of PBO, Vectran, Dyneema, or Spectra line stretches less than a foot under such load, while 100 feet of conventional polyester line stretches 3 feet. Given that a top-end line is about four times as strong as the lower-cost Dacron line, the top-end line is even more impressive in *minimal stretch* per load. I view stronger, lighter, less stretchy lines like better-quality tools: likely to be worth the investment in the long run, when used for the proper purpose. But the converse is also true, using Dyneema for docklines is like using a chisel as a screwdriver. Matching the material with the mission is essential.

There is more to lines than just tensile strength and stretch. Although stretch is an important consideration when replacing a wire halyard with rope, another important variable is the manufacturer's published ratio for line diameter to sheave radius, a measure of how much the line can bend without harming the fiber bundles. In addition, cover material is important, along with any special coatings on the line that help minimize UV damage and chemical damage caused by atmospheric variables such as acid rain.

Overall, you should consider a full range of factors when selecting cordage for a specific application, not the least being cost. The price of 7/16-inch cordage generally ranges from about one to five dollars per foot. At about the midpoint of that range one can move up from high-quality double-braid polyester to Dyneema cores for significantly improved performance.

Shock loading is difficult to quantify and hard to predict. Shock loads are short-lived spikes in the tensile load, which tend to cause more damage in cordage with minimal ability to elongate. Nylon's elasticity—an ability to stretch up to 25% without failing—makes it a superior shock absorber and load-dampener and an excellent choice for an anchor rode or spring line, though not for a halyard.

When using low-stretch cordage for rigging, choose a size with an appropriate safety factor for shock loads. For this reason, manufacturers publish safe working loads of lines for specific uses, and these numbers may be a third or less of the breaking strength. The Cordage Institute, the rope industry's technical body, specifies a 5-12 safety factor for noncritical uses: the breaking strength equals 5 to 12 times the safe working load. For lifelines, the safety factor is 15. This conservative safety margin is based on how momentary shock loads can spike in cordage under tension, especially if the rope has very little elongation or stretch. Using a line of an appropriate size such that the working load is a small percentage of the breaking strength also minimizes stretch and prolongs the line's life. A line at its breaking point has elongated as far as its elastic and plastic limits allow. Additional loading may lead to an explosive bang.

Creep (elongation under prolonged load), another mechanical factor, primarily affects lines that stay under constant load. One UK research team found that polyester rope has an expected life span of 100 years when loaded to 50% of its breaking strength by a dead weight with no inertial loads, UV exposure, abrasion, or other wear and tear involved. At a load of 64% of breaking strength, however, the life span decreased to just one year. As you can see, the inverse relationship between load and life span is nonlinear and perhaps difficult to judge.

Creep has several stages. In its primary phase, there is a relatively abrupt elongation while filaments share the loading. Then, as the load increases, a secondary phase, more linear and slower to unfold, occurs. Then in the tertiary phase, filaments can be heard snapping and elongation becomes more rapid, accelerating to the point of complete failure. We avoid creep by choosing a cordage type and diameter that keeps the working load well less than 50% of the breaking strength under even the most adverse circumstances, and to achieve true longevity, under 25%. Creep tends to be more common in olefin-based lines, including polypropylene and polyethylene (see Running Rigging Material Selection later in this chapter). Creep is almost nonexistent in high-end fibers such as Zylon-based PBO.

When choosing cordage for sheets, balance the decision making. It's good to limit stretch, but consider other factors, too. Ask those who handle genoa sheets while tacking up a tight channel, and they'll prefer the line with the best handling characteristics, including its suppleness, the ease of wrapping it around a winch, and how it grips and releases the surface of the drum. Other important considerations include how the line holds and releases from the jaws

■ *Don't purchase rope strictly by specs in a catalog, but get a hands-on feel as well. Check the slipperiness of the cover and coating used by the manufacturer, and determine how it will behave on a winch drum. Some of the strongest rope is also among the hardest to coil—that may be fine when the rope is used as the lead for an all-rope running backstay, but for a halyard, rope that coils like a tree branch has a definite downside.*

of a self-tailing winch and, for halyards and reefing lines, how the cover holds up under the repeated clamping of a rope clutch. Also test how easily the line coils and its willingness to remain hockle-free.

Racing sailors see the value of less stretch, lighter weight, and increased strength, but many cruisers need more convincing before abandoning their nylon anchor rode and dock line and their Dacron running rigging. However, a closer look sometimes changes minds. Take, for example, a Dyneema-cored (Spectra) halyard with a tough, UV-protective polyester cover and only one-third the stretch of its Dacron equivalent. An advantage of this line is how it behaves in a gust, particularly its reluctance to stretch. This keeps the sail's luff from loosening and prevents increased draft when it's least desirable. A taut luff in heavy weather is essential, and given that many cruisers run their halyard tails back to the cockpit, even a small stretch per foot of line can add up to significant luff sag.

🚩 *The Mystic Seaport Museum has a display of how natural fibers were traditionally converted to yarns, strands, and finally rope in an ingenious mechanized process—a manufacturing technique that has many parallels today.*

We also can replace wire running backstays with high-modulus cordage. Cruisers making long ocean passages benefit from the extra support and column control afforded by runners, which are mandatory when a heavy-weather forestaysail is flown. In light air, however, we like being able to tie them off near the shrouds and sailing without the runners. All-rope runners are much easier to handle and tie off than wire-in stays with rope tails.

Cruisers serious about minimizing use of their engine gravitate toward light-air reaching sails and asymmetric spinnakers. No-foil, endless-line furlers and spinnaker socks benefit from light cordage that is easy to handle. Even more valuable are light-air sheets such as Flight Line from New England Ropes, which has a polypropylene braided cover over a Dyneema core and is a strong, light line with little stretch—a big plus in ghosting conditions.

Specialized braided dinghy painters that resist abrasion and are UV-stable also feature a buoyant core, making it much less likely for the painter to wrap in the prop. Rope manufacturers are also responding to the challenges of mooring a vessel with the best possible chafe protection. Investigations of rope failures during storms have demonstrated that stretching wet nylon filaments creates friction and causes enough heat to melt these tiny fibers, so now there is a trend toward blended mooring pendants with less stretch. For example, Yale's Maxi-Moor adds a urethane jacket to a Polydyne line (braided polyester cover over a nylon core). The factory splices the line, and we can slide a piece of built-in chafe gear into position where we most need it.

When all is said and done, nylon and Dacron lines are more than adequate on a cruising boat, and they remain less expensive favorites for good reason. But worthy investments for cruisers include special-purpose, high-modulus cordage for less stretchy halyards and runners, lighter drifter and reacher sheets, and more secure mooring pendants.

Rope Construction

For centuries, cordage manufacturers used traditional construction techniques that had worked well. They spun fibers into yarns, twisted fibers (counterclockwise if the fibers were spun clockwise) into strands, and then twisted strands together (clockwise if the yarns were twisted counterclockwise) into the finished rope. The opposing twists locked the bundles into place. With tension added to the three-strand laid rope, the yarns torqued and rubbed against each other in response to elongation.

In today's running rigging, laid rope takes a back seat to braided line. With most of the twist involved

Three-strand nylon rope is composed of filaments twisted into yarns that are twisted into strands that in turn are woven into the rope. When the rope comes under load, the twisted filaments, yarns, and strands attempt to elongate, and the friction associated with this elongation is significant. Many failed nylon lines show signs of melting due to frictional heat.

Double-braid rope manufacturers often bury high-modulus, UV-degradable fibers in the core where they are better protected from sunlight and abrasion. The outer cover is comprised of tougher, UV-stable fibers, such as polyester, that add some strength but primarily protect the more costly load-bearing core. Shown here is Dyneema SK-75.

With the same amount of abrasion, the covers of these four double-braid lines behave very differently. In applications where chafe is likely, such as halyards, it makes sense to opt for a low-stretch line with a tough cover. These four polyester-covered double-braid lines were equally abraded in a controlled experiment. Note that the line third from the left, a tight 24-count braid, is the least damaged by abrasion. The looser-braided covers sustained more damage.

in laid rope eliminated, braided lines are less stretchy and the fiber bundles can be better aligned with load paths. Early Dacron braided line was usually a balanced blend, with half of the tensile strength carried in the core and half in the cover. Today's high-tech lines generally distribute the load differently between cover and core. Kernmantle rope, for example, has a braided cover and an unbraided, high-load core that carries 70% of the tensile strength. With such a line, even when abrasion jeopardizes the outer surface, the core strength can be considerable.

Rope can be engineered for anchors and moorings (and mountaineering, too, for example) with most of the tensile strength in the core, but nonetheless, once the cover of a sheet, guy, or halyard is frayed, it is time to replace the line. Urethane cover coatings help postpone that day by lessening the damaging effects of UV radiation and acid rain.

Many experts, including the technical staff of New England Ropes, still favor three-strand nylon for its toughness and ability to take physical abuse. Double-braid, single-braid, and plaited nylon docklines are more susceptible to chafe and tearing on sharp objects. For the same reason, those alternatives to three-strand nylon don't fare well as anchor rodes,

especially if rodes make contact with an underwater obstruction. They fake and coil easily, but the rode's characteristics in use are more important than in the anchor locker. In addition, you can more easily splice three-strand nylon to save the line if chafe occurs in only one point.

Steve Parola of New England Ropes tells us it's better to stuff three-strand nylon anchor rode into a bag than to coil it conventionally. The stuffing method at least eliminates the hockle-causing twists that come from coiling, and the line will be easier to deploy. Even better, you can lay the line in a figure eight before stowing it, making it fast with some short stuff or sail ties.

🚩 *Steve Parola of New England Ropes inspects a ⅝-inch nylon rope that parted just below an area of maximum abrasion damage.*

Testing Aging Nylon Lines

Nylon three-strand dock lines, anchor rodes, and mooring pendants all work to keep your boat where you want it when you're not underway. The impressive durability of this cordage, however, may encourage a belief that it's invincible and immortal. As a skeptic, I've wondered how much of their original strength old dock lines still have. Recently, in my technical editor role at *Practical Sailor*, I had a chance to find out. I rounded up a set of dock lines with a known history and tested them with the technical team at New England Ropes.

The tested lines were weathered 10- to 12-year-old three-strand nylon lines that had been used as part-time dock lines for half their life and as full-time, 24/7 lines tethering a 41-foot sloop to a fixed pier in a sheltered cove on the Chesapeake Bay for the other half. They had noticeable chafe where they made contact with chocks and cleats, but UV degradation and weathering had resulted in more insidious damage. Some of the lines had spliced ends, and others had free ends. We tested all of them to the point of destruction in the New England Ropes lab, using a hydraulic ram and a computer-recorded strain gauge.

In each test, as we exceeded the nylon's elastic deformation range, filaments began to permanently stretch, and when we removed the load, the line didn't return to its starting length. The material exceeded its limit of *elastic* deformation and moved into the tenuous realm of *plastic* deformation. Then, as the load was increased, we heard telltale crackling sounds of failure within the filaments. Before the

line's failure we saw impressive elongation, yet less than the 25% increase of new nylon cordage.

Each nylon line we tested proved that once its elastic limit has been exceeded and its yield point reached, it's only a short step before plastic deformation leads to a spectacular ending. As the filament strain reached a critical level and the line neared its failure point, everyone backed away from the ram and held their hands over their ears, prepared for the gunshot-like report as the line snapped. The spliced lines mostly failed at the throat of the splice, where the tucked strand tails enter the line. The more tapered a splice, the better it resisted failure. Even so, these tests showed a splice resulted in a 10% drop in line strength; a 30% drop occurs when a bowline is used instead of a splice. The unspliced rope ends fared better, with the lines failing in the midsection more often than not, usually at abrasion points that had been noted and marked during pretest observations.

Our results demonstrated that aging reduced the breaking strength of nylon dock lines to a startlingly degree. While experts say that nylon has great UV resistance and chemical stability, our testing revealed a worrisome trend: nylon does not age gracefully. This is an important consideration when choosing new rope for dock lines or anchor rodes.

Note that our testing measured the cordage's optimal breaking strength by delivering a straight-line pull, avoiding on-off cycle loading and minimizing chafe. Note, too, that we tested dry line, and wet nylon loses as much as 15% of strength. Yet the highest-testing line had retained only 51% of its original tensile strength, and some samples broke at only 25% of their original rating.

When new nylon line breaks, it shows extensive melting caused by the heat developed by friction

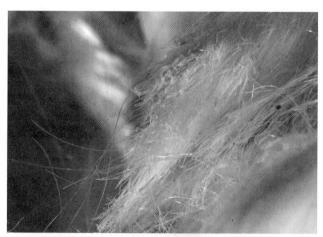

🚩 *When nylon line is tensioned near its breaking point, friction between the fibers generates enough heat to melt nylon filaments, creating additional elongation and heat and finally resulting in catastrophic failure.*

between filaments at high loads. We saw very little filament melting in the failure of these older lines because they broke at much lower loads. These test findings reinforced my belief that replacing dock lines at regular intervals is money well spent. In addition to age, look for signs of abrasion, excessive hardening, and cover deterioration. When it comes to nylon, its stretch is its big advantage; when the fibers lose that capacity it's time for new line.

Some sailors might think to downsize their nylon anchor rode and dock lines to increase their elasticity, believing that the line is more than strong enough in a diameter smaller than normally recommended. Our findings, however, suggest two significant downsides of too much rubber-band effect. First, the heat buildup associated with repeated stretching can become critical when surging stretches dock lines or gale-force gusts tension an anchor rode. Second, springy lines cause short bursts of acceleration and encourage a vessel to "sail at anchor" or saw back and forth on dock lines, thereby increasing chafe and shock loading. In addition, smaller-diameter line has less safety margin against chafe, and sooner or later, damage to the line jeopardizes the vessel.

Carefully consider your antichafe efforts. Many vessels break mooring or dock lines that were carefully covered with heavy PVC hose where they pass through chocks, as such antichafe gear can perversely hasten a line's demise. The PVC prevents dissipation of the heat generated by friction between filaments from dissipating, so although the line doesn't abrade, it melts. Carefully set up antichafe protection to allow rain to cool and lubricate the stretching and contracting fibers. Leather with a laced open top or water-permeable canvas makes better chafing gear than impermeable PVC hose. While wet nylon does lose some strength, this is a comparatively minor consideration.

Running Rigging Material Selection

As with sneakers and ice cream, a proliferation of brands of miracle high-tech lines complicates the selection of running rigging. Take Technora, for example. An aramid (lightweight, high-strength) fiber like Kevlar, Technora has extremely low stretch and high strength, it doesn't melt or creep, and it resists abrasion. Unfortunately, the fiber is UV sensitive and negatively affected by acids and salts. Therefore, the producer uses the fiber only in the core, and even though abrasion resistant, it isn't used to cover other materials.

Spectra and Dyneema are olefin fibers (*ultra-high-molecular-weight polyethylene*, or UHMWPE) comprised of long-chain molecules in a strong crystal

This section of ¾-inch nylon failed just above a spliced eye, a fairly predictable failure point, especially when a chock chafes the line as it leads over the rail.

lattice structure. These materials derive their tensile strength from long parallel bonds that behave quite differently from the shorter Kevlar molecule's bond. Creep is an issue with this fiber, and some elongation occurs under high continuous load. Many riggers have little concern about this because the safe working load is such a small percentage of the breaking strength. UHMWPE line's low density, light weight, and good UV stability make it well suited for a single-braid halyard line or the core of a double-braid line. However, its lubricity makes it slippery on winches and tricky to knot. Many racers strip the cover from the line beyond where it rides on a winch drum.

An aromatic polyester (a thermally and chemically stable component of polyester), Vectran was tough and strong enough to be used by NASA in the bounce bags for the Mars Lander. Nearly immune to creep and chemically stable, Vectran withstands UV radiation and has long-term stability. Insoluble in water, Vectran resists abrasion and has good flex and fold characteristics. In short, its blend of tensile strength, toughness, and durability makes it a standout fiber for both short- and long-term applications.

While fibers such as Technora, Dyneema, and Vectran boost the breaking strength of rope and lessen stretch, they also increase a rope's stiffness and tendency to hockle, and they coil poorly. Regardless of a rope's strength, it has little use if it slips off a cleat or refuses to be coiled. Age and environmental factors can make some high-modulus lines even stiffer—more like a dowel than a length of line. Ease of handling is important, especially when many lines lead to the cockpit. While a cantankerous halyard causes only initial problems, at least until it comes

A supple, easy-wrapping jibsheet is a line handler's best friend, especially in a shorthanded watch where one person is the sail handler, lookout, and navigator/helmsman.

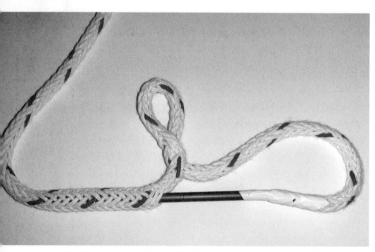

Yale's single-braid Ph.D., a high-modulus line, is easy to splice, friendly to handle, and behaves admirably as it piles up around a trimmer handling a sheet or halyard.

time to reef, sheets are handled frequently, and crew always appreciate easily coiled tails.

With so many lines spooled along chandlery walls, it's useful to consider them in groups by material and construction. Rope for running rigging can be sorted into low-, mid-, and high-performance groups based mainly on their fiber content.

Low-End Performance Materials

At the low-tech, lower-cost end of the spectrum are high-quality polyester double-braids. Most rope makers offer a polyester double-braid with excellent UV stability and handling characteristics at an attractive price. Prone to elongation under even modest working loads, these lines are less attractive for halyards, but work well as sheets on a cruising boat. Most shorthanded, long-range passagemakers aren't obsessed with continuous trimming. They turn the steering over to an autopilot and are content with an occasional look at sail shape and telltales. Eliminating the last bit of stretch from a sheet is of little advantage to them, whereas lines that resist abrasion, UV degradation, and the fatigue of days or weeks at sea are vital assets.

For halyards, many cruisers like Sta-Set X, a New England Ropes brand that encloses a core of parallel polyester fibers in a braided polyester cover. Compared to polyester double-braid, the parallel core has less stretch, and using polyester in both core and cover keeps the price down. This composition sacrifices some handling ease and abrasion resistance, the cover has an odd feel, and we find coiling not as easy as with other all-polyester lines. However, the lower stretch is important for halyards, and the tensile strength is about 10% greater.

Mid-Range Performance Materials

We find New England Rope's VPC not as nice to handle as the all-polyester braids, but we like the 50% less stretch, superior abrasion resistance, and price tag half that of high-end brands. Although stiff to handle, the company's T-900 brand offers low stretch and high tensile strength.

Yale's Vizzion is another good mid-range, low-stretch line, along with Yale's Ph.D., a single-braid, easily handled line that is easy to splice. Samson's 7/16-inch XLS line is also good to handle, grips well, eases on and off a winch drum nicely, and makes an excellent choice for sheets.

High-End Performance Materials

The sky's the limit at the upper end of the cordage range. For example, costly rope made with esoteric PBO (Zylon) finds its market primarily among top-tier racers. This synthetic long-chain polymer doesn't stretch or creep, but the mechanical properties are seriously diminished by exposure to sunlight and moisture. Coatings and covers can effectively encapsulate the fibers, however, resulting in a rope that can be used for standing rigging that provides 50% greater strength and 80% less weight than conventional rod rigging. PBO is as close to an extreme ideal as cordage manufacturers have come.

Just behind this esoteric chemistry is a group of lines with amazing breaking strength, impressive resistance to cover abrasion, and very little stretch. These include New England Ropes' Endura Braid and Yale's Maxibraid, both of which also handle well and coil nicely.

We also like Samson's AmSteel line, a single-braid, abrasion-resistant Dyneema line that remains soft and supple. Light enough to float, it's strong enough to support a pickup truck with a couple of J/24 keels in the bed. The downside is how an all-Dyneema line behaves on a winch drum. Its lubricity, or slipperiness, combined with a coating that glazes under pressure makes it difficult to set and ease on a winch drum. Nonetheless, it makes a superb halyard if used on a winch with a well-textured drum face. It's also worthwhile to keep a good supply of this line in the damage-control kit for jury-rigged lifelines, shrouds, or other vital rigging pieces.

Dyneema braid may seem very slippery, but up to a point, it holds a bowline surprisingly well. The indentation in the line is the result of a bowline pulled to 1,200 pounds of tension. At higher loads, the slipperiness of the fibers can cause knots to slip—that's why for semipermanent or permanent uses many riggers stitch the bitter end of the line to the formed loop to prevent slippage.

Rules of Thumb for Upgrading Rigging Lines

First, don't buy more tech than you're going to need. Start your upgrading with the main halyard. For the headsail halyard, unless you're a hardcore competitor, a genoa that rides in a roller-furler luff groove doesn't need as much no-stretch chemistry. When it's blowing hard and the jib is partially furled, the load dynamics spread out to the entire foil headstay and halyard, so you expect some luff sag. Those who still fly a conventional spinnaker will love the lower stretch of high-tech cordage in an afterguy. Lightweight, small-diameter light-air sheets (with no water absorption) can also improve ghosting performance. A light-weight mainsheet with good handling characteristics and a low tendency to twist may also be a worthwhile investment.

Polyester double-braid lines are just plain practical. Move up to lines with less stretchy fiber blends in the core, and you've arrived at a good compromise all around. And for those who don't choke on the prospect of spending three dollars per foot for hundreds of feet of line, there are spools of great technology just itchin' to make sailing faster and easier.

LINE HANDLING

Evaluating the Forces

For handling lines safely, the cardinal rule is to always appreciate the load on the other end—this simple physics lesson is an example of the sea sense every boater must acquire. A crewmember might be able to exert 100 pounds of force on a line with no mechanical advantage from a winch or tackle, or 1,000 pounds of tension on the same line using a large manual multispeed winch. A spring line made

RECOMMENDED RIGGING MATERIALS FOR CRUISERS, CRUISER/RACERS, AND RACERS

	Anchor Rode	Dock Lines	Sheets	Halyards	Lifelines	Standing Rigging
Nylon	C R C/R	C R C/R				
Polyester			C C/R			
Mid blend*			R	C C/R		
Dyneema				R	C R C/R	
PBO/Zylon						R

Key: C = cruiser, R = racer, C/R = cruiser/racer
*poly cover/high modulus fiber core

MAKING SURE THE RIGHT STRINGS ARE ATTACHED

Cordage and performance go hand in hand, and when replacing halyards, sheets, guys, topping lifts, outhauls, reefing lines, travelers, and downhauls, you have a great deal of cordage to choose from. The first big step is replacing conventional polyester (Dacron) main and jib halyards with much less stretchy Spectra (or Dyneema) halyards. Lower halyard stretch means less luff sag and scalloping, a big issue, especially for those using conventional piston-hanked headsails.

Another small stride forward is a new set of light-air jibsheets made of light, easy-to-handle cordage. For example, New England Ropes' Flight Line uses a polypropylene braided cover over a Dyneema core and is so light it floats. Such sheets help keep a drifter, gennaker, or asymmetric spinnaker flying in the lightest of breezes. Along with fast-action snatch blocks, they also increase a crew's ability to quickly set and jibe light-air sails.

fast prematurely while a heavy vessel still has way on can momentarily exert several thousand pounds of force to arrest the boat's forward motion.

Big-ship mariners learn quickly to respect the invisible energy that haunts a working line or tow cable. When anchored or moored in a gale or current, or when overcanvassed in a stiff breeze, recreational sailors too may glimpse the meaning of a lethal line. Surging (on/off acceleration) can cyclically load and unload lines, and crew should always stay outside the potential trajectory defined by the two points of attachment. In addition, you need to develop the ability to assess how much potential energy lurks in a line so that you can devise a plan for dealing with it.

A quick look at a line can tell you a lot about the magnitude of its load and how cautious you need to be when easing or releasing it. Always treat with respect a rigidly straight line that is "bar taut" or "humming tight." This is especially true with a modern high-modulus line holding energy at bay. I often test a line's tension by pressing its load-bearing section with my hand or foot, noting the deflection or lack of it. At the load end of the line may be a drawing genoa in a 15-knot breeze, a crewmember hoisted aloft, a pier-side bollard, or an anchor dug in against a gale. In a light wind, you might assume there is only a minimal load on a spring line you're about to adjust, but if you fail to note a 2-knot current, you could be in for a big surprise.

At sea, color-coded lines help crew pick the correct line when reefing or setting sail. As one becomes more familiar with a vessel, the lead location and terminus of a line become as relevant as its color to identify it. Rope clutches, like those shown just aft of the mast here, allow a single winch to be used for several functions, but terminating too many lines at one winch creates a log jam. Be sure that lines lead to locations where those trimming or reefing can easily handle them.

A heavy-duty anchor windlass and strain gauge allow a tester to feel how line behaves on a winch drum as tension increases. The cover material and finish of a double-braid line greatly influence its grip and its ability to be eased.

Line-Handling Tasks and Knots

We discuss a mariner's essential knots later in this chapter. First, let's look at some common line-handling situations.

Cleating a Line

When making fast a line, crew on a small craft usually first takes a single turn around the bitt, bollard, or cleat. At this point the line can still be eased or taken in, but any shock load is directed more to the attachment point than the line handler. As soon as the length of the line has been properly adjusted, the line can be made fast with a series of additional turns. Wise mariners spend little time with the line in hand but get a turn on a bitt, bollard, or cleat as soon as possible. (More on cleats later in this chapter.)

Most small-craft operators prefer a cleat for belaying a line. For decades, the Herreshoff cleat pattern has remained a favorite, and its contoured horns and widespread base mounted at four points provide good attachment. Mariners still debate whether the proper cleat hitch starts with a three-quarter turn or a full turn around the cleat to snub the line, but either way, the hitch then proceeds in a figure eight. Even in this era of rope clutches and cam cleats, it's hard to beat the never-fail conventional cleat.

Recreational mariners commonly finish a cleat hitch with an undertucked locking half hitch, but professionals on larger ships have an aversion to locking hitches. Consider a bow, stern, or spring line, for example. Unlike the situation with a jibsheet where the winch drum separates the cleat from the load, with the dock lines all of the energy is loaded directly onto the cleat; a locking half hitch can get so tight it

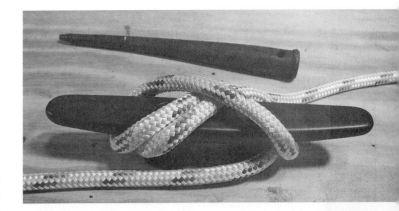

🚩 *Lines to or from large vessels are made fast on a cleat with a zigzagging figure eight that provides enough friction not to need a locking hitch. A conventional cleat hitch is often fine for small craft, but with larger vessels, excessive line tension can cause the hitch to tighten to the point of being impossible to loosen without a sharp knife.*

🚩 *Starting the cleat hitch with a full turn (bottom two photos, showing slightly varying perspectives) will resist much more pull than the three-quarter turn more commonly seen (top two photos, each from a slightly different perspective). The three-quarter turn is fine for winch-led lines; the full turn is preferable for dock lines.*

RELIEVING A LOADED GENOA CAR

The need to move a genoa sheet car under load is a frequent conundrum for line handling. Unless you've installed a car that's adjustable on the fly (for which your crew will thank you!), some ingenuity is required. In such cases I attach a line to the loaded genoa sheet with a simple rolling hitch well ahead of the car. To keep the hitch from slipping, I tie it over an 8-inch length of "split" (the fuzzy leather used to cover stainless steel steering wheels) wrapped lengthwise around the loaded sheet. The split is only wide enough to enclose the sheet's circumference. (See rolling hitch photos on page 128.)

Lashed in place by the rolling hitch, the leather prevents the temporary pendant from slipping as I ease the genoa sheet and transfer the load to the pendant. Once the load on the sheet has been lightened, the car can be easily moved. The two-turn portion of the rolling hitch should be closest to the winch, and the line of pull should be as close to parallel to the sheet as possible. I often use a secondary winch on the same pedestal to take up the load. The leather simply helps the rolling hitch gather up a better grip. This load-swapping strategy also works well when you need to relieve a sheet override on a winch.

can take a fid or knife to free it. The answer is to avoid locking hitches on cleats, especially on cleats that are large enough to take a full turn around the base followed by two or more figure-eight passes and a final full loop around the base under both horns. This approach guarantees that the line can be slipped, or released, regardless of how much tension has been put on it.

Surging a Line

Consider the *surging* (easing) of a genoa sheet under load. Because most of the load is absorbed in the friction of multiple turns on a winch drum, you should be able to release the sheet from its cleat or winch self-tailing mechanism without losing control of it. To ease the sheet, you may have to take a turn or two off the winch drum, but do this carefully and deliberately, ready to get that wrap back on if the sheet starts to get away from you. (Some sailors have been taught to press the flat of the hand against the coil of the drum to modulate friction and prevent an override on a winch. In low-load scenarios—light air—the hand-on-the-drum technique works okay, however, aboard big boats, especially when the breeze is up, this practice can turn ugly if an override sneaks into the equation or an inadvertent ease snags a finger.)

If the sheet was cleated with only one or two turns on the winch drum, uncleat it carefully, leaving a turn around the base of the cleat. Ease a little slack into that turn and note how eagerly the load on the other end consumes the slack. If you're satisfied, take the last turn off the cleat, but be ready to throw another turn on the winch drum in a hurry if needed. Such precautions allow for a controlled, gradual ease, a much better outcome than an abrupt, jerking release that pumps the rig and rigging. Just a small amount of renewed pull snubs, or halts, the surging line.

In addition, develop a feel for how fast to pay out a line to prevent its becoming heavily loaded. A hockle snagged in an undersized hawsehole, for example, will complicate the surging of an anchor rode or dock line. I always try to evaluate the required ease rate and the likely behavior of the line fairlead before I take a loaded line from its cleat. Then, if handling becomes difficult, I'm poised to quickly put a turn of line on a nearby winch, samson post, cleat, or windlass capstan. A bow pulpit, furling drum, anchor windlass, or other deck hardware can complicate such line handling, and we can encounter fairlead snafus, especially when a great deal of line needs to be paid out in a hurry. In such situations I prefer to run the line out in large fore and aft loops along the side deck rather than pay it out from a small diameter, hockle-prone coil at the bow.

In general, it's easier to surge a large line load over a short distance than to ease a more moderate load over a longer distance. The chances of an override, kink in the line, or fairlead problem increase the longer the easing process lasts. Regardless of the fall distance and the weight or force involved, however, keep a full turn—or at least a three-quarter turn—on the cleat, and be ready to add a figure eight if the load starts to slip.

Working with Power Winches

Power winches may have the energy of a fit coffee-grinder team on an America's Cup boat, but they lack the load-sensing awareness of a human cranking a handle. The operator must watch what's happening at the loaded end of the sheet, with an occasional glance at the drum. Make sure the entire crew reads the manufacturer's operating instructions for electric cockpit and halyard winches. If the written instructions are long gone, it is your role as skipper to provide adequate safety briefing regarding these winches.

When using an electric winch to hoist a crew-member aloft, don't put the halyard tail in the self-tailer jaws. A recent incident in the Caribbean illustrates why. All was fine aboard an Amel cutter when the cruising couple decided to do some work up the mast. The wife hoisted her husband aloft with the aid of an electric sheet winch, but due to a circuit malfunction the winch kept turning when she released the engage button to stop his ascent. An override of the line then occurred on the winch drum, resulting in a panic situation. While trying to free the line from the drum, she lost fingers from both hands. A crew passing by in a dinghy came to her assistance, and the runaway winch caused this individual to lose fingers as well.

This story warns us to treat power winches like any other heavy equipment. Most manufacturers recommend placing a circuit breaker nearby to cope with a switch or solenoid malfunction. Be sure to review fail-safe measures for all power-assist systems, even if they seem push-button simple.

Rigging a Bridle

A bridle can be used to hoist a dinghy on deck or to spread a towing load between two points. I'm a big believer in the bowline and its two-line cousin, the sheet bend. With these all-star knots (shown later

Power winches, like powered furling sails, do not give the operator load feedback like a manually cranked winch. Pay attention to the sail being hoisted or trimmed to make sure a snag does not occur and cause a load spike and potential damage. With a remote control in hand, a crew can adjust course, trim sails, and get a close look at sail shape in order to optimize performance.

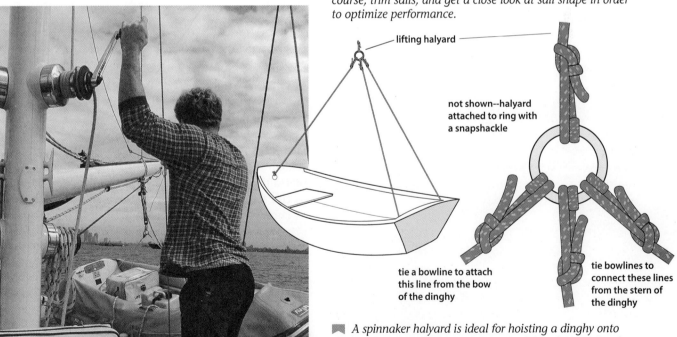

A spinnaker halyard is ideal for hoisting a dinghy onto the foredeck. Fabricating a three-point lifting harness involves attaching a center ring with a line from the stem and two from the stern quarter; onto this ring will be attached the halyard's snapshackle (or a bowline can be tied, as shown here). Tie bowlines to connect the lines to the ring. Adjust the length of the attachment lines to reach a trim parallel to the water. (Joe Comeau)

in the chapter) we can hold a harness hoisting ring in place and make no-slip junctions with or without hardware. A bowline won't slip under a heavy load yet can be untied easily when no longer needed, a part of its value.

As much as the design of the dinghy itself, the sea state and point of sail determine how successfully

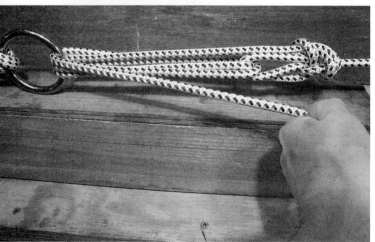

 A trucker's hitch provides a means of securing an object such as an overturned dinghy with a simple knot that can easily be tensioned. 1. Tie a mid-line bowline in the line to be tensioned. 2. Loop the bowline tail 3 times creating a block-and-tackle effect. 3. Tension rope and secure with 2 half hitches above bowline. (See bowline on a bight, bottom page 129.)

a dinghy can be towed. A Y-shaped bridle will often keep the painter following the centerline of the boat. Tie bowlines in the ends of two short pieces of line, with their bitter ends on a stern cleat at each of the boat's quarters; join the two loops together within a third loop of a bowline tied at the end of the dinghy painter. You now have a simple bridle and can adjust the length of either leg from its stern cleat. For an even easier solution, simply tie a line to the dinghy painter 10 feet from its bitter end with a sheet bend (shown later in chapter). Spread the grafted-on line and the end of the painter to opposite stern cleats. In either approach the towed dinghy can be moved to port or starboard simply by adjusting the lines.

We set bridles in two basic configurations, those that immobilize the load line at the center, as described above, or with a different approach that allows the load line to sway to either side. In most cases, we prefer the immobilized option. These fixed Y-shaped applications work well for a bridle for towing a drogue or another boat and for streaming a sea anchor from the bows of a multihull.

The other type of bridle has a midpoint attachment to the load line using a loop made with a bowline or figure-eight knot, or a more complex combination of spliced thimbles, shackles, and a ring. The latter approach provides better load handling and anti-chafe characteristics than a loop in the line. As with all bridle applications, you must prevent chafe by adding sacrificial leather or canvas or other protection.

Lashing: Dinghies and More

Regardless of your knowledge of knots and your dinghy's towing ability, the best place for a dinghy in heavy weather is upside down on the foredeck. Anchor one end of each lashing line with a bowline attached to a pad eye; pass the line over the dinghy and fasten its other end to a pad eye on the opposite side, and then secure it with two or three half hitches. Or take a turn through the pad eye and then double back to the loop of a trucker's hitch in the standing part of the lashing line, cinching through the loop and tying your half hitches there. Make sure you have a leftover rope tail long enough to prevent the knot from working loose. (Chapter 13 discusses life rafts in detail, including locations for stowage.)

Knots and lashing techniques can be critical for jury-rigging a broken boom. Although each situation may be unique, the basic goal is to splint the broken spar so that it can still handle compression and bending loads. Similarly, one may need to do lashings at the upper end of a broken mast that is to become a new masthead. With a block attached to this lashing and a jury-rigged sail, this rig may keep you homeward bound.

Line-Handling Lesson Learned: Leaving a Slip

Recently, I watched a race crew get underway from a slip, reminding me once again that a single variable, such as wind velocity, can greatly influence the outcome. The normally light wind in this yacht basin usually made getting underway a simple matter of slipping lines and backing down. On this day, however, a gusty 25-knot breeze on the beam changed all that, and the race crew soon proved less adept at tending lines in a crowded marina than sail handling around the buoys. Although the skipper understood the challenge, his line handlers appeared less aware of the forces at work.

The first sign of the impending fire drill occurred when the bowman easily removed the leeward line and moved to the windward bow line. Failing to consider the effects of the beam-on wind or the obvious tension in the line, he casually undid the cleat and was nearly sucked under the pulpit rail by the force on the line. Two other crew jumped in to help, but matters grew even more complicated when they realized that the line led under the pulpit rail. To cast it free they had to feed it through the bottom rail. Adding insult to near injury, the bitter end of the coil had yet to be undone. The skipper wanted the vessel to be kept breasted (snubbed) as long as possible to windward, but communication with his line handlers had already gone south.

The crewmembers on the foredeck were forced to release tension from the bow line in order to clear it, and as a result, just when the skipper needed the vessel as far to the windward side of the slip as possible, the bow was nearly touching the leeward pilings. A cascade of problems inevitably followed, and soon the vessel was dragging along the finger pier and leeward pilings as it cleared the slip. Fortunately, the boat's substantial rubstrake rather than its shiny Awlgripped topsides took the brunt of the abuse, and the inboard chainplates kept the standing rigging away from the pilings as the vessel backed out of the slip.

This incident illustrates important lessons. A beam wind or, even worse, a beam current changes how lines must be handled, and the skipper must choose among available options. In this situation, I often recommend using breasting lines doubled back over pilings for easy retrieval; taking the load on these allows the crew to ease the boat's working bow,

This USCG motor lifeboat is docked with double (fore and aft) spring lines and uses antichafe gear on the lines passing through the closed chocks. The combination of double spring lines better immobilizes a docked vessel, especially when fore-and-aft surging is an issue.

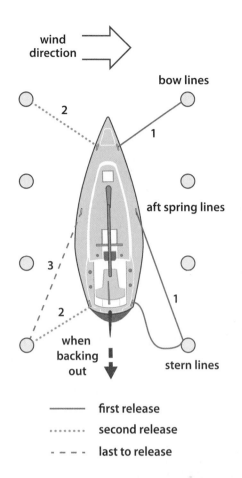

first release (solid line)
second release (dotted line)
last to release (dashed line)

With wind on the beam, a vessel needs to be breasted (pulled) to windward prior to stern-first departure out of a slip. The crew releases or retrieves leeward dock lines first, and then the crew draws the vessel to windward using the bow and stern lines, which may be tossed onto the dock just prior to departure. The windward aft spring line is the final control line (when the boat is backing out of its slip), not to be cast off until the bow clears the outboard windward piling. This last line can be "doubled back" so retrieval is possible. (Joe Comeau)

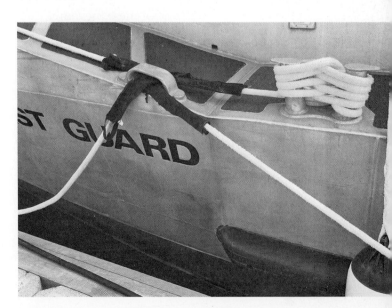

stern, and spring lines and either leave them ashore or bring them on board. Then, while still snugged to the windward pilings, with the prop already turning in reverse and the vessel ready to make sternway, you can slip the breasting lines as the vessel immediately gathers way astern, avoiding contact with the leeward pilings. Often referred to as warping, this use of secondary lines has long been a staple of sound seamanship.

Rigging a Preventer

A preventer is a line or tackle used to prevent the boom from swinging back across the boat's centerline in an unintentional jibe. Some designs are far more effective than others, and in fact one of the most common versions can pose as much of a hazard as the unwanted jibe it's meant to prevent. In its usual configuration, this version of a preventer includes a four-part block-and-tackle arrangement with a built-in cam cleat. Snapshackles at both ends of this handy-billy allow it to be rigged quickly between a mid-boom bale and a fitting on either rail. The simplicity of this arrangement is the upside. However, the downside becomes clear when a knockdown or unintentional jibe occurs and a crewmember must go forward along the upwind side deck of a deeply heeled boat to release the heavily loaded tackle. In addition, the considerable load on the boom and rail attachment points can cause unanticipated damage.

A boom-end preventer eliminates this problem. Two pendants, each half the length of the boom, extend from the outboard end of the boom toward the gooseneck and are stowed at mid-boom with shock cord. When reaching or running, you run preventer lines port and starboard from cockpit winches to turning blocks on the foredeck. To use the preventer, lead the working end of one of these preventer lines outside all rigging and, using a snapshackle, attach it to its mating pendant on the boom. The cockpit winch is used to set the preventer, and if you have to release it under load, you can handle it like any other heavily tensioned sheet. (See Chapter 11, page 327, for an illustration of rigging a preventer.)

This is a safer, more efficient preventer configuration that also avoids a load on the middle of the boom. Such a load can break the boom when the rolling motion of the boat sends it to leeward just as a steep wave face approaches. In this case, when the clew end of the mainsail drags in the water, a mid-boom preventer becomes a fulcrum, bending the boom to its breaking point. In contrast, in the same scenario, a boom-end preventer loads the boom in compression, which the boom's tube-like structure can handle much more effectively.

MODIFYING RUNNING RIGGING: LEADS AND HARDWARE

Thin, high-modulus line, as discussed earlier, can replace heavier, thicker cordage, but this becomes a problem if a small-diameter halyard goes over a sheave that is too large or, even worse, that is grooved for a wire halyard. This not only increases wear on the line but decreases efficiency. Avoid these outcomes with a close look at the masthead, the exit and lead blocks, the line organizers, and the other hardware guiding the lines up and down the mast and around the deck.

Both production and custom boat designers keep the whole in mind when they set the specs for hardware to handle the running rigging of their choice. The builder likely collaborates in those specs, but the hardware choices may change because of a favored vendor, because a specific model becomes obsolete, or for myriad other reasons. Among naval architects, differences between "as designed" and "as built" define this first round of vessel modifications. Such changes to design specs usually intend to make an existing boat even better, but unforeseen secondary consequences can take a toll, so it's necessary to consider all the implications of changes to the running rigging. When modifying the running rigging, follow the physician's oath to "first, do no harm."

A few years ago I looked over a running rigging hardware modification that had led to an unfortunate and unintended consequence. In an effort to make handling the spinnaker pole more efficient, a crew had made a small but significant change in the original hardware layout. The designer of the racer/cruiser had set up the pole downhaul with a two-to-one advantage to lessen the load to a cam cleat that controlled the down guy. However, hauling in the extra line needed for the mechanical advantage slowed the process of handling the pole. The crew's poorly considered solution was to change the arrangement to a simple one-to-one down guy, which doubled the hauling speed but also doubled the load to the cleat. The cam cleats locking the pole hoist control lines were also changed to cam cleats with much larger lead bales, a move meant to expedite pole handling. The original bales ensured that the line was well buried in the cleat jaws, while the new cleats made release much easier but also less effective at gripping the line.

This alteration worked just fine in light air, but one gusty 20-knot afternoon, the down guy came loose, the pole skied, and the flailing chute put such a load on the pole hoist line that it pulled out of the jaws and the pole shot downward. The pole smacked the bowman on the head and knocked him unconscious. Fortunately, he didn't go over the side and didn't sustain an injury with permanent damage. However, this incident underscores the need to fully understand the secondary and tertiary effects of a rigging change before you alter a vessel's initial design.

Checking Lead Angles on Fairleads and Blocks

A client once asked Tom Wohlgemuth, the founder of Chesapeake Rigging and Annapolis Spars, why an upgrade of a race boat's running rigging should include more than a cordage swap. He became animated in describing the common problem of poorly aligned lead blocks and line organizers that result in friction-induced abrasion at exit points. Experience had taught Tom that many of these key hardware components were installed in the right places but at the wrong angles, and it only takes a few degrees of offset to cause a line to rub on the wrong part of a fixed piece of hardware. Even the best roller bearings can't outwit the chafe and decreased efficiency caused by a line passing over the cheeks or cage of a block on its way to or from the sheave.

In many cases, mainsail halyard problems stem from the initial construction of the spar and deck layout. With stainless steel wire halyards, a lead that is not fair may not matter much, but unintended contact between a metal lead block and a high-modulus rope halyard is a different matter. This often results in a tough lesson for a skipper who sees a significant investment wearing out in a single season.

The best remedy begins with looking closely at how the new halyard, sheet, or guy leads from point to point as it makes its bends and turns from the snapshackle or bowline to the winch drum. The situation could require placing a beveled shim under deck-mounted hardware to generate a fair lead or may require a different style of exit block to eliminate chafe problems at the spar.

While eye-level deck hardware is easy to examine for potential causes of chafe, masthead sheaves and even the lower mast exit bocks are hidden from view. Unfortunately, we sometimes see new genoa cars, lead blocks, and snatch blocks gussie up an older race boat while apparently no one considered the well-being of the sheaves and blocks buried in the spar itself. The sea imposes cycle loads and the sail plan creates on/off forces that fatigue the system's metal and plastic hardware. Cordage vectors such forces; the less elastic the cordage, the higher the loads become at key points, especially at abrupt changes in angle.

The masthead, the line's exit at the lower end of the mast, and even the less abrupt bends in the line at deck level see significant amounts of energy transfer. The cyclic nature of these loads, especially when beating to weather in a breeze and seaway, will over time greatly reduce the breaking strength of the sheave or its framework. Fortunately, safety margins of twice the load were standard in older boats, so despite the increased load in less elastic line, we haven't seen a rash of masthead sheave failures. However, if we closely inspect the masthead sheave, we often see wear on the bearing and deterioration of the sheave, enough to have a significant impact on the efficiency of the pulley function. With no load on a halyard, the masthead sheave may roll just fine, but with halyard tension asymmetry in the bearing or sheave causes friction and perhaps even binding.

You can perform a simple test of a halyard block system with the rig up and halyards in place. With a short piece of line, connect the bitter end of the halyard to the halyard shackle in a closed loop. Carefully place a couple of snatch blocks to fairlead the new connection of the halyard ends (see diagram). An engineer can place a strain gauge between the aft snatch block and the halyard winch to deter-

Rigging a halyard fairlead test. The halyard is connected end to end, creating a continuous loop, and tension applied to the loop using a temporary boom outhaul. Rig a snatch block to the outhaul and clip it to the halyard, and incrementally increase the tension. After each increase, push-pull the halyard and note any increase in friction. If the fairlead inside the mast is not aligned or the halyard is tangled, a small amount of tension increases friction and makes the push-pull test difficult. (Joe Comeau)

this line adds tension to test the friction-free (or not) nature of the masthead sheave and exit block; pull on halyard-- downward and upward--to test

snatch block and line to outhaul

mine the amount of tension placed in the line and another to measure how smoothly the halyard can be hand-pulled while under tension. You can perform the same test without a strain gauge by starting with a mild effort on the winch handle followed by a hand-pull check for smoothness. Then, using the winch, add a little more tension to the closed loop and compare the feel of the halyard pull to how it felt with less tension in the system. If things bind up quickly, check all the fairleads associated with the snatch blocks to make sure no bowline or shackle is pressing against a block. Then go through all the contact points along the halyard route from the sheave at the masthead to the block that leads to the winch. Halyards can be twisted inside the spar or running over the wrong side of a spreader support, and you won't notice the resulting friction until a halyard is fully loaded. In the worst-case scenario, a masthead pulley problem requires unstepping the spar to implement a remedy.

Friction, corrosion, and pressure can damage a masthead sheave as well as the bearing surface it spins on. All of these shorten the life of a new halyard.

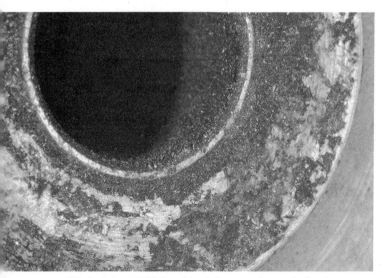

Stainless steel masthead sheave axles and aluminum bushings may not be submerged in seawater, but the ambient moisture and chloride ions from salt spray help cause galvanic corrosion.

Corrosion is an additional threat to blocks and masthead sheaves. Many a sailor has encountered a stainless steel axle and bronze bushing captured in an aluminum masthead weldment. Salty sea spray that makes its way to the masthead results in a constant march of electrons from the least noble metal—aluminum—to the more noble bronze and stainless steel. In the worst-case scenario, the weldment holding the bushing morphs into a white powdery paste (a sign of corrosion) and the bushing starts to turn in the aluminum support as the axle binds on the bushing. A noticeable increase in friction results, and if this goes unnoticed or uncorrected, you're at risk for a major failure. You can prevent this problem by regularly disassembling, cleaning, and lubricating these components; the masthead design determines whether you need to unstep the rig to do the job.

Most modern blocks have high-molecular-weight composite bearings between the sheave and the cage, thus reducing both the friction of rotation and the galvanic corrosion caused when dissimilar metals touch. At the end of the season, a good freshwater wash, air drying, and a spray with a lubricant/protectant such as McLube helps control oxidation.

High-modulus cordage has impressive straight-line strength, but every bend raises stress and drops the breaking strength. The smaller the bend radius,

Be sure line leads are fair before securing pad eyes for blocks attached to the deck. With the ability to model design details on the screen using a CAD program, misplaced lines or hatches, like the one here, should never come as a surprise to a builder.

🚩 *Rope clutches have a locking lever that causes a gripping foot to press the line against a ridged stop plate. This prevents the line from slipping under load yet allows it to be pulled toward the handler. Many clutches can be released under load, but both the line and the clutch (not to mention your fingers) do better when a heavy tension is taken up on the winch before releasing the rope clutch.*

the larger the change in direction, and the less smooth the articulation, the more negative is the impact on breaking strength. A masthead sheave that binds under load has one of the most negative effects on a halyard. The sheave may spin just fine unloaded, but it may be so worn that under load it binds against a masthead box side plate, which then acts as an effective brake. When the rig is down, check the sideways play of the masthead sheaves. This includes inspecting the sheave box sides for signs of abrasion and the bearing and sheave axle for wear.

Harken and other hardware manufacturers offer a wide array of replacement sheaves. Make sure the support for the axle remains true (perpendicular to the box) with the new sheave by checking side clearance with a feeler gauge. Overly worn sheaves and side plates can allow a halyard to jump the sheave and bind in the slot between the sheave and the side plate, creating a go-aloft nightmare, but with regular maintenance and inspections you can prevent such drama.

Deck flex is another serious consideration for how lines are run, especially when halyard leads are moved from the mast to the deck. With lead blocks

on the spar, halyard tension places a compression load on the spar, which absorbs the load effortlessly. When halyard leads are attached to the deck, however, below-deck reinforcement is needed to keep the deck from flexing under the loads. Most often, a tie rod connects the backing plate for deck-mounted lead blocks to the mast step or to a heavily reinforced portion of the hull grid. When moving lead blocks to the deck, remove any deck core material in the area of the fasteners and replace it with high-density epoxy putty, such as West System 105/205 resin with 403 filler. Then redrill the fastener holes and embed each piece of hardware in 3M 101 or a similar sealant. This retrofit prevents softer deck core material from being crushed by the tension loading of relocated halyard lead blocks.

Although it is often difficult to devise a deck layout with all sheave-to-sheave leads fair and friction-free, misalignment problems have a cumulative impact on resistance. Even high-modulus line does not guarantee immunity to abrasion damage caused by long-term, unintended contact with metal surfaces. When choosing cordage for a makeover, don't neglect the blocks and sheaves in the spar; whenever possible, choose large-radius blocks over smaller ones to make the nearly 180-degree bend a little less cramped. With any changes, carefully consider any possible downsides, especially those with safety implications.

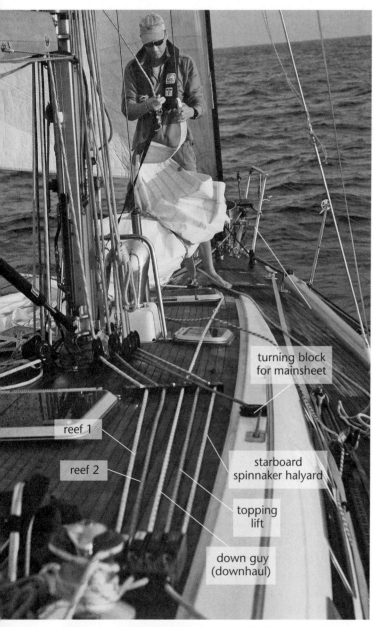

turning block
for mainsheet

reef 1

reef 2

starboard
spinnaker halyard

topping
lift

down guy
(downhaul)

🚩 *Even with the mainsheet run in a deck conduit, five halyards, reefing lines, a down guy (downhaul), and a topping lift can make line geometry a major puzzle—but one that can be solved with effective use of lead blocks and clutches.*

Rope Clutches

Rope clutches have redefined approaches to running rigging on sailboats, with a growing trend toward fewer winches, more side-by-side line leads, and lots of extra rope in the cockpit. This "all roads lead to Rome" approach is characteristic of the layout of lines on many modern sailboats, and a rope clutch helps organize the sheets, guys, halyards, reefing lines, topping lifts, and other lines led to the cockpit.

Just over a decade ago, on many boats the halyards, sheets, and even reefing lines had their own winches. Some lines were handled at the mast, others farther aft. Now one winch serves multiple lines. This multiuse approach allows the sailor to tension a line on the winch and then lock it in place with the throw of a lever. Once latched in the clutch, the line can be removed from the winch and another line wound around the drum for similar treatment. At first glance, this approach seems a win-win situation, but a few remaining questions deserve scrutiny, including the way rope clutches behave underway.

The Loads on a Rope Clutch

A line load is a specific tension measured in pounds or kilograms. The working load on sheets, halyards, runners, lifts, and reefing lines can vary from benign to lethal, as discussed earlier. So when considering a rope clutch, you must understand the load range. Equally significant, assess how quickly and how often the load may be adjusted. The bottom line remains: when handling a line under heavy load, you're always better off with wraps on a winch drum. The deck layout should ensure a user-friendly transition from a locked rope clutch to a loaded winch, along with allowing the operator to be in a good ergonomic position with a view of the sails and the vitally important room needed for easy winch grinding. In addition, the clutch must be able to hold a load without creep.

Even the best rope clutches can become hard to operate when too many lines lead to a space that is hard to work in. Juggling lines from the clutch to the winch can cause complications, and a half dozen lines piled on either side of the companionway under the dodger can block one's view of the sails. I recently sailed on a vessel where the skipper had also mounted a chartplotter perfectly positioned to be lassoed by any of six line tails.

On many multihulls, a single undersized winch is used to control both a jibsheet and a mainsheet, forcing crew to lock one or the other in the jaws of a clutch. This complicates things when the sheet load is tripled with the first puff of an approaching squall and easing the sheets becomes essential.

Early rope clutches required lines to be tensioned

on a winch when the clutch was released. Newer clutches can be released under load—a feature offering significant advantages. For example, you can handle two or three reefing lines in a slab reefing system with rope clutches and one winch. The same configuration can handle halyards set and left in place for long periods of time. But releasing a line loaded with 1,000 pounds or more of tension without first transferring the load to a winch drum is a lot like grabbing a tiger by the tail.

When releasing a tensioned line in a rope clutch, the best approach is to take a few turns on a winch to offset the tension and hold the load, and then open the clutch lever. This process does take a little time, so when you must act fast the emergency-release capability of a full-load clutch is useful. Before opening the release, be sure the line is free to run and no fingers are in the way.

Rope Clutch Considerations for Refits

After sailing aboard a wide range of new boats with rope clutches, I agree the rope clutch is a worthy innovation. However, rope clutches are like trumpets in an orchestra: a bold and powerful presence but easily overdone. Before doing a makeover using clutches, consider what you'll gain and what you'll give up. A conventional cleat is almost maintenance free, and having a sheet wrapped around a dedicated winch of ample size offers line-handling safety and simplicity.

As with other system designs, don't lose sight of the "0300 rule": the worst incidents on offshore races or cruises regularly occur in the middle of the night, when line handling is done more by feel than by sight. When these emergencies occur, you want to avoid having to fiddle with fussy lines in cute pouches while juggling six or seven lines that lead to a single winch.

In an emergency, experienced sailors would much rather have a line wrapped on a winch drum than locked in a clutch. Sailors on "over-clutched" sailboats need the dexterity of a Las Vegas card dealer to cope with the demands of switching lines on a winch, tensioning, flipping levers, and coping with extra line strewn about the cockpit. In daylight with only a moderate breeze, six or more side-by-side mounted clutches are much more user-friendly. Add some heel and raise the tension in the running rigging, however, and a winch deficit quickly causes issues.

Consider also what loads might be put on the lines that lead to a single winch. For example, you can manually manage the load on a halyard, running backstay tail, preventer, jibsheet, or afterguy much of the time and in easy conditions, but add some breeze or an unanticipated jibe or broach and all bets are off. You can release a line from a modern rope clutch with

When lines are clamped down and neatly stuffed into a nearby bin, everything looks organized, but when quick action is needed and lots of clutches lead to a single winch, you'll feel like a soldier with a single-shot rifle facing a machine gun nest. It may be better not to lead all the lines aft—some sailors keep halyards at the mast; this results in fewer lines snarling the cockpit, but crew must go forward to reef, set, and douse sails.

1,000 pounds or more of load without first tensioning it on a winch, but this situation can be scary. For example, picture a person holding a preventer line in one hand and releasing the clutch with the other to allow a backwinded mainsail to flop over and let

THE PROS AND CONS OF A ROPE CLUTCH

Pros
- Costs less than a winch
- Weighs less than a winch
- Uses less space than a winch
- Improves reefing efficiency
- Enables multiple lines to lead to the cockpit with good organization and fair leads
- Provides convenient handling for lines that are seldom used or infrequently adjusted (roller-furling headsail halyard, main halyard, reefing lines, and so forth)

Cons
- Creates congestion at one winch
- Creates a snarl of intermingled tails
- Loaded clutches can be hard to handle and potentially dangerous
- Line handling is slower than with a dedicated winch
- A multihull's genoa and mainsheets sharing a winch is a potential hazard in a strong breeze
- A clutched preventer or runner is a hazard in a jibe
- Breakdowns, the need for removal for repair (in some boats this hardware was installed before the headliner was permanently affixed, so replacing the hardware requires cutting into the headliner to access the fasteners)
- Confusing and potentially dangerous in a squall on a black night
- Causes line chafe
- Focuses loads

the boat recover from a broach. The load on the preventer line is equal to what the mainsheet was holding just a few moments before with block and tackle.

A cabintop winch intended for a main halyard load is commonly mounted with six bolts in a circular pattern, but a rope clutch dedicated to the main halyard likely has only two in-line bolts to handle the same load. This is usually sufficient for the safe working load of the clutch, but if the clutch is mounted on a cored coachroof with relatively thin FRP skins, the installation may be insufficient to handle all loads. Boat designers engineer solid FRP rather than cored skins in such highly stressed areas, and boatowners planning to retrofit an older boat with rope clutches must think in similar terms. FRP top and bottom plates should be bonded to the area to spread the load, and the core in the area must be sealed to prevent water intrusion.

Rope clutches for halyards and reefing lines certainly make a great deal of sense. Topping lifts and down guys, asymmetric spinnaker tacks, and a host of other line controls also benefit from clutches. However, using a clutch for a mainsheet or genoa sheet amounts to short-sighted thrift. Lines that are under significant load or often trimmed deserve dedicated winches for efficiency as well as safety.

OTHER RIGGING HARDWARE

Snapshackles and snatch blocks are found on most sailboats, and there's good reason to have them for quick fixes when needed, such as when the unexpected pops up and a new angle of pull or an assist with a lift is needed in a hurry. Take, for example, a rolly anchorage in which the swell and the wind direction are 40 to 50 degrees apart. A simple side load on the anchor rode can move the bow into the swell rather than the wind to reduce rolling. All it requires is a snatch block fastened to the anchor rode or anchor snubber line if chain is being used. A bowline on the end of a length of sheet-sized nylon line is locked in the snatch block's snapshackle. Using a sheet lead and a cockpit winch, the snatch block line can be used to "barber haul" the anchor rode to change its lead.

Snatch Blocks and Snapshackles

With an ordinary block, the line is roved through it end-first. However, snatch blocks are designed to pop open with a twist or button push to accept the standing part of a working line. This is convenient, and racers and cruisers alike have long loved snatch blocks. Most sailors use this hardware to lead spinnaker sheets and guys, to act as a temporary turning block for a preventer, or to provide a better angle for an outboard genoa sheet lead. Many cruisers also discover the value of a snatch block as a friction-free fairlead when kedging off a sandbar on which the boat has gone aground. A welcome addition to any gear locker, this is a versatile piece of hardware.

Tests in which I participated showed that observed signs of physical deterioration in older snatch blocks (rust stains and crevice corrosion) were correlated directly with a greater likelihood of failing at a small percentage of the block's original safe working load. Magnetic permeability, seen in some lower grades of stainless steel that can be attracted by a magnet, was directly correlated with greater susceptibility to chemical corrosion, justifying the assumption that less magnetic stainless steel (most notably Type 316 alloy) is a better choice in a marine environment.

Snapshackles are often made from 17-4 PH, 15-5 PH, or a similar precipitation-hardened martensitic stainless steel, which is magnetic, rather than the weaker but less corrosion-prone type 316. All high-strength alloys have the anticorrosion quality of type 304 stainless steel, while the 316 alloy contains a chromium-nickel ratio that all but eliminates magnetic properties and is less susceptible to galvanic corrosion. Not surprisingly, testing showed considerable corrosion and cracking around the snapshackle bodies and pivot pins of older snatch blocks, but less around their 316 stainless steel cheek plates and other parts. In an annealed (heated) state, even low-grade stainless steel (304) is nonmagnetic, but cold working and polishing can induce some magnetism in lower grades of stainless steel. Therefore, when a lower-quality metal is pressed into a complex shape and highly polished to create an initially shiny, corrosion-resistant surface, it becomes more rather than less prone to failure.

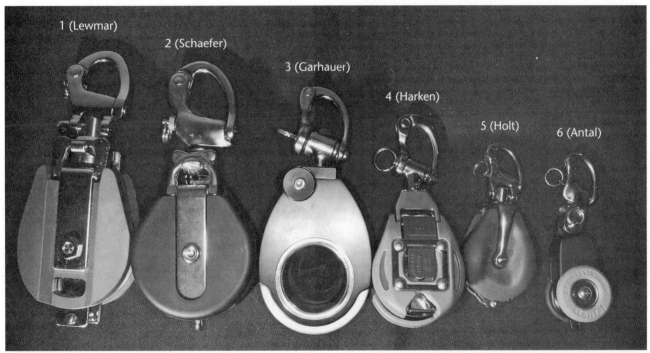

▰ *Snatch blocks are versatile pieces of hardware serving many running rigging uses. Some snatch blocks open at the top, others at the bottom. A few rotate to open for line loading. Types that open and lock with one hand can be a big plus when needed in a hurry. Left to right, 1 and 2 open via bottom hinging; 5 is side-plate rotation; 3 and 6 are top-hinging; and 4 is a bottom-opening snatch block.*

▰ *Magnetic alloys of stainless steel may be initially stronger, but they tend to corrode and are more prone to failure than type 316. (Left) Crevice corrosion caused this snatch block sheave axle to fail just beneath its bolt head as it was being unscrewed for service. (Right) The magnet test indicates that the alloy was not 316, which has a high nickel content and is not magnetic.*

Closed chocks ensure that a line will not jump free or lift out as the tide drops. They need to be large enough to accept a spliced mooring painter eye, antichafe gear, and the doubled-up lines used during stormy weather. They also ensure that no line may be mid-length inserted into the chock—not always an advantage.

Bitts and hawseholes were nearly universal on sloops and schooners designed prior to World War II.

This innovative design keeps a foredeck or amidships cleat from snagging sheets or other running rigging when a vessel is under sail. The cleat collapses and is flush with the deck.

Cleats and Chocks

On average, a sailboat used 60 times a year spends only about 6% of its annual sailing season underway. The other 94% of the time the boat is tied up, moored, anchored, or hauled out for maintenance. When the worst squalls and cold fronts batter the fleet, cleats rather than a person at the helm likely control the boat's destiny. A cleat is a most essential piece of hardware.

For centuries, timber-built craft relied upon a single post or two parallel vertical posts, called bitts, that passed through the deck from fastenings to the keelson, floor frames, and deck beams. Mariners secured lines to these samson posts, a nickname alluding to the pillars that only Samson could tear down. These bitts attached to major structural components of the vessel for the huge loads on dock lines, tow warps, and anchor rodes. Bitts and the historic craft that sported them have all but disappeared from our waterfronts, but the need for secure attachment of the cleats that replaced line-handling bitts remains as critical as ever.

In this era of stiff, lightweight, foam-cored FRP decks it is critical how energy dissipates around cleat attachment points. In areas where bolts secure a cleat to a cored deck, a higher-density material is needed between the fiberglass skins. Some builders avoid this issue by placing cleats near the toe rail mounted in solid FRP laminate rather than cored deck. If the laminate is thick enough or backed with a reinforcing, load-spreading plate or extra units of FRP, and the builder uses shoulder washers, then this approach appears adequate.

Other design problems include mounting cleats too close to the toe rail, making line handling difficult and a fair lead all but impossible to attain. Anchor lockers often lack reinforcement under the deck where the cleats are attached. A few builders have provided reinforcement of the wrong kind, burying aluminum plates in the laminate without regard for potential poultice corrosion; when aluminum oxidizes in a moist environment, a white powdery substance forms that becomes acidic and gooey, the consistency of toothpaste.

We recommend locating cleats based on safety and efficiency, along with providing fair line leads. It's easy to lose sight of how much energy a cleat must handle at times. In addition to steady-state line loads (normally in shear), a cleat must absorb the variety of angle and load oscillations associated with surging lines. Fluctuations in load intensity arise from tidal rise and fall, wind gusts, boat wakes, and even seiching, a low-frequency sloshing of the water through a basin like what happens in a bowl of soup held in unsteady hands. In many West Coast harbors, for example, submarine canyons enhance this large-scale undulation, and seiching can greatly increase the wear and tear on lines and cleats.

When conditions deteriorate, your cleats become the lynchpin of your strategy to keep the vessel where it belongs. View your cleats as unsung hardware heroes and note their location, fastening, and ability to handle the job at hand.

A variety of cleat patterns exist, including the innovative design of flip-up horn cleats. Some compromises may not pay off in the long run, however, such as recessed, hide-away cleats that must cope with water drainage and may have support structures that are less than robust. Even worse, some designers and builders apparently consider cleats passé, substituting hardware such as rings and eyes for line attachments. A few builders place cleats wherever they find room, even in some cases on the transom rather than the deck itself. This results in a new set of point loads on the hull skin and an awkward perch for line handlers. I call this an afterthought approach to placing cleats. In race boats there is a trend toward eliminating cleat clutter altogether, which occasionally results in tying dock lines to pulpit stanchions or chainplates—even stays and shrouds!

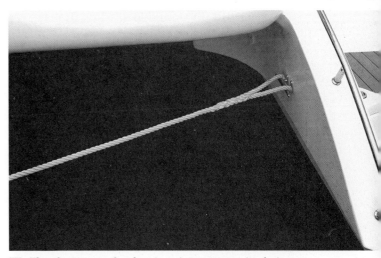

The placement of a cleat is as important as its design and construction. Forcing a crew to lean overboard to handle a line, or placing cleat loads in tension rather than shear, makes little sense—nor does simply looping a line over a cleat.

It's understandable that a foredeck crew in the midst of a spinnaker peel doesn't want obstructions in their way, especially ones with lethal horns eager to snag a lazy guy or sheet—or a boat shoe. Although a crew adjusting dock lines in a gale-swept harbor needs easy access to securely mounted hardware, it is just as important to work with a fully loaded deck cleat without sacrificing one's fingers. Cleats in the cockpit belay sheets with loads dampened by turns around a winch drum, but deck cleats must handle loads directly. The energy contained in a stretching bow or spring line goes directly to a cleat. When crewmembers have a line in hand, good cleat placement allows them to take a quick wrap around the cleat base without risk of injury. Low-profile chocks and cleats may handle braided dock lines efficiently but do not provide room for a bulky spliced mooring pendant. When a storm is forecast, you need room for antichafe gear and for doubling up the lines.

Many boats tied up in marinas display misled lines, foul leads, and incomprehensible cleat hitches—a sad lapse of seamanship.

Modern metal casting yields smooth, symmetrical hardware that needs less polishing than hardware of the past. Zinc, aluminum, bronze, and stainless steel can all be cast, but zinc, though often used with chrome plating on low-end powerboats, is too weak for sailboat cleats. Aluminum alloys are light and relatively strong as long as the casting process kept voids (air bubbles) to the barest minimum. Galvanic interaction with the stainless steel bolts securing them to the deck is one of the biggest challenges with aluminum alloy cleats. In contrast, the heavy but strong bronze and 316 stainless steel castings are less prone to corrosion.

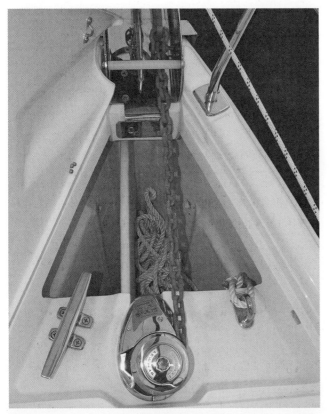

Some yacht designers and builders hide essential working gear in a well. They even place the primary cleat that's meant to hold a vessel in storm-force conditions on a flimsy FRP tray.

The cleat pattern should lock a line in place yet still allow crew to ease or snub the line. Cleats with abnormally long horns and two pedestals (rather than a single base) allow more turns of line, but these "long-horn" cleats also put more leverage on the attachment points and more vulnerable horn ends. Four-bolt open pattern Herreshoff-style cleats provide greater support, and their shorter horns are less vulnerable. Some cleats have an in-line three-bolt pattern that offers significant strength in one direction but very little strength perpendicular to the bolt alignment.

If you're retrofitting or upgrading your boat's deck cleats, pay close attention to topping and backing plates. Either plate can be made from a carefully cut and painted piece of G10 (a woven-glass/epoxy composite) or a homemade FRP layup comprised of three to five units of woven roving and mat laid up on a smooth waxed surface. This solid glass laminate is about ¼ inch thick and has enough surface area to well exceed the cleat's bolt-pattern footprint.

The exact shape of topping and backing plates depends on the available space and deck shape, but follow the principle of providing a load-spreading capacity both above and below the deck. The plates are best bonded in place with gap-filling epoxy putty before attaching the cleat. When the putty has cured,

COILING LINES

The seemingly simple art of coiling a line has an amazing array of variations. Most sailors start with a circular coil but end with something far less standardized. Many sailors simply conclude their coils with three or four turns and a single hitch to lock the corralled loops. Others use a tuck and loop over the top as shown here.

These coiled sheets (left) show one of the most common approaches to finishing a coil. A retired naval officer I sailed with made a logical pitch for a simpler, one-turn locking hitch that would let a line be returned to use a bit faster and with less chance of hockles. To tie the simpler alternative (at right), begin by grasping the line 4 to 5 feet from the cleat and coil the tail evenly. Once the bitter end has been reached, use the slack closest to the cleat to lock the coil. This involves placing a locking turn around the coil and a loop over the top to cinch the coil tight.

the cleat can be fitted, holes drilled, and a sealant used on the fasteners during the installation. If raw balsa or low-density foam core is exposed in the drilled holes, spend the time to ream out the core from a half-inch perimeter around each hole and fill that void with epoxy putty. Seal the bottom of each fastener hole before filling it with epoxy putty to prevent epoxy leaking down below. Once it cures, redrill the holes and install the cleat. Tape off areas adjacent to the holes and carefully clean up excess epoxy or sealant so that you'll have less to remove once it cures.

KNOTS TO KNOW

The following is a gallery of knots useful on sailboats. You can easily find detailed instructions for tying them in other books and online. I've intentionally not included a host of more esoteric, complex, seldom-used knots, bends, and rope-strung puzzles. I believe in knowing how to tie a few useful knots under any conditions—in the dark, on a pitching foredeck, in a howling gale, and with either your left or right hand taking the lead. If you know these knots, you won't need any others.

Remember that a knot reduces a line's strength by up to 30%. Splices preserve more of a line's strength than knots because their even taper and the elongation of the tucked tail spreads the load, creating less of a stress riser than in a knot. Often, however, the breaking load of a line is so high that the choice of a knot or a splice is not critical.

FIGURE-EIGHT KNOT. Some knots are used all over the vessel, but the figure-eight is almost solely used for sheet and halyard ends. It creates a stopper knot at the end of a sheet or halyard end that is too bulky to escape from a block, car, or fairlead. It is not used with spinnaker sheets and halyards, however, because in a really bad knockdown or emergency dousing, these lines must be free to run.

BOWLINE. This is the knot of choice for sheet-to-sail connections and many other uses where a nonslip solution is needed. The bowline is a secure knot that can be untied even after considerable tension has been put on it. The bowline tops the list of a sailor's must-know knots.

SQUARE KNOT. This knot shows up in shoe laces and reef ties and looks like two loops tucked into each other. One of its advantages is that a sailor can pull down and put tension into the knot while it is being tied, but it is not a secure knot and should be used sparingly. A sheet bend is better for joining two lines.

■ *SHEET BEND. Similar in geometry to a bowline, this knot is best used to connect one line to another. (See slip knot sequence opposite.)*

■ *CLOVE HITCH. Scouts love this knot and sailors find it handy, but it can slip under a heavy load and should not be used near the end of a line with a heavy load. If used near the end of the line add one or two half hitches to the standing part of the line to make the clove hitch more secure.*

■ *ROLLING HITCH. This is an extra-turn rendition of the clove hitch and a more aggressive grabber. Note that the placement of the double turn is toward the direction of the load.*

■ *When a line (often a jibsheet) fouls around a winch, as shown with the override here, tie a rolling hitch with a new line around the fouled winch line to release the strain; with tension off the fouled line, you can straighten out the tangle on the winch. Tying the hitch over a piece of "split" leather lessens the slip of the temporary pendant. (See the sidebar Relieving a Loaded Genoa Car on page 112.)*

SLIP KNOT. (Left) This is barely a knot, but it has certain uses on board, not only in its singular form but as a modification in hitches and reef knots. It can also be used in the process of tying of other knots such as the transformation from slip knot to sheet bend shown at left.

Form a slip knot in one line (1), pass a second line through the eye (2), pull on each end of the slip knot (3), thus transforming it into a sheet bend.

COW HITCH. Pass a bight of the line around a ring or other fixed object, then reeve both ends through the bight. (If it's imperative to maintain more strength, use a well-tapered splice for a much better option.)

BOWLINE ON A BIGHT. This bowline permutation delivers two loops that will not slip and can be used as part of a makeshift lifting harness or to help lash down a complex load. (Note that a trucker's hitch is a bowline on a bite that allows loop tensioning and ends with two half hitches.)

◣ *FISHERMAN'S BEND. Start with a couple of turns around an anchor ring or other solid object, then tuck the line under those loops before they are pulled tight and add a final half hitch to lock the knot.*

◣ *TIMBER HITCH. Some sailors use this to secure reefing lines to the boom. This keeps the loop of the line close to the boom and allows the clew to be hauled in tight.*

◣ *BUNTLINE HITCH. This hitch can be pushed close to the object it encircles. More prone to slippage than a bowline, its tail should be longer.*

1

2

◣ *TWO LINES JOINED BY OVERHAND KNOTS (1). Pull two knots together (2). A sheet bend is the preferred alternative if considerable load is to be placed on the line and untying is to follow.*

Studding Sail Bend

Camel Hitch

◣ *Extra turns and tucks are the sailor's solution to lessening the chance of slip. Specialized knots and lashings can be helpful, but proficiency with the basic knots shown here answers most of the challenges facing boaters.*

6

ANCHORS AND ANCHORING

Anchoring— the art of staying put—is much more than just securing your boat in a tranquil cove. When practiced well, your anchoring skills provide safety and comfort in anchorages anywhere in the world. Without question, a cruiser's toolbox of seamanship skills must include the ability to handle ground tackle and related secondary hardware. Anchoring skills are also a strategy of last resort when all else fails and a lee shore threatens.

Effective anchoring starts with heavy-duty ground tackle and equally rugged secondary gear. These tools of the trade come in a mind-boggling array of shapes and styles, and each manufacturer claims the best solution for keeping your boat where it belongs. This chapter examines these confusing, often bewildering claims and analyzes test data, as well as sharing the experience of other sailors, so that you can develop an approach that's right for you.

The physics of anchoring suggest that holding power is a fairly simple proposition involving two key variables: the anchor's ability to hook the bottom, and its resistance to dragging, which involves the anchor's surface area, configuration, and weight, as well as contributions made by the rode.

A change in wind direction or speed can quickly turn a good anchorage bad, so veteran cruisers monitor weather forecasts even when safely anchored. If they know when conditions likely will change, they can take preemptive action and move to a more protected bay or cove before the original anchorage turns uncomfortable. Picking a safe anchorage is as important as deploying a sound anchor and ground tackle (see page 155 for more on choosing an anchorage).

Practice may not make us perfect, but it makes us much better than we were when we started. This is especially true of anchoring. Repetition is part of becoming proficient in any skill. Cruisers become more capable by discovering ways to cope with a variety of holding grounds, weather conditions, and levels of protection. We all learn two key lessons: no one anchor is ideal in all conditions, and in extreme weather, a bigger anchor is always better.

Long-term, long-distance cruisers usually use an all-chain anchor rode and a primary working anchor that is one size larger than what is recommended in the sales brochures. As one sage voyager put it, "No boat ever dragged ashore because its anchor was too large." A second anchor, usually of a different design, is often carried at the stem of many cruising boats for a Bahamian moor or a dual anchor technique in heavy weather. On the cutter shown here, if the wind and swell were more of an issue, the crew would likely also use a snubber line to prevent chain grating noise and add shock absorption to the all-chain rode.

The longer you cruise, the bigger your inventory of challenging and unusual anchoring circumstances. My own anchoring memories include hiding from tempests in hurricane holes around the world. One of the closest to home arrived with the sights and sounds of Hurricane Irene (see sidebar, page 134).

GROUND TACKLE SIZING

Your ground tackle includes the anchor itself and the rope, chain, and attached hardware. A thimble and shackle joining rope and chain rode can be part of the ground tackle, but for our purposes we'll desig-

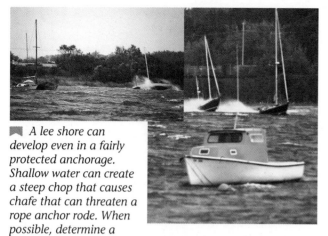

A lee shore can develop even in a fairly protected anchorage. Shallow water can create a steep chop that causes chafe that can threaten a rope anchor rode. When possible, determine a storm's likely wind direction from the forecast, and pick an anchorage with minimal fetch.

average boats in average conditions. However, these data fail to account for atypical conditions or for variations in windage and displacement among boats of similar length but dissimilar design. In contrast, the accompanying table considers other factors such as the higher payload and windage of cruising boats. Still, the necessary caveat remains: when it comes to sizing anchors and ground tackle, a little more is much better than a little less.

ANCHOR TYPES

Historically, stone weights served as the earliest anchors, which later evolved into iron hook contrivances made to engage the bottom. Nearly four millennia ago the Chinese led the development of iron anchors. They forged an iron shank and cross arm and eventually added a stock perpendicular to the flukes that positioned the anchor fluke-down. When Mediterranean influences moved the stock to the opposite end of the shaft, the modern kedge-type anchor was born.

Over time, anchors morphed into different shapes for the needs of specific vessels and anchoring conditions. In recent years, recreational sailors' desire for a light anchor with high holding power has led to several breakthrough designs. The anchor's primary attribute remains its holding power in various bottom conditions and when conditions really deteriorate.

nate a cleat, bow roller, and anchor windlass as the ground-tackle handling gear Think of your ground tackle and handling gear as components of a system ideally formulated to work in harmony. For example, first-rate BBB chain and a superior windlass can prove all but useless if the chain size and the chain gypsy casting are mismatched. Individual components are only as good as the system they're a part of—a basic tenant in the art of staying put.

Although informative, tables of data can also be misleading. For example, many anchor manufacturers provide spreadsheet data about anchor size for

GROUND-TACKLE ALTERNATIVES

Danforth H series anchors are made from high-tensile steel and resist fluke bending more than a standard Danforth of the same size—a crucial factor in a primary anchor and worth the extra expense. See text for more on anchor and chain types.

Boat	Primary Anchor	Bow Roller	Chain	Rode	Windlass	Secondary Anchor	Storm Anchor
SAIL							
30' weekend cruiser	20 lb. Danforth H-series	chock	6' (5/16")	200' nylon (1/2")	none	10 lb. Fortress FX 16	
35' summer cruiser	35 lb. CQR	single roller	50' (3/8")	200' nylon (5/8")	vertical capstan	20 lb. Danforth H-series	
45' ocean voyager	55 lb. Rocna or 60 lb. Manson Supreme	heavy-duty roller stem fitting	all chain (3/8" HT)		horizontal capstan	35 lb. Danforth H-series	75 lb. three-piece Luke
POWER							
28' express	25 lb. Manson Supreme	built-in bow roller	20' chain (5/16")	200' nylon (1/2")	vertical capstan	25 lb. Danforth S-series	
37' trawler	45 lb. CQR	single roller	all chain (3/8" BBB)		horizontal capstan	35 lb. Danforth S-series	
46' long-range cruiser	70 lb. Rocna	heavy-duty roller stem fitting	all chain (3/8" HT)		horizontal capstan	66 lb. Spade S140	47 lb. Fortress FX 85

Note: HT = high tensile

Early examples of single-fluke plow anchors on display in European ports. Crews must have done some interesting maneuvers or line handling to make sure the preferred side faced downward. These anchor configurations did prevent a vessel from swinging with the current and snagging its chain on an upward pointing fluke.

The Kedge

Known also as a fisherman or yachtsman anchor, the kedge remains symbolic of tall ships and the era of sail. These anchors evolved from crude castings with wooden stocks into much stronger, drop-hammer-forged steel designs, later coated with molten zinc to lessen corrosion. In the days of lengthy bowsprits, these anchors could be easily handled and secured to hefty timbers called catheads.

When the kedge is deployed, only one fluke engages the bottom; the other points upward, contributing weight but nothing else to the holding power of the anchor while increasing the potential for the anchor rode to foul the anchor. Professional mariners in the last days of sail nicknamed the kedge anchor the "pick" for its ability to penetrate hardscrabble bottoms, and it still leads the list of anchors capable of grabbing a hard or rocky bottom. However, its heavy weight relative to its fluke area has lessened its popularity.

Fluke shape and size are a big issue for kedge anchors, not only because softer bottoms require more surface area for the anchor to hold but also because the anchor rode can foul the unengaged fluke as the vessel swings with the current or wind. Large flukes squared off at their inboard ends tend to trap anchor rodes more frequently than flukes that are tapered at their inboard ends. (continued page 136)

The Paul Luke three-piece kedge is a modified fisherman anchor that can be disassembled for bilge storage and made ready when bad weather is forecast. I prefer to assemble and deploy the anchor ahead of time, as wrestling with it in the midst of a gale at 0300 would be daunting.

HURRICANE STRATEGIES: NOT-SO-SERENE IRENE

Each gust shook the rig, heeled the boat, and made the anchor rodes groan. The wind bore down in 60-knot crescendos, which was only half of what Hurricane Irene had doled out to those hunkered down in the Bahamas only a few days earlier in October 1999 and a lot less than had been forecast for the Chesapeake Bay. Still, I had my hands full with the conditions unfolding in this normally quiet estuary just off the bay.

In response to the forecast, I moved *Wind Shadow* from her regular space at the dock and anchored in this well-protected, dead-end arm of Whitehall Creek. I settled on a ride-it-out strategy, which I'd first used in 1976 when cyclones Kim and Laurie pinned us down in Bora Bora, French Polynesia. My favored tactic since then has been to identify the best all-around protection in local waters and settle in a day before the big event, using an overkill of ground tackle. I base my plan on the simple principle that big waves cannot build over a nearly nonexistent fetch and without waves to contend with, staying put becomes a lot easier.

Just as every storm is different, each anchorage presents its own set of challenges. In particular, when a storm is forecast, the best storm anchorages in the area become popular, so overcrowding can be a concern. Think of neighboring boats as extra shrapnel in a hand grenade. An upwind vessel dragging anchor can easily become ensnared in your ground tackle; even if your anchors hold, you'll never welcome an unexpected raft-up in a storm. Lucky is the mariner whose port in a storm is not only well protected but also thinly populated. Fortunately, in my refuge from Irene, mine was the only anchored vessel, so I had one less thing to worry about.

Setting anchors in anticipation of a tropical storm or hurricane is like making the first move in a chess match, in that seemingly minor commitments can either set the stage for success or lead to big trouble. On this occasion, I had to set up for a backing wind that would fill in from the east but eventually become just as punishing from the west during the storm's last act. On the other hand, the storm was forecast to pass to the east of us, putting *Wind Shadow* in what is euphemistically called the *navigable quadrant* of the storm. In hurricanes in the northern hemisphere, the worst wind and seas are in the right-hand quadrant forward of the hurricane, the so-called *dangerous quadrant*. This is where the storm's forward progress along its track boosts the velocity of its rotational winds. If the wind is circulating around the eye of a Category 1 hurricane at 75 knots and the eye itself is advancing at 15 knots, the wind experienced in the navigable quadrant is 60 knots; however, it's 90 knots in the dangerous quadrant—a huge difference.

Ideally, I would have set up with enough swinging room to endure the wind shift, but this creek was too tight for this ideal setup. I had to dismiss any thought of bow and stern anchoring (a tactic that's usually a mistake) because when the wind was on the beam, the windage would easily tear anchors free. Instead, I secured the two anchor rodes and line from the shore to cleats at the bow. This allowed the boat to "weathervane" (quickly change heading) with each gust.

A 41-foot sloop, *Wind Shadow* weighs 10 tons in full trim. The ground tackle I used for the sand/mud bottom included the working anchor (a 45-pound CQR plow deployed with 150 feet of 10 mm BBB chain in 12 feet of water) and a 60-pound H-series Danforth on a ¾-inch braided nylon rode. I deployed one of the anchors toward the head of the anchorage and one toward its mouth (the narrow creek trends east to west). My third line was a floating ¾-inch Poly-Dac line (polypropylene core with Dacron cover), which I secured to a stout bulkhead ashore, using the dinghy. I decided not to use the 75-pound three-piece Luke storm anchor tucked away in the bilge but held it in reserve in case I needed it. I didn't anticipate the ferocity of the williwaw-like gusts spawned in this high-banked little creek. These gusts proved the value of an all-chain rode, which helped dampen the slingshot effect that occurred between scouring gusts.

You might ask why I chose to leave the dock in the first place. For one thing, I believed I could better cope with the storm surge and rising tide in an anchorage rather than secured with lines at a dock. Some years earlier, Hurricane Isabel had created a surge and tidal rise that submerged even the tops of the pilings. Irene's arrival would coincide with a new moon spring tide, and the weather gurus had warned of a massive tidal rise. As it happened, upper-level steering currents kept the eye of the weakening storm to the east of the Chesapeake Bay, and the southerly wind that would have built a surge remained well out to sea. Fortunately, Irene entered the books as just a nasty tropical storm, not the destructive force that occurred with Hurricanes Andrew, Katrina, and Hugo and the Great New England Hurricane of 1938.

In every storm I've ridden out aboard *Wind Shadow*, I've had with me a rigid dinghy with 7-foot spruce oars. In a pinch I can row the boat into 40-knot gusts and get an anchor to windward or a line ashore (as I did this time, securing the third line). But tropical weather comes with torrential rain, which makes bailing the dinghy another part of the storm ritual. A handy 2½-gallon bucket is my tool of choice, but this time the bucket that still looked as good as new had suffered the ravages of UV degradation and its bottom let go as soon as I started bailing. Fortunately, I had a collection of gallon plastic containers trimmed for use as scoop bailers. While not as good as a 2½-gallon bucket, they beat trying to fling water with a bottomless bucket. (When tethering a dinghy in extreme weather the oars, oarlocks, and any other loose items are kept secure aboard the mothership.)

Another surprise occurred at about 0300—an hour when most snafus seem to arise on sailboats. The unrelenting northeast wind finally backed to the northwest and slackened. This allowed *Wind Shadow* to execute a nifty pirouette around the three lines and the chain snubber deployed from the bow but in the process fouled the rodes. Having learned the value of three cleats on the foredeck, I first shed the chain snubber and then one by one pulled the bitter ends of the two rope rodes around the chain and led each fairly to a cleat. On this occasion, like many others before, the ability to free each line by turn to lead it to a dedicated cleat proved valuable. Using the vessel's yawing tendency, I was able to uncleat and move each line when its load was minimal.

Anchored in a Storm:
Stay on Board or Go Ashore?

When storms approach, many sailors double up on dock lines, double-check their insurance policies, and double-time it home to stand watch with the Weather Channel. Of course, there is an ongoing debate over how actively to be involved with bad weather. Experts in mitigating risk tell us to get off our boats in bad weather and in some circumstances mandate leaving our homes too and heading for higher ground. Legislating safety through mandatory evacuation may work well in many circumstances but doesn't help cruisers or liveaboard sailors who use their boats for more than recreation.

In extreme cases, you must ask yourself if you can improve your vessel's survival odds by staying on board without excessive risk for you. In my own circumstances, there were homes nestled beneath large oaks and other hardwoods surrounding the creek where I rode out Isabel and Irene. Storms had been known to uproot trees and send them crashing on these homes, inflicting great damage, while a boat bobbed frantically but safely in the creek.

Everyone develops seamanship skills incrementally. If you have much practice with anchoring strategies, you might gain the valuable experience of riding out a gale or tropical storm in a protected anchorage using superior ground tackle. On the other hand, if you have less interest in developing this level of seamanship, you should avoid this kind of challenge and follow local advisories.

Don't get me wrong: I'm not implying that riding out a storm of this magnitude is a bucking-bronco test for thrill seekers. What I'm talking about is a hands-on, active strategy to keep you and your vessel safe in heavy weather. When riding out a storm in a fully protected anchorage, you have a chance to ease lines, replace antichafe gear, and even avoid another drag-

A delicate balance between swinging room and excess exposure must be sought when picking a good hurricane hole. At such times the versatility and abundance of good ground tackle really pays off. Deployed here are a 45-pound CQR, a 60-pound high-tensile Danforth, and a line ashore; there's a 75-pound Luke in reserve aboard.

ging vessel. You'll learn to use the lulls between gusts to haul in rode; you may even leverage a big yaw to power off to drop an anchor that was held in reserve. In short, I've found that an active response plan can be more effective for surviving a storm than simply leaving a boat to fend for itself.

With or without anyone on board, the more exposed the mooring field or anchorage, the more dangerous is the situation. In these situations it makes most sense to double up on everything before the storm threatens both you and your boat, and then head for higher ground. (See later section on doubling up anchors; for riding out a storm at sea, see Chapter 11, Handling Heavy Weather.)

Modern sailboats lack bowsprits and long over-hangs that allow a kedge to be more easily deployed and retrieved. A century ago, Nathanael Herreshoff designed the yachtsman anchor, a variation of the kedge. It featured much larger but tapered flukes and met the needs of the sloops, ketches, and schooners of that day. Larger crews and foredecks equipped with anchor davits combined to make deploying and re-trieving a yachtsman anchor a straightforward en-deavor.

Today, however, the kedge is an endangered species, rarely used as a primary anchor and sold in fewer chandleries. The innovative Paul Luke three-piece kedge is one of the last holdouts. The Luke fea-tures easy disassembly for stowage, rugged construc-tion, and Herreshoff-type flukes for holding power. A proven storm anchor, it is still favored by those voyaging far afield and facing the possibility of rely-ing on their own ground tackle to ride out a serious storm.

Navy Anchor

In the early 1800s, the U.S. Navy developed a stock-less anchor that could grip the seabed with both flukes simultaneously. Easily stowed when its shank is hauled into a hawsepipe built into a vessel's hull, this anchor eliminated the awkward and occasionally hazardous cathead-securing procedures used aboard early sailing ships. There has been a renaissance of this anchor design within the megayacht industry, and now custom stainless steel behemoths can be seen tucked into the hawsepipes of sail and motor-yachts over 100 feet long.

The early Navy anchor had to be a hefty chunk of iron because weight more than fluke area kept a warship where it belonged. The Navy anchor became the pattern of choice for both commercial vessels and Navy ships after hydraulic drives were added to an-chor windlasses. This addition enhanced crews' abil-ity to handle heavy, stud link chain rodes and heavy anchors. However, because of the weight of the de-sign, this anchor pattern holds little appeal for recre-ational sailors.

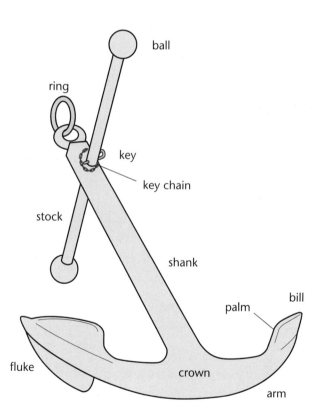

🚩 *The kedge anchor design (also known as fisherman) survived for centuries as the pattern of choice. Its main strength was its ability to take hold in a wide range of difficult seabeds, including grass, rock, and other bottom conditions that are hard to penetrate. Its two big downsides are the ability of the up-pointing fluke to snag the rode and the difficulty of handling the anchor on boats without a bowsprit. Unless a kedge anchor is "catted" to a traditional bowsprit, it is awkward to store, deploy, and retrieve. (Joe Comeau)*

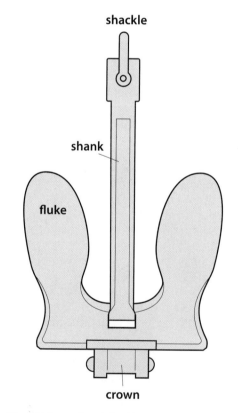

🚩 *The Navy style anchor (also known as a stockless anchor) relies more on its weight than the bottom-grabbing ability of its flukes. Designed to self-stow in a stem recess, these behemoths require a powerful hydraulic windlass and stud link chain. The combination of heavy anchor and heavy chain makes this alternative less than ideal for the fine-shaped end of a sailboat. (Joe Comeau)*

Light Anchors

What sounds at first like an anchoring heresy is actually a good example of effective engineering, proof that like better mousetraps, anchor design could still be improved. A light anchor derives its holding power from fluke area rather than weight, and the anchor must be designed so that its fluke or flukes bury in and engage with the seabed in response to a strain on the ground tackle.

The weight per cubic foot of a material is equal to its specific gravity times the weight of a cubic foot of pure water, which is 62.4 pounds. Thus, a cubic foot of granite, which has a specific gravity (SG) of 2.69, weighs 168 pounds; a cubic foot of iron, SG 7.21, weighs 450 pounds; and a cubic foot of lead, SG 11.35, weighs 708 pounds. The lower the specific gravity of a material, the greater the weight reduction it experiences when submerged in water. This means that anchors relying more on friction with the bottom than on hooking the bottom need to be made of a high-density material. Anchors made from alloys of aluminum (SG 2.64) and magnesium (SG 1.75) rely to an unusual degree on hydrodynamic function and boat pull to dig into and engage with the bottom. When a light anchor fails to set properly, its holding power based on weight alone is ineffective.

Danforth Anchor

The prototypical light anchor is R.S. Danforth's lightweight pattern, which gave the landing barges of WWII a better chance of getting off the beach after deploying troops. His landmark reimagining of anchor design used the Navy anchor concept of engaging both flukes simultaneously. He went further, however, by attaching deeply penetrating flukes to an arm mounted at the crown rather than at the head of the anchor.

Comparing a traditional kedge to a Danforth is like comparing a pickup truck to a motorcycle: both can cruise at 60 mph on the highway, but the motorcycle does it with a lot less steel.

second anchor rode

A Danforth anchor on a nylon rode in a huge scope has come to the aid of many boats caught in difficult anchoring conditions. Note the second anchor deployed from the bow in a wide, V-shaped configuration. Many vessels tend to "sail" at anchor, tacking each time the anchor rode is stretched to its limit. This dynamic yawing often puts a boat beam-to during a severe gust and can result in tearing an anchor free. A steadying sail hanked to the backstay, or in this case, an intentionally left up Bimini helps keep the bow into the wind by adding windage aft. Naturally there's a point where the wind velocity will shred a steadying sail or a Bimini into tatters. I prefer an all-chain rode and using a kellet or sentinel to mitigate yaw. A more sheltered anchorage might also be placed high on the agenda.

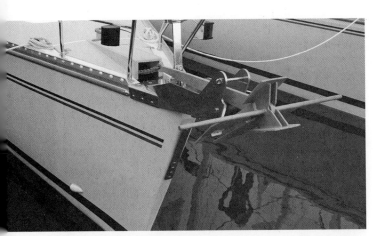

Not the most unobtrusive anchor in a bow roller, the Danforth offers excellent holding power in sandy and muddy bottoms. Its large fluke area provides a lot of contact with the seabed. Rocks and coral can foul or even damage the flukes, so the anchor is less commonly used in those bottom conditions. Note the large scoop-like opening to this anchor well, a convenience for coastal cruisers that can invite dangerous downflooding of the anchor well at sea.

The high-aspect-ratio triangular flukes of the Danforth help it dig into sandy and mud bottoms, often completely burying itself in the process. The combination of shank length and carefully controlled blade-to-shank angle causes the anchor to set efficiently while remaining easy to retrieve. However, the Danforth doesn't perform well in rocky, rubble-strewn bottoms and can be rendered all but useless if a small rock or piece of coral wedges between the flukes. The Danforth's impressively low ratio of weight to holding power was designed based on tests in sand or mud bottoms, where its large, flat flukes fully penetrate the bottom, and its holding power, especially with extra scope—a 10:1 ratio of rode length to depth—is hard to match.

The geometry of the Danforth is its main advantage as well as its Achilles' heel. Trapping the tip of one of the long, thin, flat flukes in a fissure in rocks or coral can bend or tear off the fluke, rendering the anchor useless. A Danforth well set in sand or mud easily handles the huge strain on ground tackle generated by even a small swell. However, in the same conditions, a Danforth holding only by its fluke tips stands a real chance of being damaged. For this reason, before anchoring, check the seabed type on a large-scale chart. If you're cruising in tropical waters, a swim with a dive mask answers any lingering questions. It's also a good way to confirm that the anchor(s) is well set.

Over the years, Danforth anchors have been marketed as a standard S-series anchor and an H-series anchor with higher tensile strength and a deep-set pattern. Ruggedly built with stronger steel, the H-series anchor can endure higher loads, and the greater expense of drop-forged steel pays off in the long run. You'll see Danforth copies throughout the world in every marine marketplace. The inexpensive models tend to be less well constructed; their slight design modifications, meant to improve the pattern, manufacturing costs, or both, often turn out steps backward rather than ahead.

Fortress and Guardian Anchors

The Fortress anchor is the latest version of the flat-fluke pattern. Fabricated from an aluminum-magnesium alloy with no welded seams, the Fortress has great holding power in sandy bottoms. Its large ratio of fluke area to weight makes it a good choice for mariners who stow their anchor in an anchor well or stern lazarette rather than on a bow roller. A less expensive model, the Guardian, is built from the same alloy but in a lighter extrusion and isn't anodized. It lacks all the options we find in the Fortress.

Some see the ability to disassemble the Fortress prior to stowage as an advantage, but others view it as the equivalent of a fire extinguisher that requires assembly before use. Needless to say, if the Fortress is your only anchor on board, never stow it in pieces.

The concept of a light anchor may seem counterintuitive at first, but with a fluke shape and angle that encourages setting, some sailors argue there is less need for weight. The Fortress is an adequate primary anchor for a weight-sensitive multihull or ultralight monohull, and it's useful on any boat for kedging off a sandbar or as a second anchor. Like the Danforth, it's best used for soft bottoms since rocky ledges or cobble beaches can foul, bend, or break the flukes.

The Danforth pattern anchor is a poor candidate for bow roller storage—the stock is always ready to snag a sheet or connect with a piling.

Immediate access to your ground tackle can spell the difference between running aground at 0300 on a surf-swept coastline or returning safely to port. Look at it this way: the U.S. Coast Guard considers an *uninflated* PFD not a PFD at all. Consider an unassembled anchor using that standard. On the other hand, if you've designated the Fortress as a secondary anchor or emergency kedge, you can justify disassembling it. As a primary anchor, however, it must be ready to deploy.

An aluminum alloy anchor might be pound-for-pound stronger than steel, but don't allow this fact to mislead you. By definition, steel is a more ductile, high-yield material, yield being the measure of a material's ability to cope with loads high enough to permanently deform it. The higher a material's yield, the more distortion it can endure prior to ultimate failure, meaning the range of loads that will bend it, but not break it. Steel has a much higher yield than aluminum, one reason for the ongoing popularity of steel. Many boatowners reason that a bent shank is better than a broken one. Steel has a lower strength-to-weight ratio than aluminum, not necessarily a bad thing, since much can be said for increased weight in an anchor.

Plow or CQR Anchors

The plow anchor caught on in Great Britain just after WWII. At the same time the Danforth grabbed market share in the United States, the Brits preferred more heavy-duty ground tackle. Their preference for all-chain rode and a heavier anchor that can be stowed in a bow roller reflects the wider diversity of bottom conditions and the more volatile weather patterns that characterize the British Isles.

The drop-forged steel shank of a CQR ("secure") anchor resists bending no matter what the tide or wind shift does to the angle of pull. The anchor sits securely in sand, mud, gravel, rock, or coral bottoms, and it partners well with an all-chain rode. These rugged anchors rely upon a combination of weight, fluke shape, and size for their holding ability. Though their holding power falls in the middle of the pack when tested in ideal conditions, they perform well in a variety of challenging conditions. Many CQR advocates have moved allegiance to Rocna and Manson anchors because of their higher fluke and weight ratios.

By design, a farmer's plow penetrates the earth and presents a certain amount of resistance, but not too much. It was designed to till the soil, not anchor the tractor. Despite its plowshare shape, the CQR's steep angle of attack compels it to dig in rather than drag along the bottom.

Note how the Manson Supreme fits the shape of the stem and nestles tightly into the rugged roller. There are no horns or a stock to snag spinnaker sheets or guys and the anchor can handle wave impacts without damaging the stem or breaking free from the roller. There's still room to deploy a retractable sprit for an asymmetrical spinnaker or drifter/reacher.

In ideal sandy bottom conditions, a good Danforth has more holding power per pound than a CQR plow, but the plow may perform better in less than ideal holding conditions. Consequently, the owner of one 32-footer may opt for a 20-pound H-series Danforth as a working anchor, while the owner of a sister ship may prefer a 35-pound CQR. The Danforth is light and small enough to carry forward from the cockpit, while the CQR is best deployed from a bow roller, its permanent home.

The Delta and Other Plow Anchors

Like all good inventions, the CQR plow has been imitated by other marine manufacturers. Woolsey, one of the first CQR competitors, produces the Plowright anchor, a slight variation of the original plow. In the Woolsey and other plow copies there are subtle changes, some aimed at improving holding power and others aimed at making the anchor cheaper to build. For example, the shank of the Woolsey version of the plow is made from mild-steel flat stock with welded ears or tabs to allow the flukes to pivot. The flat shank makes the anchor more susceptible to bending with heavy side loads.

The Delta plow anchor is made of cut-out metal welded into a plow-shaped anchor with good holding power. However, if you jam a CQR and a Delta side by side in a rocky fissure and put equal side loads on each shank, the drop-forged CQR would stand a better chance of retaining a straight stock.

The Delta anchor has been engineered for efficient, cost-effective construction. Flat-stock components are welded, thereby avoiding costly drop-forging.

The Delta plow has a reputation for good holding power. Its welded shank is not made of drop forged steel but seems to hold up quite well. The bend in the tie rod joining the flukes of the anchor shown here may be the result of a docking miscalculation rather than a sign of anchor inferiority.

Northill Anchor

This evolution from the kedge puts the stock at the crown and allows hauling up the anchor into a roller fitting on the stem of the boat. When stowed on a bow roller, however, the four sizable protrusions from the shank readily grab headsails, sheets, guys, and spinnakers. The Northill offers good holding power and can cope with a variety of bottom conditions, but sailors also find it unwieldy, and that limits its appeal. Some commercial fishermen and those running day tourist boats in coastal waters find it useful. There are a few backyard-welded steel renditions of this anchor, but the quality varies.

Claw, Scoop, and Spoon Anchors

Bruce Anchor

The Bruce anchor arrived on the waterfront in the mid-1970s and earned quick acceptance for three good reasons. The first involves its ability to dig in and provide respectable holding power in a variety of bottom terrains. The second is its rugged, no-weld, expertly cast construction, which in its original iteration has stood the test of time. And third, like a plow anchor, the Bruce happily nests in a bow roller, making it easy to deploy and recover. True, the two extra outboard fluke tips love to grab spinnaker sheets and guys, but nonracers and power cruisers find little to complain about.

Today, there are copies of the original Bruce anchor all over the world, but most are less expensive facsimiles that do not perform as well. The design has been fine-tuned, with glitches and flaws corrected over time, offering good reasons for choosing a proven anchor from a reputable manufacturer. Conversely, it is a gamble to join the first wave of a new design or a new builder's effort, because when it comes to anchoring, we don't consider unknown odds a positive attribute.

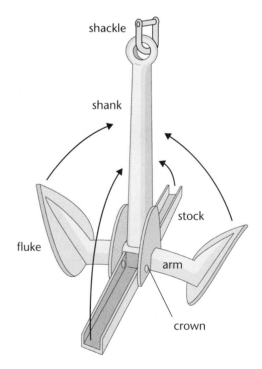

Although no longer made, treasured stainless steel folding anchors are bartered, traded, and show up at nautical swap meets. They were made by Northill, Inc., in California, designed and built to anchor PBY flying boats. (PBY flying boats are amphibious craft extensively used during WWII.) The anchor makes an ideal dinghy kedge and packs excellent holding power. They have an easy-to-fold feature which helps with stowage. (Joe Comeau)

■ *Side by side, a Bruce (port) and a CQR (starboard) sit in carefully crafted bow rollers just forward of a hydraulic anchor windlass—all indications of a serious cruising commitment.*

For example, shiny stainless steel Bruce facsimiles can be seen gleaming in bow rollers in marinas and boat shows around the world. These anchors stand out more as art installations than purposeful tools, at their best when unused and displayed at the stem like a prized piece of sculpture. While stainless steel is a great metal for certain hardware needs, anchors don't have a place on that list. For cosmetic reasons, producers usually grind unsightly welds smooth and highly polish the metal, but aside from appearance, this has no advantage for anchoring. In fact, the welds, usually done in key high-load junctions, are almost never X-rayed to check the quality of the weld. These welded stainless steel anchors work-harden over time, making them increasingly susceptible to crevice corrosion; many lack the durability of the original one-piece, carefully cast galvanized steel Bruce anchor or the even the more ruggedly built drop-forged steel CQR.

The Manson Ray anchor is a significant engineering improvement over the Bruce. In the Manson Ray the Bruce's less-than-ideal cast shank has been replaced with a much stronger forged steel shank, resulting in exemplary welded shank-to-fluke interface with superior hot dip galvanizing.

Other Single-Fluke Anchors

In recent years a new generation of single-fluke anchors have been produced, each promising to be better than its competitor. Many have an addition

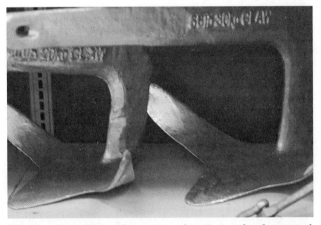

■ *The original Bruce has spawned copies made of cast steel, many of which are crudely shaped replicas. Inferior castings can create an anchor with much less strength than the more tightly controlled original castings. The relatively thin lateral appendages that form the flukes of the Bruce-pattern copy shown here are more easily damaged.*

like a roll bar meant to function like a stock, encouraging the anchor to jab the pointed end of its fluke into the bottom. Because of their sizable spoon- or shovel-shaped flukes with chisel-like points for bottom penetration, most provide stellar performance in mud and sand bottoms. Following are examples of single-fluke anchors:

- ◆ Spade: this French product, available in galvanized steel, aluminum, or stainless steel, can be disassembled.

◆ Rocna: a well-crafted anchor with a roll bar made in New Zealand, it has a single large fluke with a sharp, bottom-piercing tip.

◆ Manson Supreme: also made in New Zealand, this roll-bar anchor with carefully executed welds offers good sandy-bottom holding power. (Just before this book went to press, I switched to a 45-pound Manson Supreme for *Wind Shadow*'s primary anchor, and my initial experience with the large fluke anchor has been very positive.)

◆ Bugel: this is one of the earliest single-fluke designs with a roll bar and pointed tip.

◆ SARCA: touted as optimal for sand and rock, this Australian rendition of the roll-bar single-fluke anchor incorporates numerous slots intended to allow the anchor to break free during retrieval.

◆ Bulwagga: this triple-fluked, equilaterally shaped anchor can be set well regardless of its orientation when landing on the bottom, but its flukes are vulnerable and the anchor can be trapped in rocks.

ANCHOR PERFORMANCE IN TESTS VERSUS THE REAL WORLD

Most anchor tests are conducted on sand or thick mud bottoms—the best-case scenario. The deep fluke penetration in such tests provides higher holding power measurements, and the steady, in-line, tugboat-like pull applied to the anchor rode in such tests bears little resemblance to what really goes on in gale- or storm-force conditions. In extreme weather, especially in tropical storm conditions, wind gusts can cause a vessel to pitch and yaw at anchor, creating varied load intensities and directions of pull on the ground tackle.

Many advocates of heavy-duty ground tackle have had previous experience with lightweight flat anchors connected to little or no chain and lots of nylon rode. When such an anchor breaks free and flies across the bottom, what happens doesn't match the advertising. Lightweight anchors and rodes cre-

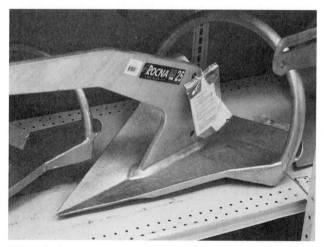

Both the Rocna (shown here) and the Manson Supreme are claw-type anchors with a roll bar, large fluke areas, and carefully executed welds.

Dave Martin rides out Hurricane Gloria aboard his rebuilt Cal 25, the vessel he and his soon-to-be wife Jaja would sail around the world, adding two new members to the family and the crew en route and a third upon completion of the voyage. Here Dave opted for his boat's ground tackle and a line to a mooring with a 500-pound mushroom anchor. Soon he would test his own ground tackle, sans mooring, in equally challenging situations.

ate little friction as they skim across the bottom, and their all-or-nothing holding power gives a crew little time to respond when the boat starts dragging. Not only does such a combination allow a boat to move quickly toward a lee shore, but the nylon rode may wrap itself in the prop just as the crew attempts to motor out of harm's way.

When things go wrong, a heavy, well-proven anchor on an all-chain rode tends to be forgiving. Its pound-for-pound holding power in a sand bottom may not be as great as a flat-pattern anchor with large fluke area, but when the chips are down its extra weight and ability to reset really pay off. Consider the wind-induced yawing that causes an anchor only partially buried in a rubble-strewn bottom to pivot and pull in a new direction. A twin-fluke flat-pattern anchor can wedge a rock or debris between its flukes in such a circumstance and may end up useless. In contrast, with a heavy plow anchor and all-chain rode, even if dragging starts, you have the extra weight to hold the vessel's bow more or less into the wind. This increases the odds that the anchor will reset, and it also makes it easier to recover the anchor and subsequently reset it.

We know of one anchor test that's never done, even though this situation is encountered in the real world. It's the pull-to-destruction test, an evaluation that begins with the pointy end of an anchor caught on an immovable object, such as a granite outcropping, a coral ledge, or the steel hulk of a sunken vessel. The next step is to incrementally add tension until something snaps, breaks, or bends. Because of their geometry, flat-pattern anchors would not score well in destructive testing, nor would anchors with a great deal of thin flat plate steel welded into complex shapes.

In many anchors the fluke is welded to the shank in a nearly 90-degree joint. Needless to say, the best weld possible is needed here. Other builders slot the shank into the fluke and pin it in place, creating a significant stress riser that could lead to potential failure. A drop-forged structure avoids these inherent weak points, but anchor manufacturers these days lean toward less expensive welded and cast alternatives. The CQR features rugged, drop-forged steel construction and an effective load-bearing shape.

The anchor and rode ideally line up with the vessel's centerline, but in a surprising number of cases an anchor gets lodged in a rocky outcropping, coral ledge, or sunken debris and then fails to pivot as a backing or veering breeze realigns the vessel. The side load on a misaligned shank separates well-fabricated anchors from those not so well made. Always look for overkill in how the shank attaches to the rest of the anchor. (Joe Comeau)

In really bad weather, company in an anchorage is the last thing you want. In congested harbors, one vessel starts to drag and takes others with it. These sailboats were driven ashore in Dering Harbor, Long Island, New York, during hurricane Robert.

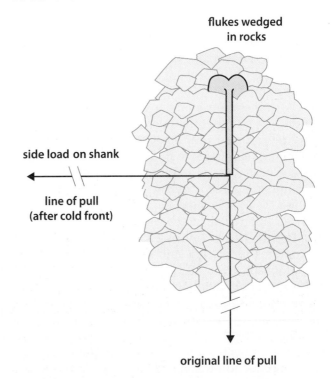

flukes wedged in rocks

side load on shank

line of pull (after cold front)

original line of pull

A close up of fluke-to-shank weld in a plow-type anchor—the inadequate hot-dip galvanizing has worn away.

Cyclical loading can cause metal fatigue, which could eventually lead to shank bending and deformation or even breakage. However, only long-term, long-distance cruisers tend to subject their ground tackle to the degree of day-in, day-out loading that causes these problems. Still, the effects of cyclical loading are cumulative, which could result in failure over time, perhaps abetted by corrosion and microcracks in welds.

An anchor's shank steers the flukes into alignment with the pull of the rode. The length of the shank and the holding power of the flukes affect how much energy is required to turn the anchor. Although less likely to bend when the anchor becomes wedged in a rocky or coral bottom, a short shank also is less likely to steer the flukes into a new alignment with a wind shift when a cold front passes. The force the rode exerts on a misaligned anchor can yank the anchor out of the seabed, completely upsetting the anchor's hold.

With these considerations in mind, I rank rugged construction higher than per-pound holding power. Yes, you can gain additional holding power with an anchor one size larger than the manufacturer's tables say you need, but the issue of weak construction is independent of anchor weight. A critical failure of the anchor itself can be more hazardous than a slow drag, which can often be halted with additional scope.

Finally, when choosing an anchor, you need to decode the marketing spin that clouds the picture. By all means, learn all you can about a new anchor pattern before buying it, but be wary of new manufacturers marketing products based only on tried and proven patterns because the design doesn't guarantee quality production. For example, the reputation of one well-respected anchor has been questioned because production was moved to China and the new

builder no longer uses the high-tensile steel that contributed to the anchor's stellar reputation but has substituted less costly mild steel. In time, we'll know how many shanks end up bending at just the wrong moment. If you already have a venerable Bruce or CQR, for example, that fits the one-size-over rule, you could do a lot worse than having it hot dip regalvanized and forget about buying the latest miracle anchor pattern.

ANCHOR RODES AND CONNECTING HARDWARE

In discussions of ground tackle, the anchor usually takes center stage, but the rode and other connecting hardware form an equally important supporting cast. From an engineering perspective, the rode acts as an energy dissipater, sharing the stress and strain between vessel and anchor. Line may seem the most convenient and cost-effective alternative, but among serious cruisers, chain continues to have strong appeal. Generations of recreational boaters have relied on a combination of chain and line. As with most compromises, there are a few trade-offs worth noting—in this section we will cover the various component parts of an anchoring system.

Anchor Well

The upside of the modern bow anchor well that houses the line and chain, and perhaps a Danforth-style anchor, is clear. For one thing, it's close to where the gear is used and keeps it out of sight when

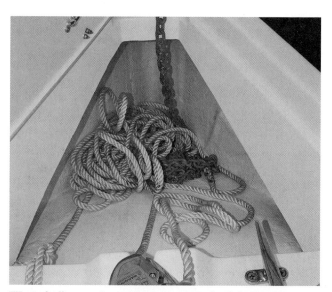

A shallow anchor well, a short length of chain, and a (no-thimble) rope-to-chain splice make a compact and convenient anchoring setup that is best for light-duty usage.

not in use. Racers and weekend cruisers appreciate a clear, unencumbered foredeck. The downside, however, involves the minimal nature of ground tackle that's both small enough to fit in a modestly sized anchor well and light enough to be lifted out and deployed by hand. When the anchor and its rode must quite literally be wrestled overboard, a lengthy chain is unwelcome.

Lightweight aluminum anchors and an all- or nearly all-line rode work well with anchor well storage and manual deployment. This is an acceptable setup for those who spend most nights on moorings or in a marina. Serious cruisers need more.

Anchor Line

The debate continues about the best rope to use for an all- or mostly all-line anchor rode. Without question, nylon's high breaking strength and elasticity are a huge improvement over the weaker, rot-prone natural-fiber ropes used for centuries. As discussed in Chapter 5, however, the elasticity of springy three-strand nylon line has both pros and cons. On the upside, the line can dissipate a positive shock load, but on the downside, this recoil effect can propel a sailboat like a yo-yo from one lateral extent of the scope to the other. The unnerving tendency to "sail at anchor" is usually more pronounced in light, agile fin-keel sailboats but might be scarcely noticed in heavy-displacement cruisers. If a gust of wind on its beam catches a boat sailing at anchor, that motion combined with the large topside surface area affected by the wind can cause the anchor to drag or break free entirely. When the anchor drags, the bow falls off and speed increases—making it less and less likely that a light anchor will reset.

For decades, conventional wisdom held that boaters should use a relatively small-diameter nylon line for an anchor rode in order to ensure maximum spring with minimum shock loading to cleats and the anchor itself. This approach still makes sense for a boat that can sit out a blow with its bow pointing constantly and sedately to windward. On the other hand, sailboats that behave like unbroken stallions when riding at anchor in a blow often do better with a one-size-larger nylon rode that both is stronger and stretches less under a given load. Taming a boat's tendency to yaw at anchor is one of the least considered and most important factors in safe anchoring. Later in this chapter, I'll discuss the yaw-dampening attributes of an all-chain rode and the use of a sentinel, or kellet.

In recent years, plaited and braided nylon ropes have increased popularity for anchor rodes. These offer the advantage of being easy to coil, handle, and

Nylon rope is a good choice for an anchor rode despite its few drawbacks. Select a bigger rode than its breaking strength alone would dictate, since chafe can reduce that strength and an undersized rode will stretch too much. If, as shown here, filaments and yarns are snagged and pulled from the bundle, don't cut or burn them off—instead carefully tuck them back into the strand.

stow. They handle as easily as a sheet and, unlike three-strand nylon, plaited or braided nylon isn't prone to hockle or to twist and kink. On bottoms clear of rocks and abrasive protrusions, three-strand nylon rodes offer a functional anchoring option. Braided rodes can also be cleaned more easily, and where muddy bottoms are the rule, their increased cost may be justified. The cover of a braided rode is highly susceptible to chafe, however, and must be protected with antichafe material wherever it passes through or over chocks and rails.

As nylon line stretches, the filaments flex, causing rubbing and friction between the fibers, leading to heat. The initial breaking strength of nylon is indeed impressive, but after a line has been rapidly cycled for hours and its filaments have heated up from rubbing against each other and a chock, the breaking strength may be reduced by 50% or more. PVC hose used as antichafe gear can have the perverse effect of thermally insulating the line and hindering dissipation of the heat, exacerbating the fibers' tendency to melt. Leather antichafe gear, laced with small stuff through punched holes around the rode, becomes wet in rain and helps to dissipate heat, thus lessening the chances of fiber failure. (See Chapter 5 for more on the aging of nylon line and the use of leather antichafe gear.)

Commercial mariners have long favored a synthetic blend of Dacron and polypropylene line called Poly-Dac (polypropylene core with braided Dacron cover), increasingly used for docklines, towing warps, and anchor lines. Not quite as strong as nylon and with a significantly lower stretch coefficient, we have

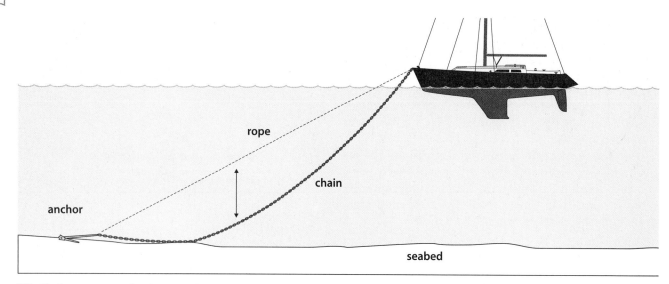

rope

chain

anchor

seabed

■ *Chain catenary—the downward curve resulting from the weight of the chain—acts like a shock absorber diminishing the spiking loads imposed by a sailboat's antics at anchor. Gusts, wave-induced pitching, and the effects of yawing at anchor are diminished by the rode's catenary. In essence, before the anchor gets a tug, the weight of the chain must be lifted. The deeper the water, the greater the catenary's effect, assuming the same scope. (Joe Comeau)*

found that when used as an anchor rode, Poly-Dac reduces a boat's tendency to behave like a paddle ball on a rubber tether. Less elasticity means not only less yawing at anchor but also less interfilament friction and less heat buildup in the line passing through a chock or over a bow roller. This decreases overall wear and tear.

The All-Chain Rode

The first advantage of an all-chain anchor rode is its catenary action. Briefly, a catenary is a curve that a hanging cable or chain forms under its weight when only the ends of the line are supported. A catenary results from the effect of gravity on the mass of chain strung from anchor to bow roller. If you're anchored in calm water without a current, much of the chain will lie on the bottom, but as wind or current increases and the vessel puts more and more strain on its ground tackle, the chain forms a sagging, inverted arc between the anchor and the bow. The energy required to pull this drooping chain straight depends on the size and weight of the chain as well as its length, which is a function of scope (discussed later in this chapter). The downward pull of this curve of the chain acts as a shock absorber and dampens a boat's tendency to sail, or yaw, during the lulls between gusts at anchor. In turn, this acts to prevent the boat from being caught beam-on to the next gust. This catenary action also makes it possible to anchor with less scope with an all-chain rode, an advantage when swinging room is limited.

The resistance to abrasion is another key attribute of an all-chain rode. A nylon rode can be cut by a sharp-edged submerged object while the crew unknowingly sleeps through a bumpy night at anchor, not anticipating what may come. An all-chain rode, on the other hand, remains impervious to granite ledges, coral rubble, or the rusted hulk that doesn't show on the chart.

Another advantage is the hands-free handling or retrieval of an all-chain rode with a well-installed bow roller and windlass chain gypsy. In heavy weather, wind gusts and waves can cause more than 1,000 pounds of tension in a rope or chain rode, so it makes sense to keep one's hands away from such loads.

Chain Quality and Weight Considerations

For centuries, metallurgists and engineers have worked to perfect the art of bending metal and welding chain-link joints. Modern robotic precision ensures uniformity without any weak links. Quality varies, however, and despite the rhetoric about a thriving global market, it's hard to beat the U.S.–made ACCO, Campbell, and Chicago brands of BBB and G4 high-tensile (HT) chain.

A short-link, low-carbon steel chain, BBB has good properties to prevent link collapse as well as a shape and size that match most windlass gypsies. BBB chain also is heavier than longer-link proof-coil chain. High-tensile G4 chain is made from higher-carbon steel (grade 40 or higher) that's stronger than its low-carbon cousin but also more prone to oxidation.

Both chain patterns rely on a hot dip galvanized coating to control corrosion. When that coating starts to wear away, it pays to promptly have the chain regalvanized. The heat of galvanization lowers

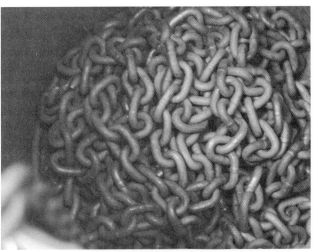

U.S.–manufactured chain is tightly controlled and uniform. Hot dip galvanized BBB or HT chain is the best choice for anchor rodes. European ISO standards also tightly control chain manufacturing and result in a product equivalent in quality to U.S. specifications. Note that European chain is metric sized, however, and the link length does not match U.S. chain gypsies. For example, 10-mm chain is a little larger in diameter than ⅜" and would likely require a new chain gypsy. New Zealand and Australia also have high-quality domestic products, but lower-quality Asian chain is increasingly seen within these markets.

Chain gypsies must be sized appropriately for the chain diameter and pattern or otherwise will jam during operation, as this unit is about to do. Many European boats come equipped with chain gypsies cast for metric-sized chains. A good windlass can be rendered inoperable by the choice of ⅜-inch rather than 10-mm chain.

the strength of some high-tensile chains but does not negatively affect BBB chain.

The weight and catenary of BBB chain are generally appropriate for a typical cruising boat. In addition to being stronger, high-tensile chain is a bit lighter than BBB of the same diameter. An all-chain rode of high-tensile chain that has a link diameter one size smaller than BBB chain will be significantly lighter. For example, BBB chain of ⅜-inch diameter weighs 1.64 pounds per foot and has a recommended working load of 2,650 pounds, whereas high-tensile chain of 5⁄16-inch diameter weighs 1.1 pounds per foot but affords a 3,900-pound working load. This weight savings and gain in working load sway many toward the more costly HT option.

Others favor BBB for its greater weight and catenary effect: 250 feet of ⅜-inch BBB short-link chain weighs about 125 pounds more than the 5⁄16-inch HT alternative. The larger-diameter BBB chain also offers additional sacrificial metal and is less prone to corrosion than HT chain. BBB chain also is considerably less expensive than HT chain.

We can compare light chain and light anchors to a light hammer: appropriate in some instances, but the wrong tool in others. One school of thought focuses on the enhanced catenary action of heavy chain, while the other school values chain primarily for its chafe resistance and the less weight of smaller-diameter high-tensile chain. Lighter chain enables

Splitting the bow locker laterally provides a bin for the chain to the primary anchor and room for the rope and/or chain of a secondary. The divider may also be a great attachment point for the forestay chainplate. The bonded-in FRP box shown here is the housing for a bow thruster; the two centerline-angled aft cables are aluminum straps securing the forestay to the bonded structure. To port of centerline aft are the windlass's electrical cables.

a cruiser to go one size up in the anchor and still carry less weight in the bow.

Because of the weight of chain, some go for the lightest chain and anchor possible. That situation is like the proverbial emperor's new clothes. Light, undersized chain has minimal catenary effect; when stretched bar taut, its breaking strength can be exceeded by the shock loads of a pitching, heaving vessel.

Always order new chain with oversized links welded on both ends. Shackles are weaker than chain of the same diameter, and an oversized link at each end enables the use of shackles one size larger than the chain itself. This practice also allows the chain to be "end for ended," that is, reversing the unused bitter end with the highly abraded working end. This can extend the rode's service life by nearly 50%. You can keep track of the abraded section of chain with paint. Simply color a one-foot section of chain every 50 feet, allowing you to note how much scope you've deployed.

Many round-the-world cruisers find that 250 feet of chain is enough to anchor safely in most harbors and coves. Just in case a deep hole becomes a necessary anchorage, they attach a 100-foot nylon pendant to the bitter end of the chain. This achieves several things. First, world voyagers find the 100-foot extension useful for anchoring in places like the Society Islands of the Pacific, where a few favorite anchorages have 80-foot depths. Second, it allows the full chain rode to exit the hawsehole in an emergency situation. You can then attach a buoy to the line and cut it away for a quick getaway, then return later to retrieve it in calmer seas.

With this type of installation, it's critical to make sure that the hawsehole is large enough to pass the spliced thimble and shackle that attach the chain to the line. Then fasten the bitter end of the nylon line to an eye or cleat in the chain locker, preventing inadvertent loss of the rode if the windlass brake is not set or a malfunction occurs.

Ground-Tackle Connections

As mentioned above, shackles are weaker than chain of equivalent diameter, which is why your shackles should be one size larger than the chain to which they're attached. All shackles used to secure component parts of a ground-tackle system should be moused, or wired, with malleable Monel seizing wire. This extra effort keeps clevis pins in place even if the tension loads carried through the ground tackle slightly loosen the screw fastener itself.

Veteran cruisers seem to agree that you're better off without any swivels in your rode since the small

upside of this hardware is more than outweighed by its downside. While permanent mooring ground tackle requires a means of unwinding tide- and wind-induced twists in the rode, this isn't necessary for anchoring ground tackle used only for shorter periods of time. You'll find a few tide cycles' worth of rotation of little consequence, with the rode unwinding itself after hoisting the anchor.

A swivel used in an anchor rode becomes a new "weak link" in an already complex system, which is the main reason to avoid it. Many assume that a stainless steel swivel is stronger and less prone to failure. On the contrary, once stainless steel is submerged, its galvanic behavior makes it more prone to corrosion than galvanized mild steel. In addition, its resistance to fatigue from cyclic loading also is not as good. More often than not, swivels are identified as the culprit in mooring failures in the Northeast. If you're intent on adding one to your ground tackle, pick a domestically produced version that's a size larger in diameter than the chain itself, and plan to replace it after a couple of seasons.

GROUND-TACKLE HANDLING GEAR

Experienced sailors consider a boat's ground-tackle handling system as important as the ground tackle itself. The more heavy duty the ground tackle, the more powerful the handling system needs to be. That's true even if the source of power is a bent-backed skipper cranking a manual windlass.

Chain and anchor windlasses are made for each other, both figuratively and literally. The combination provides the ability to handle ground tackle without getting your hands into the works—a big safety advantage. An anchor windlass is one of the telltale signs of long-term, long-distance cruisers. A flat-pattern lightweight anchor and nylon rode are a cost-effective combination for part-time cruisers, but longer-term cruisers soon come to rely on heavy-duty ground tackle and the gear that deploys and retrieves it.

Windlass

A daysailor, marina hopper, or infrequent overnighter needs neither heavy-duty ground tackle nor a heavy-duty windlass. For these sailors, a smaller windlass often works just fine. But if your cruising life calls for it, and your heavy-duty ground tackle and day-to-day anchoring form the heart of your cruising life, then you'll also want a heavy-duty windlass.

Unfortunately, over the past several years, minimum-duty windlasses have migrated from lunch-

High-quality U.S.–made Crosby galvanized shackles are a good choice for rope anchor rode thimble-to-chain junctions and seldom-seen mooring rode connections. These components are stressed by physical loads and a constant chemical assault, often for years. Equivalent galvanized mild steel ISO-compliant shackles are available throughout Canada, Europe, New Zealand, and Australia.

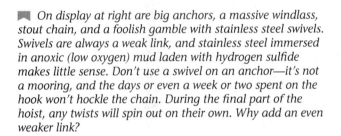

On display at right are big anchors, a massive windlass, stout chain, and a foolish gamble with stainless steel swivels. Swivels are always a weak link, and stainless steel immersed in anoxic (low oxygen) mud laden with hydrogen sulfide makes little sense. Don't use a swivel on an anchor—it's not a mooring, and the days or even a week or two spent on the hook won't hockle the chain. During the final part of the hoist, any twists will spin out on their own. Why add an even weaker link?

swivel

hook use on production powerboats to the foredecks of smaller sailboats and finally to larger sailboats marketed as "long-range cruisers." The rodes used with these units lack a traditional thimble and shackle in the junction between the chain and the nylon rode. A rope-to-chain splice without extra hardware may keep the diameter change minimal but introduces a weak link into the system. A rope-to-chain splice weaves nylon strands through chain links or simply doubles the line back once passed through the first link. The on-off tension of anchoring rubs away at the nylon and will cause the junction to fail much sooner than with a conventional thimble-protected eye splice. The additional chafe associated with the small contact area of a small-diameter windlass also shortens the life expectancy of the nylon rode.

One marine catalog states that the "strain on the windlass should be limited to the weight of the anchor and rode." Yes, under perfect conditions, the sailboat's auxiliary engine can be used to break the anchor free, and then the job of the windlass is simply to haul up the combined weight of anchor and chain from the depths. Buoyancy even helps by slightly lessening the weight of the submerged steel, and use of a combination line-and-chain lessens the

In Spanish, "entrada" is an expedition into unexplored territory. By the time the crew of this big plumb-bowed sloop, sporting neither bow roller nor windlass, have their anchor at the surface, they will indeed be entering uncharted territory.

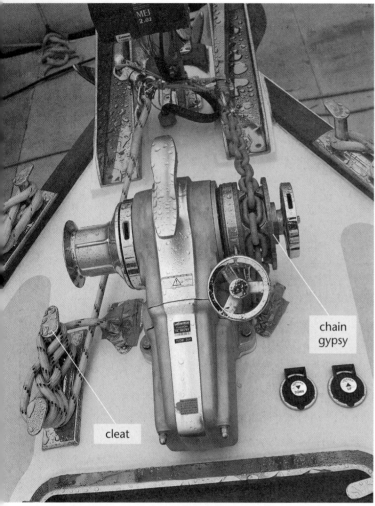

chain gypsy

cleat

A carefully installed windlass has a fair lead to the bow rollers and a straight drop for the chain to spill into the bin below. Note the handy cleat on deck that's used for a chain-snubbing line. And note the cleat on top of the windlass you can use for an anchor snubbing line, to hold a chain claw on a pendant while a rode is swapped, or for any number of other jobs. Cruisers like cleats in these locations, but racers hate them because of the potential for fouling a sheet or other foredeck lines.

weight further. This best-case scenario seems to have influenced many boatbuilders to downsize windlass power and ruggedness. After all, why put all that extra weight and sheet-snagging bulk up on the foredeck when it will rob performance, increase cost, and clutter up the limited space? This may sound great until one realizes an anchor windlass plays an important role in conditions other than optimum weather and flat seas. The worse the weather, the more important a windlass becomes, and the pitching mass of a 10- or 15-ton cruising boat under the influence of gale-force winds and building seas puts strain on an anchor rode measured in four-digit, not three-digit, numbers. A robust, rock-solid anchor windlass qualifies as safety gear and acts as an insurance policy for many

long-term, long-distance voyagers. We count on its reliability in rough, gale-swept anchorages, situations when being able to handle an oversized anchor and a hefty all-chain rode is critical.

When the chips are down and the primary anchor is fouled on a discarded bucket or abandoned scrap of twisted steel on the seabed, the ability to clear the fluke and rapidly retrieve the anchor can mean the difference between safety and dragging ashore. For a serious cruiser, skimping on the windlass makes no sense at all. Those determined to have less weight in the forepeak can move the windlass farther aft and install a chainpipe that leads deep into the bilge well aft of the stem.

Anchor windlasses come in an astounding array of shapes, sizes, and durability. The best are powerful, hold each chain link like the jaws of a great white shark, and release it like a toy from the mouth of a submissive puppy. When picking the right windlass for your boat, consider the speed of chain retrieval and the pulling capacity of the unit.

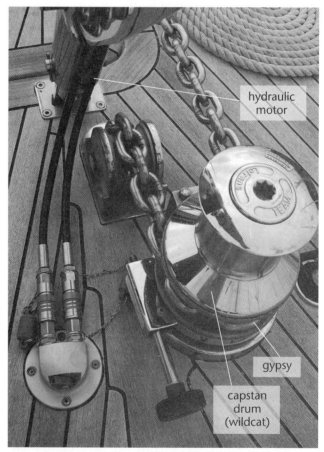

hydraulic motor

gypsy

capstan drum (wildcat)

A vertical-capstan windlass can be elegantly compact, but you must take care to provide effective chain stripping with a fair lead into a deep locker. Vertical seals on the drive shaft tend to be more prone to leaks, but the powerful, hydraulically powered unit shown here is more immune to this problem than an electric drive would be.

All anchor windlasses function in a similar fashion. A power source—electric, hydraulic, or human arm strength—rotates a drum-like structure that engages the rope, chain, or both. The case, or housing, transfers the load from the ground tackle, making it necessary to mount the case to the boat with bolts that penetrate the deck and backing plates that spread significant loads. Many manufacturers use a cast aluminum housing secured to the deck with stainless steel machine bolts, but the dissimilar metals and abundance of seawater cascading over the stem lead to galvanic corrosion that can damage these attachment points. Most alloy housings now incorporate sleeved bolt holes that use a dielectric plastic to eliminate metal-to-metal contact. Adding a sealant to the bolt also helps to lessen the chance of corrosion.

Both vertical- and horizontal-capstan windlasses are geared to change the moderate torque, high-RPM motor spin into high-torque, low-speed drum or gypsy rotation. (The cast bronze gypsy deploys and retrieves chain, while the drum handles rope.) In the best models the gears and other rotating parts are submerged in an oil bath that lubricates the gears and heavy-duty bearings. The housing must be strong enough not to deflect under the full range of working loads. Smaller units use alloy-cased angle drives with reduction gears, but their continuous load-carrying capability is much less than the rugged drivetrain of a premium unit, such as the Ideal Windlass BHW vertical-capstan windlass. In addition, when problems arise with smaller units, particularly when cruising, you might find parts difficult to find.

The best drive systems engage the rope or chain drum to the shaft with a clutch system. This allows the anchor and rode to be dropped quickly from a free-spinning drum rather than slowly deployed with a "power-down, power-up" drive that's permanently engaged. The always-engaged drive type is less expensive to produce because no clutch is necessary; however, if you use a clutch-less windlass, you'll likely find an emergency recovery and reset in the middle of a stormy night especially challenging.

The chain and the chain gypsy on the anchor windlass must be carefully matched. Some windlass manufacturers request a foot-long sample of your chain so they can match it to the gypsy's sprockets and link pockets; others offer a universal gypsy that, in theory, fits all variants of a given chain size. The former practice ensures a better fit because the match is actually tested.

It's sad to see large, cast-bronze chain gypsies giving way to small-diameter alternatives. These smaller gypsies engage fewer links and are more prone to problems caused by twists and tension changes during recovery. For long-term cruisers, a unit that functions

Seawater often finds its way into a vertical-capstan windlass, and the corrosion it spawns is no friend to an electric motor. Careful cleaning with a stainless steel wire brush and emery cloth can often cure the ills. Replacing the carbon brushes and perhaps installing a new bearing and seal complete the mini-makeover.

flawlessly in calm wind and flatwater may fall short when caught in a midnight squall dragging toward a hungry lee shore. In such conditions, a chain that jumps its bow roller or binds in the chain gypsy can add up to the loss of fingers—or much worse.

Vertical-Capstan Windlasses

The windlasses on the market have either a vertical or horizontal capstan. Vertical-capstan windlasses place the drive motor and reduction gear below deck, leaving only the gypsy and capstan drum, or wildcat, above deck. Some boatowners prefer this type as a way to reduce deck clutter. Others note that a vertical-capstan windlass binds more frequently and relies on a vulnerable deck seal to keep water out of the reduction gear and electric motor below.

Horizontal-Capstan Windlasses

A horizontal-capstan windlass combines drums and/or chain gypsies on either side of a housing that contains the electric motor and reduction gears. The combined above-deck unit is much larger than the above-deck profile of a vertical windlass. Racers and those with considerable foredeck action usually prefer a vertical windlass. But if you want maximum

This horizontal-capstan windlass is mounted far enough aft to provide a deep vertical chain fall that reliably strips chain from the gypsy during recovery and keeps the chain weight farther aft. The shaft seals are well above the deck and less likely to leak than a vertical-windlass seal. When necessary, servicing or replacing the unit is generally a straightforward task.

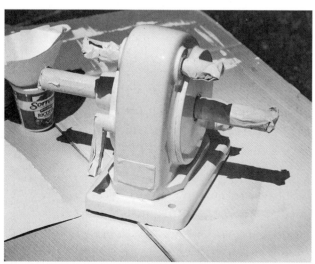

A simple two-gear hand-cranked Nilsson windlass is spruced up with a fresh coat of paint. The big, fishing reel–like mechanism works just fine for my 10-mm chain rode and 45-pound CQR anchor, and like my reliable servopendulum steering vane, it draws no electrical current at all.

control over anchoring and see the windlass as an essential ally in your cruising routine, give a horizontal windlass primary billing on your foredeck.

Manual Windlasses

We see significantly fewer hand-operated mechanical windlasses today. Their disappearance coincides with the trend to add more complicated energy-consuming equipment to small and midsize cruisers. In reality, the job of an anchor windlass is not to pluck a deeply buried anchor from the seabed; it's intended to recover the chain and hoist the anchor once the engine and the boat's buoyancy have broken the anchor free. The vessel itself does the heavy lifting.

With that job description for the anchor windlass, retrieval loads are or should be modest, and a manual windlass can perform well on cruising boats up to about 40 feet. In addition, a manual windlass is much more reliable and simplifies rather than complicating anchoring. Granted, my stance on this runs counter to mainstream wisdom, but I've seen too many small boats overburdened with unnecessary equipment. When it comes to an electric windlass, there is more to consider than how the unit will be bolted to the deck.

A few savvy old salts still row their dinghies and hand-crank their anchors and chain. Some view these stoic traditionalists as more penny-pinching than practical, but others consider less complexity and more reliability in keeping with the enjoyment of sailing as a physical activity rather than button-pushing experience. Not only are manual windlasses a viable alternative for small cruisers, but they're durable and can be rebuilt, allowing them to easily stand the test of time.

Back in the late 1970s I changed my priorities during an extended Pacific cruise. While in New Zealand, I swapped the Brooks & Gatehouse wind instruments I'd never installed for an all-chain anchor rode and a hand-cranked Nilsson windlass. Since then, the windlass has been unbolted from *Wind Shadow*'s foredeck a couple of times to be sanded and repainted, and we've replaced its aluminum mounting feet with a solid FRP base. The oversize reduction gear and large, double-cone clutch on the Nilsson make chain handling safe and easy, and the horizontal pattern allows chain stripping and fall without assistance. A simple rotary cranking motion with a 10-inch radius handle provides enough force to manually retrieve a 45-pound CQR and ⅜-inch BBB chain. I use the boat's engine and buoyancy to break the anchor free.

When surging loads are transferred to the windlass, its extra-heavy-duty structure and design have paid off. Robust solid bronze castings, a substantial main shaft, and the large chain gypsy and rope drum

Anchor windlasses exert a heavy current draw, and all conductors that lead amps to the beast need to be up to the job at hand. The wire diameter must be increased according to the distance run, and when selecting the correct wire gauge the voltage drop calculation requires using 2 times the distance between the battery and the component as the total wire length. Here we see a set of high current carrying 12-volt DC terminal strips and a fused junction supplying power to a windlass and bow thruster: one lead goes to the windlass (W), two go to the bow thruster (T), and two are auxiliary (A) power for furling and pumps.

diameters are signs of a well-made and useful piece of gear, regardless of whether it's manually, electrically, or hydraulically powered.

Power to the Windlass

To develop the hoist power required to retrieve ground tackle, most manufacturers of electric windlasses use a motor the size of a diesel auxiliary starter motor. Bearings are used instead of bushings, and the unit's output and duty cycle are matched to the longer run times required of a windlass motor. This means that in a 12-volt DC system, the windlass may draw 100 to 150 amps of current. Breakers that can handle 150 amps make sense, along with similarly rated solenoids.

This kind of current may require 2/0 or 4/0 cable running through a conduit to the bow, an effort and expense you'll find more palatable if your boat also has a bow thruster and these heavy-capacity conductors can do double duty. A 24-volt system uses only half the amps and thus allows for a smaller wire gauge, but this adds charging complexity and other undesirable constraints. A third option is to place an auxiliary battery close to the windlass and route forward smaller wires capable of carrying a charging current for this battery, but what is saved in wire ex-

pense is more than made up for in charging complexity and issues with another battery. Most pros continue to recommend welding-size cables from the main battery bank to the windlass, protected with a fuse or circuit breaker close to the battery terminal.

If a sailboat under 40 feet has power winches in the cockpit, an electric windlass forward, an electric refrigerator/freezer, a watermaker, and an electronic autopilot, it has the system complexity of a larger vessel—but it likely lacks the room needed to house the batteries needed. As a result, storage space is lost and displacement has been increased, nipping away at light-air sailing performance. Both designers and owners should understand the mission of any given boat and incorporate systems in keeping with that mission. Moderate- to heavy-displacement cruisers are popular because they can carry larger systems and payload weights, larger engines, and bigger tanks for diesel fuel. To gain these advantages, however, they sacrifice the ability to sail well in the lighter airs that dominate coastal regions over much of North America. And that leads us back to recommending a manual windlass as a viable option for a cruising boat under 40 feet long.

Electric windlasses normally use 12- or 24-volt DC series-wound or permanent-magnet motors. The

When a deck drain, low-guttered locker lip, windlass motor, high-current wiring, connections, and relays all cohabit one of the wettest parts of a boat, ocean passage-making will not be kind to the electrical components.

permanent-magnet motors can work in forward or reverse with a simple change of polarity. Like starters on diesel engines, windlass motors have grown smaller over time. They produce more torque per unit of size than older technology, but the small motors also tend to produce more heat.

In the early days of electric windlasses, manufacturers used automotive starter motors with a longer armature shaft and a ball-bearing race to carry thrust loads. Their heavy, rugged cases, stout commutators, and brush assemblies made for a reliable, long-term power source that could be rebuilt in any automotive electrical shop around the world. Today's smaller windlass motors with a higher ratio of torque to weight appear more thoroughbred in nature and have less tolerance for overheating and excessive strains than their plow-horse forerunners.

A large engine room and space for ancillary systems offer a cruiser the option of a hydraulic system to power a serious anchor windlass along with a bow thruster, tender hauler, and other equipment. Hydraulic power can't be beat as a source of high-torque, low-speed energy—just what an anchor windlass needs. We find nothing more reassuring than stepping onto a foredeck and seeing a big, hydraulically powered horizontal windlass on a hefty pedestal leading chain fairly to big bow rollers.

Bow Roller

At the heart of a chain-and-anchor retrieval system is what New Zealanders for over a century referred to as a "spare man," that is, the stem rollers fitted to the sides of their bowsprit. At one time, New Zealand's commercial scow crews put their "spare man"

to use in their coastal waters. Today sailors gain just as much advantage from rugged, line-capturing bow rollers as those bygone Kiwi coastal scow crews once did. The bow roller redirects the anchor chain from its primary alignment between the anchor and the stem of the vessel to its final, fair lead to the windlass. Best of all, it's able to do this in a pitching sea or when current forces the vessel out of alignment with its rode. High cheek plates and a straight or U-shaped overbar are usually incorporated to prevent the chain from jumping out of the slot, and the rugged, stainless steel channel holding the roller is strong enough not to deform under load. The chain gypsy of the windlass aligns laterally as well as vertically with the roller, and this fair lead is essential to the grab and subsequent release of each link of recovered chain.

Bow shape and overhang have much to do with the ease and efficacy of anchor handling. The fickle whims of yacht design have increased maximum static waterline length and made plumb bows popular again. Valid reasons exist for a plumb bow, but anchoring is one of the downsides.

We saw a case in point in Bermuda a couple of years ago. The crew of a 50-foot modern racing sloop attempted to deploy a bow anchor and back stern-first into a Mediterranean mooring at the Royal Bermuda Yacht Club (see Chapter 4 on Med mooring). The crew deployed a light but awkward flat-pattern anchor, but unfortunately it dragged, which meant hauling it up and resetting it. Unfortunately, this maneuver inflicted about $1500 worth of cosmetic damage to the glistening dark-blue plumb-bowed hull. The stem-mounted bow roller let a short shot of chain chew away at the topsides, and as the anchor was finally manhandled over the bow pulpit, further gouges were cut into what had been a perfect finish. Mud slopped on the deck, too. All in all, a boat built for line honors is not necessarily designed to be easily anchored.

In such a case, the problem can often be prevented with a long, odd-looking roller extension or a permanent bowsprit with a roller mounted well ahead of the stem. This solution has to include a bobstay, and crew sleeping forward at anchor will learn what chain grating on a stainless steel bobstay sounds like. Those who consider a bow overhang passé seldom recall how efficiently it works with a bow roller and is a convenient platform for anchor retrieval. As well, it serves as a place to nest a CQR plow or, for that matter, a Rocna, Manson, Spade, or other pattern currently in vogue.

Plow-type anchors have gained wide acceptance, one of the important reasons for this being how well they fit on the bow roller and vessel's stem. Once retrieved, these anchors ideally sit so firmly wedged into the roller channel that boarding seas have no effect on their security. This storage method means the anchor is always ready to go, a secondary advantage. If the engine stalls in a windless, current-ridden channel, the crew can safely anchor before the vessel is swept ashore.

Deck Washdown Pump

The foredeck crew's best friend is a deck washdown pump for rinsing mud and muck from the chain as it rises out of the water before it reaches the roller. These saltwater washdown systems seldom have the volume and pressure of a city water supply, but it's amazing how even a small stream of water can dislodge the varied bottom sludge found in most harbors. In some cases you may need a scrub brush to handle the worst of the muck. A few veterans actually power ahead at a slow speed with their plow-pattern anchor just below the surface, a cleaning system using the flow of water over the anchor. This practice requires enough bow overhang or a bowsprit to keep the anchor from hitting the boat as it gathers way. A few minutes of this slow-speed drag cleans the anchor and aligns it with the roller, and it should come aboard easily for stowage.

ANCHORING TACTICS

Choosing an Anchorage

The suitability of an anchorage is relative and involves the present and short-term influences of bottom characteristics, wind, waves, current, tide, boating traffic, and other changing influences. As long as the skipper understands the variables that may intrude on the apparent tranquility, all is well. Disre-

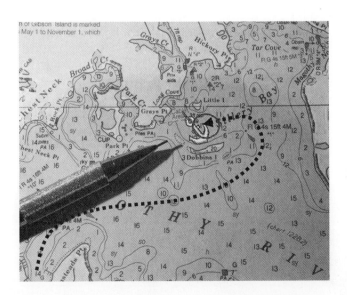

 Shown is a prime example of a carefully executed set of anchor rollers combined with a sprit extension for the furling headstay. It's a mirror-shiny example of stainless steel craftsmanship, but another foot of deck length with a less nearly plumb bow might have been a more logical and perhaps even less costly solution.

A deck washdown pump is worth its weight in gold. If you need to justify the cost of the components and installation, add an interior switch and faucet, and with a flexible garden hose you've added considerably to your firefighting capability. The two-for-one functionality is well worth the expense.

A well-chosen anchorage affords appropriate protection for the prevailing weather and for the weather forecast for the immediate future. The holding ground and water depth should be appropriate for your ground tackle, the vessel's draft, and the expected tidal range.

Developing versatile anchoring skills along with a sound ground-tackle setup encourages exploration off the beaten path. "Bulletproof" ground tackle adds a unique sense of security. This is the Bay of Islands, New Zealand.

garding an approaching cold front and dropping the hook in what seems to be a millpond may quickly prove problematic, and being forced to get underway at 0200 due to a 180-degree wind shift arriving with a squall is an unpleasant experience best avoided.

Choosing an anchorage involves analysis of multiple variables but need not be difficult. Begin with the largest scale (greatest detail) paper or digital chart that you have showing potential anchorages. Download, record, or write down the wind and wave details forecast for 24, 48, and 96 hours. Then spend some time noodling over what each potential anchorage can provide in the way of holding ground, swinging room, and protection for the forecast conditions. An ideal bottom, such as evenly contoured sand, is not of much value if a forecasted cold front passage results in your boat facing out into miles of open ocean with a swell intent on driving you ashore.

Nearing arrival at a new landfall, I scrutinize the forecast, and if bad weather is in the offing, I check out each anchorage with a simple wind rose overlay. First, I overlay each potential anchorage with a set of bearings showing wind direction on arrival and how it will back or veer over the next 24 hours. If the long-range forecast is reliable, I create a multiday wind rose with vectors showing where the most wind is likely to be found. Over the years I've learned the value of

ferreting out information about the orographic wind effect of coastal mountain ranges and passes between high islands, along with other factors that affect wind direction and velocity. *Sailing Directions* or *Coast Pilots* can be a good source of such information. Finally, if the forecast looks bleak, I'll plot the bad weather bearings on the chart comparing where I might hypothetically anchor and how much protection each alternative would offer.

At times, the best holding ground does not coincide with the best protection from wind and sea, so when seeking shelter from a storm, favor limiting the fetch (distance over which a wind blows) over finding the ideal bottom in which to bury your anchor.

In fair weather conditions, the options are many and there is less threat in an open span of water. But as the forecast becomes more bleak, the priority of finding better protection (less exposed water) grows exponentially. Even long-valued hurricane holes like the bay of Ensenada Honda near Culebra, Puerto Rico, can become a roiling caldron if a hurricane's wind finds its narrow entry slot. The island's steep-sided harbor—protected for 330 degrees—became a wave tank of epic scale during hurricane Hugo, and over 100 boats were driven ashore. In addition to wind and waves another villain the locals call "boat bombs" took their toll, as poorly anchored bareboats, hurriedly shuttled to Culebra by a plethora of Virgin Island charter companies, turned the hurricane hole into a really bad bet. The right answer in this case is simply not to be in the Caribbean during hurricane season.

Setting the Hook

We hear wide debate among sailors over the best anchor or anchors to use but also find many points of agreement about how to get the most from the anchor(s) you use. First, take the time to make sure the anchor is securely set before turning your thoughts to exploring ashore or delving into other boat projects. The secure setting of an anchor begins at deployment, which should be a controlled lowering rather than abruptly dumping the anchor and rode into the water.

As mentioned earlier, I believe a windlass with a well-designed clutch offers the best option for efficiently using your ground tackle and operates better than one that only operates in power-up or power-down mode. To gain the best chance for an efficient anchor set, maneuver the vessel head to wind or current, whichever is stronger. Just as the vessel loses headway, lower the anchor toward the bottom using the clutch on the windlass to slow and stop the rode as the anchor reaches its destination. It's important to prevent an all-chain rode from castling, or

A length of nylon three-strand line hooked to the chain about 8 feet below the bow roller places the load on the cleat rather than the windlass. This snubbing line is a last line of defense against shock loading when the forces of wind, wave, and current prove great enough to straighten out the chain. The snubber also silences grinding noises by relieving tension from the chain in the roller.

When anchoring in marginal conditions, it pays to note the GPS position, take visual bearings, and jot down a radar range on a nearby beacon. The reef to starboard in this photo can't be seen at night, and the fix and bearings may come in handy if the sailboat begins to drag its anchor.

piling up on top of the anchor, during this part of the anchoring process.

If all goes as planned, the boat will start to move astern just as the anchor begins descending toward the bottom, and this directional change causes the rode to lay out to leeward (or downcurrent) across the bottom. When you've released a 2:1 or 3:1 scope, gradually tighten the clutch, slowing the release of the rode and then stopping the boat's sternward progress. This causes the anchor to set and the boat to fetch up on the ground tackle, pulling the rode into a line with its endpoints at the bow and anchor.

More often than not, this first pull is enough to start the anchor-setting process and stop the vessel's sternward movement. The larger the anchor, the more likely this first pull accomplishes the set. Final scope (the ratio of rode length to water depth plus freeboard) should be a ratio of 3:1 to 5:1 (all-chain rode) or 7:1 to 10:1 (rope or rope-and-chain rode). At this point, make a final half-throttle backdown test. If the anchor holds without dragging, once the yawing settles down, take bearings on shoreside landmarks and/or record a GPS position. To eliminate noise and shock loads, you can set up a nylon snubber on a chain rode (see photo on page 157). Make a quick check of the windlass to ensure that the brake is on and all pawls are in place.

In tight anchorages, the scope of an all-chain rode can be as little as 3:1 if the water is deep enough to afford some useful catenary effect. However, in depths of less than 15 feet, be sure to add more scope, since the catenary effect will be minimal. The scope for an all or mostly rope rode varies depending on the holding ground and the effectiveness of the anchor. As a good rule of thumb, avoid short scope anchoring (less than 5:1) with an undersized anchor. Boats with smaller anchors need an anchorage where scope can be increased to 10:1 if a thunderstorm or longer bout of bad weather rolls in. It can be difficult to achieve and maintain greater swinging room in crowded anchorages, another reason all-chain rodes are popular today.

Keep in mind that the calculation for scope ratio includes the height of the bow roller above the water, and in addition to water depth, take into account the tidal rise for the lunar period. In heavy weather, the depth estimate might also include a storm-surge rise in sea level.

Line snarls, hockles, and twists—the bane of every mariner—can be especially challenging when it comes to using ground tackle. Any time you need to pay out line under load, experienced mariners put little faith in drawing directly from a narrow-diameter coil, because the cordage must have been twisted to form every loop of a perfect coil. When the line pays out, these twists have no place to go but into the straightening line. For this reason, old salts prefer a figure-eight coiling technique (see Chapter 5) or, even better, faking the line along the deck to make its run as hockle-free as possible.

So for a 5:1 scope in rope rode for a short stay in 20 feet of water + bow height, use 100 feet of rode; for a 7:1 scope for an overnight stay in 20 feet of water + bow height, use 140 feet of rode; for a 10:1 scope

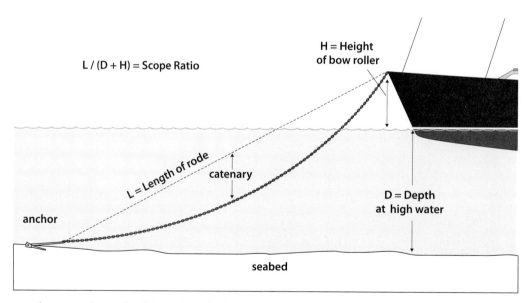

Adding scope decreases the angle of the rode to the bottom, which improves an anchor's holding power. Greater scope also lessens the force that lifts an anchor out of the bottom and increases the pull force more in line with the bottom. Unfortunately, crowded anchorages often prevent the use of extra scope; as an appropriate response, choose a larger anchor or an all-chain rode. (Joe Comeau)

for heavy weather in 20 feet of water + bow height, use 200 feet of rode. For a 3:1 scope of all-chain rode with a catenary in 20 feet of water + bow height, use 60 feet of chain.

Doubling Up Anchors (or Doubling Down?)

Two anchors of inadequate size don't add up to the holding power of one substantial anchor deployed on a strong rode with generous scope. On the other hand, the use of two appropriately sized anchors and rodes can offer an extra degree of security, especially in situations influenced by tidal currents, shifting winds, or limited swinging room.

The real art of using two anchors involves picking the right location for each and setting both effectively. The pattern and order of the set is dictated by weather and anchorage conditions. As your goal, you want two anchors deployed in a V-pattern off the bow, with the angle of the V determined by various factors, such as the angular difference between the old and anticipated new breeze or between ebb and flood currents.

There are two ways to implement this strategy, and in both the primary anchor is set first. The most often used version begins with setting the first anchor in a location that affords the best shelter and swinging room when the breeze clocks and rises to its maximum. This could be a different wind direction from what prevails at the time of anchoring. Once you've deployed the anchor, back down carefully to set the anchor in line with the anticipated new breeze or current, as described above. An all-chain rode needs less scope than a nylon rode, but the working all-chain ratio of 3:1 should be increased to 5:1 or more if heavy weather is anticipated.

You then set the secondary anchor in a V angle with the first and in accord with the wind or current prevailing at the time of anchoring. To easily carry out this task, pay out additional scope on the primary anchor and then steer under power upwind and slightly away from the location of the first anchor. Once you're over a point that will put the anchors 30 to 45 degrees apart, drop the secondary anchor. Twin bow rollers really help in such an endeavor. A good compromise anchor rode for this secondary anchor is 50 feet of chain and 250 feet of nylon rode. The rope rode can be snubbed around the windlass as scope is paid out, and once a 7:1 ratio is reached, you again use the back-down routine to set the anchor. Note that the mostly line rode of the secondary anchor needs more scope (assuming the primary anchor is on an all-chain rode) and should be set accordingly. Carefully placing each anchor and appropriately ad-

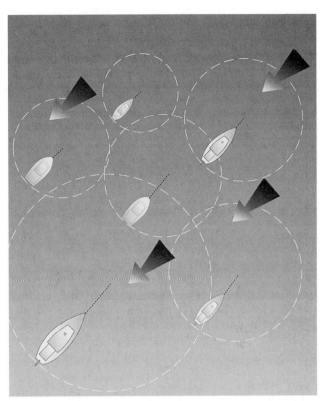

Vessels behave differently at anchor, sometimes because of the type of rode used, or design of the keel, and various other reasons. In light air some sailboats are more influenced by current than wind, which causes an intrusion into the swinging room of other vessels that might have an opposite tendency. Allowing for adequate swinging room and enough extra space to increase scope should conditions demand it is an essential consideration when choosing an anchorage.

justing the scope should result in having your boat where you intended to put it, plus allowing it to safely swing to the anticipated new breeze or current set. If a gale is forecast, the anchors should align effectively with the strongest anticipated wind. Of course, you should choose an anchorage that provides the best protection in gale conditions. If possible, you want room astern that's free of catastrophic consequences, with the holding ground a good match with the anchors used.

Deploying the Second Anchor with a Dinghy

Sometimes it makes sense to set the primary hook as described above and then use a dinghy to set the secondary anchor. One of the biggest mistakes made when rowing out an anchor, especially when there is a current, is to attach the bitter end of the secondary rode to the boat and then try to tow the rode through the water with the dinghy. This greatly complicates getting to the drop point and even raises the chance of the crew getting swept overboard during the deployment effort.

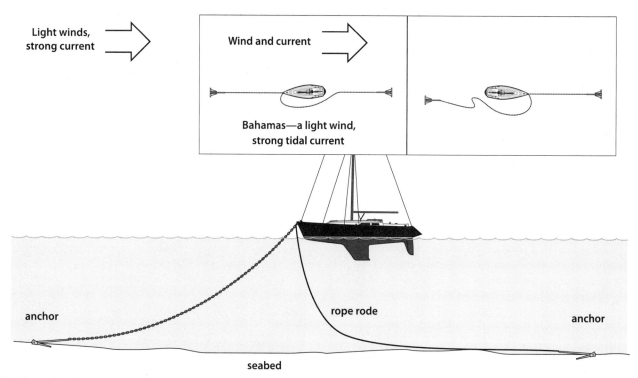

Light winds, strong current

Wind and current

Bahamas—a light wind, strong tidal current

anchor

rope rode

anchor

seabed

The Bahamian moor uses two anchors set 180 degrees apart in opposition. Both anchors are deployed from the bow, and the vessel swings on the current, which like clockwork flows on and off the sandy banks of the Bahamas. The rodes will twist, so it's best to have one anchor on a chain-rope rode that allows you to tuck its bitter end around the all-chain primary anchor to remove twists. Quite often the boat does a good job of preventing twist by rotating in opposite directions on its own. (Joe Comeau)

It's much easier to put the anchor and all of its rode in the dinghy and motor or row a little upwind or upcurrent the desired distance. Row cross-wind or -current to achieve some offset for the V-shaped set and lower the second anchor. The dinghy will drift back as you pay out scope. The wind or current may carry the dinghy back to the boat or you may have to row a few strokes to come alongside. A flat-pattern anchor such as a Danforth or Fortress is a good choice for the second anchor deployed by dinghy on a sand or mud bottom. Smart skippers carry a 50-foot length of light line with them just in case they have slightly underestimated the distance from the drop point to the boat.

Finally, take the bitter end of the rode or the makeshift extension aboard and pull it in hand over hand or with help from the windlass until the slack is removed, the extension (if used) is untied, and the scope is properly adjusted. The secondary rode is then given the same half-throttle back-down that set the primary anchor.

Bahamian Moor

The most extreme version of this pattern is the 180-degree separation of two bow anchors used in a Bahamian moor, an anchoring tactic devised to cope with tidal changes in current set. You can also use this two-anchor tactic in the Intracoastal Waterway, where you often find changing currents along with limited anchoring room.

Maintain an Anchor Watch

As previously mentioned, once you've set the anchors, you can attach a nylon snubber using a chain hook to an all-chain rode, and then set antichafe gear on all lines in contact with metal surfaces. The final nuance in the art of anchoring involves noting the vessel's position either casually—by referencing landmarks and other boats—or more formally with bearings and a GPS position. (Many GPS units also allow you to set an anchor alarm that will warn you if you start to drag.) This extra step helps you determine if you're dragging in the middle of a pitch-black, squally night.

In addition, if you're not in a designated anchorage, a day shape (ball) should be hoisted forward of the mast during the day and a 360-degree white anchor light at night. Large tidal ranges need to be considered, and that means more than making sure

THE ANCHOR WON'T HOLD—DEPLOYING A KELLET

Unfortunately, no anchor comes with an "always will hold" warranty. In fact, those who haven't dragged their favorite anchor just haven't been at it long enough. So I add one more tried and proven aid to staying put. Earlier we looked into response to dragging such as adding more scope and setting a second anchor. The kellet or sentinel solution uses the existing anchor and rode and augments its holding power by sending additional weight part way down the rode. This is easy to accomplish on a rope rode by attaching a snatch block to the rode with a control line affixed to the block along with a weight equivalent to the already deployed anchor. This new addition to the rode is paid out a length that's just a little more than the sum of the depth and height of the roller above the WL.

This added weight contributes two important anchor performance enhancing characteristics. The most important is its contribution to the catenary effect. As the boat surges sternward with each wind gust the rope rode straightens out and the angle of pull abruptly elevates. The geometry created through the use of a kellet or sentinel makes the angle change less abrupt and the shock-dampening effect is beneficial. Secondly, the heavy kellet weight in contact with the bottom slows the rate of yaw and lessens the tendency to sail at anchor. It's important to note that the lead or steel weight does not have the physical shape to act as an anchor, and many sailors say that opting for a larger anchor in the first place is a much better long-term solution.

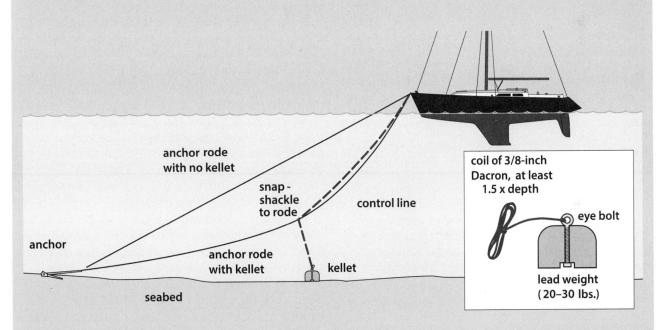

anchor rode
with no kellet

snap-
shackle
to rode

control line

anchor

anchor rode
with kellet

kellet

seabed

coil of 3/8-inch
Dacron, at least
1.5 × depth

eye bolt

lead weight
(20–30 lbs.)

Adding a kellet to your anchor rode lessens sailing at anchor and can reduce the chance of dragging. Attach a snap shackle from the kellet to the rode, then lower the weight to the bottom or approximately 1.25 × depth. As tension on the anchor rode increases, the kellet lifts off bottom, taking pressure off the rode. (Joe Comeau)

there's water under the keel at a spring low tide. It can also mean that there will be a big scope ratio reduction at high tide. The upside here is that the catenary increases with the deeper water. But the circle of swing radius will increase at lower tide—all play into the formulation of a sensible anchoring plan for a given body of water.

When conditions really deteriorate it may require an anchor watch. Having foul-weather gear and boots at the ready is imperative, and if conditions really deteriorate a dive mask becomes a very welcome way

to quell sideways blowing rain. In the worst weather it may become necessary to start the engine and use some low RPM forward propulsion to take some load off the ground tackle.

Quite often a vigorous cold front will pass with a rapidly veering breeze that will change the line of pull that your well-set anchors have adapted to. Most modern claw-type anchor designs and older plows respond well to abrupt wind shifts. Naturally this is contingent on being set in a good substrate. If you start to drag, add more scope and be ready to deploy

RETRIEVING A STUCK ANCHOR

More often than not, we have a very incomplete idea of what we are getting into when we drop anchor. At least that's the case outside the tropics where turbidity makes seeing the bottom unlikely. On one hand the bottom may be a perfect substrate, but every so often the anchor hooks onto the scuttled remnants of an old boat, or finds an abandoned mooring cable or a granite ledge full of anchor-swallowing crevasses. The net result is an anchor that's unwilling to break free.

In such cases, abandonment of the ground tackle is the least attractive option, but if it becomes necessary, leave the ground tackle attached to a float or marker so you can return to retrieve it later. Most of the time there are a few tricks that are likely to loosen the entrapped anchor. The first involves simply paying out scope and motoring a short distance, 180 degrees away from where you have been streaming. Then simply fetch up on the rode and see if the anchor breaks free. A little winching and backing with this new angle of pull often does the job. The Manson Supreme actually has a slotted shank that allows the rode shackle to pull to all the way to the crown of the anchor in this 180-degree break-free maneuver.

Another worthwhile plan is to use a marker float and line attached to a portion of the anchor (at the opposite end of the shank) that, when tugged on, will dislodge the flukes. It's necessary to have all the load off the rode when hauling in on this break-free line. It can be done from a dinghy or the bow of your boat by motoring over to the float and picking it up with the boat hook, while at the same time slacking the anchor rode. The direction and angle of pull will usually free the flukes from their entanglement. Only on three occasions during our cruise around the world did I have to don dive gear in order to clear a hopelessly fouled anchor. About a half dozen other times it took some work from the dinghy to extricate ourselves from snagged cables and lines. We were able to hoist the anchor to the surface but had to use a hacksaw and a sharp serrated knife to cut away the wire rope and hawser-sized rope.

a second anchor. Use the engine to lessen the strain on the rode but be sure not to override a rope rode and snag it in the prop. The bottom line is it's difficult to retrieve rode(s) and anchor(s) in the middle of the night and re-anchor expecting better results. This is why anchor overkill makes sense and avoiding the drama of dragging undersized ground tackle around the anchorage is a big step forward.

WEIGHING ANCHOR

I often prefer to sail out of an anchorage as much for fun as for the practice. This is another advantage of an easy-to-handle, all-chain rode. The process begins with a quick look at the true wind direction and what challenges lie off to port and starboard. Next comes a leisurely walk forward with a stop at the mast to make sure the mainsail is ready to hoist. After that it's up to the foredeck and a slow but steady bit of cranking to shorten the scope to just a little more than a 1-to-1 ratio. With a short-scoped rode and the anchor still well set, it's time to hoist the mainsail, keeping the sheet slackened and the sail luffing. Then it's back to the stem and the final few cranks of the windlass that tensions the chain and allows the buoyancy of the bow and slight pitching moment to break the anchor free. As the bow falls off an effective wash-down pump proves its worth. Now the multitasking really kicks in. The anchor needs to be retrieved just as the boat begins to gather way. This is another moment when not being a singlehander has a real up side. When there's a shipmate to take the helm and handle mainsail trim, anchor retrieval becomes no big deal.

My approach is to put *Wind Shadow*'s bow overhang to good use and actually tow the anchor slowly for a short period in order to give the last few feet of chain a chance to "auto clean." The overhang keeps the chain from touching the hull, and Lenore trims to spill breezes and keep us moving at just a couple of knots. A fringe benefit of this tow-the-anchor technique is that the flukes align with the flow and when the shank reaches the roller, the flukes face down and the anchor is ready to snug itself into the roller.

This approach works even better with a power windlass with a push button instead of a big crank hauling in the chain. But because running the electric windlass consumes quite a bit of energy, many skippers start the engine to put the alternator(s) in play and feed current back into the battery bank. With either approach, before leaving the foredeck make sure that the anchor is locked in the roller using windlass pawls, a chain brake, or a simple straight-forward lashing. An unintentionally deployed anchor when sailing along at hull speed can be more than a minor embarrassment.

A look at the remains of a good boat after it has dragged onto a nasty lee shore is all it takes to understand why serious cruisers usually opt for primary ground tackle comprised of heavy-duty anchors and an all-chain rode. Whether it's a surprise thunderstorm in the middle of the night or a cold front that arrives with more vigor than anticipated, anchor overkill can keep you

🚩 *When an owner, designer, and builder collaborate on ground tackle ahead of time, some great examples of form and function often result. Palawan VI is a Sparkman & Stephens 60 built by Abeking & Rasmussen. You see a CQR plow anchor in the port bow stem roller of this custom alloy cruiser. Below that, built into the stem, you find a hawsehole for the custom Bruce-pattern primary anchor. Don't skimp on any aspect of your anchoring gear. Ground tackle, like storm sails, provides a vital line of defense.*

from dragging ashore and jeopardizing your boat and crew—and other boats and crews as well. Over time, and through trial and error, we've seen the evolution of the long-distance, long-term cruiser's preference for a one-size-larger anchor, plenty of chain, a good windlass, and a strong bow roller.

Anchoring is indeed all about staying put, and the challenges in doing so are many. But there's no

better feeling than the confidence that experienced cruisers gain in knowing that there's overkill in the anchor inventory, and their anchoring techniques are up to the challenge of a 0300 squall. In the next chapter we'll look at the flip side of staying put and examine how sails and sail handling afford an entirely different approach to coping with that very same 0300 squall.

7

SAILS AND SAIL HANDLING

Poets and engineers find common ground in the art and science of sailing. John Masefield's most anthologized poem, "Sea-Fever," portrays the feeling of wind in the sails, while mathematician Daniel Bernoulli theorizes the fluid dynamics of lift. Masefield speaks for both when he refers to a schooner as "so much chaos brought to law."

SAILING SCIENCE

Before we dive into choosing, setting, trimming, and changing sails, we need to understand how an invisible moving air mass leads to the visible motion of a sailboat.

Lift from Sails

Eighteenth-century mathematician Daniel Bernoulli postulated that the pressure of a stream of fluid or gas decreases as its velocity increases. The nine-teenth-century physicist Giovanni Venturi observed this phenomenon and backed up the claim. Bernoulli's principle is revealed in the way a sail responds to the pressure of wind. Except when sailing downwind, in which case the wind pushes the sail forward, a sailboat is actually pulled forward by the lift from the sails. Consider how an airplane wing generates lift to raise the plane in the air. Air is flowing on both sides of the curved wing, but the longer curved surface of the upper wing forces the air to flow faster than the air on the bottom of the wing. This faster moving air has lower pressure, thus "pulling" the wing upward. The curve of a sail works similarly (see illustration on air flow). The angle of the sail produces a force that can be understood in two vectors—forward and leeward—but the keel and rudder (foils themselves) resist much of the sideways force vector, allowing movement mostly forward and to a lesser extent to leeward.

A foil, in this case a sail, constricts the flow of a fluid, in this case air, as it approaches its leading

If you get an opportunity to go sailing with a sailmaker, take it. When Butch Ulmer of UK Sails holds a "School-of-the-Boat" session, sailors learn the nuances of reefing, trimming, and how to optimize what's been engineered into the fabric and shaped into your sails.

edge; it then encourages rapid divergence of the flow around the foil, followed by an increase in flow speed (wind velocity) over the leeward surface of the foil. That greater velocity on the leeward side of a sail then creates an area of low pressure.

Critical to developing this flow pattern is a foil's so-called angle of attack to the approaching fluid—again, air. When a boat is pointed head to wind, the sails' angle of attack is zero. An equal amount of breeze traverses each side of the sails, causing them to flog like flags in the breeze. Bear off on a tack, however,

and the sails will fill, creating an unbalanced flow over the sails. A convergence of air occurs at the luff, or leading edge, of each sail; a divergence of air occurs as the breeze moves toward the leech, or trailing edge (see illustration). This results in an increase in air velocity and decrease in pressure on the lee side. This developing mini-low on the convex side of a sail enhances the convergence at the sail's leading edge, causing more of the approaching air to find its way onto the "back side" of the sail. This, in turn, further decreases the lee-side pressure (continued page 167)

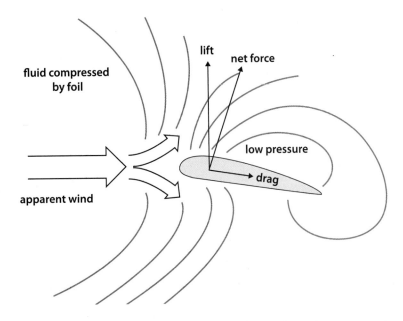

◀ *Air flow over a curved surface slightly misaligned with the flow—like this airplane wing—can create a pressure imbalance, resulting in lift. (Joe Comeau)*

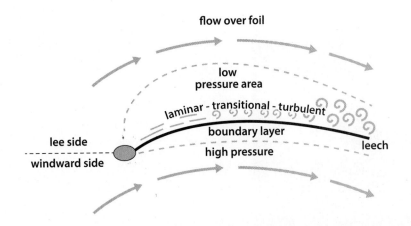

◀ *We can also view a sail as a soft wing with lots of challenges when it comes to draft control (draft is the maximum depth in the sail). Trimmed and shaped just right, the apparent wind splits to both sides of the sail, speeding up as it passes over the convex curve of the leeward side in order to meet up with air moving in a straighter path along the convex surface on the windward side. The lower pressure on the leeward surface results in aerodynamic lift. To increase this beneficial force sailors attempt to maintain laminar or smooth airflow over as much of the leading edge as possible. Shown here between the smooth laminar flow desirable at the leading edge of the lee side is a transitional area, followed after by a turbulent area at the leech on the lee side. Turbulent flow creates vortices that decrease lift and impede performance. Telltales provide important feedback that helps maintain a smooth flow. (Joe Comeau)*

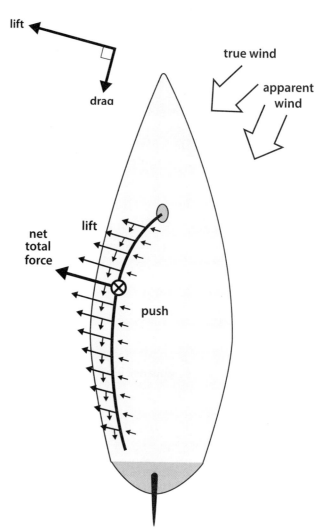

The view aloft from the foredeck of a boat sailing off the wind under pole-set spinnaker and well-eased main. Lift and drag are still operative off the wind. On a broad reach, you ease the mainsheet, adjust the traveler to leeward, and add tension to the boom vang. Here we see the spinnaker's leading edge trimmed so it's just shy of collapsing, and lift is maintained. Only when running dead downwind, square to the apparent wind, is a modern sailboat pushed by the breeze.

Air flow over a sail creates both lift and drag; for centuries, if not millennia, sailors have been trying to maximize the former and minimize the latter. The sail plan and hull are inanimate dance partners responding to aerodynamic and hydrodynamic forces. A well-designed sailboat places the center of effort, or net effect of the sail plan, in just the right fore and aft location on the hull. Sailing to windward benefits from just a little weather helm, a tendency of the boat to turn more into the wind. The corrective offset of the rudder increases its lift, and when sails are trimmed correctly the combined lift delivered by sail plan, keel, and rudder work together to increase boat speed. The total force created by a modern, well-trimmed sail is the sum of the push effect on the windward side of the sail and the pull or suction force that develops on the leeward side. (Joe Comeau)

When your sails are in balance with the lateral plane of the boat and properly trimmed for your point of sail, steering is easy, the boat's motion is kind, and progress is good. Note the well-tensioned luff on the reefed mainsail. (Note also that reefing points on a main should not be tied around the boom.)

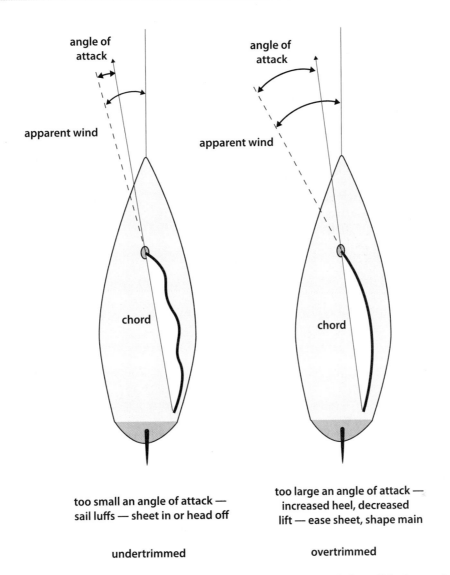

angle of attack

angle of attack

apparent wind

apparent wind

chord

chord

too small an angle of attack — sail luffs — sheet in or head off

too large an angle of attack — increased heel, decreased lift — ease sheet, shape main

undertrimmed

overtrimmed

The undertrimmed sail (left) flutters and flaps while the overtrimmed sail (right) chokes off the breeze flowing over its foil-shaped surface. We best discern overtrimming by telltale behavior. With the correct angle of attack, the bits of yarn or nylon on both sides of the sail and on the trailing edge flow aft evenly, but in an overtrimmed sail the leeward telltales flutter or droop. When overtrimmed, ease the sheet to a better angle of attack with smooth laminar flow (thus maximizing the forward vector of the lift). Easing the sail too much, however, will stall the sail. It usually takes mainsail shaping as well as sheet trimming to coax all telltales to behave. (Joe Comeau)

and increases the speed of flow to leeward, and on we go. Since air cannot be compressed at the low speeds involved in sailing, these pressure imbalances create the almost magical effect of lift.

A modern, well-trimmed sail creates a total force, the sum of the push effect on the windward side of the sail and the pull or suction force that develops on the leeward side. It may seem counterintuitive, but when sailing above a beam reach, the force developed on the leeward side is about twice as strong as the force created on the windward side.

A sail's angle of attack, the angle between the sail's leading edge and the apparent wind direction, is critical. Given a proper angle of attack, achieved by means of helm, sheet, and traveler, even a sheet

of plywood canted to the breeze can be used on a dinghy in lieu of a sail to make progress, albeit poorly, to windward. Telltales (on the leech of a main, for instance) are a good starting point for discerning the flow of air along the sail. You can use telltales in conjunction with the look of the sail to confirm the correct angle of attack, as described later in this chapter.

The vertical sheer, or gradient, of a surface wind complicates correct sail trim. This occurs because of the universal tendency of wind speed to increase with height above the water (see illustration on page 179). Friction between wind and water reduces wind speed at the wave tops, but that friction falls off rapidly with altitude, so the wind speed at 30 feet might be 50% higher than the speed at sea level. The stronger wind aloft will appear to blow from farther aft (or, if you're close-hauled, from a broader angle on the bow) because its velocity is greater relative to the boat's forward speed. Put another way, the apparent wind is typically farther aft aloft than on deck, and considerable leech twist may be needed to keep all the telltales streaming correctly.

The angle of attack is the angle between the chord of the sail and the apparent wind direction. The optimum measure of this angle depends on the type of sail plan and how the sails have been shaped and set. For example, a flattened shallow-draft (draft is the curve of a sail) mainsail and a jib set with lots of halyard tension perform better on slightly smaller angles of attack. Telltales attached in several points up and down the luff of the headsail and leech of the mainsail help you to fine-tune sail trim. Note that if the mainsheet is overly eased the sail will luff

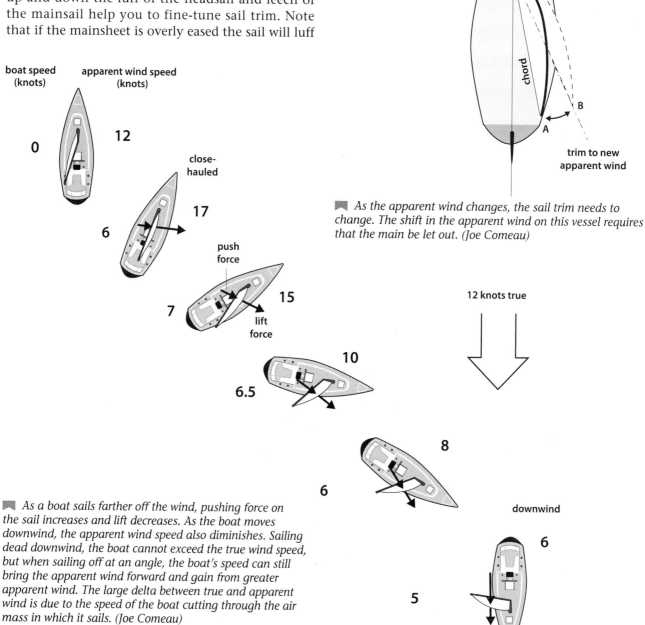

As the apparent wind changes, the sail trim needs to change. The shift in the apparent wind on this vessel requires that the main be let out. (Joe Comeau)

As a boat sails farther off the wind, pushing force on the sail increases and lift decreases. As the boat moves downwind, the apparent wind speed also diminishes. Sailing dead downwind, the boat cannot exceed the true wind speed, but when sailing off at an angle, the boat's speed can still bring the apparent wind forward and gain from greater apparent wind. The large delta between true and apparent wind is due to the speed of the boat cutting through the air mass in which it sails. (Joe Comeau)

—a sure sign of turbulent flow. (When the mainsail is overtrimmed, heel increases, lift is diminished, and leeward telltales stall.)

Lift from Keel and Rudder

A sailboat deploys foils in two realms: sails in the flow of air and keel and rudder in the flow of water. A sailboat's unique occupancy in air and water makes the science of sailing more complex than the science of flight. By slightly angling a foil to the direction of flow (the angle of attack), lift is generated in both air and water.

Unlike a sail, a keel (or centerboard or daggerboard) remains aligned with the boat's centerline at all times on most boats. How, then, can a keel acquire the necessary angle of attack to generate lift? The answer involves the way boats move under sail. All boats under sail make a certain amount of leeway, meaning they sideslip, often called "crabbing." This crabbing to leeward creates an offset angle of attack. The boat's course made good may only be 2 to 4 degrees to leeward of the course steered, but that's enough to cause the flow of water to impinge more directly on the keel's leeward surface. The windward surface of the keel experiences a faster flow and therefore a lower pressure. This results in a lift to windward that helps counter the leeward vector of the sails' lift. When thought about this way, leeway is not a flaw (unless excessive) but rather a vital component of a sailboat's ability to make progress to windward.

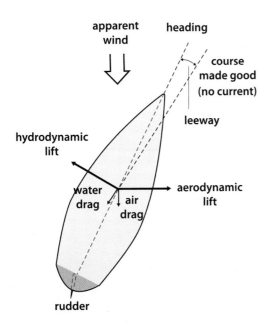

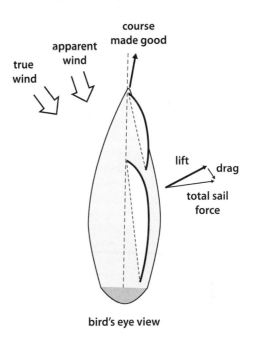

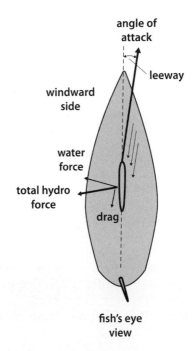

🏴 *The combined effect of the forces on a sailboat both above water and below water. Above the waterline, the deck, the sails, rig, and rigging influence drive, and freeboard and poorly trimmed sails increase drag. Below the waterline, the keel, rudder, and hull shape contribute to both hydrodynamic lift and drag. The rudder's angle corrects against the forces of weather helm to keep the bow down and adds lift, but excess angle increases drag. (Joe Comeau)*

🏴 *Shown at right are both a bird's eye view of the forces at work above the water, and a fish's eye view of the forces below the water. The interactive effects of a vessel's sails and its underwater foils produce forward progress and leeway. Enhancing the lift of underwater foils while lessening leeway is one of the goals of yacht design. Drag is a parasitic effect that's influenced by the boat's underbody, superstructure, and rig. (Joe Comeau)*

A sailboat's performance on all points of sail is much affected by its fore-and-aft and athwartship trim. A balanced sail plan is important too; when your sails are properly balanced and you're not overpowered, you should need minimal rudder offset to maintain a straight course. Rudder offset creates drag, and drag reduces speed. Note the streak of rudder-induced turbulence behind this boat, indicating that it is overpowered and attempting to round up.

A high-aspect rudder kept slightly angled to offset weather helm is also a lift-creating foil. Three to 10 degrees of rudder angle is ideal; any more than this and the flow of water past the rudder blade is disrupted, at which point the rudder stalls and becomes more brake than steering foil.

Yacht designers carefully assess the interplay between the lift forces of the sail plan and the lift-inducing characteristics of the underbody. They see the balance of a vessel as based on the rig's center of effort and the underbody's center of lateral resistance, a dynamic balance that may also include fins and foils to develop lift. (See Chapter 12 for more on yacht design.)

Sail Shape

Just as angle of attack is critical for generating lift, foil shape is also vitally important. Aerodynamic engineers have studied sail shapes in varied wind velocities and in turbulent and laminar flow, defining what shapes work best in each condition. Laminar flow, the most efficient lift producer, also is the hardest to retain over the curve of a foil. Even a well-shaped, well-trimmed sail can maintain laminar flow only on the forward part of the foil, one reason why high-aspect sails are generally more efficient. A low-aspect sail is shaped with greater area toward the bottom of the sail, giving it less heeling effect than a high-aspect sail, but also less lift.

In a nutshell, sailors tend to prefer more draft, or curvature in the sail, in light air because a sail with deeper draft has relatively more power. Less draft is used as the breeze increases, because a flatter sail has less power. Although a sail's shape is determined on

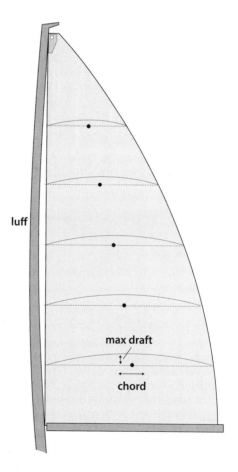

luff

max draft

chord

The fore-and-aft location of the maximum draft is also important. Jibs and genoas are usually built to carry their maximum draft 33% to 40% aft of the luff, while the deepest draft on a mainsail is usually around 40% aft of the luff on a rig without an overlapping jib, but closer to 50% in a rig featuring a big genoa. The draft is more forward on the top of this main. (Joe Comeau) the sail loft floor, the crew can still do much to shape draft and experiment with it as conditions change.

The last century has seen dramatic changes in sail materials, but the basic concept of turning flat cloth into a controlled curved surface remains the same. This is achieved with a process called broadseaming, which mates the flat edge of one panel of cloth with the curved edge of the next panel, thus coaxing a two-dimensional material into a three-dimensional shape. The shape of the curved panel's edges dictates the amount of draft placed in a sail and the fore-and-aft location of deepest draft.

To visualize draft, imagine a soaring seagull's view of a horizontal cross section through a sail. Now imagine a straight line—called a chord—connecting the ends of that curved cross section. And now, in your mind's eye, construct perpendiculars at intervals between the chord and the sail's curve. Each perpendicular represents the depth, or draft, of the sail at that point along the chord, and the longest perpendicular represents the sail's maximum draft at the height of the cross section. Divide that maximum draft by the length of the chord for the ratio that describes the sail's curve, or camber. A simplified rule of thumb equates more draft with more power, a shape optimized for light air. Flatter sails with less draft tend to point higher and perform better in fresh breezes. A sail with a maximum draft of 1:20 is cut very flat, and one with a draft of 1:6 is very full.

Sailmakers consider the sail area, the two-dimensional shape (aspect ratio) of the sail, and the draft created through broadseaming. Sailmakers also factor in the stiffness of the headstay and shape the leading edge of a headsail accordingly. This shaping involves building in some hollow to cope with headstay sag and counter the negative effects of a leeward-curving luff. The more headstay sag a rig happens to have, the more hollow should be cut into the leading edge of the sail.

The leech of a headsail or mainsail involves more nuances in the sailmaker's craft. We gain extra sail area, and thus extra drive, through the roach of a mainsail, defined as additional material extending aft of a straight line between the head and clew of the sail (see illustration). Battens are used to help support the extra material of the roach. (Designers have carried this concept to extremes in modern racing multihulls and America's Cup vessels, which place considerable sail area aloft through the use of battens and special headboard designs. In the 2013 Cup series the boats used rigid wing sails. These double-sided rigid foils had greater lift per square foot of area but also a complexity that could allow the big multihull to become an unguided missile. The mainstream sailing community is unlikely to see

Draft control bands—the solid lines on this headsail—give the trimmer a good idea of the draft shape at different heights above the deck. We can use jib leads and barber hauling in conjunction with sheet trim and halyard tension to control headsail draft. (Barber hauling adds windward tension to the slack jibsheet.)

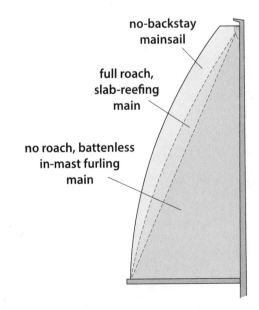

no-backstay mainsail

full roach, slab-reefing main

no roach, battenless in-mast furling main

Large full battens are used to support extra roach, and multihulls and some monohull race boats unencumbered by a backstay use a mainsail with an especially full head. (Joe Comeau)

Cruising catamarans rely on massive mainsails with a large roach and full-length battens (like those visible here) to support the leech. Such mainsails with a high aspect ratio and full head are possible when there is no permanent backstay. Some high-performance monohulls have also eliminated the permanent backstay, trading the upside of more sail area aloft for the downside of a commitment to backstays.

Ted Hood bridged the gap from sailmaker to sailboat designer (and later power cruiser designer), always showing a flair for integrating the component parts of a vessel. His early pioneering efforts with roller furling and roller reefing redefined sail handling.

rigid wing sails on production sailboats, but a few smaller performance multihulls will hit the market sporting hydrodynamic lift foils as seen also in these Cup boats. These daggerboards combined with the rigid wing sails lifted both hulls out of the water when the boat was moving fast enough, and the 72-foot catamarans literally flew on top of the water.)

As mentioned earlier, having a lot of sail area aloft is an advantage because the breeze is stronger higher up in the wind gradient. However, one downside to such high-aspect sails is the cost of the complex tracks and batten-car systems used to support a massive roach. On conventionally rigged vessels, the backstay limits the size of the roach and headboard.

MODERN SAIL CLOTH TECHNOLOGY

Over three decades ago, the late Ted Hood, known as the "Man from Marblehead," innovated sail making. Beginning by turning sand into dollars—forcing fine silica into tightly woven, dimensionally stable Dacron—his 18-inch-wide signature sailcloth panels kicked off a technology race that propelled sail development for decades. The quest for better sail materials continues at an even more fevered pace today, with the latest buzz focused on membrane laminates and molded wing sails. These materials are engineered for the load developed in a sail.

Lab tests and post-regatta feedback demonstrate that the most shape-stable lightweight sails are made

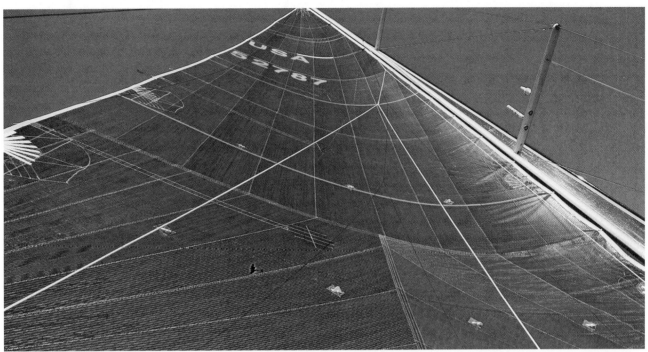

High-modulus materials allow sails to be made lighter, stronger, and more resistant to stretch. This 48-foot cruiser/racer's triradial-cut, carbon-fiber-composite mainsail is half the weight and twice the cost of a Dacron alternative. Cost, durability, and performance are competing concerns, and each sailor must decide on the right balance between them.

of laminates and are molded rather than woven. These composite nonwoven sails outperform their conventional woven counterparts. North Sails has taken the build-in-place concept furthest, creating seamless sails on a camber-changing mold. In their 3DL product line, they take the approach of controlling draft and adding carefully engineered load-path reinforcements all at once. They do this in much the same way a custom boatbuilder reinforces high-load regions of a hull. In their approach, high-modulus "strings" covered with adhesive film are positioned across the mold. The mechanical properties of the yarns used and the added extra layers provide support exactly where it's most needed. Equally important is the ability to lower the yarn density in regions with less load. Once the grid-like reinforcement is in place over a scrim (thin covering layer) and a veil of thermoset film completes the sandwich, pressure and heat are applied, thermoforming three layers into one sail.

Many other top-end sailmakers use Dimension-Polyant films and yarns to build up a load-path-engineered sail on a flat surface. Australian Bob Frasier developed this D4 version of sail engineering, and Doyle Sails introduced it worldwide. It incorporates a laminate buildup that is shaped on a flat laminating table rather than a curved mold. Large sections of a sail developed with a computer-aided design system are made by building up a sandwich of different laminates. These laminates range from a simple film

Laminated sail material strung with high-modulus carbon fiber is akin to high-tech laminates in boatbuilding, a means of deriving better strength-weight ratios and less stretch—but leaving less money in the bank! The result is a winning edge for racers but a bit frivolous for all but the most performance-oriented cruisers.

SAIL MATERIAL CHOICES

In sails, as in ropes and lines, it can be difficult to understand high-tech fabrics clouded by acronyms identifying a growing array of fancy fibers, resulting in a mire of fact, fiction, and superstition. To help prevent that, I'll offer a thumbnail sketch of the properties of each of these yarn products.

Traditional polyester fibers tend to earn low to moderate marks for strength and stretch resistance. Their grades on durability and handling are much higher, and Dacron often leads for best price.

More esoteric filaments tend to be a bit more quirky, such as solar-phobic aramids (with a light weight but high strength). These include several iterations of Kevlar, Technora, and Twaron, all of which are tough, stronger than steel, and less stretchy than Dacron by a factor of five or more. The downside (in addition to cost) is how quickly sunlight, flexing, folding, and flogging deteriorate these materials.

Spectra, Dyneema, and Certran are tough, high-modulus, polyethylene derivatives that can put up with UV exposure and flex. Their Achilles' heel is a mechanical property known as creep, another form of deformation under load. The result is a shape-robbing tendency that makes the material less appealing.

The liquid crystal polymers PBO and Vectran have huge tensile strength and great creep resistance but relatively poor UV stability. Burying these and or aramid fibers under UV-blocking taffeta can be a solution to that issue but adds unnecessary weight to the sail. Cuben Fiber, another special iteration in the ultra-high-molecular-weight plastic revolution, uses thin treated Spectra filaments that all but eliminate creep. North Sails now owns this product.

And finally there's carbon fiber, a costly but UV-immune, high-tensile-strength superstar with almost no stretch at all. And there's at least one more miracle yarn that trumps carbon, known as boron fiber, a thin film deposition filament manufactured by Textron Specialty Materials that's gotten the nod from aerospace engineers and can be found in the tail of F-14s, shaft of high-end golf clubs, and the spinnaker pole of the 12-meter boat *Intrepid* (quickly deemed too high tech by the race committee). But at $500 a pound it may be a while before boron fiber is "strung" into high-end sails.

The quest goes on for higher and higher modulus materials and there's often a willingness among racers to forego durability in favor of performance. The flip-side view among cruisers is equally polarized. Many see the sweet spot as either high-quality premium Dacron or one of the more durable, less esoteric composites.

When evaluating new sail material, always consider the stretch characteristics, which result from the traits of component yarns and the construction of the fabric. Consider two categories of stretch: deformation (permanent stretch) and elasticity (temporary stretch). (Because it's so elastic, nylon is not used for mainsails and jibs, although it's strong enough.) When bundles in a loosely woven fabric shift or when individual fibers exceed their yield point, permanent deformation occurs in the sailcloth. Low-modulus (stretchier) fibers tend to stretch permanently when stressed beyond their yield points, whereas higher-modulus materials often break when transitioning from elastic to plastic deformation. Laminate bonds and fill resins can also deteriorate, causing material stretch that robs a sail of its shape. Another factor in premature sail shape degradation involves material that's too light for the righting arm of a given vessel or the type of sailing the crew engage in. In short, durable strength in sail cloth is important, but dimensional stability is just as vital.

reinforcement to a film bundle or a more complex layup of taffeta, film, string reinforcement, film, and taffeta.

Whatever the laminate materials, the objective includes carefully aligning reinforcement with expected stresses, squeezing the layers together without disrupting the string geometry, and then applying heat to create a composite structure. Once cured, the sailmakers put sail sections on a plotter/cutter to be broadseamed. They're eventually moved to the pit or loft floor for stitching or seam sealing, and the final result is a lightweight, dimensionally stable composite jib or mainsail.

The upside of the laminating process includes the ability to align high-modulus fiber reinforcement with the load patterns in a sail. This places more shape-stabilizing material where it's most needed and also saves weight. Pre-impregnated films and yarns are bonded by heat in the final structure, which also eliminates the crimping associated with woven materials. The vacuum squeeze or debulking part of the process that precedes the heat sealing minimizes air voids, thereby lessening the chance for moisture intrusion and delamination. Keep in mind that these custom materials and methods can double or triple the cost of a sail. Consider, too, that one-off design and manufacturing can have issues of quality control, an argument put forth by sailmakers who use traditional fabric panels. These manufacturers contend that better laminate material is produced under optimum factory-controlled conditions.

When it comes to choosing sails, how high-tech do you need to go? The answer involves the way you sail as much as how much money you're willing to spend. For example, if you're a serious racer with a well-trained and capable crew and have already painstakingly faired the keel and achieved a wickedly smooth bottom, you're ready for membrane sails. But if you love to cruise, have roller-furling headsails, and sit under a bimini while letting the autopilot do the steering, then don't get all worked up over high-performance alchemy.

How About Dacron?

Let's assume you're a cruising sailor and don't want to pay double the price for sails with reduced stretch and a little less weight. In this case, good-quality woven Dacron and the less esoteric laminate panels offer fine choices. Lingering nostalgia for the old days aside, this isn't only my opinion. Quantum Sail designer and materials specialist Doug Stewart may give you the same advice, for he always asks customers about the way they sail, not just the type of boat they own. In many cases the sailor's answer about sail inventory leads him to develop a functional midlevel product, not a performance-enhanced package. Based on the cruiser's priorities, such as well-reinforced reef points, UV stability, mildew resistance, and modest cost, he suggests *polyethylene terephthalate*—the most common polyester (Dacron)—as a logical cruising alternative.

Woven polyester material has a good track record amassed from decades of development and use, but how the material is woven is more important than the yarn itself. Low-end sailcloth often has big-bundled, uneven weaves with inconsistent stretch characteristics, which allow these sails to lose their shape in a season or two. Other Dacron products, such as those from Bob Bainbridge's Challenge Sailcloth, include a wide range of tight, well-controlled weaves and careful approaches to resin finishing. To ensure dimensional stability, Challenge uses the Dupont 52 and Honeywell 1W70 yarns that feature tight crimps and a structure that relies less on resin and more on the quality of the weave.

Woven sailcloth is engineered in a grid construct. The warp yarns run the length of the cloth in an over-and-under shuttle around the fill yarns at a 90-degree angle. When the cloth is comprised of heavier-denier fill and lighter-denier warp yarns, it is considered "unbalanced." (Denier is the mass of fiber in a given strand length.) This means the woven material conforms better to specific load paths. Conventional crosscut sails make good use of this weave pattern, but the right material must be used for more complex panel layouts in radial-cut sails.

We still hear plenty of debate about the right sail material for any given vessel. After an inordi-

High-tech sails make sense on a high-tech boat for the same reason that a high-quality lens belongs on a high-quality camera. But high-tech sails are not an essential component of a great cruise.

Wedged between rolls of laminate sailcloth you can see a good example of tightly woven polyester fabric (Dacron)—a cruising sailor's best bang for the buck. High-quality woven Dacron has some durability plusses that are hard to ignore.

The jib on this seagoing little cutter is looking good, but the mainsail has seen more than enough time at sea. Perhaps more batten extension would clean up the leech, but when the camber shifts aft in a sail, drag increases and lift diminishes.

leech hook

The end of the black band indicates a hooked leech caused by overtensioning the leech line, probably in an attempt to quell leech flutter in this reefed mainsail. A sailmaker may be able to nip and tuck the sail back to life, but if the surgery is too extensive, a new sail may make more sense.

nate amount of research and sea trialing, I've concluded that no one product serves all uses, but certain points must be emphasized. First, before you commit to a new set of sails, pin down your priorities. Sailors might list shape-holding ability, light weight, strength, UV stability, flex tolerance, mildew resistance, flaking ease, longevity, and low cost. However, you'll find some of these attributes mutually exclusive, particularly in regard to price, so pick the two attributes that are most important to you and that offer the greatest benefit and put them at the top of your list, and proportionately discount the other features.

Sadly, too many sailors keep ancient sails they think still have life left in them just because the material appears more or less white and hasn't torn from luff to leech when jibed with gusto. These old sails often have stretched and the point of maximum draft has moved too far aft. Such a sail creates heel and drag—and not much else. The shape-holding capacity of the cloth is long gone even if strength and rot-resistance remain.

MASTHEAD VERSUS FRACTIONAL RIGS

In a masthead rig (sometimes called a full rig), the headstay runs aloft to the masthead and effectively opposes the backstay tension. In a fractional rig, the headstay usually attaches an eighth to a quarter of the way down the mast. The choice between full and fractional rig comes down to the characteristics you value most.

Most racing sailors favor a fractional rig. It permits a taller mast, a higher-aspect mainsail, and use of an adjustable backstay that is not directly opposed by the headstay to induce mast bend, thus altering the mainsail shape to match conditions. Since race boats almost always fly a conventional or asymmetrical spinnaker off the wind, the smaller headsail of a fractional rig doesn't hinder performance. On the contrary, the taller mast allows a crew to choose either an oversized masthead spinnaker in light air or a more moderate fractional-hoist kite in a fresher breeze.

Many daysailors and weekend cruisers also lean toward the versatility of a fractional rig. With an efficient slab-reefing system and a small roller-furling jib, the mainsail and primary headsail take care of winds of 10 to 30 knots. This eliminates sail changes within the wind range typically experienced by a daysailor or coastal cruiser. In addition, fractionally rigged sloops often perform well under mainsail alone. A fractionally rigged mast is stepped farther forward, so it moves a little more of the mainsail area ahead of the center of lateral resistance. This is why the vessel can be better balanced under mainsail alone, especially when reefed. In heavy weather this allows some fractionally rigged sloops to make way upwind or even heave-to under deeply reefed mainsail alone. However, we see a catch-22. In a fractional rig the mainsail must be a premier example of engineering and design in order to serve as the primary heavy-weather sail while also allowing the sail to retain the shape required for light-air sailing. This makes a good case for using higher-modulus, more dimensionally stable, and ultimately more costly sail material for the mainsail and an even better case for including a storm trysail in the sail inventory.

When sailing in less than 10 knots of wind, a weekend cruiser might turn on the engine, but that's a less attractive option for a long-distance cruiser with limited fuel. Above 30 knots, we could see a problem if the second reef in a two-reef system fails to decrease enough of the fractional rig's larger mainsail area. This often leads the crew to strike the mainsail and sail under a small portion of the partially furled headsail, a poor alternative at best. In such a case, the center of effort is so far forward that upwind sailing becomes all but impossible.

Many long-term cruisers prefer the added versatility and complexity of a masthead rig with a double-headsail sloop or cutter sail plan. The masthead rig offers more drive for a given mast height, an important consideration in places like the Intracoastal Waterway with its fixed bridges limited to 65 feet of

Many modern coastal cruisers (both masthead and fractional rigs) lack a deep (or third) reef in the mainsail, and in about 25 to 30 knots of wind, crews find themselves out of options to reduce sail. An extra set of reef points could easily solve this problem, lessen heel, and make life aboard more inviting.

SAIL REPAIR

We don't practice the art of repairing sails at sea as much as we used to, thanks mostly to better materials and excellent engineering approaches. Nevertheless, those headed across an ocean or on a lengthy coastal voyage need a few sailmaker's tools, including an awl, needle, and thread. Long-distance cruisers also need to understand a few key techniques, such as handling 3M Fast Cure 5200, which can fix many problems arising from chafe, sudden squalls, and poor reefing techniques.

Sail repairs at sea usually involve lessons in patience, ingenuity, and resourcefulness, and while woven Dacron is easiest to stitch back together, high-tech materials can also be hand stitched, glued, and put back into action. Tears often occur in areas other than seams, and patching may entail holding a covering piece of material in place while stitching away without the advantages of a sail loft pit and sewing machine.

Use alcohol to clean the repair area, and once dry, coat the patch and sail with contact cement. The adhesive allows you to stick the patch in place and keep it from moving during the hand stitching. Double-sided sailmaker's tape will do the same job for small patches,

but contact cement has a more tenacious grip. Alternatively, you can use 3M Fast Cure 5200 to bond the patch in place. This approach harnesses the serious sticking quality of this polyurethane adhesive-sealant and lessens the need for multiple rows of hand stitching (in high-stress sail areas, e.g., around reef points, use the sealant and stitches). The cure time for regular 3M 5200 is a day or more, however, which limits its use, but Fast Cure 5200 will speed up the process. Ideally, use scrap lengths of the same material your sails are made from to execute the repair.

Your sail repair ditty bag should contain an array of sail needles and palms for lefties as well as right-handers, and several awls or punches to make penetrating thick, multilayer sail corners and reef points a little easier. You'll also need thread and twine of different deniers and strengths to use along the edges of nylon webbing, along with sticky-back nylon cloth for spinnaker repair. Choose other tools of the trade that fit both your budget and tool locker. For example, I've always carried a hand-cranked sewing machine for long-term cruising, as much for repairing awnings and sail covers as for sails. While not a necessity, it comes in handy more often than you might think.

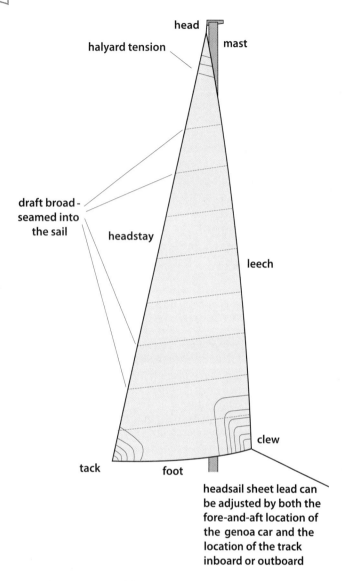

head
halyard tension
mast
draft broad-
seamed into
the sail
headstay
leech
clew
tack
foot
**headsail sheet lead can
be adjusted by both the
fore-and-aft location of
the genoa car and the
location of the track
inboard or outboard**

🏴 *There are several factors that influence sail shape. Sails,
like the headsail shown here, have draft built into them
so that drive and force can be adjusted. Using the right
combination of halyard tension and sheeting angles for
different conditions separates the novice from the advanced
sailor. (Joe Comeau)*

overhead clearance. But for me the key variable involves how much mainsail area a crew can handle.
Reefing a bit ahead of time is a noble goal, but sooner
or later a crew is caught with the boat on its ear, dras-
tically overcanvassed. On a fractionally rigged boat
with its big mainsail, the resulting fire drill can be
daunting. If we divide the sail plan into a somewhat
smaller mainsail, a headsail with masthead hoist,
and a staysail on a stay landing partway up the mast,
we end up with a more manageable sail area. The
reaching ability and versatility of a double-headsail
rig with less mainsail area also makes sense because
cruisers set spinnakers less frequently.

Even rigid commercial aircraft wings undergo significant shape changes as a pilot adjusts flaps and transitions from takeoff to cruising mode. Likewise, sailors
have a variety of sail-shaping options to fine-tune
the shape the sailmaker cut, sewed, or molded into
the sail. For example, halyard tension controls luff
sag on a variety of sails, and on a headsail the sheet
lead angle affects the shape of the sail. The nuances
of these and many other controls are the mark of a
seasoned sailor.

Mainsail Controls

The sheet, outhaul, traveler, and vang make up a useful foursome in the mainsail-shaping routine. In a
fractionally rigged boat, adjusting backstay tension
also helps shape the sail.

Mainsheet

The mainsheet is as elemental to sailing as a spoon
to a kitchen. Its primary role is to control the mainsail's angle of attack. As every sailor knows, when the
sheet is too loose the sail flogs, and when hauled in
too tightly, air flow over the leech becomes turbulent
and the sail stalls. The trick is finding the sweet spot
between these two easily defined trim points and
maintaining that angle as the breeze heads, lifts, increases, or decreases and as the boat intentionally or
inadvertently changes course.

Telltales are the mainsheet trimmer's best friend
when sailing close-hauled or on a close reach, but
there's plenty of debate on how many should be
stuck on a sail and where they should go. I am happy
with three or four telltales equidistantly spaced on
the leech. Some sailors prefer several rows flowing
and fluttering telltales at equal heights along the
body of the main. A good rule of thumb is to not
stick more on the sail than you actually use to make
performance decisions. If you sail with in-boom or
in-mast furling, telltales will be hard to maintain.

Sail shaping and trim upwind focuses on using
all the "strings" available to coax all the telltales
into even, parallel, fore-and-aft streaming, which
indicates a smooth flow of air over the foil. When I
say "all the telltales," I include both the windward-
and leeward-side telltales of each pair sewn or taped
into the body of the sail.

Telltales become less useful when you're sailing
deeper than a beam reach—especially if the mainsail
is restricted by swept-back spreaders—unless your
boat has a freestanding rig as in a Nonsuch catboat.
Such a boat can keep lift in the equation and fly the

telltales on a broad reach. And extremely fast boats, such as agile, light multihulls, can head 150 degrees off the true wind yet keep the mainsail trimmed for a beam reach and the telltales streaming happily. They accomplish this because they pull the apparent wind forward by virtue of their speed (one of the reasons no one builds spinnakers for iceboats).

Important mainsail trim factors include the location and geometry of the mainsheet. As a convenience for the crew moving about in a cockpit, many cruiser/racers prefer a mid-boom sheeting arrangement that keeps lines and blocks out of the way. This arrangement places the traveler forward of the companionway hatch, where a dodger or bimini doesn't intrude on the movement of the mainsheet. Unfortunately, because of the location

of the attachment of the blocks to the boom, this configuration provides less leverage. In addition, it places the sheet blocks too close to the vang attachment for either to have maximum effect. This is why end-boom sheeting evolved as the preferred option among performance sailors and many long-distance passagemakers.

The mainsheet tackle arrangement and its location in the cockpit also comprise an important safety consideration. Research shows that the boom and related tackle are the major cause of serious sailboat accidents at sea. In fact, accidental and intentional jibes lead the list of hardware-induced sailboat fatalities. Boats with the traveler placed nearby aft of the companionway hatch are especially prone to such hazards.

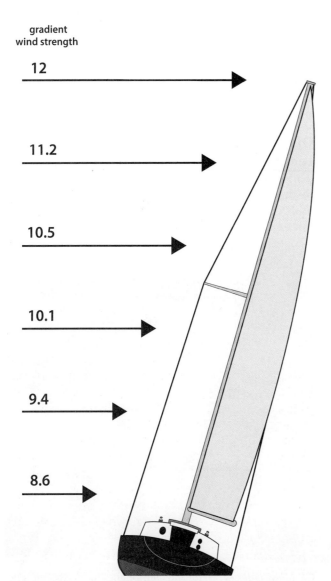

gradient wind strength

12

11.2

10.5

10.1

9.4

8.6

The gradient wind strength is the velocity distribution between the base of the sail plan and the masthead. The wind is usually stronger aloft than at deck level. (Joe Comeau)

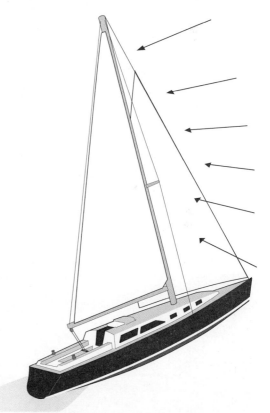

Because the wind is stronger at the masthead than at deck level, the resulting vertical gradient affects apparent wind and is consequently an important trimming issue. Wind shear causes changes in velocity and direction related to the height above the deck. Optimum sail power often requires adding twist to maintain an efficient angle of attack at differing heights above the deck. Twist is added by easing the vang, hauling the traveler to windward, and easing the mainsheet. This combination loosens the tension in the leech and allows the upper part of the sail to twist to leeward and trims to the wind-shear-affected direction change. Note that the angle of attack is actually more obtuse than it would be if increased velocity aloft were the only factor involved. On the other tack, the extreme wind shear would have the opposite effect and require a tighter leech and eased vang.

The U.S. Naval Academy's 44-foot sloops designed by McCurdy and Rhodes provide a case in point. These rugged, seaworthy vessels have a mainsheet traveler mounted on top of a bridge deck just aft of the companionway. In numerous documented instances, disoriented crew coming on deck for a night watch have ended up tangling with a sheet during a tack or jibe. These incidents have resulted in several serious head injuries. If your mainsheet and traveler are similarly located, then carefully train crewmembers about this potential hazard. The end-boom sheeting, longer boom, and lengthened mainsail foot of the David Pedrick–designed Navy 44 MKII have resulted in improved sail handling and created a safer, more obstacle-free passage between cabin and cockpit.

Some designers address the mainsheet and boom hazard by elevating the boom and adding a multipurpose arch at the stern that keeps the traveler and sheet well above the cockpit. This solution imposes extra weight and windage, however, and it also sacrifices mainsail area unless the rig is made taller to compensate. In that case, however, we see an undesirable rise in the centers of effort and gravity.

Outhaul

The outhaul is another important sail-shape control. Tension this outhaul to flatten the sail (reduce its draft) in a fresh breeze, and loosen it to increase draft in light conditions. A rough rule of thumb defines a flat mainsail as one with less than a 1:10 ratio of depth to chord length, while a full shape ratio is

◖ *A custom International Measurement System (IMS rating rule and handicap system) race boat with end-boom sheeting has its traveler just forward of the helm, giving mainsheet and jib trimmers some needed room between each other. Dual sheet-lead complications can accompany this setup, however.*

◖ *Mid-boom sheeting aboard this Island Packet 460 does not control leech twist as effectively as boom-end sheeting, but does clear the tackle from the cockpit and lessens the hazards caused by an uncontrolled jibe.*

◖ *Many cruisers run all sail control lines to the cockpit, and the outhaul control line (far right in photo) offers an easy response to oscillations in wind velocity. (See Chapter 6 for more on rope clutches.)*

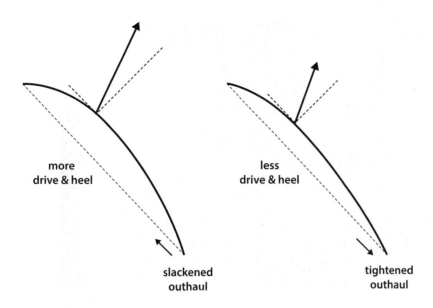

more drive & heel

slackened outhaul

less drive & heel

tightened outhaul

The outhaul is a key power-up and power-down control for mainsail shaping. You can increase the draft of your mainsail in light air by slackening the outhaul (left-hand illustration), providing more drive and heel. The more tension you apply (right-hand illustration), the flatter the sail becomes, depowering it in a building breeze, lessening the driving force of the sail, and reducing the vessel's heeling angle. (Joe Comeau)

about 1:6. Flatter sails usually point a little higher but produce much less lift.

The best outhaul configuration is a line run in the boom using a multipart tackle to make it easier to tension the foot of the sail. The mainsail clew-attachment hardware, especially on a loose-footed sail, endures considerable loading, and when it's time to flatten the sail, it's best to ease the sheet enough to depower the sail—spill the breeze—prior to hauling on the outhaul tackle. An exit point of the outhaul line on the bottom of the boom and within a few feet of the gooseneck allows crew to easily use it from the cockpit on either tack and on any point of sail.

Traveler

The mainsheet traveler allows more shaping control of the mainsail but often involves compromise. The traveler carriage, or car, moves athwartships along the traveler track, allowing the mainsheet attachment point to be moved to either side of the vessel's centerline. This configuration improves the shape of the main on various points of sail. Some smaller sailboats don't come with travelers, but as you evolve as an experienced sailor, you'll want to seriously consider adding one.

The ideal traveler is curved and runs from rail to rail, a combination that's hard to fit on anything but a hardcore race boat or a multihull. A typical compromise uses a shorter traveler—usually straight. But when the traveler's length shrinks to around 2 feet, the cost-versus-usefulness calculation swings in favor of no traveler at all.

Trimming only with a sheet jointly affects both the mainsail's angle of attack and the downward pressure on its leech. This secondary effect of straightening the leech becomes more pronounced as the boom approaches the centerline, and depending upon the wind conditions, you'll find the effect either welcome or undesirable. The traveler provides a way to fine-tune the leech. In light air, for example, with the vertical gradient of the wind most noticeable (see illustration on page 179), you might find an open leech and lots of mainsail twist helpful; in this situation you'll want to minimize leech tension, best accomplished by moving the traveler car to windward and lightly trimming the sheet. (A sail with a lot of twist is more open at the upper part of the leech; see the illustration on page 182.)

Since a traveler involves compromise, put a great deal of thought into setting it up the right way. Despite decades of attempts to streamline the process of hauling the carriage from one side to the other, a block and tackle remains the best answer. Cars on ball bearings have less friction and make hauling the boom toward the weather rail feasible, even with the sail trimmed while beating to weather in a breeze.

Boom Vang

The boom vang is the unsung hero of mainsail shape. Its major role is to control the boom's vertical angle to influence leech twist. In essence it behaves like an accelerator, allowing a crew to flatten the leech and power up when sailing off the wind. On the wind, the mainsheet and traveler can control the vertical

A well-constructed, ball-bearing traveler car allows a mainsail under load to be hauled in or eased without adjusting the sheet. This maintains leech tension and twist while allowing the sail's angle of attack to be altered.

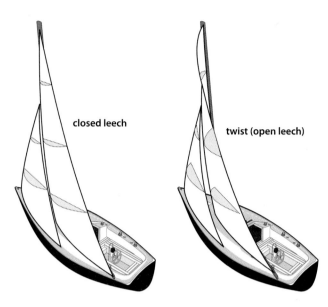

A sail with lots of twist is open at the upper leech, spilling power aloft. A sail with little twist is more powerful, but in light air one way to drive the boat forward is by encouraging the right amount of sail twist. (Joe Comeau)

mainsheet traveler to leeward

As seen on this Alerion Sport 33, on a deep reach or run, the traveler is "dumped" to leeward. It takes a long traveler across a wide deck to get an optimum mainsheet lead. The less distance the traveler extends from the centerline, the more leech twist develops, which then necessitates more vang tension to reduce the twist.

and horizontal boom angles, influencing the sail's angle of attack, its leech shape, and even its draft or fullness.

The vang, nevertheless, also plays a role on a weather leg. One-design sailors learned the art of vang sheeting long ago. It involves a heavy-air technique in which vang tension flattens the sail through mast bend while at the same time removing twist from the leech and shedding excess wind. Depowering a mainsail can be accomplished in several ways. An

often seen approach twists off the top by easing the vang. However, in a really strong breeze that can lead to too much flutter, even flogging aloft, some sailors prefer instead to flatten the sail shape with outhaul and vang and ease the sheet to spill breeze along the entire leech. This is the Rod Stephens approach to trimming *Puffin*'s mainsail, as noted in Chapter 1. With this trimming technique, you use the mainsheet only to control the horizontal boom angle. Through a proactive approach to using a vang, a crew can help tame rolling, lessen seam chafe, and work miracles to help keep the top leech telltale flying. A rigid vang can also unload the boom in light air, opening up the leech of the sail to give it more power and twist.

In essence, the boom acts like a lever being lifted by the energy of the mainsail; the vang attachment point becomes a fulcrum for that lever. When used with a mid-boom mainsheet, the vang attachment must be even closer to the gooseneck than the sheet block. This gives—literally—the short end of the stick and a correspondingly higher load. Most manufacturers try to incorporate a 30- to 45-degree vang-boom angle. However, on long booms this angle range can still leave the vang unfavorably leveraged, requiring a larger vang and stouter mast and boom support points.

Overtensioning an adjustable backstay and/or hauling in on the vang tackle (and mainsheet tackle) can overbend a mast, causing performance-robbing wrinkles to radiate from the clew of the sail. For this reason, many crews handle on-the-wind heavy air with an eased vang instead of using the dinghy sailor's technique of vang sheeting. An eased vang also allows the crew to depower the mainsail by using the sheet and traveler to trim the lower portion of the sail while the top portion twists open, spilling the breeze. However, when the need to depower the main becomes so great that you're applying enough backstay or vang tension to cause distortion wrinkles, it's time to reef the sail.

When reaching in light or heavy air, however, the vang owns the show and controls twist to keep the top batten parallel to the boom. The wider the sheeting angle (the horizontal angle of the boom), the less effectively the mainsheet controls the boom's vertical angle. This simple geometric fact justifies the addition of a boom vang. In addition, the ability of a rigid vang to "float" or unload the weight of the boom from the sail during light-air ghosting has significant value as well as making reefing and sail dousing easier.

When used in conjunction with the traveler, a boom vang goes a long way to help the crew cope with wind sheer, which can cause the apparent wind direction to vary over the short distance from deck to masthead. By carefully controlling leech twist with the traveler/vang combination, the mainsail trimmer can shape the sail and coax all the trailing-edge telltales to stream aft. Without question, both cruisers and racers have a close friend in the vang. When faced with the choice of a simple block and tackle, a

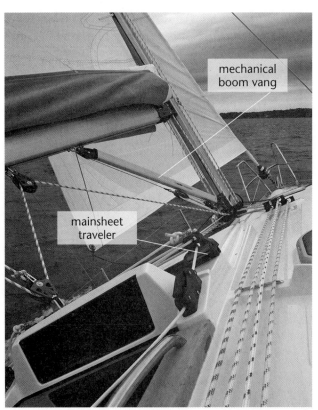

A mechanical boom vang can flatten the leech of a sail on a reach or run, but its role on the wind is limited if the mainsail has mid-boom sheeting, as shown here, because its boom attachment is too close to the gooseneck and the sheet's net effect is in part a vang-like function.

A rigid vang is usually comprised of a heavy-duty stainless steel spring held inside a telescoping tube. A block-and-tackle arrangement vangs the boom when needed to tension the sail leech, and when released, the compressed spring expands, turning the strut into a boom support.

rigid vang, or a high-end hydraulic system, the rigid vang is the right path for those looking for a significant performance upside, modest to moderate cost, and user-friendly simplicity.

Dual Sail Trim—Main and Headsail Telltales All Streaming

Jib or genoa trim often receives more attention than mainsail trim. Most sailors trim the headsail and steer to its luff telltales. However, tandem sail trim is a better approach: considering the air flowing over all sails and examining how each foil shape interacts with the other(s). When sailing upwind, for example, it makes sense to trim the jib initially and then fine-tune the mainsail. The sail plan is properly trimmed when headsail luff telltales and mainsail leech telltales all stream aft. To accomplish this, it may be necessary to twist the mainsail leech or change the position of the genoa car. Ideally, this dual trim effort is performed while holding the boat close to its desired course.

It's worth repeating that the first step in setting up the headsail(s) in cruising trim is making sure the vessel is on course when the sail(s) are set. This may seem too obvious to mention, but it's surprising how easy it is to wander 10 or 15 degrees off course while

TAKING CARE OF YOUR VANG

When the sail is furled, a rigid vang becomes a gas-cylinders-and-spring-equipped compression strut supporting the weight of the boom. A rigid vang should not be used to support the weight of a doused and covered mainsail, however. Rather, before leaving the boat, a main halyard or topping lift needs to be set up at the end of the boom and tensioned to lessen the compression load on the rigid vang. This will decrease the chances of "spring memory" problems or damage to the seals in a gas cylinder. Otherwise, prolonged boom weight induces downward pressure that over time can damage a mechanical vang's internal components.

Gooseneck, mast, and boom attachment-point failures are usually associated with poorly engineered and installed reinforcements. All such hardware must effectively spread the loads associated with using a vang, including both wind- and seaway-induced forces. Not only is it vital to keep the stress and strain well within the confines of the hardware's safe working load ratings, but it's also vital to consider a mechanical vang's duty cycle. Ocean racing on a 24/7 basis requires a heavier-duty unit than you'd need for club racing on occasional weekends. The real enemy is metal fatigue caused by cyclical loading. The more hours the gear is in use and the more oceanic the conditions encountered, the more logical it is to choose the next size larger vang and fittings, which are more rugged than those associated with inshore use.

Many booms have welded lugs for vang attachment; this is a good mounting approach as long as these anchoring points spread vang loads over a sufficient area. Welded lugs eliminate the need to drill holes in the boom or spar, and a topping plate or internal doubler eliminates a potential point of additional stress. Many slotted spars come with sliding lugs for vang and sheet attachment, which are adequate in some cases and not in others, depending on the forces involved and the ruggedness of the sliding lugs. More often than not, additional mounting hardware is needed, and most rigid-vang manufacturers offer custom fittings to mount their products. Thin-walled masts and booms need attachment plates of larger surface area to more effectively spread the compression and tension loads of the vang. If you have carbon spars, you should consult with the manufacturer for detailed hardware mounting guidelines.

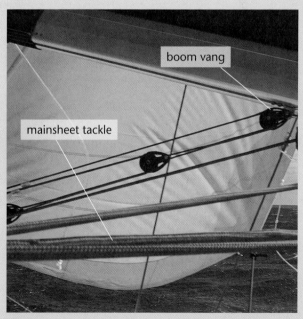

Vang and sheet loads can be significant, and the hardware they attach to must be capable of at least handling the safe working load of the line used. In this case, a slot in the underside of the boom carries eye fittings for the boom vang and mainsheet tackles. Boom types abound: cast alloy boom ends and extruded slots (top and bottom) are found on many production boats. Much more expensive custom alloy spars use machined and welded ends and fittings, creating lighter, stronger spars. Even more costly autoclaved carbon spars have a still higher strength to weight ratio.

boom vang

mainsheet tackle

you're trimming the headsail. A seasoned trimmer checks the course with the helmsman or looks at a handy bulkhead-mounted compass just before putting away the winch handle.

Headsail telltales fly with the apparent wind and let you know when sails are in trim. The luff telltales, usually three groupings ascending the leading edge of the headsail, communicate whether you're under- or overtrimmed and whether the sheet car lead needs to be moved to revise sail shape. All's well when all telltales on both sides stream in resolutely fore and aft. When the windward telltale yarn tips up, you're undertrimmed or pinching too high, so ease off your steering or trim in the headsail. When the leeward telltales start to misbehave, you're either overtrimmed or steering too deep. Breaks in telltales near the top of the sail (when lower telltales are streaming) indicate shear aloft that's a header; tightening the leech by moving the jib car forward a bit may solve the problem.

In light air, moving the genoa sheet car forward tightens the leech and, in conjunction with slightly easing the sheet, powers up the sail. Moving the car aft tightens the foot and loosens the leech; in heavy air, this allows the top of the sail to twist open, spilling air and depowering the headsail.

As a roller-furling sail is reefed, the sheet-lead geometry changes and you'll likely need to reposition the genoa track car. If you don't do this repositioning, then the leech or the foot of the sail ends up either too slack or too tight. Start with a quick bit of sheet trim that gets most of the telltales aligned horizontally, then fiddle with the car lead to align all the telltales even better. Before fine-tuning the trim, check with the helmsman or the autopilot to ensure the vessel holds a steady course.

Shorthanded cruisers tend to leave much of the steering offshore to an autopilot or self-steering vane, so it's especially important to balance the helm. More often than not, you'll use a slightly more eased mainsail than when hand steering to reduce the load on the drive system of the vane or autopilot. On many boats meeting this goal might require reefing and reducing headsail area a bit earlier than when hand steering.

Around-the-buoys racers trim and shape sails constantly to compensate for shifts in wind direction and velocity, while cruisers are usually less concerned about reacting to shifts and minor anemometer fluctuations. On the other hand, many sailors find reasons to add various hardware: a genoa track that's adjustable under load, barber-hauler hardware to adjust the jib lead inboard and outboard, a sprit for setting light-air sails, or an endless-line furling gennaker. But ask yourself if you and your crew are ready for the string pulling and attention to sail shape such

A skilled sailor looks at the sails, not the winch, when trimming. At the same time, he or she checks with the person on the helm or takes a peek at the compass to make sure the vessel is on course. Some cruisers like winches close together, while racers cringe at the thought.

installations demand. If the answer is no, you'll likely be better served by gear that delivers more efficient line pull, offers ways to easily secure and free lines, and provides nearly friction-free line movement over blocks (discussed later in this chapter).

Summary of Sail Shaping

Now that the sail controls have been introduced, let's put them to work.

Good sail trim is like a good snapshot—both mark a moment in time when all variables are in harmony. But there's also a moment just before and just after trimming that constantly reshuffles the variables, and recognizing the changes taking place is as important as knowing the strings to pull or the tight lens to use.

The interplay of sheet, traveler, outhaul, vang, halyard, and backstay tension and how to power up in light air and depower in a fresh breeze are critical skills that go hand in hand with noting the factors

SAIL SHAPING AT A GLANCE

Light Air Means Loosening up the Mainsail
- Ease the sheet until the sail luffs and then add a small bit of trim
- Ease the outhaul and the halyard, developing maximum draft
- Ease the vang and twist the leech with the traveler to make all batten-tip telltales fly
- Minimize backstay tension

Light Air Headsail Logistics Mean Optimizing the Lead
- Ease the halyard to add draft
- Set the car lead so all telltales fly
- Move the lead inboard or out (barber haul) according to the point of sail

Increasing Breeze Means Depowering the Sails and/or Adding a Reef
- Tighten the halyard, tension the outhaul, pump up backstay tension
- Twist off the top of the mainsail by easing the vang and sheet and haul the traveler to windward
- Option two: tighten the vang, flatten the sail, ease the sheet to spill the breeze along entire leech

Depowering Headsails (Often Better to Reef or Change Down In Sail Size)
- Flatten the sail with halyard tension and increased backstay tension
- Move the lead car back to open up the upper leech and spill the breeze
- Overtrim when heading on a deep reach

Coping with Swell or Chop
- Don't reef deeper than necessary
- Use the sails to dampen roll moment
- Usually one tack affords better motion than the other
- A small change in boat speed can make motion more tolerable

Off the Wind Trim
- Ease the halyards and trim to the telltales; set a preventer
- Often add more sail area
- Ease tension of the backstay
- Avoid dead downwind sailing; deep reaching is more efficient

Larger Changes in Wind Velocity and Sea State
- When cruising, don't wait too long to reef and/or change sails
- Use heavy-weather sails that are cut and set flatter and built stronger
- Make sure the tack and clew are well secured

in play. The accompanying sidebar summarizes how to respond to changing wind and sea conditions in order to keep the telltales streaming.

DOUSING AND REEFING THE MAINSAIL

The mainsail remains the beating heart of most sail plans and the bane of many shorthanded cruising sailors. Today, boat buyers look for bigger boats, and the larger designs have modern rigs that sport larger mainsails than ever before. This trend toward putting more sail area in the mainsail allows one jib to serve a larger wind range, which can be a good thing. But the flip side is that handling the larger, heavier mainsail becomes a greater chore. While all sailors become familiar with setting and dousing the main, many become anxious when facing unanticipated reefing or the fire drill of having to suddenly douse the main in a thunderstorm.

At the active, go-for-it end of the spectrum are racers and young, fit cruisers who lean toward a "stick shift" version of simplicity afloat. Their boats sport a mainsail equipped only with a halyard, topping lift (or vang support), and slab reefing, without sail setting or flaking aids and furling gizmos. This is the lightest, fastest, least complicated mainsail setup. It's at its best with the sail hoisted and the vessel and crew happily underway. When it comes time to reef or douse the sail, however, this configuration is less desirable when it imitates a bedsheet on a clothesline levitated by a gale. As crew release halyard tension to drop the sail, only wind direction determines where the leech will go, and mainsail reefing and flaking becomes a substantial chore, especially with a bolt-roped main whose luff also is not held captive.

At the other end of the spectrum, a cruising couple can become daunted by the overpowering heft of a very large modern mainsail. They may end up day-sailing their boat with only the jib unfurled. Others spend tens of thousands of dollars to automate mainsail furling with a specially designed mast or boom. In addition to the considerable expense, these in-mast and in-boom furling systems add more weight and complexity to a boat's rig while decreasing the efficiency of the sail plan. Such trade-offs can make sense on large boats, but less costly and more sailing-friendly alternatives exist for 30- to 45-foot boats, stacking the odds in your favor when the time comes to wrestle the mainsail into repose.

In the battle to tame the main, lazyjacks, sail cover/lazyjack combinations, and Dutchman systems continue to grow in popularity. These are cost-effective solutions for small and medium-sized sailboats.

Lazyjacks

For centuries, sailors have appreciated the value of lazyjacks, a set of light lines on both sides of the sail that catch the mainsail as it's lowered and coax it into a stack on top of the boom. When you release the halyard, the sail settles itself on the boom as if guided by an invisible hand—or at least that's how it works when all goes well. When lazyjacks are properly set up and you follow a few simple guidelines, they're your friend, every bit as much as they were to the shorthanded schoonermen who coasted New England a century ago.

On the other hand, a lazyjack may snag a batten tip when the sail is hoisted. A loose lazyjack can even snag a spreader tip just before the crew jibes in the middle of a dark night, and in the moments that follow the crew rapidly becomes jaundiced about the system. While I don't use lazyjacks on my own boat I frequently run across them on other boats. The bottom line is, if you don't want to chafe your sails to an early death, you gather the lazyjacks and bring them forward to the mast when you're underway. They slat against the spar and all too often tangle up, making redeployment something between a nuisance and a nightmare. But once back in place, they make dropping a mainsail a whole lot easier.

The irony is that lazyjacks are assumed to be a merit badge of the open ocean voyager, when in truth they are sailors who hoist and douse sail the least. Some like the foot-of-the-sail-gathering convenience offered by lazyjacks, but they can be nothing but trouble when it comes time to hoist a storm trysail. If you decide lazyjacks are a must, you need a routine for setting and unsetting the "jacks" in order to minimize sail chafe and eliminate snags on spreaders or other protrusions. You'll also need to keep the boat or at least the boom headed exactly into the wind when hoisting and (to a lesser extent) dousing sail. One $10 mini block slamming against an alloy spar can ruin a $1,500 paint job.

Sail Cover/Lazyjack Combinations

Lazyjacks used in conjunction with a canvas hammock on the boom make mainsail dousing more user-friendly. When you release the halyard, the lazyjacks guide folds of the mainsail into the waiting canvas cradle. A full-length zipper turns the slab sides into a sail cover; in theory, the need to wrestle the sail into flakes over the boom is gone. As with all too-good-to-be-true innovations, however, there are downsides. When the sail is set, the canvas and lazyjacks remain exposed, hanging unused, causing chafe and some windage. When hoisting the main-

sail, care is needed to avoid catching a batten end under a lazyjack or part of the canvas pack. When and if it comes time to hoist a storm trysail, you must clear the tackle associated with the lazyjacks out of the way. For many sailors, the convenience outweighs these concerns. More and more boats use these pack-and-jacks combinations.

How big a mainsail a crew can handle depends on their size and physical abilities and the automation aboard. A decade ago, cruising sailors began to switch from slab reefing mainsails to roller furling mainsails at about 500 sq. ft. Today, boatbuilders have dropped the size to about 350 sq. ft. Megayacht crews like the ones on this 140-foot ketch become familiar with their furling systems and have backup plans should the system foul.

A sail cover/lazyjack combination makes good sense for coastal cruisers and daysailors. Many long-distance voyagers, however, prefer to do without the chafe and nuisance of the extra gear. They only set the main on departure, and unless the storm trysail is needed, it remains up for the duration of the passage.

The Dutchman System

The Dutchman furling system simplifies the lazyjack concept and makes mainsail handling even more user-friendly. It does require some additional sail work and minor rigging additions, but the cost-benefit trade-off seems a bargain. At the heart of the system are three or four monofilament lines clamped at their top ends to the topping lift and descending vertically through fairleads in the sail to small tabs at its foot, just above the boom. The mainsail is fitted with grommets that allow these lines to be laced through the sail. The doused mainsail simply slides from full hoist to the boom as efficiently as a fireman sliding down a brass pole. If lazyjacks can tame a bucking-bronco main, a Dutchman system turns it into a lamb.

Simple and functional, the system can even be retrofitted on a boat with a rigid or high-tech hydraulic vang that supports the boom when the mainsail is

The nearly invisible monofilament lines of the Dutchman system cause a mainsail to behave like a cooperative puppet on a string—flaking itself submissively while being lowered. The downside some sailors and sailmakers complain about is stitch and sail cloth chafe, a particular issue for sailors who spend days, weeks, seam months underway. As well, if the sail cloth is as stiff as plywood, all bets are off.

stowed—simply rig a topping lift to attach the Dutchman lines. The best bet is a topping lift that functions like a conventional halyard and can be set up, taken down, and adjusted at will. This setup is better than one with a fixed attachment near the masthead, which would eliminate the Dutchman's adjustability. A topping lift can become wedged under the main halyard and headboard, and even prevent the mainsail from lowering when you release the main halyard. This doesn't happen often, but when it does, you simply release the topping lift and the sail will drop despite the jam. (With a topping lift fixed at both ends, you'd need to send someone aloft to free the jam; if it is fixed only at the top but can be loosened at its boom end, the jammed line at the top can be freed.)

True, the Dutchman system has some flaws, some of which are shared with other systems. A batten can snarl on the topping lift during a tack, and the monofilament lines can and do occasionally snap, requiring a repair that is easy but one you must be prepared to make.

Dousing Systems
—Sail Cover, Reefing, and
Storm Trysail Implications

Once the sail has been lowered, both lazyjacks and the Dutchman system require a modified sail cover. For the Dutchman system there's usually a series of small secondary zippers that accommodate the vertical monofilament lines; with lazyjacks, you may need to ease the lazyjack hoists a little in order to fit a conventional sail cover. There is no such problem with a hammock-style jack-and-cover system (see above).

Either system allows easy use of reefing lines. A stack of luff cars on the mainmast track can get pretty high, however, making a boom attached reefing hook impractical for securing the reefed tack. A good way around this involves running a tack pendant through a reefing block attached to a well-reinforced ring in the sail's luff near the reefed tack position; the tack pendant is tightened and secured in a rope clutch anchoring the tack. Make sure the line leads are fair and chafe is minimized. Outhaul and halyard loads should be entirely on the reefing block, not on the mainsail slides, slugs, or track cars.

In many of these setups, the real challenge is how the crew would cope with extreme conditions and the need to set a storm trysail. The Dutchman system, when set up with an adjustable, halyard-like topping lift, allows the easiest transition to a storm trysail. Once we've lowered the mainsail, we need only slacken the topping lift and gather up the loose monofilament lines. This clears the area aft of the mast and allows you to set a storm trysail. The same can be done with lazyjacks but in both cases you're left with a lot of failing cordage ready to snag the head of the storm trysail as it is being hoisted.

Most sailors can handle mainsail sizes up to about 250 or 300 square feet easily enough, with flaking aids optional rather than essential. From the top end of that range up to about 500 square feet, lazyjacks or a Dutchman system can be as valuable as an extra crewmember. In one extensive test series with which I was involved, the Dutchman system got our crew's most enthusiastic nod of approval, even though both systems improved mainsail handling significantly.

Roller-Furling Mainsails

Furling mainsails originated as modified headsail furlers attached aloft to an aft extension on the masthead and below to a beefed-up bracket at the gooseneck. These first units were relatively inexpensive, and the mainsail furled and unfurled relatively easily. Unfortunately, however, the aerodynamics and engineering left much to be desired. With only top and bottom attachment points, sailing loads tended to bow the mast and cause it to pump, placing excessive loads on the tack and head attachments along with the lower rear shroud. Along with these detrimental rig loads came another unwelcome byproduct, a luff sag that made the flat, roachless mainsail even less efficient. All in all, the first round of mainsail furlers gave a good idea a bad reputation.

The next development came in the form of an add-on housing surrounding a furling rod that attached to the original mainsail track at the trailing edge of the mast. These systems transmitted mainsail loads along the entire column. While Selden and others developed and pioneered this second generation of mainsail furlers, Ted Hood introduced his revolutionary in-mast Stoway furling system; this idea mainstreamed the concept of mainsail furling.

In simplest terms, retracting a mainsail inside a mast is a challenge not unlike retracting a window shade, easier to describe than to engineer. The foil in the center of the sail housing holds the luff much as a headsail furler does. A swivel at the top allows the gearing or other twisting mechanism at the base to wind up the sail as a window shade rolls up for storage. The mast must also provide for rigging attachments, spreader connections, and electrical wire runs and be able to resist the compression and bending loads caused by the interplay between the sail's power and the vessel's righting moment. And a mast slot size that might be optimal in other respects can cause a harmonic whistling that would drive a crew nuts. With a hand in both mast building and sailmaking, Hood was better positioned than anyone to develop

Ted Hood mainstreamed in-mast roller-furling, developing the Stoway concept from his background as a sailor-sailmaker-boatbuilder. The downsides—sail shape and extra weight aloft—are offset by the likelihood of having the right sail area set. We still see many of his 1970s-era rigs in use today, like the one shown here, with the main partially furled.

FURLING MISHAPS AND POWER WINCHES

I recall a sail up Lake Michigan aboard the Harken 60-foot prototype *Procyon*. The crew was deploying the huge freestanding furling mainsail when the inhaul abruptly locked up while the outhaul power winch continued to operate. In little more than a second or so, tension increased to the point of tearing the clew and all its reinforcement off the sail. During a transatlantic crossing, the crew of a sloop named *Harmony II* developed a similar issue when water got into the furling relay box and short-circuited the outhaul winch, leading to mainsail damage and a small electrical fire. Many savvy skippers install a kill switch in the cockpit just in case a power winch malfunctions. Large, shiny power winches seem benign when the power is off. But once the power is on they exert tremendous torque, and serious injuries can occur if a piece of clothing or a hand is caught under the line wrapping around the drum. With a little extra vigilance, a power winch can be as useful and welcome as an extra crewmember.

Early drive mechanisms for boom furlers were exterior to the spar, and were coupled via a universal joint to a spindle running through the mast to the slotted boom. Later models have the motor inside the boom. The foot of the sail is attached to the spindle, and the sail is hoisted, furled, or reefed simply by hauling or easing the halyard to rotate the spindle. Note the "sunhat" shielding the exposed head of the sail from harmful UV rays.

The infinitely reefable in-mast furling mainsail can be fine-tuned for existing conditions—such as the gusty ones of this day—and readjusted with the push of a button or pull on a manual reefing line. Hanging halyard tails on mast-mounted winches remains a valid way to cluster seldom-handled running rigging.

a successful system, and he captured a new market in sailboats ranging from 35-footers to megayachts.

The next advance in furling technology came from Hood again, this time stemming from his interest in improving the aerodynamics of a furling mainsail. His StoBoom furler was another version of window-shade engineering. In this case, the wind-up action takes place around an in-boom furler rather than an in-mast furler, and the main is hoisted with a conventional halyard system. An electric or hydraulic winch can provide the hoisting power, but it is critical to ensure all aspects of the furling system are aligned and behaving appropriately.

This rendition of mainsail furling gear has the advantage of working with a full-battened, big-roach mainsail along with operational flexibility. Even if the furler fails, for example, the sail can be lowered in the conventional fashion. The downside includes the heavy, large-diameter boom. As well, the sail luff must transition from its fully rolled-up boom stowage to the track on the trailing edge of the spar—a trip prone to snags.

The smooth operation of mainsail furling systems depends on a few distinct variables, including the obvious: the design and the engineering quality of the equipment. Fortunately, the industry in general did a good job of picking the right materials for component parts and building the gear with effective quality control. Each design seems to have its own strengths and contingent small set of weaknesses, which quickly surface if users fail to operate the system 100% correctly. Some operational problems can be traced to faulty installation or not matching the size of the unit to the vessel.

When selecting the size of gear to use, the length of the vessel is only a starting point. It's just as important to assess the type of cruising you'll undertake and how hard and how long you'll sail the vessel. The higher and more prolonged the sailing loads on the gear, the more important it is to choose the next larger unit, especially if your boat is near the upper end of the size range for the unit you're considering. Whoever installs this gear needs to be familiar with its nuances, so it's usually better to enlist a rigger who's a rep for the product rather than leaving the job to your local boatyard crew.

Using Mainsail Furling

When you're setting sail with in-mast or in-boom furling, following a few basic rules helps prevent significant problems. The most obvious but most often neglected precaution involves making sure you or some member of the crew watches the sail as you raise/set or douse the sail. This is imperative when you're pushing a button rather than grinding a winch. Traditional winches provide direct feedback, with increased resistance acting as an early warning that a line is not running freely or the sail is snagged. On the other hand, a power winch continues to tension a line until either the switch is released or a circuit breaker blows—or something breaks. The motor won't recognize a hockle in a line or a luff tape that has just pulled out of the mainsail track. The operators of heavy equipment facing similar issues have been trained to visually confirm what's happening around them. Absentmindedly pressing an electric winch button can turn a convenience into a significant disaster very quickly.

Getting along with a modern mainsail furling system includes some key guidelines, one of which involves making sure the sail is neither wildly flogging nor powered up while it is being set or doused. Find the sweet spot between these extremes by controlling the sail's angle of attack with steering and sheeting. A head-to-wind attitude reduces the angle of attack to zero and depowers the sail, but if the mainsheet is tight, falling off just a little will cause the mainsail to begin to fill and power up. Or, you can ease the mainsheet and steer slightly to one side or the other of head to wind (no more than 30 degrees). These strategies help avoid the serious problems that can develop when a powered-up sail is hoisted or doused.

To keep the furled sail compact and prevent loose sail material from jamming in the mast cavity, in-mast furling systems need a small amount of tension on the outhaul as the main is rolled into the spar. A crucial point in the operation of in-boom furlers literally revolves around the tension and feed angle of the luff tape as it ascends toward the track at the gooseneck. Placing too much tension on the halyard may cause the sail to bind in the boom, or failing to ease its furling line smoothly can place an excessive load on the feed point of the track. In both cases, damage can occur. The potential for damage increases if the crew doesn't watch the feed—or can't adequately see it—while a powerful electric or hydraulic winch is engaged (see sidebar page 189). If a large dodger or a pilothouse obscures your view of the mainsail, then move the control lines and pushbuttons to a location with a better view.

In addition, work with your sailmaker to customize a new mainsail for the furling system you intend to use. For example, in-boom furlers allow use of full horizontal battens, a sizable roach, and more draft than an in-mast mainsail can carry. However, the battens must be absolutely parallel to the rotation axis

of the in-boom foil, and the furled sail diameter must fit inside the boom cavity. Sail material matters, too. An in-mast roller-furling mainsail should be made of stiffer yarn-tempered polyester or a higher-modulus material that resists wrinkling. The material, panel pattern, and location of chafe patches on the sail can also be optimized for the furling system.

Associated equipment such as the boom vang or boom support also becomes strategically important, especially with an in-boom furler, which relies on careful control of the angle of the boom to the mast. As this angle varies above or below 90 degrees, the luff of the sail feeding into the track tends to move forward or aft in the boom cavity. For some time, owners of Hood's StoBoom, for example, have sworn that 86 degrees is the optimum boom-mast angle, providing a good lead angle for furling and hoisting. The best boom angle for your system goes hand in hand with developing or maintaining the right halyard tension on the luff as the sail feeds onto or off the track.

In-mast furling is not as sensitive to a few degrees of boom angle one way or the other, and with negligible roach in the sail a topping lift is often ample boom support. Mast bend must be avoided with in-mast furling because the rotating luff rod

The behavior of the luff tape during an in-boom furling process is related to the boom angle. If the tape walks too far aft or forward, track and sail damage can result. Note the preventer tail at the bottom of the picture. Furling booms are heavy, making an unintentional jibe even more dangerous than with an ordinary boom, thus the need for an easily rigged and regularly used preventer.

would contact the slot walls at mid-luff and the foil, part of the mainsail, or both might end up jammed in the slot—a major inconvenience.

Vertical battens allow an in-mast furling mainsail to sport a positive roach, but they also increase the risk of a hang-up in the furling mechanism. If the vertical battens are lengthy and a furling problem occurs at sea, you can imagine what it would be like to try to douse the mainsail. If you choose in-mast furling, consult with your sailmaker about a no-roach mainsail made of stiffer cloth and cut specifically for the furling system.

Mainsail Reefing

Whether cruising or racing, you need someone in charge of sail-area decisions. The skipper, watch captain, or a designated person in charge needs to welcome discussions about whether it's time to tuck a reef or change a sail. However, one person must be responsible for making the call and be accountable for the outcome. Most cruisers sail shorthanded, so the dialogue is streamlined, but the primary challenge involves getting the job done just ahead of the time that it's absolutely necessary. Too much sail area causes high-anxiety fire drills, but too little causes the boat to wallow along underpowered.

Knowing what to change is as important as knowing when to change it. If you're heeling a little too much in a slowly but steadily building breeze, you may simply need to tuck the first reef in the mainsail. But let's say you're ghosting along under full main and genoa and see a fast-moving line of thunderstorms headed your way. At that point, you might need to drop the main entirely and furl up much of the genoa before the line squall rolls over you.

When you see potential for trouble it makes sense to prepare for the worst and see what happens. It's always easier to set sail in response to a storm that fails to materialize than to claw down a sail or roll it in when the gusts approach 50 knots. The skill is knowing how much wind to expect from the towering thunderheads headed your way and how your boat behaves in 30, 40, or 50 knots of wind.

Think of reducing sail like shifting gears on a bicycle. Consider how difficult your situation becomes when you're peddling uphill and have waited too long to downshift. This is why virtually all experienced sailors advise shorthanded cruisers to reef or change sails early. The calculation becomes more complicated for Grand Prix racers, who hate to reef a mainsail. Instead, they depower with vang, mast bend, outhaul, halyard tension, and traveler, shaping the sail with a draft like a sheet of plywood and enough twist to spill much of the breeze. In the worst

gusts, they ease the sheet until the sail teeters on the verge of being flogged to death. When even this fails to depower the rig sufficiently, an exercise in disaster management follows as the crew attempts to get the sail down with battens, seams, and stitching intact. On the other hand, cruisers never relish the thought of having to accomplish such a feat.

When developing your own sail-management plan, first consider your boat's rig and sail inventory and your crew's strength and skill. Then add in the volatility of wind and sea conditions and wild cards such as darkness, heavy rain, and cold air temperatures. The result should be a solid plan for matching the sail area to the conditions.

If you formalize this plan in a written table format, include rows for "on the wind/upwind" and "off the wind/downwind" and columns for various combinations of wind and sea states. In the column for winds under 10 knots you might also include sail material: nylon, lightweight Dacron, or even a high-tech composite spinnaker, gennaker, or drifter/reacher and code sails. Or it may include the phrase "turn on the engine." Toward the other end of the list the storm jib and storm trysail are included. In between, consider the series of sail changes that make sense for both the crew and the design of the vessel. The table on page 195 is an example of one such plan for a moderate-size cruising sailboat.

Slab Reefing

One of the original three sailor competencies (hand, reef, and steer), conventional reefing continues to be highly significant today. Nothing shy of steering clear of a surf-swept reef trumps having the right sail area in play. Too much and a good boat takes on bad habits, and too little and the roll becomes intolerable and the progress abysmal. The pathway to slab reefing success begins with the skills of steering and trimming.

The golden rule of reefing is that it is always easier to shake out a reef than it is to tuck one in, especially if you waited a little too long to reef or forgot to run reef lines before leaving the dock. In fact, if you're sailing shorthanded or singlehanding and the forecast promises a building breeze, you might consider setting a reef before you hoist the sail. If the forecast fizzles and the promised breeze never materializes, simply shake out the reef.

The goal of the reefing process is to depower the main without letting it flog. Cruisers often prefer bearing off a bit to reef, while racers tend to head up and tuck in a faster reef. Offshore, a building seaway makes the technique of turning into the wind to tuck a reef much more problematic. However, by bearing off a bit, the crew keeps the jib driving, and then easing the main allows a balance between fully spilling breeze and flogging the mainsail. Whether there's one person to reef while the autopilot steers or a half dozen crew on hand to speed up progress, the steps are the same. The steps also remain the same whether all of the lines lead to the cockpit or the crew does the reefing at the mast. A topping lift or rigid vang to support the boom when you release halyard tension is a great friend while reefing.

To slab reef, follow these steps:

1. Steer between a close and beam reach—depower the mainsail by easing the sheet.

2. Release the boom vang—an essential step. When this is missed, excess clew pressure can be placed on the sail as the reefing line is tensioned with a winch. Those with a topping lift can haul it up to tip up the outboard end of the boom, thus making reefing easier.

3. Ease the halyard—carefully ease the halyard enough to put the reef tack ring over a horn or haul down the new tack with a reefing line; secure that tack line. Retension the halyard.

   Some sailors prefer a single reefing line that snakes its way from the boom-end clew reef point to the gooseneck where it engages the reef tack ring. In this approach one line hauls down both ends of the sail; it sounds good in theory, but this method makes it difficult to get a properly set sail. This is due to the single reefing line load going to both the tack and clew at the same time and resulting in neither setting snugly in place. Add to this the overly long nature of a single reefing line and you can see why stretch and abrasion become a factor. Worst of all is the tendency with this approach to end up with the tack of the reefed sail set well aft of where it belongs, and excessive loads placed on the cars, slugs, or slides just above the tack. With single-line reefing, a fixed horn or hook is not used and the afterward pull of the combined reef and tack line keeps the tack from ending up right at the gooseneck.

4. Take up the reef—with separate tack and clew lines, a flatter sail shape (essential in heavier weather) is easier to achieve. Prior to pulling home the clew's reefing line, make sure you've fully re-tensioned the main halyard so the luff is tight. If you skip this step, you might end up with the sail's slides, slugs, or the bolt rope torn from the mainsail since the reefing line tension can pull mainsail slides above the tack and cause them to tear free from the sail.

   As the reef line is being winched in, make sure the person handling the sheet has eased the sail to the point where it is on the verge of luffing. The photograph on page 164 illustrates a well-set reef. Note how Butch Ulmer has taught his crew to haul the new clew in so it tightly sets against the boom and the reefed mainsail is flatter than when not reefed.

5. Tension the clew's reef line—use a winch to tension the reefing line, keeping in mind that a big powerful two-speed winch or an even more aggressive electric winch can put a load on the sail that alters its shape or damages the clew. Experienced cruisers use the roll of the vessel to assist the reefing process. By hauling in on the reefing line during the phase of the roll that depowers the sail and pausing as the opposite phase of the roll increases load, less effort accomplishes the task.

6. Gather the foot—the excess sail cloth now at the foot of the sail should be neatly rolled up parallel to the boom and secured with reef ties, using a reef knot but making sure that these reef ties do not encircle the boom. If the clew reef line breaks or is inadvertently released, these ties can damage the sail. When this happens, all of the clew load moves to the light reef tie and the cringle nearest the trailing edge of the sail. The result is often a big hole in the sail, and as the load shifts to the next tie in the sequence, the same thing happens. However, tucking these reef ties around the rolled-up foot and not the boom means that when and if the clew's reefing line lets go, it's easier to control a brief period of non-damaging sail flogging.

7. Tie in an earing—this is a centuries-old trick passed on from schooner sailors. The art of tying

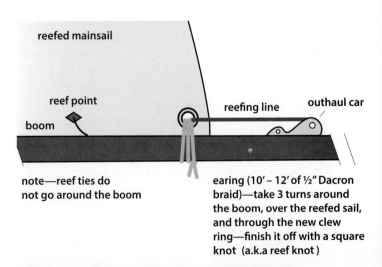

reefed mainsail

reef point

boom

reefing line

outhaul car

note—reef ties do not go around the boom

earing (10'–12' of ½" Dacron braid)—take 3 turns around the boom, over the reefed sail, and through the new clew ring—finish it off with a square knot (a.k.a reef knot)

⚑ *When tying in an earing, set the reef using the reef line, and tie the earing as described in text and shown here. Ease the reefing line so the load is taken by the earing. (Joe Comeau)*

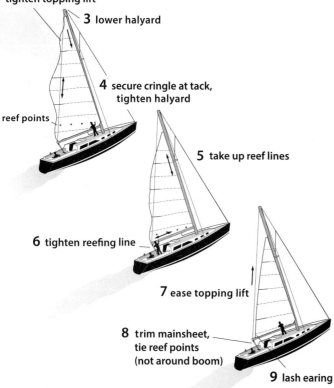

1 ease mainsheet

2 release boom vang, tighten topping lift

3 lower halyard

4 secure cringle at tack, tighten halyard

reef points

5 take up reef lines

6 tighten reefing line

7 ease topping lift

8 trim mainsheet, tie reef points (not around boom)

9 lash earing

Reefing a main under sail using a single-line reefing. (Joe Comeau)

in an earing keeps a reefing line from chafing and guarantees that even if the reef line is inadvertently released or parts, the reef remains set. Run an 8- to 12-foot piece of ½-inch Dacron line through the reefed-down clew and around the boom three times, cinching it up with a square (reef) knot. This new lashing (called an earing) takes the load, so you can then ease the reefing line. Sailing 24/7 with a reef set can cause considerable chafe to a long reef line, but diverting the load to the earing protects the reef line from wear and tear.

8. Clean up—as a final step, coil up the lines, reset the boom vang, and trim the mainsail once back on course. A good ball-bearing block on a strong piece of webbing, instead of reef point clew rings, makes the reef line run more smoothly. When reefing, remember to treat your big winches with respect, and make sure the halyard is taut before hauling home the reef line.

The right hardware and rigging make the reefing process a much easier process:

- Mainsail with heavily reinforced reef points
- Reef tack points with rings and proper setback
- Attached webbing and ball-bearing blocks used as clew points rather than rings
- Tack hook at gooseneck or snapshackle on short pendant
- Boom-end reef lines routed to cockpit or winch near mast

SETTING, DOUSING, AND REEFING HEADSAILS

Roller furling has pushed piston-hanked headsails to the brink of extinction. Today's well-engineered slotted-luff roller furler offers the wonderful compromise option of an easily handled 120% to 135% genoa you can roll out or in to match 12 to 25 knots of breeze. Modern composite materials are better suited for a wide wind range than the Dacron sails of a generation ago. These modern materials, together with improved furling systems, make shorthanded sailing simpler and more fun. We may not always have in place the optimum sail material or shape for a given wind velocity, but except when racing, most crews don't change hanked headsails to match every 5-knot fluctuation in wind velocity.

In light air (below 10 to 12 knots) or heavy air (above 25 to 30 knots), the primary roller-furled genoa no longer works well, so another approach is needed. Before exploring those alternatives, however, let's recap how roller-furling technology got where it is.

Choices in Roller-Furling Units for Headsails

In the late 1970s and early 1980s, Hood, Hyde, Merriman, and Schaefer pioneered the idea of a headsail with window-shade furling. Some of the earliest systems lacked luff-tape foils, relying instead on head and tack drum swivels and a faux headstay sewn into the sail luff. Headstay tension on the early bearing systems accelerated fatigue, resulting in dramatic failures in the form of more than a few dismastings.

During a stormy passage around Africa's Cape of Good Hope I watched a nearby ketch spectacularly flailing its furling headsail from the masthead after the tack drum jaw failed. An inner forestay kept the rig on the boat, but I'll never forget the sight. The marina buzz that resulted from incidents like that provided a boost for a resurgence of interest in piston-hanked sails. Fortunately, Ted Hood and others saw the sense of installing an extruded foil over an existing headstay to allow the latter to hold the mast up while the former handles the furling.

SAIL COMBINATIONS UNDER VARIOUS WIND SPEEDS

Wind Speed Knots	Under 10	11–15	16–20	21–25	26–30	31–35	Over 36
Upwind							
Racer	LT#1/FM	H#1/FM	#3/FM	#3/1RM	#3/2RM	#4/2RM	#4/SJ/ST/3RM
Cruiser	GEN/MS/FM	GEN/FM	GEN/1RM	RGEN/2RM	S/S/2RM	S-S/ST	SJ/ST
Downwind							
Racer	C/A/S/FM	C/A/S/FM	C/A/FM	A/1RM	#3/1RM	#4/2RM	S-S/SJ/ST/3RM
Cruiser	A/S/MS/FM	A/GEN/FM	GEN/1RM	RGEN/2RM	S/S/2RM	S-S/ST/3RM	SJ/ST

KEY
LT#1: light weight 160%
H#1: heavy weight 150%
#3: small genoa
#4: small jib
GEN: genoa
RGEN: reefed genoa
MS: motorsail
FM: full main
1, 2, 3RM: reefs in main
SJ: storm jib
ST: storm trysail
S-S: Solent or staysail
C: code sail
A: asymmetrical spinnaker
S: symmetrical spinnaker

Eventually, the early "roller-fooling" gear evolved into the reliable roller furling in use today. Short-handed crews in a building breeze realized they could handle more sail area with a sound furling unit than by wrestling with piston hanks on a plunging foredeck. Today almost every new cruising boat over 35 feet comes standard with a roller-furling headsail. Top refit priorities for an older boat include the addition of roller furling. Nineteen out of 20 cruisers now sport one or more headsail-furling systems.

Modern headsail furling systems work so well that some sailors ignore routine maintenance, leaving the fittings, end terminals, and central wire or rod to endure year-in, year-out usage without close inspection. However, bearing materials vary from one manufacturer to another. In the early days, rust-prone high-carbon steel bearings were used in housings protected by plastic seals. When these deteriorated and allowed water in, the system would no longer rotate smoothly. If this happened at sea, a dramatic situation likely developed.

To avoid trouble with your present gear, take a close look at the spec sheet for your system and note the bearing descriptions for the top swivel unit and the lower drum. Read the manufacturer's prescribed maintenance procedures, and carefully inspect the system from stem to masthead. Also use the manufacturer's website as a good starting point for technical information.

We view the growth of a keep-it-simple style of roller furling, once the sole domain of Cruising Design, Inc. (CDI), as a pleasant surprise. As a result, integral-halyard furling systems without an upper halyard swivel now comprise about a third of the units seen on 30- to 35-foot sailboats. These furlers attach the head of the jib to a built-in halyard or a fitting at the top of the foil section. All but one of these systems completely eliminate ball and roller bearings and instead rely on simpler bushings to offset thrust

It takes some dedication to find piston-hanked headsails in use these days, but they are cost-effective, reliable, and easy to maintain and replace. The crew of Goshawk—a brand-new classic yacht—sets a high-modulus headsail on a rod-rigging headstay using venerable piston hanks.

There are two categories of furling headsail systems with luff groove extrusions: those that use an existing jib halyard to hoist a head swivel, and a simpler design that builds in a halyard at the top of the luff extrusion and does away with the head swivel. The latter requires a heavier extrusion to handle the compression caused by the built-in halyard's tension. The unit on the far left and the two on the far right are of this design. These units are generally used on smaller vessels, and the majority of the industry remains committed to swivel-headed systems.

The top portion of a furler without a head swivel contains a single or double pulley used in the built-in halyard system. In a DIY installation your first tasks include threading the headstay through each segment of the foil, affixing the bushing, and connecting the segments together.

and axial loads. All these units put the foil sections in compression and have an external halyard directly connected to the top of the upper foil.

Tried and proven at sea, the conventional bearing and head-swivel systems made by Furlex, Harken, Profurl, Reckmann, Schaefer, and others remain the top choice among offshore cruisers and racers. When considering furler options, consider how loads migrate from the line to the drum and into the foil itself. Most manufacturers have worked hard on corrosion abatement in bearings and linkages, picking the right metal for the job and developing foil interlocks that better hold sections together. Concerns about fastener freeze-up over the long term led one manufacturer to take an extra step of using Helicoils for stainless screws. This feature alone increases the chance that owners will be able to carry out maintenance tasks.

A rigger friend showed me a scrap heap that spoke loudly about sources of furler failure. The heap included many rusted and frozen bearings, foils that wouldn't stay together when a sail was hoisted, and first-generation composite bearings degraded by UV. Various owners have told me about halyard wraps, rotating drum guards, and twisted foils.

Boatbuilders and boatowners both must make choices about the system that's right for them. Which system should they choose:

- One that allows them to wash off plastic bearings with a hose?
- One that relies on permanently sealed high-carbon steel bearings?
- One that incorporates open-race stainless steel bearings that occasionally need cleaning and lubrication?
- One that has no ball bearings at all?

Such decisions always involve price issues, and there is a 400% spread in price from the least to the most expensive units. Having sailed with all the brands, I've concluded that the most efficient and best built among them is the Reckmann system, which also happens to be the most expensive. However, other systems costing half as much deliver almost as much capability.

A perfect blend of low price and top performance may not exist, but for those headed offshore or on an extended coastal voyage, don't bargain hunt with this rigging gear. For all-weather ease of furling, a unit with efficient ball bearings is best. Furlers without ball bearings use larger-diameter drums to compensate for some of the added friction. The net effect is like sailing with a longer tiller: furling takes a little harder pull, but for smaller boats the load is completely acceptable. Weekend cruisers and daysailors don't need a heavy-duty headsail furler, and one of the simpler systems does the job nicely.

One of the biggest upsides of roller-furling headsails is the ability to incrementally reef the sail area. The downside is that the smaller the sail becomes, the more its shape is compromised. Not only is there a bundled roll of cloth at the leading edge of the sail, but the shape of the sail (draft) is quite distorted. Even so, the advantage of quickly controlling sail area wins out with cruising sailors.

When sailing with a reefed headsail, keep a few things in mind. First, understand your boat's sail plan limitations and don't be caught without sail change options. For example, those who reef a 150% genoa down to a scrap-sized working jib but still need a smaller headsail to cope with a rapidly building breeze face a real dilemma. If there's not another stay on which to fly the smaller sail, they must unfurl the big genoa to get it down and attempt to hoist another sail in the slotted luff track. This is why heavy-weather staysails and Solent sails have become such favorites of offshore sailors (see Chapter 11).

Light-Air and Heavy-Air Headsail Options

Does one size really fit all? The cruising sailor with a single roller-furling headsail soon sees the folly of this concept. For example, a midrange genny is neither a working jib nor a light-air-optimized headsail. While a 135% genoa can be reefed to 110% and still retain an adequate shape, further reduce it to the size of a 100% working jib and you'll see it's baggy and inefficient at that size but still not big enough for light air when unfurled. In addition, if you'll use the same sail for a wide range of wind velocities, you're forced to choose a sail cloth that is heavier than is optimal for light air. Because it must be cut flatter than a hanked sail in order to furl smoothly, it provides a little less drive than you would get from a hanked headsail of the same size. And any idea of making your workaday roller-furling headsail a 4-ounce 150% genoa designed for light-air sailing defies all principles about shape and material constraints.

A single roller-furling headsail is a big win for ease of sail handling but a significant loss for light-air efficiency compared to a light number one genoa or a drifter/reacher. These light-air sails of old have become orphans without a stay on which to be hanked. This leaves sailors with a need for other options for light or heavy air.

The first alternative that comes to mind is simply to douse the midsize genoa and, depending on the situation, replace it with a light 165% drifter or a heavy working jib. However, this means peeling a boltrope-fed genoa out of the furler slot and then slotting in the replacement sail. Cruising sailors have to perform this task without a dexterous foredeck crew, a challenge that may make them long for piston-hanked sails.

In light air another dilemma may soon appear: after taking down and bagging the 135% genoa and wrestling the 165% light-air reacher into the roller-furler foil, a gusty afternoon 20-knot sea breeze may appear. Overpowered in this new snootful of

The foredeck crew is happy about having the afternoon off while the roller furling handles the work. Note how the furling line maintains a fair lead to a turning block fastened to the bow pulpit. Minimizing abrupt angle changes in such line leads lessens unwanted friction.

Winding up the large genoa and sailing under a reefed main and forestaysail is a good way to maintain drive and reduce heel. Increased tension in the main and staysail halyards would remove the luff wrinkles shown in both sails.

wind, the big, fragile headsail must be furled up, leaving the sloop rig one sail short. Changing back to a smaller, heavier headsail requires unfurling the reacher and peeling it out of the luff groove—a process that redefines both mechanical friction and

Completely unwound, a furling jib sets nicely and is nearly as efficient as a hanked-on headsail. Swept-back spreaders are a mixed blessing—they offset forward mast bend—but are no friend to a well-eased mainsail—chafe can become a big concern on long passages.

When reefed to the size of a working jib, a midsize genoa (135%) has acceptable but not stellar sail shape and drive.

Large furling headsails survive longer on the head- and forestays if a UV-protective cover is sewn to the leech and foot. Note the dark narrow UV bands on the genoa, and see how the concept works on the furled forestaysail.

crew discontent. These sails of course lack hanks and don't stay tethered to a headstay when doused. Lightweight, loose-luffed sails just itch to find their way over the side. Singlehanded ocean racers often opt for two or three independent furlers to avoid just such sail-shuffling snafus, fully deploying the one that best matches the prevailing breeze. But most coastal cruisers reluctantly accept the poor light-air performance of a fairly heavy, flat-cut furling genoa and make up for its shortfalls with diesel fuel.

Foil-Less Furling Headsails for Light Air

One response to this light-air situation involves re-fining foil-less systems with a swiveling head and tack. In the bad old days, such a system allowed sails with wire luffs to function as both the furling mechanism and headstay. We saw the technology reemerge in the infamous prestart sequence of race two in the 2000 America's Cup, when the Kiwis dragged a bag onto the foredeck of their boat and set a sail that established a new standard in light-air performance.

The crafty New Zealander crew baited the stylish Italians aboard *Prada* into following them on a slow amble away from the starting line in a light breeze. But as soon as the Kiwis tacked back toward the line, they hoisted a furled-on-itself lightweight headsail they called a *code 0*. It unrolled with a whoosh, and the New Zealand rabbit left the Italian tortoise in their wake. Just shy of the line, the crew rewound the code 0 and quickly dropped it to the deck and switched back to their upwind sail plan.

The Kiwis proved to be a smart rabbit, never giving back the gain they had made with their code 0 and consummate sailing skills.

This technology trickled down to grand prix racers and eventually to recreational sailors around the world. A straightforward assumption is operating here: if light-air sails could be made easier to handle and offer even better performance, more cruisers and daysailors would expand their sail inventories. Asymmetrical spinnakers, gennakers, and good old lightweight drifter/reachers have been around for a while. But the latest trend involves a tame version of a bowsprit-mounted roller furler that promises to spice up the average sailor's light-air experience. We also see a return of the much-maligned bowsprit in a configuration that's more demure. In fact, many are removable, eliminating the protrusion whenever it isn't needed. When it comes to performance, a longer foretriangle base and longer luff possible with a bowsprit add value. But when the breeze is blowing, there's an advantage being able to get the extra bits and pieces out of the way.

If you enjoy the time spent under sail and you're willing to invest in aftermarket equipment to take better advantage of breezes under 10 knots, you can avoid much of the sail-swapping hassle by using one of these new furlers. Modern fractionally rigged boats with masthead halyards can supersize their light-air headsails, and owners of older, low-wetted-surface, light-air-efficient, masthead-rigged boats will benefit just as much.

Many old Cals, Rangers, Ericsons, and Pearsons have narrow, light-air-efficient, easily driven hulls with fairly small sail plans. However, if retrofitted with conventional extrusion-over-headstay roller-furling headsails, their compromise genoas are both heavier and smaller than desirable for light-air sailing. In such cases the trusty 165% 2-ounce Dacron drifter/reacher is left in the basement along with the ability to enjoy a 7-knot breeze blowing over smooth water. If your priority involves eking out more light-air performance from your boat, and you don't have a couple of teenagers or a hyperactive sailing partner on board to wrestle with a conventional spinnaker, you could find your answer in a foil-less furler, especially when the apparent wind is at 50 to 110 degrees.

Handling Light-Air Sails

These foil-less furling systems are designed for nylon and other lightweight off-the-wind sails dubbed A-stars, gennakers, asymmetrical spinnakers, and other appellations referring to light-air, curved-luff sails. The furling units that tame them give us a chance to hoist a cloud of nylon under complete control. During the hoist, the sail is fully furled, and

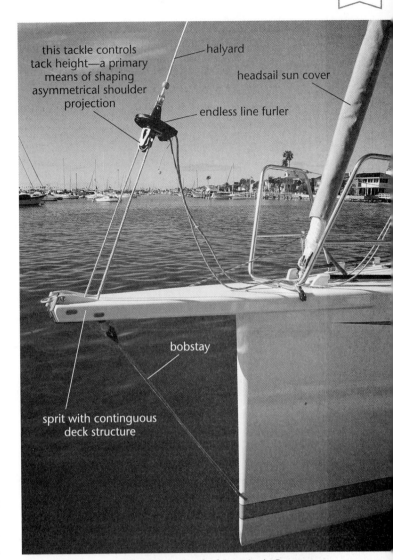

Offshore racers followed the lead of America's Cup racers and fitted endless-line furlers to stem extensions, minisprits, and other devices that extended the J dimension (the fore-and-aft base of the foretriangle) and projected a light furling headsail into clean air ahead of the headstay. A top-down endless-line furler allows a shorthanded crew to cope with an asymmetrical spinnaker. The system winds the sail onto a torque rope from the top swivel downward to the base. Once the sail has been furled it can easily be lowered to the deck. Even more convenient is the reverse process of setting the spinnaker via a simple pull on the sheet that unfurls the sail.

once up, with sheets run and the crew at the ready, the sail can be easily unfurled via a tug on the sheet. Furling winds up the sail with reduced spinnaker anxiety. The process begins by steering 90 to 120 degrees off the apparent wind, easing the sheet, and yanking away on the line to the endless-loop furling drum. In no time at all you have a snuggly rolled up spinnaker that's ready to be lowered to the deck and stowed away in its turtle or bag. With the loose nylon plunge toward the sea eliminated, spinnaker fire drills become a thing of the past, and shorthanded cruisers can cut their engine run time in half and double the pleasure of being under sail.

As long as you don't carry the light-air canvas too long in a building breeze, hoisting a sprit-set roller-furled sail and then lowering it at your convenience takes 95% of the drama out of light-air sail handling. As with all large sails, you need to recognize that modest increases in true wind velocity can

🏴 When hoisted the spinnaker is restrained in a full-length nylon sock. To deploy, the sock is hauled to the head of the sail, as shown. To douse, the downhaul line pulls the sock down as the sail is blanketed by the main and the sheet is released.

🏴 (Top) Aboard my sloop Wind Shadow, I've found an anti-torsion rope foil-less furler a valuable aid in handling a large asymmetrical spinnaker. (Above) Note how the sail is tightly furled around the torque rope. Care must be taken to keep the lazy sheet from being bundled into the twisting sail.

🏴 Asymmetrical spinnakers and other light-air sails are easily set on sprits, especially when handled using an endless line furler or a sock-type snuffer device. It's a lot easier to set and douse a sail that's rolled up or under wraps.

add up to large increases in sail power. Boat motion in a seaway can also influence the load on the sail and rigging; therefore, every crew needs clear guidelines about the gear used in varying wind velocities and points of sail.

Furling gear is not meant to reef down a light-air sail. With a conventional midsize genoa furled on the headstay, don't hesitate to roll in a light reacher or gennaker as soon as the breeze fills in and swap over to the heavier headsail. When facing an increasing breeze or an imminent threat of heavy weather, it makes sense to lower the tightly wound sail, bag it, and stow it below, a process that's streamlined by its rolled shape. Likewise, it makes sense to lower and stow the sail when you're away from the boat to protect it from UV and eliminate the risk of a squall peeling open an upper portion of the leech and causing problems for the sail as well as the boat.

When tacking, a shorthanded crew can coax a big gennaker or drifter through a 2-foot slot between the headstay and the spritsail's tensioned luff. Alternatively, it's a snap to furl the sail, tack the boat, and unfurl it on the other side. To greatly improve light-air sail handling, you can add a set of lightweight sheets, such as polypropylene-covered Dyneema, cordage that floats and sheds water like a duck. Some prefer to set up the sheet leads to jibe (rather than tack) with the clew forward, the way an asymmetrical spinnaker is handled. Given how easy it is to simply haul in the sail using the endless-line furler and reset on the other tack, however, it's not necessary to deal with these complications.

Sail furlers are far more than a marketing fad. If you're a cruiser, daysailor, or point-to-point racer who sails shorthanded, these furling systems can make light-air sails as user-friendly as the trusty old genoa wound up on the headstay.

Sprit-Set Light-Air Sails

Big sprits, massive sail area increases, and tricky sailing seem to go hand in hand with high-end race boats, but it's easy to overdo these features. Many a retrofit aimed at turning a nonsprit boat into a speedster wielding an asymmetrical spinnaker and code 0 served up new loads that could break things. For example, the sprit itself, usually made of an alloy or carbon-fiber tube, handles compression loads better than bending loads. Unfortunately, many sailors want a sprit without a bobstay, thus placing a significant bending load on the tube where it contacts its midlength bearing point, whether that's a support in the hull or a fitting on deck.

Consider the wave-induced loading associated with pitch, roll, yaw, and heave, motions that can momentarily double the prevailing loads (see illus-

A star-cut spinnaker (a style of spinnaker that aligns the thread lines with the major load) can be flown on a reach from a small removable sprit. This sail is set using a sock, and when a jibe becomes necessary, dousing the sail with the sock and opening it up on the opposite tack often works best. Just aft of the removable sprit is a conventional midrange roller-furling genoa for 12 to 25 knots of wind. The stay in the foreground is a removable forestay used in heavy weather with opposing running back stays. This is an optimum point to fly a hanked-on heavy weather staysail or storm jib.

The ability to hoist a rolled-up, ready-to-unfurl sail, put it to good use, and refurl it prior to dousing makes setting the sail more of a walk in the park than a climb up a steep mountain. This catamaran is flying a lightweight reacher with a torque rope luff.

tration in Chapter 4). Add in the effect of rooting the bow into a wave or a wave breaking in the foot of the sail, and you'll find it easy to believe the horror stories about code 0 misadventures. If you wait too long to close down the show, especially with the breeze forward of the beam, you take the chance of blowing out a light-air sail or perhaps even breaking the sprit.

Good engineering always pays off. I recall a day spent sailing aboard a 60-footer with a freestanding sprit (no bobstay). While we were close-reaching down Narragansett Bay, the hefty-looking carbon-fiber/E-glass tube began flexing as the wave-induced roll of the boat added more and more energy to the equation. Finally, with a sound like a gunshot, the one-piece pole became two when the spar exceeded its plastic phase of fiber elongation. Since then, I've better comprehended the loads that torment such appendages. Now I understand why many sprit manufacturers add two bold comments in their literature: "must be professionally installed" and "not for code 0 sails."

Once you get a feel for the wide range of sprit types, you'll understand why removable freestanding sprits should be limited to off-the-wind sailing, and in some cases to winds less than 12 knots. Freestanding sprits are a mini-version of a freestanding mast, which must be designed to take bending rather than compression loads, whereas conventional wire-supported masts and sprits endure more compression loading than bending.

Heavy-Air Headsails and Solent Stays

For offshore and long-range cruising, you may want to add a furling Solent stay with a dedicated working jib inside the furling genoa. The Solent stay is a removable secondary headstay that attaches to the mast just far enough below the headstay landing to clear the headstay furling system. At the same time it's close enough to the masthead or the headstay tang on a fractional rig that you don't need to add more support to the spar with runners or checkstays.

This higher attachment point distinguishes the Solent stay from the more familiar inner forestay. Another difference is the Solent stay's tack point on deck much closer to the stem. Set up in this way, the Solent stay becomes an ideal wire for a high-cut heavy-weather jib that's bigger than a storm jib but smaller than a number 4 genoa or working jib. The combination of two or three reefs in the main and a small headsail hanked on a removable Solent stay gives a sailboat the ability to beat to weather in near-gale-force conditions without reverting to the storm trysail and storm jib. However, if conditions continue to worsen and storm sails become necessary, you won't regret having already set them up when the process was easier. A storm jib can be hanked on in advance under the lowest hank of the Solent sail and left at the ready (still bagged) with sheets attached. The storm trysail's slugs or slides can be affixed to its independent track (on the mainmast) and the sail remain in its bag at the ready. When it's time, simply swap the main's halyard and the sheets and hoist away.

When the Solent stay is set, the furling headsail can no longer be tacked without first being furled. For this reason, many sailors still opt for a traditional cutter or double-headsail sloop rig. In this arrangement, a midsize genoa and a slot spacing of 6 feet or more usually allows the headsail to be tacked, but it may take a bit of coaxing.

Solent stay with roller-furling jib

A Solent stay is a good option for offshore and long-distance cruising. Once a Solent stay becomes permanent with a roller-furling system, it cannot be removed for light-air sailing—every tack of the genoa/reacher requires rolling up/furling that sail.

A versatile, well-designed rig for a shorthanded crew. Other than UV protection for the exposed bit of mainsail, not much needs to be added to this well-appointed cruiser. Two furling headsail options and a roller-furling in-mast mainsail make sail handling a push-button and pull-strings operation. (With automation comes the need for tip-top preventive maintenance and careful use of power winches.) A separate track for a storm trysail on the mast and a removable staysail stay for a storm jib would complete the long-distance cruising package.

As mentioned earlier, the mainsail and roller-furling/reefing genoa have become the inshore sail plan of choice, but it's not a versatile or rugged enough combo for offshore use. So we have looked into how many extra sails and stays you really need. For those crossing oceans or engaged in high-latitude sailing, a storm jib and storm trysail are "must have" additions. Adding a separate track for the storm trysail on the mast and a back-from-the-bow stay for the storm jib make handling storm sails in a serious blow a much more user-friendly experience. (See illustration on page 335 in Chapter 11.)

A Solent stay can be used to hoist a storm jib, but once you add a roller-furling system you hinder this dual purpose functionality. Trying to pull down a foil slotted Solent jib and feed in the luff tape of a storm jib when the wind is trying to peel the paint off the mast is a tough challenge aboard a full crewed race boat, and an even a more daunting challenge for the doublehanding cruising couple.

To solve this challenge, those with larger boats (over 45') add a removable forestay in addition to the furling equipped Solent stay. Running backstays may be needed to offset the bending load on the mast column. The fact that the Solent stay hinders the tack-

ing ability of the larger genoa set on the headstay makes this rigging approach less than perfect. Thus, the conventional cutter rig remains a valid alternative, especially for those short-handing cruisers not excited about increased sail area in the mainsail.

The current trend in sail plans is toward a large mainsail and smaller headsail combo, along with a removable Solent stay on which you can also hank a heavy-weather headsail or storm jib. On mid-size cruisers sailing offshore in the summer months, but not crossing oceans, this can be a simple and suitable combo for passagemaking—especially when a separate track for a storm trysail is added to the mainmast.

The long-term, long-distance cruiser also needs to have a means of sailing in light air, and if handling large, light-weight nylon sails is not in the picture, extra fuel tankage and a reliable diesel and drive train will be called upon. In either case, this is how we deal with getting from A to B, a challenge as well as a delight. Nowhere is the hand, reef, and steer depiction so relevant, and in the next chapter you'll see why I call navigation a seamless link between where you are going and how you will get there. The sails drive the vessel, but the navigator tells us how to put them to best use.

8

NAVIGATION

Navigation is typically defined as the science of getting a vessel from place to place. Experienced navigators might add that this science is also an art, with the relative portion of each changing with both the waters they travel and the weather they encounter. A recreational sailor enjoying a clear summer afternoon on a local bay practices intuitive navigation without benefit of charts or instruments. In this situation visual piloting skills prevail, and knowing where you are and where the hazards lie are taken for granted.

When we modern sailors venture beyond the familiar, we call on science and technology to replace this intuitive navigation art. We use charts to help our visual piloting on coastal passages, and today, radar and GPS also become key players. When sheltered waters give way to open seas, the navigator's role changes once again. On long ocean passages, navigators spend more time tracking weather systems and determining the influence of currents than plotting fixes. But whether we're sailing in familiar coastal waters or on ocean passages, the practice of navigation remains both art and science.

Little more than two centuries ago, navigators learned to check ill-tempered chronometers with lunar-distance calculations when determining longitude, and they checked their celestial fixes whenever possible with soundings data and dead reckoning. Most important of all, they gave visual watchkeeping the highest priority. We might think of navigating as an easier endeavor now, but experienced navigators remain a skeptical breed, always questioning the validity of a fix that looks just a little too good to be true. And radar and GPS fixes should augment piloting, not replace it.

In this chapter we'll explore the gamut of navigation alternatives, including networked do-it-all electronic charting and digital information systems (ECDIS). Contemporary hardware and software technology is getting closer and closer to giving us an artificial-intelligence navigator that needs neither a good bunk nor rum drinks after landfall. But the human navigator still encounters plenty of challenges to decipher, and doing the job with a facile hand is what the game is all about.

The bottom line facing every mariner is how to answer just three simple questions:

- What risks lie ahead? How will I track them?
- Am I fully leveraging available navigation information in my decision making?
- Where am I?

When informed crews put the answers to these questions in play, they should be able to avoid unwanted situations or at least be aware of what lies ahead. This forehandedness gives the crew a chance

Radar and digital chartplotters are effective innovations in navigation science, forever redefining the navigator's routine. Their contributions to safe passagemaking are considerable, but they have yet to make the navigator obsolete or paper charts irrelevant.

to react to a changing status quo on their own terms. Preparation prevents being surprised by waves breaking on a nearby shoal or finding ourselves pinned on a lee shore by a side-setting current.

The best navigators have a complete understanding of the vessel they're guiding, its abilities under sail and power, its capacity to handle heavy weather, and its performance strengths and weaknesses in a wide range of conditions. They're aware of the boat's structural integrity and the crew's ability to cope with the job at hand. Their comprehensive knowledge includes the ability to acquire data from multiple sources, compare and contrast its significance, and perhaps most important of all, judge its validity.

Good navigators use weather forecast information as part of passage planning (see Chapter 10). They're also aware of oceanographic conditions ahead and gauge the influence of shifting sea conditions on the navigation routine.

In short, navigators' skills extend well beyond fixing a position and include planning a passage, designating a route, timing departure, and continuously changing passage dynamics during each cruise or race. It's this comprehensive job description that causes many shorthanded crews to treat the navigator and skipper's roles as one and the same.

ELEVEN KEYS TO NAVIGATION

We discuss each of these keys in this chapter, which together form a baseline for both electronic and traditional pencil and paper chart navigation.

- Pay heed to the depthsounder.
- Use 7 × 50 binoculars.
- Understand the threat posed by a lee shore.
- Treat GPS and digital charting system (DCS) data with deep appreciation but constant skepticism.
- Practice with radar in good visibility to build your skill.
- Update the weather forecast daily, and monitor local VHF weather broadcasts.
- Carry paper charts and use them in conjunction with DCS equipment.
- Jot down fixes at regular intervals and note buoys passed.
- Carry *Sailing Directions, Coast Pilots,* cruising guides, a nautical almanac, and other publications.
- Use a bright spotlight at night to spot marks and obstacles.
- If crossing oceans, carry a sextant and calculator or sight reduction tables and a nautical almanac.

Dead Reckoning
Determining a position by plotting courses and speeds from a previously known position.

Piloting
Navigation using visual sightings of fixed objects to determine position.

Celestial Navigation
Using the sun, moon, planets, and stars to determine position

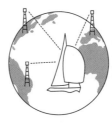

Radio Navigation
Using one of several different types of radio signals to determine position and relay your position to others.

Radar Navigation
Using a pulse modulated signal, radar measures range and bearing to targets that reflect the signal. Valuable in avoiding collisions with other vessels.

Satellite Navigation
Using orbiting satellites to determine position.

▨ *Over time the methods of navigation have changed: the most basic type is dead reckoning, followed, in order of sophistication and historical development, by the other methods shown here. Satellite navigation, also known as GPS, remains the most popular method today, but as its owners—the U.S. Department of Defense—say, "it's not a standalone means of navigation."*

A NAVIGATOR'S DAY'S WORK AT SEA

Let's take a then-and-now look at navigation by comparing a typical routine today with a navigator's routine at sea aboard a shorthanded sailboat at sea 30 or 40 years ago. We can begin by noting changes in both technique and technology. Even with the differ-

With sextant in hand and well-honed sight reduction skills, a navigator has a completely autonomous backup means of position fixing.

A nautical almanac provides the location of celestial bodies at any given second over a given year—this information is needed for celestial navigation, which involves calculating the relative position of the celestial objects and the boat, using fixes (a fix is obtained by deriving two or more lines of position [LOPs]). These fixes require solving the sides of a celestial triangle: one corner is the geographic position of the sun, moon, planet, or star; another is the assumed location of a vessel; the third is the closest pole.

ences brought by modern tools and technology, the deck of a sailboat remains more or less the same today as yesterday. The work flow may be faster today, but the definition of a job well done hasn't changed.

A Day's Work Then

As mentioned earlier, almost four decades ago, in the pre-GPS days, my wife Lenore and I and our two young children, Tara and Eric, sailed our sloop *Wind Shadow* around the world. On that voyage external factors determined my navigation routine: weather conditions, sea state, the proximity of land, and the visibility and availability of stars, planets, sun, and the moon. In 1976 I handled a sextant and acquired a sight in much the same way navigators had in 1876. My preferred routine included an early start to the day, when I hoped for a clear enough sky to shoot a round of sights in the morning twilight just before dawn; this is a time when the delineation between ocean and sky has just begun to unfold. During those precious predawn minutes I'd shoot lower-magnitude stars in the east first, while the ambient light was weaker, saving brighter planets and first-magnitude stars until last. This approach worked because we can see brighter planets and stars even as the ambient light of approaching dawn increases and the horizon line becomes more and more prominent.

Working out a three-body fix using a nautical almanac and Sight Reduction Tables HO 249 Volume 1 consumed a half hour, and by the time the lines of position (LOPs) were plotted and had been double-checked, the sun was above the horizon and night had transitioned into a new day. For a celestial navigator, starting the day with a good three-star fix holds the same importance as a good breakfast. It sorted out the vagaries of night-watch steering, vane or autopilot anomalies, and the accumulated divergence of the dead-reckoned (DR) track from the vessel's actual track over the prior 12 hours. The closer we were to landfall, the more important this morning fix became.

In overcast conditions, I found it impossible to get a three-star fix; even a single line of position could prove elusive. At such times our uncorrected DR track continued to grow in length and decrease in accuracy. Our worst luck with overcast conditions coincided with a trade-wind reach through the Lau Group of Fiji, a region known for cross-equatorial tidal currents, low-lying atolls, and surf-swept coral reefs. Overcast conditions forced me to run on a crumbling DR plot for three days. Fortunately, I'd acquired a midday sun LOP on the second day and used it to tune up the DR with an estimated position (DR crossed with an LOP).

The experience underscores why sun sights between 1000 and 1400 hours are a celestial navigator's best friend. The bright disk of the sun often shows itself at least momentarily during this period, giving us a usable shot and a reliable LOP. If it makes another cameo appearance a couple of hours later, we can grab a second LOP and calculate a running fix.

Once I transferred the midday position update to a small-scale offshore chart (small scale = small detail over a large area), I turned my attention to acquiring or decoding weather updates received via single-sideband (SSB) radio forecast transmissions. I preferred the voice version of the National Weather Service high-seas forecast, but at the time I also taught myself to use a tape recorder and struggle through Morse code numbers to develop a weather map. Knowing where weather systems were headed and what their intensity would be was nearly as important as knowing where the boat was positioned and headed.

In the early afternoon I'd take another sun sight and work out an LOP I could use to create a running fix. All I had to do was advance the morning sun line along the DR track and cross it with the afternoon LOP, a process identical to constructing a running fix from two time-separated bearings on the same object ashore, as described later in this chapter. Finally, at dusk, I'd shoot another round of star sights and "reduce" the sights using HO 249 Volume 1 (a shortcut to the sight reduction of selected stars). With a clear sky and a smooth sea, I could get a very accurate fix.

When I later welcomed a TI–59 calculator aboard, I felt I'd been given a magic touchstone. The gadget soon led to dust collecting on my sight reduction tables. But I eventually replaced it with a Celesticomp and finally the versatile Star Pilot software on a laptop. And just as celestial navigation became easier than ever, along came Loran-C, SatNav, and then GPS—the final nail in the sextant's coffin. Today, some liken celestial navigation to Sanskrit, but others find the endangered technique a valuable backup talent for a well-prepared navigator.

We know for sure that with an accuracy of a mile or two under good conditions and ten miles in heavy weather, celestial navigation created a cult of anxious practitioners. Doubt and a healthy dose of skepticism made for attentive watchkeeping and the navigator's tendency to double-check worksheets and plotting.

Like many offshore navigators, I grew accustomed to the skyscape, often finding myself steering toward a setting star with a declination similar to my latitude rather than continually peering at the compass. When I reached deep, open ocean water, a stretch of sea unencumbered by land, I breathed a sigh of relief, knowing that the next big navigation challenge would coincide with landfall.

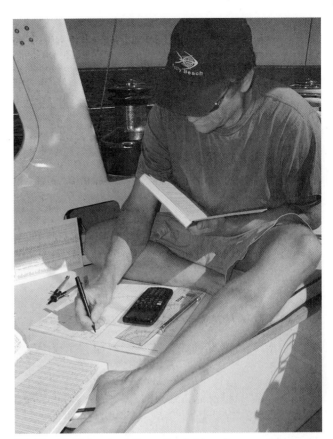

The GMT date and time of a sight and name of the body are used to locate the correct page in the almanac and acquire declination and hour angle calculations necessary for a celestial fix.

A Day's Work Now

Writing as a navigator who started crossing oceans with essentially the same tools Captain Cook used centuries ago, I'm keenly appreciative of the electronic revolution. It's reshuffled how I spend time offshore, and for every shorthanded crew, this means more time for other vital tasks and even better accuracy in your primary role of getting a boat and its crew from here to there.

Navigation technology has changed my daily offshore routine, and the keypad and touch screen on a multifunction display (MFD) have become more familiar than the feel of the sextant in my hand. However, although enjoying a cup of coffee in the cockpit has replaced the morning star sights, the sextant remains on board and I still note the location of familiar friends like Vega, Antares, and glistening Venus. But I'm much like a player who's become a spectator as I passively peer at a screen as it provides a satellite fix. No calculations necessary. Reduced to a symbol on the center of the screen, *Wind Shadow*'s relationship to the route I've programmed appears on a chart, but without the touch of dividers or parallel rules. I appreciate my electronic assistant, but I admit to a bit of nostalgia about the old days, and although I embrace new technology I also still hear the old navigator's refrain.

The multifunction display (MFD) is the digital clearing house for a networked navigation system: inputs from the GPS antenna, fathometer, anemometer, radar, AIS, and other data-gathering-sensors get processed and displayed on this screen. Multiple MFDs can be set up so those at the helm or in another part of the boat can tap into the same information.

Aboard Wind Shadow, I utilize a built-in fixed GPS/plotter, plus a laptop with digital charting software to add a level of redundancy to the electronic navigation system. Even so, I continue to carry a "just in case" set of routing and safe-haven paper charts that will get me from here to there if all the gadgets give in to Murphy's Law. Perhaps this is overkill, but relying on only one piece of electronic equipment to pinpoint your location and store all the charts you carry on board is far too optimistic an outlook.

Still a skeptic, before I sign off on an electronic fix, I scroll through the menu on the GPS or chart-plotter and go to the "Satellites" page and check the quality of the signals received. Factors such as "signal-to-noise ratio" and "dilution of precision" affect the quality of the fix. Important, too, are the heights of the satellites above the horizon and their angular separations from one another. When stars are selected for a fix, important criteria include declinations and angles of separation. Likewise, position accuracy degrades when satellites are too close to the horizon or have too small an angle of separation. I regularly check the small box on the screen that tells me if I'm receiving the Wide Area Augmentation Signal (WAAS) or the unit is working as an autonomous GPS receiver. The WAAS yields a much more accurate fix and corrects for small variations in GPS data.

The new routine aboard our old sloop *Wind Shadow* involves continuous navigation rather than episodic updates of a DR plot. Digital charts and electronic navigation software afford accurate position finding at a glance and the ability to steer a preset route. Despite this quantum leap in electronic navigation accuracy and convenience, I maintain a backup plan that some might consider common sense but others write off as a quirk. But I'm not alone. As one gifted navigator has said, "All electronic aids will fail at some point. You just don't know when."

My hedge against inevitable electronic glitches and outright failure leads me to jot down hourly GPS lat/lon coordinates and carry enough paper charts and ChartKit booklets to cover the waters I'm cruising. (Even though NOAA has now discontinued the governmental printing of paper charts, the agency updates digital charts and provides the information

Smart phones and tablets can augment the navigator's routine, but when they completely replace it, bad things can happen.

to commercial vendors who will no doubt continue to print and make paper charts available for the foreseeable future, as they have already for decades.) My backup plan then allows me to segue seamlessly into conventional DR piloting and celestial navigation when and if the lights go out. I suppose one could consider this overkill if we're transiting the ICW or engaged in coastal cruising, but ocean passages require a different approach.

True, some navigators simply carry a couple of handheld GPS receivers and plenty of spare batteries in case their primary GPS unit packs up. However, what would happen if there's an interruption in the GPS signal? The U.S. Air Force maintains the GPS and clearly states that the system is not meant to be a stand-alone means of navigation. GPS is a global system and its fix accuracy remains consistent as long as all satellites in the constellation are in play. In all regions, there are some fluctuations in accuracy due to satellite geometry.

In a sense, navigators are always on watch. Underway, they hold a 24-hour everyday job. Before getting into their bunks, they double-check the last fix and/or DR position, contemplate its accuracy, and note nearby obstacles, sharing these concerns clearly with those on watch. They factor the implications of the most recent weather forecast into the equation and also consider the longer-term weather patterns. Before turning in, navigators also consider the vessel's present location and project the location of the vessel a few hours ahead when they wake.

In the pre-GPS era it was good to doubt the absolute accuracy of a fix. Even today, many veteran passagemakers still feel a twinge of anxiety right up until they make landfall or a visual fix confirms their location.

Aboard small craft, the dual responsibility of skipper-navigator can prove quite functional. Of course, we don't see this kind of streamlining aboard U.S. Navy warships, for example, where navigating, watchkeeping, weather forecast tracking, and combat information tracking are separate roles performed under the command of the skipper. Segmenting responsibilities has the advantage of efficient information gathering; the challenge involves integrating the information and reliably delivering it to the decision maker. On vessels with large crews, the skipper, executive officers, and their lieutenants like to glance at the electronic chart display to see for themselves what's going on. Obviously, the Navy's navigation needs are inextricably linked to their need to track multiple combatants, both friends and foes.

Regardless of the differences between the demands of naval ships and typical commercial or recreational craft, all skippers need to view their vessels

The navigation process on large commercial ships is more formalized than what goes on aboard recreational craft, but a dual paper-and-digital approach is common to both.

as a three-dimensional box defined by draft and vertical clearance above the waterline and the surface area needed to maneuver at a given speed. The crew always focuses on what's approaching or moving away from that imaginary space. Every vessel operator can use this valuable construct.

Small-boat navigators face the challenge of abbreviating the navigation process while simultaneously retaining most of its integrity. By contrast, aboard a warship, for example, a sailor on each bridge wing shoots bearings for a quartermaster to plot, a cabin full of combat information center staff tracks contacts, and a bridge team and engine room watch ready to implement the officer of the deck's commands. Fortunately, aboard recreational craft, there is no need to calculate firing solutions against enemy craft—although offshore racing is nearly as combative!

Navigators also need to keep track of nearby vessels, and aboard a 30- or 40-foot sailboat or trawler one or perhaps two individuals on watch likely steer the boat, trim sails, navigate, and monitor the engine and other systems, not to mention thinking about what they'll make for lunch. The need to multitask has driven the recreational boating industry to make sail handling, steering, and navigation as streamlined and automated as possible.

The marriage of GPS and digital charting is among the most widely accepted feats of automation. We've seen the technology improve with advancements in chip capacity, processing speed, and graphic display capability. As a result, a network of instruments and computer power allows the crew to interface position information with digital cartography. This means real-time progress tracking on a flat screen, plus the capability of interfacing the data with the brain of an autopilot to synchronize steering with pre-plotted heading information.

The NMEA (National Marine Electronics Association) 2000 network, an offshoot of automotive electronics, provided a bus for lashing a wide array of information sensors to a single processor and multiple flat-screen displays. Wireless networks are already available in wind and speed instruments, and we'll see further digital advances in the future. (See Chapter 14 for more on wi-fi technology aboard.)

Proportionately, of the time gained from automated position fixing and course plotting, I spend a surprising amount of it checking and maintaining these systems. In addition, managing power has become a much bigger concern. Consider that the 2 or 3 amps per hour required by a GPS/plotter/AIS system add up to 48 to 72 amp-hours per day. When we add to that total power demanded by an autopilot and refrigeration system (together, another 120 amp-hours), lights, pumps, watermaker, and communications, the power drain approaches 200 to 300 amp-hours per day. Hence, you might easily eat up the time you saved by streamlining navigation in carrying out your new role as systems technician and power plant operator. This gives new meaning to the adage "No such thing as a free lunch." However, the comfort, convenience, and accuracy of electronic navigation offer a fair trade. After all, *knowing where you are is the first step in safely getting where you want to go.*

ELECTRONIC NAVIGATION

Electronics have redefined our approach to navigation in the same way that the personal computer has revolutionized the writer's craft. Typewriters and taffrail logs are now museum pieces and the "glass helm" has made its way from power cruisers onto more and more sailboats.

Empowered by GPS, digital charting systems, and radar, an increasing number of recreational sailors are venturing in and out of unfamiliar harbors at night and in the fog in places where even local experts hesitated to go a decade or two ago. This new wave of navigation technology is one of the few things in boating that's getting both better and less expensive. By understanding both its lengthy list of advantages and the short but imposing tally of consequences, we can put this important aid to navigation to maximum use.

In the late 1970s, a Transit satellite navigation receiver retailed for over $18,000. Today's GPS/plotter with hundreds of NOAA charts installed sells for less than one-tenth of that price, plus they're many times

more accurate and reliable. Although miraculous on its own accord, the stand-alone GPS receivers needed a navigator to plot the latitude/longitude position on a paper chart using dividers and pencil. When GPS is integrated with a digital charting system (DCS), however, even that task is eliminated. Meanwhile, radar has become more sensitive and selective, lighter, more compact, less electricity-hungry, and easier to operate; a radar unit now costs less than the power-hungry dinosaurs of the 1970s. In short, navigation electronics offer more bang for the buck than ever before.

Digital charting systems fall into three distinct categories:

- ◆ Dedicated chartplotters with built-in GPS capability.
- ◆ Versatile software programs running on a conventional laptop or PC that receives input from a cable-connected or Bluetooth GPS receiver.
- ◆ A smartphone or tablet like an iPad with a built-in or external GPS and a digital charting app.

Chartplotters are generally user-friendly and more weather resistant and can be mounted on deck, whereas computer software affords more options, making a navigation computer easier to use for route planning, accessing tide and current information, creating a voyage log entry, and so forth. Many of the latest chartplotters allow data sharing with PC-based cartography and route-planning software as well as NMEA 2000 networking. NMEA 2000 is a standardized network connection that's used to link electronic components. It's taken directly from the automotive industry's Controller Area Networking (CAN) bus and helps create interoperability among components from many different manufacturers.

A big advantage of a digital charting system is its conversation of a GPS signal into a symbol marching across the screen, providing a direct, real-time, visual representation of your boat's location on the surface of the earth. Most systems allow the user to center the vessel on the display with an easy keystroke or dedicated button. The display can be zoomed in or out, along with many other functions as well. Users can move a cursor to any location on the screen for a display of range and bearing and scroll the chart in any direction. If the vessel symbol moves off the screen, a simple button or click brings it back. Multifunction touch screen displays as well as smartphones and tablets add further versatility to data access.

Still, paper charts and the ability to use them are anything but obsolete—see A Few Chart Basics (Paper or Digital) on page 223 for more on charts and the wealth of information they provide. A paper chart can be carried up on deck and rotated to align with what lies ahead. Zooming in is as simple as moving your face closer to the paper surface or using a magnifying glass. To pan from side to side, simply turn your head—much faster than moving a cursor. The chart is omnipresent, not a temporary vestige of an electron dance on an LCD stage. As a big advocate of digital charting and the convenience it offers recreational boaters, I still believe you need to keep paper charts (or chart books) on board to complement digital chart navigation.

By itself, the small display size of a typical digital chart for recreational use is a good reason to keep a paper chart at hand. Commercial digital charting systems offer greater detail and a wider visual field, which can lead to safer navigation. Even a so-called "big screen" for a recreational boat is only half the size of what's used in the commercial world, and this holds true until the price tag approaches five digits. For example, a new 19-inch digital display appears crisp, bright, and the epitome of what a chart display or radar screen should be. But, at a suggested retail price of $12,000, its path to the bulkheads of many boats less than 45 feet long will be slow indeed.

Some believe the zoom function makes a large-scale digital chart fully viewable on a small screen, and that's true to an extent. However, when a paper harbor chart has shrunk for a 7-inch screen, the user must either zoom way in to see details or way out to gain a wider perspective. (See the Overzooming sidebar.) The screen can only display a small amount of data before graphic clutter overwhelms the viewer. In a way, this is like the predicament faced by radar users: they get the best close-in detail from a short-range setting, but they need to select a longer range to see what lies at greater distance.

Most vector digital chart systems allow users to layer more or less detail on the screen to keep the information as readable as possible. They differ from raster charts, which are equivalent to a photograph of a traditional paper chart that does not allow any data layering. When using vector charts, however, we must take care not to eliminate vital information. For example, I once used a vector chart with one layer of detailed text description intentionally toggled off, leaving only a tiny dot with a PA (position approximate) designation beside it. Assuming it was a private buoy or mark, I later was shocked when out of the hazy dusk I faced a cluster of 35 pilings comprising a fish trap. Had I been looking at a paper copy of the same chart or a raster digital sequel, I'd have clearly seen the fish trap designation. Once again, I proved to myself the value of a best-of-both-worlds approach of DCS used in combination with large-scale paper charts.

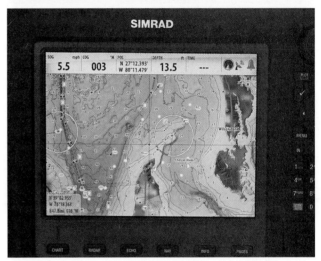

Digital charting systems—whether in a dedicated chartplotter, computer software, or device app—have come of age. Chartplotters are more weather resistant and lend themselves to secure bracketed mounting. Laptop and desktop software excel at helping mariners plan routes, scrutinize weather, and handle navigation information.

OVERZOOMING

Avoid overzooming on a small-scale raster chart, such as a routing chart. Small-scale raster charts lack crucial soundings and benthic and shoreline detail. Overzooming on these charts is like looking at a printed page with a magnifying glass: the letters look larger, but you won't find additional information. Furthermore, minor errors in perspective can be exaggerated through zooming. Therefore, for detailed views, use large-scale charts. Some digital charting systems include programming that make the screen go blank when overzoomed; others present a text warning. Vector cartography seamlessly switches scales.

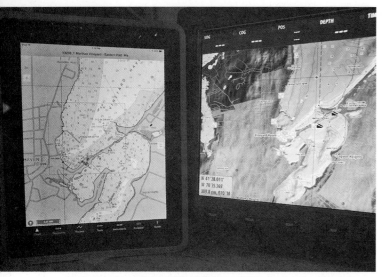

NOAA's release of free digital charts covering all U.S. domestic waters in both raster (left) and vector formats (right) is one of the best values in digital charting. All it takes is a program decoder, available as a free download at the NOAA website. Add a GPS receiver to your laptop and you have a portable nav station. You can even miniaturize the concept with a smartphone or tablet.

Another reason for a continued commitment to conventional charts is the growing trend to network all types of data on a common bus and display the information on the DCS screen. One look at how diminutive a 7-inch or even 10-inch LCD screen becomes when it's split to display radar on one side and a digital chart on the other provides reason enough to hang on to paper charts. If we add a data strip across the bottom with engine vitals, boat speed, wind info, and water temperature, the already small DCS chart and small radar image get even smaller.

When using a digital charting system, you must also consider chart orientation. Most software packages and dedicated chartplotters allow either a north-up or heading-up alignment of the chart; some even offer a course-up option. A north-up chart is easy to read when sailing or powering on a northerly heading, because the vessel symbol on the chart and the bow of the boat are nearly aligned. When heading south, however, the symbol progresses toward the bottom of the screen, which means that a course correction to port causes a turn toward the right-hand sector of the display. Navigators accustomed to turning their paper charts to a heading-up orientation may want to select that option on their chartplotter, thus ensuring that the boat's bow is always pointing toward the top of the display. In such a configuration, what lies ahead is visible at the top of the screen. A third display mode is referred to as course-up, and it keeps the screen epicentered on the route that has been entered as waypoints.

As this book was about to go to press I looked over *Wind Shadow*'s networked 12-inch MFD linking radar, AIS, depth, digital compass, and autopilot inputs. It's not the latest touch-screen model, but at sea I prefer its dial over touch-screen inputs. I favor its fixed location, waterproof architecture, and rugged construction. My iPad with the iNavX app augments the system; its graphic display is superb and the portability feature has appeal. I've trialed apps that allow the tablet to interface with the onboard MFD and control the networked equipment, but my own preference is to keep the iPad as a stand-alone device.

Chart Precision, or Lack Thereof

The big challenge is how to avoid being mesmerized and seduced by the apparent precision and certainty of a DCS display. Elsewhere, I've mentioned the dilution of precision in a degraded GPS fix, but we must also recognize that some cartography is simply more accurate than others. The translation of latitude and longitude coordinates into a cartographic representation is by no means straightforward. The offsets required to adjust for the earth's imperfect sphere involve a complicated algorithm, or datum. The GPS unit must recognize this in order for the vessel's symbol to appear in the right spot on the chart and yield the system's accuracy within a few meters. (See A Few Chart Basics and the section on Datum page 225.)

For over a decade the U.S. Department of Defense has been scrambling to develop charts as accurate as a typical GPS receiver. The U.S. Navy's shift to using electronic charting and digital information systems (ECDIS) for primary navigation has been delayed in part because of the need to increase the accuracy of 5,000 paper charts and convert them to digital format. The National Geospatial Intelligence Agency has been using synthetic-aperture radar, another Star Wars spin-off, to gain the accuracy needed. Meanwhile, commercial and recreational boaters must recognize that their cartography, especially that depicting remote regions, provides nowhere near the accuracy of the GPS location coordinates etched onto the screen or plotted onto paper.

We often speak of the accuracy of a chart in terms of a zone of confidence (ZOC). We ascribe grades A, B, and C to charts accurate to within 5, 50, and 500 meters respectively. Navigators must be aware of the gamble they're making if they count on absolutely accurate position information to negotiate a pass for a night entry into some off-the-beaten-path Indian Ocean landfall. Just as an uncharted seamount sealed the fate of the submarine *San Francisco*, a cruising sailor faces the same risk when blindly depending upon the cartography of Captain Cook. The imprecise charts that worked just fine in an era of sextant

▰ *Perhaps if the crew of this ketch had attempted their nighttime harbor entry in the present age with GPS and digital charting, they'd have had a better outcome. But even with modern instrumentation, such disasters continue to occur, although more often caused by a decision-making shortfall than a navigation-system failure.*

▰ *The ability to network an autopilot control to follow a route laid out on a digital chart is among the features offered by electronics manufacturers.*

accuracy and big doses of navigator anxiety can cause trouble when used with the few-meter accuracy of GPS.

The Right Charting System

All digital charting systems have numerous features in common, and you can compare one unit or software package to another based on their commonalities. For example, it should be easy to move from one location to another on the virtual chart, zoom in for more detail, and shift the cursor to read bearing and range information. Likewise, the system should move seamlessly from one chart to the next.

Be honest about your own nav-a-geek proclivity. If you have programmed scan channels into your handheld VHF, have delved deeply into the submenus of your handheld GPS, and operate your smartphone like a trained jockey, you're likely to use the more complex features of a digital-charting navigation software package. But if you're after simple and easy commands that a new crewmember can cope with and you're unlikely to spend time composing complex tide- and current-based routing on your PC, a user-friendly dedicated unit might be a better choice.

In the commercial maritime world, where chart updating must be carried out on a regular basis, the once-arduous task of hand-lettering *Notice to Mariners* updates on paper charts has been automated by new DCS equipment. Recreational sailors also gain from this value-added DCS feature. Although not mandatory for recreational sailors, the extra cost of having

▰ *Waterproof multifunction displays readable in bright sunlight reside in the cockpit as happily as they do below. The helmsperson has a new wealth of information available, but we must lower the brightness level at night in order to maintain night vision.*

the latest cartography can pay off in the long run. It's true that coral reefs and granite ledges don't change much over short periods of time, but sandbars shift

■ Make sure the connection cables in a navigation network are as watertight as possible. When contacts oxidize in a marine environment, resistance changes and the operational reliability of equipment falters. Invest wisely in a system with sealed plugs and a waterproof rating.

■ A 3D view has a video-game feel to some and a flight-simulator authenticity to others. The angle of view is adjustable. As we creep closer and closer to virtual-reality navigation, however, keep in mind the requirements of visual watchkeeping.

and buoy numbering systems often change from year to year. Therefore, it makes sense to buy a digital charting system that provides updates to its cartography.

Networked Navigation Systems

Navies, coast guards, and commercial shipping have led the way in the latest revolution in navigation, electronic networking. The big players in networking include Furuno, Garmin, Raymarine, and Navico, whose lineup includes the Brooks & Gatehouse, Simrad, Lowrance, and Northstar brands. Each of these manufacturers expanded from stand-alone electronic navigation equipment to integrated systems, although their array of hardware varies a bit in electronic architecture. However, all the systems incorporate multifunction displays and high-data-rate cable links that can access information from radar, GPS, depthsounder, sonar, masthead instruments, and other sensors. This gives users fingertip control of more information than ever before.

Many DCS manufacturers and software-only producers offer 3D forward-looking and top-down views in their premium cartography. Featuring preloaded domestic NOAA charts (raster, vector, and bathymetric), this approach completely changes the way navigators view their surroundings. The resulting screen image is a blend of raster, vector, and bathymetric charts that allows satellite photos, weather maps, and even radar overlays to augment the picture. Just short of being a holographic image, this kind of picture highlights channel boundaries and navigation hazards like the granite ledges of Maine, the shoals fringing Cape Hatteras, the entrance to San Francisco Bay, and so forth.

Furuno, Garmin, Raymarine, Simrad, and others offer a wide range of cartography for regions outside U.S. territorial waters. The chip cost for the charts needed by a long-distance cruiser can be significant, especially if you're coastal cruising (with large-scale charts) extensively rather than planning long-distance passagemaking. In cruising grounds closer to home, with less demanding itineraries, you'll end up with more reasonable costs. Many vendors offer regional package pricing that helps to cut the cost of digital charts. But make sure that you have all the charts you need for a voyage, because counting on at-sea chart downloads is never a good gamble.

The first generation of networked systems involved some voodoo, but the networks have since improved. We consider Garmin's installer-friendly plug-and-play network architecture representative of what's available today. Sensors connect to multifunction displays through a proprietary Ethernet cable or, in some cases, a serial cable. You'll find a straightfor-

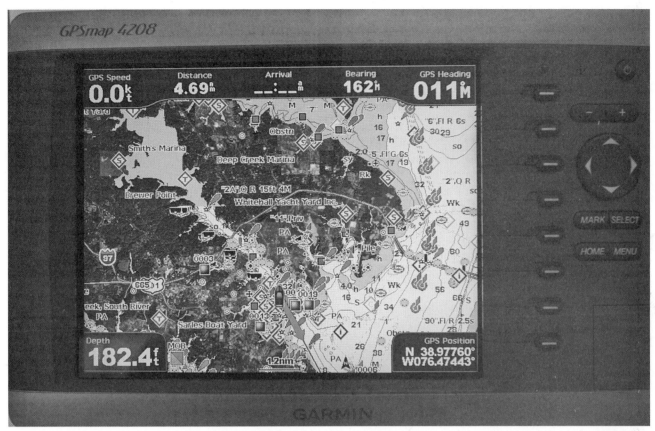

🚩 *Each manufacturer of multifunction-display (MFD) digital charting systems uses a slightly different architecture and often different cartography. You want a system that's user-friendly and information-rich, but extra bells and whistles don't necessarily get you safely from here to there; it's the extra detail on a radar screen or the accuracy of the blinking cursor on a digital chart display that does that. A great deal of nonessential high-contrast color on this display can lead navigators to lose sight of more essential constraints such as soundings, symbols indicating obstructions, and unlit marks. For example, Garmin's proprietary vector scan cartography incorporates land-based graphics, marina data, and symbols not found in NOAA Chart 1. Although helpful to some, navigators accustomed to NOAA raster charts find the bold graphics and superfluous data distracting. Fortunately, vector charts allow you to turn off layers of information, but you need to take care not to remove crucial soundings or other information about navigational hazards.*

ward do-it-yourself network assembly. You start with a MFD—such as a 3205, 3206, or 3210 chartplotter or the CANet—and link a couple of other input devices (radar, depthsounder, and so forth) to it with quick-connect cables. To add more sensors, add a network port expander and additional MFDs. Each MFD in the network is capable of calling up data from every sensor, even those linked via a NMEA 2000 link. The third generation of networked MFDs offers a yet wider range of installer-friendly, plug-and-play add-ons. Two displays can be connected with cables and couplers; you can add sensors using the manufacturer's router. These might include radar, a chartplotter, a depthsounder, a Sirius satellite weather receiver, AIS, FLIR thermal imaging sensor, and much more. No latency problem occurs with integrated instrument signals and autopilot commands, and most networks can handle NMEA 0183 and NMEA 2000 interfaces with a wide array of non-manufacturer equipment.

🚩 *You can network an infrared camera to a multifunction display, making its see-in-the-dark capability available to the navigator.*

Such systems also provide a convenient way of wiring engine-monitoring sensors to a navigation network. You can link video signals for live engine-room monitoring, deck views, infrared video, and even satellite TV, a feature many navigators are unhappy to see gaining access to the bridge. Well-sealed cables are costly, but will prove to be money well spent as they keep moisture intrusion problems to a minimum. And as most pros will claim, the failure of an electronic device often results from a faulty connection rather than a flaw in the device itself; self-sealing factory-made cables are a big step forward.

As with all good things, there are downsides to networked electronics—beyond their hefty price tags, of course. Sensory overload stemming from an avalanche of data is one of the biggest drawbacks. This overload can cause the navigator to lose sight of the forest in the trees, a situation we avoid by understanding how to manage the incoming information, sifting out the inputs of most immediate importance, and sidelining the rest. In poor visibility, for example, you want a detailed radar picture, and modern digital radar offers the sensitivity and selectivity to reveal a small skiff or lump of granite shrouded in fog. Unfortunately, a small display screen cluttered with radar, DCS plotter graphics, fish-finder info, and a virtual dashboard showing engine instrumentation makes radar signals difficult to discern. As in a good restaurant, a menu full of options makes picking and choosing as important as knowing what's available.

Anti-networkers make an interesting case for stand-alone chartplotters, radar units, depthsounder displays, and engine sensor readouts. With dedicated displays and no interconnecting cables, you have uncluttered screens and, above all, you have continuously available full-screen radar and chartplotter images. These voyagers also cringe at the thought of a TV program playing on their radar screen and have no interest in an arcade-like graphic dashboard showing a digital picture of an analog dial. When it's time to log the engine oil pressure, they don't mind looking at the instrument panel, and their radar troubles don't interfere with their chartplotter, and so on.

We find merit in these arguments. But many small-craft navigators steer a middle course and carefully determine what appears and what's excluded on a given monitor. Although costly, adding multiple monitors can increase safety as well as user-friendliness. Within the past few years, I sailed aboard a cruising ketch with two Raymarine C80 flat screens mounted side by side under a hard dodger and a third at the nav station below. The two on deck provide dedicated screens for radar and a digital chartplotter. This arrangement makes tricky passages in tight confines much easier, especially in bad weather, plus adding valuable display redundancy. It also makes sense to buy the biggest display you can afford and have room for. I recently added a 12-inch monitor to *Wind*

This medium-sized cruiser has enough room on board to set up dedicated screens for digital charting and radar. Choose the optimal screen size for viewing—smaller units with split screens and function-bar displays can clog up quickly with nonessential information, leaving little room for an effective radar display. The two-screen approach is both versatile and user-friendly.

Shadow and find that I use the split-screen function (displaying radar and the chartplotter) some of the time, but when I need more detail, I toggle to a single-screen radar or plotter view.

Radar in pea-soup fog and the omniscient GPS-guided boat symbol marching across an LCD screen have proven themselves as useful a pair of electronic aids as ever trickled down to the recreational boater. In limited visibility we should welcome any equipment that adds valid and reliable information to the navigation process. But networked electronics represent only a facsimile of the real world; we're heading in the wrong direction if we shortchange visual watchkeeping and choose any navigation routine that favors screen gazing. Better to use the black boxes as intended to augment the navigator's craft but not replace it. The art of navigation comes in how we evaluate, prioritize, and accept or reject data as we make decisions about where we are and where we're heading. Fixes and images on a screen don't constitute the final test of navigators' skills. We find those tests in what we do with information—from all sources—to provide safe passages for ourselves and our crew.

Marine Radar

As noted in the sidebar (Radar—A Brief Background), radar has developed into affordable equipment that is practical for almost all cruising sailboats. Contemporary units have a more compact size, lower power consumption, and a more modest price tag than in the past and have become mainstream in the recreational boating market. Radar still depends on transmitting and receiving radio-frequency pulses via a sweeping antenna, and as in the past, larger, more metallic targets generally yield stronger reflected signals.

Radar can now be networked with chartplotters and depthsounders, as discussed above, allowing the display of signals on numerous *(continued next page)*

RADAR—A BRIEF BACKGROUND

Beginning in 1928, financier Alfred Lee Loomis turned significant stock equity into enviable liquidity, ready to weather the crash that he was sure was coming. Over the next decade he acquired a significant lock on electrical utilities, devised the concept of the holding company, raced J-boats against the Vanderbilts and Astors, and purchased most of Hilton Head Island. However, these excesses couldn't fulfill this Yale-educated mathematics scholar who saw physics as the heart of knowledge. Hard science remained his true love, despite studying law and becoming the editor of the *Harvard Law Review*. By the late 1930s, his fortune intact, he spent his weekends consulting with groups of scientists, becoming both patron and participant in pure and applied research.

His mansion in Tuxedo Park, New York, became a private laboratory and impromptu conference center with a "who's who" guest list that included Albert Einstein, Niels Bohr, Werner Heisenberg, Enrico Fermi, and an ongoing string of researchers engaged in pushing the boundaries of physical science.

With the onset of WWII, Loomis committed his efforts to strategic research and soon headed the National Defense Research Committee's Microwave Committee, collaborating with the British Tizard Commission in a mutual quest for radar. The Brits had developed a revolutionary cavity magnetron with which to generate high-energy microwave pulses, while Loomis's team had already built a prototype radar they carried around in the back of a truck.

Loomis organized, initially *(continued next page)*

■ *Since the Navy installed this first radar aboard the battleship* USS New York *in 1938 radar technology has been continually refined and universally applied.*

RADAR—A BRIEF BACKGROUND, CONTINUED

capitalized, and led the civilian radar research effort in the United States. Inevitably, his crew eventually outgrew their digs in Tuxedo Park and he set up a new facility at MIT, the Radar Laboratory, or Rad Lab as it became known. Advances in technology came quickly. Bell Labs, General Electric, and a handful of other players joined the combined military and private sector project, moving to the prototype phase and on to production in a matter of weeks and months rather than years. Many believe this rapid development of radar proved even more important to the Allied victory in WWII than the rapid work involved to develop a nuclear weapon. In any case, A.L. Loomis was in on the ground floor of both efforts.

In addition, Loomis also devised Loomis Radio Navigation, what eventually became known as LORAN. As a lifelong sailor, precise navigator, and scientific visionary, Loomis created far more than a financial legacy.

After the war, radar quickly proved its value as both a navigation tool and an asset in the quest to avoid collisions at sea. Ships could use radar signal returns, the energy bounced back from targets, to modulate an electron beam scanning a phosphorous screen. This cathode-ray-tube plan position indicator (PPI) revealed targets as bright spots or semi-differentiated blobs on the screen—the larger and denser the target, the brighter and larger the image on the display. The signal attenuated with distance, and rain and the state of the sea further degraded performance.

Before long the industry began standardizing features and providing filters to cope with rain and sea clutter. Range resolution, a unit's ability to discern multiple targets in close proximity, steadily improved; bearing resolution, the ability of a unit to separate two targets at the same range but slightly different bearings, improved as well.

It also quickly became clear that the height of the antenna helped a crew see farther. Units operating at higher frequencies proved better able to discern smaller targets, while lower-frequency systems afforded longer range. To this day, ships at sea rely on the superior range of S-band equipment, while inshore recreational boaters favor the improved signal detection of X-band radar.

We've left the bad old days of PPI radar behind, along with the days the operator needed to wear a hood to see the screen in daylight. Around 1980 more viewer-friendly raster units hit the marine market; the older power-hungry magnetrons were replaced with light, small-diameter domes and solid-state circuitry with lower current demand. These new X-band units originated as weather radar in aircraft and became instant hits among sailors and power cruisers alike.

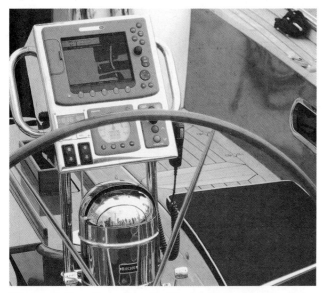

At one time, the sailor aft of the binnacle did most of the navigation with the compass. Today, we accomplish more and more with the gadget that's perched above. On some cruises the compass binnacle never slides open. Without traditional piloting skills and practices, however, you'll lack a backup plan, plus you won't realize when the electronics are steering you wrong.

monitors around the boat and, if desired, overlaying radar information on a digital chart. The flat-screen LCD is compact, viewable in daylight, and energy efficient. Small-diameter 2-kilowatt radomes have the smallest current draw of any magnetron-based system and are a good choice for sailors on a tight dollar and energy budget. However, you'll find a noticeable improvement in sensitivity, selectivity, and image resolution from a 4-kilowatt unit used with a larger open-array antenna.

Broadband Radar

Navico's line of Simrad, Northstar, and Lowrance radars have turned the page on single-frequency magnetron-based microwave radar. Their approach is based on a broadband frequency-modulated, continuous-wave (FMCW) system that uses a tiny fraction of the power of conventional radar. Other advantages include exquisite detail at close ranges. Broadband radar also eliminates the difficult choice between auto-tune image compromise or manual-tune complexity.

Broadband radar returns automatically display digitally as crisp, sharp, detailed images. In addition, the radiated energy is more than a thousand times less than with conventional radar, which lessens concerns about microwave effects on human tissue. The lower power consumption is also an important factor for vessels under sail.

Originally used in radar altimeters, the sensitivity and selectivity of broadband radar gives an operator crisp target discrimination at ranges as close as 100 feet. This close-range discrimination, along with the instant-on feature and the ability to flip quickly through always-tuned ranges, provides major advantages for avoiding collisions and navigating in close quarters.

The drawbacks of broadband radar number few, but they're significant. First, acquiring targets and presenting target detail drop way off in a range beyond 6 miles. Second, FMCW radar has a blind eye to all racons (radar beacons). (Racons, important aids to navigation in coastal waters, paint a distinctive return on a conventional radar screen. We consider it a shortfall if you lack an ability to detect them.) Finally, broadband radar shows a heightened preference for hard targets and a poor ability to discern large soft targets like rain-laden thunderstorm cells.

You should weigh these shortcomings against broadband radar's very real advantages. For example, poor performance when you're trying to avoid a squall could be offset by the excellent close-in maneuvering data displayed in overcast conditions. Some see broadband radar as an ideal way to augment a conventional X-band system, especially aboard a sailboat where energy efficiency is needed. Switching to broadband radar can cut current consumption considerably.

Weighing the Radar Choices

X-band small-craft radar still represents a functional amalgam of refinement and operational reliability. For example Furuno's radar models use dual bandwidths, narrow pulse lengths, and changes in antenna rotation speeds at different ranges in order to achieve optimal resolution of nearby and distant targets. Raymarine's simple plug-and-play networking makes it easy to add monitors on deck and below, and their MARPA autotracking makes monitoring contacts easier than ever. Garmin brings aviation-proven technology to the boater. All these systems remain X-band based.

Phased array radar is the cutting-edge technology adopted by the U.S. Navy, but it is unlikely to be seen on recreational boats in the next couple of decades. Commercial ships carry X- and S-dual-band units; the former provides more detail at closer ranges (less than 36 miles), while the S-band has greater range but would have to be mounted at the masthead to offer any advantage.

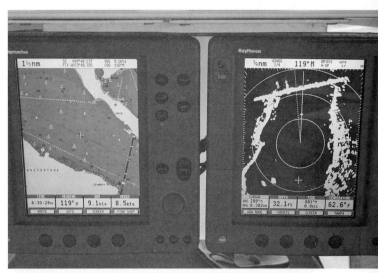

A modern digital radar unit displays contacts on an LCD screen. Automatic tune, gain, and sea clutter controls take the tricky tuning out of range changes. The radar image, in heading-up mode (right) reveals the banks and a bridge across the Chesapeake & Delaware Canal; the chartplotter, in north-up mode, also shows the bridge, although in a different orientation.

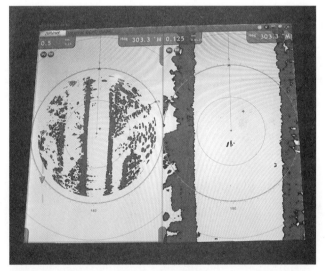

An example of a digital radar display on an MFD screen (ranging in size from 2 to 25 kilowatts) and equipped with true dual-range function. These units simultaneously transmit and receive on both ranges. In other words, they operate as if they were two independent units. For example, dual-range radars can simultaneously show both ½-mile and 3-mile range images on a split-screen display.

Both broadband and X-band radar units offer easy-to-use electronic bearing lines and variable-range markers with network connectivity, and AIS contacts and vessel information can be overlaid on the screen. With all this relevant data—and much more just a button push away—sensory overload can become an issue. It's imperative to prioritize what the screen

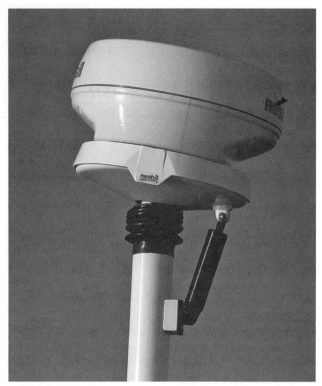

⚑ *One of the best ways to improve the performance of pedestal-mounted radar on a sailboat is to provide a tilt control for leveling the antenna when heeled and beating to weather.*

displays. Each bit of eye-grabbing information could eclipse or hide a weak, intermittent target, probably nothing more than a seagull floating on the surface but maybe this time kids in a skiff. That's why many professional navigators put their radar display on a simplicity diet and eliminate any information not part of the target-detection process. This approach may seem draconian to some, but you're asking for trouble if you attempt to use a 6.5-inch screen as both chartplotter and radar display.

Obviously, for radar to be an asset, you have to turn it on and then monitor it. Some years back, the cruising sailboat *Melinda Lee* approached landfall in New Zealand in squally, overcast conditions. Despite being only 30 miles from the coastline, the crew, a family of four, chose not to turn on the radar in order to save battery-bank energy. A Korean merchant ship failed to spot the yacht crossing its path, and in extremis, neither vessel made appropriate collision-avoidance maneuvers. The yacht was run down, and only the mother survived the ordeal. Here's the vital lesson from this tragic episode: if you have radar on board, use it.

With that in mind, select a unit with a manageable energy appetite. For example, 4 or 5 amps of current draw seem minimal until you multiply that by 10 to 12 hours of dusk-to-dawn operation. Broadband

radar might prove the best choice for those with limited ability to generate electricity or the need to feed the amp-hour appetites of a refrigerator, an autopilot, and incidentals such as instrumentation and lighting. A powerful X-band unit requires much more electricity, but putting the unit in standby mode or turning it off for long periods prevents you from collecting useful information. Ideally, budget permitting, install a hefty DC power system and have both broadband and conventional X-band radar units.

Automatic Identification Systems (AIS)

Recreational sailors and commercial mariners alike consider avoiding collisions a big deal, and all mariners benefit from the international effort to implement the Automatic Identification System (AIS). Initially mandated by the International Marine Organization (IMO) for vessels over 300 tons, AIS (Class A) spawned a second generation of transceivers (Class B) for small craft. The system ties together a two-channel VHF communication capability (AIS 1 and 2), GPS location and vessel movement information, and vessel registration details. These capabilities then create a digital location/identification signal that can be broadcast to other vessels within range. The electronic line of sight between AIS-equipped vessels is a nominal 20 miles in open water but often quite a bit more. And vessels in the same area automatically comprise a virtual network, advising each of the other's location, identity, course, and speed.

Today, commercial vessels operate AIS-Class A transceivers that incorporate 12-watt transmitters and a more detailed, more rapidly updated data stream than the Class B units used aboard recreational vessels. Class B units function with a 2-watt transmitter meant to radiate a less detailed, shorter-range signal. The more capable Class B units use twin receivers and respond to the alternating-channel AIS signals much more quickly. As an important byproduct of AIS reception, the unit can compare one vessel's projected course with that of other AIS broadcasting stations in the vicinity. Many of the latest versions feature alarm signals that sound when the unit perceives a collision course with another vessel or when a vessel enters a preselected alarm range. Some systems allow networking the AIS signal to remote MFDs around the boat; however, others are stand-alone units with an independent antenna.

If you've equipped your boat with a Class B AIS receiver and you receive data from a large merchant vessel, don't assume they see your own AIS signal. Merchant ships must be equipped with a Class A transceiver, and although the newer of these detect and display Class B signals, older models do not. In addition, merchant ships often find inshore waters so choked with AIS signals they intentionally filter out the clutter of small craft.

AIS information can be displayed as text, as blips on an LCD screen, or as a vector layer overlaid on a digital chart. As more sophisticated algorithms show up in digital charting software, the ability to analyze vessel movement and calculate a predicted closest point of approach (CPA) increases. But each calculation represents only a snapshot that is no longer valid if either vessel alters course or speed. Many AIS receivers include the ability to prioritize the display of a contact that poses a potential collision risk, and some allow the user to select a CPA alarm radius. A typical AIS receiver can handle 2,000 or more contacts at once.

Screen display size and contact clutter influence the degree of an AIS unit's user-friendliness. In congested areas where you have room on the screen for only the most threatening contacts, an abrupt change in your course can shuffle the deck, presenting a whole new set of closing contacts that need visual identification. For example, let's say your display is full of contacts even after you've chosen a small CPA range of, say, 0.5 nautical mile. In that case, a simple course change to respond to a meeting, crossing, or overtaking situation might add a new grouping of contacts to the screen. If one of these was 0.6 mile away before your turn, it may go from not being displayed on the screen to being a significant collision hazard that prompts essential evasive maneuvering.

We can easily see such relationships with other vessels on radar. In addition, vessels, buoys, and other obstructions not radiating an AIS signal usually show up just fine on radar as well. The combined use of AIS and radar is a powerful way to double-team collision avoidance, and radar doesn't rely on satellite transmissions or equipment aboard other vessels. The assumption that AIS renders radar passé is both misleading and fundamentally incorrect.

Many sailors opt for receive-only AIS, which doesn't communicate your position to others. Like the AIS Class B transceiver, you can use a receive-only unit either as a stand-alone navigation aid or networked with a plotter, electronic compass, radar, etc. Receive-only units may not offer the complete answer, but they provide a big step in the right direction. Knowing who you want to avoid gives you more than 50% of the informational value of AIS. Then, at a later date, you can add an AIS transponder.

Most major electronics brands offer black-box plug-ins that detect AIS signals and route the data to multifunction displays. In addition, it's often possible to use a NMEA 0183 or 2000 interface to shunt

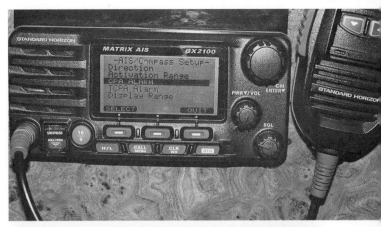

The AIS Class B equipment used by recreational mariners and other small-craft operators interfaces with the Class A (commercial) system, but Class B units are not as powerful, fast, or detailed in data transmission or reception. On top is an AIS-equipped VHF radio; a stand-alone AIS unit (above) provides larger screen graphic displays of target.

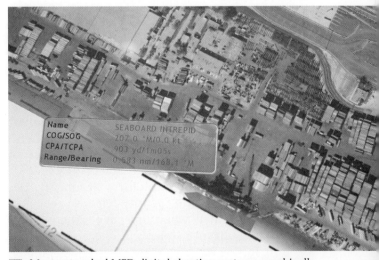

Most networked MFD digital charting systems graphically display AIS contacts, including vessel name, position, current course and speed, and other useful data. The system also calculates the closest point of approach (CPA) along with the time it will occur—information that changes if either vessel alters course or speed.

📕 *Electronic aids to navigation such as radar and AIS can assist in collision avoidance, but neither replaces visual watchkeeping during times of good visibility. AIS can be a help when we're trying to identify a ship and make bridge-to-bridge VHF contact.*

data from an AIS receiver or transceiver to a display of a different brand. Many networks allow the user to overlay AIS vessel locations on a digital chart or radar display, and you can watch in real time the relative motion between your boat and the AIS-equipped fleet. Advocates of stand-alone displays prefer to have the AIS signal displayed on a screen of its own, just as they prefer separate displays for radar and a digital chart. Either approach is valid as long as all inputs are monitored regularly.

Though billed as a collision-avoidance aid, in the long run we're likely to view AIS as much more multifaceted. At this writing, the U.S. Coast Guard is in the process of implementing the Nationwide Automatic Identification System (NAIS), a vessel-tracking system that homes in on AIS signals. Eventually, this new capability will use a satellite array that can detect AIS signals from up to 2,000 miles away. A necklace of sea buoys around the coastline and shoreside Rescue 21 towers will be integrated into the vessel-movement big picture. The Coast Guard's stated purpose is "a focus on improving security, navigational safety, search and rescue, and environmental protection services," which goes well beyond avoiding collision. The Department of Homeland Security refers to the NAIS program as one that "will complement other surveillance and intelligence systems in identifying vessels requiring further investigation and action."

For the time being, at least, recreational boaters can decide their commitment to both track and be tracked. At this point, AIS equipment is mandatory for large commercial craft and fast motoryachts over 65 feet; it remains optional for small craft. We've already seen advisories about shutting off AIS in waters with reported pirate activity. Questions also arise about the legality of selling the tracking information the system collects.

Today, the Coast Guard's NAIS Phase I plan is in play, as reported: "Since September 2007, increment 1 of the NAIS project—receive capability only—has been deployed to 58 ports nationwide. This first increment of the system allows the Coast Guard to receive signals out to 24 miles from shore. The next step, which will continue through 2014, is to deploy permanent transceivers at these 58 sites, extending the receive range to 50 miles, and adding the ability to transmit information out to 24 miles from shore." On the upside, this means expediting responses to calls for help. Rescuing vessels no longer need to spend precious time using radio direction finding for a vessel in distress; rather, the system allows GPS coordinates to be displayed along with vessel details and a graphic position on MFDs aboard search-and-rescue vessels and aircraft.

Regardless of electronic advances, no matter how impressive, most of the time we keep visual navigation rules in play. Watching a screen is not an alternative to keeping a good lookout, even if boating statistics show that other types of vessels rarely run down sailboats. Rare is not never, though, and every year commercial craft do run down recreational boats or these boats run into each other, and still others disappear mysteriously during a passage. Sailors who have experienced close calls too often say they "never noticed" another vessel that remained on a constant bearing with decreasing range until they had barely enough time to avoid the collision and live to tell about it. A small number of the more unfortunate incidents cost lives. Legal settlements following collision incidents usually include gag orders preventing other sailors from hearing about the lessons learned. In such cases, however, we know AIS could have made a profound difference.

Sailing offers a chance to taste freedom and get away from it all. At the moment, we see AIS as a nonintrusive safety asset, not a means of surveillance—being tracked seems like no big deal. We hope never to see a time when the nation's quest for security requires us to switch the unit on before leaving the dock and leave it on throughout the voyage. As with all promising technology, how it is used determines its final story.

PILOTING WITH PAPER CHARTS AND SHIP'S COMPASS

A printed copy of a Mercator chart remains a mariner's best friend, and if a picture is worth a thousand words, the worth of the right chart figures beyond calculation. Navigation using your boat's compass and paper charts remains a foundation skill and the failsafe option to fall back on when the electronics malfunction. But paper charts also offer some advantages over their digital counterparts. In the follow-

ing sections I delve into chart basics, explanations of navigation aids, compasses, dead reckoning, and other fundamental piloting skills that are critical to seamanship. I assume readers have at least a working knowledge of how to navigate with a chart and compass.

A Few Chart Basics (Paper or Digital)

A large-scale chart shows a small area in great detail (epitomized by a harbor chart), whereas a small-scale chart shows a large area with minimal detail (epitomized by a sailing chart). A large-scale view shows less of the planet's surface, so it involves less curvature and distortion than when a spherical shape is translated into a flat, two-dimensional configuration. Perhaps the biggest advantage of Mercator projections used for charts comes from the expanded longitude, thus allowing us to accurately measure directions and distances on all but small-scale charts (on which the shortest distance between two points is not a straight line). The downside of Mercator projections shows up as the distortion of coastline shapes, especially in high latitudes and on very small-scale charts. (Mariners navigating polar regions need an alternative to the Mercator projection. The more favored options include the modified Lambert conformal, gnomonic, and stereographic projections. Fortunately, for everyone else, the Mercator projection does the job nicely.)

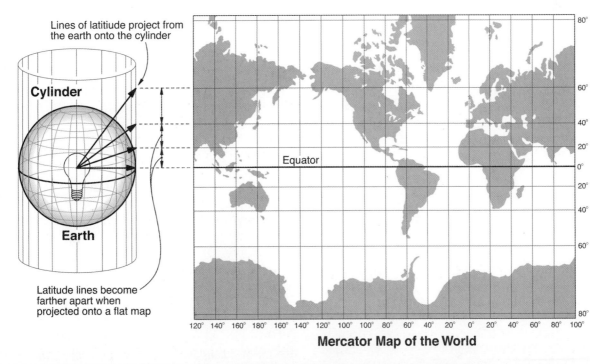

Mercator Map of the World

A Mercator chart is a cylindrical projection, a mapmaking technique that delivers accurate directions and distances while distorting landmasses closer to the poles. The smaller the scale, the more noticeable the deformation becomes. An X, Y Cartesian grid is defined on the chart by lines of latitude and longitude that cross at right angles.

Geographers define a great circle as any circle whose plane cuts through the center of the earth, separating the planet into two equal hemispheres. The equator is a good example of a great circle, with a clear location perpendicular to the earth's axis. Other great circles (an infinite number, in fact) can be formed by planes that bisect the planet perpendicular to the plane of the equator; these serve as the y-axis of the Cartesian grid and are known as lines of longitude, or meridians. Meridians appear as straight, vertical lines on a Mercator projection.

Meridians of longitude are numbered from the prime meridian—an arbitrary starting point, 0 degrees of longitude. Centuries ago, national egos weighed in on the designation of prime meridian, with the English, French, Spanish, and others insisting that the prime meridian (0 or 360 degrees of longitude) run through their own backyards. Finally the world's maritime interests agreed on Greenwich, England, as the common starting point.

All lines of longitude are great circles, because their circumference equals all other great circles, including the equator. Lines of latitude are considered small circles—except at the equator—because the planes they define do not transect the center of the earth, splitting it into equal halves, nor do they have the circumference (approximately 21,600 nautical miles) of a great circle. One degree of latitude represents a distance of 60 nautical miles on the earth's surface, whether measured in the tropics or in Nova Scotia—good news for navigators. Therefore, each minute of latitude equals one nautical mile.

This precision makes a minute of latitude a handy reference gauge, from which we can derive all kinds of angle and distance relationships. When we relate these angle and distance relationships to the rotation of the earth on its axis, we can make some interesting observations, as noted in the sidebar, Earth's Rotation and Time Zones.

Unfortunately, the earth has less than perfect spherical shape. Thanks to the effects of gravity and centrifugal force, our earth is an oblate spheroid that's fatter around the middle. This causes some problems for the neat grid we try to plaster atop the misshapen sphere. Corrections made through cartography and celestial navigation account for the plan-

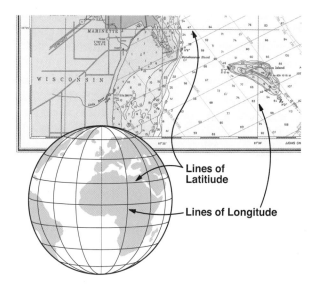

Lines of latitude and longitude create the grid that makes up the nautical chart.

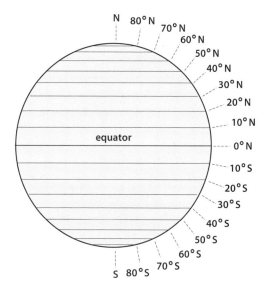

Parallels of latitude are measured north and south from the equator, which is designated as 0°N.

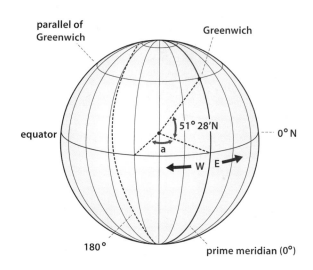

The meridians of longitude, all great circles with equal circumference, are measured east and west from the prime meridian, located at Greenwich, England, and set as 0°. Angle "a" in the drawing represents a west longitude.

et's less-than-perfect shape, the wobbles in its orbit, and its elliptical course around the sun.

Chart Datum

In the bad old days of imprecise navigation, no one worried about small errors resulting from the assumption of the earth as a perfect sphere. The navigator's wobbly arm or bad eyesight when attempting to shoot star sights on a rolling deck introduced enough error to mask the variation between perfect X, Y coordinates and the bulging waistline of this planet we call home. Today, accuracy of electronic position finding within a meter has exposed the nightmare of cartographic inaccuracy. In essence, the GPS signal references the coordinates of a perfect sphere, while imperfections in the earth's surface introduce minor but measurable discrepancies. Old-fashioned measurement methods also introduced inaccuracies, adding to the scramble to improve chart accuracy over the last decade or so, and the process continues today.

This arcane world of imperfect chart rendering has been helped through the use of datum and offsets that act as corrections to better align the cartography with the graticule (the earth's Cartesian grid of latitude and longitude). To paraphrase Bowditch, a datum is any numerical set (horizontal and vertical quantities) that may serve as a reference for other quantities. If you look closely at a printed chart you can see a designation telling you what datum was used to prepare it. But how does your GPS unit know what datum was used on the charts it is linking your position to? Fortunately, most GPS units automatically select the WGS 84/NAD 83 datum, also used by most U.S.-produced charts. The longitude and latitude grid—graticule—is shifted to coincide with the datum employed. Although it's highly unlikely you'll ever use a chart with a datum other than the two named above, if you do, you'll need to select the new datum from the GPS menu. If you can't do this, you can manually insert a lat/lon offset in order to calibrate the GPS-derived coordinates with the graphic detail of the chart. The bottom line is that the chart and the instrument yielding the fix need to reference the same grid representation (datum) of the misshapen earth.

Chart Scale

The ratio between the real world and its two-dimensional representation on a paper surface or digital screen defines how "zoomed" in or out the chart seems to be. Consider what's meant by a 1:1 ratio using a photographic analogy. With a 1:1 relationship, the size of the object photographed is identical with the size of the image on the camera's sensor. It delivers great detail of a very small area. The same is true

Paper charts and traditional piloting skills remain a valuable part of navigation despite all that automation and digital charting deliver. Dividers, parallel rules (shown here), and a sharp pencil are the tools of paper navigation, and you need no power supply to use a printed chart. Zooming and panning occur instantaneously and without thought. Don't leave port without them.

EARTH'S ROTATION AND TIME ZONES

While sailors use GMT, on land we carve up the earth into time zones—how they are calculated takes us back to solar time and longitude. Each time zone encompasses 15 degrees on average (allowing for a few gouges, bulges, and jogs due to political expedience) because the earth rotates about 15 degrees in an hour. Think of it this way:

- 360 degrees of longitude takes you around the world;
- the earth turns through 360 degrees in a day;
- 360 degrees divided by 24 hours is 15 degrees an hour.

By dividing 60 minutes of time into 15 degrees of arc, we can find out how much angular rotation takes place in one minute of time. The answer is 15 minutes of arc, and on the equator, which happens to be a great circle, that amounts to 15 nautical miles.

Dividing the earth's approximate circumference at the equator by 24 hours, we can see how fast a person on the equator is moving because of the earth's rotation: 21,600 nautical miles ÷ 24 hrs = 900 nautical miles per hour.

From this calculation we can determine that, on the equator, the earth moves 15 nautical miles in one minute of time. Therefore, the circumference of the earth at the equator equals a simple rate-times-time calculation ($D = R \times T$).

The resulting solution (24 hrs x 60 minutes × 15 mpm = 21,600 nautical miles) is the circumference of the equator and every other great circle on the planet.

A large-scale chart depicts a small area in significant detail. Often called a harbor chart, the information offered includes soundings, secondary buoyage, and special anchorage locations. (If this chart were electronic we would call it a raster depiction because it is non-layered and uses a printed chart as its basis.)

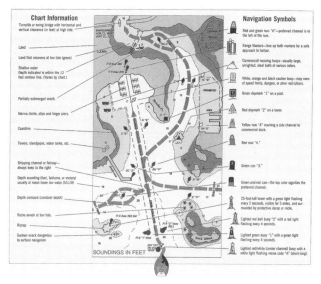

Nautical charts contain a wealth of data—get to know their symbols, some of which show features above the water, and some below.

of charts with smaller ratios. For example, a 1:50,000 scale chart delivers more detail than a 1:500,000 scale chart. One inch of distance on a 1:50,000 harbor chart represents 50,000 inches (4,167 feet) in the harbor itself. One inch on a 1:500,000 sailing chart represents 500,000 inches (41,667 feet or 6.94 nautical miles) on the earth's surface.

The smaller the scale, the larger the area covered by the chart, and the more inaccurate a pencil line or point becomes. Cartographers call the process of showing more area and less detail generalization. We use generalized charts to plan voyages, referring to them as sailing or planning charts, with a scale even smaller (usually) than 1:500,000. This small scale renders the charts all but useless as a tool for approach-

ing a landfall. Sailors use charts falling into a range of 1:150,000 to 1:500,000 for coastal navigation beyond the 10-fathom line or at least well outside reefs and the sand shoals of river mouths.

For more inshore navigation, approach charts fall into a range from 1:50,000 to 1:150,000 and show more detail. Large-scale harbor charts at scales of 1:10,000 to 1:50,000 are used when threading tight confines choked with obstacles to navigation because harbor charts show a very small area in great detail.

Chart Symbols

To get the most from a chart you need to understand the symbols and abbreviations used to depict everything from bottom type to shoreside towers, water tanks, and government aids to navigation. NOAA's *U.S. Chart No. 1: Symbols, Abbreviations and Terms used on Paper and Electronic Navigational Charts* (http://www.nauticalcharts.noaa.gov/mcd/chartno1.htm) is the key to all other charts rather than a chart itself. It identifies the pictographs and symbols used on modern American (and most international) charts. Most symbols are intuitive, like the anchor shape used to designate an anchorage, but many stretch the imagination, which is why every navigator should have a copy of this decoding book handy in a chart table drawer or shelf. You can acquire enhanced editions of Chart No. 1 from commercial publishers, including Nigel Calder's *How to Read a Nautical Chart* (see A Sailor's Library).

For centuries cartographers have refined how they present vital graphic information without cluttering the chart and risking obscuring the most significant features, such as geologic and oceanographic features that can threaten the well-being of a vessel and crew. Half-tide ledges, isolated rocks, shoal spots, coral reefs, and surf-swept sandbars are primary examples of mariners' greatest concerns, so secondary information is presented in a way that avoids obstructing the visibility of the critical features. A larger-scale chart that covers a smaller area allows more space to clearly define bottom contours and other hazards. Because of the need for detail when maneuvering in close quarters, we suggest that you don't use small-scale routing charts for this navigation.

Chart Plotting on a Paper Chart

We've established that on a Mercator projection, lines of latitude are parallel to each other and the distance between them remains consistent from the top of a chart to the bottom. One minute of latitude equals one nautical mile in the tropics or the arctic, and the latitude scale along the edge of a chart can be used to measure distance along a course line or on a projected track. Meridians (lines of longitude) are all great circles that converge at the poles, meaning that they're not actually parallel even though they are drawn that way on a Mercator chart. As we move away from the equator, the distance between adjacent meridians decreases. Only at the equator does a minute of longitude equal one nautical mile, and it diminishes to nothing at the poles.

To plot a position using X,Y coordinates of latitude and longitude, locate the latitude on the latitude scale in the left or right chart margin, then draw a horizontal line from that point across the chart, parallel with the nearest printed line of latitude. (Parallel rules are ideal for this work.) Now locate the longitude on the longitude scale at the chart's top or bottom margin, and draw a vertical line from that point, parallel with the nearest meridian, so that it crosses the latitude line you just drew. The intersection of the two pencil lines is the point in question, your plotted fix.

Anyone can learn to plot a course and position information on a chart. The skill involved is by no means irrelevant in an age of electronic precision. It trains sailors to think spatially and be more aware of their surroundings, and it provides a backup plan if the electronics fail. It's a talent—or skill—that benefits from a precise approach and attention to detail. Routine double checks also improve accuracy. When plotting a course from a previous dead reckoning (DR) point or fix to the current location, navigators use information they gather from the instruments and observations the crew noted in the deck log or passed

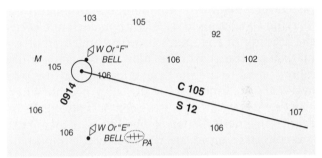

■ *Course and speed are indicated on a line segment that's a vector representation in scale with the chart. The 0914 fix, indicated by a dot within a circle, was based on the close proximity of a government mark used to indicate a sunken wreck. From there we're steering a course of 105° true (courses not labeled as magnetic are assumed to be true) at a speed through the water of 12 knots, and we begin the next leg of our DR plot accordingly.*

■ *Dividers and a hard graphite marking pencil remain a navigator's best friend, and a gum eraser also comes in handy.*

	U.S.	U.K.
dead reckoning		
estimated position		
fix		
fix by position lines		
range (distance)		
transfered position line	R Fix	
course to steer and water track	C	
ground track	TR	
current vector	S / D	
electronic fix		

■ *Standard chartplotting symbols appear here. Your own practices may differ from what's shown here. That's okay— just be consistent.*

along verbally. Calculated from speed and direction, a DR omits influences of current, leeway, steering error, and so forth. Traditionally the boat's DR position is indicated by a half circle with the time in four digits (using the naval 24-hour clock) written next to it. The line leading from a previous fix or DR calculation represents the assumed track of the vessel. The letter C appears above the line, along with a three-digit number defining the average course heading sailed, marked with an M or T for magnetic or true.

Professional mariners operating ships equipped with gyrocompasses read headings in true degrees, while recreational boats rely upon magnetic or flux-gate compasses, the readings from which, once adjusted for deviation, provide magnetic headings. Marking DR courses in magnetic nomenclature keeps the reading of the boat's compass and the course marked on the chart consistent. Most recreational sailors prefer to use the magnetic compass rose (see page 237), the inner ring on the chart, because when properly swung, their vessel's compass also reads in degrees magnetic. When comparing true, magnetic, and compass courses, always consider the important issues of variation and deviation.

How to graphically identify a fix, a DR position, or a bearing line varies slightly from one navigator to the next and are covered in more detail later in this chapter. Regardless, it is critical to use symbols consistently and make all markings legible.

Knowing Your Aids to Navigation

Like road signs on a highway, lateral and cardinal navigation marks warn mariners away from hazards, and you should know the meanings of the colors, shapes, and symbols used to designate safe passage. In 1980, the International Association of Lighthouse Authorities (IALA) reached agreement on buoyage by conforming to an IMO request for consistency—or at least this *almost* happened. However, instead of closing the session with one system of worldwide buoyage, the IALA closed it with two. Ever since, we have to assess whether the particular waters we're sailing are covered by IALA Region A or Region B buoyage. One difference involves a complete color reversal of lateral marks. For example, a couple of decades ago, sailors headed into Roadtown Harbor in the British Virgin Islands mistakenly used the old Yankee habit of "red-right-returning" and ended up stranded on a shoal rather than inside a friendly harbor.

Most of the world adheres to IALA Region A standards, which put red marks on the port side of a channel when entering from sea. North and South America and a handful of other nations adhere to Region B "red-right-returning" standards. Fortunately, for Americans, the Caribbean now adheres to IALA Region B regulations.

In U.S. waters, the Coast Guard maintains most placed buoys and fixed aids, but states and local municipalities place and maintain some additional marks. All parties involved generally make a concerted effort to conform to IALA guidelines, which also include design and engineering specs for buoyage.

Buoys have five basic shapes: can, cone or nun, sphere, pillar, and spar. The first three have lateral significance. "Cone" and "conical" have replaced the somewhat politically incorrect term "nun buoy." (While it's difficult to break lifetime habits, it still seems to me that the word "nun" offers a clearer contrast with a "can" shape than the word "cone.")

These floating and fixed aids to navigation perform a variety of jobs, but the vast majority fall into one of three categories: marking the sides of channels; identifying rocks, reefs, wrecks, and other hazards to navigation; and identifying safe waters for navigation. Although buoys and fixed marks have other uses, these are the primary ways in which we count on them as navigation aids. In daylight, the shapes, colors, and topmarks of these aids define how they should be approached; at night, those with lights convey their identities through the period (intervals between or number of flashes), color, and characteristics of their beacons.

Ground tackle consisting of chain and a cast iron or concrete weight hold navigation buoys in place with a usual scope of about 3:1. This means a buoy's position is less accurate than the GPS coordinates that define its location. Chain weight limits the depths in which conventional marks can be moored to about 200 feet. Inshore aids to navigation consist of small floating buoys similar to those in deep water, fixed marks on single pilings (day beacons), or more complex structures.

Used in conjunction with a chart and visual piloting skills, these marks provide what we refer to as level-one piloting skills, a process in which navigators can fix their position on a chart by identifying one or more specific navigational aids near the boat. We recommend establishing a fix using an array of identifiable marks and fixed features rather than relying on one buoy. But if the buoy's location and identification number agree with other data such as soundings and perhaps a radar image of a jetty or other prominent shoreside feature, consider the visual fix reliable.

All navigators learn to be skeptical, which is why prudent navigators, much like good scientists, prefer making decisions based on multiple indicators that point to the same conclusion rather than rely on a single piece of information, even if it appears definitive. Buoys can move, GPS fixes can go awry, and DR tracks can be inaccurate, but when all three put you in the same place, you can conclude that's where you must be.

Develop the habit of noting the time you pass a mark close at hand, using a pencil to write down the four-digit local time using the 24-hour clock directly on the chart beside the mark; or if you keep a deck log, record the information there. Put a dot in the center of a small circle to indicate your fix: where you were in relation to the mark at the time you passed it. If your visibility later decreases because of fog, nightfall, or a torrential squall, your recent fix might become extremely valuable, even when you're in familiar local waters.

GPS units, even the handheld devices, can record a breadcrumb-like trail depicting the vessel's track over the bottom. If you find yourself in zero visibility, this feature can help you safely return to port. On the other hand, don't let this electronic convenience lure you away from the practice of noting buoy passage times on a regular basis.

The need for frequent fixes depends on your speed and any immediate threats. When you're piloting reef-strewn coastal waters, you plot fixes every 10 or 15 minutes rather than the customary hourly plot you'd normally use in coastal waters.

As discussed earlier, digital charting systems display a real-time image of a vessel's location as well as a line astern marking the course made good. They can also project a line ahead that represents the outcome of the current steered course. While this instantaneous information can lead to safer navigation, in an instant you could lose the visual display, and in that situation, navigators are back to square one. For this reason, we recommend regular pencil and paper notes to provide backup information.

Lateral Marks

Lateral marks define channel boundaries. In IALA Region B areas such as North America, a boat approaching from seaward encounters a pathway bordered on the starboard side with numbered red marks (often nuns, but sometimes bells or daymarks), which increase in even numbers. Numbered green marks (cans, bells, and daymarks) appear on the port side, with increasing odd numbers. The most seaward of these channel marks are often larger deep-water marks; often a bicolored buoy (red and white, often a pillar-shaped gong buoy) with a flashing white light for Morse code A (dot-dash) defining the seaward start of the approach channel.

As mentioned, "red-right-returning" is the slogan passed along to every fledgling navigator in U.S. waters and applies to nun buoys or triangular marks

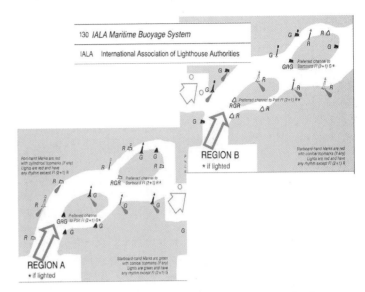

IALA regions A and B flip-flop the "red-right-returning" rule.

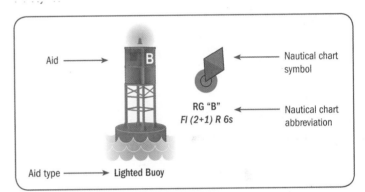

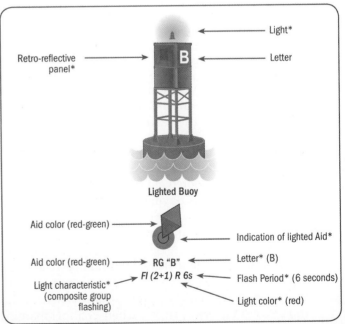

Lighted buoys are shown on charts with the color and characteristic of the light clearly defined.

When approaching from seaward, keep red, even-numbered lateral marks in IALA B waters to starboard. They mark the right-hand side of a channel and may or may not be equipped with a light or sound device, as on number "14."

Marks on a single piling (beacon) dominate shoal waters and may be lighted or unlighted. Their locations don't vary like buoys because of the scope of ground tackle, and they occasionally do double duty as a perch for an osprey nest.

—always red and even-numbered. Remember always to check the regional *Sailing Directions* elsewhere in the world for how the red and green marks are used.

Daymarks Fixed navigation aids, including a single piling or more elaborate structure, afford a more precise location than a moored aid that swings on its scope. Often referred to as daymarks, each has a topmark shape that groups it with either nuns (triangle) or cans (square). Like nuns and cans, when returning from seaward, these marks are odd-numbered and green on the port side of a channel and even-numbered and red on the starboard side. These are more common than buoyed aids in shallow-water estuaries such as the Intracoastal Waterway (ICW), where channel margins are shallow and sand or mud bottoms prevail.

In the ICW, yellow squares and triangles on marks differentiate them from the channel marks and buoy-

age used to delineate the inlets, harbors, and rivers that transect this waterway. For example, a small yellow triangle on a red mark indicates that we should leave the mark to starboard on a cruise south toward Florida or west toward New Orleans. A green mark bearing a small yellow square means we should leave it to starboard during the opposite trip east or north.

Sea Buoys The most seaward marks in the coastal zone tend to be large bicolored buoys (red and white vertical stripes) with a Morse A light (indicating a safe-water mark, safe to pass on either side) and a sound-making device. We see big pillar whistle, gong, and bell buoys replacing spherical marks because the pillar buoys tend to be visible from a greater distance. These buoys lead a vessel to an entrance channel.

Sailors progressing without their engines running find the distinctive sounds of traditional bells, gongs, and whistles quite valuable. Just a few decades ago, and for centuries prior to that, mariners regarded each buoy's sound, like its light characteristic, as familiar as a close friend, especially in coastal waters plagued by overcast or foggy conditions. Bell buoys rely upon wave motion to swing a heavy clapper into a bronze bell, yielding a single pitch. A gong incorporates multiple bell shapes and radiates several different tones. The whistle buoy also relies on wave motion to force air through a tubular-shaped whistle, yielding a baleful moan. These devices sound louder in rougher weather than in light breezes.

Electronic navigation equipment may have given way to the lat/lon readout on a GPS unit or a symbol on a chartplotter's LCD screen, but buoy identification remains a good secondary means of position confirmation. As previously mentioned, we recommend using a paper chart to jot down the time you visually identified a mark. It's an important part of the navigator's routine.

Special-Purpose Marks Unnumbered, bicolored center-channel marks designate the preferred side for passage with the topmost color band in their topmark.

A red-over-green combination means that the buoy should be left close to starboard, when entering from seaward.

A green top band signifies that the buoy should be left close to port when entering from seaward.

Isolated danger marks are black and red. They are unnumbered but may be designated by letters.

Special yellow marks can signify a no-go area or a special restriction zone; on large-scale charts their significance is indicated.

Large, buoy-type weather stations, also painted yellow, appear on charts.

The Cardinal System

Cardinal marks are the equivalent of a seagoing metric system. Popular in Europe, often seen in the Caribbean, but used infrequently in U.S. waters, I found mastering them less intuitive than other systems. However, once you memorize the stripe and topmark designations, you'll find them much more understandable.

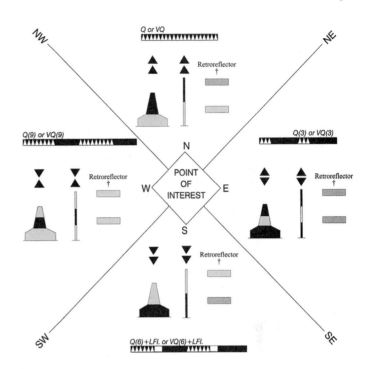

Cardinal marks denote the locations of specific dangers via their topmarks, color bands, and light characteristics.

You'll see cardinal marks placed in the quadrants surrounding a rock, reef, bar, or other obstacle. Note that they're named after the four cardinal points of the compass: N, E, S, and W. To use them, follow the guiding rule: pass the mark to the same side as its designation. For example, when you see a north-designated cardinal marker, you'll find a safe passage to its north.

Atop each cardinal mark note two black conical shapes arranged in one of four possible patterns. Pointing up designates a north mark (a mark that is north of the danger), while pointing downward designates a south mark.

The two cone bases are joined on an east mark, and the cone tips touch on a west mark. Some sailors use the slogan "north up and west is a wine glass" to remember the cone and cardinal point relationship.

You must memorize the colors appearing in horizontal bands, along with light characteristics. The accompanying table summarizes the information provided by cardinal marks.

CARDINAL MARKS CHARACTERISTICS

North	Cone tips up	Black over yellow	Even flashing
South	Cone tips down	Yellow over black	6 flashes in group + 1 long
East	Cones base to base	Black yellow black	3 flashes in group
West	Cones tip to tip	Yellow black yellow	9 flashes in group

You might find the light pattern characteristics initially confusing: quick flashing or very quick flashing. However, if you imagine a compass rose superimposed on the face of a clock and see east as 3, south as 6, and west as 9, you'll find them easier to recall. The

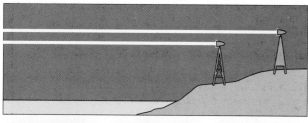

left of range, turn to starboard to return to range on range line

on range line

right of range, turn to port to return to range

🚩 *The more distant range light is always higher than the closer one. If they slip out of alignment, always turn the wheel toward the lower light. If the lower light appears to the right of the upper light, steer right, and vice versa.*

long flash in the south pattern helps to distinguish it from the 9-flash pattern of the west designation.

Ranges Back in our school days we learned one of the first rules of geometry: two points define a straight line and only one line. Consequently, only one specific line of bearing can connect two points on a chart. This simple but irrefutable fact, at least when it comes to close-quarters navigation, gave rise to an ingenious use of two marks aligned as leads, or range marks. Range marks are used to designate a preferred, center channel for the deepest water. In tight estuaries like the Delaware River or the Upper Chesapeake Bay, bow and stern ranges aid commercial as well as recreational sailors as they transit these narrow channels.

Once the range marks or their lights come into view, their use becomes a simple matter of stacking one topmark or light above the other. The higher mark and its light are always farther away. When the bottom mark seems to be drifting left of the upper mark, you'll steer the vessel to port to realign the two; when the bottom mark is drifting right, steer to starboard. You can also use these aids for back bearings by aligning them astern as you sail or power away from them. If, when facing sternward, the front range mark seems to be moving right, you must turn the boat to port to realign the range.

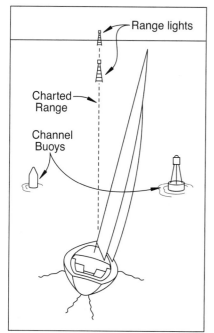

RANGE LINED UP, BOAT IS IN MIDDLE OF CHANNEL

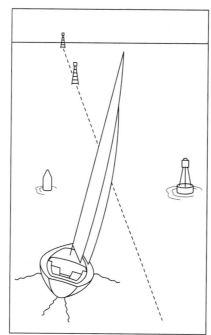

RANGE TO STARBOARD, BOAT IS TO PORT OF THE CHANNEL

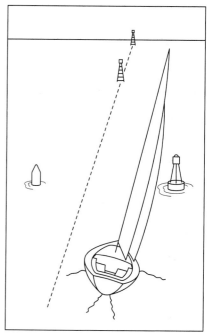

RANGE TO PORT, BOAT IS TO STARBOARD OF THE CHANNEL

🚩 *The range will be lined up when you're sailing on the correct approach. They will appear out of line when you are off course. Keep in mind that often when you are perfectly aligned with a range you are also on a collision course with large, deep-draft commercial traffic, and must be extra vigilant with watchkeeping and collision avoidance.*

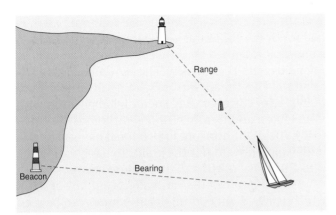

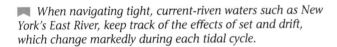

A simultaneous range and bearing can lead to an accurate fix. Any two charted objects can constitute a range; here, a conical buoy is aligned with the more distant lighthouse. To plot the range, simply draw a line from the lighthouse to the buoy and extend it to your estimated position. A compass bearing to a third charted object (in this case a daybeacon) can then be crossed with the range line to fix your position. You can also measure the bearing of the range to double-check the accuracy of your hand bearing compass. (Accuracy will be influenced by the scope of the buoy's ground tackle and your proximity to the buoy.)

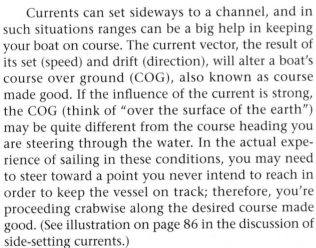

When navigating tight, current-riven waters such as New York's East River, keep track of the effects of set and drift, which change markedly during each tidal cycle.

Currents can set sideways to a channel, and in such situations ranges can be a big help in keeping your boat on course. The current vector, the result of its set (speed) and drift (direction), will alter a boat's course over ground (COG), also known as course made good. If the influence of the current is strong, the COG (think of "over the surface of the earth") may be quite different from the course heading you are steering through the water. In the actual experience of sailing in these conditions, you may need to steer toward a point you never intend to reach in order to keep the vessel on track; therefore, you're proceeding crabwise along the desired course made good. (See illustration on page 86 in the discussion of side-setting currents.)

Put simply in a statement of comparison, the lower the ratio between your boat speed and the current's set, and the more nearly on your beam the current's drift happens to be, the more radically the current will set you off course. The best way to stem the effect of a side-setting current is keeping range marks aligned. Both the speed and direction of a current can change rather quickly and lead you to alter the amount of steering offset required to stay on course. You can also find the right course that yields the desired course made good on your GPS screen or chartplotter.

Ranges can inadvertently cause dangers, such as the tendency for recreational craft to follow them blindly, failing to recognize that they're right in line with commercial traffic using the area. If no merchant traffic is using the main channel, then go ahead and sail the safest deep water. However, when a ship comes into view, it's the responsibility of the shallow-draft boat to move as far to the right-hand side of the channel as possible. If you discern you have enough water just outside the lateral channel marks, as is often the case, that's the best place to be.

Lights and Lighthouses

Tourist attractions, artists' subjects, postcard adornments—lighthouses come in great variety, many of them iconic. But their configurations came from more than architectural whim. The design of each is based on the site, the range of its light, and the conditions the structure must withstand.

These stately giants of the shoreline have been standing vigil ever since the light at Alexandria called mariners home from the sea. Their role is as a primary beacon, with their location clearly shown on charts and their light characteristics so specific that it cannot be confused with any nearby light. Three decades ago, electronic navigation was in its infancy

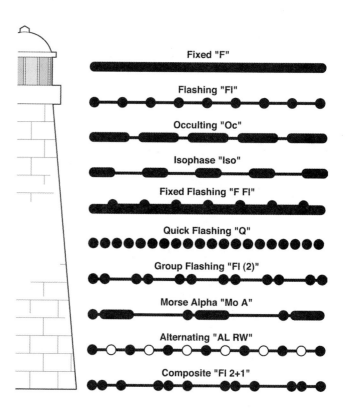

and the great lights still reigned supreme, as they had for over a thousand years. Today they have been somewhat sidelined by the electronic symbol marching across the LCD screen. The new allegiance may be to the GPS signal, but savvy old salts understand the value of corroborating their digital position with visual fixes, and clearly visible lighthouses continue to dot the night horizon. Professional navigators also understand how to put these aids to navigation back into a primary role if a digital failure occurs.

The curvature of the earth affects our line of sight, which is why lights on higher structures can be seen farther offshore. Thanks to the French and their development of the Fresnel lens, low-candlepower light sources have provided great beacons for nearly two centuries now. This carefully cast glass lens combines circular rows of prism-like rings that magnify the light source and focus it in a narrow band on the horizontal plane. Using a mirror to further intensify the light, and rotating its beam through a 360-degree arc inside the cylindrical Fresnel lens, designers could transform the lamplight into a carefully timed rotating beacon. The last of the oil-lamp lighthouses remained in operation on islands off the northern Australia coast until about 1980. (continued page 236)

Fixed "F"

Flashing "Fl"

Occulting "Oc"

Isophase "Iso"

Fixed Flashing "F Fl"

Quick Flashing "Q"

Group Flashing "Fl (2)"

Morse Alpha "Mo A"

Alternating "AL RW"

Composite "Fl 2+1"

Three iconic lighthouses: Execution Rocks in Long Island Sound; Little Gull Island Light in Block Island Sound; Thomas Point Light on the Western Shore of Chesapeake Bay.

Lighthouses and lighted beacons are designated by range, color, and light characteristics. The height of the light above the sea surface is another significant variable. Nautical charts show this information, and the USCG Light List offers more detail.

SPOTTING BUOYS

Two important pieces of gear help in spotting buoys.

Spotlights. A bright spotlight and a good pair of 7 × 50 binoculars make nighttime buoy spotting much easier. Your spotlight should cast a narrow, highly concentrated beam. Although not as portable as battery-operated units, plug-in or permanently connected 12-volt spotlights yield maximum brightness each time the unit is turned on and are usually more powerful than portable alternatives. Almost all navigation aids are equipped with reflective paint, tape, or other means of improving their reflectivity when illuminated by a spotlight. For a spotlight to be effective, it must be bright and free from any floodlight effect. If part of the light beam disperses at a wide angle, the ambient moisture in the surrounding air greatly reduces the effectiveness of the spotlight.

Binoculars. Unlike abuse-resistant boating gear such as winch handles, binoculars don't take to being bumped and dropped. You want to protect this precision optical instrument from falling off the chart table or being stuck in a salt-encrusted corner of the cockpit. Falls and neglect can damage even the best rubber-coated, water-resistant binoculars. To retain a high performance level, keep the optics clean and free from the misalignment blunt trauma can cause. Binoculars belong in an easy-access box, hung around a user's neck, or in hand at eye level. Adhere to this "three-places rule," and when they're not in use, keep the lens caps on. You'll extend the life and maintain the operational efficiency of this essential piece of equipment. The same goes for a night-vision monocular that can extend even further a sailor's visual acuity in darkness.

■ *A good pair of 7 × 50 binoculars enhances light gathering at dawn and dusk and makes navaid identification much easier. A built-in compass adds a magnetic bearing to the sighting.*

■ *Numbers on all government aids to navigation are created with reflective tape or paint and react to spotlight beams with even small amounts of light. Lateral buoy number 4 is lighted and has a bell (not a gong).*

■ *Left to right: 7 × 50 binoculars with a built-in compass, a Generation 3 night-vision scope, and 10-power image-stabilized binoculars. These sea-trialed instruments help you pick out hard-to-find targets in varying degrees of darkness or overcast. An infrared monocular (page 254) is also a handy aid.*

Electrification gave lighthouse designers much greater ability to create unique light patterns for mariners to better discern one beacon from another. Lights are defined according to their nominal range (the distance they can be seen in conditions of normal visibility), their color, and their characteristics (a combination of timing and tempo of the on-and-off phase).

Note that the geographic range of a light is sometimes shorter than its nominal range. A 150-foot lighthouse has a horizon distance of 15 miles at sea level; if your height of eye above the water surface is 9 feet, your own horizon distance is 3.5 miles. Thus, a 150-foot light dips below your horizon at a distance of 18.5 miles even if its nominal range is 22 miles. On a practical note, if you're making landfall on that light and haven't yet picked it up 19 miles out, don't panic.

Piloting Skills—Compass Headings

A vector describes both direction and distance, the essential factors for charting progress over any surface. At sea, with no need to address changes of altitude, we can describe movement as a specific heading and speed. Ever since the Chinese developed the magnetic compass, sailors universally reference movement to a magnetically aligned grid. More recently the gyrocompass, an instrument that can be aligned with true north, converted naval and commercial mariners from magnetic to true courses and from the inner to the outer ring of a chart's compass rose. As noted earlier, most sailboat navigators still live and work on the compass rose's inner, magnetic ring.

True, or geographic, north and south lie at the north and south poles, where the lines of longitude converge and where we would see the earth rotating on its axis if that axis was like an axle. Located at the northern and southern confluences of earth's magnetosphere, the magnetic north and south poles meander a bit with time. A compass needle seeks to align with these magnetic lines of force, the north-seeking end of the needle (actually the south pole of the magnet needle) being attracted to magnetic north pole, and vice versa in the southern hemisphere. "Compass north" is where a magnetic compass points, but compass north often does not agree precisely with magnetic north. The term *deviation* refers to the magnitude of the disagreement; the cause of deviation

SWINGING A COMPASS

Every magnetic compass can be adjusted (called swinging the compass) by a compass adjuster or patient crewmember. The swinging process first determines the amount and direction (east or west) of error on numerous points of sail, usually at 15- or 30-degree intervals. Most marine compasses carry small magnets in their base you can use to nullify some or all of the error. When you measure deviations of more than a couple of degrees, however, a discrete and correctable cause usually exists, such as audio speakers mounted in the cockpit or stainless steel fasteners with high ferrous content used to secure a bracket on the binnacle. You can easily find the latter, by the way, once you remove the compass, by checking the binnacle area with a magnet.

Developing a deviation table (card) showing the number of degrees of deviation to add or subtract from the course steered in order to correct any residual error is the most important result of swinging a compass. This deviation card gives a helmsperson the offset necessary for any given heading. Choose the deviation associated with the heading that's closest to the course you want to steer.

Here's a simple way to check your compass's accuracy. Find a pair of landmarks you can line up with the vessel. Choose landmarks far enough apart that a small amount of vessel movement won't result in misalignment. Align these two landmarks on a chart and measure the compass rose magnetic bearing with parallel rules or a course plotter. Place your vessel on this line, moving toward the aligned landmarks, and then reverse course and head away, checking your compass. Ideally it should display the bearing and its reciprocal (the bearing plus or minus 180 degrees), matching what you read on the chart's magnetic compass rose. Do the same with the vessel aligned on another range approximately—perpendicular—to the original bearing line. (A compass adjuster measures magnetic compass readings at 15- or 30-degree intervals, using a pelorus to shoot bearings on a range while the vessel crosses the range on headings that increase by a set amount [15 or 30] of degrees with each pass.) The bow, stern, and beam test mentioned above provides a rough idea of the instrument's accuracy, but a full "swing" and a deviation card with 15-degree intervals remains the gold standard.

Another useful means of checking compass error involves calculating the sun's azimuth just as sunset or sunrise is about to occur. (A nautical almanac affords a navigator a means to calculate the azimuth of the rising or setting sun anywhere on the surface of the earth.) Then you compare it to your compass reading when you momentarily head directly at the sun. Don't forget to convert your compass reading to degrees true, since that's the way azimuths are calculated.

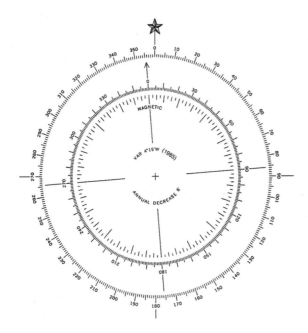

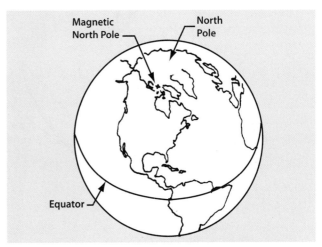

The relative positions of the true and magnetic north poles. In 2007 an expedition located the magnetic pole at 83.95°N/110.8°W.

The compass rose on a nautical chart contains true and magnetic bezels aligned with true north and magnetic north. Both are divided into 360 degrees, with 90-degree quadrants between each of the four cardinal points: north, east, south, and west. Local variation (the angular difference between true and magnetic north) is listed in the compass rose and/or the chart's legend along with its annual rate of change. Most small craft navigators refer to magnetic headings, bearings, and courses. With an accurately "swung" and compensated magnetic compass or fluxgate, the maximum deviation can usually be held to a couple of degrees, and the compass reading becomes the lingua franca of the boat.

usually is ferrous metal or electrical equipment in the vicinity of the compass.

The compass remains an instrument of primary importance to every boater, and even a sailor with a digital charting system running on an electronic rendition of the magnetic compass should have a conventional backup compass at the helm. Regularly glancing at the compass reassures the helmsperson that electronic data and the magnetic compass are in reasonable agreement. Keep in mind, however, that if the DCS displays course over the ground (COG) rather than a simple heading, you'll likely find a discrepancy between the two readings. This reflects the cumulative effects of current, leeway, and steering error. The magnetic heading tells us where the vessel is pointing, but not necessarily where it is going.

With three versions of a heading available to mariners—true, magnetic, and compass—confusion comes as no surprise. In sight reduction tables for celestial navigation, current and tide tables, and in *Sailing Directions* and other marine publications, headings are given in degrees true. Therefore, a small-craft sailor staring at a magnetic compass needs to easily convert from magnetic to true and back again. For-

Compass cards behave as an analog device, and like a speedometer needle, they show the rate of change. When the lubber line is aftmost, the compass card rotates past the lubber line in the direction the bow of the boat is turning. When the primary lubber line is forward, as here, the card rotates in the opposite direction from the boat's turn. There are devotees of both alternatives.

tunately, there is a fairly straightforward relationship among the three heading types.

You can ignore the deviation error of a small-craft steering compass if it's been corrected to a degree or two on all headings, which is usually possible. This is true whether you're using a conventional magnetic compass or a state-of-the-art fluxgate electronic compass networked into all the instruments on the boat. This correction then circumvents the nuisance of converting compass courses to magnetic again and

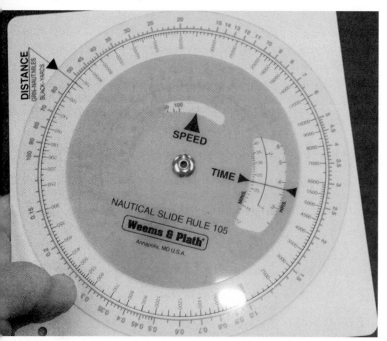

A nautical slide rule is a calculator that uses no batteries. The circular slide rule solves D = RT equations, is waterproof, and easy to use. This is why, even in a digital age, they're still produced and sold.

again. Instead, you can assume they're one and the same.

Classroom-trained purists who are perhaps unaccustomed to the one-armed-paper-hanger routine of a shorthanded crew at sea might cringe at this kind of shortcut. They'd likely point out that it could induce a steering error of a degree or two. However, we also know that even the best helmsperson has a hard time reducing steering error below 5 degrees, and with regular plotting and course checking, a 1- or 2-degree error fades into background noise. When you take bearings and plot courses in degrees magnetic (using the inner ring of the compass rose) and assume that your compass readings are likewise in degrees magnetic, your need for conversions is significantly minimized.

That said, when the time comes for absolute, no-holds-barred accuracy, you can easily revert to the traditional routine of working from compass to magnetic to true headings; you reverse the process to convert in the opposite direction. For example, to plot a bearing on a chart that only has a true compass rose, a navigator would first simply take the compass reading and add or subtract the correction on the deviation card. The local variation is then added to or subtracted from that magnetic bearing to arrive at the true bearing.

A wide array of magnetic compasses are available these days. The most traditional are the Danforth-type dome instruments with a forward-reading lubber line and often a pair of secondary lubber lines used when the helmsperson sits to weather or leeward

while steering. In an aviation or bulkhead-mounted compass the lubber lines are attached to the aft edge rather than the leading edge of the compass bowl. Each design takes some getting used to, but each claims its fans. Other mariners like digital fluxgate compass displays or even the steering graphic displayed by a GPS receiver or digital charting system.

Piloting Skills—Dead Reckoning

If the point on a sharp pencil breaks, a pocketknife or a piece of sandpaper can restore it to full functionality, but when a networked MFD quits or the iPad screen goes black, there's usually no quick fix, and a back-to-basics backup plan should be in every navigator's tool kit.

To calculate a DR position, you need only a compass, timepiece, and means of measuring speed. The old D = RT (also shown as D = ST) formula defining the relationship among distance, rate of speed, and time forms the basis of deduced reckoning, com-

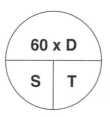

Another method to help compute time, speed, or distance. The relationship between the three is shown in the illustration. To use this handy illustration, cover the answer you need. The formula for the answer remains uncovered. To find time, cover the T. The formula is $60 \times D \div S$. To compute speed, cover the S. The formula is $60 \times D \div T$. To find the distance traveled, cover the $60 \times D$. You have S and T left. Distance equals $S \times T$. Divide the result by 60. T = minutes; S = knots; D = nautical miles.

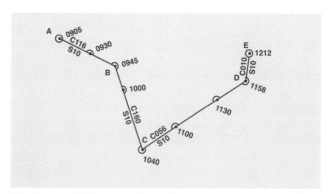

A typical DR plot. A DR plot is a vector diagram in which both line segment length and direction convey meaning. The plot is based on speed, time, and direction measurements and, when all goes well, the graphical construct is a scaled-down replica of the track of the vessel during the time period indicated.

monly known as dead reckoning or DR. In most cases navigators express distance in nautical miles, speed or rate in knots (nautical miles per hour), and time in hours. You'll find the arithmetic simplicity of one nautical mile equals one minute of latitude delightfully easy to use. At a speed of 6 knots, a vessel will advance 6 nautical miles in an hour, or a mile every 10 minutes. DR plots ignore the effects of current and leeway and assume that the helmsperson steers a straight course.

Good, experienced navigators always think about progress down the DR track, thus developing a feel for their location on the chart—and without even picking up a set of dividers or a parallel rule. We recommend that prior to plotting a fix or DR position you develop the habit of drawing a small, light, erasable pencil mark where you assume you're located and compare this guess to the formal plotting that follows. As you become a skilled navigator, you'll gain this kind of feel for your surroundings and an intrinsic ability to gauge progress. You'll likely be able to estimate speed through the water to a half-knot accuracy.

Piloting (as opposed to navigating) is all about guiding a boat through close-quarters situations and involves using all data sources at hand, along with the navigator's and skipper's ability to make prudent decisions. In such situations, you may need to correct your DR plotting with fixes every 15 minutes rather than hourly or even twice a day (the norm during ocean crossings). Sure, inshore sailors don't face the threat of rogue waves, but granite ledges can be equally consequential. Even if you follow a breadcrumb trail on a DCS screen, you should double-check your progress with bearings, buoy identifications, and identified landmarks.

Piloting Skills—Taking Bearings

A bearing is an angular measurement within a specified frame of reference, typically magnetic or true north. With a steady hand and some practice, your hand bearing compass becomes a good friend. Skilled navigators discover a multitude of ways to put bearings to good use, each one based on a few fundamental principles.

It's important to keep in mind that bearings can reference true north, magnetic north, or even the fore-and-aft centerline of the vessel from which we take the bearing, known as a relative bearing. We most commonly use a relative bearing to track another vessel in order to avoid a collision. A relative bearing of 90 or 270 degrees means that the target is on your starboard or port beam, regardless of your

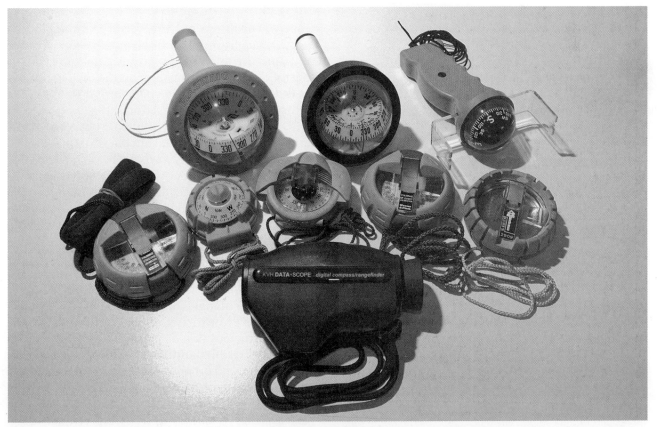

Hand bearing compasses come in a variety of shapes and small sizes, and many sailors find them quick and easy to use.

heading when you take the bearing. If an approaching vessel maintains a constant relative bearing as the distance between you shrinks, this indicates a collision course.

On the other hand, when we want to determine the bearing of a fixed object ashore, or navigation mark, we use a true or magnetic reference. These bearings relate to true or magnetic north as the starting point of a 360-degree scale. They define a line connecting your boat with the sighted object at the time the bearing was shot in terms of the angle it makes with either magnetic or true north. To be most useful, you should plot the sighted object on the chart.

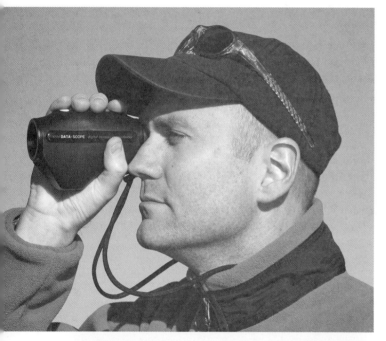

This digital hand bearing compass combines a monocular and a compact fluxgate compass. The unit brings targets closer into view and can even record bearings.

If you are using an electronic device with a keypad or touch screen, you can simply select the reference point on the screen and a bearing will be drawn from where the GPS, or other satellite navigation system, calculates your location to that object with range and bearing automatically appearing on the screen. Compare this bearing with the one you have taken from your actual location just to keep your hand in the game. This use of bearings helps to identify your position, not avoid collision. You can plot a line of position (LOP) by using the compass rose on a paper chart, and setting your parallel rulers to the measured true or magnetic bearing. Next move the ruler and strike a line through the object on the chart. The bearing has become an LOP, and you are located at some point along this line.

We can most easily measure magnetic bearings using a hand bearing compass or a compass-equipped monocular or binocular. The navigator keeps the hand bearing compass level with the sea surface and aligned with the object. This human gimballing helps prevent the compass card from dragging on its housing, thus yielding an inaccurate reading. Yaw, pitch, and roll are destabilizing factors that can complicate your ability to take an accurate bearing, so in difficult situations, take three or more shots of the object and average the results.

Multiple Bearings Make a Fix

Once you acquire a bearing, you'll find the plotting process straightforward. Simply use the compass rose to define the angle, align either parallel rules or a roller plotter with the reading on the rose, and transfer the bearing across the chart until it transects the sighted object's charted location.

One bearing provides a line of position; at the moment the bearing was taken, the vessel was located somewhere on that line. A second bearing taken close on the heels of the first, using an object at least 45 and preferably nearly 90 degrees offset from the first, creates a second LOP that crosses the first. This intersection results in a fix of your vessel's position. Additional bearing lines plotted in the same time frame, using other recognizable landmarks, would ideally intersect the first two LOPs at the same point, but seldom is the process that exact. The three lines usually create a small triangle (often referred to as a "cocked-hat triangle") in which you can confidently assume that your true position lies.

Clearly visible landmarks such as lighthouses, water towers, and other fixed structures included on a large-scale chart are the best choices for a fix. Moored navigation aids provide less accurate but nevertheless valid bearings. When taking a bearing, one of the biggest potential errors involves misidentifying a land-

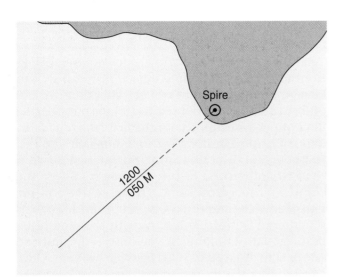

A compass bearing in degrees magnetic describes a line from the compass to the object. When the bearing is plotted, write a four-digit time reference on top (1200) of the line and the three-digit bearing below the line (050M).

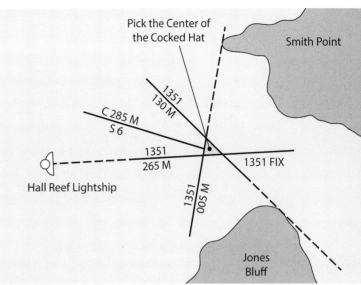

To plot a fix, you can use two or more bearings taken almost at the same time on different fixed objects or landmarks. Here we have three magnetic bearings: one on the end of Smith Point, one tangential to Jones Bluff, and one on Hall Reef Lightship. They form the familiar cocked-hat triangle, and we plot our fix at the center of the triangle. From there we are steering a course of 285° magnetic at a speed through the water of 6 knots. (Note, however, that lightships and buoys are not fixed objects; estimates of being tangent to a bluff and where the exact end of a point lies are not as precise as using a lighthouse, water tank, or radio tower. Fixes using the former are often a little less accurate, and the enclosed area of the "cocked hat" grows larger.)

mark. For this reason, we recommend taking more than two bearings; if any falls way out of concurrence with the others, you've probably misidentified one of the sighted objects, indicating a need for another round of bearings.

A digital charting system presents a facsimile of your surroundings, while visual and radar bearings reference your actual surroundings. DCS positions are highly accurate almost all the time, but when wrong they can be very wrong. Visual and radar bearings are almost never as precise, but they're seldom flat-out wrong. When the Department of Defense advises GPS users not to make the system a stand-alone form of navigation, they mean we should use bearings to double-check our DCS.

Day or night, we can easily compare compass bearings taken on a lighthouse with bearings taken on an LCD screen. The bearing to the lighthouse shown on the screen should be the same or very close to that of the bearing shot with a hand bearing compass. A couple of degrees difference can result from the vessel's deviation, a time lag between taking bearings, or user inaccuracy. However, you need to check larger errors with additional bearings or another means of fixing your position.

Bow-and-Beam Bearings

When sailing or powering along a coastline on a steady course and speed, you can shoot two bearing lines on the same object at two different times to acquire a quick and easy fix. One of the most useful, the bow-and-beam bearing, calls for taking the bearing shot on an object first when it's 45 degrees off the port or starboard bow and again at 90 degrees. You

note the time as each of these relative angles is met. Then convert the time elapsed between the two readings to a fraction or decimal representation of an hour and multiply it by the boat speed. The solution of this D = RT equation provides the distance covered between the first and second sight. Thanks to the geometric relationship of the sides of a 45/45/90-degree right triangle, the distance traveled between the two bearing measurements equals the distance from the sighted object at the time of the second bearing.

Doubling the Angle on the Bow

If you take a first bearing on a charted object when it's close on the bow, and then take another bearing when the object's angle on the bow has doubled, your distance traveled between the bearings will equal your distance off the object at the time of the second bearing. For example, let's say you sight a charted object ashore when it's 20° off the bow and again when it's 40° off the bow. If you traveled .05 nautical mile between the sights, your distance off at the time of the second sight is .05 mile (see illustration). Naturally, current set and errors such as inattentive steering and errors in recording your speed can affect the accuracy of these fixes.

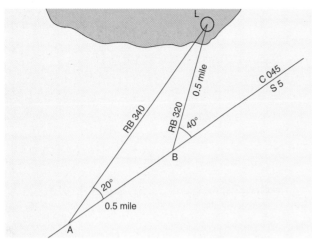

📄 *Doubling the angle on the bow, you can put basic geometry to good use when you keep a straight course and maintain an even speed. A bow bearing on a fixed object is recorded (at A) and again when it is doubled (at B), and the distance run since the first bearing (A to B) is equal to the distance off the charted object (B to L) at the time of the second sight.*

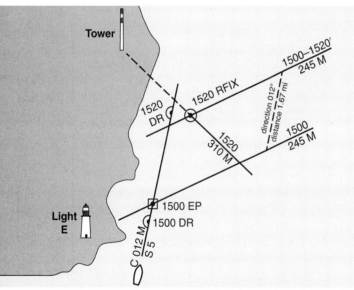

📄 *Since obtaining a fix at 1400, you have run an hour at a speed through the water of 5 knots on a course of 012 degrees magnetic. Even with poor visibility, at 1500, through a momentary break in the fog, you sight a bearing on a lighthouse and establish an estimated position (EP) where the bearing LOP crosses your DR plot. Your 1500 EP is approximately ¼ mile ahead of your 1500 DR, and you update your DR plot accordingly, but you can't yet fix your position because you can't see another charted object on which to sight a crossing bearing. You continue at 5 knots on a course of 012 for another 20 minutes, at which point another break in the fog gives you a view of a distinctive water tower at 310 degrees magnetic. After plotting that bearing, you advance your 1500 bearing 1.67 nautical miles (the distance traveled in 20 minutes at 5 knots) to cross the second bearing line. This is your 1520 running fix, which is approximately ¼ mile east of your 1520 DR. You will now begin your next DR plot from the running fix.*

Piloting Skills—Running Fix

You can use a running fix to create two useful LOPs from only one discernible object. A useful skill to have when taking bearings on objects ashore, it's also one of the most often used techniques in celestial navigation. Take and record the first magnetic bearing to a landmark along with the time and the vessel's course and speed. During the interval between the first and second bearings, it's best to keep the course and speed constant. The more uniform the rate of advance and the course, the more accurate is the interim DR calculation. As with bow-and-beam bearings, with a running fix you convert the time and rate data to distance traveled between bearings. Once you've taken the second shot of the same landmark and you've calculated the distance and direction traveled between bearings, you advance the first bearing along the course line to the point designated by the DR plot between bearings. Make sure you keep the advanced bearing line parallel to the original bearing line, accomplished with parallel rules, a course plotter, two triangles, or other means of advancing a parallel line. Your running fix is the point where the advanced LOP and the second bearing cross. Although a running fix is not quite as reliable as a three-point fix from simultaneous bearings, you'll still find it a valid way to obtain an accurate position, especially when you take care to be as precise as possible with the between-bearings DR.

Additional Piloting Inputs

Piloting skills are much more than rote procedures based on distance, rate, and time. Dead reckoning does play a role, but the pilot is actually acting as a clearinghouse of data, interfacing information in order to get as precise a position and as accurate an awareness of the vessel's surroundings as possible. One of the most important skills to master is self-doubt, the enduring value of which has been threatened by GPS and digital chartplotters.

For example, DR positions have value, but good navigators learn to keep track of the quality of the data being processed. When traversing current-bound waters in overcast or foggy conditions, prudent navigators always doubt the accuracy of a DR plot. To paraphrase one old salt: beginners mark their location with a sharp pencil point, intermediate navigators indicate location with a thick finger and less certain words, while experienced voyagers center their palm over the pencil point and use terms like "vicinity" to define their DR. The longer a navigator goes without a fix, the more suspect the DR becomes.

Tides and Currents

The moon and to a lesser extent the sun exercise a gravitational attraction on the earth's oceans. Gravity is assisted by the centrifugal force caused by the earth's rotation to create a predictable surface bulge called the tide. Twice-monthly spring tides occur during the new and full moons, the times of greatest tidal range. The sun and moon are aligned during these times, that is, the moon is either between the earth and sun (new moon) or on the opposite side of the earth from the sun (full moon)—and their gravitational effects are additive. In the moon's first and third quarters, midway between the new and full moons, the moon and sun pull at right angles to one another and we experience the smaller-than-average tides known as neap tides.

The moon's greater influence stems from being so much nearer the earth than the sun. A tidal day spans 24 hours and 50 minutes, the time required for a given point on earth to complete one spin around earth's axis (24 hours) and rotate a little farther to overtake the orbiting moon and once again be directly beneath it (50 minutes). The 29.5-day lunar month is another key repeating cycle. In addition, the earth's year-long orbit around the sun involves some changes in distance from the sun and declination of the three bodies involved. When our planet comes closer to the sun or moon, each exerts greater influence.

The times and heights of high and low tides vary from place to place because of factors other than lunar and solar alignment. For example, the shape of ocean basins and confines of sounds, bays, and estuaries create intricate patterns of tidal flow. Water

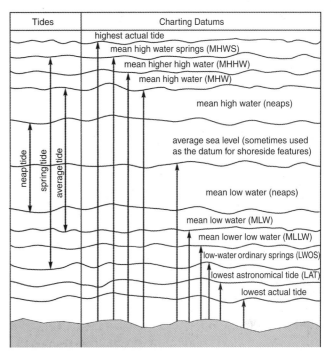

The tidal range depends first and foremost on the phase of the moon, but in many areas local weather anomalies and basin shapes can have significant effects. The state of the tide will affect what obstacles are visible or not, and nautical charts use various abbreviations to indicate the state of the tide an object is charted at.

The moon is approximately 25% the size of the earth and only 238,855 miles away, so its influence on tides is primary. Our sun, though massive by comparison, is 93 million miles away, and this distance lessens its effect upon our tides. The moon's influence on navigation and visual watchkeeping is significant; a full moon is also the right time to put 7 x 50 binoculars to good use.

moves on and off the banks of the Bahamas, raising and lowering the sea level only a small amount, while farther north, scouring tidal currents rush into the Bay of Fundy lifting boats over 20 to 40 feet in a single tide.

Along with variations in the range of the tide from place to place, there are also differences in the period of tidal activity. For example, some regions see a semidiurnal rise and fall with two high and two low tides over a 24-hour, 50-minute period; slightly more than six hours separate each change of the tide. In a regular semidiurnal pattern, the AM and PM high and low tides are about equal in height.

Other coastlines in North America and elsewhere in the world see mixed tides, meaning one of the day's high tides is much higher than the other. Some regions have diurnal (once-daily) tides, with approximately 12 hours, 25 minutes between successive highs and lows. Still other areas experience no perceptible tide at all, at least during neap tides. All these variations can be accounted for by a fluid-dynamics version of energy trading. In essence, the tide is a long-wave-length, low-amplitude form of energy transfer, and the pressure gradient between low-tide and high-tide regions changes on a regular basis.

Bay sailors often see a tidal current associated with the tidal rise and fall. On eastern Long Island

Sound, for example, a rising tide is associated with a west-setting flood current, while a falling tide produces an ebb that sets eastward. Note, though, that the rise and fall of the tide is seldom precisely in phase with the resulting tidal current. The tide may start rising as the current still ebbs, something seen particularly in river mouths and estuaries, and the converse is also true. Basic laws of motion come into play here. A huge mass of water moving in one direction must feel a significant change in force to stop and then reverse motion. For this reason, tide tables and tidal current tables for a single locale, though related, are unlikely to be in phase. Therefore, planning a coastal passage around favorable currents requires the use of tidal current tables, not merely tide tables. (See the following sidebar on Navigation Publications and A Sailor's Library for more on how and where to find these tables.)

Many navigators consider the tide and tidal current information offered by digital chart systems and many smart device apps an added value for coastal cruising. The slower a vessel travels, the more important a tidal current becomes. Measured in set (direction) and drift (speed), a current is either fair or foul, but that doesn't mean it's always going to be directly astern or ahead. We can best understand its net effect

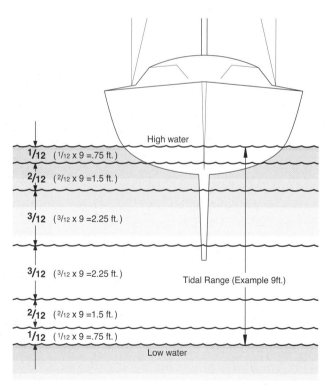

High water

1/12 (1/12 x 9 =.75 ft.)

2/12 (2/12 x 9 =1.5 ft.)

3/12 (3/12 x 9 =2.25 ft.)

Tidal Range (Example 9ft.)

3/12 (3/12 x 9 =2.25 ft.)

2/12 (2/12 x 9 =1.5 ft.)

1/12 (1/12 x 9 =.75 ft.)

Low water

The tide rises or falls more rapidly around mid-tide than it does near the times of high and low water. Indeed, half of the total change in height occurs in the middle two hours of each six-plus-hour rise or fall. The "rule of twelfths," as illustrated here, codifies this pattern.

by using vector diagrams, much as we do with the influence of wind on sails or a boat.

Wind and weather systems can also influence tidal flow. For example, strong northerly conditions in the Bahamas, known as a rage, can blow surface waters off the banks and keep a low tide in place for days. The same holds true for the upper Chesapeake Bay when a strong winter northerly can maintain a day-long extremely low tide. At the other extreme, the combination of low atmospheric pressure and onshore wind can cause flooding of coastal lowlands during a storm high tide. *Sailing Directions* and cruising guides offer a deeper understanding of the interplay between weather conditions and tides in given areas.

To estimate the impact of a known tidal current on your course over ground, draw a vector on a piece of graph paper or directly on the chart in the direction of the course steered with a length scaled to the boat's speed through the water. When drawn on the chart, this vector coincides with a DR plot. From the tip of this arrow, plot another vector representing the set (in degrees) and drift (in knots) of the current. Your vessel's course and speed over ground are then defined by a third vector connecting the origin of the first vector with the end point of the second. The length of this third vector indicates your speed over ground, or SOG; its direction indicates the course over ground, or COG. (See the illustration.) This information can also be obtained from a chartplotter; simply call up functions such as tacking angles and current graphics and you'll see how your boat is moving relative to course and speed over ground (COG/SOG). But if you lose electricity you'll also lose this option, so backup plans remain an important priority.

When you calculate your progress along this COG vector after a given time—say 20 minutes or an hour—you're calculating an estimated position. Unlike a DR position, an estimated position attempts to account for the influence of current and perhaps leeway. However, the estimated position is based on a predicted average current set and drift. And just as high winds tend to be gusty, strong currents tend to vary in velocity and direction over brief spans of time and distance.

Alternatively, and perhaps more commonly, let's say you steer a given course at a given speed through the water. Then, when you obtain your next fix, you find you aren't where your DR plot says you should be. In this case the vector difference between your actual position and your DR position represents the current set and drift.

The most recent development in monitoring set and drift involves networking a vessel's knotmeter with other electronics, allowing you to compare speed through the water (STW) *(continued page 246)*,

NAVIGATION PUBLICATIONS

Mariners have always valued collected wisdom. Among the most useful tools for recreational and commercial mariners are the various regional volumes of the *Coast Pilot and Sailing Directions*, which describe coastline features, prevailing weather, currents, and factors such as fog and ice. They present information about seasonal changes in conditions and their effects on navigation, along with detailed directions for entering specific ports. Professional maritime experts carefully vet these publications, which generally are subjected to much more scrutiny than privately written cruising guides and books on voyaging. (See A Sailor's Library for more about these publications.)

We also recommend the annual compilations of tide and tidal current tables. These government publications provide authoritative predictions well worth the space they consume on your bookshelf, especially if you're headed off on a lengthy voyage. Navigators with less far-reaching plans can often do just fine with an annual almanac such as *Reed's Nautical Almanac* for UK waters and Europe or the *Eldridge Tide and Pilot Book* for the U.S. Northeast. These volumes contain tide tables and current diagrams for key locations in the covered regions, plus light lists and vital information about bridge openings, canal regulations, weather broadcasts, and more.

Over the years cruising guides have evolved into a major segment of marine publishing. They range from pithy little volumes describing a small segment of the Maine coast to multivolume encyclopedic tomes covering coastal voyaging from New England to the Gulf of Mexico, delineating every mark and marina along the way. Some sailors lament that these publications rob us of a sense of exploration, but as soon as they get confused by the array of marks ahead, these same sailors grab their guides for directions to the municipal fuel dock in Timbuktu.

Printed copies of key publications remain important references and must be ready to access and use. You can use digital forms of secondary references, but the worse the weather becomes, the more you will welcome a printed copy of a Coast Pilot or cruising guide.

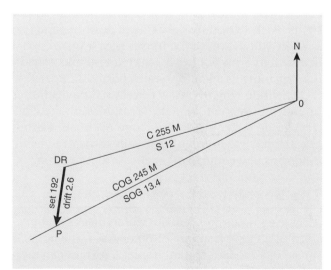

The helmsperson has been steering a course of 255 degrees magnetic, and the boat speed has been 12 knots. During the transit from O to P, however, the actual COG was 245 degrees magnetic at an SOG of 13.4 knots. The cause of the disparity is the current set (in degrees true) and drift (in knots), and this simple vector diagram illustrates both.

A good-sized diesel auxiliary can move a sailboat at hull speed. Factor a favorable current into the mix, and speed over ground can approach double digits. Running onto a sandbar at such speeds can make extrication difficult; the impact of a rock ledge can cause significant hull damage.

as measured by the knotmeter, with SOG, as measured by GPS. This results in continuously updated information on current set and drift based on real-time data rather than current diagram projections or hour-old data.

Sailors often think of tidal currents only in coastal waters. However, these currents have open-ocean counterparts in the form of the great ocean currents, described as wind-driven rivers in the sea, and even different density water masses interacting with each other. Such gyers help shape global climates and act as either a boost or a barrier to progress. Every navigator learns to double-check current diagrams and think twice before embarking on a passage that puts the bow into a serious ocean current without first researching the pilot charts. These month-by-month profiles of wind and current give us a good idea of varying ocean circulation and wind patterns.

With modern communication equipment and high-seas Internet access, some oceangoing motor-sailer skippers download the location of the fickle Intertropical Convergence Zone (ITCZ). The ITCZ is a thin band of light wind and countercurrent between the tropical trade-wind easterlies of the northern and southern hemispheres, and skippers put their downloaded information to good use. Originally known as the doldrums, the ITCZ offers an eastbound motor-driven vessel a respite from the easterlies that dominate the latitudes between 20° north and south.

Navigator Steve D'Antonio using a David White Navy Mark II sextant, the instrument that guided the U.S. fleet of WWII.

The countercurrent and variable winds of this band afford calm conditions and smooth seas right in the heart of the tropical latitudes, just the right stuff for tallying miles under power and making significant progress to the east. Of course, using this strategy assumes plentiful fuel and a propulsion system up to the 24/7 demand of continuous powering.

CELESTIAL NAVIGATION

Given the current state of technology, many mariners argue over relevance of celestial navigation, the art of shooting the sun, planets, moon, and stars; reducing the sight data to lines of position (LOPs); and plotting a resulting fix. Is this system outmoded? Should we relegate the sextant to museums, displayed alongside the lead line, the taffrail log, and the windup chronometer?

Even the U.S. Naval Academy continues to vacillate on the need for a sextant and the skills needed to use it. On the other hand, the commercial world still requires all who hold advanced licenses to prove their proficiency at celestial navigation. As I've suggested earlier, sailors crossing large expanses of open ocean should think twice about calling a couple of handheld GPS units sufficient backup for a digital charting system.

Here's a fair compromise: carry a plastic sextant with a micrometer drum and a programmable calculator (or smart phone or tablet) that automatically reduces celestial sights. This combination, along with an inexpensive but accurate electronic wristwatch, enables you to take sun, moon, planet, and even star sights. Each sight provides a line of position, and two or more will provide a fix. In this way, a small capital investment arms you with a very useful and reassuring capability as an autonomous position finder.

The following overview of celestial navigation is intended only to provide its flavor. A complete practical guide falls outside the scope of this book, but celestial navigation is not especially difficult to learn, as long as you commit to practice and repetition.

The Sextant

A circle contains 360 degrees, which means that one-sixth of a circle is an arc of 60 degrees, the angular spread of a modern sextant frame. A sextant can measure angles up to 120 degrees by the use of two mirrors—the index mirror and the horizon "glass." Since the zenith (the point directly overhead) is 90 degrees above the horizon, 120 degrees is more than enough to measure the altitude of any celestial body. Thanks to the elegant geometry of a sextant's two reflecting

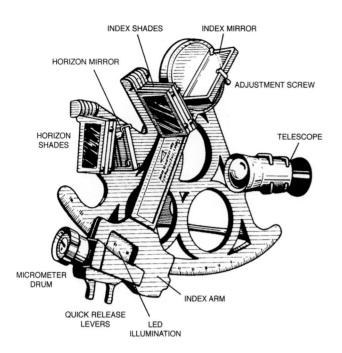

INDEX SHADES   INDEX MIRROR

HORIZON MIRROR

ADJUSTMENT SCREW

HORIZON SHADES

TELESCOPE

MICROMETER DRUM

INDEX ARM

QUICK RELEASE LEVERS   LED ILLUMINATION

All modern sextants have a micrometer drum that allows angular measurement to the nearest tenth of a minute.

mirrors, the altitude (angle above the horizon) of the celestial body you're observing is twice the angle of inclination between the two mirrors of a properly adjusted sextant.

The process of measuring altitude involves "bringing down" a celestial body to the horizon, accomplished by using a sextant's two "sight lines." The first is a direct view of the horizon, and the second is a reflected view of the celestial body. By moving a swinging arm (called the index arm) on the sextant's protractor-like frame, we can lower the view of the star, moon or planet so it appears on the horizon.

In essence, a sextant is a protractor with an articulating ruler arm and an ingenious dual mirror sighting system. All celestial sights involve locating the horizon in the clear portion of the horizon mirror. Next, adjust the index arm so that the celestial body appears on the silvered half of the horizon glass. When both the celestial body and the horizon line coincide, you find the altitude of the body displayed on the index arm and micrometer drum. It's also worth noting the *azimuth*, or bearing of the body relative to your position. The observed altitude (Ho) of a celestial body is its angular height above the horizon and the azimuth is the true bearing of the celestial body. (See illustration on page 252.)

The better the sextant, the more precise you'll find its adjusting mechanism, and the more immune its frame is to any twisting or torque-induced inaccuracy. On early sextants, vernier-type sliding-scale final adjustments were used to add a more precise reading capability to the angle measurement. However, a micrometer drum adds even more accuracy and stands as the measurement scale of choice.

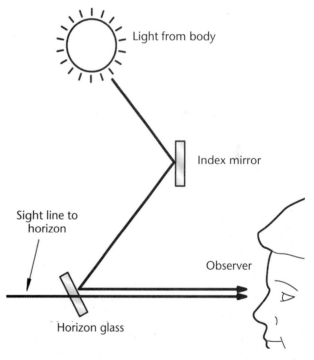

Light from body

Index mirror

Sight line to horizon

Observer

Horizon glass

The sextant is essentially an expensive protractor with optics. The angle it measures is made by two imaginary lines that join at the instrument's optical center. One is a line from the sextant to the celestial body observed, and the other is a line from the instrument to the horizon. When the index arm is properly adjusted, the mirrored half of the horizon glass (which is perpendicular to the sextant frame) reveals the celestial body (star or planet perched on the horizon and moon or sun with either upper or lower limb just touching the surface). Some sextants use semitransparent horizon mirrors rather than the traditional split mirror. These instruments afford easier acquisition of the celestial body but not as crisp a delineation of the body and horizon.

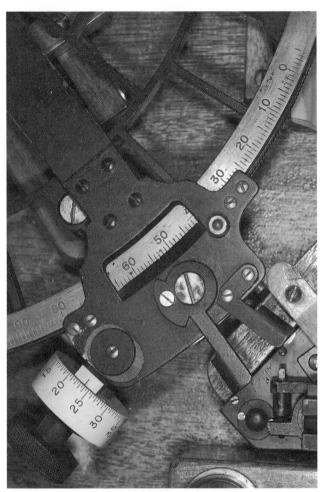

🚩 *Early sextants (top) lacked a micrometer, and users took readings directly from a minutely engraved index scale. The micrometer drum (above) is mechanically linked to the degree scale, and the drum itself is divided into 60 minutes. To read minutes and tenths of a minute (right), users look at the hash marks on the vernier scale just to the right of the drum (next to the pointer with the dot) to answer two questions: (1) which hash mark on the drum falls at or just above the pointer on the vernier scale, and (2) which vernier-scale hash mark comes closest to connecting with a mark on the drum. In this case, the 1' mark on the drum is just above the vernier pointer, and the ²/₁₀ths hash mark on the vernier scale comes closest to a mark on the drum. Thus, the sextant height, or H_S, is 74º 01.2'. Worrying about the tenths reading has caused many a navigator to misread the index and get the tenths of a degree reading perfect while missing H_S by a whole degree!*

🚩 *Filters pivot in front of the mirrors to lessen the glare of sunlight. In overcast conditions, with a poor outline of the sun, we can use an amber high-contrast filter to sharpen the edge of the sun's upper or lower limb.*

Correcting Index Error

Sextant errors can occur for several reasons. Among the most common is index error, which we compensate for by adding or subtracting a small correction factor during the sight reduction process. In essence, index error involves how accurately the index scale agrees with what we're actually observing. The easiest way to check this is to set the sextant reading to 00 degrees, 00 minutes of arc, and sight the horizon on a calm, clear day. If the horizon runs as a seamlessly straight line between the mirrored and clear halves of the horizon glass, no index error exists. If we view a step-like transition between the mirrored half and the clear glass, an index error exists, and we can easily read its magnitude on the micrometer drum. Determining whether to assign it a positive or negative value demands a little more consideration.

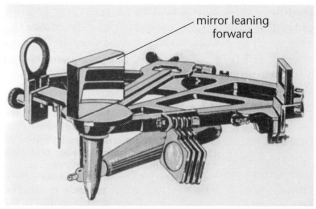

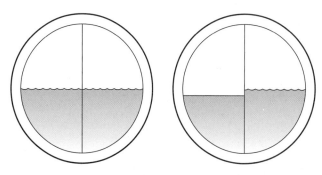

🚩 *Index mirror perpendicularity check. A step between the actual and reflected edges of the limb indicates the index mirror is tilted. Misalignment will seldom be this dramatic. (Courtesy Defense Mapping Agency)*

🚩 *The sextant needs adjustment when the mirrors aren't parallel to each other and perpendicular to the frame of the sextant. The horizon glass can be tested by sighting on a star as described in the text. Alternatively, set the index arc to 0 degrees and use the micrometer drum to align the horizon so it extends in a straight, uninterrupted line from the clear portion to the silvered portion of the glass. Then rock the sextant laterally with twists of the wrist and look for an abrupt break in the horizon line where the clear and silvered portions of the glass meet. If you see no break (left) the horizon glass is properly aligned. A break in the horizon (right) is a sign of misalignment. Solve the problem by using the screw-like adjusters on each mirror mount. Unless you carefully research that process, however, you're better off leaving these adjustments to a technician, who will check over the entire instrument.*

Like the "red-right-returning" rule, an aphorism reminds us how to handle the value of an index error. Here's the slogan to memorize: "If it's off, add it on, and if it's on, take it off."

Note the micrometer drum reading of the index arm pointer when you have readjusted it to even out the horizon line. If the pointer registers above 00 degrees, 00 minutes, you are on the scale and must take off, or subtract, the minute and tenths correction from your sextant height (H_S) in order to get your observed height (H_0).

Conversely, if the pointer is off the scale—that is, if it reads less than 00 degrees, 00 minutes—you need to add the correction to the reading. This makes sense in practice and quickly becomes familiar.

Mirror Adjustments

Sextant accuracy also involves aligning the mirrors. Light rays passing from the index mirror to the horizon glass should be parallel with the plane formed by the sextant frame and index arm; this means the mirrors need to be perpendicular to the sextant body. You can do a quick check of the index mirror by setting the index arc to 35 degrees and laying the sextant on a table so that you can sight along the index arc, or limb, while at the same time observing the arc's reflection in the index mirror.

The index arc should merge seamlessly with its image in the index mirror, just as the horizon and its reflected image merge when testing for index error. If there's any offset, turn the index mirror adjusting screw to eliminate the step-like misalignment and return the mirror to a perpendicular position. With some sextants, this task is probably best left to a technician.

Likewise, the horizon glass can move out of its perpendicular position relative to the sextant frame,

resulting in side error. Test for this by "rocking" (or "swinging") the arc as shown in the diagram, or alternatively, by simply setting the index arc reading to zero and sighting on a star. In the latter instance, you turn the tangent screw (located on the lower end of the index arm, near the micrometer dial) back and forth past zero to move the reflected image of the star up and down. If the reflected image, in its vertical travel, passes directly over the star's directly observed image, no side error exists. If the reflected image passes to one side of the directly observed image, however, the sextant has a side error you can eliminate by adjusting the screw on the horizon-glass frame.

The central axis and optical path of the telescope should be parallel with the sextant frame, at which point the light traveling through the scope is properly collimated, or aligned. The classic test for collimation involves setting the sextant on its legs on a flat surface across the room from a perpendicular wall. Carefully sight along the frame of the sextant and place a mark on the wall. Measure the distance between the sextant frame and the center of the telescope collar and plot a second mark on the wall above the first mark by the distance just measured. If the optical path is parallel with the sextant frame, the second mark appears in the center of the telescope's field of view. If the mark doesn't appear in the center of the field, make an adjustment to the telescope mount. Scopes with nonadjustable mounts are seldom out of alignment. However, if you discover an alignment problem in yours, find a technician who can fix the problem.

Nonadjustable errors also can occur in these instruments, and you'll find them noted on the factory test data sheet. When you take a sextant to a technician for service, the instrument shop usually returns it to you with updates to this record and specific correction offsets to use in altitude calculations.

Using a Sextant

Navigators recognize the distinction between tools and instruments. They use elegantly designed and engineered winch handles and socket wrenches for specialized tasks, but their rugged construction identifies them immediately as tools. However, because of its complexity and relative fragility, they identify a sextant, also a task-specific piece of gear, as an instrument, not a tool. Handling it carefully, including faithfully returning it to its box whenever it's not in the hands of the navigator, helps prevent the almost inevitable mishaps that cause damage.

Heavy weather makes all aspects of celestial navigation more difficult. We know the difficulty of grabbing a sight as the sun peeks out between clouds, for example. Likewise, we might face the challenge of trying to stabilize the sun's lower limb as you bring it down to the horizon while the boat bucks like a mechanical ride at an amusement park. Because of these potential difficulties, experienced navigators develop a sight-taking ritual. For example, they always shoot sights from the same location on board, braced against a familiar piece of rigging or other source of support. They use a second crewmember to track the time and a "ready" and "mark" set of commands to indicate each observation made. The sight may then be reduced, or worked, with a programmed calculator, a computer program, or printed sight reduction tables and a pencil and paper. Whichever option they choose, they don't vary their routine; they prove the adage that repetition is the best teacher. Eventually, their second-nature familiarity with the process enables navigators to generate an accurate fix even in unfavorable conditions.

Many small-craft navigators prefer to use a sextant without a telescope. For sights of the sun and moon, a telescope magnifies motion, even as it increases the diameter of the body being sighted. Some navigators consider this a slightly positive effect, but others see it as a wash at best or even a slight negative. For star sights, however, a scope causes magnified motion and a greatly reduced field of view without also increasing the diameter of the body sighted. This occurs because with the exception of the sun, stars are too far away across vast depths of interstellar space to be brought any closer by a small-magnification telescope. Many

Early brass sextants well over 50 years old with a micrometer drum can still deliver accurate measurements. The keys to longevity include protecting the sextant when not in use, removing salt spray to minimize corrosion, and treating all optical components like a camera lens.

skilled small-craft navigators thus prefer a hollow "peep sight" to a telescope, especially in rough seas.

Here's another trick of the trade: turn the sextant upside down for the start of a star sight, bringing the horizon up to the star rather than the star down to the horizon. Once you've made a rough adjustment and see you have the right celestial body in sight, you turn the sextant right side up for the final micrometer drum adjustment. Some sextants are equipped with a lenticular mirror that turns a pinpoint of light into a thin, straight line, which helps you place a star on the horizon.

We can take a sun or moon sight using either the lower or upper limb of the body as a reference point. We apply a correction called the semi-diameter to change either of these readings into a measurement of the angle at which the center of the body touches the horizon. This reading would be difficult to capture accurately by direct observation.

In light winds and calm seas, taking a sight involves fairly straightforward eye-hand coordination. When wind and sea conditions deteriorate, however, the accuracy of a sight degrades. In these situations, all the negative influences simultaneously accelerate and increase your boat's pitch, roll, yaw, and heave. For example, heaving changes the observer's height of eye, or dip, a key factor in the sight-reduction process. The angle variations associated with pitching, rolling, and yawing changes your sextant reading session altogether. It's like trying not to slosh coffee from a cup as you bounce on a trampoline bolted to a flat-bed truck careening down a bumpy road! Add a partially overcast sky and you can easily understand why pre-GPS navigators became intimately familiar with anxiety. In optimum conditions, a good navigator can reduce a celestial fix to an accuracy of about one mile. Aboard a 40- or 50-foot vessel maneuvering through a rough seaway, that accuracy deteriorates to 5 to 10 miles. Fortunately, in the open ocean, we can usually declare that good enough.

The Time of the Observation

The accuracy of the observed sextant height (H_S) is critical, but accurate time-of-sight readings hold equal importance. The time of the sight is adjusted to Greenwich Mean Time (GMT), also referred to as Zulu or Universal Corrected Time (UTC). It makes sense to keep an accurate quartz timepiece permanently set to GMT. Then you regularly confirm its accuracy by tuning an SSB receiver to WWV or WWVH on 2.5, 5, 10, 15, or 20 MHz, along with listening to the English voice broadcast time ticks.

As mentioned earlier, if you can, enlist another person to help you note the exact time of a sextant

During the final phase of bringing a celestial body down to the horizon, navigators rock the sextant, a process called swinging the arc, accomplished by pivoting the wrist. The object in the mirror sweeps an arc and should just touch the horizon at its lowest point.

We can easily tune a single-sideband (SSB) marine transceiver to receive time ticks on the frequencies mentioned in the text. Offshore sailors often have their best luck on 10 and 15 MHz.

observation. Use the verbal prompt "ready, mark" to mark the moment you make an accurate reading. However, if a second person isn't available, you can use an accurate wristwatch. You must be especially careful when reading the minute and second hands of an analog timepiece, and many navigators find a digital timepiece easier to read. In addition, be aware of the error rate of your timepiece (if it has one), and always read the seconds before the minutes simply because the seconds change more rapidly. When you're timing your own sights, an inevitable lag exists between the moment the celestial body is aligned with the horizon and the moment you read the time. You can calculate a correction factor and subtract that small lag from subsequent "watch times" in order to acquire actual "fix times."

Today's inexpensive quartz watches and the time ticks available from WWV can obviate the need for chronometer corrections and translations from zone

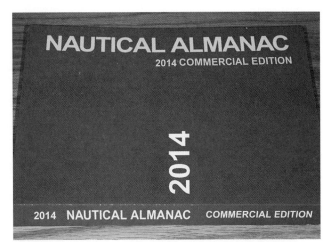

The nautical almanac is basically a celestial calendar that allows a sailor to calculate the geographic position of the sun, moon, planets, and selected stars at any given time during the year.

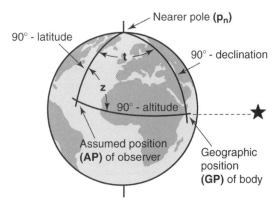

z = azimuth angle

t = meridian angle

The navigational triangle consists of three points: the nearer pole, the assumed position of the observer, and the geographic position of the body. Angles used in celestial navigation are the meridian angle "t" and the azimuth angle "z." The earth's rotation and revolution, the orbital behavior of the moon and planets, and your boat's progress across the ocean ensure that the latter two points of the celestial triangle are in constant motion. A sight leads to a line of position much as a compass bearing does. In essence, you come up with an imaginary line that intersects your location at the time of the sight. But you don't know where you are on that LOP until you cross it with another LOP.

time to Zulu. Keep a watch set to Greenwich Mean Time and be done with it.

Working the Sight

A working understanding of celestial navigation depends on a perception of the universe as a sphere surrounding the earth, with the earth at the center (according to our magical thinking). In this view, we see all the celestial bodies as embedded in the surrounding celestial sphere, with all of them equidistant from earth. For our purposes as navigators, it's irrelevant that the moon and Alpha Centauri are not even remotely equidistant from the earth. This geocentric myth establishes a correlation between latitude and longitude on earth and the declinations and hour angles of bodies in the celestial sphere. In essence, we project the equator outward as a plane merging with the equinoctial, or equator, of the cosmos.

Astronomers had hoped for a clockwork precision to the solar system, and they almost got one. But axis wobble, orbital anomalies, and planetary bulges caused by gravity and centrifugal force all complicate things. We can account for these influences on the solar day through a nifty equation of time and by using a nautical almanac, a particular type of calendar. The nautical almanac forecasts what spot on the earth's surface will be directly beneath the sun, moon, the planets, and more than 50 key stars at any time of day, any day of the year. Taking the sun as an example, a laser beam from the center of the earth to the center of the sun would penetrate the earth's crust at a precise location at any given instant of time. We refer to that location as the geographic position (GP) of the sun for that instant, and a nautical almanac provides the location at the instant of your sun sight.

This GP defines one corner of the celestial triangle (also called the navigational triangle or PZX triangle), while either the north or south pole and your boat define the other two corners. The three sides of the navigational triangle are as follows (see illustration at left):

- One side of the triangle is defined by an angle that equals 90 degrees minus the latitude of your boat;
- The second side is defined by an angle that equals 90 degrees plus or minus the declination of the observed body (its angular distance north or south of the equinoctial—in effect, its celestial latitude);
- The third side is defined by an angle that equals 90 degrees minus the observed altitude of the body above the horizon.

A trigonometric relationship results, allowing a navigator to derive a line of position from a sextant reading, the time of that reading, and the DR position at that time. The nautical almanac provides a means of calculating the body's GP at the time of the sight; you can do the math, called the sight reduction, with a calculator or computer, using sight reduction tables, or through a couple of spherical trigonometric equations. (Most sailors opt for calculators and computers—or smart phones and tablets—as the easiest method.)

From each sight comes a line of position—more precisely a circle of position—with your vessel located somewhere on the circle. Because the circle's diameter is thousands of miles and you will only be plotting a short arc of that circle, you can plot it as a straight line without introducing noticeable inaccuracy. To define your location on the LOP you need a second LOP to cross with the first one, just as with coastal piloting, and that requires a nearly simultaneous sight on a second celestial body. Although the intersection of the two LOPs can yield a fix of considerable accuracy (although far less than GPS provides), several opportunities for errors exist when we take and work the sights. For this reason, we recommend taking a third sight for confirmation.

You can accomplish sight reduction using the "plug and chug" method of posting data in a form that prompts the navigator through the process. Site Reduction Tables H.O. 249 and H.O. 229 are most often used, and the following outline generalizes the

CELESTIAL NAVIGATION STEP-BY-STEP

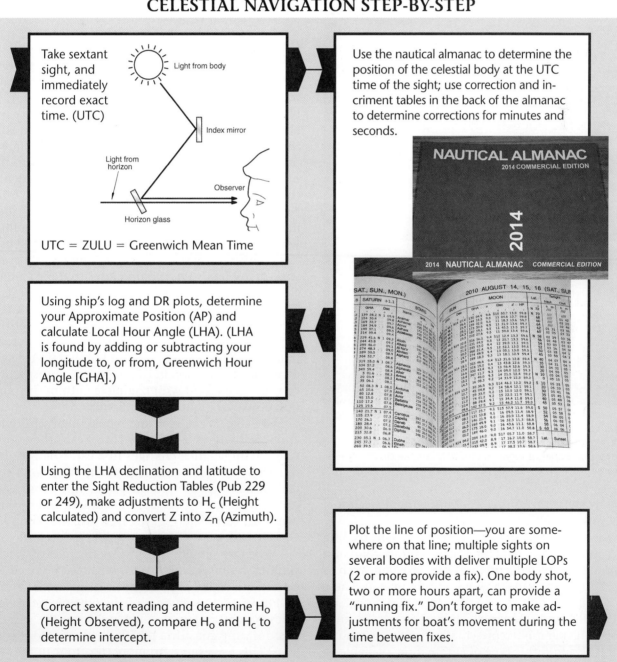

Take sextant sight, and immediately record exact time. (UTC)

Light from body

Index mirror

Light from horizon

Observer

Horizon glass

UTC = ZULU = Greenwich Mean Time

Use the nautical almanac to determine the position of the celestial body at the UTC time of the sight; use correction and incriment tables in the back of the almanac to determine corrections for minutes and seconds.

NAUTICAL ALMANAC
2014 COMMERCIAL EDITION
2014

2014 NAUTICAL ALMANAC COMMERCIAL EDITION

Using ship's log and DR plots, determine your Approximate Position (AP) and calculate Local Hour Angle (LHA). (LHA is found by adding or subtracting your longitude to, or from, Greenwich Hour Angle [GHA].)

Using the LHA declination and latitude to enter the Sight Reduction Tables (Pub 229 or 249), make adjustments to H_c (Height calculated) and convert Z into Z_n (Azimuth).

Correct sextant reading and determine H_o (Height Observed), compare H_o and H_c to determine intercept.

Plot the line of position—you are somewhere on that line; multiple sights on several bodies with deliver multiple LOPs (2 or more provide a fix). One body shot, two or more hours apart, can provide a "running fix." Don't forget to make adjustments for boat's movement during the time between fixes.

Although a costly addition to navigation kits, a handheld infrared scope/camera is a potentially life-saving tool for spotting a crew overboard at night, plus it helps locate lobster trap buoys at night. Shown here are the views from an infrared scope.

step-by-step process involved in solving the celestial navigation riddle.

Here's another option: enter the sextant reading (H_S) and time and date information into a computer running a sight-reduction software program, such as Star Pilot, also available as a smartphone app. These programs crunch the numbers for you, come up with LOPs, and compare them mathematically, thus providing a graphic representation and a lat/lon fix. You'll also find this type of automation available in handheld programmable calculators that carry out the same function.

Using a programmable calculator with a sextant makes sense for those who are looking for an emergency navigation backup but who aren't intrigued by the skills and lore of table-driven sight reduction. Always bring spare batteries for the calculator and remember that what's easy in a warm, dry classroom can become challenging at sea. Those of us taking sights only infrequently should set up our sight-reduction process to be as easy and user-friendly as possible.

PRUDENT SEAMANSHIP —WEAVING THE OLD AND THE NEW NAVIGATION

GPS information should be used as an aid to navigation, not as the sole means. The military employs inertial guidance systems and other electronic means to locate position in order to augment and double-check GPS fixes. However, many boaters have put all their eggs in one basket, albeit a good basket. Still, things happen. A few years ago, for some unknown reason, the GPS signal shut down for boaters in the mid-Atlantic region of the U.S. East Coast. Suddenly, the sportfishermen who routinely charge out from New Jersey harbors to deep-water canyons a hundred miles or so offshore had no satellite guidance for their return trip. Their handheld GPS receivers proved useless. The resulting scattergram of landfalls said it all, with many boats ending up closer to Cape Cod or Cape Hatteras than to their New Jersey home ports.

The grounding of the *Queen Elizabeth II* a few years ago is another illustration of the potential downside of blind allegiance to one data source. In that case, the GPS signal was lost but the GPS receiver continued to function in DR mode. The unsuspecting crew plowed ahead with complete faith in the position displayed by the GPS equipment.

GPS signals are weak and require high sensitivity and selectivity in a receiver. This means they don't tolerate impedance changes in a cable or antenna caused by moisture and corrosion. They don't tolerate other intrusions, either, including those associated with weather-related P-static or intentional jamming. Fortunately, newer DCS displays post a NO GPS SIGNAL alert when the satellite lock is lost.

When we simultaneously play the roles of watchstander, helmsperson, and navigator, we need an easy-to-use digital charting system and radar combination to help us navigate. This type of system enables watchstanders to quickly discern the vessel's position, the coastline profile, and any radar contacts. This leaves us with more time to scan the waters ahead and behind. Visual sighting remains the ultimate way to identify targets. Too often, crews get wrapped up in what's on a screen and fail to keep the cockpit or pilothouse dark enough for enhanced night vision. Then they're surprised when they hit the unlit mark they used as a waypoint when programming the route.

For good reason, radar is every commercial navigator's best electronic friend. Although automatic tune and gain adjustments do a good job of allowing a user to switch from one range to the next, careful manual tuning and gain control give you an even better rendition of what surrounds you. Radar is not known for its ability to discern a small fishing skiff or sea kayaker, however, especially in rain. Never assume your radar screen fills the role of an all-seeing eye of providence. Likewise, never underestimate the power of what the navy refers to as the mark 1, mod 1 human eyeball. Watchkeepers' best friends include visual acuity and a good pair of 7×50 binoculars.

Thanks to the need for better battlefield night vision, new technology has improved ways to enhance human visual acuity. The current generation of light-gathering night vision scopes can, for example, help a crew avoid crab or lobster pots or, more critical, find a crewmember who has gone over the side. I also use them to spot lit and unlit marks. Image-stabilizing binoculars, which eliminate roll-induced blur, deserve similar kudos. Forward-looking infrared scanning units continue to become more popular, and this technology's ability to discern small temperature variations is quite useful. For example, a person overboard in cold water presents a stark heat signature easily seen on a FLIR thermal imaging display.

Boat technology is in full swing—a headlong charge to network sensors of every variety: boat speed, wind speed, water depth, engine coolant temperature, even the volume of liquid in a holding tank. With a NMEA 2000 network we can share data among an array of devices. We can monitor a vessel like a car on a lift or a patient in a hospital bed. We can handle huge amounts of data and see the information displayed on screens connected to the network. But here's the rub: screens can become so overloaded with data that we lose crucial navigation information. On most boats paper charts are bigger than the navigator's work surface, which can be annoying. However, now we might see a 10-inch LCD screen split in two, with radar on one side and a digital chart on the other. More networked data appears across the bottom of the screen. This either informs or distracts watchkeepers—probably both in turn. In such busy displays we can find it too easy to overlook critical but hidden or even missing cartography.

As mentioned earlier, I prefer a stand-alone radar display unencumbered by strings of unrelated data across the bottom. And although I lay out tracks on my digital chartplotter and use it as my primary source of position information, I keep a chart book or a large-scale paper chart of the area handy for reference. And I keep in mind that although two GPS receivers provides some redundancy, they still operate on a single global satellite system that the Department of Defense states emphatically is not a stand-alone means of navigation.

We mentioned early in the chapter the eleven keys to safely navigate each time you cast off. Savvy mariners, especially navigators, should also maintain a two-tiered approach to seamanship and specifically to navigation, as discussed in this chapter. The first tier involves a deep appreciation for the tools and instruments on board and their contribution to safe and comfortable cruising and fast, tactically astute racing, as well as accurately knowing where you are and where you're heading.

The second tier involves your ability to carry on a safe and functional shipboard routine despite the failure of all electronics on board. The elegant simplicity of a sailboat is sometimes obscured by the quest for comfort and convenience. When and if you experience an electronic failure, the transition back to the bygone days of traditional navigation should be smooth and seamless.

9

SHARING CROWDED WATERS

I once knew a Chesapeake Bay sailor who applied his own collision-avoidance rule to any commercial traffic he met. Calling it his "law of gross tonnage," he likened it to a little dog giving a wide berth to big ones. His rule included an equally straightforward nighttime counterpart: the more lights a vessel displays and the brighter they appear, the livelier his avoidance response.

True, this idea of steering clear of big dogs appears grossly deficient in the details of the navigation rules drummed home in USCG-approved training programs and in naval and merchant marine academies around the globe. On the other hand, we see simple logic in the guiding principle to steer clear of the big boats, regardless of who has the "right of way" (a concept no longer recognized under the rules, as explained below). In short, you want to avoid proximity. When you have the room to put distance between your boat and the big boys, take advantage of the opportunity.

We offer a corollary piece of homespun wisdom: steer clear of the main channel when possible and work the shallower waters outside the channel instead. You'll find this feasible more often than you might think. If you're sailing the Chesapeake Bay or Long Island Sound, for example, even in a boat drawing 7 feet, you can cover most of the distance outside the main channel, although extreme shoal water may chase you back into the channel in the northern part of the bay or the western sound.

It's safe to say that when the depthsounder reads 12 feet, no ship will run you down. However, remember this one big caveat: tugs and barges are a different story. For nearly a century, these commercial vessels have been working the shoals to stay clear of big-ship traffic. This means small-boat operators must watch out for tugs and barges when outside the deep-draft channel.

Here's another truth for avoiding collision, and it has particularly hard edges: *when the bearing to an*

🚩 *Operating at night among bright, confusing background lighting tests a sailor's understanding of navigation rules. Navigation lights can be all but obscured by shore lights. Those who sail congested waters learn to watch for relative motion between fixed and moving lights.*

approaching vessel remains constant while its range decreases, you are on a collision course. Simply put, collision is the eventual endpoint of any constant-bearing, decreasing-range (CBDR) scenario. (See Chapter 8 for more on bearings.) To prevent it, one or both vessels must take evasive action. Therefore, if we come down to the final moments prior to an inevitable collision, and the give-way vessel has not maneuvered to avoid collision, the stand-on vessel must make an effort to get out of the way. In this "extremis" situation, under the rules, both vessels are obligated to take evasive actions.

THE NAVIGATION RULES: AN OVERVIEW

Some recreational boaters harbor the dangerous misconception that navigation rules, unofficially known as the nautical Rules of the Road, apply only to commercial traffic. Like the Chesapeake sailor I mentioned earlier, these sailors think that to hold up their end of the bargain, all they have to do is stay away from ships. Steering clear of other traffic is a good start, but situations involving meeting, crossing, and overtaking inevitably arise. In these situations, understanding what you need to do requires a grasp of what for decades have been known as the International Regulations for Preventing Collisions at Sea, or COLREGS. The first rule in the COLREGS begins with the clear message that, "These rules shall apply to all vessels."

The COLREGS apply to waters seaward of river mouths and the entrances to harbors and embayments (indentations in the shorelines smaller than harbors and bays but large enough that navigation regulations apply). The International Maritime Organization (IMO) established the demarcation lines between inland and international waters. The IMO maintains and oversees the COLREGS, which allow each treaty nation to modify the rules for its inland waters. Many countries simply use the International Rules also in inland waters, while others add small changes—but no more than necessary to accommodate a special condition or circumstance.

You can refer to the magenta demarcation lines on coastal charts to determine which set of rules apply where you happen to be. These lines often run from headland to headland or follow short segments between prominent navigation aids or landmarks. However, sometimes you'll locate the demarcation line farther inshore than you'd expect to find it, such as near the head of a bay, for example, or inside the mouth of a major estuary.

In 1972, the COLREGS were established by international treaty. In 1980, the U.S. Congress followed

Hugging the sides of a channel or, when depths allow, running just outside it will keep you away from draft-constrained ships. Likewise, running down a set of range lights or following a digital plot up the center of a channel will put you right in the midst of commercial shipping traffic.

Ships entering coastal waters switch from the International to the Inland Rules as they cross the COLREGS demarcation line. New Homeland Security regulations aimed at enhancing port security impose added constraints on shipping traffic in U.S. waters, including required stand-off distances around naval warships and strategic installations.

with the U.S. Inland Rules, which merged the previous Inland, Great Lakes, and Western Rivers rules and, for the most part, they continue to conform to the International Rules. Although only a few differences remain between the International and U.S. Inland Rules, it's important to understand them. The

U.S. Coast Guard administers and enforces the Inland and International Navigation Rules in U.S. waters. In this discussion we follow the Coast Guard convention of referring to the two related sets of rules collectively as the Navigation Rules.

Today, collision-avoidance maneuvering rules, lighting standards, sound signals, and other stipulations of the Navigation Rules guide all mariners. In many ways, these are like roadway traffic laws. On highways, vehicles range in size from small motorcycles to eighteen-wheel trucks, while on the high seas the size disparity is even greater. The authorities responsible for making the rules are charged with developing equitable navigation rules for vessels as small as rowing dinghies and as large as aircraft carriers and supertankers. For centuries, the international community has wrestled with the complex and demanding challenge of determining the roles and responsibilities of all vessels during close-quarters maneuvering.

Those who sail non-commercial "uninspected vessels," a category comprised mostly of recreational boats, don't need Coast Guard licenses. In general, it's likely these recreational boat skippers are not as well versed in the Navigation Rules as licensed skippers. However, we can name at least two good reasons every recreational skipper needs a working knowledge of the rules. First, when we share the water with merchant ships, fishing vessels, and tugs pushing or towing barges, understanding the rules that govern their maneuvers is key to predicting the way these vessels will behave—for our own safety. Second, as any admiralty lawyer will note, failure to conform to the rules becomes a major factor in the outcome of any litigation following an accident at sea, including those involving recreational boats.

A TOUR OF THE RULES

One of the most appealing aspects of the Navigation Rules is their commonsense presentation. Organized in an identical manner, this feature of the Inland and International Rules varies only occasionally. To streamline this tour through the rules, we'll cover the Inland and International Rules together, noting major differences where they apply. These 38 rules include prescriptions for every close-quarters maneuvering situation, along with some details to help you fine-tune your collision-avoidance responses.

Part A: General Rules

Part A of the rules includes Rules 1 through 3, which set the stage for the rules that follow. Rule 1 makes clear that the rules apply to all vessels from kayaks to ocean liners. Rule 3 defines terms such as *give-way vessel, stand-on vessel, vessel not under command,* and *vessel restricted in her ability to maneuver,* among others. (We define these terms in context below.)

And Rule 2, perhaps the most important of the rules, states that nothing in the rules exonerates a vessel or skipper from the consequences of neglecting any precaution required *by the ordinary practice of seamen.* In other words, follow the rules, yes, but above all else, avoid collisions. If you must break a rule to avoid a collision, you're both allowed and required to do so. Rule 2 prevents any argument that deems any party to a collision faultless on principle.

Part B: Steering and Sailing Rules

Part B of the COLREGS and the U.S. Inland Rules collects the Steering and Sailing Rules, Rules 4 through 19. You don't need to memorize these rules, but you need to understand and have the ability to paraphrase each, thereby having the intent of the rule and the desired response at your disposal and immediately ready to implement.

The steering and sailing rules are grouped into three sections:

Section 1, "Conduct of Vessels in Any Condition of Visibility," includes Rules 4 through 10.

Section 2, "Conduct of Vessels in Sight of One Another," includes Rules 11 through 18.

Section 3, "Conduct of Vessels in Restricted Visibility," comprises Rule 19 alone.

These rules go straight to the heart of a vessel's responsibilities when another vessel approaches. As you see, this section uses long-standing nautically accepted traditions of personifying the vessel with the pronouns "she" and "her." This convention adds some seafaring flare to what could be an otherwise dry code of the high seas.

Part B, Section 1: Conduct of Vessels in Any Condition of Visibility

This group of rules applies at all times, whether you are piloting by eye in clear weather or by compass, GPS, or with radar in a thick fog.

Rule 5: Lookout. Paraphrased, Rule 5 mandates that *every vessel* shall at *all times* maintain a proper lookout. Further, we can carry out the lookout's duties by way of sight and sound and by any other available means on board, including radar, AIS, and VHF communications.

This regulation gives singlehanders and short-handed cruisers nightmares. Intentionally vague, the regulation uses the term "proper" without defining the scope of the term, probably to cover a wide range of vessels under a single rule. In admiralty court, the crew-by-crew definition of what constitutes a proper lookout is one of the most tested matters.

Rule 6: Safe Speed. This rule also is, as it should be, a major concern among recreational mariners, because excessive speed turns up as a factor in many marine casualty cases. As a general guideline, do not exceed a speed that effectively avoids collision and allows the vessel to stop within a safe distance. The rule goes on to enumerate the conditions that require reduced speed: reduced visibility, vessel traffic, the boat's maneuverability, light clutter at night, and wind and sea state. The rule even includes your boat's draft relative to the surrounding water depths, because draft can influence hydrodynamic effects in a shallow basin and the effect of your boat's wake on other craft.

This rule represents another example of the "all vessels shall" mandate, framed broadly enough to apply to sailboats and supertankers alike. Admiralty courts have ruled repeatedly about safe speeds in restricted visibility and defined it as a speed that allows stopping within half the range of visibility.

Rule 7: Risk of Collision. This rule charges vessel operators with using every means appropriate under prevailing conditions to determine the risk of collision. The well-defined, classic method is the navy's use of the acronym CBDR (constant bearing, decreasing range), four words that describe a collision in the making. As noted previously, when the relative bearing of another vessel remains constant as its range decreases, you know you're facing an imminent collision unless at least one of you changes course, speed, or both. The rules that follow spell out collision-avoidance actions.

"Every means appropriate" includes radar, if fitted and operational. And the rule cautions us that risk of collision may exist even if we see the bearing of the approaching vessel changing but the vessel is large, or close, or has a barge or another vessel in tow.

Rule 8: Action to Avoid Collision. When we must act to avoid another vessel, the response must be early, decisive, and, whenever possible, readily apparent to the other vessel. For example, the best action involves a change in our course that reflects both good seamanship and our clear intent. To avoid a collision, skippers may need to reduce speed or completely stop the vessel. To prevent confusing the other vessel, avoid a series of small, incremental changes in course, speed, or both.

Rule 8f (iii) contains one of the most important caveats in the International Rules, though its impact is

The phrases "every vessel" and "at all times" set the stage for the rigorous requirement of watchkeeping. Single-handed sailors, like all mariners, operate in this context, and need to use all available means to keep a continuous lookout.

Any vessel operating on U.S. waters inshore of the demarcation line is regulated by the U.S. Inland Navigation Rules, including those rules related to the definition of a safe operating speed. An appropriate speed in an open, unobstructed bay likely becomes too fast when you're maneuvering around other boats. You're responsible not only for avoiding collisions but also for the wake you produce and its effects on other craft.

obscured by the language used: "A vessel, the passage of which is not to be impeded remains fully obligated to comply with the rules of this part when the two vessels are approaching one another so as to involve risk of collision." Later rules describe the roles of *give-way* and *stand-on* vessels, but Rule 8 means even the stand-on vessel—sometimes misunderstood as having an absolute "right of way"—carries a responsibility to avoid collision. However, as a caveat, the rule also says that the stand-on vessel should not take avoidance maneuvers that would cause an allision with a fixed object or a collision with another vessel.

In effect, Rule 8 establishes the scaffolding on which later rules are built. The rule puts the onus for early action on the give-way vessel, but if that action fails, both vessels must take responsibility to avoid collision. By "early action," the rule means that the give-way vessel should change course and/or speed soon enough to make its intention clear.

This third "all vessels shall" rule builds on the previous two (Rule 5, Lookout, and Rule 6, Safe Speed). Rule 8 establishes the manner in which we should engage the following maneuvering rules (12–18) and calls for the skipper or watchkeeper to make significant decisions. Risk management in a collision-avoidance context requires a cultivated sea sense as well as a clear understanding of the rules. For example, sailors and power cruisers accustomed to minimal current drift can be surprised by how quickly a simple crossing situation deteriorates into an emergency when slack water gives way to a powerful ebb or flood. For this reason, professional mariners calculate their closest point of approach (CPA) and treat close-quarters maneuvering with deference. Staying "well clear" means maintaining a safe distance from other craft.

Rule 9: Narrow Channels. Often called the "stay-to-the-right rule," Rule 9 is intuitive for U.S. mariners because it's consistent with our roadway rules and treats channels like two-lane roads. When moving in opposite directions, vessels ensure safe passage if they keep to the starboard side of a channel.

Rule 9 also assigns a pecking order of vessels not to be impeded in a narrow channel. For example, no vessel engaged in fishing may impede the progress of

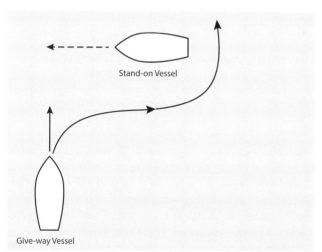

Rule 9 requires you to stay to the right-hand side of a channel. Another handy "right rule" (Rule 15) is that when two vessels under power are on crossing courses, the vessel that has the other on its starboard bow is the give-way vessel and should alter course to the right (starboard) so as to pass astern of the stand-on vessel.

any other vessel navigating the channel, nor may a vessel crossing a channel impede the passage of a vessel that can't navigate safely outside the channel. A vessel less than 20 meters in length or a sailing vessel must not impede the passage of a ship that can operate only within the channel, a critical element of the rule for recreational boaters. As mentioned, one of the small-craft mariner's most helpful but least used strategies involves simply staying out of a ship channel whenever there's enough water to do so.

One caveat of the Inland Rules applies specifically to the Great Lakes and Western Rivers. It mandates that because of their diminished maneuverability, downbound vessels operating with a following current shall have right of way over upbound vessels. This is one of the few times the phrase "right of way" appears in the latest Navigation Rules. In other situations, the *right-of-way* vessel—a nautical status that sounds somehow analogous to "diplomatic immunity"—has become the *stand-on* vessel instead, with its own set of responsibilities.

Any channel narrow enough to restrict a vessel's maneuvering options is, at least to that vessel, a narrow channel. The USCG has classified many river segments in inland waters as narrow channels.

As prescribed under Rule 34, when in a narrow channel it's a good idea to use VHF radio communication or a whistle to signal an intended course change. In international waters the whistle signal indicates a planned maneuver, not the start of course change. Prior to executing the change, the other vessel must agree with the planned maneuver. Once the give-way vessel (presumably) has made the course change, a favorable bearing change results. A change in speed resulting in a favorable bearing drift also gives us another useful tool to avoid collision. Later rules spell out which vessel is responsible for taking the initial action to avoid the other.

Rule 34 also specifies at least five short whistle blasts to signal one's confusion about another vessel's intentions. Though sound signaling can itself cause confusion in crowded waters, it also helps to prevent mishaps in a narrow channel.

Rule 10: Traffic Separation Schemes. This rule establishes vessel behavior within the traffic separation zones found in the approaches to major seaports. As in narrow channels, vessels under 20 meters long and sailing vessels must give way to larger vessels transiting these lanes. When possible, recreational craft should avoid these designated lanes. If you must cross one, do so on a course as nearly perpendicular to the traffic lane as possible.

Transiting in and near these zones requires heightened vigilance, and it's best to enter or leave at the start or end of the zone to preserve the traffic separation pattern and minimize divergent maneuvering. However, if you need to leave or join a lane from the side, do so at as acute an angle as possible, as you do when merging with highway traffic from an on-ramp. Bridge-to-bridge communication on VHF Channel 13 helps to clarify another vessel's intentions. In addition, radar, AIS, and other aids also identify targets and their movements within a traffic separation scheme.

Part B, Section 2: Conduct of Vessels in Sight of One Another

Prior to the 1972 COLREGS, whenever two vessels approached one another, one of them was deemed the *privileged vessel* and maintained the right of way, while the other was the *burdened vessel*, required to keep clear. But the latest version of the Navigation Rules does not use the terms "privileged" and "burdened," nor does it acknowledge an absolute "right of way" in these situations.

The rules now replace this concept with the notion that when vessels approach in sight of one another, one should *give way* and the other should *stand on.* We can liken each vessel to an actor with an assigned role. But if the give-way vessel shows no sign of maneuvering to stay clear, the stand-on vessel must do so, and in extreme situations, it must take all possible evasive actions. In poor visibility, assuming the two vessels are not in each other's sight, the rules instruct both vessels to take primary measures to avoid collision.

The rules in this section, 11–18, assign stand-on/give-way roles to vessels that have each other in sight in most but not all close-quarters situations. Vessels approach one another in one of three ways: they meet head on, their courses cross, or one overtakes the other. Each crew must determine what the other vessel is doing, and you must know if you are overtaking or being overtaken, crossing or being crossed, and whether a CBDR (constant bearing, decreasing range) situation exists.

Rule 11: Application. This rule states that rules in Section 2 apply to vessels that have each other in sight, meaning under visual observation rather than radar. The entire stand-on/give-way construct becomes irrelevant when fog, smoke, smog, or heavy rain restrict visibility. Under low visibility conditions Rule 19 takes over, and each vessel "shall" assume a primary role in maneuvering to avoid collision. Put simply, in moderate visibility, vessels under visual contact should act in accordance with Rules 12–18, while those observing each other through electronic means revert to Rule 19.

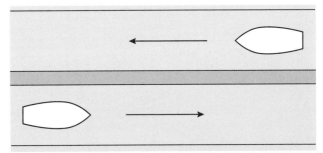

Traffic separation zones are set up like highways with an invisible barrier between the lanes. Often leading to major ports, these designated approaches require traffic to pass port to port and to navigate on the right-hand side of the designated area. When crossing these inbound/outbound lanes, a boat should steer clear of traffic using the lane, proceed on a course that's perpendicular to the traffic, and maintain both an active radio and visual watch.

The officer of the watch aboard a commercial vessel continuously evaluates contacts on a give-way/stand-on basis. Inshore the officer monitors VHF Channels 13 and 16 and transmits an AIS signal that identifies the vessel, provides its course and speed, and even yields a CPA based on the SOG and COG of both vessels.

Rule 12: Sailing Vessels. When two vessels approach each other under sail on opposite tacks, the port-tack boat shall keep clear of the other. When the boats are on the same tack, the windward boat shall keep clear of the leeward one. When a leeward port-tack vessel can't discern the tack of the boat to windward, the skipper must assume that the boat is on starboard tack and give way accordingly. (A common question among new sailors is which tack a boat is on when wing-and-wing downwind—the tack is the one opposite the side that the boom is on.)

You may see exhaust smoke from an approaching sailboat or even hear its engine running, but don't assume it is motorsailing. The skipper may well be running in neutral to charge up the batteries, and under the rules, the boat is proceeding under sail and retains its status as a sailboat.

A boat under sail on port tack must be ready to give way to a sailboat on a starboard tack, assuming the vessels are in sight of one another. When sailing in restricted visibility, both boats must maneuver to avoid collision.

When a craft approaches from just abaft the beam, it can be difficult to determine if the vessel is overtaking or crossing you. Overtaking vessels fall into the sector of the stern light as they approach, but in a borderline situation, you may think you're being overtaken when the other skipper thinks the two boats are crossing. At such times, a whistle signal (see Rule 34) or radio communication may clear up any confusion. In the absence of a response, initiate a maneuver to avoid the other vessel.

Rule 13: Overtaking. You're overtaking another boat if you approach within the arc of the boat's stern light; the arc extends from 22.5 degrees abaft its port beam to 22.5 degrees abaft its starboard beam. Without exception, an overtaking vessel must give way to the vessel being overtaken. Even if you're under sail and overtake a power-driven craft, you become the give-way vessel.

Other variations can come up. Let's say you approach another vessel from slightly (say 10 to 15 degrees) abaft its starboard beam. In this case, you're the stand-on vessel and it's a crossing not an over-taking situation. It's important that both parties perceive either of these situations in the same way, so use Channel 13 for bridge-to-bridge (vessel-to-vessel) radio confirmation of your status and intention. This represents sound practice and good seamanship.

Rule 14: Head-on Situation. When two pow-er-driven vessels approach on reciprocal courses, both should alter course to the right so as to pass port to port. Both sidelights on the other vessel will be visible when it approaches you head-on at night, and a larger motor vessel will show near alignment of its masthead lights; as you carry out the maneuver, the green side-light of the approaching vessel disappears, its red light remains visible, and its masthead lights separate.

A port-to-port passing is often termed a "one whistle" passing because under Rule 34, one whistle is the signal for a course alteration to starboard. On inland waters, where obstacles may prevent a port-to-port passing, a "two whistle" starboard-to-starboard passing may be initiated instead. Given that many recreational boaters don't know the meanings of various sound signals, we advise you to use radio communication and initiate early and unambiguous maneuvers.

Rule 15: Crossing Situation. When power vessels of the same standing find themselves in a crossing situation, the vessel having the other on its starboard side is the give-way vessel (see illustration page 260). It should alter course to starboard, slow down, or both, if possible, in order to cross astern of the other craft. Of course, you need enough room to carry out this maneuver.

Whenever a chance of collision exists, this rule supersedes the "do not impede progress of larger vessels" regulation that's in play in narrow channels and traffic separation zones (Rules 9 and 10). As long as you have room and depth to maneuver, even a large ship and a small craft treat each other as equals. Both parties must take responsibility for avoiding collisions, and early in the process your best bet is to engage in clear, decisive bridge-to-bridge radio confirmation of an agreed-upon maneuver.

Rule 15 applies only when you have visual contact with the other vessel. A clear and distinct radar image is no substitute for a visual sighting. When vessels are unable to maintain visual contact, Rule 19 comes into play and supersedes Rule 15. (See discussion below.)

At night, if you can see only one sidelight of an approaching vessel, you're involved in a *crossing* situation. You are *overtaking* the other vessel (Rule 13) if the stern light is visible (or was visible initially). A *head-on* meeting (Rule 14) is in progress if you see both sidelights consistently or intermittently. As noted above, in a crossing situation you must determine whether you are the stand-on or give-way vessel and act accordingly.

Rule 16: Action by Give-Way Vessel. In almost any situation, other steering and sailing rules designate the stand-on and the give-way craft (formerly called the *burdened vessel*). Rule 16 clarifies the actions required of the give-way vessel, and its singular role involves staying out of the way to prevent a collision. To accomplish this, the give-way vessel should take decisive and obvious action, such as an easily noticeable and identified change in course, speed, or both.

The give-way vessel must also remain "well clear" of the stand-on vessel. If you decide to pass ahead of an oncoming stand-on boat, usually the least desirable option, you assume the responsibility to remain a safe distance from the stand-on boat during the maneuver.

Rule 17: Action by Stand-On Vessel. A stand-on vessel should hold its course and speed but also carefully monitor the actions of the give-way vessel. If the actions, or inaction, of the give-way vessel appear to threaten a collision, then the stand-on vessel is mandated to respond with collision-avoidance actions. If the give-way vessel lies to port, then avoid steering to port. These last minute—in extremis—actions taken by the stand-on vessel don't remove the primary obligation to avoid collision assigned to the give-way vessel.

More complex than the previous give-way statutes, this rule requires that the stand-on vessel make a decision that it may or even must take evasive action. In essence, the crew of the stand-on vessel must determine that the give-way vessel's inaction has substantially raised the risk of collision and, therefore, the stand-on craft must initiate a decisive maneuver.

Sounding five or more short whistle blasts, as prescribed by Rule 34(d), the stand-on vessel makes the maneuver that provides the best chance to avoid a collision or minimize the impact if contact appears unavoidable. VHF bridge-to-bridge communications often help prevent such encounters.

Timing means everything. For example, a large stand-on ship could take action while still 2 miles from the give-way vessel. Small craft in tight confines have the benefit of greater agility in their maneuvers, but time remains of the essence.

When several vessels converge, avoiding dual conflicting designations might prove impossible. In this case, the middle vessel (we'll designate it vessel B) in a three-way convergence may hold stand-on rights over vessel A but have give-way responsibility to vessel C. Such situations put you between a rock and a hard place, forcing you to disobey one or more rules in order to satisfy others. This is why Rule 2 includes a clause about "special situations" and makes clear that to "avoid immediate danger" you can and should substitute good sense for the letter of the rules.

Large container ships maneuver with difficulty, take up to a mile to stop, and have trouble seeing small craft because of the stacks of containers piled high on their decks. Giving these vessels a wide berth makes plenty of good sea sense.

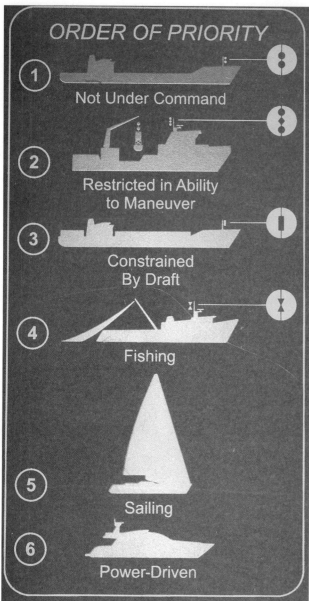

ORDER OF PRIORITY

1. Not Under Command
2. Restricted in Ability to Maneuver
3. Constrained By Draft
4. Fishing
5. Sailing
6. Power-Driven

◆ You'll find a reminder plaque defining the stand-on/ give-way pecking order a handy addition to any nav station. In most cases it's logically based on a vessel's ability to maneuver. In this graphic the far column indicates the vessel's prescribed day shape pattern.

Rule 18: Responsibilities Between Vessels. In framing the Navigation Rules, a key challenge involved defining the pecking order that gives one vessel stand-on priority over another. It oversimplifies the situation to use the law of gross tonnage as the guide, yet it's a fact that a large tanker, freighter, or warship can have difficulty stopping in less than a mile, and even minor course corrections take time. Therefore, common sense and logic about a vessel's ability to maneuver underlies the hierarchy of privilege. In descending order of privilege, the hierarchy looks like this:

- ◆ Not under command
- ◆ Restricted maneuverability
- ◆ Constrained by draft
- ◆ Fishing and trawling
- ◆ Under sail
- ◆ Motor vessel
- ◆ Seaplane (on the water)

You can't assume that a boat under sail is always the stand-on vessel. In fact, that assumption is far from the truth. Yes, sailboats under sail have rights over motorboats, but as soon as you fire up your auxiliary engine and put it in gear, the sailboat becomes a motorboat, even if the sails remain set. The rights of fishing vessels pertain only to commercial craft, not recreational fishing. A fishing vessel has stand-on status relative to motorboats and sailboats only when actively engaged in trawling, setting nets, or other activities that restrict its maneuverability. When a fishing vessel is working, the crew should show a day shape comprised of two cones aligned vertically apex-to-apex; at night, they use red-over-white (fishing) or green-over-white (trawling) lights, visible all around at 360 degrees.

According to the rule, skippers correctly display these lights and shapes *only* when gear in the water constrains the vessel. Unfortunately, many fishermen leave the day shape permanently affixed in the rigging and switch on their "engaged in fishing" all-around lights as soon as they leave the dock, actions that wrongly bend the rules. Rule 26 clearly spells out that unless a fishing boat has gear in the water, it is treated as a motor vessel with the attending privileges and responsibilities.

One of the difficulties of maneuvering near a working fishing boat involves predicting its course, often anything but straight. A dragger towing a net frequently changes its headings as it tows. Draggers and trawlers often work in a circular pattern, and the change in their navigation-light configuration can be deceiving as they turn through 360 degrees. At such times, you'll find radar a valuable tool. It provides an accurate means of tracking the distance to the contact and eliminating the confusion caused by the fishing vessel's changing light configurations.

Confusion can have consequences; many collisions have been caused by the shifting light patterns of trawlers at night. Perhaps the give-way vessel fails to notice the green-over-white or red-over-white all-around lights and, while trying to make sense of the circling vessel, continues to close with it. In their confusion, the give-way crew ignores the fundamental CBDR principle.

In the case of the circling trawler, the changing light pattern can create the illusion that separation is occurring when it's not. Seeing a stern light appear can bring momentary relief, but it also can cloud rational thinking, and as the trawler continues its circular track, the potential for collision returns. Radar, and perhaps an AIS signal, allows you to continually monitor the range and bearing of the target. It also makes sense to establish bridge-to-bridge VHF radio contact and confirm the other vessel's intentions.

Other conditional issues influence the fundamental fishing vessel-sailboat-motorboat hierarchy. For example, we may encounter *severely restricted maneuverability* caused by a specific operational procedure such as dredging, laying cable, or towing a barge or other vessel. A tug towing a barge in a narrow channel is normally classed as a motor vessel of its given length that, therefore, must give way to a boat under sail or a fishing vessel with nets out. However, special circumstances associated with tow dynamics can significantly restrict the tug's ability to maneuver. In this case, it can display a ball-diamond-ball day shape (vertically stacked with the diamond in the middle) or red-white-red lights at night. The tug's restricted maneuverability gives it the right of way, or, more accurately, a stand-on designation over the sailboat or fishing vessel.

In any event, out of courtesy and respect, if not statute, sailors should give tugs and their tows as wide a berth as possible. Tow cables are true hazards, and under no circumstance should a vessel ever choose a shortcut that leads between a tug and its tow.

Draft is another significant constraint, especially in narrow channels. Sailors should note that only power-driven vessels can be designated as *constrained by draft*. An auxiliary sailboat cannot be so designated when operating under sail alone; the engine must be on and the drive train engaged. Note that there is no mention in the U.S. Inland Rules of a vessel "constrained by draft."

Vessels "not under command" top the pecking order of privilege. This designation refers to an exceptional circumstance such as a steering or propulsion failure.

As noted above, regulations associated with narrow channels and traffic separation lanes (Rules 9 and 10 of the COLREGS and U.S. Inland Rules) further condition the standard right-of-way pecking order. Vessels' relative headings upon approach and how well give-way vessels handle their role also add conditions. For example, as we've seen, an overtaking vessel is always deemed the burdened or give-way vessel, regardless of size or method of propulsion.

Once you understand the rules you'll know in any situation the designation of your boat as either

In this close-quarters maneuvering situation, a fishing trawler is underway with its booms lowered but shows only the running lights of a motor vessel of its size, indicating that its nets are not deployed and it is not engaged in fishing. Therefore, this trawler is required to give way to a vessel under sail.

When operating under power or under a combination of power and sail, a sailboat is considered a motor vessel under the Navigation Rules. The rules require a sailing auxiliary to display a conical shape (apex down) in the rigging when operating under power by day. We seldom see this requirement followed, however.

the stand-on or give-way vessel, along with your appropriate response. Under some circumstances, however, such as a strong current, a mechanical failure, or operator error, the give-way vessel may fail to take action to avoid a collision. In the extreme situation of imminent threat of collision, the stand-on vessel must also act to avoid it. Then, should a collision occur anyway, admiralty law steps in to handle litigation, assign proportionate responsibility for the mishap, and place blame where justified. If an accident occurs, even the captain of the stand-on vessel may be held accountable for failing to act in a reasonable manner and not following some stipulation of the Navigation Rules.

Part B, Section 3

This section of Part B consists only of Rule 19.

Rule 19: Conduct of Vessels in Restricted Visibility.

This rule preempts and nullifies the give-way/stand-on premise developed in the preceding rules. It applies when conditions limit our ability to see other vessels, leaving us with sound signals, radar, AIS, and other instrumentation to track these vessels.

As a cardinal rule in these conditions, proceed at a safe speed dictated by the state of visibility around you, stopping distance, and your ability to maneuver. You must execute maneuvers early and make an effort to avoid turning to port in order to steer clear

The large screen of a commercial ship's radar offers a detailed picture of what lies ahead, but compared with a visual view in clear weather, it has significant limitations.

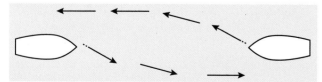

In the classic port-to-port or "one-whistle" response to a head-on meeting situation (Rule 14), both vessels alter course to starboard and maintain safe separation.

of vessels forward of the beam in all but overtaking situations. Avoid altering course toward a vessel in an attempt to cross ahead of it. Fog may dictate that you reduce speed to the minimum you need to maintain your ability to steer. Prepare your crew to stop the vessel to avoid collision or to clarify a sound signal.

Although often equated with a fogbank, restricted visibility also includes mist, haze, downpours, snowstorms, sandstorms, and even volcanic ash. On the open ocean, visibility less than 5 miles is considered restricted; in inshore waters, where we assume slower transit speeds and increased traffic, the restricted visibility range is cut almost in half.

Rule 19 includes this key provision: when vessels involved in close-quarters maneuvering are not in visual contact, consider the visibility "restricted." This means you can operate in full sunlight with a blue sky overhead, but restricted visibility rules apply if an adjacent fogbank obscures a ship or sailboat less than a half mile away. If other vessels are in your blue-sky donut hole and can see each other, navigate according to Rules 11–18 rather than Rule 19. However, you must respond to unseen vessels in the fogbank according to Rule 19, thus ignoring the statutes laid out in Rules 11–18.

Part C: Lights and Shapes

The next 73 pages of the COLREGS (Part C) describe the lights and shapes carried by every imaginable class of vessel, including aircraft capable of landing on the water and submarines running on the surface. Commercial mariners need to know every combination, and the most diligent recreational boaters might follow suit. However, most of us are satisfied with knowing the lights and shapes most often seen on our local waters but carry a copy of the Navigation Rules as a handy reference we can pull out when needed.

Fortunately—and logically—a great deal of overlap exists in running lights displayed on all vessels, from runabouts to supertankers. We welcome the similarity in the way sidelights and a stern light split up the 360-degree perimeter around a vessel. Each 112.5-degree sidelight arc extends from dead ahead to 22.5 degrees abaft the beam, and the stern light arc fills in the remaining 135 degrees of the complete circle around the vessel, forming a wedge centered on the stern. The consistency of this pie-shaped light puzzle allows mariners to discern a rough heading for nearby vessels. The near universal use of side and stern lights is the foundation for safely maneuvering at night.

You likely feel some anxiety when you see red and green sidelights side by side on an approaching

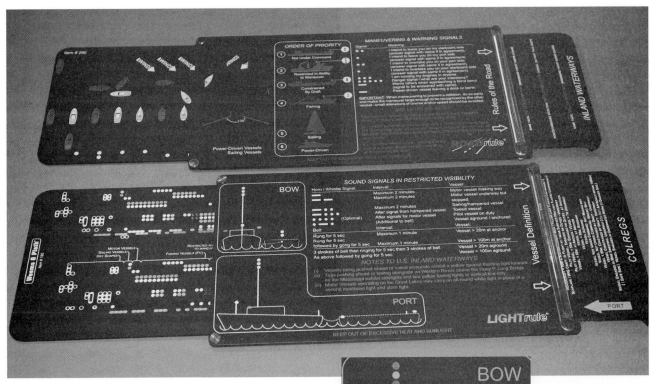

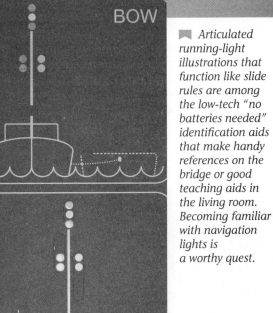

Articulated running-light illustrations that function like slide rules are among the low-tech "no batteries needed" identification aids that make handy references on the bridge or good teaching aids in the living room. Becoming familiar with navigation lights is a worthy quest.

vessel, but rest assured, all who go to sea experience the same angst. Larger vessels incorporate a second white 225-degree masthead light abaft and higher than the forward one. When these are in line and both red and green side lights are visible, you're facing trouble and it's time to use whistle signals, bridge-to-bridge VHF contact, a range check via radar, or AIS. The preferred action calls for both vessels to use a "one-whistle" starboard course change that allows for a safe port-to-port passing. Maintain a safe passing distance and heave a sigh of relief when a single white light, the vessel's stern light, recedes astern toward the horizon.

Recognizing and interpreting navigation lights can be challenging, because diverse vessels engaged in various activities show diverse light patterns. These patterns change as our perspective as observers change. We must interpret the relative alignment of the lights on board a vessel as it changes course but momentarily retains the same bearing to your vessel. Imagine that vessel you're observing sits on a lazy Susan, and as it gradually rotates, its navigation lights change their relative positions and one or more may appear or disappear as their viewing sectors come into play or are eclipsed.

Say, for example, that you're on the open ocean in a nighttime crossing situation and a vessel is moving on your port side. Rule 15 makes you the stand-on vessel, but will the ship give way? Does the crew even know you're there? Looking for clues, you anxiously study the vessel's lights and its relative bearing. Then, although the bearing doesn't noticeably change, you see—or think you see—the separation between the forward and aft masthead lights narrowing. Is the vessel turning? A moment later, you confirm this when the masthead lights come into alignment and both sidelights come into view. Before this, you could see only the green. Now you conclude the vessel is heading directly at you, which, if the turn continues, could be a good thing. Sure enough, a moment later his green sidelight disappears and the higher, after masthead light moves to the right of the lower, forward masthead. As the gap between these masthead lights continues to widen, you know the ship has altered course to pass behind you, and you soon confirm this when the vessel's relative bearing moves sternward.

Most ships and commercial vessels sail with a plethora of non-navigation lights, posing additional challenges. At times these lights become more indicative of the class of vessel encountered than the vessel's navigation lights. For example, cruise ships and navy cruisers are similar in size, but you'll see the cruise ship lit up like a small city, while the navy cruiser may sail with no lights at all.

To become more familiar with the way vessels appear at sea, create a set of cards illustrated with dots showing the various navigation light patterns as they appear when viewed from port, starboard, astern, and ahead and/or download a useful nav-light app. These simple cards and apps illustrate the relative differences in height, separation on deck, and sector visibility. For example, tugs and tows carry lights that indicate the way a barge is lashed to a tow or, if it's towing astern, the length of the hawser.

Rule 20: Application This rule specifies that the lights prescribed in Part C shall be carried from sunset to sunrise or whenever restricted visibility deems them necessary. Vessels must also carry specific shapes during daylight hours. Part C describes both lights and shapes for each class of vessel.

Rule 20 contains a few interesting nuances, including a mandate that bad weather doesn't excuse us from using our navigation lights. In other words, we must replace blown-out bulbs, even in less than ideal conditions. In another important caveat, we can't allow non-navigation lights to confuse or obscure the lights mandated by the rules. One short clause points out that any light impairing the vision of a lookout violates the navigation rules. Shorthanded vessels on which the helmsperson is also the lookout need to be mindful of the brightness of digital chartplotter screens and other LCD displays mounted on the binnacle. We can easily lose our night vision when nearby lighting causes the pupil of the eye to constrict.

Rule 20 also mandates compliance with Annex I of the Navigation Rules, which offers technical details about luminosity, atmospheric transmission ability, and other arcane details of navigation light performance. Annex I also includes details about light placement and position. You can ignore the formulas, but take heed of the useful details about lamps, bulbs, housings, and screens. Make sure that a new lamp or bulb conversion yields a fixture that has USCG-type approval.

Rule 21: Definitions We routinely see these principal lights:

- ◆ Masthead light: A fixed white light that shines over a 225-degree arc bisected by the centerline of the vessel, the masthead light shines unbroken from dead ahead to 22.5 degrees abaft the beam on both sides of the vessel.

- ◆ Sidelights: Red and green sidelights that shine through an arc of 112.5 degrees from dead ahead to 22.5 degrees abaft the port (red) and starboard (green) beam.

- ◆ Stern light: The 135-degree arc of this white light shines directly astern, with 67.5-degree subarcs extending on both sides of the vessel. The lamp housing is near or on the transom.

- ◆ Towing light: A yellow light that shines astern through a 135-degree arc.

- ◆ All-around light: A light that shines through a full-circle arc of 360 degrees.

- ◆ Flashing light: A light with a pulse rate of 120 or more flashes per minute.

- ◆ Special flashing light (Inland Rules): A yellow flasher with a rate of 50 to 70 pulses per minute placed forward on a barge. Its arc is 180 to 225 degrees, centered over the bow, with no intrusion

Bright, low-power LED lights have revolutionized running lights for sailors. No longer do we worry that a night under sail means flat batteries in the morning. Replacing incandescent running lights with LED alternatives can turn a 2-amp 12-volt DC current drain into an energy-saving 0.4-amp current drain.

RULE 22: VISIBILITY OF LIGHTS

LIGHT RANGE IN NAUTICAL MILES

Vessel Size	Masthead	Sidelight	Stern	Towing	All-Around	Special Flashing
>50 meters	6	3	3	3	3	2
12m–50m	5	2	2	2	2	2
<12m	2	1	2	2	2	2
Object towed					3	

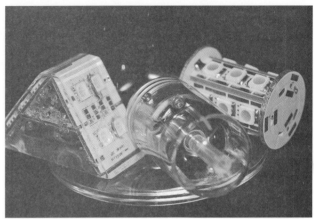

A conventional long-filament incandescent bulb (left) consumes 25 watts per hour, while the same brightness can be delivered from an LED fixture (right) for 3 to 4 watts per hour. Make sure the light manufacturer approves of the LED bulb replacement.

beyond 22.5 degrees abaft the beam on either side of the barge.

Sailors sometimes struggle with seeming confusions in navigation light requirements. For example, a light mounted on the leading edge of the mast, usually one-third to one-half of the spar's height above deck is called the steaming light because a sailboat using its engine at night must display this light. On the actual masthead usually is an all-around white lamp used when anchored. Some sailboats also have a combination of sidelights and stern light at the masthead housed in a single fixture.

Rule 22: Visibility of Lights The accompanying table summarizes Rule 22's provisions.

Rule 23: Power-Driven Vessels Underway A power-driven vessel underway is the light configuration most often seen. Its combination of masthead, sidelights, and stern light provides the lighting foundation for most vessels (see illustration page 270). On vessels greater than 50 meters in length, a second masthead light is displayed aft of and higher than the forward masthead light. On the Great Lakes only an all-around light may be substituted for the after masthead light and the stern light. Vessels 50 meters and under may display a second masthead light at their discretion.

Power-driven boats less than 12 meters long may substitute an all-around light for the masthead and stern lights in both international and inland waters but still need the sidelights. Boats less than 7 meters long traveling at 7 knots or less must display an all-round white light; however, under the International Rules only, they may dispense with sidelights if these are impractical.

Special-purpose and smaller motor vessels often carry additional lights. Hovercraft, for example, must display an all-around flashing yellow light when operating in nondisplacement mode. Submarines have the same requirement when operating on the surface.

BARGE LIGHT CHARACTERISTICS

Barge Lighting	Sidelights	Stern Light	Special Flasher
Inland Tow Alongside	x	x	
Inland Pushing	x		x
International Alongside	x	x	
International Pushing	x		

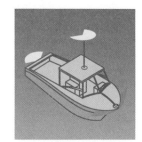

▰ *One of the most often seen light configurations consists of a masthead light, two sidelights, and a stern light designating a powerboat making way. (Middle) A sailing vessel underway with separate sidelights.*

▰ *A sailing vessel underway with separate sidelights.*

▰ *At night or in overcast conditions, a vessel of less than 20 meters making way under sail only must show either independent red, green, and white lights of approved sector coverage, color, and brightness or an all-in-one tricolor masthead light. These independent lights can be used in conjunction with a mid-mast "steaming light" when motorsailing or proceeding under power alone. However, the tricolor option is not used in conjunction with a steaming light.*

Rule 24: Towing and Pushing It's easy to spot tugs and their towing lights, but slight differences in light combinations indicate the nature of the tow itself. For example, in both inland and international waters, three stacked masthead lights forward, sidelights, and a yellow towing light above the stern light indicate a towing vessel of less than 50 meters hauling a tow of over 200 meters in length. Removing one masthead light indicates a tow of less than 200 meters. Add a masthead light aft and the towing vessel is 50 meters

long or longer. The barge displays sidelights and stern light in all cases when being towed (see table).

A tug of less than 50 meters pushing ahead or towing alongside in most inland and in all international waters displays two stacked masthead lights forward, sidelights, and a stern light. On western rivers below the Huey Long Bridge (which crosses the Mississippi River in Louisiana), two stacked yellow towing lights replace the masthead and stern lights. The tow displays sidelights only if being pushed, and sidelights and a stern light if towed alongside. On inland waters only, it also displays a flashing yellow light.

When a tug and tow are rigidly joined bow to stern in a "composite" configuration, the lights convey a motor vessel equivalent to the combined length as prescribed in Rule 23.

Rule 25: Sailing Vessels Underway and Vessels under Oars The Inland and International Rules allow vessels of less than 20 meters to display either a tricolor masthead light or sidelights and a stern light. In addition to these options, a sailing vessel using the stern and sidelight alternative may also display two all-around lights at the top of the mast in a red-over-green configuration.

A boat under sail or oars and less than 7 meters in length may substitute a flashlight or lantern if not equipped with the lights listed above; keep these alternative lights ready to be displayed when you need a collision-avoidance signal.

Rule 26: Fishing Vessels A vessel underway engaged in trawling displays all-around green-over-white lights in addition to sidelights, stern light, and a second masthead light if the vessel is over 50 meters long. The rules require red-over-white all-around lights aboard vessels engaged in commercial fishing other than trawling. Recreational fishing vessels require no such lights, and these vessels do not have special rights.

As mentioned earlier, once a commercial fishing vessel halts the trawling or other fishing activity, it no longer has special rights and the crew must extinguish the green-over-white or red-over-white lights.

Rule 27: Vessels Not Under Command or Restricted in Their Ability to Maneuver

"Red over red, the Captain is dead" is a morose but effective mnemonic aid that helps mariners recall lighting for not-under-command situations. Whether or not the vessel is making way, the two all-around red lights are the only masthead illumination shown.

A combination of red-white-red all-around lights stacked vertically signifies a vessel's limited ability to maneuver. For example, a working buoy tender may display these lights. Likewise, a tug towing in a situation where its ability to alter course is severely limited also would use these lights. Restricted-maneuverability lights are also used during dredging, diving, or other underwater operations.

Though potentially visually confusing, lights added to a dredge make good sense if we keep in mind that the off-centerline all-around red over red and green over green behave like traffic signals. They tell us that we'll find safe passage on the side of the vessel marked with the green light, while the red defines the location of the obstruction.

We seldom see triple green all-around lights in a triangle pattern, but this configuration tells us a mine-clearing effort is underway and we should stay at least 1,000 meters from the craft.

Rule 28: Vessels Constrained by Their Draft

Deep-draft vessels confined to a narrow channel must display three red, vertically stacked all-around lights indicating that even a small change in course will lead to a grounding incident.

Rule 29: Pilot Vessels

All-around white-over-red lights designate a pilot boat engaged in piloting activities. When it's underway, the vessel also displays running lights according to its size.

Rule 30: Anchored Vessels and Vessels Aground

Vessels at anchor are required to display one white all-around light in the forward portion of the vessel and another all-around white light near the stern. Vessels less than 50 meters in length may substitute a single all-around white light placed where best seen. Vessels over 100 meters long must display deck illumination as well as the fore-and-aft all-around lights.

A vessel aground displays an anchor light(s) required for vessels of its length, along with the red-over-red all-around not-under-command lights.

Rule 30 of the Inland Rules gives vessels the right to ignore the anchor light requirement if they anchor in a special anchorage. You'll find special anchorages clearly designated on large-scale charts.

Day Shapes Rules 24 through 30 also mandate black day shapes to signal operational status for various situations. For example, by day you can't always easily tell if a commercial fishing vessel is headed home or engaged in fishing. The answer is provided by the prescribed day shape: two black vertical cones hoisted in the rigging so they touch apex to apex, indicating the boat is actively fishing. However, some crews often leave the cone-to-cone shape or the basket (an approved substitute for fishing boats under 20 meters long) hoisted, even when they aren't fishing.

Another common day shape is the black ball that boats under anchor are required to display in their rigging—a requirement, by the way, that is routinely ignored by legions of sailboats and power cruisers. More mariners need to become aware of the requirements and hoist the proper day shapes.

We often see the trawling shape rigged on fishing

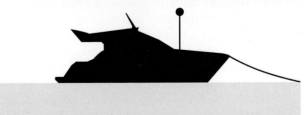

Day shapes are underused and misused. On top is the correct signal for a vessel trawling; in the middle is the day shape displayed by a sailing vessel under both power and sail; and on bottom is the shape for a vessel at anchor.

SOUND SIGNALS

Maneuver	Inland	International
Meeting and Crossing: Port to Port/Starboard to Starboard	1 short / 2 short	1 short / 2 short
Affirmative Response	1 short / 2 short	1 short / 2 short
Overtaking to Port/to Starboard	1 short / 2 short	Prolonged-prolonged-short / prolonged-prolonged-short-short
Affirmative Response	1 short / 2 short	Prolonged-short-prolonged-short
Leaving Slip	1 prolonged	
Bend in River	1 prolonged	1 prolonged
Danger / Failure to Understand	5 or more short	5 or more short

boats tied alongside the dock, clearly a misuse of the signal. Not using a designated shape or incorrectly showing one can become a big issue when authorities investigate an accident.

Part D: Sound and Light Signals

Part D of the COLREGS pertains to sound and light signals meant to show the location of a vessel or indicate its intended action in a developing situation.

Rule 32: Definitions What sounds like a horn is defined as a "whistle"; Annex III of the Navigation Rules spells out sound-producing characteristics. All signals are comprised of short (about 1 second's duration) and prolonged (4 to 6 seconds) blasts.

Rule 33: Equipment for Sound Signals A mouth-blown whistle or gas canister-operated horn meets the federal sound signal requirements for vessels 12 meters and under. Vessels over that size must also carry a bell. Stricter sound level and tone regulations apply to commercial craft.

Rule 34: Maneuvering and Warning Signals The bureaucrats faced a small battle of semantics when they settled on signals in this group (see table). The internationalists saw the sense in a proactive "I am" approach to sound signals and what they mean. One short blast of the whistle means I am turning to starboard, two blasts means I am turning to port, and three blasts indicate I am going astern. We see the logic in this approach. At sea, we carry out the signal-and-maneuver process as soon as vessels come into visual contact, while we still have sufficient sea room to monitor inaction, thus prompting the stand-on vessel to prepare to respond.

In inland waters, however, a single short blast means "I intend to leave you on my port side," and the vessel receiving this signal must respond before the maneuver can begin. If the receiving vessel agrees with the proposed maneuver, its crew gives an in-kind response. If the crew sees danger, disagrees, or is in doubt about the proposed maneuver, they respond with the danger signal, five or more short blasts.

The difference between these two rules is essentially "I am" versus "I would like to." Further, in inland waters, the signaling process for vessels meeting or crossing is held until they are within a half mile of each other. This proximity allows for better sound transmission and increases the chances that both vessels will understand the maneuvers the other intends to carry out in crowded, obstacle-strewn waters. The double round of whistle signals also provides information to other vessels in the vicinity about what's about to transpire.

You'll find the inland/international dichotomy less confusing if you remember that wherever you happen to be, in meeting and crossing situations one short blast means a port-to-port passage, two short blasts mean starboard-to-starboard, and three short signals of the whistle or maneuvering lights indicate that the signaler either is or intends to operate astern.

The sound signals may be supplemented with light signals of similar duration and character. (Rule 34 is also discussed on page 260.)

Rule 35: Sound Signals in Restricted Visibility In conditions of restricted visibility, sailors unencumbered by a pilothouse or the rumble of an engine can make the most of other vessels' fog signals. Unfortunately, there is virtually no chance that crew aboard a merchant ship will hear the relative weak signaling sounds generated by small-boat portable sound-generating equipment. This is an additional reason that radar and AIS have grown so popular for collision avoidance.

The table shows required sound signals in restricted visibility; these should be repeated at intervals no greater than 2 minutes.

A vessel anchored in the fog should ring the ship's bell for 5 seconds once a minute and may also use a short-prolonged-short whistle signal. A vessel aground incorporates three strikes of the bell before and after each 5-second ring. These signals are not required of a vessel less than 12 meters; however, boats in this category must make some sound signal at intervals of no longer than 2 minutes.

Rule 36: Signals to Attract Attention We can use light or sound signaling to gain the attention of another vessel as long as the signals can't be mistaken for those specified in the rules or appear to be a navigational mark.

SOUND SIGNALS IN RESTRICTED VISIBILITY

Power Vessel	prolonged
Power Vessel, Stopped	prolonged-prolonged
Sailing	prolonged-short-short
Fishing	prolonged-short-short
Not under Command	prolonged-short-short
Restricted Maneuverability	prolonged-short-short
Last Vessel in Tow	prolonged-short-short-short

■ *Pneumatic horns are not easy to fit aboard a cruising sailboat, but if you spend much time in foggy conditions, you'll find an automated foghorn a useful addition. On this vessel, a small, electric air compressor sends air aloft to the horns via tubing routed up the mizzen mast; an automated digital intervalometer times each signal accurately.*

■ *Ships operating in coastal waters are asked to change their whistle etiquette as they cross the demarcation line separating inland from international waters. If you end up confused, VHF radio contact is less ambiguous. Use Channel 13 for normal bridge-to-bridge contact, and Channel 16 if there's no response and a collision seems imminent.*

Rule 37: Distress Signals This rule requires a vessel in distress or needing assistance to use one of the sixteen distress signals included in Annex IV of the rules. These include commonly used Mayday calls, EPIRBs, and flares, as well as the more arcane use of November Charlie code flags, dye markers, and arm waving. The only difference in inland distress signaling is the additional approved use of a white strobe light flashing 50–70 times a minute.

Part E, Rule 38: Exemptions

This rule targets owners more than crew. It's a vestige of the time that the navigation rules were new and older vessels were given some leeway in compliance. A vessel whose construction started prior to 1980 (1977 in the International Rules) and is compliant with the rules in place prior to the 1972 COLREGS has a grandfathered exemption from certain navigation light specifications, though not from showing the lights themselves.

Annexes and Notes

The rules are followed by five annexes.

Annex I is a compilation of technical data defining navigation light characteristics and how installations should be configured;

Annex II specifies additional light signals for vessels fishing in close proximity;

Annex III specifies technical details of sound-signal devices;

Annex IV lists distress signals;

Annex V lists pilot rules for inland waters and provides details and locations of the demarcation lines separating inland from international waters.

Embedded near the tail end of the Navigation Rules is section 2304, "Duty to provide assistance at sea." Its straightforward text states that a vessel shall render assistance to "any individual" in danger at sea as long as the effort does not pose "serious danger" to those rendering assistance and their vessel.

This rule stands out as the opposite of what prevails on land, where, for example, no legal statute compels a physician to stop at an accident scene and render assistance. In fact, statutes exist that protect physicians and others from liability if they don't administer emergency treatment in such situations. On the other hand, mariners are part of a culture that expects us to look out for each other. The principle has roots as far back as pre-Roman times, and the present AMVER (Atlantic Merchant Vessel Emergency Reporting System) voluntary safety program provides a good example of such cooperation.

Carrying the Navigation Rules

U.S. federal regulations mandate that all vessels over 12 meters (39 feet and 4.4 inches) in length operating in U.S. waters carry a copy of the Navigation Rules.

◤ *For all vessels to coexist on the water, it's paramount that we understand our rights and responsibilities, whether as a recreational boater or the master of an unlimited-tonnage vessel. The crew of this sloop should be getting ready to push on the tiller and tack over, lessening the chance of an unpleasant encounter.*

All sailors will find it a useful reference when faced with quickly identifying an unusual set of lights or unfamiliar sound signals. While some complain that the rules read as if written in a blend of old English and obfuscating legalese, these 38 vital rules define close-quarters collision avoidance and lights and signaling, making the Navigation Rules a vital reference. (There are more user-friendly versions of the rules that fulfill the requirement, among them Charlie Wing's *One-Minute Guide to the Nautical Rules of the Road*.)

Regulations Unique to the U.S. Inland Rules

Following are examples of stipulations that appear in the U.S. Inland Rules but not in the International Rules:

- In western rivers and the Great Lakes, those headed downcurrent have right of way over vessels heading upstream.
- Vessels crossing a river give way to vessels headed up- or downstream.
- Tugs pushing or towing alongside must display a forward-facing flashing yellow light that is visible through 180–225 degrees.
- Submarines display an amber all-around light flashing three times every 3 seconds while operating on the surface.
- When barges are towed alongside each other, each outboard barge shall show a stern light, but only one sidelight will be displayed on each side of the combined tow.
- A vessel pushing ahead exhibits two towing lights above the stern light.

In most other significant respects, the U.S. Inland Rules are quite similar to the International Rules.

MAKING LANDFALL

As mentioned in Chapter 4, making landfall brings big changes to the routine of an ocean passage. Days or even weeks at sea, scanning an empty horizon, often leave a crew hoping to see more rather than fewer vessels. The shift from wide-open solitude to shoulder-rubbing close-quarters maneuvering can be abrupt, and now we urgently need a clear understanding of the navigation rules.

The entrance to a busy seaport is no place to ask yourself whether the ship crossing your bow is the give-way or stand-on vessel. Ships, boats, and barges converge from all directions, establishing a pecking order in which some must steer clear of others. The rules in this seafaring dance become as important as knowing your boat's position and course. Sail trim, wind shifts, and other elements of your open-water routine take a backseat to avoiding collision.

Your ability to remain aware of each unfolding situation demands constant vigilance and an ability to track—at least roughly—the relative movements of a wide variety of other boats. A funnel-like convergence takes place at nearly every major port, packing arrivals and departures together. Inbound and outbound vessels, heading in opposite directions, often line up on the right-hand side of a traffic-separation zone.

Planning an approach route ahead of time and plotting it on a paper chart or digital screen takes some of the pressure off navigators. I prefer to head first for the outer sea buoy, not directly to the inlet jetty or river mouth. This gives me a chance to confirm my navigation while still in deep water with relatively few obstructions, and it also allows me to align with most of the inbound traffic and with vessels heading out to sea.

As mentioned earlier, when you enter a deep-water commercial port, try to avoid making your approach through the center of the main channel where you'll find the deep-draft traffic. Better to plot a route that skirts the side of the channel or uses a secondary channel. When you're in 10 feet of water just outside the main channel, you won't be run down by a 900-foot tanker that draws 35 feet. Should you need to enter the channel to avoid running aground, looking astern for overtaking ships becomes as important as being aware of what lies ahead.

I customarily pre-enter waypoints on the digital chart display: the outer sea buoy (flashing Morse "A") that marks the seaward end point of the approach channel, selected lateral marks leading up the main channel from the sea buoy, and so forth. In addition to remaining on guard against the unexpected, I also try to time my landfall so it occurs in daylight. Nothing is certain, however. In one recent landfall, a fog-bank descended with little warning, shutting off the sunlight and rendering everything beyond the bow of the boat invisible. At such times visual navigation yields to the dictates of Rule 19, which mandates that all vessels take on give-way responsibility.

Radar, AIS, and VHF radio become primary tools. In addition, if you're under sail, you'll find it easier than on a motor-driven vessel to discern the proximity and direction of other boats' sound signals and propulsion noises. Of course, the cacophony of a Detroit diesel in a small dragger moving at 6 knots may outstrip the noise of a 500-footer running at 12 knots. Multiple sources of noise can quickly confuse you, so in these conditions, designate radar as one of your best friends. A digital chartplotter shows your position relative to charted features, but only radar shows you vessels moving toward you or crossing your course.

AIS receivers (see Chapter 8) show nearby AIS-equipped vessels according to the collision risk they pose, a helpful feature of this technology. Seeing the name and call sign of a boat on screen allows you to make VHF contact and reach an agreement about the way each vessel will maneuver in order to avoid a collision. But this process can become cumbersome in highly congested waters with many vessels hailing each other on Channel 13.

In addition, since many boats in the area don't have AIS, you may need to rely on radar, sound signals, or a last-minute visual sighting. In zero visibility, a Sécurité call (a method of calling attention to an important message, as discussed in Chapter 14) on the VHF radio announcing your position, course, and speed could prove helpful to others in the area. Shoal-draft tug and barge captains use Sécurité messages regularly, and like most commercial mariners inshore, they describe their location by bearing and distance to a known landmark rather than by latitude/longitude coordinates.

As a general rule of thumb, when sailing in poor-visibility conditions, I try to avoid crossing ahead of other vessels, especially in tight confines. I also keep a handheld VHF in the cockpit, ready for close-quarters bridge-to-bridge radio contact. I prefer this approach over using a remote-access microphone for the primary VHF radio because I can leave the primary VHF in receive mode. In addition, the handheld's short range is just right for communicating with a nearby vessel without interfering with communications 10 miles or more away. The handheld is also more portable and versatile than a remote-mounted microphone.

As electronic aids to navigation become increasingly sophisticated, a crew needs to understand their strengths and limitations. On a recent nighttime entry into a crowed port I monitored progress via radar and a detailed view on a chartplotter screen. The AIS unit revealed several close-in contacts, but the radar also showed a row of unlit marks to one side not identified on the AIS. A look through a handheld FLIR unit (infrared scope) revealed that the closest contact was two fishermen in an unlit skiff. The AIS had not hinted at their presence. You get the point, I'm sure. If I'd relied totally on any one electronic aid to navigation I could have been on my way to a collision or allision. At night, my last line of defensive navigating in tight quarters is a bright spotlight and slow speed—a process that allows visual confirmation of what lies ahead.

10

READING THE SEA AND SKY

Benjamin Franklin, a constitutional framer and endearing Francophile, understood good wine and bad weather. He researched the Gulf Stream and coined the phrase "the weather wise and the otherwise." More than two centuries later, mariners can still be grouped accordingly, and the former are still safer and continue to get more enjoyment out of their time on the water.

Knowing what lies ahead is perhaps even more important than knowing what's causing the good or bad weather of the moment. This is especially true for sailors. It's hard to outrun bad weather at the speed of a slow jogger; the better bet is not to be in the neighborhood.

The more volatile the climate and the higher the latitude or the closer you are to hurricane season, the more advantageous a heads-up weather-driven game plan becomes. The good news for contemporary sailors is that more weather information than ever before is within easy reach of those poking along coastlines or sailing thousands of miles from home. There's only one catch: if you're after more than a look at how the barometer is trending, where the clouds are coming from, and which way the wind is blowing, you're going to have to make some decisions about hardware and software and ask yourself how much of an investment weather wisdom is worth to you.

There are three schools of thought when it comes to weather awareness. The first is exemplified by a dwindling group of stoics who prepare for weather contingencies, pick the right season for a passage, and endure what comes their way. Communication equipment takes a backseat to storm sails, vessel stability, and structural integrity for this group. Their gamble is one of higher stakes and greater challenges, as it was centuries ago, and the wise among them improve their odds with the sort of seamanship skills that were common in bygone centuries.

The second school of thought among passagemakers is a do-it-yourself approach that combines a "Weather 101" level of knowledge with a familiarity with what it takes to receive VHF, cellular, SSB, and satellite voice and data broadcasts. This approach as-

Knowing whether the clouds rolling by are the harbinger of an approaching cold front or the welcome departure of a low-pressure system is part of a sailor's weather awareness. A lot can be ascertained from trends in wind direction, barometric pressure, and cloud cover.

sumes that the onboard decision maker can read a surface weather analysis chart, evaluate 24-, 48-, and 96-hour forecasts, and make sense of the contours of a 500-millibar chart—topics we'll discuss later in this chapter.

The third option is to relegate some or all of the weather strategizing to an expert who is not onboard. With an abdication of weather planning comes complete reliance on a communication link that could fail when you need it most, but those who can afford to have a full-time meteorologist on call can also afford redundant communications capability. The value of access to such unquestioned expertise is understood by commercial maritime ventures that enlist such services.

Climates vary with latitude, but equally as important are the influences of air masses and currents such as the Gulf Stream or Kuroshio Current that shunt warm or cold water into a region. This uptick in ocean-to-air heat transfer can result in fog and turbocharge a developing low. Assuming that regions of equal latitude will have similar climates can be a big mistake.

Many weather-wise passagemakers see the ideal approach as an amalgam of all three philosophies.

DEVELOPING WEATHER AWARENESS

Most sailors don't need to be told why weather is so important. Although you may not have experienced every meteorological danger, you've likely heard and read about them. Here's the short list of what mariners should understand:

- Gales
- Secondary lows
- Squeeze zones
- Gusts
- Squalls and thunderstorms
- Lightning
- Tropical storms and hurricanes
- Waterspouts
- Fog
- Waves

The Inuit people of the Arctic never studied thermodynamics or took a course in atmospheric science. Their weather awareness is intuitive and passed down, learned from direct observation and cataloged as folk wisdom. Living in their laboratory 24/7, they have survived by heeding the lessons learned. A more scientific approach to meteorology and oceanography can work for mariners, but it works best when linked to the sea sense accumulated from experience.

All it takes to get started is an understanding of a few general concepts regarding highs, lows, and frontal boundaries. Once you've mastered a few basic principles, you'll be ready to leverage forecast data. We'll cover the basics in this chapter; a text such as Jack Williams's informative and well-illustrated *Ultimate Guide to America's Weather* is a great source of more detailed explanations.

You can develop your weather awareness anytime—on the deck of your boat or while commuting to work. Start by paying attention to morning and evening map discussions on the Weather Channel broadcasts and website. Correlate what's in the forecast for your area with the clouds you see, the direction they're moving, and local changes in temperature and humidity. Phase two is to track barometric changes. Note several readings each day; when a deep low approaches or is replaced by a high-pressure system, try to note hourly readings.

The next step in this home-brew Weather 101 course is to look at weather maps on the Ocean Prediction Center website. The OPC, a division of the National Weather Service (an agency of the National Oceanic and Atmospheric Administration, or NOAA—see more on government forecast resources later in this chapter), generates analyses and 24-, 48-, and 96-hour forecasts for surface maps; equivalent analyses and forecasts for 500-millibar maps; and wind-wave chart analyses and forecasts, all of which are also broadcast via single-sideband radio (SSB) weather fax. We'll discuss these weather products later in the chapter; you can look at them compared with what's going on outside your office window and with the Weather Channel's latest update. Such comparisons of weather analysis maps and forecasts with direct observations help instill the seaman's habit of feeling the weather continuously, knowing when the atmosphere is unstable, and noticing when the tempo of a cold front has reached its crescendo and when the first hint of a wind shift to the north (in the Northern Hemisphere) is about to occur.

The third phase of home study is to check your weather-guessing accuracy and that of the pros at NOAA and the talking heads on the Weather Channel against recorded observations. The National Data Buoy system provides just such observations, and by scrolling through the 24-hour profiles on each buoy's web page (accessed from the National Data Buoy Center website), you can test and refine your Monday-morning quarterbacking. Keep in mind that wave reports are based on significant wave height, which is the average of the highest one-third of waves recorded over an hourly period. Statistics show that in open ocean areas, during a 24-hour period, there's at least one wave that's twice as high as the significant wave height.

Buoy data comprise a powerful tool that can confirm the passage of a cold front or the location of a low. Equally useful on a local scale is Doppler radar imagery, which highlights the rain in clouds and defines the intensity of thunderstorm cells. It also depicts the direction and speed of movement of these systems. These images can be found on the National Weather Service (NWS) website, the Weather Channel's home page, or Weather Underground's informative home page.

Of course, this home weather study can and should continue on the boat. Indeed, one of the best ways to cultivate weather awareness is by comparing the information from a VHF weather broadcast with direct observation of what's happening in the atmosphere around you. This look-listen-learn approach field-tests a forecast even as it gives you a preview of the weather changes waiting in the wings. Ongoing practice will give you more and more confidence when it comes to discerning the likelihood of thun-

VHF weather broadcasts are familiar to us all, but many of us underutilize them. They can be a great instrument for honing your weather knowledge. Try linking the cloud cover you see around you with the local VHF forecast. Listen for buoy reports, note wind directions, and see how your barometer compares with the atmospheric pressure reported from a nearby weather buoy.

derstorm development on a hot, humid summer afternoon or how a veering breeze (shifting clockwise) can announce the approach of a fast-moving cold front in the Northern Hemisphere. Comparing VHF weather broadcasts with careful 360-degree scans of the horizon gives a mariner a feel for the climate and the day-to-day weather changes each season holds.

REALLY UNDERSTANDING THE CAUSES OF WEATHER

A weather-wise sailor views local conditions both close up and in the big picture—a full three-dimensional perspective. Although the wind on the surface rules a sailor's life, it's often what's happening midway up the atmosphere that drives these surface conditions. Newspaper weather maps, in contrast, are two-dimensional, but adding an understanding of the vertical dynamics pays off. The place to start is with an understanding of global circulation, fronts, pressure gradients, etc.

Surface Weather Systems

The atmsphere is a veil surrounding the planet, so thin that if the globe were reduced to the size of a softball, the atmosphere would have the thickness of an onion skin. Most weather takes place in the bottommost layer of the atmosphere, a roiling mix of gases—most notably nitrogen, oxygen, and carbon dioxide—called the troposphere, which varies from about 10 miles thick at the equator to about 5 miles thick at the poles. Above the troposphere, extending to an altitude of about 30 miles, is the stratosphere, which contains the ozone layer that prevents the most harmful of the sun's radiation from reaching the earth's surface.

Global Circulation Patterns

Just under half of the sun's incoming short-wave energy is reflected back to space or absorbed by the atmosphere. The rest passes through the thin atmospheric envelope and heats the land and oceans (the latter more slowly), which then re-radiate longer-wave, infrared energy back into the lower atmosphere. The equatorial regions soak up more energy from the sun than they re-radiate back to the atmosphere and would thus become hotter and hotter if this excess heat were not transported toward both poles via the atmosphere and ocean currents. Polar regions, meanwhile, absorb less heat than they lose by re-radiation and would thus become ever colder but for the heat received from lower latitudes. In effect, the oceans and atmosphere are sun-driven heat machines perpetually engaged in redistributing heat energy, and the result is weather, which is greatly influenced by seasonal changes in the sun's declination. Evidence continues to accumulate that global warming from human causes is leading to long-term changes in weather patterns. As warming proceeds, the earth's weather is becoming more volatile.

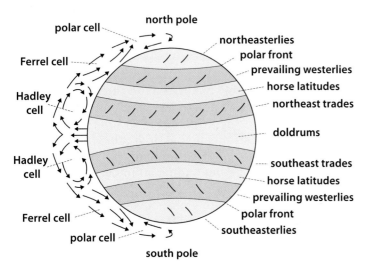

The best way to conceptualize the heat-driven winds of the planet is to stop the earth's rotation and visualize the hot tropics and cold polar regions. They are linked by a thermal transfer system in the form of wind belts. Hot, light air at the equator rises and is displaced by colder, denser air arriving from the poles. Add the earth's rotation and its attendant Coriolis effect, and the big belts become a series of smaller loops encircling set regions of the planet. The picture is further modified by seasonal changes and by the five ocean gyres that harness the major currents of the world.

At the center of the weather-making machinery is the simple fact that hot, less dense air rises while cooler, denser air sinks. This simple dance plays out on a global scale, with warm air rising at the equator and forming a persistent band of low pressure around the equator known as the Intertropical Convergence Zone (ITCZ), or in popular parlance the doldrums. The width of this band is about 15 degrees of latitude, varying seasonally. The risen air moves toward higher latitudes aloft, some of it becoming cool and dense enough to subside at about 30 degrees north and south, forming bands of persistent high pressure there. These bands are the subtropical highs, or more popularly the horse latitudes. Since air flows from regions of high pressure to regions of low pressure, a portion of this sinking air flows back toward the equator along the earth's surface, and this return surface flow constitutes the northeasterly trade winds of the Northern Hemisphere and the southeasterly trades of the Southern Hemisphere.

The rest of the air that subsides at 30 degrees north and south flows poleward at the planet's surface: the prevailing westerlies of the northern and southern temperate zones.

While some air sinks at 30 degrees north and south, the rest remains aloft and continues to flow poleward before descending over the arctic and antarctic regions. The result is the prevailing easterly surface winds of the polar regions—northeasterlies in the Northern Hemisphere, southeasterlies in the Southern Hemisphere—and these meet the mid-latitude prevailing westerlies at the so-called polar fronts—from 40 degrees (winter) to 60 degrees (summer) north and south—where the warmer air of the temperate-zone westerlies is forced aloft. As always when warm, moisture-laden air ascends, the results are instability and storms along the dynamic polar fronts.

Taken together, these circulations comprise three belts in each hemisphere, referred to as the Hadley (tropical), Ferrel (middle latitude), and polar circulation loops or cells. The Hadley and polar loops act as thermally driven conveyor belts, while the ball-bearing-like Ferrel loop separates the two and is significantly affected by the behavior of the jet stream. Within the Ferrel cell, the dry continental and moist maritime air masses march generally west to east, interacting along their boundaries as they go. Annual changes in the sun's declination drive the seasons and the locations of the cell boundaries.

Thus, air is set in motion within the great planetary circulation loops by the heat differential from the equator to the poles, and the spinning earth deflects the moving air (and ocean currents) to the right in the Northern Hemisphere and to the left in the

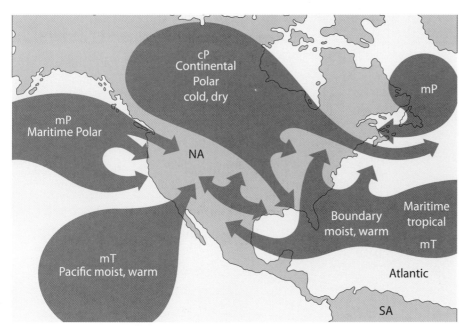

Key: mP = maritime polar; mT = maritime tropical (moist, tropical); cP = continental polar (cold, dry)

Wind belts and upper-level dynamics corral air masses and keep them in place long enough to acquire specific heat and moisture characteristics. Along the frontal boundary between two significantly different air masses—such as when warm, moist air from the Gulf of Mexico meets cold, dry air from Canada, shown along the Gulf coast here—the stage is set for extreme cyclogenesis and the birth of a classic extratropical low.

Southern Hemisphere, a phenomenon known as the Coriolis effect. These cells are a simplification of the complex thermodynamics in play. Storms help with thermal transfer between cells, as exemplified by hurricanes, which can extract heat from tropical Atlantic waters and take it all the way to England across two cell boundaries. Indeed, a hurricane can be thought of as a mechanism for heat distribution—a violent, short-lived atmospheric counterpart to the great equatorial ocean currents such as the Gulf Stream and the Kuroshio Current, which are the greatest heat-transfer mechanisms of all.

Frontal Boundaries and Low-Pressure Systems

Because warm and cold air masses are reluctant to mix, frontal boundaries—zones of rapid transition in temperature and pressure—occur wherever they meet. Such boundaries are prevalent in middle-latitude regions (30 to 60 degrees north and south), where warm and cold air masses most often meet, which is why temperate-zone weather is so dynamic. In particular, warm air masses meeting cold air along the polar fronts generate most of the strongest middle-latitude storms.

Imagine, for example, a cold continental air mass moving southeastward from the Canadian Shield and meeting a warm, moist, maritime air mass that is moving northeastward from the Gulf of Mexico. In this familiar scenario, at the frontal boundary between the two air masses—which is in fact along the polar front—the cold, dense polar air burrows beneath the warm, moist air, forcing it aloft, and clouds and precipitation develop. The boundary is not ver-

tical; rather it slopes gently upward when viewed in cross section, gaining anywhere from a half mile to 2.5 miles of altitude across 100 miles of horizontal distance. Nor is the boundary sharply defined, although, for convenience, meteorologists speak as if it is; rather, there is substantial mixing along the boundary. Still, it is a boundary.

What happens next is determined in significant measure by wind streams aloft, at midheight in the troposphere, about 18,000 feet above the planet's surface (near the 500-millibar level, as we'll see later in the chapter). This band of high-speed winds flows west to east in a series of waves, with troughs extending toward lower latitudes and crests projecting toward higher latitudes. These are not the infamous jet stream that makes an airline flight from New York to London significantly faster than one in the opposite direction; the main axis of the upper jet stream lies at 30,000 feet, near the top of the troposphere, and also flows west to east. The jet stream links to these midlevel steering currents, which link in turn with surface frontal boundaries, intensifying them. It is these midlevel steering currents that are tracked by 500-millibar weather charts.

When these midlevel streamlines move smoothly west to east without pronounced troughs, the flow is called zonal. The associated surface weather systems can be expected to be relatively weak and will move quickly west to east at one-third to one-half the wind speeds in the overlying steering currents. But sweeping dips in these streamlines toward lower latitudes—creating meridional (north-south) flow and upper-level troughs—are not just a harbinger of bad weather but one of the contributing causes, because the southward-dipping loops in the flow (north-

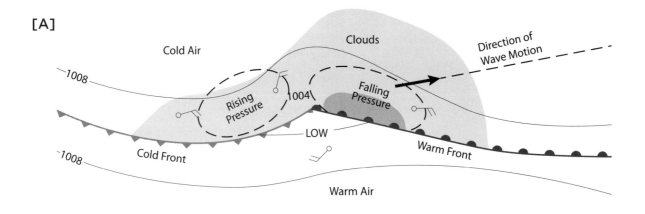

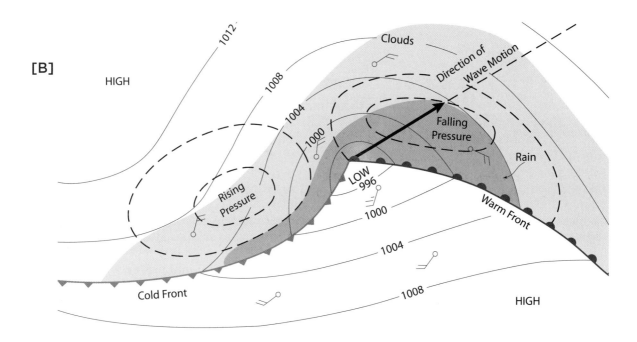

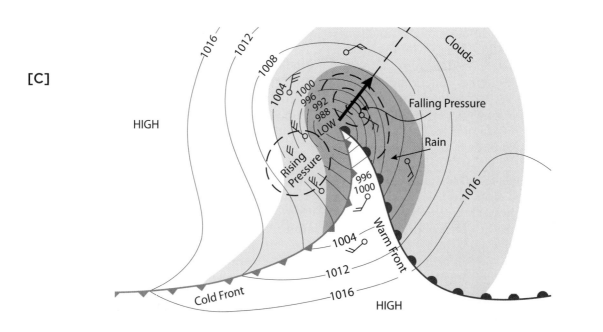

[D]

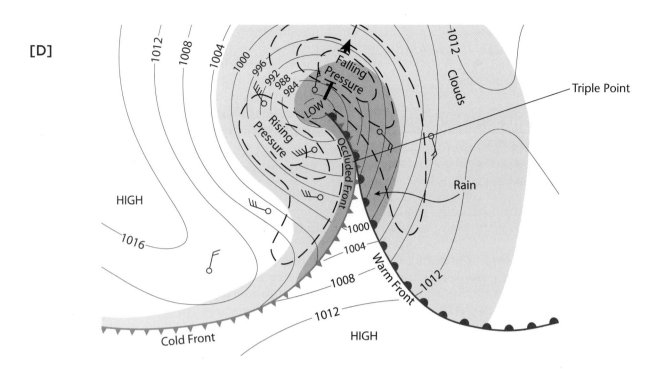

(Facing page and above) The birth of a midlatitude low. A. With a little twist induced by upper-level dynamics, the boundary between two air masses pinches into a wave shape and gathers a cloud field indicative of falling pressure in front with rising pressure behind. This is the first step in extratropical cyclogenesis, the formation of a midlatitude low. B. As the central pressure deepens and winds start to flow counterclockwise (clockwise in the Southern Hemisphere) around the developing low, distinct warm and cold fronts develop and are drawn along with the developing system. This frontal formation is termed frontogenesis. Isobars begin to pack in tighter, a sure sign of a developing low with a core of cold air pinched off from the polar air mass. C. As the low matures, the cold front catches up with the warm front, a process known as occlusion. Winds strengthen (up to 30 knots, as shown by the increasing number of tails on the wind arrows) and the central pressure continues to drop (down to 988 mb). When such a low develops at sea and a nearby high-pressure system lies just to the northwest (southwest in the Southern Hemisphere), a steep pressure gradient can result, causing the clockwise winds around the high to be turbocharged by the counterclockwise flow around the low, resulting in storm-force conditions and hazardous seas. D. A fully developed extratropical (cold-core) gale has a comma-shaped occluded front. The area near the center of the low, the origin point of the comma-shaped cold front, is the spot a mariner most wants to avoid. As the storm grows more intense and the pressure rapidly drops (now at 984 mb), warm air twists around the cold core (which has been pinched off from the cold air mass), and winds in this region are often the highest, reaching gale, storm, and occasionally even hurricane strength. There can also be violent squalls at the "triple point," the location in a mature low-pressure system where the cold front is occluding (overtaking) the warm front and where new secondary lows can develop.

ward-dipping in the Southern Hemisphere) jumpstart surface low-pressure systems.

Let's return to the frontal boundary between our cold polar and warm subtropical air masses. The boundary runs more or less west to east, and if the overlying steering currents are likewise flowing smoothly west to east, lows are less likely to develop along the boundary, and those that do develop are likely to be comparatively weak. But a trough in the overlying steering current can instigate a kink in the frontal boundary, twisting it into a closed cell in which air flow wraps around a low-pressure core. That wind circulation is counterclockwise in the Northern Hemisphere and clockwise in the Southern Hemisphere.

As the surface low matures, its central pressure drops and the isobars that connect areas of equal pressure move closer together. When coupled with an upper-level trough, the low can deepen rapidly and become a dangerous middle-latitude storm system.

Cyclogenesis is the term for the formation of an extratropical low, and the result is a low-pressure cell with a cold core pinched from the cold air mass. A warm frontal boundary and trailing cold front are formed (in the process called *frontogenesis*) as the low matures and the central pressure drops. In contrast, a typical warm-core low forms on an easterly wave (also known as a tropical wave), usually in tropical latitudes north or south of the ITCZ. Warm-core lows lack frontal boundaries and, when fully developed as tropical storms and hurricanes, reach into the stratosphere. Indeed, new research shows that the vertical development of a tropical low can be rapid enough to eject ice crystal cirrus clouds through the tropopause and beyond the earth's atmosphere, causing the moisture to dissipate in space.

Pressure Gradients and Surface Winds

A high-pressure system develops through a process called *subsidence*, in which cooler air aloft falls to the surface, increasing the density of the air on the ground. As air molecules are compressed by this process they tend to warm adiabatically, and clear skies and fair weather result from this high-pressure, or anticyclone, cell formation.

Together, highs and lows form giant air-shuffling machines that operate in a coupled relationship. Air converges aloft, subsides, and diverges at the surface in a high, while a low is like a stack in which air converges at the surface, rises, and diverges aloft. Wind blows from high to low pressure in a manner reminiscent of water spiraling around a bathtub drain, with the low acting like the drain (but ejecting its in-gathered air upward rather than downward). The wind would blow parallel with the isobar curves in a frictionless world, but due to friction with the ocean surface, it crosses the isobars at a 15-degree angle, bent inward toward a low and outward from a high. The steeper the gradient, the stronger the flow.

When meteorologists refer to a gradient, they are speaking of the magnitude of pressure differential over a given distance. Tightly packed isobars can occur within a high-pressure or low-pressure system, and in either case the result is strong winds. Some of the worst conditions of all occur when a deep low develops just to the east of a large high-pressure system, creating a very steep gradient. A vessel caught in the squeeze zone between the two can encounter hurricane-force winds caused by the rapid change in pressure over a very small horizontal distance.

Meteorologists measure atmospheric pressure in millibars (mb), and each isobar line on a map represents a 4 mb change in pressure. Unfortunately, the United States still clings to inches of mercury for pressure measurements, and many boaters have barometers that read in both scales. The most important measurement, however, is not the absolute value of a single reading but the change in atmospheric pressure over time. A rapidly falling barometer is another sure sign of strong wind and bad weather on the way.

A rapidly rising barometer is likewise predictive of strong wind, though this is less intuitive because rising pressures herald fair weather. But sunny gales can occur without a cloud in the sky. The California coast from Santa Barbara northwest is notorious for strong high-pressure gales, and in Southern Califor-

nia, off Mexico's Gulf of Tehuantepec, and elsewhere, high pressure inland and the effects of mountains can create a turbocharged wind that can gust to 100 knots without a cloud in the sky. High winds are most often associated with low-pressure systems and cold fronts, but not always, and fair-weather gales can be a big obstacle to progress to windward.

Thunderstorms and Squalls

Thunderstorms offer a vivid display of atmospheric forces at work. A local thunderstorm cell often arises independently of larger-scale weather systems, usually quickly and with little warning. Thunderstorms constitute the worst weather many sailors will ever experience.

A thunderstorm develops when warm, moist, unstable air rises. When cooled at high altitudes, the now-denser moisture-laden air plunges back to the surface. This updraft-downdraft conveyor belt transfers huge amounts of energy, and the interface between the updraft and downdraft is the most dynamic part of a thunderstorm. If you're in the presence of a fully vertically developed cumulonimbus cloud and notice intermittent pulses of cold air—even if rain, lightning, and thunder have yet to materialize—you should realize that you are likely only seconds, or minutes at the most, from a potentially hazardous outflow of wind. Strong wind gusts —"microbursts"— can reach hurricane force, and these dense cold outflow winds often precede torrential rain and hail. The storm's onset can occur with little or no warning. Given such harbingers, it makes sense to deeply reef or drop sails and lash down whatever is loose on deck.

A thunderstorm cell is also a conveyor belt for moisture, which is carried aloft in the warm, moist updraft and then returns to earth as precipitation. The result is a rain signature on radar that causes the cell to show up clearly. Mature storms carry warm, moist air to astounding heights—35,000 to 50,000 feet—and they not only convert water vapor into rain but in many cases cause raindrops to coalesce into icy pellets of hail that grow larger and larger as the pellets shuttle up and down in vertical loops. Eventually the towering anvil-shaped thunderhead becomes unstable, and the vast amounts of water and ice held aloft yield to gravity, causing powerful downbursts and outrushings of rain- and hail-laden wind that can momentarily exceed 100 knots. These terrific bursts of energy often occur in the vicinity of what's called a shelf cloud, and except for a direct lightning strike, they constitute the most destructive feature of a thunderstorm.

When an isolated thunderstorm is spawned on a hot summer day, it is usually *(continued page 287)*

WIND AND SEA STATE

The Beaufort scale links wind strength with resultant sea state, an important consideration for those headed offshore because swells and breaking waves must be reckoned with. Sustained 28- to 33-knot winds (Beaufort Force 7) may raise only 4-foot seas, short-period chop, and spray in a protected bay where fetch is limited, but similar wind velocities at sea, where the fetch can be measured in hundreds of miles rather than hundreds of meters, can raise 13- to 20-foot seas. The Beaufort scale depicts sea states on the open ocean with unlimited fetch, and it further assumes that the wind blows long enough from a given direction at the given velocity for the seas to become fully developed. Tables of significant wave height (the average height of the highest one-third of waves) as a function of wind velocity, fetch, and time are also useful but don't seem to account for background swell effectively. The Beaufort scale is useful because it's more descriptively qualitative than deceptively quantitative. It worked for the sailing navies, and it still works.

THE BEAUFORT WIND SCALE

Force		Wind (knots)	Classification	Appearance of Wind Effects on the Water
0		Less than 1	Calm	Sea surface smooth and mirror-like
1		1–3	Light Air	Scaly ripples, no foam crests
2		4–6	Light Breeze	Small wavelets, crests glassy, no breaking
3		7–10	Gentle Breeze	Large wavelets, crests begin to break, scattered whitecaps
4		11–16	Moderate Breeze	Small waves, 1–4 feet, becoming longer, numerous whitecaps
5		17–21	Fresh Breeze	Moderate waves, 4–8 feet, taking longer form, many whitecaps, some spray
6		22–27	Strong Breeze	Larger waves, 8–13 feet, whitecaps common, more spray
7		28–33	Near Gale	Sea heaps up, waves 13–20 feet, white foam streaks off breakers
8		34–40	Gale	Moderately high waves (13–20 feet) of greater length, edges of crests begin to break into spindrift, foam blown in streaks
9		41–47	Strong Gale	High waves (20 feet), sea begins to roll, dense streaks of foam, spray may reduce visibility
10		48–55	Storm	Very high waves (20–30 feet) with overhanging crests, sea white with densely blown foam, heavy rolling, lowered visibility
11		56–63	Violent Storm	Exceptionally high (30–45 feet) waves, foam patches cover sea, visibility more reduced
12		64+	Hurricane	Air filled with foam, waves over 45 feet, sea completely white with driving spray, visibility greatly reduced

🚩 *Nothing demonstrates the volatile dynamics of the atmosphere-ocean interface better than a classic thunderstorm cell. Each of these independent air circulations is a thermal engine transferring heat energy vertically, creating massive static electrical buildups, and triggering blinding displays of high-voltage cloud-to-cloud and cloud-to-water energy transfers. The gust front emanating from a single cell can stir a flat, calm sea instantly to life. A thunderstorm at sea is a lesson in storm genesis on a microscale.*

🚩 *A lightning strike is not comprised of a single arc of current but rather involves a series of leaders arising from the ground or sea surface as well as originating in a cumulonimbus cloud.*

LIGHTNING STRIKES AND GROUNDING YOUR VESSEL

🚩 *If thunderstorms have been spotted on Doppler radar and you are in their path but not yet underway, stay put, go below, and remain clear of the mast and chainplates. If the boat is struck by lightning, check the crew first, and then look in the bilge for any sign of a leak. When lightning strikes, your vessel becomes part of the conductive pathway. The strike ionizes a column of air normally so high in resistance that it's a good insulator. At such extreme voltages, lightning can jump gaps and find its way all around the boat. Providing as direct a pathway to the water as possible seems to lessen damage.*

Most cloud-to-cloud and cloud-to-ground (or sea) lightning bolts are massive static electrical discharges caused by the friction associated with air movement in a thunderstorm cell. Oppositely charged particles array themselves on cloud surfaces, and as the charge differential increases, a point is reached at which the insulating property of the intervening air is overcome by the voltage between the charges. A leader, an ionized pathway through the air, bridges the gap, followed by a huge energy transfer over that path linking the two opposite charges.

The American Boat and Yacht Council (ABYC) recommends that all boats have a grounded and bonded electrical system that drains all static charges to a common ground point in contact with the sea. The purpose of this wiring is to make the charge state of the vessel electrically identical to the surrounding sea surface rather than standing out as a statically charged hotspot. As a secondary safety feature, this wiring also helps to guide a direct strike toward the sea, but because lightning can ionize an 8-inch-diameter column of air, it is ridiculous to think that it will be carried safely to ground via 8- or 10-gauge wire. At best, the grounding system may help guide the lightning along a path of least resistance, thus causing less damage.

short-lived due to its fast rate of advance and the relatively short lifespan of most individual cells.

Thunderstorms can also be embedded in warm fronts in the summer and in cold fronts year-round, and they are also a component of troughs (on NWS forecast maps), tropical waves, depressions, storms, and hurricanes. When associated with fronts or systems, thunderstorms can become both more numerous and more violent than an isolated cell developing from local heating of surface air. The cold air/warm air interface along an advancing cold front turbocharges the instability upon which thunderstorms thrive, as the cold wedge bulldozes under the warm, moist air ahead and forces it aloft. A fast-moving cluster of storms is referred to as a line squall and is usually found in the warm sector ahead of the advancing cold front. The involvement of multiple cells can prolong the bad weather.

The presence of a low-pressure trough is another key factor in the development of severe thunderstorms. People often visualize weather in two dimensions, neglecting the profound impacts of rising and descending air regionally (around highs and lows) and locally (in a thunderstorm cell). Near a surface trough of low pressure, which forms beneath a U-shaped dip (toward lower latitudes) in the upper-level jet stream, the instability of the surface air is increased, and thunderstorms are often more volatile. This is especially true when warm, moist Gulf of Mexico air is drawn into the equation and wind shear (directional changes with altitude) exists. This vertical twist can cause a rotational influence, leading to a tornado or waterspout. Although such twisters can also be generated in bands (continued page 289)

■ When the anvil-like cloud tops of a squall line begin to shear off, it's a sign that the cells are past their peak and the vertical heat transfer is starting to break down. Before heaving a sigh of relief and calling friends over for cocktails, make sure no new cells are building up and the squall line is moving away from your location.

WATCHES AND WARNINGS

One of the least understood facets of a marine weather forecast is the difference between a weather watch and a warning. Severe weather watches are issued when conditions are ripe for thunderstorm development. This does not mean that any storms have developed in the watch area; rather, it's a precautionary advisory justifying extra vigilance. When a warning is issued, it means that severe thunderstorms have been sighted in the watch area, and this should be a red flag to those about to leave the dock and a game-plan changer to those already underway.

■ Hot, humid, calm summer days are ingredients for local thunderstorm development. More often than not these single cells towering toward the stratosphere peter out at about 30,000 feet, making them relatively minor examples of convective activity that nevertheless pack a big punch in the gust-front region. Storms that continue to develop vertically, reaching as high as 50,000 feet, can deliver microburst gusts of 100 knots. Steering clear of such a cell is worth a substantial diversion from your course. Keep in mind that such cells regularly travel at 35 knots, so taking evasive action does not always result in avoidance.

THE CAPSIZE OF *WINGNUTS*

In a thunderstorm in the 2011 Chicago Mackinac Race, the 35-foot sloop *WingNuts* capsized, resulting in the loss of two lives. I was involved in the later analysis of the incident, contributing a weather appendix to the report commissioned by US Sailing. A pair of causal factors rose above the rest: thunderstorm development and vessel design. We'll look at the first now and the latter in Chapter 12.

Localized severe weather was a primary cause of the *WingNuts* capsize at about 11:00 p.m. central daylight time on July 17, 2011. The Independent Review Panel convened by US Sailing noted that the development of thunderstorms in the waters west of Charlevoix, Michigan, generated localized storm-force wind gusts. The squall line was not associated with a low-pressure system or related warm or cold fronts, but formed on a weak surface boundary amidst a very unstable atmosphere.

One of the hardest weather phenomena to fore-cast a day or more in advance is the severity of the thunderstorms that are likely to track through a given area. On the afternoon of July 17, Doppler radar picked up developing thunderstorm cells over Wisconsin and the Upper Peninsula of Michigan, and forecasters monitored their progress. The forecast for northern Lake Michigan grew worse throughout the day, but the dynamic nature of a thunderstorm's vertical development and the relatively short time interval during which a fully developed cell is at its most destructive made a precise forecast difficult. A severe thunderstorm watch was issued at 7:25 p.m. (about 3½ hours before the capsizing), meaning that conditions were right for wind gusts of gale force and higher to develop. As the cluster of thunderstorms moved over the waters of Lake Michigan, the National Weather Service issued a special marine warning, saying that wind gusts over 35 knots were being recorded and that dangerous cloud-to-water lightning was affecting the area.

WingNuts *under sail. Vessel design was a major factor in her capsize when a fast-moving thunderstorm overtook the fleet of the 2011 Chicago Mackinac Race. Note the wide deck with minimal corresponding hull volume beneath. This design characteristic emphasizes the need for movable crew ballast, rather than buoyancy-induced form stability. The net result is a precipitous drop off in righting moment at angles less than 80 degrees—just when it is needed most. (See Chapter 12 for a fuller discussion of stability and vessel design.) (Courtesy Hubert Cartier)*

It is clear from available NWS data that the duration of the worst weather varied from 10 to 45 minutes for the racing fleet, depending on each vessel's location. The highest gust measured by a calibrated NWS anemometer was 64 knots, and sustained winds of 40 knots or more were reported over a wide area of the Upper Peninsula. According to the meteorologists with whom the Independent Review Panel spoke, a bow echo (a Doppler radar image in the shape of an archer's bow, associated with a line of convective thunderstorms) containing a supercell thunderstorm (the most severe type, characterized by a rotating updraft and often called a rotating thunderstorm) developed west of Charlevoix and likely resulted in a downburst with wind gusts of 70 knots. The cell passed close to the recorded position of *WingNuts* at the time of the capsizing. Wind direction depended upon where a vessel happened to be located in relation to a specific cell, but the general trend was a breeze veering from southwest to northwest. The cells were moving at 30 knots, and not long after midnight the system had exited the region. Severe though it was, this weather event was hardly unusual for this region or, for that matter, for many locations up and down the East Coast and across the Gulf of Mexico.

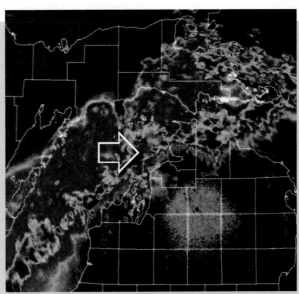

This Doppler radar image from the time of WingNuts' *capsizing shows a line of thunderstorms moving across northern Lake Michigan. The arrow shows* WingNuts' *location in the heart of a severe thunderstorm cell. The worst of these supercells approached 60,000 feet in height—with that much vertical development the downbursts were of storm- to hurricane-force. (Courtesy National Weather Service)*

of severe thunderstorms, they are more likely to be generated by isolated cells than by bunched cells in a densely packed line squall. A tornado that moves over water becomes a waterspout, and these can cause significant damage to vessels, though such incidents are infrequent. Course changes to avoid these often slow-moving spouts make sense, as does carefully tracking them on radar. Small-craft radar operating on the X-band do a great job of picking up the large water droplets associated with squalls, waterspouts, and thunderstorm cells, not only warning of their presence but also indicating their direction of movement.

An AM radio is a good way to know lightning may be coming, as it picks up the static caused by lightning discharges, with more static indicating a more severe storm. An inexpensive battery-powered portable radio can thus provide an early warning and is a useful piece of safety gear on board. When the underside of towering cumulonimbus clouds take on a rolling, lumpy, or fragmented appearance, sometimes with a visible green tinge, you are in the presence of cumulonimbus mammatus, another strong indicator of an imminent storm that will likely include hail. You may see a descending shelf cloud on a cell's leading edge, and yet another sure sign of an impending

gust front is a wisp of noticeably colder air on a hot, sultry day.

Thunderstorm Seamanship

Avoiding a severe thunderstorm is always the best option, but being caught in shoal water or in a nasty inlet while attempting to get to safe shelter can be far worse than encountering the same conditions with sufficient sea room to keep free of collisions or running aground. Attempting to outrace a squall line with a mad dash toward the harbor is a gamble. It may make better sense to head for a part of the bay with less traffic, fewer obstacles, and a fair distance from the nearest hungry lee shore.

Know how fast you and your crew can react. If a blistering hot summer day is already punctuated by cold wisps or gusts, you've probably already waited too long to get rid of the genoa and prepare to reef or strike the mainsail. Prudent sailors often douse the mainsail and let the tempest pass while reaching along with a scrap of unfurled jib, a storm jib, or engine power and bare poles. Powerboaters may power slowly into the wind and developing seas or run before the wind under such conditions. Faster vessels may be able to avoid the worst of these severe thunderstorms by taking evasive action. Short-lived winds in excess of 50 knots can push a moderate-displacement vessel at 6 knots with no sail set. If the seas are flat at the onset of a line squall or an encounter with a single cell, there's little time for seas to build, so the sole threat is the wind itself.

When a cold-air warning bell catches you at anchor, it's time to add more scope and get ready to cope with storm-force gusts. If the lunch hook is down, big problems await, especially if a heavier anchor isn't ready to be released from its bow roller. Running the diesel and shifting into forward during the gusts can take some of the load off the ground tackle. A dive mask (or ski goggles) for the helmsperson may be needed when a gust front or microburst rolls into view.

Along the U.S. East Coast, most of the vigor of these thunderstorms dissipates before they move offshore, but they can be quite intense right along the coast. Typically they won't spin back up until the moist air reaches the thermal boundary along the north wall of the Gulf Stream.

Air-mass thunderstorms are hot air events, not obviously a time to be reminded about hypothermia, but cold fronts can often be punctuated with violent convective activity and the air behind this band of thunderstorms is often much colder. Dressing for the deluge involves foul-weather gear with good seals at the neck and wrists, boots to keep the socks dry, and perhaps a wide-brimmed hat. The post cold-front chill is best warded off with a dry watch cap and gloves. Remaining damp as temperatures drop and the cold dry nor'westerly wind takes hold instigates hypothermia—preventing it from getting a foothold through layering and opting for moisture wicking layers is much easier than trying to warm up after the fact.

Fog

Fog is caused by a stratus cloud formation on the sea or land surface. West Coast and New England boaters have plenty of fog, with its obvious implications for navigation and collision avoidance. Many offshore sailors are surprised to discover that fog doesn't only occur with a calm sea or calm wind. On both U.S. coasts, fog can coincide with winds of 25 knots or greater and significant seas, making watchkeeping even more challenging.

Fog genesis involves an air temperature and dew point that are within 4ºF of each other; water vapor coalesces around tiny dust or salt particles. Fog becomes mist when the dew point is very close to the temperature, affording even lower visibility than fog. The Grand Banks off of the New England Coast has earned the title of the foggiest locale on the planet.

California's advection fog is also known for its tenacity and unwillingness to yield, even during warmer summer months.

Radiation fog occurs more often inland and in coastal areas where diurnal cooling (day to night temperature changes) are more extreme. Fall is a classic time for such cooling, and as the air temperature drops during the night and approaches the dew point, fog develops. When this occurs on a bay or in coastal waters, it's often called sea smoke.

Advection fog involves warm and relatively dry air masses moving over cold water. As the air temperature approaches the dew point, fog forms and can become so dense that even a 25-knot breeze will not disperse the surface cloud. Contributing factors such as warm and cold currents meeting exacerbate the situation. Extreme examples include the Labrador Current's confrontation with the Gulf Stream and the collision of the Benguela Current with the Agulhas Current at the tip of South Africa.

New Zealand, Argentina, and Chile, as well as the Arctic and Antarctic waters, all have regions where maritime fog banks are a persistent challenge. Interestingly, breaking waves in an active surf zone put more salt into the air, and these minute hygroscopic particles attract water vapor that thickens the fog in an area that's most threatening to a sailor.

Upper Atmosphere Troughs and Ridges

Thus far we have focused mostly on surface analysis and how surface features impact the world of the mariner. Once the surface maps and their related wind and wave imagery have become familiar friends, it's time to look aloft and see what's happening where the average barometric reading is 500 millibars. This is an active part of the atmosphere, where north-folded ridges of high pressure and south-folded troughs of low pressure move westerly across North America under the influence of a band of high-speed winds traveling west to east. These midlevel steering winds are, in effect, the linkage between the overlying jet stream and the underlying surface air masses. As mentioned earlier, directional changes in these midlevel winds are what fold a straight-line frontal boundary into a classic surface low, and the north-south depth of a midlevel short-wave trough exercises great influence over how violent a surface storm will become and where it will go.

500 Millibar Charts

To better understand what's going on in the mid-level atmosphere, meteorologists map the atmosphere with isoheights, or curves of equal altitude—essen-

■ *Advection fog, a dominant feature of West Coast boating, is caused by the cold California Current flowing south down the coast. (This cold flow is the descending portion of the Pacific gyre fed by Japan's Kuroshio and Oyashio merging currents.) The prevailing westerlies arrive on the coastline cool and dense after blowing over this cold water, keeping warm desert air from moving offshore.*

tially the mirror image of the contours of equal depth shown on nautical charts. Meteorologists sample the atmosphere with weather balloons equipped with sensors that transmit pressure, temperature, altitude, wind speed and direction, and other data to receiving stations—and use these data to make what amounts to an atmospheric topographic map (see the sidebar Unlocking the Mystery of the 500 mb Chart). Tighter gradients mean stronger winds—just as with the isobars on surface maps—but the streamlines or flow directions of these midlevel winds more closely follow their contour lines.

The flow is called zonal when these streamlines move west to east, and if the flow is not strong, bad weather on the surface is reduced. Winds of 100 knots or more do occur in zonal 500 mb flows, however, and when they do, hurricane-force surface lows—called right-movers by meteorologists—can result. More commonly, though, pronounced upper-level troughs in the 500 mb charts—dipping deep to the south—cause surface lows to develop and intensify. These upper-level troughs often appear as a rather innocuous dashed line on surface analysis and forecast maps; lacking the shark's teeth-like jagged triangles of a cold front notation, the symbol seems rather benign. But a steep isoheight gradient aloft associated with a deep-dipping trough intensifies a surface low and can turn run-of-the-mill bad weather into a

gale-, storm-, or hurricane-force low. See the sidebar for rules of thumb for using the 500 mb chart as a weather routing tool.

One look at the map shows that the regions north of 40 degrees north have a justified reputation for bad weather. Adventure sailors seeking record-breaking east-to-west transatlantic runs often try to place themselves smack in the middle of this heavy-weather superhighway to harness the nor'easters spawned there. Those headed in the other direction attempt to stay below the lows, looking for the southerlies in the warm-core segment between the warm and cold fronts. The high pressure that follows the cold front delivers a favorable westerly breeze, dries out the crew, and allows spinnakers to fly. But most crews know to head more northerly to avoid being caught in the windless center of these systems.

The upper-level flow shown on a 500 mb chart also features ascending (north-curving) loops that form ridges, and these are associated with surface high-pressure cells and fair, tranquil weather. Ridges develop between troughs in a 500 mb chart, and troughs develop between ridges. Such meanders in the flow move eastward in two separate wave patterns, featuring long- and short-wave troughs. Long-wave troughs have a lot to do with seasonal pattern changes (and sometimes with El Niño or La Niña climate cycles). Short-wave troughs move faster and are

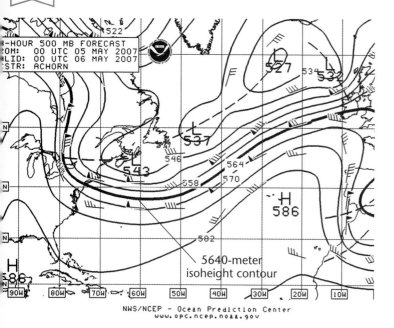

NWS/NCEP – Ocean Prediction Center
www.opc.ncep.noaa.gov

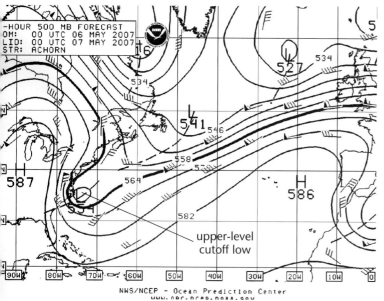

NWS/NCEP – Ocean Prediction Center
www.opc.ncep.noaa.gov

▨ *On this 500 mb 24-hour forecast chart the streamlines and wind arrow are exiting the U.S. East Coast in a zonal flow trending west to east, and the midlevel winds are moderate. This chart was issued at 7 p.m. on May 4, 2007. In less than a day a trough will develop, and the map below shows how abrupt a change takes place.*

prime instigators of surface weather, directly influencing system formation, movement, intensification, and decay. When long-wave and short-wave troughs get in phase and their wave amplitudes become resonant, the tight band of the midlevel high-speed wind belt is intensified. This condition can give rise to the most violent surface lows, sometimes referred to as meteorological bombs.

Between upper-level short-wave troughs lie upper-level ridges, and the associated dynamics of the atmosphere's midlevel winds are impacted by these north-south twists and turns. Stronger winds occur in the hard bend just east of a deep trough because the left-hand turn about the axis of the trough is enhanced by the Coriolis effect and the energy derived from our spinning planet. Thus, when a surface low lies just a little east of an upper-level trough axis, it will be significantly intensified by its interplay with the trough, which enhances the vertical convection of surface air and resultant instability.

A *cutoff low*, another unwelcome weather development, occurs when an upper-level trough pinches off near its southern extremity (continued page 294)

▨ *This 500 mb 24-hour forecast chart (above) was issued a day after the one shown at top. In the intervening 24 hours, the zonal flow over the U.S. East Coast has been replaced by a deep-diving upper-level trough, which has been pinched off to form a cutoff low high above Cape Hatteras. When this happens, a developing surface storm quickly begins to intensify. Some 32 hours after this chart was issued, subtropical storm Andrea overwhelmed the 54-foot sailboat Flying Colours, whose story is told at the end of this chapter. Comparing this chart with the surface analysis (next chart), revealing the actual weather that evolved, we can see that it is already too late to be seeking shelter. Some private weather routers saw this cutoff low developing in the 500 mb chart shown 24 hours earlier and started warning their clients.*

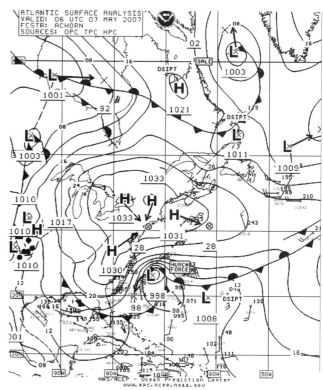

NWS/NCEP – Ocean Prediction Center
www.opc.ncep.noaa.gov

▨ *The surface level analysis showing the low that Flying Colours encountered (see page 314). Note the hurricane-force wind warning, a feature confirmed by local buoy reports.*

UNLOCKING THE MYSTERY OF THE 500 MB CHART
Lee Chesneau

Safe and prudent navigation decision making at sea begins with a fundamental understanding that weather is a dynamic three-dimensional process. The 500 mb atmospheric pressure level is about halfway up the atmosphere at roughly 18,000 feet (5,487 meters), and the air flow at this altitude can be considered as the basement layer of the jet stream. The jet stream core is higher, between 300 (polar jet stream) and 200 (subtropical jet stream) mb, but both jet streams are mirrored at 500 mb, especially in the winter months, and the impact of 500 mb dynamics on surface weather is quite significant.

A 500 mb chart is simply a map of the elevation contours in a surface of constant pressure. These elevation lines reflect the north-to-south temperature differences of their underlying air masses. A 5,400-meter-tall column of cold high-latitude air and a 5,700-meter-tall column of warm low-latitude air may weigh the same, both exerting 500 mb of pressure on the underlying sea surface. The elevation lines are called isoheights and are drawn at intervals of 60 meters. Winds of 30 knots or more are displayed between the isoheight contours on Ocean Prediction Center (OPC) 500 mb charts at intervals of 5 degrees of latitude and 10 degrees of longitude. These symbols are displayed as if the winds were horizontal, when in actuality their stronger component is vertical, especially when the isoheight gradient is steep (i.e., the isoheights are close together). A horizontal display makes it easier to locate strong wind belts or corridors aloft and thus to determine the location and track of a surface storm and its breadth across the ocean surface. This enables a navigator to plot a route that will avoid the heaviest winds and seas.

In this way, 500 mb charts provide important information about how the major synoptic-scale surface-weather systems (i.e., the everyday low- and high-pressure areas seen on surface maps) will form, move, and weaken or dissipate. Providing a macro picture of the wind energy aloft, its orientation, where the resultant worst surface conditions will be, and what changes to expect as much as 120 hours into the future, 500 mb charts comprise an important tool for weather forecasting and routing decisions.

Rules of thumb have developed *(continued next page)*

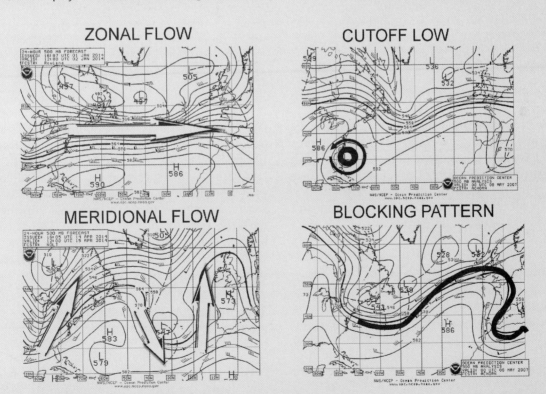

Characteristic flow patterns on 500 mb charts. Counterclockwise from top left: west to east zonal flow; north to south meridional flow; a blocking pattern and a cutoff low. The blocking pattern, a classic Omega block in the midlevel of the atmosphere, initiates a flow pattern that looks like the Greek letter Ω. Its main significance to surface weather is the way in which it impedes the movement of surface systems, resulting in high and low pressure cells making little westward progress. A midlevel cutoff low can enhance the volatility of a nearby surface low.

UNLOCKING THE MYSTERY OF THE 500 MB CHART, CONTINUED

from decades of observation and practice, beginning in the 1950s when commercial weather routing services were established. These rules are built around the following recognizable flow patterns in the embedded upper-level short-wave troughs and ridges: west-to-east zonal flow, north-to-south meridional flow, blocking ridge patterns (which deflect wind energy and storms north and south), and cutoff lows (which are at lower latitudes than blocking ridges—say 25 to 40 degrees latitude—and move little over days to a week or more). There may be more than one flow pattern overlying any given ocean basin at a given time.

A primary rule of thumb is that surface storms will track parallel with the isoheight contours above and will blow at one-third to one-half of the 500 mb wind speeds in a corridor ranging from 300 to 600 nautical miles poleward of the 5640-meter isoheight contour, which is always highlighted in bold on a 500 mb chart. The 5640 contour therefore reflects the southern extent of Beaufort Force 6/7 westerlies in summer and Force 7/8 westerlies in winter. As used here, the term "westerlies" indicates that the only part of the storm track impacting the 5640 isoheight will be the cold front that usually extends north-south across latitude lines, producing a wind shift from southwest, to west, to northwest as it passes. The strongest winds (gale-, storm-, and hurricane-force) and heaviest seas are very likely to be north of the 5640 isoheight line in the Northern Hemisphere. (Captain Ma Li Chen, who with me coauthored the book *Heavy Weather Avoidance*, uses the more conservative 5700-meter contour rather than the 5640-meter contour to define the poleward edge of the "available zone" within which vessels can safely navigate.)

A second rule of thumb is that up to 50% of the 500 mb wind speeds behind a short-wave trough (i.e., to the west of the trough in the colder air) can be expected to translate to the sea surface. If you see 80 knots on the 500 mb chart, prepare for 40 knots on the sea in the west-to-southwest quadrant of a Northern Hemisphere middle-latitude extratropical cyclone, where the tightest pressure gradients and the strongest winds and heaviest sea states are located.

Lee Chesneau is a marine meteorologist who for years signed many of the Ocean Prediction Center's weather fax charts that scrolled out of printers aboard sailboats, powerboats, and commercial ships. On one particularly lumpy transatlantic, Chesneau charts won our crew's "Gifted Meteorologist" award for nailing the intensity and duration of the gales and storm that stalked our route. In later years, I worked with Lee at sailing seminars, and he proved as gifted at teaching weather awareness as he was at divining where the nasty lows were headed. He holds the view that every sailor benefits from understanding what lies ahead.

(in the Northern Hemisphere), and the short wave that spawned it separates, shifts north, and moves on to the east, leaving the pinched-off low behind. To understand the dynamics of a cutoff low, one must think in three-dimensional terms. Like uneven ground, the atmosphere arranges itself in mounds of air with valleys between, as depicted in upper-level (500 mb) charts. The cutoff low can remain nearly stationary, and a trough of low pressure on the surface will be turbocharged by this reluctant-to-move upper-level low. In the mid-Atlantic region of the United States, surface lows often form on these trough boundaries and move eastward over coastal waters, intensifying as they reach the warmer north wall of the Gulf Stream. This pesky, slow-moving weather feature can spawn a week's worth of bad weather. During some summers, the effect sets up over the Great Lakes and extends a surface trough along a line from 30 to 40 degrees north about halfway to Bermuda, creating a gray, lumpy sea passage all the way to or from the island.

Sailors in the Northern Hemisphere seeking kinder, less gale-ridden adventures know that when they see a deep hitch in the 500 mb chart, setting up a trough over the East Coast, it's best to find a safe haven or be ready for a dose of heavy weather. When this happens in the early spring or late fall, low-pressure systems developing off Cape Hatteras or elsewhere along the East Coast mix cold continental air with the warm, moist air over the Gulf Stream, turbocharging an already eruptive atmosphere. Phrases such as "rapidly intensifying low" and "developing storm" are often associated with such preconditions.

Tropical Weather Patterns

One of the best bits of weather news for those headed for trade-wind latitudes is the farewell they can bid to the unending march of cold fronts and baroclinic lows across the temperate regions of the globe. The tropics are dominated by easterly trade-wind belts. As mentioned earlier in this chapter, the northeasterly trades of the Northern Hemisphere and the southeasterly trades of the Southern Hemisphere are separated by the Intertropical Convergence Zone (ITCZ) and are bounded on their higher-latitude edges by

■ *Persistent squally weather, as seen here, can last for several days. As the trough or cutoff low strengthens and an interacting surface low deepens, the wind increases, turning calm seas into gale-force conditions. An upper-level cutoff low behaves like its creator, the upper-level trough; both are linked to unsettled weather. Surface low-pressure systems often develop on an upper-level trough and move in a northeasterly direction in the Northern Hemisphere. This weather pattern can set up and remain stalled over coastal waters for days, often linked with an upper-level atmospheric phenomenon known as an Omega block—a ridge bounded by two upper-level lows near its base that create the shape of the Greek letter omega: Ω.*

the semipermanent subtropical high-pressure belts known as the horse latitudes, where upper-level air subsides and spreads equatorward to feed the trade winds and poleward to feed the temperate-latitude westerlies. The ITCZ is a band of low-pressure troughs (the doldrums) extending around the globe near the equator where the convective rising of heated equatorial air produces widespread showers, thunderstorms, and frequent lightning.

The aptly named easterly trades act like a conveyor belt across the oceans. In the Northern Hemisphere they fill in around Christmas and remain steady in direction (though not in velocity) for months at a time. Atypical conditions caused by El Niño and La Niña events can alter the pattern, resulting in a cessation of the easterlies in one area and a strengthening in another. These climatic perturbations can also change the dynamics of the flip side of tropical paradise. Summer in the trade-wind belt brings a lessening of the prevailing easterly, a decrease in wind shear, and sea surface temperatures of 80°F or higher to depths of 150 to 200 feet. These hot, humid conditions, a thunderstorm-ridden atmosphere, a lack of wind shear aloft, and a maritime

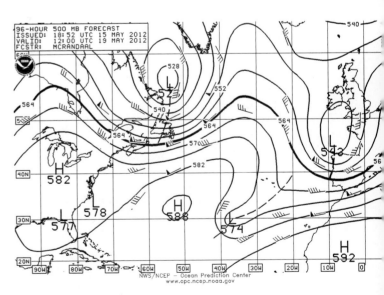

■ *This 96-hour 500 mb forecast from May 2012 shows the development of an upper-level ridge in the mid-Atlantic, with isoheight lines warped from a west-to-east zonal flow into a more meridional configuration with north- and south-flowing legs. We can expect an Omega block to develop in the midlevel atmosphere, slowing the progress of surface weather systems and tending to move bad weather into higher latitudes.*

heat source are the required conditions for tropical storm development.

Tropical Cyclone Genesis

Tropical waves can be thought of as upper-level disturbances that cause an increase in thunderstorm activity at the surface and more often than not are linked to the creation of tropical depressions, the fledgling phase of a hurricane. These swirling masses

of low pressure have a warm-air core and are not associated with a front—unlike extratropical lows. Like extratropical lows, however, they rotate counterclockwise in the Northern Hemisphere and clockwise in the Southern Hemisphere. Called typhoons, cyclones, and hurricanes in different parts of the world, their effects are felt in every trade-wind region except the South Atlantic, which is *almost* completely hurricane-free. (Note the emphasis on "almost;" in March 2004, cyclone Catarina proved that, contrary to the prevailing assumption, even the tropical South Atlantic is not immune.)

Anatomy of a Tropical Storm or Hurricane

As mentioned earlier, hurricanes are really thermal-transport mechanisms that transfer poleward heat energy generated in the tropics. Although a complete understanding of these devastating weather events still lies well down the road, meteorologists have a good idea about what must be present for tropical cyclone formation to take place. A handful of key criteria can be directly linked to summer conditions in the hemisphere.

The stage is set for tropical storm formation when the water temperature is above 80°F to a depth of 150 to 200 feet. An unstable atmosphere with high humidity also needs to be in place, as occurs during the summer months in the tropics more than anywhere else in the world. Low wind shear is another vital ingredient, because the vertical development that establishes the water vapor condensation heat engine can be torn apart by winds that vary in direction as altitude increases. Strong west winds aloft stifle tropical storm development much as rain stifles a forest fire.

Tropical storm development also requires a preexisting weather disturbance in the form of a band of thunderstorms or an upper-level tropical wave, the latter being linked to most tropical storm development in the Atlantic, while ITCZ thunderstorms are the primary causal agent in the Pacific and Indian oceans. Another fascinating needed ingredient is at least 4 or 5 degrees of latitude for the rotation to begin. The Coriolis effect is zero at the equator, but just a few degrees north or south, the effect of the earth's rotation is strong enough to spin convective activity first into a tropical depression and eventually, if conditions continue to favor, into a tropical storm and finally the infamous eye of a hurricane.

Winds increase as the barometric pressure of a warm-core storm drops. The stages of development are defined by the Saffir-Simpson Hurricane Wind Scale shown in the accompanying table (see the sidebar Tropical Storm and Hurricane Development).

Like a giant vortex in the atmosphere, a tropical storm reaches upward to the tropopause, establishing an eye wall and a central region of extremely low pressure and calm wind. In the Northern Hemisphere, the highest wind gusts in the cyclonic (counterclockwise) flow are usually found just outside the eye wall on the right-hand (northeasterly) side of the advancing storm, where the speed of advance is added to the embedded wind speed. In the Southern Hemisphere the flow is clockwise, and the strongest winds are found on the left-hand (southwesterly) side of the advancing storm.

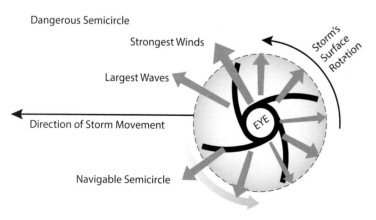

Waves generated by a hurricane rush out in all directions, organizing into deep ocean swells that move much faster than the storm itself. When a hurricane speeds up, its forward progress reinforces the waves moving ahead of it along the storm track, creating much larger seas in that direction.

The concentric nature of hurricanes and tropical storms derives from a series of spiral bands wrapped around a central core or eye wall. The heaviest weather and highest wind velocities are found along the perimeter of this cylindrical inner eye wall, the diameter of which can range from 2 to over 100 miles. Eye wall regeneration occurs in stronger hurricanes, sometimes multiple times. What takes place is a significant but short-term abatement of the high winds and convectivity in the eye wall that can be clearly noted in the storm's radar signature. Barometric pressure remains the same or continues to drop and a new, more intense, eye wall develops. Between the concentrically wrapped spiral bands lie gaps of lower wind and less violent convective activity, and in the eye itself are found calm wind, bright sunlight, and clear sky, a result of the massive central downdraft of dry air pumped down by the heat engine effect of the storm. In essence, the very center of the storm is a chimney in reverse.

MOST INTENSE ATLANTIC HURRICANES, BY PRESSURE (NOT PROPERTY DAMAGE)

Rank	Hurricane Name	Year	Pressure (hPa; note 1 hPa = 1 mb)
1	Wilma	2005	882
2	Gilbert	1988	888
3	"Labor Day"	1935	892
4	Rita	2005	895
5	Allen	1980	899
6	Katrina	2005	902
7 (tie)	Camille	1969	905
	Mitch	1998	905
	Dean	2007	905

(Courtesy Hurdat)

TROPICAL STORM AND HURRICANE DEVELOPMENT

Tropical storms can go through four phases of development that are linked to pressure minimums and wind intensities. The diameter of the storm and the area it covers are not as closely associated with storm intensity as one might suppose. Andrew, the brutal Category 5 hurricane that struck south Florida in 1992, had a relatively small footprint, while Gilbert, a Category 4 hurricane upon landfall (Category 5 earlier), impacted a much larger area. The four phases of development are:

- **Tropical disturbance**—an organized cluster of showers and thunderstorms over tropical or subtropical waters.
- **Tropical depression**—a counterclockwise (Northern Hemisphere) closed rotation around a defined low-pressure area with sustained winds less than 34 knots. This weather event is given a number but not a name.
- **Tropical storm**—when a tropical depression increases to maximum sustained surface winds of 34 to 63 knots, it becomes a named storm.
- **Hurricane**—when the wind speeds in a tropical storm intensify to 64 knots or more and the convection becomes better organized with a well-defined eye, the storm becomes a hurricane.

THE SAFFIR-SIMPSON HURRICANE WIND SCALE

Category	Mean Central Pressure (millibars)	Wind Speed	Surge (feet)	Damage	Example
1	980 or more	68-82 kts 119-151 km/h	4-5	Minimal	Agnes 1972
2	965-979	83-95 kts 152-176 km/h	6-8	Moderate	Kate 1965
3	945-964	96-112 kts 177-209 km/h	9-12	Extensive	Elena 1985
4	920-944	113-136 kts 210-248 km/h	13-18	Extreme	Hugo 1989
5	less than 920	> 136 kts > 248 km/h	> 18	Catastrophic	Gilbert 1988

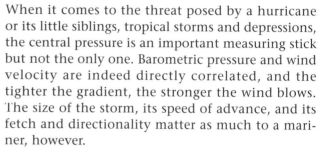

HURRICANE/TROPICAL STORM SEAMANSHIP

When it comes to the threat posed by a hurricane or its little siblings, tropical storms and depressions, the central pressure is an important measuring stick but not the only one. Barometric pressure and wind velocity are indeed directly correlated, and the tighter the gradient, the stronger the wind blows. The size of the storm, its speed of advance, and its fetch and directionality matter as much to a mariner, however.

Tropical storm avoidance depends upon understanding the timing and geographic extent of hurricane season and closely tracking weather developments during the season. Staying out of the tropics during the height of the hurricane season has always been and continues to be the mariner's best bet, but some sailors today, relying on satellite storm tracking and better long-range forecasting, venture into waters visited by hurricanes using some form of weather routing. It may be unwise, but it's not uncommon to see vessels sailing across the Atlantic from Africa and up to the northeastern U.S. during hurricane season (roughly June to November).

Hurricanes behave something like big jellyfish

Commercial mariners know the value of a good, carefully calibrated aneroid barometer like this one. Pressure readings provide information regarding the passage of lows—it is the trend, or rate of change, that best predicts wind velocity. Many sailors have added an electronic barometer/barograph that is able to profile the rate of change.

LA NIÑA AND EL NIÑO

The children, as these two weather events are called, aren't as exact in their arrival and departure as the seasons. These events, referred to as the Southern Oscillation by scientists, involve atmospheric and oceanic factors that are not yet completely understood. Thanks to satellites and data buoys, however, we know more than we did just a few years ago.

El Niño arrives with a subsidence in the Pacific's easterly trade winds and a redistribution of rainfall across the Pacific. There is a cessation of the upwelling of nutrient-rich water along the west coasts of North and South America—a critical loss for the marine food chain in those regions—and warm water invades the western Pacific, causing fish stocks to crash. The phenomenon has been recognized ever since farmers and anchovy fishermen from California to Chile noted that once in about every 10 years their lives and livelihoods were significantly threatened. More recently, the cold cycle La Niña, the flip side of these El Niño events, has come under scrutiny.

These two faces of a climate cycle affect where low-pressure centers track and are associated with a long-term shift in sea surface temperature and midlevel wind patterns. A few general trends are important to

mariners. For example, during La Niña events, massive amounts of warm, moist Gulf of Mexico air are advected into low-pressure systems over the United States, causing an increase in the severity of thunderstorms and lows that develop along the East Coast. There is often a split in the jet stream, and the lower, subtropical portion can dip all the way down to the Gulf and then snake its way northward just off the East Coast. The warm moist air it ushers up toward cold-core lows can turn such storms into what forecasters call a "bomb." With the Gulf Stream further instigating this eruptive cyclogenesis, there's good reason for sailors to have deep respect for Cape Hatteras. These conditions can last for over a year. El Niño conditions, on the other hand, warm up the eastern portion of the Pacific and move tropical cyclone activity farther eastward. They clamp a lid on the conveyor-like reliability of the Pacific trade winds and place those hiding from tropical cyclones in the eastern Pacific more at risk. Such major climate shifts impact passage planning and up the ante for long-distance cruisers attempting to avoid heavy weather. "Safety valve" passagemaking, comprised of shorter hops between all-weather anchorages, can be a viable option during periods of increased volatility.

VOYAGE PLANNING BASED ON CLIMATE AND WEATHER CYCLES

During my family's westabout voyage around the world, we handled ocean-to-ocean passage planning in a finish-to-start process. Arrival dates at landfalls were planned before the onset of the hurricane or cyclone season in that part of the world, and from there we worked back to our starting point to set departure dates that would allow us ample time to make trade-wind transits avoiding hurricane seasons. For our passage across the Indian Ocean from Darwin, Australia, we set up a timetable that would get us into Durban, South Africa, in early November, which marked the onset of the summer cyclone season in the south tropical Indian Ocean. Each stop we made along the way was governed by a timeline that held us to that arrival date.

Then the rudder failed 300 miles from the island of Mauritius, and we made landfall in the independent island republic under jury-rigged steering. Ex-tracting the rudder with the boat in the water was easy, but rebuilding the rudder with little material available was a lot harder. Long days, a few engineering shortcuts, and a local shipyard's willingness to do some welding solved the problem and let us keep on schedule. The sprint around Madagascar to Durban took us through a storm-tossed Southern Ocean, but we were not yet into the cyclone season. The same good fortune did not hold for the crew of the Cal 34 *Drambuie*—whom we met in Chapter 2—a small sloop a month behind us, who chose to chance a cyclone-season passage through the western Indian Ocean. Their last radio message spoke of mountainous seas and knockdowns. At the time they were 400 miles from the center of cyclone Claudette, a storm that would eventually cross their track. Friends waited for them at the dock in Durban, but *Drambuie* never made landfall.

in the atmosphere, except that they are steered by upper-level winds rather than sea currents. The direction they take is determined by the trade winds in the tropics and weather systems in the temperate zones, and forecasters have gotten good at predicting and computer-modeling their tracks. Even so, gambling on your ability to route your boat away from a developing storm can make Vegas odds look good.

The wind field around a tropical storm or hurricane is unbalanced because of the storm's own speed of advance, which lessens the wind velocity on one side of the storm and increases it on the other. Add to this the snowplow effect of storm-generated seas, and it's easy to understand why the right-hand forward quadrant of a Northern Hemisphere tropical storm or hurricane is the most dangerous. If the counter-clockwise circulation (Northern Hemisphere) generates wind speeds of 50 knots and the storm is moving westward at 25 knots, a vessel caught in the forward right-hand quadrant of the storm would experience winds close to 75 knots and the largest seas associated with the system. Furthermore, if the boat sets a drogue and runs off before the wind (see Chapter 13), it will be drawn deeper into the heart of the advancing storm in this quadrant. On the other hand, a vessel in the left-hand rear quadrant will find the wind closer to 25 or 30 knots and the seas less dangerous. This is why one of the mariner's golden rules in the Northern Hemisphere is never to sail into the right-hand semicircle of a tropical weather system.

Things get dicey when a storm reaches the western basin of the North Atlantic and in many cases become "extratropical," or what the National Hurri-

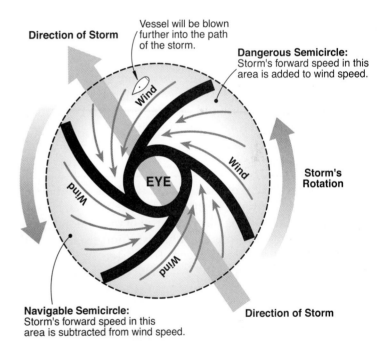

In the dangerous semicircle of a tropical storm or hurricane, wind strengths are enhanced by the storm system's speed of advance. A 70-knot wind blowing from the south in a northern-hemisphere hurricane moving northward at 20 knots will feel like 90 knots to any boat unfortunate enough to experience it. Where the rotational wind is blowing from the north in the hurricane's navigable semicircle ("navigable" being a relative term here), the effective wind strength will be 50 knots. What makes the leading quadrant in the dangerous semicircle even more dangerous is that a vessel running before the onslaught in that quadrant is actually heading into the heart of the storm.

cane Center now calls "post-tropical." During such a change, the intense hurricane wind speed seen only at the eye wall lessens, but as the warm core characteristic of the storm dissipates, warm and cold fronts develop and a cold core transition takes place. The result is a much larger diameter storm with high wind readings over a wider area. These transitioned cold core storms can cause horrific damage ashore and at sea—post-tropical storm Sandy was a classic example of such a transition. This in no way is equivalent to falling apart. In fact, many a weak tropical storm has become turbocharged while losing its warm core, and has subsequently spread out, picked up fronts, and gone on to shred the maritime interests of temperate latitudes.

WEATHER PREDICTIONS

The first half of this chapter has only summarized some of the key factors and variables that influence weather. Meteorologists study these plus additional factors, employing sophisticated computer modeling to arrive at forecasts issued to mariners and the public. But it's important still for sailors to understand these basic causes of weather—and to understand that forecasts at best are only more and more accurate estimates of the weather that may actually arrive. Still, government and private forecast services play an important role in safe voyaging.

Government Forecasts

The Ocean Prediction Center (OPC) is a branch of the U.S. National Weather Service (NWS), an agency under the administrative control of the National Oceanic and Atmospheric Administration (NOAA), and it's the boater's best friend. Forecasters in the Camp Springs, Maryland, NOAA Science Center analyze a stream of data from buoys, weather stations, direct satellite feeds, and ships at sea, massaging this information into a variety of forecast products that offer mariners reliable short-, medium-, and long-range looks at the weather ahead. This is a great example of tax dollars at work for the good of all boaters, commercial mariners, and coastal residents.

Weather forecasting and atmospheric sampling are generally conducted nation by nation, although there are many independent sources that compile an array of global forecast data. A good rule of thumb, however, is to always include information from the internationally recognized weather forecast source for each area in which you sail.

Like most scientific endeavors, the meteorologist's tradecraft has been revolutionized by computer technology. Rather than replacing human forecasting, however, computers have enhanced it. Today's forecaster uses data-crunching programs that offer a big picture as well as small snapshots of what's going on from the sea surface to the roof of the atmosphere. With such detail come more accurate and specific forecasts, a big plus for those poised to take advantage of a weather window or preparing to cope with a storm at sea.

Unfortunately, there are so many dynamic factors involved in weather that computer forecasting models cannot address all possible variables. Different computer models also produce different results. The forecaster plays a vital role in tweaking and interpreting the model output.

For example, when a steep-gradient high-pressure system follows a vigorous cold front over the mid-Atlantic region of the U.S. East Coast, the breeze builds and veers from southeast to southwest to west-northwest, and the intensity of the shift is impacted by temperature and pressure differences as well as by the rate of advance of the weather system. An accurate prediction of whether the worst winds will be encountered in a pre-front trough, in the cold-front boundary itself, or during the cold insurgence of northwest winds behind the front requires that the data be decoded with the experience and intuition of an expert. When raw model output is downloaded as a GRIB file by the mariner (see below), the meteorologist's interpretation is missing.

Sometimes a computer model produces a forecast that's well off the mark. These hiccups are most often manifest as mistakes in predicted wind velocities, which can be disconcerting or worse to sailors. A sustained 20-knot sea breeze on a day when 5 to 10 knots was forecast can be caused by a fairly small change in the pressure gradient or by a thermal enhancement to the sea breeze that's greater than what was expected. In some areas, high islands or coastal mountains will cause an orographic wind increase, and a skilled forecaster will know when such conditions are likely to occur.

Ship reports still play a vital role in evaluating computer-generated forecasts, and an array of coastal sea buoys provides further direct feedback and model input. Sea state reports from satellite radar imagery also help with real-time feedback to the prognostications of computer algorithms. Meteorologists have developed a reliable system that uses satellite radar images to correlate sea-surface texture with wind strength and direction. The result is a real-time ability to measure wind and sea conditions associated with specific weather events, another great tool to help evaluate a forecast. Using such techniques, meteorologists have raised model tweaking to a fine art. Trend

ONLINE SOURCES OF WEATHER INFORMATION (NORTH AMERICA)

Ocean Prediction Center
  http://www.opc.ncep.noaa.gov/
National Hurricane Center
  http://www.nhc.noaa.gov/
National Data Buoy Center
  http://www.ndbc.noaa.gov/
Weather Underground Marine Weather
  http://www.wunderground.com/MAR/
Oceanweather Inc.
  http://www.oceanweather.com/data/
Storm Prediction Center
  http://www.spc.noaa.gov

The staff at the Ocean Prediction Center evaluate the weather picture unfolding in the Atlantic and Pacific oceans. Forecasters feed satellite, ship, and other data to various model algorithms, interpreting the results with a human awareness of an algorithm's attributes and potential short-falls. They fine-tune GRIB file information and send forecasts and analyses to the OPC website, to fax broadcasting stations, and to numerous other consumers of their work.

analysis from these forecast/feedback loops also helps programmers improve the computer models and lessen the effects of inaccurately weighted variables. As time goes on, forecast models will become even more reliable, but for now the OPC forecast is a blend of human and machine.

One of the best services of the OPC is its continued commitment to providing online and at-sea weather fax forecasts. A full range of graphic and text products can be downloaded from the OPC website (www.opc.ncep.noaa.gov), with detailed current weather conditions as well as 24-, 48-, and 96-hour forecasts for East and West Coast offshore sailors.

This suite of weather forecast products can also be received at sea without costly satellite Internet equipment and service charges. Thanks to USCG communications stations in Marshfield, Massachusetts, and Point Reyes, California, all it takes to get these graphic and text forecasts at sea is a single-sideband (SSB) receiver and a laptop with an inexpensive weather fax decoding program or a dedicated marine weather fax receiver. This service shouldn't be taken for granted; funding was in question just a few years ago, and some private forecast interests lobbied to keep the detailed forecasts from being offered to the public free of charge. Hopefully, no future efforts will be made to limit access to this vital information.

OPC personnel developing a wintertime forecast for the North Pacific—a lesson in isobar compaction. Low-pressure systems dominate this part of the Pacific, and the waves generated by these storms torment mariners from Hawaii to the Gulf of Alaska. Avoiding midlatitude storm seasons as well as hurricane season is a key component of sensible passage planning.

The National Buoy Data System

The National Buoy Data System is another means of checking a forecast and learning more about what the graphics on the screen or on a printed chart mean for those at sea. All you have to do is point and click your way through the National Buoy Data System website, covering U.S. coastal waters, to get

a feel for how conditions at sea are affected by the proximity of a front or a low-pressure system. Use the wind speed, wind direction, and sea state information from a buoy to verify the location of the fronts and the high- or low-pressure system. You'll soon notice that short-range forecasts are more accurate than mid- to long-range forecasts, but the accuracy of the latter two has greatly improved in the past few years thanks to the efforts of teams like the meteorologists at OPC and the global recognition by SOLAS and other international bodies that weather forecasts are a vital safety link for those at sea.

GRIB Weather Data and Files

The acronym GRIB stands for gridded binary files, referring to a compressed information format favored by meteorologists for transmitting weather information digitally. GRIB has become the favored buzzword of the weather-worried, but experts continue to debate the value of GRIB interpretation by nonprofessionals. Lee Chesneau, an ex-OPC meteorologist and now an engaging weather seminar speaker (and contributor to this chapter), tells mariners to be very careful with the raw model data that GRIB files graphically provide. First look closely at the forecasts, surface analyses, and 500 mb information broadcast by the U.S. Coast Guard, downloaded free from the web, or received via SSB or weather fax receiver. The GRIB files most often used by sailors are computer model generated graphics that show wind speed and direction as wind barbs overlaid on a chart and designated for a specific time and date. The data is derived from mathematical models, and the forecast has not been developed by a team of meteorologists. GRIB forecasts derived from different models often differ significantly, and a forecaster using the data develops a "feel" for which model tends to yield the most reliable information under a specific set of conditions. Sailors tapping into these data sources seldom have the same level of insight. Forecasters looking at major storms often allude to diverging model data or converging information. The latter indicates that storm tracks shown on various GRIB sources are coming together, that is, are in better agreement as to a likely storm track.

GRIB data are based solely upon model-driven calculations using complex algorithms—they reflect absolutely no human intervention, not even a look out the window. What's amazing is how accurate these computer-crunched projections can be. In fact, those cruising in remote Southern Ocean regions have been shocked by how often the GRIB file forecast matches local conditions even though weather stations and sampling are scarce. This fact alone is a great testimony to how good the models are getting, but despite this glowing upside, there are times when the models are 180 degrees out of sync with each other, one calling for calm seas and sunshine and another placing a rousing gale in your path. The GRIB charts generated will be equally contradictory, and there's no human element ready to add an expert's opinion.

Forecast Models. NOAA sifts data from the atmosphere via weather stations, weather balloons, ship reports, satellites, and ground radar. Their models (GFS, AVN, and the Wave Watch 3 wave model, also known as WW111) give a shorthand digital summary of the information tweaked by weighted mathematical formulas. For example, the GFS model covers land and sea areas and generates wind vectors at a 10-meter height over a grid with a resolution of 0.5×0.5, 1.0×1.0, or 2.5×2.5 degrees. The data include wind speed and direction, temperature, pressure, humidity, and much more.

WW111 offers high-seas data in a much smaller file, limited to oceanic wind waves and ocean current data. It's updated at 3-hour intervals, and the model is run four times a day. Its grid size is 1.0×1.25 degrees, meaning that each data point is for a rectangular area of sea surface roughly 60 miles by 45 to 75 miles (depending upon the latitude of the cell).

The navy has also put models such as NOGAPS and COAMPS in the public domain, and more and more data are being shared worldwide.

Acquiring GRIB files. People with a high-speed Internet connection can snappily download GRIB files, but it's a much slower world at sea with baud rates that make a 1990s dial-up connection seem impressive. Sailors either spend a huge amount on satellite phone, Inmarsat, or other provider of air time, or purchase a plan with a provider such as WeatherNet, which compresses GRIB files and provides them via SSB or satellite service. A few competitors in a recent race from California to Hawaii spent as much as $2,000 on air time for weather information downloads!

Also needed is a GRIB file reader, a software program that turns the binary files into a color chart depicting wind velocity and sea state as well as other vital meteorological data. GRIB Explorer or another Windows program running on your PC is linked to your communication gear. Ashore, GRIB files can be downloaded by a landline, cell phone, or wi-fi. At sea, an SSB with a digital Pactor III modem can do the job, as can Sailmail and other email/SSB links. Inmarsat and Iridium and other satellite systems also can connect the GRIB file reader in a laptop with a service provider. Ham operators use products such as Ugrib and Pactor-equipped transceivers to circumvent the costs of a commercial service, but the process is less user-friendly and the products are not quite as easy to handle.

Ideally, GRIB files should be used as one more input for forecast development, much like a trend in barometric readings or a shift in wind direction. Basing a forecast solely on a *(continued page 304)*

WEATHER ADVICE IN THE CARIBBEAN 1500 RALLY

In lieu of reading Hiscock, Street, and Moitessier (see A Ship's Library) and using their cumulative wit and wisdom as a primer to traditional voyaging, Caribbean 1500 event organizers offer entrants a fast track to the fun and fraternity of passagemaking en masse, from Hampton, Virginia, to Tortola, British Virgin Islands. This approach to leaving winter astern and fetching up at a landfall surrounded by blue water and palm trees holds much appeal. The pitch is compelling, and the package promises much more than token handholding and a little help getting your boat from here to there. The pre-departure shoreside support process includes a vessel inspection for readiness, a chance to gain knowledge in formal lectures, and the weather wisdom of Ken Campbell, one of the best storm guessers in the business. The rally also has a safety-in-numbers appeal for many first-timers anxious about ocean voyaging.

November's weather near Cape Hatteras, like its springtime sequel, is a fickle crapshoot that features two extremes—calms and gales—the only sure thing being that current conditions won't last long. The answer is to clear out on the heels of a cold front with a high-pressure system and westerly winds hopefully hanging around for a while. During these precious few days of good weather, the herd stampedes east and south. There's no dilly-dallying in light air; instead, you crank the diesel and push on toward lower latitudes anytime progress drops below your normal cruising speed. The secondary challenge complicating this plan is the need to put as much easting in the bank as possible before reaching 25 degrees south, at which point you'll likely encounter easterly trade winds that have pushed waves all the way across the Atlantic and can turn an eastward slog into an unwelcome ordeal.

You may not be able to outwit Mother Nature, but if you're a gifted meteorologist you can gauge her mood shifts, and that's just what Ken Campbell of Commander Weather did the day before the scheduled start of the 2006 Caribbean 1500.

A week before the start, a brutal cold front had plunged southward out of a low-pressure system punishing the Northeast. The cold, unstable air mass left a remnant of its ferocity sitting aloft over Texas. This upper-level cutoff low looked to Ken like a candidate for intensification, and despite the fact that on the day before the start of the Caribbean 1500 this undeveloped weather system had hardly any clouds and moisture, one of the computer models was hinting of significant development. Unfortunately, another major weather model and source of GRIB data showed a high-pressure system in its place and nearly optimum conditions for a great getaway.

Campbell staked his call on the Canadian model and his wealth of weather experience. He understood how cold air and warm water off Cape Hatteras can behave like a match in an almost-empty gas tank. Facing a room full of cruisers eager to hit the road, he explained why he had advised race organizers to postpone the start for three days and demonstrated how he had used web-based data to keep current on conditions. Two vessels, *Between the Sheets* (a Hallberg Rassy 62) and *Faraway Eyes* (an Amel 53) shoved off anyway, seeing a 24- to 36-hour window of light, favorable winds in which to sprint south and east, but the rest of the fleet heeded Campbell's warning and stayed put for the next three days.

In retrospect, staying put *(continued next page)*

■ *A 30-knot northwest wind at Cape Hatteras. This view is westward into Albemarle Sound, well away from the reach of ocean swells.*

WEATHER ADVICE IN THE CARIBBEAN 1500 RALLY, CONTINUED

turned out to be the right choice for the majority of the fleet. The phantom low materialized, and 24 hours after the postponement the buoy off Cape Hatteras showed south-southeast winds at 20 knots; the next day at 2130 EST, a southeast headwind had freshened to 33 knots, gusting to 42, and seas were approaching 20 feet. As Campbell had predicted, by Wednesday the low was on its way to New England, and a northwesterly brought clearing skies and a good reason to get going.

Such weather guidance is worth its weight in diesel fuel. It makes little sense for most cruising boats to beat into 25- to 35-knot winds; progress is poor at best, and the toll on gear and crew morale can be significant. It's one thing to cope with a gale during a passage, but sailing into one that can be avoided makes little sense at all.

Professional routers like Rich Shema and Ken McKinley also provide commercial and recreation clients with custom-tailored forecasts, and as long as one realizes the need for solid communications gear and a backup plan in case communication is lost, engaging a weather guru can make sense.

When a well-prepared vessel and crew head to sea, the forecast has been checked and the departure date is based on the weather rather than a mark on a calendar. Decks are ready for breaking seas, and the sail plan is matched to the passage at hand.

GRIB file is dangerous. For example, as mentioned already, models that are spot on with wind velocity predictions for one type of weather system often miss the wind velocity implications associated with another. Information garnered from the GFS model are regularly tweaked by meteorologists when developing a forecast. They look at satellite photos of the Gulf Stream's constantly changing north wall conditions, for example, and check ship reports and note how other models read the situation. Leaving a forecaster entirely out of the loop is a gamble with a serious downside. GRIB files should be another tool in the box—not the only tool available.

Private Weather Services

Do-it-yourself amateur weather forecasters believe that NOAA/NWS has done a pretty fine job of sampling and evaluating the dynamics of the atmosphere and putting that information at the fingertips of the boating community. So why pay others to process the same model data and charts? Unfortunately, this argument only holds water for those who have done their homework and can decipher the information on weather fax 24-, 48-, and 96-hour forecast charts and understand why a teardrop-shaped isoheight line on a 500 mb chart is an alarm bell for the formation of a cutoff low. For predeparture planning, if you want GRIB files, satellite radar analysis of the sea surface, and its associative relationship to wind speed, it's all on the web, but Ben Franklin's wisdom quoted at the start of this chapter about the "weather wise and the other wise" seems to sum it all up. It is best to be informed and to have an onboard decision-making process whether or not you plan to sign up for a weather router's service. At sea, a ship with a 22-knot cruising speed can steer clear of a lot of developing weather, but the sailor plugging along at 6 knots may need to prepare to be in harm's way as well as learn how to avoid the worst weather. A satellite weather radio receiver networked to a multi-function device makes sense, and if a private weather-routing service is in the budget, so much the better. Just don't use the money for the new storm jib and trysail to pay for a weather router.

Most professional weather routers willingly admit that they base their advice on the same model information and forecast data that NOAA/NWS provides for free in voice and digital format. Their added value can be twofold: they focus on conditions in their client's vicinity, and they are often experienced small-craft mariners themselves. Their understanding of weather model shortfalls and their familiarity with the unique conditions of a specific water body can be of considerable value. Such expertise is exactly what's missing from every GRIB file.

Most manufacturers of network-capable multifunction displays offer a satellite weather service that can display forecasts, GRIB files, and other useful weather information.

PUTTING IT ALL TOGETHER: INTERPRETING YOUR WEATHER AND GAUGING OTHER FACTORS INFLUENCING WEATHER AND SEA STATE

Even when you understand what causes weather and know how to obtain forecasts, you still need to know what to do with this information—how to interpret forecasts and use what you see in your local conditions. This includes interpreting clouds and other weather signs, understanding local impacts on wind and sea conditions, and the nuances of forecasts.

Clouds and Other Weather Signs

We have seen how, as a cold-core low develops in the temperate regions of the world, it folds what was a more or less straight-line frontal boundary between warm and cold air into a twisted boundary. As the developing system moves west to east, comparatively warm, moisture-saturated air is in the vanguard. Due to the characteristic slope of a frontal zone, that moisture-laden air will be high overhead long before the warm front arrives at ground level, and it will announce its approach with a distinctive cloud cover. Looking west, a boater can often see high cirrus clouds and cirrostratus mare's tails that are made up of ice crystals and foretell the approach of severe weather.

As the warm front draws closer at ground level, it is usual to see a descending deck of gray stratus clouds. You may see a sun dog—a refraction of light that can mimic a second, usually smaller, sun-like disk—through this gray veil, often accompanied by a rainbow-like arc or halo around the true sun. Growing cloud cover and gentle rain typically follow. A warm front's benign demeanor should not be taken for granted, however; volatile air masses can sometimes spawn severe thunderstorms or even tornadoes along a warm-front boundary, though fortunately this is an infrequent exception (more likely in late spring and early summer) rather than the rule.

When a low-pressure system, approaching from the west, will pass to your north, and you are in the Northern Hemisphere, you can expect a veering easterly to settle in the southeast. It will often remain light during the approach of the warm front, as moist air and rising temperatures make the atmosphere more volatile. And as you move into the warm sector between the warm and cold fronts the veering breeze moves to the SW just ahead of the cold front passage (signified by an abrupt wind shift to the NW). (When an extratropical low passes to your south in the middle southern latitudes—the equivalent Southern Hemisphere scenario—you are likely to experience a northeast wind backing into the north and northwest as the warm front approaches.)

Warm fronts often arrive unnoticed. Occasionally, local heating provides the lift needed for cumulonimbus clouds and squally rain showers to develop; the more vigorous the heating, the higher the clouds rise, and thunderstorms with pronounced anvil tops can develop. These taper off quickly, however, with the passage of the warm front and the arrival of the warm sector.

The cold front in a well-developed low races to catch up with the warm front that precedes it. The classic baroclinic low (i.e., a middle-latitude low with its characteristic associated fronts) features a central point of lowest pressure from which two comma-like legs extend toward the south. These represent the folded warm-front and cold-front boundaries

A high layer of thickening cirrus and cirocumulus clouds align with upper-level winds and indicate the direction from which the next low-pressure system is approaching. These clouds usually precede a warm front by a day or so, and after the warm sector passes by a cold front will usher in the next high-pressure system. This west-to-east flow pattern is typical in the temperate latitudes, but a variety of twists and turns modify this pattern. (One dramatic example is the retrograde movement of a coastal low discussed earlier in this chapter.)

separating the air masses that spawned the low. At times, when a powerful high lies to the west and the temperature differential is large, a low-pressure system can grow very deep (with a central pressure less than 975 millibars) and the associated cold front can be very long; over the U.S. East Coast during the winter, the cold front associated with one of these "mega–lows" can stretch all the way to Cuba or even, occasionally, to Panama. Such turbocharged fronts can bring the dangerous conditions known in various parts of the world as bombs, southerly busters, black nor'easters, or equally descriptive titles.

As a cold front approaches, pre-front squalls can be vicious. The worst example of this scenario plays out along the north wall of the Gulf Stream in early spring and late fall, when cold continental air masses push volatile fronts quickly over warm Gulf Stream waters. Avoiding such encounters should rank right up there with avoiding tropical storms and hurricanes. Heaving-to away from the Gulf Stream— essentially parking your boat to allow a cold front to cross the Stream—is better than meeting the front in the middle of the Stream.

The good news is that the cold front's approach is usually well telegraphed, and knowing what to look for can lessen the chance of being overwhelmed. As one sails or powers through the warm sector, the wind continues to veer to the south, and by the time it reaches a southwesterly heading, meanwhile increasing in velocity and ushering in more numerous squalls, it will be clear that the cold front is close at hand and its passage may be minutes, not hours, away. The worst weather may precede the frontal passage, especially if an upper-level trough has set up in the vicinity to complicate the issue. More often, however, a cold front's fury is focused on the minutes-long passage of the cold front—i.e., the boundary between the warm and cold sectors of

EARLY INDICATIONS OF WEATHER CHANGES (NORTHERN HEMISPHERE)

Approaching warm front: high cirrus, mare's tails, wind backing or veering to south, falling barometer.

Weather as the warm front passes: increasing humidity, showers, overcast, may have scattered thunderstorms (can be volatile especially if there's an upper-level trough).

Weather to expect in the warm sector: southeast winds veering to the south and southwest, rising temperature and humidity.

Weather as a cold front passes: increasing squally winds southwest veering abruptly west and northwest; rapid drop in humidity and temperature, strong thunderstorms on frontal boundary, potentially violent weather when temperature/pressure gradient is steep.

What to expect with an occluded front: the worst weather is at the triple point where the cold front catches up with the warm front.

First sign of a new low: a falling barometer, red sky in the morning.

the low. Screaming winds that double the velocity of the sustained winds experienced an hour before, whiteout conditions caused by blown spume, spray, and torrential rain, and thunderstorms with 50,000-foot cloud tops capable of 100-knot downbursts and hail occur in the very worst of these conditions.

With the frontal passage can come an immediate shift in wind direction to the northwest at a velocity equivalent to the punishing gusts that preceded the shift. In open ocean conditions, this can be an awe-inspiring sight. In an instant the seas generated by pre-front winds are blown flat before your eyes, while sunshine dominates a fractocumulus-dominated sky. In the Gulf Steam, the spectacle can be a crescendo announcing that things are about to go from bad to worse because that northerly wind blowing directly against the north-flowing current will cause waves to stand on end. Waves weighing as much as a bulldozer can drop on a vessel caught in such conditions. This is another good reason to cross the Stream in stable weather if you possibly can.

The progression is very different when a low approaches to your south in the Northern Hemi-

A circle around the sun and the formation of a sun dog (to the right of the sun) are prime indicators of the approach of a warm front. Normally less volatile than a cold front, this boundary normally ushers in warm, moist air, and gentle rain. Infrequently, in the presence of sufficient upper-level instability, powerful thunderstorms can arise.

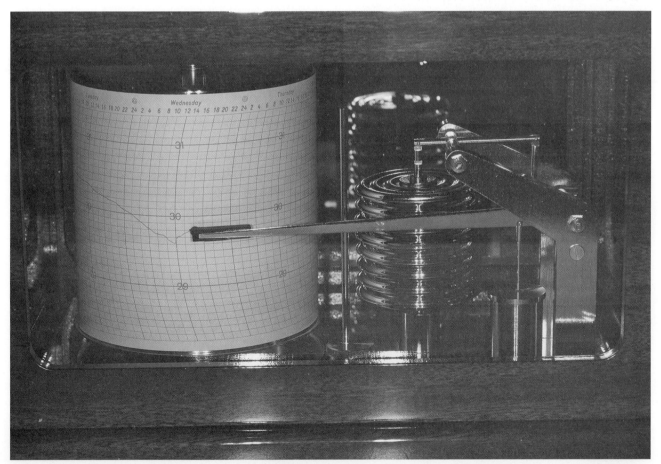

A recording barometer (barograph) tracks the approach of a low-pressure system. The more precipitous the fall, the stronger the expected gale. The tiny uptick shown for Wednesday at 1200 local time coincided with the passage of a cold front and a shift in wind direction from southwest to northwest at 45 knots.

sphere. The wind will back from the east into the northeast as the low approaches. You are likely to experience steady rain, and the cool air preceding the low may cool further as it passes south of you. You will experience no frontal passages. The wind will slowly back into the northwest and the pressure will climb as the low departs.

Low-pressure systems can settle over an area and make boating a rough-weather experience for several days in a row. Deep low-pressure systems are more common in the late fall, winter, and early spring but can occur at any time of the year. On the U.S. East Coast, pay special heed to forecasts that allude to nor'easters and alter your sailing plans accordingly. On the West Coast, keep a weather eye on wintertime Aleutian Gulf lows that can cause gale-force conditions in Southern California. Savvy Florida and Gulf Coast boaters watch every easterly wave that heads across the tropical Atlantic during the hurricane season, and Great Lakes sailors and power cruisers check the pressure gradients of the fall lows that stalk their waters starting in August.

Local Oceanographic Impacts on Wind and Sea

We voyagers tend to think of the sea as a two-dimensional construct and plot our progress with the X/Y coordinates of latitude and longitude. But we should also consider the Z axis, the vertical dimension of the sea beneath us. The configuration of a basin, for example, changes the behavior of the water it contains, defining its tidal range and period as well as current set and drift. Wave development is directly related to seafloor topography. In this section we'll look at how coastal and inshore sailors as well as ocean passage-makers can be influenced by an unseen seafloor or bottom feature. Just imagine what a midocean range of completely submerged seamounts, some nearly as tall as Mt. Everest, can do to a deep ocean current and its influence on nearby surface waters. Or envision what happens when gale-spawned seas rushing westward collide with shallow water and an outgoing tidal current over the sandy shoals off the mouth of the Delaware Bay. Benthic configurations can have a dramatic effect upon wave dynamics.

Wave Dynamics

Sailors nearing the Gulf Stream, rounding Cape Hatteras, or transiting Georges Bank are often shocked at how quickly a friendly rolling swell changes into a vessel-threatening seaway. In the first instance the root cause is a wave train in opposition with a vigorous current; in the latter two instances, a shoaling seafloor is to blame.

But we should begin where waves begin, at the air/ocean interface. Energy is transferred from the atmosphere to the sea surface by wind, and partially because water cannot be compressed, the energy radiates efficiently away from the source, organizing into geometrically ordered swells. This is similar to what happens when a large rock or calving iceberg enters the sea. The initial chaotic splash indicates potential energy becoming kinetic, but thanks to gravity, surface tension, and the viscosity of water, this kinetic energy is quickly reshaped into organized waves moving away from the initial source. The bigger the rock, iceberg, or wind, the larger the swell. In the wind-driven energy transfer, there's a frictional relationship between air and water, and fluid dynamic principles prevail: the stronger the wind, the longer the fetch, and the greater the time duration, the larger the waves. Mariners need to keep in mind that storm-created waves are shaped not just by the nearby weather event, but also the swell influence from more distant gales.

In deep water away from the storm source, the energy becomes mostly benign, long swells with modestly sloping wave faces. The wave energy in a rolling swell passes through the water column in an almost purely oscillatory manner. As a wave moves past, the water particles themselves move up and down in a vertical circle and wind up almost precisely where they were before the wave arrived. There is almost no net forward movement of water, and a cork floating on the surface would bob but remain in the same location. (The true picture is a little more complicated, of course. In reality, the lead wave in a set will dissipate while another is formed at the trailing end of the set.) As mentioned above, time, distance, and opposing wind and wave energy all affect ocean swells.

A wave train in deep water is analogous to wave energy moving down the string of a musical instrument; the vibration is a manifestation of energy transfer, but the string remains in place. As long as the water depth remains hundreds or better yet thousands of feet deep and there's no influence from a current or strong breeze moving in the opposite direction, the swell retains an oscillatory nature (not steepening into a breaking wave) and will appear to roll on smoothly. A 15- or 20-foot ocean swell with a long period can be gentle enough to pose little threat. Those who have made the downwind run from the U.S. West Coast to Hawaii probably recall such conditions.

As long as the swells travel over the open ocean's abyssal plain—a monotonously flat seabed devoid of shoals, seamounts, and contravening landmasses—they continue to behave as sinusoidal deepwater waves. But the deep-looping oscillations in a fast-moving long-period swell begin to feel the frictional drag of a shoaling bottom at the outer edges of the continental shelf, when the water is still hundreds of feet deep, and the result is a slowing of wave speed, an elongation of the ocscillations into unstable ellipsoids, and a corresponding heightening and steepening of the seas. As the steeper faces of the once fast-moving ocean swells move toward even shallower water, their speed slows further, and trailing waves crowd the slower, destabilized waves ahead of them. This confluence of energy creates even larger waves. Finally, gravity transforms the steep, overcurling swell into a breaking wave. The highest waves—those magnified to the greatest extent by the amplitude harmonics of overtaking waves or crossing seas from a different wave train—break on the reefs and off-lying sandbars farthest offshore, and when they do, tens of thousands of gallons of water, weighing more than 8 pounds per gallon, plummet downward from the breaking crests at speeds that can exceed 40 knots. In a worst-case scenario that breaking sea can land on the deck of a sailboat caught in the wrong place at the wrong time, and a sailor on such a boat will not be consoled to think that he has just witnessed a transformation of energy of oscillation into the kinetic energy of moving mass.

Breaking Seas. Energy of translation is the kinetic energy of water in linear motion—as opposed to the oscillatory motion of gentle swells. It can be seen even when small wavelets crowd into each other as the wind velocity increases. Whitecaps form and dissipate as they splash down the faces of the unstable waves formed by a building breeze. The phenomenon is supersized in the avalanche-like conditions created by large breaking waves. In Beaufort sea states over Force 5 (about 20 knots—see page 285), there's a very noticeable combination of breaking wave faces and oscillatory rolling swells. The more predominant the energy of translation becomes, the more dangerous the sea state. Wave theories vary somewhat, but all show a relationship among three key factors: wave height, H (the vertical distance between trough and crest); wave length, L (the horizontal distance between successive crests); and wave period, T (the time in seconds between the passage of one crest and the passage of the next). The ratio of wave height to wave length is the primary measure of steepness, and when a wave gets steeper than 1:7—or said another way, when its crest angle becomes less than 120 degrees—it will become unstable and start to break.

Breaking seas may also result when an ocean swell's lengthy passage interacts with wave energy from another storm system. When a crest in one wave train meets a trough in another, the two par-

tially cancel one another. But when two crests converge, the result is additive. The overall result is a chaotic sea in which some swells nearly disappear while others grow mountainous in size.

Finally, big waves may break in deep water when slowed and steepened by an opposing current. It has been estimated that a 1-knot opposing current doubles the height of a wave, and this effect is magnified further by stronger currents. Given that the Gulf

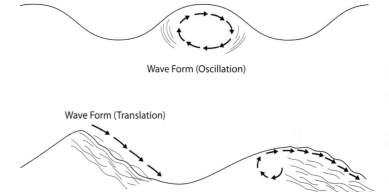

Wave Form (Oscillation)

Wave Form (Translation)

Breaking Crests

When waves become steep enough to break, the benign energy of oscillation is transformed into the violent kinetic energy of moving mass.

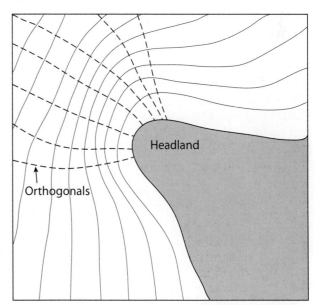

Headland

Orthogonals

Wave energy is refracted toward a headland—a good reason why bluewater sailors give a wide berth to geographic locations that begin with the word "Cape." The dashed lines are orthogonals, or wave rays, crossing each crest at a 90-degree angle. The ratio of the distance between two adjacent orthogonals offshore to the corresponding distance at the beach is a measure of the degree to which wave energy is focused on a headland or other shore feature.

SHIP KILLER WAVES

In the late 1990s a cruise ship in the North Atlantic east of Cape Cod (nearing Georges Bank) encountered a rogue wave of 90 feet associated with a fairly run-of-the-mill storm of tropical origin. The huge sea would not have been predicted by the storm's central pressure alone, but when its track and rate of advance were added to the equation, the reason for huge waves became clearer. A Category 1 hurricane had dissipated, turning into an extratropical low complete with a cold core and a frontal boundary weather system. Its northerly rate of advance as it turned post-tropical was an extraordinary 35 knots, and its course and speed had kept it resonant with its wave train. The net result was much more energy being imposed upon the swell moving away from the storm, and just as the cruise ship was making her way toward the abruptly shoaling Georges Bank, the swells and the storm arrived together. Massive waves that had been unfettered by the friction of a shallow bottom now stood on end as they piled up on the steeply rising seabed. Such bottom conditions focus wave energy as a lens focuses light. When a mariner faces heavy-weather decision making, avoiding the worst sea conditions becomes paramount; as discussed on page 299, in a tropical storm, deep water and the "navigable-quadrant rule" (the left-hand quadrant in the Northern Hemisphere) are first considerations.

Breaking surf caused by shoaling water is a good example of the oscillatory energy in an ocean swell being transformed into water cascading shoreward in a wave of translation. In 2012, a Sydney 38 in the Farallones Race and a Hunter 376 in the Ensenada Race navigated into the surf zones of offshore islands and were ravaged by the concentrated wave energy unleashed when ocean swells steepen, refract, and break. In the two incidents together, nine crewmembers were lost. A rocky lee shore and a large swell send experienced mariners on a quest for sea room.

Stream flows at speeds up to 4 knots or more, it's little wonder that breaking seas kick up when a strong northerly opposes the Stream.

Wave Refraction. Light is refracted, or bent, as it passes through a concave or convex piece of glass, and when the energy converges on a focal point, there's increased light and heat caused by the increased photon density. Something similar happens when a swell approaches a jutting headland with an associated offshore reef structure. The portion of a swell crest approaching the headland first slows down and steepens due to the frictional effects of the rising bottom. Meanwhile, off to the right and left, the portions of the crest still in deeper water do not slow down and thus outrace the middle portion. This causes the "wings" of the swell crest to bend in toward the headland and in this way focus the energy on the headland.

Wave dynamics in shoal water have been well described by oceanographer Willard Bascomb in his 1964 classic *Waves and Beaches,* a must-read for all serious cruisers coastal sailing or headed for distant landfalls. One of its best explanations is how an orthogonal (also called a wave ray—a curve drawn on a wave diagram so as to cross each successive wave crest perpendicularly) can be used to depict a wave train's energy dispersal or concentration as it approaches a coastline. When waves bend, or refract, toward a prominent headland, the orthogonals converge toward shore, as shown in the illustration on page 309. Dividing the distance between adjacent orthogonals in deep water by the corresponding distance at the beach gives you the refraction coefficient; the higher the coefficient, the more the wave energy is focused. The point of greatest focus of the orthogonals is where the largest waves and the most dangerous plunging breakers will occur. Reefs lying just off such headlands deserve to be given a wide berth. The Potato Patch off the mouth of San Francisco Bay is just such a situation; swells passing over deep submarine canyons to seaward approach the rocky headlands, and the first shallow spot to intrude on the energy flow is this offshore cluster of reefs covered by as little as 24 feet of water. In light air and flat seas, a fair-weather shortcut nips inside the Potato Patch, but when the swell is up it can be a dangerous gamble to sail there.

Effects of Seabed Topography

Along the U.S. West Coast, submarine canyons over a thousand feet deep come almost to the beach in some areas, and jagged headlands like Point Conception jut seaward. This abrupt sea/land interface concentrates wave energy almost as effectively as the Hawaiian islands, which are actually the tips of volcanic seamounts. These coastlines offer very little wave abatement and do even less to slow down the shoreward progress of powerful ocean swells. In seconds, these huge mounds of dense blue water morph into towering giants as plunging breakers. Big-wave surfers speak with reverence about the power of thick, fast-moving Hawaiian waves or the abundance of energy found in a Northern California winter swell.

The East Coast and its adjacent seafloor are much older geologically than the West Coast, and like the rounded, eroded, worn-down mountains of the East, the seabed has less precipitous peaks and valleys. The East Coast is rimmed by a continental shelf 100 to 200 miles wide—a sandy aggregate of glacial moraine and riverine sediment that has built its way out toward the edge of the abyssal plane or deep oceanic realm—and the submarine canyons are a hundred miles offshore. The wide coastal zone of relatively shallow water causes waves to slow down much farther at sea, dissipating much of their potential energy. Unfortunately, this coastal zone within the 10-fathom depth contour can turn into a tempest when a gale stirs the waters. Building seas become highly unstable, and shallow water increases the likelihood of encountering a breaking crest. Wise mariners seek deep ocean water when they are unable to find a safe harbor.

Currents

The Gulf Stream emanates from the North Equatorial Current and runs northward from the Florida Straits along the U.S. East Coast and then easterly across the North Atlantic. As discussed elsewhere in this book, it is one of the major ocean currents in the world and has a huge impact on local weather systems. One of the reasons that this part of the Atlantic

Cutting corners too closely when a big swell is running can claim a terrible toll. The crew of Low Speed Chase *passed over shoal water as they rounded the Farallones Islands and were caught by a large breaking wave that capsized the boat, killed five of the crew, and left all sailors to ponder the need for sea room. (Courtesy Sophie Webb)*

has such a history of savage weather is the confluence of cold and warm air masses meeting just offshore in proximity with the warm water of the Gulf Stream. Hot, moist tropical air from the south is often dragged up the coast in warm fronts associated with rapidly deepening lows, and when dense Canadian cold air forces this warm air aloft, convective activity becomes eruptive, spawning thunderstorms with 50,000-foot cloud tops. Not only does the north wall of the Stream constitute a unique physical boundary between the warm Gulf Stream and cooler inshore and Labrador Current waters, but the heat it radiates also boosts the volatility of warm, moist tropical air and the intruding cold Canadian air associated with each cold front. Satellite imagery reveals towering cumulonimbus buildups along the edge of the gyre and pre-front squalls of epic proportions.

Things get even trickier when a low passes just south of a vessel in the Gulf Stream. The vessel encounters northeast winds, and if the gale or storm has been blowing for a day or two, the resulting seas are mountainous. Their size would be problematic in any event, but the real challenge comes from the opposing current, which steepens the wave faces and makes them dynamically unstable, resulting in dangerous plunging breakers. The prudent mariner

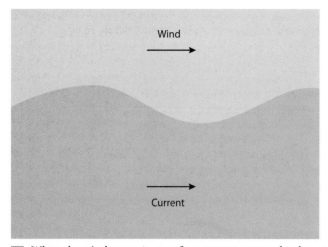
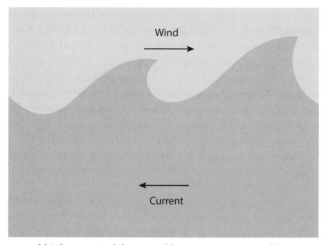

When the wind opposes a surface current, waves develop steeper and higher vertical faces and become more unstable. Breaking crests are more numerous, and the threat of capsize greatly increases

avoids entering the Gulf Stream when such conditions are predicted.

The same phenomenon can occur elsewhere around the globe where strong currents are present—whether an ocean current or tidal current. At sea, wind against the current, especially near a continental shelf, can double the size of the waves and cause them to steepen and become much more dangerous. A strong northerly in the Gulf Stream or when crossing Africa's Agulhas Current is something to avoid—if not, it's an experience one never forgets.

Currents and the Sea Floor. Littoral currents are a wind- and wave-driven sand transport system that scours every coastline. Along the New South Wales coast of Australia, for example, shallow water and a tenacious downcoast current can cause northbound sailors to take note of the relationship between sea and seabed. In this region, the friction between moving water and a shallow bottom diminishes the drift. The sandy bottom also weakens the current by sapping energy as tons of sediment are lifted and carried down the coast. Savvy Aussie sailors take advantage of this region of diminished current and sail with "one foot on the beach." Doing so overnight is far too anxiety provoking for most cruisers headed north toward the Great Barrier Reef, however, and a tack offshore with a dawn return toward shallower water seems to make sense. At least that's what I thought some years ago during a passage from Sydney to the Great Barrier Reef. At dusk we headed offshore, beating into a headwind and a significant downcoast current. Staying clear of land in the darkness and returning on the opposite tack the next morning, I was dismayed to see the same lighthouse that we had bid farewell to the previous evening. The name of the headland was Tacking Point; once again Aussie humor prevailed,

and "one foot on the beach" sailing to stay out of the current was the lesson learned.

Today I cope with such situations—whether in Australia, Baja, or just off the New Jersey coast—by short tacking in shallower water with appropriate caution applied to good navigation and a perpetual stare at the depthsounder. Another alternative is to motorsail to weather, staying well inshore and capitalizing on the lighter breezes of early morning. Or you can anchor or visit a new port and wait for a favorable wind—often the cruiser's most delightful prerogative.

Shoals and Inlets

In New England and the Middle Atlantic region, gales mean easterly winds, and many harbor entrances take on a dangerous lee shore demeanor. Waves pile into the coast, causing gutter rips that move sand out to offshore sandbars that are constantly migrating in much the same manner as barrier islands themselves are moved. In an easterly wind the entrances to shallow, sandbar-choked small-craft harbors along this stretch of coast can look like a "ride the wild surf" movie. Sailboats attempting to negotiate these channels are in danger of being spun broadside and in really bad weather can be swamped by breaking seas. The condition is exacerbated by strong shifting winds that steepen already unstable wave faces.

It makes sense to keep careful track of soundings and bottom contours, plot your course on a large-scale chart, and recognize the risk associated with bad weather and breaking seas. Those who cruise the skinny waters of Delmarva and the sand shoals of coastal North and South Carolina should pay special heed to chart updating. Many software programs and apps include free chart updates, and for chartplotters chip updates are often available at reduced price. (See Chapter 8 for more information on digital NOAA charts.)

All navigators learn to pay close attention to coastline features, but experienced voyagers also track bottom contours, soundings, and other benthic features, noting their likely effects on sea state and factoring this into surface and 500 mb weather forecasts. The resultant picture of likely sea-state dynamics is as complete as a sailor can manage. The process blends the sciences of the oceanographer and the meteorologist with the art of seamanship.

Global Weather

Just as American sailors need to understand the weather patterns around North America and the causes of changes in the weather, cruisers elsewhere around the globe should study local weather patterns and possibilities. Following are just a few general examples of other global weather patterns.

Easterly trade winds persist for a good part of the year on either side of the equator in every ocean. They tend to blow a consistent 10 to 20 knots and give rise to equatorial currents that can boost a vessel's daily westerly progress by 20 to 30 miles. The eastern basin trade winds are lighter in all oceans, while those sailing the Caribbean, the western Pacific, and the east side of Africa often find "enhanced trades" (winds over 20 knots) not that uncommon.

The Med is a feast or famine for sailors who prefer to make passages under sail. Local winds coming off the desert of Africa or from higher snow-clad mountains in Europe often play havoc as the crew scurries to take in sail. The best way to avoid being surprised is to read local cruising guides and discern how the northerlies (the tramontana winds of Spain, the mistral of France, and the grigal of Greece) blow during winter and the southerly Sahara sand-carrying sirocco can dust those anchored in France. There's even an easterly levanter that scours mountain passes and blows across the straits of Gibraltar causing rough seas in the western Med. The fickle katabatic meltemi wind of Greece and Turkey slams down from mountain peaks and can easily reach gale force without a storm in sight.

High-latitude sailing is energized by the Roaring Forties and Furious Fifties, a region in the Southern Ocean where waves literally circle the globe ahead of huge low pressure cells. Ice, short days in winter, and snow squalls that blow sideways keep the region's population low and yachts transiting the region to a minimum. *(continued page 317)*

■ *Cape Horn on a moody gray day. The only certainty in these latitudes is that the status quo of weather and wind will not last long.*

WEATHER CASE STUDY: THE *FLYING COLOURS* INCIDENT

The foundering of *Flying Colours*—and the loss of three other vessels in the same storm—southeast of Cape Hatteras in the spring of 2007 provides a classic lesson in how volatile middle-latitude spring and fall weather can be. We can analyze this incident in hindsight to better understand the weather concepts and realities we have been discussing.

As mentioned throughout this chapter, early spring and late fall weather is highly volatile in the middle latitudes. During seasonal changes, the mid-level streamlines, especially the strong-wind belt, migrate north and south. During the Northern Hemisphere summer, the flow is centered at about 50 degrees north latitude, while in winter it can shift as far south as 30 degrees north in El Niño years. In spring and fall, the main axis is centered around 40 degrees north, just where and when many cruisers are considering a passage north or south between the Caribbean and the U.S.

For such passages, one wise precaution is never to put to sea when a tropical storm or hurricane is south of your latitude. Another is to beware of the double-barreled impact of a deepening surface low sliding off the coast of Cape Hatteras when the lower branch of a split jet stream is near the same latitude, as described earlier. And the third caution is to respect the venomous nature of the north wall of the Gulf Stream and its ability to boost convective activity by injecting warm, moist air into already-unstable air masses. Any

mariner making a spring or fall sprint between the U.S. East Coast and the Caribbean needs to watch for and guard against these weather-making elements. A crewmember of an Island Packet 38 was lost in late October 2011 when the NARC Rally encountered the unstable boundary between a tropical system and a temperate air mass, turbocharged by the Gulf Stream. But nothing more clearly demonstrates the dangers of this volatile weather brew than the tragedy of the *Flying Colours*.

In May 2007, the crew of *Flying Colours,* a Hood Little Harbor 54, was making a transit from the Caribbean to the vessel's home port in Annapolis, Maryland. The four on board included Trey Topping, the vessel's professional skipper, another licensed captain, and two others who had also worked in the Caribbean charter trade. On May 3, a high-pressure system was moving southeastward from the Great Lakes into New England, and a weak frontal boundary extended west to east off the Carolina coast. A new low-pressure system was forecast to develop on this frontal boundary, but the Ocean Prediction Center indicated that it would dissipate over the next 24 hours as it moved east.

The May 4 forecast retained the weak stationary frontal boundary off the Carolina coast and introduced a new, very weak low (1014 mb) moving eastward out of the area. The high by this time was centered off the mid-Atlantic states, and a modest pressure gradient dominated the region. In a nutshell, there was not

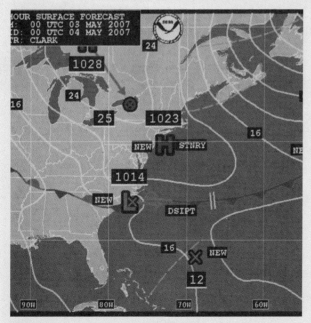

This weather fax of the OPC's 24-hour surface forecast for May 4, 2007, showed a benign weather pattern off the U.S. East Coast. A new low-pressure system off the Carolina coast was expected to dissipate as it moved offshore. (NWS/NCEP)

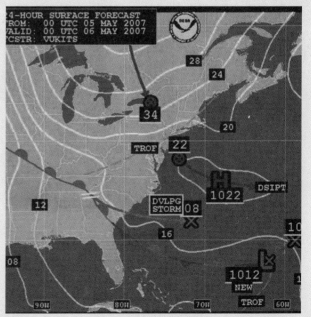

This 24-hour surface forecast—issued 48 hours after the former one—warned of a developing storm that was forecast to move east. (NWS/NCEP)

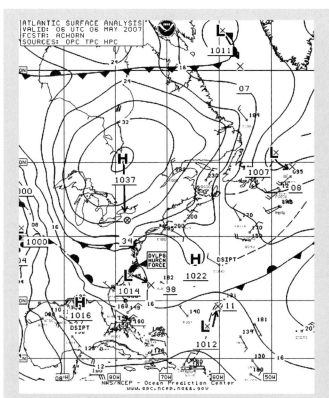

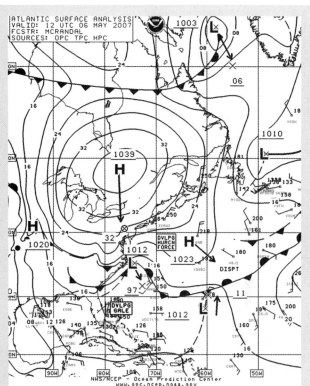

■ *This May 6 surface analysis from OPC shows that heavy weather has become even worse as three atmospheric instigators coincide. High pressure to the north has steepened the pressure gradient on the deepening coastal low. An upper-level cutoff low (not visible in this surface analysis) has stopped the eastward movement of the system. A surface analysis is not a forecast; it is a representation of what is actually happening at the time and date indicated. (NWS/NCEP)*

■ *This surface analysis issued 6 hours later shows that the rapidly deepening low, the approaching high-pressure ridge, and the Gulf Stream's proximity are creating a veritable weather nightmare. Of the four yachts that issued distress signals off Cape Hatteras, two were driven ashore and their crews rescued by the U.S. Coast Guard, and one was capsized and sunk (its crew also rescued by the USCG). Unfortunately, the 54-foot* Flying Colours *was caught in the center of the storm and disappeared along with its four-member crew. (NWS/NCEP)*

much to make a mariner apprehensive. But seasoned sailors understand that the weather in this region is volatile in early spring and that Cape Hatteras is notorious for its fickle mood shifts. Recall also the influence of the Gulf Stream as described earlier.

On May 5, the OPC reset the stage by placing in its 24-hour surface forecast a small rectangle between the dissipating high-pressure system off the mid-Atlantic states and the pesky frontal boundary now sliding southward into Georgia and off toward the southeast. In the rectangle was printed DVLPG STORM, one of the most unwelcome warnings a sailor can imagine.

On May 6, the 24-hour surface analysis changed the rectangular box warning to HURCN FORCE, leaving no doubt that bad had gone to worse and that anyone caught in the vicinity was in for trouble. This is what forecasters call extratropical cyclogenesis, meaning the development of a middle-latitude (i.e., extra-

tropical) storm with potentially hurricane-force winds. The key culprits were a mid- to upper-level cutoff low, which did not show up on surface charts, and a rapidly building high-pressure system to the north. Some private weather routers recognized as early as May 5 the implications of the cutoff low and how it would interact with the massive 1034-millibar high moving into New England waters, and they began telling their clients to alter course and stay away from the area. The wind field of the counterclockwise-rotating low would be bolstered by the clockwise rotation around the high to the north, and anyone caught in the resulting nor'easter would be in big trouble.

The forecast was vindicated on May 6 and 7. An offshore buoy well away from the worst of the storm reported 65-knot winds and 39-foot seas. *Flying Colours,* the well-built, well-maintained Hood Little Harbor sailed by Trey Topping and his crew, was caught in a very bad part of (continued next page)

WEATHER CASE STUDY, CONTINUED

This 24-hour surface forecast—issued 12 hours prior to the surface analysis immediately previous—predicts that the low will deepen even further, from 1012 to 1002 millibars, and winds of storm and hurricane force will engulf the region from Cape Hatteras east to 70 degrees west longitude, some 300 miles offshore. And the worst of the weather will be encountered in enraged Gulf Stream seas. (NWS/NCEP)

the ocean, and early in the morning of May 7, the Coast Guard received an EPIRB distress signal from the vessel. *Flying Colours* was not the only vessel sending distress signals—early on May 7, the U.S. Coast Guard had their hands full with EPIRB signals from vessels across hundreds of miles of storm-swept ocean. A container ship outbound from Savannah, Georgia, en route to Norfolk, Virginia, lost 21 containers in the rapidly growing seas. The delivery crew of the 67-foot alloy cutter *Illusion* was only about 50 miles from the EPIRB signal sent by *Flying Colours*. The crew of *Illusion* was spotted by a C-130 and rescued by a Coast Guard HH-60 helicopter. Closer to the coast, a crew was plucked from a vessel in vicious seas off Frying Pan Shoals. The first distress signal, however, had been issued by an EPIRB the Coast Guard thought was aboard the *Lou Pantai*, although the distressed vessel that actually sent the signal, which was sinking 225 miles southeast of Cape Hatteras, was actually the *Sean Seamour II*.

Sean Seamour II owner Jean Pierre De Lutz and his crew had departed Saint Johns River, Florida, on May 2 aboard a well-equipped Beneteau Oceanis 44 and were headed across the Atlantic. One of the communi-

cations upgrades on the vessel was an Iridium satellite phone linked to a computer with MaxSea software. Chopper and OCENS software were also loaded in order to decode weather maps and GRIB files. The skipper had been checking weather patterns since April 25 and did not notice any alarming change in the GRIB data until May 5, when they were approximately 200 miles along their route. The skipper chose to maintain his north-northeast heading, and that fateful decision would put him in a battle for survival two days later.

On May 7, *Sean Seamour II* was 217 miles east of Cape Hatteras, running before mountainous seas with a scrap of inner forestaysail unfurled and a drogue towed astern. As the seas grew larger and more unstable, the vessel was violently driven down by breaking crests. At 0245 hours, a severe knockdown occurred, the drogue parted, and the vessel no longer responded to steering. Less than 10 minutes later the sloop was capsized by an even larger breaking sea, dismasted, and severely damaged. The water in the cabin was up to the knees of the crew, and the life raft was over the side and tangled in the rigging.

To make matters even worse, the ACR GPIRB (an emergency position-indicating radiobeacon, or EPIRB, with a GPS chip) flashed for a short period and then seemingly ran out of battery power and stopped flashing. Fortunately, the owner had brought along a second EPIRB that had belonged to his prior boat, *Lou Pantai*, which apparently had been activated when it was torn from its mount inside the hard dodger when *Sean Seamour II* was first knocked down. The crew knew they were in dire straits and were unable to keep up with water entering the sinking vessel. Hoping to hold off abandoning ship until dawn, they feverishly pumped and bailed, but another breaking wave added 18 inches more water to the downflooding disaster.

At about 0520, they began the process of abandoning ship. They freed the raft from the tangle of standing rigging, which had damaged the raft's canopy, and clambered into it, watching the Beneteau fill with water and soon sink. The raft was capsized and rolled but was righted by the crew. Then the effects of hypothermia began to set in. Between 0600 and 0700, the crew spotted a fixed-wing aircraft, and around 0830, a USCG HH-60 helicopter reached them and rescued all three on board the raft.

During this same period, the crew of *Flying Colours* were also fighting for their lives. Caught in the maw of fierce weather, their larger, more ruggedly built Hood Little Harbor apparently also became a victim of the wind and waves. The rescue coordination center began receiving EPIRB position reports at 0330 on the morning of May 7, but the signals ended abruptly at 0700. At about 0930, a C-130 reached the last known position of *Flying Colours,* initiated a search pattern, and dropped a buoy to track the current. The active sea-and-air search continued until May 12, but no trace of the missing vessel or the crew was ever sighted.

Such tragedies often leave us pondering, but one thing the crew of *Sean Seamour II* was certain of was that the old EPIRB the owner had brought along as a backup saved their lives. The cause of the signal failure in *Sean Seamour II*'s primary GPIRB may yet be discovered, but why the position reports from *Flying Colours* stopped will probably never be known.

The *Flying Colours* incident leaves more questions than answers. The spotty EPIRB transmissions from *Flying Colours* placed the boat near the north wall of the Gulf Stream and in the current's influence when the storm overwhelmed it. No one knows what decision-making process caused the crew to sail into the heart of the rapidly intensifying storm. Did they have a communications system failure that left them unable to receive weather forecasts? Had an engine problem rendered them unable to make a motorsailing sprint to Beaufort during the two days of calm weather preceding the storm? The answers to these and other questions remain a mystery, but this tragedy underscores the risks of rounding Cape Hatteras and other notorious capes worldwide that are confluences of wind, wave, and weather.

Not only was the storm unusually intense, but it was unusual in other respects as well. Instead of behaving like a normal, rapidly developing coastal low and speeding off to the northeast dragging its attendant cold front across the region, this deepening springtime low moved southeastward in its fledgling phase, and on May 7—while at its worst—it made an abrupt 90-degree course change to head southwest (toward *Flying Colours*), giving it what is termed a retrograde track. On May 8 it veered even more westward, and by May 9 it was headed northwest. Instead of dissipating normally, the low shed its cold front on May 9 and replaced its cold core with warm air, developing a more symmetrical cross section and the vertical profile of a tropical storm. This prompted the National Hurri-

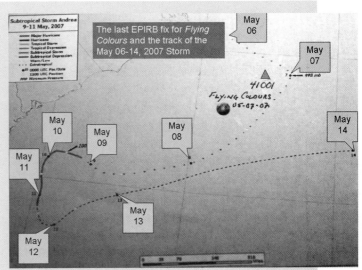

Note the retrograde movement of the storm to the west-southwest between May 7 and May 12 and its un-usual morphing into a tropical storm on May 9 and 10. The pressure at the center was 998 mb at 0000 UTC May 7, which was 7 p.m. on May 6 for boats off the U.S. East Coast. The EPIRB signal from Flying Colours was activated at the position shown 8½ hours later, at which point the storm had moved southwest and was almost on top of the boat.

cane Center to open shop a month early and name the storm Andrea, crowning it the first tropical storm of the season—although there was some grumbling among weather agencies as to whether or not this transition from a cold-core low to a warm-core tropical storm (i.e., *baroclinic* to *barotropic*) was quite that complete. (The Ocean Prediction Center handles forecasts for extratropical cold-core lows, but the National Hurricane Center handles tropical and subtropical warm-core storms.)

Turning south on May 10, the storm skirted the Georgia and Florida coastline for two days before turning eastward and leaving the region as, once again, an extratropical weather system. Coastal residents and structures were mostly spared.

The pot of gold at the end of the ordeal is the Antarctic Peninsula, a transition zone with a summer hint of green and a few days when 50-degree temperatures thaw a little ice. Good weather is fleeting, the forecasts are often inaccurate, and risk factors are elevated. Summer in the Arctic is a little less brutal, but a cruise to these waters is an expedition, and one should read about what happened to Shackleton and his crew before even pondering such a voyage.

INTERPRETING FORECAST DATA

By now you should see weather should never be treated lightly—and also that it can be unpredictable and not always follow the forecast. Be cautious and never assume the best, and study weather patterns well before heading out to sea. Even then, stay cautious with how you interpret forecasts.

THE DANGER OF CUTOFF LOWS

The rescue of the crew from *Sean Seamour II* and the tragic loss of *Flying Colours* illustrate several salient points. The first is that a storm at sea can claim even well-found yachts with experienced hands. Another is how important it is to make use of as much weather information as possible and to obtain updates at least daily. Finally, in the case of the May 7 storm, long-range forecasts and model data didn't come into agreement until May 5, and even when the storm's severity was recognized, its retrograde motion and transition into a tropical storm were completely unanticipated.

The bottom line is that cutoff lows are a significant threat, and their development needs to be closely monitored. Looking at surface forecasts right up to May 5 would not have alerted a crew to the imminent danger ahead. The best early warning came from the upper-level, 500 mb behavior of the atmosphere and model predictions of how an upper-level low and the massive high-pressure system to the north would affect the surface low. A close read—a 2-day warning of a very bad storm but not a perfect picture of what lay ahead—reveals there was enough evidence to cause a prudent skipper with the May 5 forecast in hand to head for a safe haven, or at least get clear of the Gulf Stream's influence.

Even when you have the best data-reception capabilities and hired professional guidance, there remains a significant risk of encountering bad weather. The spring of 2007 had been cold and stormy in the mid-Atlantic region, and the volatile start to May was more typical of early April than mid-spring. Atmospheric volatility also increases in areas such as Cape Hatteras, where weather systems and the Gulf Stream meet. An apex of the infamous Bermuda Triangle, this part of the ocean has a deservedly dangerous reputation—but more due to weather extremes than mystical legends.

Getting and Using Forecast Data

A major goal for sailors is to better understand the material generated by the OPC, and as mentioned at the start of this chapter, one of the best ways to improve your skills is to seek confirmation of your weather chart reading. It can be as simple as downloading a set of charts and imagining the weather coming. Then compare your forecast with the Weather Channel forecast. Study weather graphics online to recognize the value of the 24-, 48-, and 96-hour surface forecasts and their associated wind/wave maps. Notice the direct correlation between isobar gradients and the size of the seas that are generated. The tighter or steeper the gradient, the more feathers on the wind arrows and the larger the sea state number. Your skills will grow from such basic observations to a more detailed familiarity as you practice reading these graphic forecasts during your shoreside life. In a way, all this is like installing radar on your boat. Hooking up the unit is only the start, and if you wait until you're in zero visibility to turn it on, you'll probably not gain much benefit from it. But if you practice when it's clear and can confirm what you see on the screen, you'll make better use of the equipment when the time arrives to use it in earnest. The same holds true for the weather information provided by OPC; the more familiar you become with how charts compare with actual weather, the better you'll be able to interpret the new chart scrolling out of the weather fax machine.

During many of my early voyages I looked at the sky and wished I had a large-scale weather map perspective of what an approaching cold front looked like and how fast it was moving. Today, we can print out graphic forecasts and compare the squiggly lines with the cloud cover and trends indicated by the barometer. Add to this the wind speed and direction as well as the sea state and ocean swell dynamics, and you can get a really good feel for the implications of a weather chart. It's a lot like looking at a large-scale harbor chart of a new landfall and feeling as if you already know what the anchorage looks like.

What to Do with Your Forecasts

A forecast means different things to different crews. The gale that a cruising couple wants to avoid at all costs can be just what the crew of an 80-foot transatlantic record breaker is looking for. The first requirement for making optimal use of forecast information is a working understanding of the sea conditions generated by a given weather system and what that means for your vessel and crew.

Some years back I was aboard a 60-foot sloop enjoying the final day of a three-week springtime transatlantic passage to England. We had been tormented by two gales and a storm that hammered us with relentless easterlies, and the prospect of landfall was welcome. As the Lizard came into view, our young-eyed helmsman saw something in the distance: a small speck that looked initially like a rock awash in an angry sea. But as we drew closer, the rock turned out to be a 28-foot pilot cutter slogging upwind with a hardy British crew awash in the cockpit. What to us was a miserable day at sea was a normal sailing day to these voyagers from the storm-tossed Hebrides. Be aware of your crew's comfort threshold.

You should also be aware, of course, of how much punishment your boat can handle and in what weather conditions you're likely to see wind and sea that challenge the boat's survival. This is a matter of sea sense, the point where the meteorologist's expertise leaves off and the sailor's skill takes over. During the transatlantic crossing mentioned above, we received weather guidance from the U.S. Navy, and at one point the forecaster advised us to head 2 degrees (120 nautical miles) south to get away from the 50-knot blow that was assaulting us. The problem was that the wind was out of the south, and the prospect of beating into 50 knots of wind was a lot less appealing than reaching under storm sails and making 9 knots in the direction we wanted to go. An aircraft carrier and a 60-foot sloop have different needs and capabilities when it comes to making way to windward, obviously. We held our course and safely reached on toward our destination.

Picking the best time of year to make a passage remains a sailor's best bet. This is usually summer in temperate parts of the world. But hurricane activity usually ramps up in August and September, and finding your boat in the crosshairs of even a tropical storm can do more than dampen enthusiasm.

As mentioned earlier, the weather window approach to passagemaking can give you a few good days to clear the shoals, cross the Stream, and gain sea room, but if your destination lies a couple thousand miles away and "safety valve" landfalls are few and far between, you and your crew need to be ready to handle heavy weather if and when the need arises. Regardless of your weather router, a 6-knot sailboat will have a hard time avoiding a big low or tropical storm moving at 25 knots. Knowing what lies ahead helps you prepare for the worst. The next chapter discusses how to handle heavy weather.

11

HANDLING HEAVY WEATHER

During the squally 1982 Bermuda Race, I learned a worthwhile lesson in how to press on in heavy weather—something that isn't a must-have tactic in every cruising sailor's bag of tricks. Sailing aboard the 47-foot yawl *Puffin* (introduced in Chapter 1), I experienced firsthand the way Rod Stephens liked to handle vicious Gulf Stream squalls. Each of these hot-water turbocharged thunderstorms packed a short-lived 50-knot punch, and in order to cope with the lighter air that immediately followed, Rod pressed on

Training a crew to handle a gale at sea begins with implementing the "hand, reef, and steer" tradition. The "hand" part includes learning how to move around the vessel safely in a seaway, which includes clipping in a harness tether and watching for breaking waves. The "reef" portion involves fine-tuning the sail plan to match the demands of wind and sea. Learning how to make the transition from a deep reef to a storm trysail is an important rite of passage. And the "steer" portion of the apprenticeship builds the necessary skills to keep the boat on track, avoid a broach, and allow the off-watch to get some vital sleep.

through the gusty squalls without reducing sail at all. As each violent encounter occurred, he had me steer the well-built yawl on a beam reach and signaled trimmers to ease sheets until the flattened main mizzen and high-cut number 2 genoa were on the verge of flogging. Trimmed to spill most of the wind, the big yawl still sprinted off like a scared cat. Because of the acceleration, the apparent wind shifted forward and the sails hinted at flogging, signaling me to bear off a bit and keep the wind on the beam.

We sailed on a razor's edge: too much trim threatened a knockdown and too little violently flogged the sails. When these 15-minute tempests subsided, leaving light air in their wake, we hauled in the sheets and lost no time continuing our sprint to Bermuda.

When the other watch crew tried the same tactic, however, someone failed to ease the mizzensheet and the boat spun up into the wind, allowing storm-force wind to raise havoc with the flogging sails. A chaotic fire drill ensued, and by the time the genoa and mizzen were down and the yawl was again under control, the wind had dropped to 10 knots.

When cruising with my wife, Lenore, aboard our sloop *Wind Shadow*, we use an alternate approach. A shorthanded crew can't afford such an on-the-edge response to Gulf Stream squalls. Instead, we put a reef or two in the mainsail and set a small, high-cut staysail before a squall hits. Then, in the light air between squalls, we hoist (or unfurl) a larger headsail that we're always ready to douse or furl before the next gust front hits.

As mariners quickly learn, "heavy weather" is a relative term. Crew size and skill, along with a vessel's strength, stability, and sail-carrying ability, play into decisions about when to reef, when to switch to storm sails, and when to initiate extreme heavy-weather tactics (including forereaching, heaving-to, and running off—covered later in this chapter). The convergence of crew skill and the boat's characteristics helps us determine even whether to go to sea at all. We also need to factor in the willingness of those on board to endure the pounding and exaggerated motion of pressing hard in a seaway. Racing sailors with large, experienced crews and fleet rankings at stake will likely push a boat more aggressively than cruising sailors are inclined to do. A large crew likely has a capable navigator to assess what the weather is about to bring, but a cruising couple must cope with all such exigencies on their own.

Heavy-weather boat-handling tactics and skills can be explained, as I'm doing here, but what really counts is implementing the skills. Experience leads to adjustments in our attitude that are less easy to characterize. By that I mean that ocean sailors gain confidence and coping mechanisms by weathering gales and storms at sea. Still, old salts and neophytes agree that avoiding a tempest always trumps being trapped in one.

THE HEAVY-WEATHER THRESHOLD

Every crew needs to identify where on the Beaufort scale heavy weather begins for them (see page 285). Many sailors define it as the point where their vessel is overpowered, despite being double-reefed and flying a very small jib or heavy-air staysail. The threshold for heavy weather typically falls somewhere between Force 7 (28 to 33 knots) and Force 9 (41 to 47 knots) depending on the related issues of the boat's tenderness and the experience of the crew.

A secondary swell or a strong ocean current can substantially lower the threshold. As mentioned earlier, a situation of contrary wind and current, such as a northerly blowing against the north-flowing Gulf Stream, makes the wave period shorter and the wave faces steeper, as much as twice as high when opposed by a 1-knot current.

When heavy weather threatens, having an updated forecast in hand allows you to assess if the blow will likely be short-lived or will continue to build. The duration of a strong wind is as important, if not even more important, than its velocity. The longer a gale blows over an open sea, the larger and more unstable are the waves it generates. As noted in Chapter 10, the sea states described in the Beaufort scale are fully developed seas, unlimited by wind duration or fetch.

When you're sailing offshore, keep up with the 96-hour long-range forecast, along with the 48- and 24-hour forecasts that give you the most accurate picture of nearer-term weather. When you become a savvy weather-forecast watcher, you'll also look at the 500 mb chart features and note the locations of troughs and upper-level cutoff lows (discussed in Chapter 10). When you see that a developing surface low is associated with an upper-level cutoff low and a nearby high-pressure system, you're looking at the

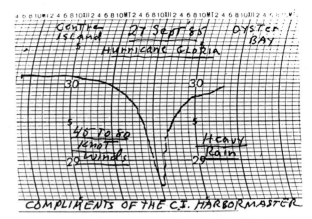

A barograph tells the story of a direct hit by hurricane Gloria in September 1985, in Oyster Bay, New York. Southeast winds reached 80 knots as "the bottom fell out of the glass." A dead calm ushered in the eye (lowest reading), followed by hurricane-force northwest winds. (See Chapter 10.)

conditions for a serious blow. In this situation, you face the decision to either tuck into a safe anchorage (if possible) or head away from the worst of the expected blow, shoal water, and the threat of a lee shore.

Experienced mariners keep a constant eye on the weather, and long-term, long-distance cruisers don't suspend their weather-watching routine when they make a landfall. To avoid a battle with the bad stuff, your best heavy-weather tactic of all involves keeping track of weather systems and safe havens.

On the other hand, exercising *excessive* caution can keep you from venturing to the destinations you hope to visit. In addition, if caution slows your escape from an expected seasonal deterioration of local weather, you could end up deeper in harm's way. For example, lingering in the Caribbean until you're well into June and the hurricane season, or dawdling about New England into November, doesn't meet the definition of a safe sailor.

No Name Harbor, a well-known and convenient little anchorage in Biscayne Bay, Florida, is one of the best places to observe risk-averse sailors. Referred to by many locals as "Coward's Cove," this harbor offers a temporary home for sail and power cruisers waiting for the perfect weather window for a Gulf Stream crossing and entry into the Bahamas. Now, it's logical to want to avoid a cold-front passage in the Stream or, even worse, a full-blown coastal low that can turn the Gulf Stream's hypnotic turquoise water into a seething cauldron. We've also seen our share of hyperactive adventurers, sailors who ignore common sense and depart prematurely, often facing the fickle Gulf Stream's severe punishment. Their tales of woe have the power to make those whose anchor rodes are growing barnacles become even more anxious about what lies ahead. Some end up spending more

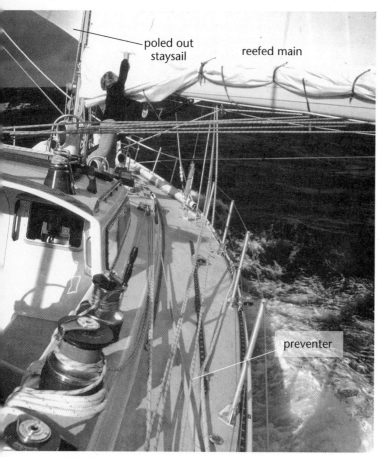

In moderate conditions, reefing the mainsail, setting a preventer, and poling out a staysail can be the best bet for making smooth progress on a broad reach. Running dead downwind is usually a slower point of sail and a hard course to steer for a windvane, autopilot, or helmsperson.

of the season in and around Biscayne Bay than in the Bahamas. We know it's difficult to find perfect conditions for crossing the Gulf Stream, although we can confidently say that too little wind is better than too much. In addition, beware of jumping on a favorable southerly or, even worse, a southwesterly, because wind from that quadrant promises an imminent cold front, usually less than a day away.

Regardless of destination, the right weather window can promise only a day or two, maybe three, of favorable conditions. As a good friend once said, "Take a look at the weather today, and realize that unless you're sailing in the trade winds, tomorrow's weather is likely to be quite different." With this sage advice in mind, you can see why we urge you to keep up with essential forecast data.

Pressing On or Turning Back

Perhaps the hardest decision you'll face when heavy weather is forecast involves the choice to abandon progress and find shelter, ride out the weather, or turn around and sprint back to where you've just been. When headed north from the Caribbean in midspring, you may be called upon to consider those choices. As mentioned elsewhere in this book, the situation arises when a rapidly deepening low moves off the U.S. East Coast and the bottom falls out of the barometric reading. Running into a full-blown Cape Hatteras low is an experience well worth avoiding. If you monitor the forecast carefully, you can get a two-day warning, allowing you to seek sensible safe havens in ports such as Charleston, South Carolina, and several places in the Georgia sounds. These are much better choices than a risky rush to round Cape Hatteras.

If neither heaving-to (discussed later) well south of such a storm or finding safe shelter is a feasible option, get away from the Gulf Stream's wave-boosting northeasterly flow and also avoid the shoals found west of the Gulf Stream. This means heading east into the deep water on the south side of the Stream, farther from land and your destination port.

When in the thick of severe weather, you don't have the option to choose strategies to avoid the storm in the first place. This makes decisions based on weather that hasn't arrived yet even more difficult, especially when you need to sail away from your desired track. More often than not, this need to implement a course change occurs when you're sailing in bright sun on calm seas. A situation that looks so ideal also can lull a skipper into believing that the approaching weather system won't be so bad after all. However, it's a risky gamble to talk yourself into thinking that the 50-knot storm forecast to cross your track in 48 hours will turn out to be just another 35-knot borderline gale.

Trying to second-guess the weather or otherwise rationalize a decision to downplay what's coming your way is especially risky if you're sailing in an area known for vicious, rapidly developing storms. Granted, changing course and instituting your storm-avoidance plan while pleasantly sailing on a sunny afternoon may not be popular with your crew, but such decisions usually pay off in the long run.

COASTAL WATERS AND SEEKING SHELTER

As noted in Chapter 10, large swells that are stable and less threatening in deep water become more dangerous when they start to "feel" the bottom and steepen over the continental shelf—and an opposing current can also cause wave faces to steepen.

The building seas and breaking waves associated with a gale on the continental shelf raise the stakes for those attempting to seek safe shelter in a coastal harbor or estuary. "Any port in a storm" is a popular adage, but those are misleading words, to say the least. Don't attempt to enter a lee-shore harbor in a full-blown storm unless it's an all-weather harbor with a deep, wide entrance devoid of offlying sandbars and rocky reefs. In addition, steer well clear of any harbor with migrating sandbars in its approaches. Knowing or sensing when a harbor is not a safe haven is an important tool in your seamanship inventory. As a helpful rule of thumb, look for deepdraft commercial ports, which, by definition, tend to be free of breaking bars and shoaling entrance jetties.

Running an inlet plagued by breaking waves is a big gamble for most sailboats and only a slightly better bet for the average power cruiser. Channeling a great deal of swell energy between two jetties raises steep seas, especially when a strong ebb current is flowing out through the entrance—particularly with an opposing wind. In that circumstance, you might see standing waves breaking over shallower spots, and those waves can broach or even capsize a vessel. Many coastal radio broadcasts give warnings about breaking bars and inlets that are closed by breaking waves. Attempting to enter an inlet under such conditions, especially at night, is like trying to cross a busy highway with your eyes closed.

Even deep rivers like the Hudson and Delaware are fraught with outlying sand shoals and lower bays etched with navigable channels running amidst shoal water. Seeking shelter from *(continued next page)*

RALLIES HEADING OFFSHORE—WHO'S IN CHARGE? YOU ARE

Facing rough seas shortly after their November 4 departure from Hampton, Virginia, for the Caribbean, participants in the 2013 Salty Dawg Rally faced tough conditions in the Gulf Stream waters east of Cape Hatteras. Two boats lost steering, two were dismasted, and one suffered a sheared hull-to-deck joint. Many sailors were violently seasick and found themselves unprepared for the offshore conditions. The Caribbean 1500 fleet, another group also leaving from the same area, had left a day ahead of schedule to avoid the approaching weather. All of that fleet made it to and through the Gulf Stream without incident.

Two years before, a rally departing from New England in the autumn was caught in the crosshairs of a bad low and the fleet was pounded for several days. A crew member on one boat was washed overboard and lost (as described in Chapter 10). Two incidents don't make for definitive findings, but there are some underlying issues worth noting. The first is that fall in the northeast is a volatile time of year, and no matter how well the pros scrutinize forecasts, one must be ready to handle heavy weather. Fall is earmarked by rapid changes in the weather—fronts move quickly and carry with them strong winds. Everyone hopes to find a window of fair weather and moderate breeze, but there are no guarantees it will play out that way. More often than not, sailors heading off this time of year will be dodging the effects of late-season tropical weather or violent early season nor'easters.

The second observation from these incidents is the reminder that a shakedown cruise is needed before any offshore trip to validate the readiness of the boat and those on board. Unfortunately, many new offshore cruising sailors, with brand-new boats, use such rallies as a de facto shakedown cruise instead of undertaking a lengthy summer sail in light to moderate conditions,

overnighting in coastal areas where one can rest and regroup or repair if necessary. Many crews have hardly finished fitting out newly purchased sailboats and preparing for a great escape and have had little or no time underway with the new boat.

Herd-like groups can't make up for shortfalls in crew skill and vessel readiness. Nor does sailing in a rally change the equation for who is responsible. Each captain must recognize that he or she along with the crew are on their own once the dock lines are slipped and the sails hoisted. When all the chips are handed over to someone else to make the decision to depart, one still needs to be ready to handle the consequences. Leaving in a hurry can cause Caribbean-bound sailors to get caught in headwinds or a contrary Gulf Stream current mixed with cold nights and shorter days. When these challenges are confronted by experienced or inexperienced sailors in untested boats, it's like taking a final exam before enrolling in the course.

Coast Guard Advice: Be Prepared!

After a busy couple of years coming to the aid of sailors in distress, the Coast Guard has begun issuing specific advice pertaining to the issues that caused the problems. Following the Salty Dawg Rally rescues in the fall of 2013, the Coast Guard issued a bulletin on being prepared for offshore sailing, emphasizing preventing or managing rudder loss, which plagued several of the Salty Dawg sailboats. Knowing how to jury-rig a rudder, or sail without one, is a key practice of seamanship. (See Chuck Hawley's comments on jury rigging a rudder in Chapter 13.) The following is excerpted from that bulletin:

The Coast Guard strongly recommends that owner/operators of offshore sailboats ensure proper maintenance *(continued next page)*

RALLIES HEADING OFFSHORE, CONTINUED

and repair of their critical mechanical systems to reduce the possibility of failure during stressed operating conditions.

Operational limitations of the systems must be understood.

Sailors should have the repair manuals associated with their important propulsion and steering systems onboard and be able to detect oncoming failures and perform emergency repairs.

Adequate tools, hardware, and an array of fasteners should be kept onboard.

Common spare parts that are known to fail on a particular system should be kept onboard.

If mechanical ability is lacking, additional training should be taken to provide minimum skill sets.

Regular inspection and prompt corrective action of all steering gear components including linkages, ram assemblies, controls and cables, in addition to engine systems, should

be part of getting underway and day-to-day operations.

Equipment should be tested before getting underway, noting variations in movement, feel, sound, and resistance.

Flooding and damage control kits should be kept onboard.

Sailors should contemplate and envision ways to fabricate a temporary emergency rudder using components (table tops, cabinet doors, spinnaker poles, etc.) already onboard.

Make sure all EPIRBs, PLBs, are registered, operational, and available. Ensure your VHF radio is fully functional.

Lastly, always file a float plan with family or friends ashore *before* getting underway. Float plans are simple tools that help rescuers locate stranded boaters in distress, and may be printed from the following site: http://www.floatplancentral.org/download/USCGFloatPlan.pdf

Seldom is a capsize and 360-degree rollover caught on camera, but the crew of the USCG cutter Alert filmed the rolling and dismasting of this small schooner while they launched a RIB to rescue the singlehanded skipper. The rescue crew of the RIB used boat speed and maneuverability to avoid the breaking crests and adroitly recovered the sailor, who had swum clear of the capsized schooner. Note the schooner's beam-on orientation to the seas, which contributed to the rollover. (Courtesy USCG)

a gale that's already raging obviously requires careful navigation. It's also necessary to consider powerful side-setting currents before undertaking a heavy weather plan that brings you closer to shore.

Sea Room

Mariners in the Age of Sail understood that land isn't necessarily synonymous with safety. Gloucester fishing schooners would run for home before a northeasterly gale, but only because they had fish for market and were out there to make a living or die trying. They also knew they'd likely find refuge because the New England coast is dotted with sheltered bays and harbors that can be entered in any weather. What was risky for them would be untenable on most lee-shore coastlines, and sailors should recognize the difference. The unobstructed sea is often the safer haven when heavy weather threatens and sea room becomes the vital commodity. Lacking the ability to claw off a lee shore to windward, the sailors of square-rigged ships knew precisely how valuable sea room could be.

Sea room remains a vital concept today, despite our close-winded boats, auxiliary engines, and high-tech weather forecasts. The open sea often means deeper, less current-affected water, plus more stable deep-water waves less likely to tumble onto the deck of a vessel caught in a gale at sea. With ample room to leeward, you can run before a storm (see later section) without fear of fetching up on a lee shore.

Still, offshore cruisers will likely face critical points at which they must decide if their soundest strategy involves racing for shore to seek safe shelter ahead of an approaching gale. Being caught in shoal water outside safe shelter is the worst of the possible options. For example, Cape Hatteras has earned its nasty reputation "between a rock and a hard place." Inshore we find sand shoals over which seas break in a blow, and offshore we face the added volatility of the Gulf Stream. In 1980, revered yacht designer Angus Primrose and a crewmember were caught in a nasty situation in shoal water. During the melee of a Gulf Stream storm, Primrose's Moody 33, *Demon of Hamble*, a sloop of his own design, was capsized, inverted, and eventually sunk. His crew was rescued, but Primrose was tragically lost at sea. (His young partner at the time, Bill Dixon, took over Angus Primrose Design and changed the name to Dixon Yacht Design.)

I've already alluded to the toll Cape Hatteras can take on sailors trapped in one of its brutal spring or fall gales. With a lack of any safe shelter between the mouth of the Chesapeake Bay and the inlet at Moorhead City and Beaufort, North Carolina, the trap offers no easy choices, making it essential for anyone headed offshore to pick an appropriate weather window. If a vessel's draft and mast height can be accommodated in the Intracoastal Waterway, consider that inshore route as an attractive alternative to rounding Cape Hatteras.

Because of the paucity of safe shelter, West Coast sailors need to plan judiciously when headed west-northwest up the coast around Point Conception. The route leads toward San Francisco or Seattle, and Point Conception divides the normally more tranquil Southern California waters from more volatile Northern California coastal conditions. Keeping track of impending weather systems must be a key component of your heavy-weather planning. Your best strategy remains a summer transit and a keen eye on forecast low-pressure development.

PREPARING FOR HEAVY WEATHER AT SEA

Avoiding heavy weather is usually feasible for coastal cruisers. But bluewater passagemakers commit themselves to lengthy offshore voyaging, so sooner or later (barring extraordinary luck) they'll be forced to contend with heavy weather. Offshore sailors can try to stack the deck in their favor by picking the best season for a given voyage. In addition, they can minimize the time spent as a proverbial sitting duck. For example, in areas such as the north cape of New

When a crew makes landfall in rough weather, no room for error exists. Running aground on a sand shoal or rocky ledge has dire consequences, and even though fatigue levels may be high, this is a time for the lookout, the navigator, and those sailing the boat to be at the top of their game. If the approach is at night, it's often wise to wait for daylight, as is carefully assessing tide and current.

Zealand or the approaches to South Africa, a day or two less time at sea can make the difference between avoiding or encountering the next in the unrelenting series of cold fronts that parade out of the storm-tossed Southern Ocean.

While it is often inevitable to encounter a storm at sea, as mentioned frequently, keeping abreast of the weather systems' movements allows you to react appropriately as the fronts strengthen or weaken. Weather routing is an asset for Volvo race boats and container ships that travel at speeds that allow choices of where to maneuver in respect to highs and lows, but this is seldom a choice open to most cruisers. Minimizing contact with heavy weather is the name of the game. The average eastbound cruisers transiting the temperate region of the North Atlantic are regularly overtaken by leaden gray skies, buffeted about for a couple of days, and finally spit out into a sea full of sunshine and a helpful west-northwest breeze. For the following day or two crew spirits are buoyant, and then the next eastbound weather system starts to take hold. This is the cadence of the extratropical lows that march across the middle latitudes. During summer their grip (continued page 327)

HEAVY WEATHER AT ANCHOR

An option sometimes available in heavy weather is to seek or remain in an anchorage. As discussed in Chapter 6, it's essential to choose an appropriate anchorage and to have the right ground tackle before trying to ride out a storm.

In the tropics, easterly trade winds dominate for more than half the year. However, tropical (easterly) waves and tropical weather systems become a major concern during the wet season, when warm ocean water and massive amounts of convective activity develop into tropical systems. If you stay in the tropics during the summer months, you're forced to play the odds on avoiding weather, so you'll constantly track tropical systems and note the locations of ever-elusive "hurricane holes." You'll make monumental decisions and tough calls about where to hide from an approaching hurricane. Even a shallow, confined bay can develop 4-foot waves when an 80-knot wind churns the water.

In addition, we recommend avoiding anchoring in a roadstead (a sheltered area outside the confines of a marked harbor or cove) with open fetch in one or more directions. As a tropical storm passes by, the wind changes direction, and even a small sector of open fetch can erupt into chaos. The anchorage on the island of Culebra, an island off the coast of Puerto Rico and near the Virgin Islands, was once assumed to be a safe hurricane hole because it was sheltered from three directions. However, that myth was exposed when hurricane Hugo drove more than a hundred boats ashore.

The mizzen of this 50-foot ketch unfurled while in the grasp of hurricane Gloria, and the boat began dragging its 1,200-pound mushroom anchor. Fortunately, the sail disintegrated and the vessel came to a halt before running into the boats moored and anchored astern. The importance of taking down sails, bimini, and dodger prior to a hurricane can't be overstressed, whether at anchor or at sea. Insurance companies, boatyards, and marinas are beginning to mandate this.

Large swells arrive in advance of a developing storm and can be a somber harbinger of what lies ahead. With big seas making up and a gale on the way, make sure the crew is rested, loose gear stowed, and harnesses, tethers, and jacklines rigged and checked. Large swells also mandate a careful lookout, for both breaking waves and any sea traffic.

is weakened, but during winter and the shoulder seasons their effect on sea state is dramatic.

When heavy weather is expected, it's time to prepare both the boat and the crew for what may be coming.

Boat Preparations

Preparing the boat for heavy weather involves several steps, including setting a preventer and running backstays (when appropriate), taking down cockpit canvas, installing jacklines, and preventing downflooding.

Preventer

The ability to avoid an unintended jibe is a key safety issue when handling heavy weather. Some say that the best preventer is a skilled helmsperson, and there's certainly much truth in that statement. But in a rolling, rough sea a breaking wave crest can pivot the boat despite the rudder position, and the result is often an unintentional jibe of the mainsail and heavy boom. Keeping the boom from inadvertently careening from one side of the vessel to the other is more

An inflatable dinghy hung in davits can be a real convenience for a coastal sailor, but heading to sea with such a rig is risky. If you're caught in heavy weather, a breaking wave can easily carry away the RIB and all of that cantilevered tubing at the stern, not to mention the windvane and radar. Access to a life raft is vital offshore, however—see Chapter 13.

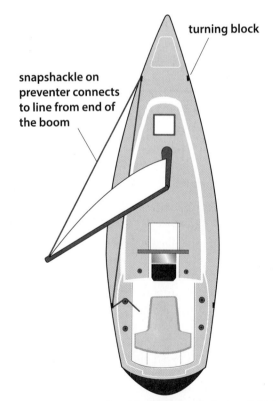

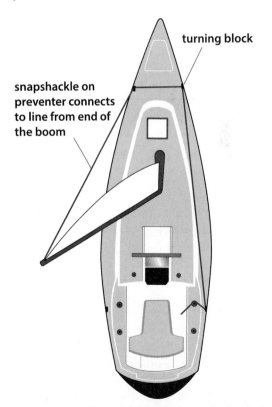

A preventer may be only lightly loaded when initially set, but if the mainsail is backwinded it can take on the load of a single-part mainsheet and be dangerous to release unless controlled on a winch drum. A boom-end preventer eliminates this problem. Two pendants, each half the length of the boom, extend from the outboard end of the boom toward the gooseneck and are stowed at mid-boom with shock cord. When reaching or running, you run preventer lines port and starboard from cockpit winches to turning blocks on the foredeck. To use the preventer, lead the working end of one of these preventer lines outside all rigging and, using a snapshackle, attach it to its mating pendant on the boom. The cockpit winch is used to set the preventer, and if you have to release it under load, you can handle it like any other heavily tensioned sheet. The windward winch (right) is preferred; if that one is not available, run the preventer to the cockpit winch on the leeward side (left). (Joe Comeau)

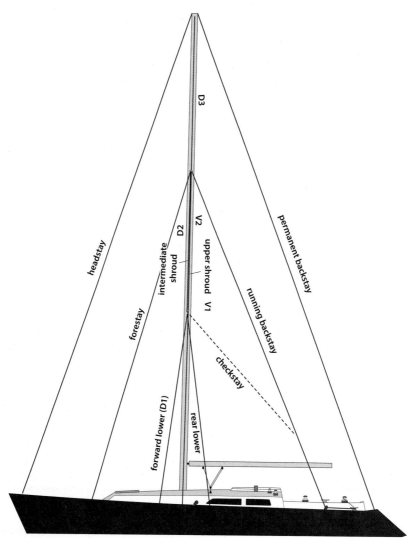

Checkstays are used aboard race boats with tall, light, bendy rigs. Running backstays ("runners") offset the load of forestay on double-headsail-rigged cruising boats. Each tack requires a swap of running backstays. When no sail is set on the forestay no runner is set. (In the diagram, the "V" designation before a shroud indicates vertical load; the D indicates diagonal.) (Joe Comeau)

than a helmsman's responsibility. The best ways to accomplish this is with a preventer. The preventer tackle is comprised of a line clipped to the outboard end of the boom and run forward on the leeward side to a block on the foredeck, returning to a cockpit winch. This setup allows the crew to lock the boom in place and hold a backwinded sail rather than allowing it to unintentionally jibe, as described in detail in Chapter 5. Inshore racing sailors often find a preventer an unnecessary encumbrance, but as soon as they take their talents offshore and the reality of long tacks and large seas sets in, the use of a preventer becomes a sensible tactic, at least in heavy-weather situations.

Running Stays

Running backstays and checkstays offset the load of a headstay or forestay. Some modern race boats do not have a backstay and depend solely on port and starboard runners or checkstays to keep the headstay tight and the mast in place. Runners are also used to provide secondary support for the mast with a cutter rig or double-headsail rig. When the breeze is up and no sail is set on the headstay, the inner stay or forestay often carries a high cut staysail or a storm jib. The bending load is lower on the mast, and a port or starboard runner is used to keep the spar in column. When a storm trysail is set, both runners can be set up since the boom is not in the way.

Cockpit Canvas

Cockpit canvas—a dodger, bimini, lee cloths, and more—offers protection and convenience in settled weather but becomes a liability in heavy weather. Such canvas both creates unwanted windage and can be easily torn away, with associated damage, by wind or boarding waves.

Lee cloths—which are rigged on stanchions and keep spray out of the cockpit—are a nice addition on aft-cockpit boats with low freeboard—at least until a boarding sea bends the lee cloths and lifeline stanchions level with the deck. The best way to avoid such drama and damage is to remove rail canvas as heavy weather approaches or use lee cloths with snap fittings or low-strength lashings that let the bottom edge break away if a breaking wave strikes the cloth. This is a delicate balance: too strong a bottom connection will lead to stanchion damage, and too weak a fitting and the cloths will simply fly like a flag in the wind.

Although most dodgers are stronger than lee cloths, they too cause windage and can be ripped off in a storm, causing injury and/or boat damage. In most cases it is best to fold down and secure the dodger or remove it entirely. The same is true of a bimini—and especially the "Florida room" cockpit enclosures that create a nautical nightmare if a wave breaks over it. Even a large bimini can usually be collapsed and lashed down, creating less surface area potentially impacted by boarding seas. (Dodger removal leaves the helmsperson vulnerable to boarding seas and spray—wearing a dive mask or ski goggles improves visibility in these conditions.)

Finally, take a look around the deck and cockpit for anything else that can be damaged by heavy seas, and remove it. Bagged sails that have been left on deck are easily washed overboard along with other loose gear. Rail-mounted solar panels and similar items are also prime targets for boarding seas.

Jacklines

Install jacklines *before* the weather arrives, and make sure crewmembers are hooked in via tether as they move about the deck in deteriorating conditions. A breaking wave hitting you squarely in the chest can make the stream from a fire hose seem like a water pistol. The big risk in heavy weather is not an unanticipated capsize but rather a crewmember being knocked over the side while not hitched to a jackline. No matter how well your crew-overboard rescue techniques seem to work in moderate conditions, all bets are off when gale- to storm-force weather tears up the sea surface. See Chapter 13 for more detailed information about jacklines.

Downflooding Prevention

When water enters the interior of a vessel, gravity pulls it toward the lowest point, resulting in a double-barreled negative impact on stability. When the boat is upright the water heads for the bilge, but as soon as the vessel begins to heel the water migrates

When forecast information promises a significant weather event, it pays to get ready beforehand. A gale will soon overtake this transatlantic passagemaker, and the crew has already hanked on the storm trysail, leaving it in its bag with the sheets attached. The preventer is set, the running backstay is in place, and the jacklines are run. Note that the crew is clipped in and wearing an inflatable PFD.

toward new low points. These de facto sumps may be found in lockers, behind berths, or worst of all, in the cabin trunk itself. Water trapped inside the hull reduces buoyancy by an equal amount, and when a vessel downfloods, the righting moment is greatly diminished, along with creating a large and rapidly growing negative area in its stability curve (see the explanation of stability in Chapter 12). To survive a bad storm at sea it's vital to keep water out.

Consider the big issues, such as your coachroof structure and the integrity of hatches and ports. Well before heading to sea, fit storm covers for your big windows and have a plan for responding to a breached port or hatch. Storm preparations while at sea may include dogging (tightening down) ports and hatches and fastening large window-covering plates you had made ahead of time and stowed for this purpose. Ports in the hull are a real concern, and many ISO Category A approved options—further explained in Chapter 12—involve using storm cover plates. Outboard coverings that are flanged over recessed windows need to be installed well before you find yourself in the grip of storm-force conditions. Many bluewater veterans place these covers over large windows before leaving on an ocean passage.

Mike Keyworth, a consummately experienced ocean sailor and boatyard manager from Rhode Island, often tells passagemakers about a client who refused to cover the large cabinhouse windows of his 58-foot cruiser. A fall gale caught the client and his crew at sea en route to the Caribbean, and the windows were breached. Tragically, the vessel foundered and lives were lost.

Professor Paul Miller, a naval architect with a doctorate in engineering and a keen focus on mate-rial structures, provides another eye-opening example. Miller was contracted to calculate what thickness of tempered plate window glass was needed to make a large cabinhouse window as strong as the cabinhouse itself. The vessel in question was a high-tech 70-footer, and when the number crunching was done, it was calculated that the tempered window glass would have to be 2 inches thick. At that point, the builder, owner, and designer agreed to segment the aperture into smaller windows and integrate plenty of carbon fiber into the surrounding molded framework.

Keeping the companionway closed and latched with hardware that can be opened from both on deck and below remains a challenge that few builders adequately consider. Despite the ISAF rules mandating this, most production boats don't offer a companionway hatch system that can accomplish this straightforward feat.

The counterargument is that bulletproof hatches and ports may be fine for a crew off to see penguins in Antarctica, but why burden the average ocean cruiser headed for Bermuda and the Caribbean with such overkill? The answer is probably best supplied by incidents such as the disappearance of the Little Harbor 54, *Flying Colours,* and the entire four-person crew in a storm, described in detail in Chapter 10. We'll never know for sure that the vessel was lost because of downflooding—whether caused by dismasting, a companionway hatchboard washing away, or cabin window damage from a capsize—but we can say that flooding of some sort is the most likely reason for a boat to disappear so quickly without a trace.

More is known about the losses of the tall ships *Pride of Baltimore* and *Marques.* In both instances the vessel was proceeding in heavy weather when gusts of wind much stronger than the sustained winds drove the boat down on its beam, and inadequately closed hatches allowed seawater to rush below. In the case of the *Marques,* a cargo hatch cover was breached and the 120-foot vessel sank in less than a minute, tragically claiming the lives of nineteen of the ship's twenty-eight crewmembers.

Because of these and other instances of downflooding, ISO stability calculations factor hatch and port size and location into stability index ratings (more on this in Chapter 12). Apertures higher and nearer the centerline add points to the overall stability rating; opening ports in the hull and offset hatches and vents detract from stability ratings.

Heavy weather raises the potential for both flooding caused by a crack or hole in the hull and downflooding from sea-driven water finding entry through poorly sealed or slightly opened hatches, lazarette lids, ports, and other deck openings. Chapter 13 addresses

This single-piece, circular, poorly hinged, extruded-frame forward hatch may have all kinds of aesthetic appeal, but it's one errant sheet away from being rendered useless and creating some significant downflooding worries for the crew. Storm preparation includes imagining the worst that can happen and taking measures to prevent the same. In this case having a damage control plan to seal the hole if this hatch is damaged is a high priority.

MANAGING HEAVY WEATHER ANXIETY—OR ITS ABSENCE

Freud saw anxiety as a sensible neurosis linked to self-preservation. At least that can be the case when it exists in small amounts and can be ameliorated through planning and preparation. Consider the saber-toothed tiger effect: no caveperson fretted over becoming dinner while running full tilt away from a predator—it was during quiet walks through the woods that such thoughts occurred.

The same goes for controlling anxiety levels in heavy weather. During a storm, the crew is too busy to dwell on what might happen. The real storm worry problems arise prior to the onset of strong winds and heavy seas. Anxiety is more closely linked with the anticipation of the unknown. Over the years, I've found that there's nothing better when it comes to anxiety abatement than being proactive before the bad weather arrives. I look closely at the forecast, tracking cloud cover and barometric trends to get a feel for what's on the way. But it's the methodical preparation of the vessel that seems to be the best anxiety ameliorator.

There are two kinds of heavy weather encounters. First are the unanticipated, quick-onset episodes such as high-octane squalls that can blow hard enough to sting the skin. They can be part of a fast-moving line squall, a pre-front trough ahead of a cold front, or just simply a vertically developed single-cell thunderstorm. The second type are better forecasted weather events such as classic warm front/cold front low-pressure systems and can take a day or two to arrive and just as long to exit. Knowing the severity of a weather system underscores the aphorism "Knowledge is power." And once you are aware of what defines an upcoming heavy weather event, you're more likely to make effective preparations.

Keeping the entire crew engaged in these preparations and building a realistic awareness of the challenges ahead are essential for reducing anxiety. As crewmembers dig out the storm sails, set up a trysail at the base of the mast, and clear the deck of extraneous clutter, they benefit from being positively engaged in doing something about their future worry. This process improves a sailor's ability to handle heavy weather and lessens the concern about the unknown.

Encourage dialogue concerning tactics and focus discussions on storm preparation. These can be as simple as how to lash an overturned dinghy on the foredeck or as complex as planning the course during different phases of the approaching storm. Use the heavy weather anxiety as a growth experience for the entire crew. Often what we fear is much larger than the actual storm—beforehand allow the crew to express their concerns and take purposeful action to prepare themselves and the boat. Gales at sea are an opportunity for the entire crew to become more comfortable and acclimated to the conditions that arise during bad weather. When the approaching low-pressure system, tropical storm, or severe cold front finally rolls through, the crew should have a déjà vu feeling following these preparations. As soon as conditions abate and the routine returns to normal, it's time to go over what transpired. Begin with a careful critique of any assumptions that had been made about the weather pattern and how it actually played out. Make sure the entire crew analyses and responds to any disparities between the two. Finally, take a detailed look at what worked really well and what didn't work. This debriefing session can be one of the most important learning experiences a crew can have. The more involved and experienced each sailor becomes, the more comfortable he or she will be when handling the next heavy weather challenge, and the less anxiety-provoking these interactions become.

The flip side of suffering from too much anxiety is being plagued by too little. Those who feel no trace of anxiety or concern about an approaching gale or storm are like Icarus flying toward the sun. Worse still, eagerness to face the next storm-tossed sea can become an addictive adrenaline rush, fraught with plenty of pitfalls. Every heavy-weather encounter ups the risk and increases the number of variables that can affect the outcome. Great sailors like Mike Plant and Alan Colas were lost at sea engaged in high-stakes single-handed racing. Their vision of the balance between risk and reward was different from mainstream voyagers'. Where they pushed the limits, others dialed back. There's nothing wrong with a little anxiety, especially when it can be harnessed as a voice that speaks out a little ahead of time, encouraging reefing or heading for deeper water.

how to cope with such situations and the approaches one should take when it comes to extracting water from the hull. Here, stopping or at least slowing a leak is the primary concern. Ideally, both prevention and dewatering can proceed concurrently, but with a very small crew, stopping a serious leak takes precedence. Early warning of a leak is paramount, and that's done nicely with a simple bilge alarm—little more than a float switch wired to a loud horn.

Protecting Boat Systems

Earlier chapters have described the many kinds of power equipment included on many modern sailboats. When choosing such equipment, make sure that it's reliable and robust enough to cope with the loads imposed by heavy weather. You also need to ensure enough electrical energy is available to cope with the demand. Take, for example, what can happen during a long ocean passage under sail. The engine

Watchstanding under the protection of a rigid dodger can be a big plus, especially if it offers all-around visibility and allows a crew to be just a few steps away from the sheet winches and the helm. With an autopilot remote control, radar, and digital charting display packed into the same protective shelter, the watchkeeper has a first-rate perch from which to conn the vessel. Take care to ensure that any dodger is robust enough to handle the gale, and if not, stow it before the blow.

is used routinely to generate enough power to run everything, and at times the battery banks may come close to being overly discharged. This can become a real problem during heavy weather if you abruptly need high-capacity electric bilge pumping or to keep the autopilot running while you attend to emergency measures. Although many boats now carry a generator, those without one depend on their diesel auxiliary for needed electricity. The engine must be well maintained to ensure it doesn't break down just when it's most needed. Similarly one should have a contingency plan to keep the batteries well charged in heavy-weather situations.

Crew Preparation

Your crew, regardless of its size, is a critical variable in coping with heavy weather. An experienced skipper always manages these human resources in order to keep up their energy reserves and fight the onset of fatigue. Little things help, such as preparing a supply of sandwiches and reviewing damage-control strategies before the weather completely deteriorates. In addition, review crew-overboard and abandon-ship procedures (covered in Chapter 13). These steps show a level of preparedness—and management—that consider existing and developing conditions, which in itself develops confidence.

The rising anticipation and anxiety of waiting for bad weather to arrive can put the whole crew on edge (see the sidebar on how to prevent this).

Unfortunately, by the time the weather finally comes, fatigue levels are already high, even before especially challenging watches and poor sleeping conditions further exhaust all on board. It's essential to keep the off-watch crew in their bunks (secured with lee cloths) and maintain regular eating and hydration routines. If possible, pair new sailors with experienced crew and shorten the watches, perhaps expanding from a two-watch to a three-watch system. The off-watch crew have the highest priority for sleep, and your next-up team is ready to be called on deck if conditions and sail handling warrant.

Dressing for Heavy Weather

Every shorthanded crew knows fatigue is the biggest adversary, and nothing speeds up the onset of fatigue quite like being cold and wet during lengthy night watches. In really bad weather, wrist and neck seals on foul-weather gear prove their worth. Additional items such as sea boots with good grip, wet suit gloves, and a neoprene hood/hat round out heavy-weather gear. A dive mask (or ski goggles) for the helmsman helps take the sting out of spray in a 50-knot gust. In addition, a waterproof headlamp allows a crew to put a beam of light where they want it and still leave both hands free. Dressing for safety is covered in more detail in Chapter 13. In addition to a well-fitted harness and PFD, those facing survival conditions may want to have a personal locator beacon (PLB) tucked into a pocket just in case things go from bad to even worse (see Chapter 14).

MOTORING THROUGH HEAVY WEATHER

Many safety seminar attendees ask if it makes sense to drop sails and motor through heavy weather, and the answer is usually no. Those who drop the sails, take refuge in the cabin, and attempt to power through a storm often get so seasick that their decision making is hampered. A sailboat is a poor platform when the sea is roiling and no sails are set. The low center of gravity and hull shape are designed to react to the heeling moment of the sail plan. Problems arise when that force is eliminated, and the huge unchecked righting moment causes the boat to dance a jig. The boat's buoyancy attempts to keep pace with the sea's dissonant cadence, resulting in a whiplash roll that harasses the crew.

One way to tone down the fury is to motorsail with a storm trysail set. While I prefer sailing, motorsailing with a trysail does have a couple of upsides. Motorsailing at a low RPM, with low fuel consumption, provides good directional stability and a chance to move diagonally away from a breaking crest (when forereaching); at the same time you are charging the batteries and providing plenty of current for an autopilot that may or may not be up to the challenge. Well-charged batteries are always a plus when it comes to running pumps, communications equipment, navigation lights, and so on. Motorsailing is not as appealing when deep reaching or running, however, simply because the nauseating diesel fumes that come into the cockpit with the howling wind over the stern can make crew seasick. Keep a deck bucket handy and dissuade a seasick crew member from hanging over the side.

Heavy-weather boat gyrations not only affect the crew's appetite but also tend to stir up tank detritus and clog fuel filters when motorsailing. Regularly shine a flashlight beam through the primary diesel filter to check for clarity and any sign of water at the bottom. One of the grand design features of a sailboat is its elegant simplicity for handling both calms and gales under sail with human-powered hardware.

A forestaysail and deeply reefed main can carry a crew through a strong wind and into the early stages of gale-force conditions. But once the spray really begins to fly, the need for storm sails becomes apparent. On this 60-foot sloop, American Promise, the foredeck dorade vents face aft to keep waves rolling down the deck from soaking the accommodations below. Aft of the mast, forward-facing dorades are able to shed spray and allow only air below, delivering welcome ventilation in a seaway.

Well-maintained roller-furling sails can be a real friend to shorthanded sailors offshore, but they need to be cut flat, and an in-boom or in-mast mainsail furling system must be handled carefully. A separate storm trysail track and a removable forestay—not seen in this photo—are always good additions on a long-range cruiser.

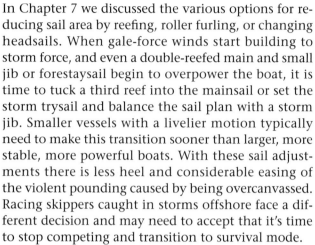

STORM SAILS

In Chapter 7 we discussed the various options for reducing sail area by reefing, roller furling, or changing headsails. When gale-force winds start building to storm force, and even a double-reefed main and small jib or forestaysail begin to overpower the boat, it is time to tuck a third reef into the mainsail or set the storm trysail and balance the sail plan with a storm jib. Smaller vessels with a livelier motion typically need to make this transition sooner than larger, more stable, more powerful boats. With these sail adjustments there is less heel and considerable easing of the violent pounding caused by being overcanvassed. Racing skippers caught in storms offshore face a different decision and may need to accept that it's time to stop competing and transition to survival mode.

The anxiety of a threatening forecast and a low deck of stratus clouds can cause many sailors to sail undercanvassed as they await more volatile weather. This could make sense when a cold front is powering down on a shorthanded crew. However, an undercanvassed vessel wallowing in a seaway makes life more uncomfortable than when more sail is set. Today's trend toward roller-furling headsails and a removable inner forestay allow for some functional compromises, especially for a shorthanded crew that prefers to reef before conditions completely deteriorate.

Reaching under a reefed main with forestaysail set, this double-headsail sloop powers along, and if the breeze lets off a bit, the crew can deploy a little of that tightly furled jib.

Multihull sailors have a particularly keen interest in matching sail area to wind conditions. Catamarans and trimarans lack the heeling reminder that warns a monohull sailor well ahead of time of the need to reef and change headsails. Waiting too long to reef, especially in gusty conditions, is challenging for monohull sailors, as seen in the photograph on the right. However, it's even worse for those aboard a multihull. When a multihull leaves a rooster tail like the one shown above, it is time to reef, or have skilled crew aboard ready to react.

In such situations you can reef the main and set the inner forestaysail, preparing the crew for an encounter with winds of 25 to 30 knots or more. If the wind drops to 15 knots between squalls or while awaiting the passage of a cold front, you can easily unwind your furled headsail, thus restoring adequate sail area with the sail that's easiest to furl. When the next batch of dark clouds descends and the anemometer starts to spike, a quick haul on the furling line or a push of the autofurl button tightly winds the headsail around the furling foil. Make sure you have enough sheet tension to create a neat, tight furl, and secure the sheets and reefing line. Some sailors use a rope clutch and a slip knot to make sure the furling line can't be inadvertently released.

Triple-reefing a mainsail is a shortcut to handling heavy weather, but it comes with more risk than reward. You might think that it's much faster to take a third reef and easier than setting a storm trysail. After all, the process should be no different from taking the first and second reefs (described in Chapter 7). But triple reefs might not be as easy as they appear.

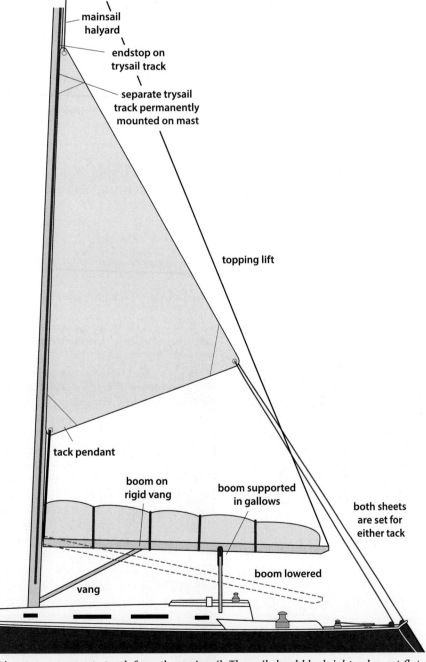

A storm trysail is set on a separate track from the mainsail. The sail should be bright color, cut flat, and made out of triple-stitched heavy premium woven Dacron. The ISAF Offshore Regulations stipulate that the trysail is not greater than 17.5% of P x E (P = mainsail hoist; E = mainsail foot). (Joe Comeau)

Few booms are rigged with three reefing lines. This means most mainsails with a third reef require a hoist pendant to shuttle an unreeved first reef line up and through the third reef position. You'll find this more than a minor challenge at 0300 in gale-force winds and sweeping seas.

There are several additional reasons to avoid tackling a serious gale with a triple-reefed mainsail. The first is the weight and strength of the mainsail; even if all goes well, the experience permanently alters the shape of this essential sail. Building the mainsail from heavier, higher-modulus material may help, but then the sail would be less efficient for 90% or more of its normal use. And if it's damaged in the storm, you're left without a mainsail when the wind drops and large, unstable seas roll through.

Another downside is that the main, reefed or not, is tacked close to the deck, where breaking seas can damage it. A storm trysail is tacked free of the boom on a pendant that's 6 feet or more above the gooseneck (see illustration page 335). In this position, it avoids breaking seas and still provides drive as the boat settles into deep troughs between swells, without the danger of an unintentional jibe that can injure crew.

The justification for a dedicated storm jib follows similar logic. Its flatter shape, heavier construction, and bright orange color or head patch all contribute to the job at hand, plus its higher cut and high tack make it less vulnerable to breaking seas. In addition, when it's set on a forestay well aft of the headstay (perhaps a moveable inner stay), it pairs up with the storm trysail to consolidate the center of effort in the middle of the vessel. This is a well-balanced sail plan that's less likely to create unwanted yawing when gusts hit the boat.

A yawl that relies on a jib-and-jigger placement of storm sails has a vulnerable sail plan. The mizzenmast of a yawl is seldom as well stayed as the mainmast, a potentially significant issue in breaking seas. Ketches have a mizzenmast with much stronger stays, but a storm trysail attached to a separate track on the mainmast still usually offers the best choice for heavy weather. A schooner, on the other hand, offers flexibility for adjusting sail area and balance. Many schooner sailors cope with a gale by striking the large mainsail and proceeding under a forestaysail and reefed foresail.

The storm trysail and storm jib are also the best bet for heaving-to in high winds (see the later section

BOAT DESIGN AND STORM TACTICS

A modern race boat with a fin keel and canoe-shaped hull, if deep-keeled and heavily ballasted, may be able to forereach (move with a combined forward and sideways motion, as described later in reference to heaving-to) under storm trysail alone. These often fractionally rigged sloops have much of the working sail area in the mainsail. In lighter air they can be sailed to weather under main alone, so the sailor may feel an urge in a storm to simply deep-reef the mainsail, douse the headsail, and sail a close reach. But as explained earlier, sailing with a deeply reefed main is not the best choice. But this type of boat may balance well under a storm trysail alone, without a storm jib, and point high enough to forereach. It's critical in such conditions that the boat not fall off enough to get beam-on to the approaching seas. You're most vulnerable when you expose your beam to steep, breaking seas.

The forereaching tactic is usually inappropriate for wide-beam, shallow-draft vessels that lose substantial lateral plane with only a small amount of heel—they give up too much leeway when forereaching. These wide cruisers have a high risk of ending up beam-on to a breaking sea. This design characteristic often coincides with lower ballast ratios and a low limit of positive stability (as discussed in Chapter 12). Combined, these factors create a boat with a greater tendency to capsize and less ability to recover. Therefore, it's imperative that you keep the long axis (the centerline) of the vessel pointed toward or away from the approaching seas.

Fortunately, climbing over wave faces in a forereaching attitude is not the only alternative. Traditionally, mariners with sea room ahead ran before breaking seas, often the best alternative for a wide-beam, shallow-draft vessel. Indeed, many modern racers and cruisers can admirably maneuver in this way. The best performers in these circumstances are boats with moderate length-to-beam ratios and enough hydrodynamic lift designed into the bow to overcome wide, flat stern sections. However, boats that are quick to plane but tend to root the bow (bury it in the back of the sea ahead) can be a handful when running before the short, steep seas of a rapidly deepening low.

Many cruisers with less beam carried all the way aft handle heavy weather best while running before a blow. You can maintain even more control by tackling wave faces the way a skier traverses a slope, using maneuvers that avoid the straight downhill schuss. A high-windage production cruiser may gather too much way while running down a wave face, even when running under bare poles. Your boat might behave much better if you stream a drogue device astern, which will slow it down (as discussed later). And some multihull sailors who have endured storms at sea seem to favor streaming a sea anchor on a bridle from the bows (see below for a discussion of sea anchors).

on heaving-to). In less volatile conditions a reefed main and forestaysail work well for this tactic.

Regardless of the sails used, you'll need enough winches and rope clutches to handle all the sheets, runners, and preventer lines required for sailing in heavy weather.

STORM TACTICS

Setting the right amount of sail area begins the process of handling heavy weather, but the point of sail is equally important. As you might expect, it makes sense to choose a heading that avoids the worst of the weather while also keeping the vessel as far from beam-on to the approaching seas as possible, thus avoiding capsize conditions. (Navigating to avoid the worst of a storm is especially important with tropical storms and hurricanes. As noted in Chapter 10, a tropical storm system's forward motion along its track reinforces the rotational wind speed on the dangerous side of the storm and lessens it on the more navigable side.) Unfortunately, there is no fixed rule to find the best heading to accommodate your vessel's stability and seaworthiness. The naval architect's vision, the boatbuilder's hand, and the sea state you're dealing with all play key roles in the way you handle heavy weather.

When you have sufficient crew for effective watchkeeping, it makes sense to carry on under reduced sail, and eventually with storm sails, especially if you're progressing away from the worst of the weather. You could reach a point, however, at which carrying on no longer seems tenable. For example, an exhausted crew or worsening seas may mean it's time to take further measures. A boat staggering under the assault of a storm—especially when the weather forecasts predict more to come—might also force assessment of your options.

Effective heavy-weather tactics include *heaving-to/ forereaching, running off, running off with a drogue, lying to a sea anchor*, or *lying ahull*, described in the following sections. While all are widely discussed, no single heavy-weather tactic fits all situations or vessel designs (see sidebar). Whatever tactic you choose, you need to devise a plan to implement it after carefully considering the decision. Timing is everything, so don't wait too long to deploy a drogue or sea anchor if that's part of your "worst weather" plan.

Trial and error, and practice help, too. Take your boat out in a Force 6 breeze and practice setting your storm sails. Try forereaching and heaving-to or running before the breeze. Try deploying a drogue or sea anchor if you think you might use that tactic in a storm at sea. See how your boat—and you—perform.

AT THE HELM IN HEAVY WEATHER AT NIGHT

Even on a moonless night, breaking wave faces can be seen. Often it's the bioluminescent plankton firing off like a strobe in the tumult that mark the wave face. The sound can be nerve wracking but is a helpful indicator of trouble on the way. When running off at night, I am always attentive to waves that are abnormal in both size and direction. My strategy when deep reaching in the dark is simple: I steer to avoid a wave on the beam. If I'm going to get clobbered by a breaking crest, I want the long axis of the boat as perpendicular as possible to it; this makes a broach much less likely. Those sailing heavy-displacement boats with a fine entry may also have to contend with the boat's tendency to root, or bury the bow—a trait that can lead to a broach or pitchpole in the worst of conditions. If my course is to weather in the dark, I close reach under storm jib and storm trysail, paying heed to how well the boat is climbing wave faces. If "stall-out" or loss of way starts to become an issue, I turn tail, run out the drogue, and head downwind at slow speed. Those with a light boat with a large volume aft may not find this technique appropriate and may want to forereach into the tempest or deploy a sea anchor (a tough task when conditions are already violent and at night). Racing crews aboard soundly built lightweight flyers often use boat speed as an ally, harnessing maneuverability to steer clear of wave-face dangers. However, it's a hard tactic to implement at night and requires a number of skilled, adroit helmspersons ready to handle short, attentive stints at the wheel.

In gales in the Southern Ocean, long-period swells interact with energy from a secondary wave train to create a dangerous energy transfer from wave to boat. At night, a peaking crest is difficult to avoid.

When you carry out various tactics, you'll learn a great deal about what might work for your boat and crew when it counts.

Whatever your tactic, you don't want to be on a wave face when it becomes so vertical that gravity causes the crest, and the boat with it, to drop into the trough. Such destabilizing conditions occur only in violent storms at sea or on breaking bars and shoals, and the storms that generate such conditions are rare. As mentioned earlier, steer clear of shoaling coastal areas and be cautious about conditions where the wind confronts a strong current in heavy weather. The likelihood of encountering such a storm increases in high-latitude sailing, above 40 degrees north or south, especially outside the more benign summer months. Likewise, the seas generated by hurricanes and even some tropical storms can become steep and unstable to the point they can cause a capsize.

Heaving-To and Forereaching

Heaving-to is a heavy-weather tactic for some boats, especially when using a storm trysail and storm jib. The technique is to tack yet leave the jib backwinded

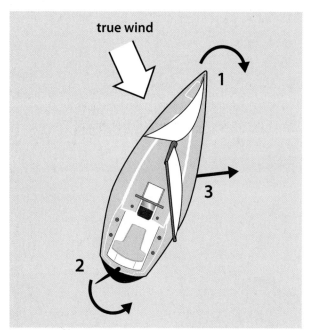

true wind

1

3

2

◀ In a heave-to position, the backwinded headsail (1) tries to force the bow away from the wind, while the wheel, turned hard to windward (2), causes the rudder to attempt to force the bow into the wind, opposing the back-winded jib. Meanwhile, the reefed mainsail or storm trysail is eased to the point where it spills most of the breeze (3), but does not flog and maintains enough movement through the water to allow the rudder to function. (Each sailboat behaves a little differently: longer keel boats are less finicky about the sheet ease and traveler position, while shorter lateral-plane keels often need more tweaking to behave while hove-to.) (Joe Comeau)

and ease either the triple-reefed mainsail or storm trysail so it is feathered but not flogging. As the vessel settles onto the new tack, the helm is turned as if to induce another tack, but the backed headsail prevents the bow from turning through the wind. The resulting movement is called *forereaching*—meaning a combined sideways and forward motion. In this case, the forward component of the vessel's motion is intentionally minimized by easing the main or storm trysail. This causes the sideways movement (leeway) to increase. (The forereaching tactic mentioned earlier on page 336 involves more drive and less leeway, and with both sails trimmed close-hauled, the boat points higher.) In heave-to trim, the keel stalls and leaves a vortex of disturbed water to windward. Some believe that this turbulence helps prevent breaking waves. Maybe. We do know for sure that heaving-to provides easier motion, a feeling that someone has just shut off the "storm switch."

Many modern sloops with the mast stepped quite far forward can heave-to under a deeply reefed mainsail alone. (Because the main is so far forward, when eased, its drag rather overwhelms its lift, allowing the bow to blow to leeward. The rudder, lashed as if turning into another tack, tries to turn the boat to windward, and when these forces are equal the boat stays in a slightly forereaching, hove-to position.) Some sailors find they can keep the bow closer to the wind this way than when heaving-to under jib and main. Boats with a modern, high-aspect spade rudder might not need the helm hard over to heave-to. In fact, the significant amount of lift that such a rudder generates may cause the vessel even with a backed jib to turn its bow through the wind. Discovering the ideal sail plan and rudder position for heaving-to takes a bit of trial and error, but when well executed, the tactic allows a crew to leave the helm unattended and establishes a stable platform on which to prepare a meal or get some essential rest.

When choosing the tack for heaving-to, give thought to wind and wave geometry and pick the tack that best keeps the swell from approaching beam-on. This will lessen the possibility of a steep, short-period breaking wave inducing a knockdown. Naturally, you also want to be on a tack that affords ample sea room.

Running Before the Storm

The hardy fishermen who once sailed Gloucester schooners to the Grand Banks used to speak of "squaring the sails and scudding for Squam," referring to running before an easterly blow in order to reach the sheltered bays, coves, and fishing ports that dot the New England coastline. The tactic is equally

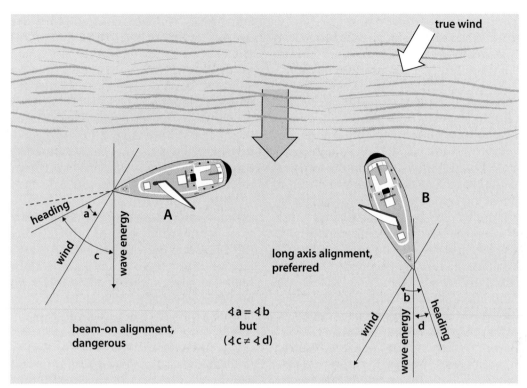

true wind

heading

wind

a

c

wave energy

A

beam-on alignment,
dangerous

long axis alignment,
preferred

B

b

d

wind

wave energy

heading

∢a = ∢b
but
(∢c ≠ ∢d)

Both boats are sailing the same broad-reach wind angle while running off, but on opposite tacks. The vessel on the right is sailing with the seas approaching from the stern quarter; the motion on board will be kinder and the potential for capsize lower. The vessel on the left, though carrying an identical apparent wind angle, experiences nearly beam-on seas that aggravate the vessel's roll motion and potential for capsize. Plot the location of the weather system and its movement prior to choosing your course, which should carry you away from the worst of the storm while keeping the seas astern. (Joe Comeau)

viable offshore when the desired route keeps a building breeze on the stern.

The first question about this heavy-weather tactic involves how much speed to carry. The glib—but honest—answer is to carry as much as you and your vessel can handle safely. For a shorthanded crew, the answer usually is determined by how well the self-steering gear behaves. Most start to get squirrelly when hull speed is approached, and the rolling motion of a deep reach or run further influences steering dynamics. Larger race boats with an abundance of skilled crew for the helm can avoid self-steering limitations, but they must still contend with regular transitions from displacement to planing mode. This ups the ante, and those who plane down the faces of large, storm-tossed seas must continuously make calls about wave-face stability and the threat of burying the bow in the trough or back of the wave ahead.

Modern, light race boats behave much better at planing speeds than older racers and cruisers; their flatter canoe bodies, wide sterns, and big rudders make wave riding a prolonged rather than intermittent capability. With speed comes maneuverability, lower apparent wind, and great progress toward wherever the bow is pointed. Many modern, flatter-bottomed racing sailboats switch into prolonged planing stints

When experiencing heavy weather offshore, be prepared for breaking seas that are offset to the prevailing wave train. An alert helmsperson can turn the boat just enough to avoid a beam-on encounter. More often than not, a 30- or 40-degree approach angle to the wave face is optimal. The same geometry holds true for waves approaching the stern. The delicate balance is between avoiding a beam-on boarding sea capsize versus burying the bow and broaching by driving straight down a wave face. When there are enough crew aboard to have a wave spotter on watch, surprise wave bashings diminish and hailing "Wave!" lets everyone know to hang on.

with great helm control and little or no tendency to root the bow. With careful steering and attentive watchkeeping, heavy-weather downwind sprints have led to 300-, 400-, and even 500+-mile daily runs.

For a variety of reasons, this white-knuckled side of sailing is for record breakers and should carry a "do not try this at home" warning. The crew is just one bad turn away from a violent broach. At that point the boat's 20-knot forward velocity can instantaneously become a 15- to 20-knot increase in apparent wind speed just as the vessel and crew are pinned in the trough of a breaking sea. At some point, changes in wind strength and wave-face steepness make most sailboats start to misbehave, so even the most avid competitor must eventually slow down to survive.

Cruising sailors, in contrast, need to get to know certain thresholds for their boat and themselves. One of the most important pieces of information involves understanding how fast your own boat should go when running in heavy weather. The answer varies and often depends on keeping the vessel easy to steer by autopilot, windvane, or attentive crew. A dead-downwind rhythmic roll is not the ideal course; rather, put your boat on a deep reach that keeps wind and sea on the quarter and avoids putting the bow on a perpendicular descent into the trough of every wave.

Wave crests are seldom perpendicular to the wind vector, because waves move much faster than weather systems. You can be tormented by the winds of one low-pressure system even as you are tossed about in waves created by another. For example, sailors headed west across the Indian Ocean toward Durban, South Africa, often learn what it's like to be propelled by 30-knot easterlies down the faces of trade-wind generated swells, smack into the face of a diagonally moving contradictory swell spawned deep in the Southern Ocean. The feeling is like sailing downwind and beating at the same time, and as torrents of indigo water roll from bow to stern, all ports, hatches, and even Dorade vents must be plugged and dogged.

Most of the time, the axis of the wave crests is offset no more than 20 to 30 degrees from the perpendicular to the prevailing wind vector. However, this modest offset is significant when attempting to run before heavy wind and seas. The diagram on page 339 illustrates how important it is to pick the tack that allows a vessel to hold building seas on the better stern quarter while running off. The port-tack boat in the diagram is deriving full benefit from its fore-and-aft stability, while the starboard-tack boat, though sailing an identical wind angle, meets the swells and breaking waves almost beam-on. The starboard-tack boat is more prone to capsize because of the reduced stability of a vessel when beam-on the seas.

At some point when running, yaw increases (see Chapter 4 for a discussion of a boat's motion). Despite your best efforts (or those of the autopilot or windvane) to prevent it, the bow begins oscillating from side to side around your nominal heading. When that happens, reefing and reducing the headsail area restores a good degree of control while sacrificing only a little speed. If you've changed down to storm sails but still find yourself hauling along faster than hull speed, it's time to consider other options in case conditions worsen. You could sail with bare poles (running before the storm with no sail set), and you might further enhance this tactic and prevent pitchpoling by towing a drogue astern. Note, however, that many ocean-voyaging veterans

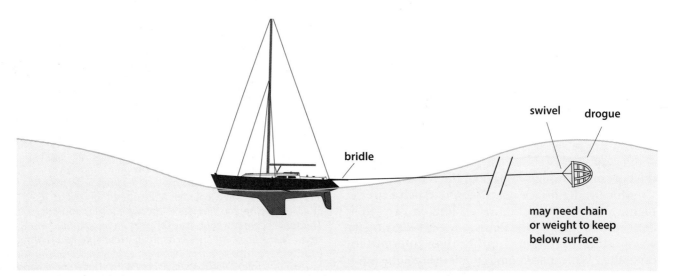

🏴 *With a Galerider drogue set, the boat is deep reaching or running off before the storm under greatly reduced sail or bare poles. Check regularly for chafe at the quarters, and pick the tack that keeps waves more perpendicular to the vessel's centerline. (Joe Comeau)*

are unwilling to strike their storm sails because of the violent motion that prevails when no sail is set.

Running before the storm assumes there is abundant sea room to leeward and progress is away from the worst of the weather. Companionway washboards, aft-facing ports, cockpit lockers, and sliding hatches must be ruggedly constructed, positively dogged, and able to withstand breaking seas.

Towing a Drogue

A drogue is towed from the stern to slow the vessel and add directional stability. A drogue is not a sea anchor (see below) and is designed for bare-poles or off-the-wind sailing. The loads on the rode are significant, and in addition to using a bridle and providing plenty of antichafe padding, the strength of the drogue rode must be equal to your primary anchor cable.

This setup is usually one of the last-ditch efforts of a crew caught in especially violent weather. A drogue dampens the violent yawing motion associated with high-speed running and it keeps the long axis of the boat better aligned with the wave energy, thus increasing the boat's stability and its resistance to broaching and capsize.

The Galerider drogue produced by Hathaway, Reiser, and Raymond is a clever web basket with a circular stainless steel wire clamped around its open mouth. The towline attaches to a swivel whose opposite end gathers the smaller lines from the drogue's individual pieces of webbing. When towed, water passes through the device as if through a perforated

■ *Turbulent flow through the conical webbing of a Galerider drogue causes significant drag and adds directional stability to a vessel running before heavy wind and seas.*

funnel, creating a significant drag. When properly sized for a given vessel, the drogue can cut a hull-speed run under bare poles down to a more sedate 3 or 4 knots.

The Jordan series drogue accomplishes a similar feat using multiple small cones lined up along the rode to induce a cumulative drag. The manufacturer believes this configuration makes it less likely a breaking wave face will destabilized the drogue, while increasing its ability to load and unload gradually and smoothly as seas overtake the vessel. A series drogue is also more likely to remain submerged, even when the vessel accelerates in extreme wind gusts and seas.

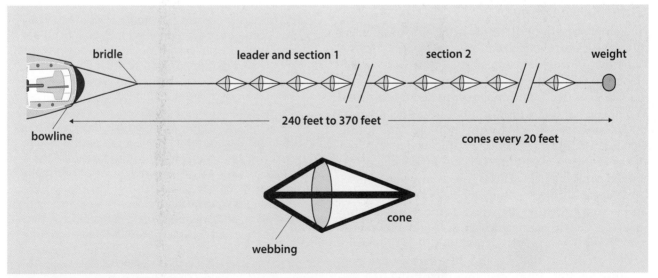

■ *The logic behind this series drogue design involves spreading frictional contact with the sea over the entire length of the warp. The assumption is that by doing so, there's less likelihood of complete loss of drag if and when some part of the drogue encounters an aerated breaking wave face. The down side is the chance of snagging one of the mini cones as the drogue is deployed and the inability to winch in the last 200 feet of rode when the storm abates. (Joe Comeau)*

🚩 *Fifty knots of wind can damage a 40-foot yawl anchored in a partially exposed cove. Imagine what the same vessel might do in 30-foot seas and winds of hurricane force when tethered to a sea anchor. One thing is certain: if you decide to use a sea anchor, be sure the hardware attaching it is up to the job.*

Launching a Drogue

In heavy weather offshore, drogue users generally praise both configurations, the series and the Galerider. With either system or a homemade equivalent, the real challenge occurs when you attempt to get the gear overboard in storm-tossed conditions. When the wind is strong enough to propel a vessel under bare poles at 4 to 5 knots or more, attempting to launch a high-resistance towable device tethered to the end of a 300-foot rode can have some unintended consequences. This is true even when you set up a proper bridle, carefully fake (lay out) the warp, and attempt to slow the vessel as much as possible first. If a hockle or snag occurs during deployment, the drogue goes into action and hundreds of pounds of pull are felt in the line and on whatever inadvertent fitting, stanchion, or human hand the line has snagged.

Every crewmember should practice a drogue launch on a flat calm day, using the engine to main-

tain a 2-knot speed. During this exercise, try laying out all the tackle so that it runs cleanly from a faked figure-eight line or layout of the rode on a side deck. Be sure there's no snafu over or under a pulpit. But if you do encounter a problem during the process, all it takes is a shift to neutral to eliminate the load. Once you've perfected the process in flat water, perform a sea trial in 25- to 30-knot conditions and you'll develop a feel for vessel surge and the wind force.

Some crews prefer to deploy a drogue by taking a few turns on a large primary winch and then gradually easing out the rode. The big challenge with this is the final transfer from the winch to the bridle at the stern. With all the lines in place, when the wraps are cast off the winch the rode runs free and fetches up on the already-configured bridle. But snag a cleat or a man-overboard pole and this elegant load transition turns into a fire drill.

Some crews find it necessary to weight the drogue with a shot of chain to keep it from pulling free from the water as the vessel surges. A short shot (20 feet) of heavy ½-inch chain usually does the job, placed between the drogue's swivel and the thimble of the eye splice at the end of the rode, attached using shackles.

The bridle and rode are best set up in a three-way junction. You can use three bowlines, but this causes considerable chafe. A hardware connection is better; ideally, three thimbled rope ends are connected to a

TOWING WARPS AND IMPROVISED DROGUES

The principle behind any towable drogue device is to increase drag. In addition to the Galerider and the Jordan series drogue, trailing warps (usually lines, sometimes even an anchor as weight) is another way to a similar outcome. But it doesn't take complicated mathematics to see that it would take much more line to create the same amount of drag as commercial drogues. Still, towing warps delivers a bit more directional stability and helps lessen yawing. Some sailors stow a homemade drogue device, such as an automobile tire on the end of a long warp. The tire scoops water to increase drag and is tough, making it a valid candidate for a homemade drogue. Weight is usually added to keep the tire from skimming over the surface. Though inelegant on a yacht, an automobile tire can double as a towable drogue as well as a makeshift fender against a concrete quay. Drill a few large holes to drain water when stowed, add a good quality swivel for attaching it to a warp, and perhaps even wrap the tire with nylon webbing or rope to prevent smudging the topsides when used as a fender.

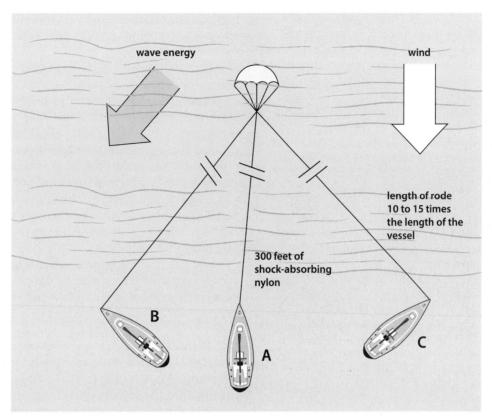

wave energy

wind

length of rode
10 to 15 times
the length of the
vessel

300 feet of
shock-absorbing
nylon

B

A

C

A vessel that behaves as shown in A, retaining a bow-on attitude toward the wind and sea, is a prime candidate for a sea anchor. However, if the boat yaws back and forth while sailing under bare poles (boats B and C), there's a good chance it may be hit broadside by a breaking wave and suffer a knockdown or damage when tethered to a sea anchor. (Joe Comeau)

common ring via shackles, forming a Y-junction at the bridle's apex. This arrangement minimizes line chafe, and because the two bridle legs are trimmed independently, the crew can load one quarter more than the other, thereby optimizing the stern's orientation to the overtaking seas.

Retrieving a Drogue

As the effects of the storm abate, the wind settles down, and the seas dissipate, it's time to retrieve the drogue, a fairly straightforward process. At this point you're usually undercanvassed and it's easy to heave-to, easing most of the tension on the drogue. The crew then hauls in the line slowly, usually taking figure-eight coils in the cockpit or on the afterdeck. The manageable size of the drogue itself and the fact that it sheds all water makes the Galerider easy to recover. A simple twist of the mouth decreases its diameter and makes it easy to fit it in its pack.

Sea Anchors

There are many sea stories both for and against the use of a sea anchor. This piece of gear that looks like a nylon parachute is set from the bow, tethered to a lengthy rode. Its effectiveness depends on the design of the vessel, making it a good heavy-weather survival technique for some boats but not for others.

Streaming to a sea anchor in storm-force seas is like a boxer trading blows toe to toe with his opponent rather than bobbing and weaving to duck and deflect blows. Ideally, the sea anchor holds a vessel head-to the seas, and like the boxer, the vessel must be strong enough to take the impact. When it works, this tactic aligns the boat's long centerline axis with the storm, providing the most stable and least capsize-prone angle of attack while offering the least resistance to a breaking sea.

The tactic works best with heavy, long-keel vessels and catamarans that have good directional stability and tend to remain where they have been pointed. In contrast, light, lively fin-keelers yaw back and forth like a puppy tethered to a stake; streaming from a sea anchor can cause the vessel to swing nearly beam-on to breaking seas. The vessel then suffers the worst of both worlds: maximum exposure to the sea, but minimum stability. The load of the sea anchor adds another force as breaking waves accelerate the boat. Adding in the "lull effect" of wave troughs and the regular velocity changes in gusty storm-force conditions, many light vessels streaming a sea anchor be-

MANEUVERING A SEA ANCHOR

Adding a breast line to the sea anchor's rode, hauled on a primary winch, shifts the load from the stem to the forward quarter. The result is increased load on the rode and the centerline of the boat no longer being head to wind. In essence, the boat takes on more of a hove-to angle of attack. This may be desirable on some long-keel heavy vessels or in conditions where the wind and waves are not aligned. Skewing the bow to face the wave energy makes sense. But this technique doesn't work well with boats prone to "sailing at anchor." Such boats can be accelerated by a gust, come to the end of the yaw, and tack over with the breasting line now under the forefoot of the boat. A good way to test how well your boat would behave with a breasted sea anchor is to rig up a breasting line on rope anchor rode with a 10:1 scope, and note how the boat behaves in a windy anchorage. Make sure it's a big anchor and the holding ground is good, because breasting the boat exposes more surface area and with more windage comes more load.

have like a yo-yo on a string. If your boat yaws back and forth on its mooring or anchor, it won't ride well to a sea anchor either.

Multihull sailors find the sea anchor a valuable tool, and using it can help keep a catamaran or trimaran right side up in survival conditions. Multihull sailors still debate whether to stream the sea anchor from a bridle at the bow or stern. Those advocating streaming from the stern argue that less stress is put on the rudders. However, too many multihulls have huge sliding "patio" doors and a vulnerable hardtop at the stern, and facing such structures into breaking seas simply asks for trouble and is a much bigger gamble than keeping the bow facing the seas and risking more rudder loading.

Deploying a Sea Anchor

Despite the challenges in survival conditions, a sea anchor can prove helpful for traditional long-keel boats and multihulls. However, getting a sea anchor into position is even tougher than launching a drogue. Slipping a parachute-like device over the side and keeping all the lines from twisting into a big snafu is no minor accomplishment. In 50 knots of wind, the sea anchor can behave like an unbagged spinnaker caught by a gust. Indeed, when you finally need a sea anchor, the conditions make simply being on deck a challenge.

Think about setting a conventional anchor with your vessel hauling along at 3 knots or more. When

the anchor sets, the vessel puts serious tension in the rode—and the same is true when deploying a sea anchor. When the canopy opens, the rode comes under terrific tension and the vessel pivots head to wind and stops dead.

Getting a sea anchor safely over the side in heavy weather generally requires steering onto a more beam-on position. Although you'd find better protection on the leeward side of your boat, that is a poor option because of the likelihood of running over anything deployed from the leeward side. That means you must launch the sea anchor from the windward rail, somehow managing to get it over the side without twists or hockles that prevent the canopy from opening.

You begin deploying a sea anchor by dousing storm sails and lashing down or eliminating deck clutter. Clear deck space to fake out the nylon rode, making sure it can run clear and free. Most manufacturers describe the next step with phrases like "head into the weather" or "slow the vessel to a stop." However, these feats become more and more difficult as wind and seas increase. In 40- to 50-knot conditions, turning into the seaway often results in waves sweeping over the vessel, carrying away anything not well secured, including crewmembers and the sea anchor. Clearly, deploying a trip line (used to recover the sea anchor after the blow), sea anchor, and rode on the windward side of your boat is easier said than done, especially if you've followed a logical heavy-weather strategy. That means you've downshifted from reefed sails to storm sails before opting for the sea anchor in still-worsening conditions. One manufacturer bluntly states that a crew should deploy the sea anchor early and not wait for the onset of storm-force conditions—a tough call when you're trying to sail away from the worst of the storm.

Once the sea anchor goes over the side, the next challenge lies in paying out rode quickly enough to avoid full tension on the line. Any hockles, snarls, or snags can lead to injury or gear damage. You're dealing with multiple, cyclical forces. At their peak, these forces result in loads much greater than what an anchor rode endures in a sheltered cove under similar wind velocities. The dynamic loads caused by the seaway are added to the baseline wind-pressure loads. When the breaking face of a 20-foot wave cascades over the boat, the shock-absorbing effect of the nylon rode helps dissipate the energy, but ports, hatches, and gear attached to the deck, as well as the hull and deck itself, must be able to sustain repeated assaults. Because movement to leeward is constrained by the pull of the sea anchor, more of the wave energy will be dissipated through the vessel's structure itself.

To put adequate distance between the sea anchor

and the boat, use a minimum of 300 feet of shock-absorbing nylon rode, preferably 10 to 15 times the length of the vessel. The rode should be secured to a very robust set of cleats or other means of attachment, such as secondary lines forward from the primary winches. Each surge of the vessel causes a tug on the sea anchor; the more violent the conditions, the greater the rode tension generated. Once the rode has been carefully paid out, add antichafe protection.

Pay attention to the slingshot effect, which is greater with smaller-diameter rodes with more stretch. Not only might the vessel be accelerated into a beam-on position during a momentary lull, but a light-displacement, fin-keel, spade-rudder boat could move over the rode and catch it with the prop shaft or rudder. Some mariners suggest setting a tiny backstay-hanked riding sail to keep the bow from falling off the wind, but others see the extra windage and the complication of a riding sail as more hindrance than help. But if a tiny scrap of sail keeps a vessel headed to the wind and minimizes yawing, it's a complication worth having.

Once you've set up the sea anchor with appropriate scope and antichafe gear and you've secured all sails and gear, lash the rudder amidships, preferably with a well-secured emergency tiller rather than by locking the wheel. As the vessel accelerates sternward, the rudder blade is subject to significant force; securing it in place with a lashed emergency tiller prevents these loads from damaging the vulnerable steering linkage and cables.

In the midst of a gale, a sea anchor cannot easily be hauled back in and redeployed, so if it fouls during the initial deployment, you'll likely have a major fire drill. For this reason, practice setting the sea anchor in more modest conditions when you can develop a sense how and where lines should be run. Practice also provides your crew with a sense for how long you can wait to set the device in deteriorating weather.

A shorthanded crew needs a more cautious approach. When caught in gale-force conditions that are forecast to become worse overnight, it's usually best to deploy the sea anchor in daylight. Otherwise, you risk having to deploy it at 0300 with seas and rain blowing sideways—conditions that increase the chances of encountering problems.

Recovering a Sea Anchor

Recovering a sea anchor can be a serious challenge. More often than not, the wind lets off after a serious storm more quickly than the waves subside. As described, the functionality of the sea anchor depends on the wind's pressure on the hull and rig to keep the vessel's centerline streaming with the wind and sea.

When the wind lightens or stops completely, the sea anchor and its rode are more of an impediment than an advantage, and the lack of wind does not mean that recovery of the tackle is a walk in the park. The process can be complicated by large waves and even breaking seas. Many sailors have noted the most dangerous sea state conditions sometimes occur just after the wind abates. Determining the right time to haul in a sea anchor is as important as knowing when to deploy it in the first place.

During recovery the load on the rode should be as little as possible, and it's critical to always know the location of the rode relative to the propeller(s). The initial rode recovery is the easy part. Slowly motor toward the sea anchor, putting the shift lever in neutral whenever there is a threat of overriding the pendant line. Most modern sea anchors have a recovery line that allows the nylon chute to be pulled in its opposite side with a collapsed rather than open mouth. At the last stage in this process large swells and breaking waves can be a significant hazard. Be ready to quickly put turns of the rode on a cleat or let go if a lift of the bow threatens to load the sea anchor. Once the sea anchor's recovery line has been tensioned, the anchor should no longer be open, but careful boat handling is still needed to keep breaking waves from shoving the boat over the sea anchor.

Sea anchor recovery can fail, and as a last resort it may become necessary to cut the anchor free.

Lying Ahull

When a sailboat or power vessel is left to survive or founder on its own after the crew has been rescued, a surprising number of abandoned boats weather the blow. Some sailboats have found their own way to Bermuda, for example, and a few crewless cruisers manage to make it all the way across the Atlantic. Indeed, an abandoned boat's prospects for remaining afloat are so good that search-and-rescue teams often ensure a through-hull is open to sink the abandoned vessel before it becomes a navigation hazard.

When a vessel lies ahull—that is, tiller lashed, with sails down—abandoned or not—it usually assumes a beam-on attitude to wind and sea—the least stable orientation. Some offshore sailors, such as experienced ocean voyager and sailboat designer Steve Dashew, see advantages in this orientation for shoal-draft vessels with high freeboard. Dashew believes that a shoal-draft hull will skid to leeward, a highly underrated attribute of seaworthiness. On the other hand, vessels with deep fin keels can "trip" on their keels and be rolled. High freeboard adds buoyancy and a positive righting moment, though the wind-

 Seeing the approach of a Gulf Stream squall or any line squall, skippers weigh the threat, have a measure of their crew, and prepare to reef deeply or sail the fine edge between full speed and being knocked flat.

age it creates has a countervailing negative effect. Tank tests addressing the seaworthiness of a shoal-draft, high-freeboard hull have had ambiguous results. Many wide, shallow-draft vessels have survived brutal conditions, but capsize data show a direct correlation between a low limit of positive stability and a significant increase in capsizes (see Chapter 12).

There are several major problems with lying ahull, the first being the horrific motion of the vessel whiplashing its crew as it is buffeted by wind and sea. Abrupt changes in wave face angles alter the center of buoyancy and fling the boat about. Despite the sideways skid referenced by Dashew and others, there remains an increased likelihood of a capsize substantial enough to dismast the vessel. Following a dismasting, remnants of the spar connected to the rigging can hole the boat or damage the prop shaft and rudder. Most experienced voyagers prefer to keep the long axis of their vessels more or less aligned with the seas.

STAY ONE STEP AHEAD

Boats, like their crews, have a wide range of aptitudes and agility. Some vessels run well before building seas, happily planing down wave faces and generat-

ing enough lift in the forward sections to keep the bow from rooting in the wave troughs or burying in the swell just ahead. A surfer understands the consequence of running directly down the face of a steep wave and burying the surfboard's nose; as undesirable as that experience is on a 15-pound surfboard, it's far worse for a sailor aboard a 15-ton sloop. A plunge like that can cause the boat to broach in the trough, leaving it beam-on just as the overtaking wave may be starting to break. Much of the art of big-boat surfing involves gauging how much to angle away from a direct descent to avoid burying the bow in the trough or being caught beam-on to a big sea.

A controlled high-speed broad reach works best in daylight, when unstable wave faces are easier to spot and speed and maneuverability let you steer out of harm's way. On dark, stormy nights, the same strategy is like driving down a mountain road with your headlights off. There are times to slow down, and feedback from the boat and the crew can tell you when you've reached your limits.

Whether you're sailing coastal waters or crossing an ocean, keep alert to wind and sea conditions. The art of staying one step ahead of the next vicious squall can help you avoid at least some encounters with heavy weather.

THE BOATS WE SAIL

Futurist and outspoken advocate of human ingenuity R. Buckminster Fuller may have said it best: "The sailboat is humankind's most noteworthy invention, an elegant machine that continues to harness renewable energy."

Seamanship trumps boat and gear when it comes to safety at sea, but a sound and seaworthy vessel is seamanship's best friend and sometimes even its replacement: sailors caught out in heavy weather have occasionally survived thanks to their vessel's design and construction rather than their own actions.

Sailboats that durable are exceptional, however. The trend in production sailboat design is toward higher volume with an escalation of creature comforts while shaving structural weight to the minimum. Racing sailors seek and are getting better performance, but achieving a high-volume interior and performance at the same time is always a challenge. Designing and building a roomy, good-performing sailboat that is also offshore-capable is an even greater challenge, especially if the boat is to be affordable.

To evaluate the suitability of any boat, start with a realistic idea of your boat's purpose, the conditions you're likely to encounter, and your crew. Being honest in this analysis is essential. The optimum vessel for a voyage around Cape Horn is seldom the best choice for a transit down the Intracoastal Waterway. A voyage from Seattle through the Inside Passage to the southern tip of Alaska spans hundreds of miles of often dead-calm flat water with fast-moving currents. High-latitude cruising it may be, but most of it is not open-ocean voyaging, and motorsailing range and speed will likely play a more significant role than the vessel's ultimate seakeeping ability. The next section of this spectacular coastline, however, requires crossing the fickle and often volatile Gulf of Alaska, a passage that can test a boat's seaworthiness and seakeeping ability.

Ken Read's Volvo 70 (top) and descendants of the venerable Westsail 32 (right) mark the outer extremes of offshore sailboat design.

Here's a pair of bookends depicting a century-long evolution in naval architecture. The double-ender with a long run of keel will have a kind, easy motion, while its boatyard neighbor with deep keel plus bulb attachment will get you where you want to go in a hurry. Which boat would be better for you depends on your voyaging plan and boat-buying budget. It's clear which one needs more water to float in!

What constitutes the consummate cruising sailboat is a matter of debate, and multihulls like this catamaran are the latest to enter the fray. Advocates point out that the only lead on board is in the batteries (and these days that may not even be true), while detractors allude to their immense stability—upside down as well as right side up. More on this debate later in the chapter.

A cruiser appropriate for offshore passagemaking is strong enough to handle a tough blow and agile enough to sail in a variety of wind and sea conditions. Note the small, seaworthy ports, versatile headsail combination, and substantial bow roller and stem fitting.

The folly of selecting a vessel for the average conditions it will face will become apparent the first time you're caught in extreme conditions. On a run across the Gulf of Alaska or a fall or early spring sprint around Cape Hatteras, you're at sea with no shelter, despite (in the latter instance) your proximity to land. In both instances the vessel must be able to sustain a serious pounding.

Virtually all production builders target an audience of inshore and coastal cruisers: 90% of production sailboats in the 30- to 40-foot size ply the lakes, bays, and nearshore waters of North America, the Caribbean, and Europe. As a result, the stability, structural scantlings, and even the accommodations plan of a typical production sailboat are anything but open-ocean optimized. These coastal cruisers tend to have high volume for interior roominess, shallow draft, low-to-moderate ballast ratios, and modest scantlings and stability. There is nothing at all wrong with this—why build a platform capable of an Atlantic crossing for a crew who will never leave Montauk Point astern?

Complicating the planning of a potential long-distance voyager is the marine industry's habit of lumping all sailors who don't race under the label "cruiser," regardless of whether the cruising involved is an ocean passage, an overnight sail, or simple enjoyment of home-port and local waters during fair weather. The implied common bond among all sailors is a nice sentiment, but it clouds the sales pitch.

In order to better clarify the offshore attributes of a vessel, the Europeans have developed the International Standards Organization (ISO) approach to boatbuilding, which provides valuable design and building guidelines based on sound engineering. The ISO standards may be a little tainted by nationalism, boatbuilder lobbying, and special interests, but they're the best small-craft guidelines available; we'll delve into the specifics in this chapter.

In the United States no clear demarcation separates inshore from offshore sailboats, nor is there a willingness among most American builders and brokers to draw such a line. Nor does the U.S. government present marine manufacturers with as many building codes as European authorities. As long as a U.S. boatbuilder doesn't plan to sell in Europe, he or she has far fewer regulatory challenges. Consequently, one U.S. builder's version of an ocean-capable boat

A watershed design of 1963, the Cal 40 represented a confluence of performance under sail, a fiberglass structure strong enough to race offshore, and a cost that opened up ocean racing and cruising to a much wider audience.

Imagine this vessel in the grip of a knockdown and a breaking wave: things would go from bad to destructive quickly. The designer of this vessel never envisioned the stern accouterment, and the builder didn't plan for 10,000-pound point-loads being imposed on the deck and transom when a wave takes the dinghy on a ride in a different direction. Counting on never broaching or being knocked down at sea is like assuming your anchor will never drag.

may be and usually is quite different from another's. This shifts considerable responsibility to the sailor to understand what differentiates a perfectly acceptable inshore cruiser from an oceangoing vessel. (There are, in the U.S. many organizations that do speak out on best practices for boatbuilding, however. These include the ABYC [American Boat and Yacht Council], ABS [American Bureau of Shipping], and US Sailing, to name just a few. We will also touch upon some of their insights in this chapter.)

■ *The 33-foot* Araminta *ketch (top) was designed by L. Francis Herreshoff, son of Nat (the Wizard of Bristol). Though not as prolific as his father, L. Francis drew some astounding vessels, including the revered* Ticonderoga *(above)—built in 1936 and still going strong today. The* Araminta *design is suited for inshore daysailing with some short-term cruising capability. However, the low freeboard makes the small ketch a wet boat offshore.* Ticonderoga *may appear to be a scaled-up* Araminta, *but the increased LOA, higher freeboard, and displacement make for a splendid passagemaker—and a race boat to reckon with, then, and now.*

■ *Design and building techniques have migrated from ships to small craft and vice versa through maritime history, with small craft all over the world still harnessing the wind's energy. At top is a replica of the shallop Captain John Smith used to explore the Chesapeake Bay in the early 1600s. At bottom is a lateen-rigged double-ender typical of those sailing the coastal waters of Sardinia and the eastern Mediterranean for hundreds of years.*

It's impossible to judge good and bad boats simply by rig or number of hulls. Yes, a practiced eye can read a story in a hull shape, and good bridgedeck clearance, designed into this multihull, is a welcome sight. The moderate-displacement cutter (or double-headsail sloop, as shown on right) remains a favorite of shorthanded ocean passagemakers; large, agile catamarans have also gained a dedicated following.

Stability and structural strength are at the core of staying afloat and are very difficult attributes to retrofit. Unfortunately, many sailors looking for an ocean-capable cruiser focus on the refrigeration system, electronic navigation equipment, and other features of secondary or tertiary importance rather than assessing these less noticeable attributes that can make or break a heavy-weather encounter. Poor electronics, worn-out sails and canvas, and even a tired engine are relatively easy shortcomings to cure, but too low a limit of positive stability (LPS) or too few layers of fiberglass over a wide span of unsupported sandwich structure is not nearly as easy to remedy. In the following sections we'll explore how to understand a vessel's stability and structural attributes.

STABILITY

Staying upright and afloat leads the list of desirable yacht characteristics, and stability has a big role to play in that. Comprised of multiple components, stability is usually misunderstood. To sort it out, let's look first at form stability and ballast stability and see what staying upright is all about.

Form stability derives from a vessel's shape. A wide, short, hard-chine skiff has an abundance of *transverse form stability*—you could stand near the rail and not fear capsizing. This is a plus, but if you try to row the boat, there will be so much skin drag from its wide, flat bottom that it will be like rowing a barge. A longer, leaner, round-bilge Whitehall skiff might send you for a swim if you stand near the rail, but she will row like a dream (she will also refuse to go on

STIFF OR TENDER?

A sailboat that can carry a lot of canvas in a strong breeze is called stiff, while one that heels early to a freshening breeze is referred to as tender. Stiffness derives primarily from form stability and is not necessarily an indication of ultimate stability—the resistance to capsize. Either a stiff boat or a tender one can be a good sea boat if other criteria are met.

plane even with an outboard—a big plus in a dinghy being towed). From these simple shape comparisons you get a hint at the design compromise every naval architect faces: simply put, form stability comes with more low-speed resistance.

Form stability is the largest component of *initial stability*—the sailboat's resistance to heeling. When a boat heels, its center of buoyancy (CB) shifts from the centerline toward the leeward side. The more form stability a hull possesses, the farther outboard the center of buoyancy will move with each added increment of heel, and thus the longer the lever arm, or righting arm (GZ), that resists further heeling. The result is that a beamy boat tries harder to stay perpendicular to the water surface (upright)—which is great when the water is flat, but not as comfortable, or safe, when breaking waves are present.

Form stability's dance partner is *ballast stability*, which derives from the amount and placement of ballast and its effect on a boat's vertical center of gravity (VCG). Working together, these two sources

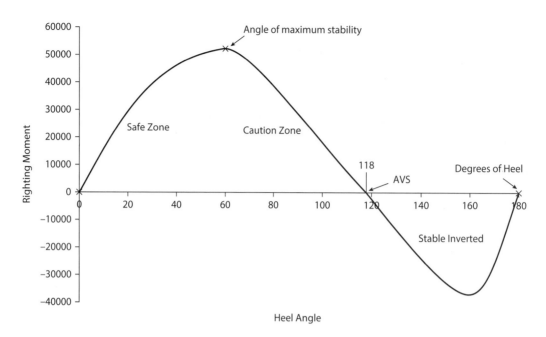

A static stability curve (for a Sabre 426) shows how much resistance the vessel generates to avoid capsize at varying angles of heel. This boat develops its maximum righting moment at 60 degrees of heel and loses all tendency to stay upright at about 118 degrees of heel. When interpreting a stability curve, consider how it was measured. Including the reserve buoyancy of a large, boxy cabinhouse will increase the limit of positive stability (LPS), for example (because the house, if submerged in a knockdown, increases the boat's effective beam—but only if no water floods below), while including the weight of tanks other than half-trim weights will reduce it if the tanks are situated above the center of gravity. We'll explain more about the importance of the areas inscribed by the positive and negative portions of the curve later in this chapter.

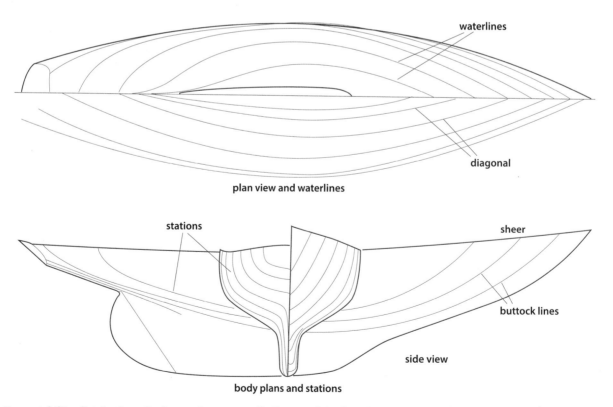

Form stability, distribution of volume, placement of ballast, and freeboard all contribute to a boat's ability to stay upright, and all are defined in two dimensions although they exist in three. Depicting three dimensions on a two-dimensional sheet of paper requires that lines be drawn from multiple vantage points. End, side, and plan views are represented by sections, buttock lines, and waterlines, respectively. (Joe Comeau)

of stability produce a *righting moment* (righting arm × the boat's displacement) that works to return a heeled boat to an upright position. As seen in the static stability curves shown here, the righting moment varies with heel angle. What is less obvious is that the relative contributions of form stability and ballast stability also vary with heel angle. At small angles of heel, form stability provides the lion's share of righting moment, but form stability reaches its maximum at less than about 40 degrees of heel and decreases at larger heel angles, even as ballast stability continues to increase. By the time a ballasted boat heels to its limit of positive stability, its remaining righting moment is due entirely to ballast stability.

Further, the relative contributions of the two types of stability vary with the boat. A narrow, deep, heavily ballasted boat emphasizes ballast stability, while a beamy, lightly ballasted boat depends more on form stability. The former is likely to be more tender but have a greater limit of positive stability—i.e., a greater resistance to deep knockdown and capsize.

Think of a seesaw: you can increase the leverage of the person at one end by increasing his weight, moving him farther from the seesaw fulcrum, or a combination of both. The skinny kid held aloft on the seesaw is like the heeling moment delivered by the wind on the sails and hull, and the big kid weighing down the other end is like the hull's shape and the location of its center of gravity. At least that's the way it is when the righting moment overshadows the heeling moment. But as sails experience greater and

SAIL AREA/DISPLACEMENT RATIOS

The sail area/displacement (SA/D) ratio tells a boat buyer or owner how much emphasis has been placed on light-air performance under sail. The higher ratios (20 and above) are found aboard light displacement race boats while heavy displacement cruisers with smaller rigs will fall into the 10–15 range. Many capable cruisers tally a 16–19 score. Calculating SA/D can be done with a fairly simple equation SA/D = Working Sail Area/(Displacement in cubic feet)^2/3.

BALLAST RATIO

The ballast ratio, also known as the ballast-to-displacement ratio (B/D), is derived by dividing the weight of the ballast by the half-load displacement, then multiplying by 100. A higher number indicates a greater secondary righting moment—such boats have a greater ability to recover from a deep knockdown. Rules of thumb are that a ballast ratio over 40 indicates a stiffer boat, able to stand up to more wind. A current trend by boatbuilders is to drop the B/D to 30 and increase beam—this provides form stability, which, as noted elsewhere in this chapter, is a type of righting moment that disappears at deep angles of heel.

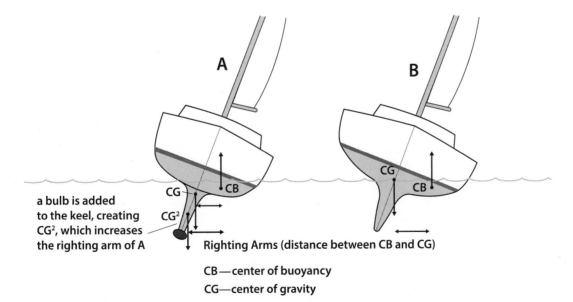

The effect of beam on static stability. Boat B depends more on beam (its form) than ballast for its stability. Boat A has less form stability and thus a shorter righting arm from its narrower beam (assuming it is similar to Boat B in all other respects) but can make up that shortfall with a lower center of gravity (CG). One way to achieve this is with a ballast bulb on the keel as shown. Despite the differences in their form stability, once the bulb is added, these vessels have equal righting moments. (Courtesy Paul Miller, redrawn by Joe Comeau)

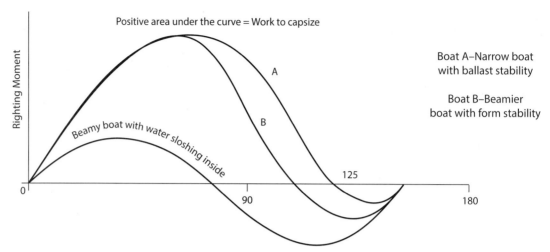

The static stability curves (also known as righting moment curves) for Boats A and B in the previous illustration might look like this. Boat A, with greater ballast stability, maintains a substantially higher righting moment at high heel angles (over 125) and also has a higher limit of positive stability than Boat B that depends more on form stability. There is a third curve shown here of a beamy boat that is downflooded—you can see its righting moment is dramatically decreased (the curve is very small) at all angles of heel. The larger the positive area on the curve, as with Boat A, the more work it takes to invert the vessel. (Courtesy Paul Miller)

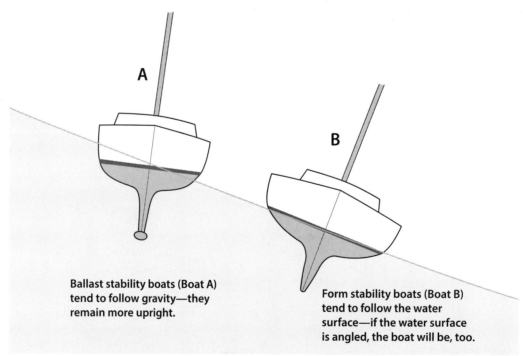

Dynamic stability is an important characteristic of an offshore boat. Boat A, with ballast stability, fights to keep upright regardless of what the water surface is doing, but Boat B, more reliant on form stability conforms to the water surface even if that surface is a wave face sloped well away from the horizontal. The greater your boat's dependence on form stability, the more careful you should be to avoid presenting your beam to a steep sea. (Courtesy Paul Miller, redrawn by Joe Comeau)

greater pressure from a building breeze, the heeling moment continues to build, and that skinny kid becomes more and more formidable. That's why we reef and change down to smaller headsails.

Another key factor of stability is a vessel's ability to resist wave-induced capsize. A vessel possesses *ul-timate stability* when it stands up well when moving water and the energy of a breaking sea hits the hull, superstructure, and perhaps even the sails, attempting to drive the vessel down to leeward. The force to be resisted grows in proportion to the severity of the storm. In severe conditions, *(continued page 357)*

DESIGN CHANGES THAT MODIFY STABILITY

The GZ curve (also known as the righting arm curve, or stability curve) offers a valuable snapshot depicting sailboat stability. Three of the most critical factors revealed are a boat's limit of positive stability (LPS), it's point of maximum righting arm (GZ), and the very important relationship between right side up and upside down stability. The latter is defined by the ratio of the areas of the two arcs comprising a GZ curve.

In order to focus more attention on the importance of stability, Dr. Paul Miller and I have simulated a sailboat we can modify one attribute at a time. We start out with an 18,000 pound (9-ton), 40-foot sailboat with a 42% ballast-to-displacement ratio (B/D) and a displacement-to-length ratio (D/L) of 158. In our first modification we lower the CG by increasing the draft—hull shape, ballast weight, and keel configuration remain unchanged. With increased draft comes a

greater LPS, and a more seaworthy ratio between the area under the positive and negative portions of the GZ curve.

In Boat 1, 6 feet of draft delivers a healthy 120 LPS and a stability curve that's widely accepted as a valid representation of an ocean-going sailboat. Even better is Boat 2 with its 127 LPS, the result of a 7 foot draft. A fringe benefit of this keel configuration is better windward sailing performance. The downside of the latter is its inappropriateness when it comes to shoal water cruising. For those more intent on coastal cruising, there's a shallower draft 5 foot keel with a 113 LPS designated as Boat 3. The range of stability in this shoal draft option is appropriate for inshore sailing but less than optimum for offshore passagemaking.

Next we compared two identically shaped hulls that have a 10% variation in ballast- (continued next page)

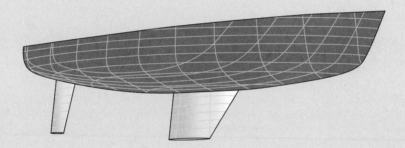

We created a hypothetical boat with identical hull shape and modified certain draft, ballast, and keel shape parameters to better understand their effect on stability.

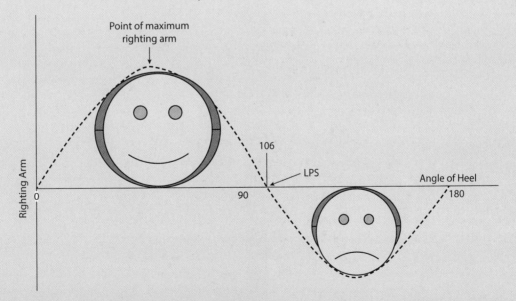

A GZ curve (also known as a right arm curve, or stability curve) encloses area above and below the zero-degree axis. Comparing the two areas reveals a sailboat's ratio of positive to negative stability. The higher the ratio the more likely a boat is to recover from a capsize.

DESIGN CHANGES THAT MODIFY STABILITY, CONTINUED

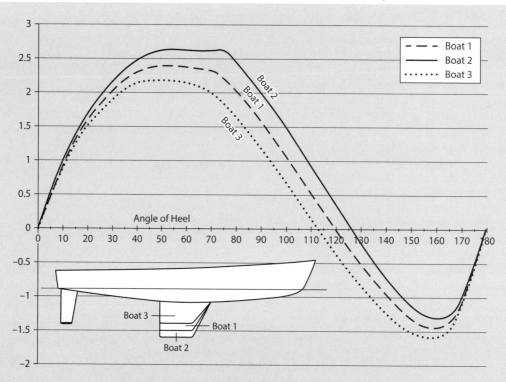

Variations to a vessel's draft (when linked to the location of the VCG) has a profound effect on stability. Boat 1 represents a stable offshore boat, with 6 feet of draft. Boat 2, with 7 feet of draft, shows an improved LPS, and an ability to recover from even larger angles of heel. Boat 3, with only 5 feet of draft, drops in LPS and displays a GZ/righting arm curve appropriate for coastal cruising, not offshore sailing. Note that as positive stability decreases negative stability increases—a doublebarreled disadvantage.

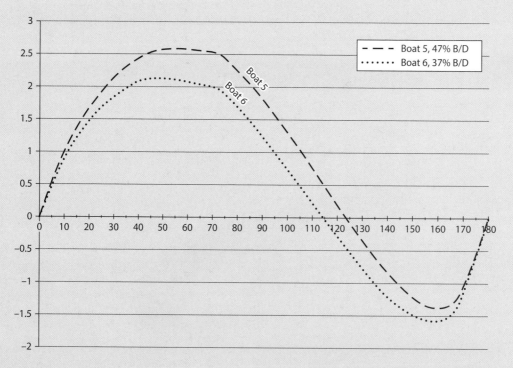

Modifying ballast-to-displacement ratio from 47% (Boat 5) to 37% (Boat 6) lowers a monohull's stability.

DESIGN CHANGES THAT MODIFY STABILITY, CONTINUED

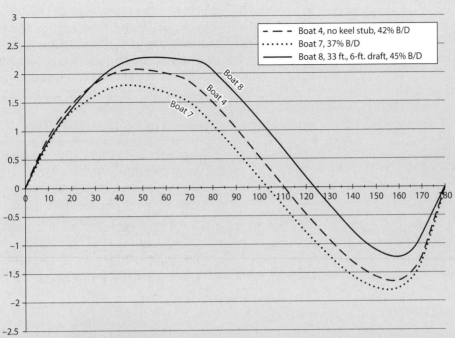

Effect of other changes in ballast on stability: removing a keel stub (Boat 4), altering ballast-to-displacement ratio (Boat 7), and shortening the vessel but increasing ballast (Boat 8).

to-displacement ratio: Boat 5 has a BD of 47%, Boat 6 of 37%. The GZ curves show a 9-degree variation in LPS which is a distinct switch between an LPS appropriate for offshore sailing and one more suited to coastal cruising.

Lastly we modified other attributes to see how they affect stability. For Boat 4 we eliminated the keel stub (a heavily reinforced hollow structure that acts to attach the ballast to the hull). We designed Boat 7 identical to Boat 4, but with a 37% ballast-to-displacement ratio instead of 42%. The reduction in ballast results in an 8 degree decrease in the LPS (111 to 103).

Boat 8 is a heavy displacement 33-foot sailboat with a 45% ballast-to-displacement ratio and 6 feet draft. Boat 8 compares favorably with Boat 1—because they are the same displacement their GZ curves can be directly compared. The point here is that a boat 20% shorter than those above can have equally as good righting moment.

Our simulations make it clear that ballast ratio and draft directly correlate with LPS angles—that's why adding more ballast is the way many designers cope with LPS shortfalls linked to shoal draft keels. Another interesting modification to increase the LPS without either adding ballast or increasing draft is to deepen the keel stub/sump and configure the ballast into a bulb or anvil shape, thereby lowering the CG.

it's the sea, not the wind, that becomes the mariner's worst enemy. Being knocked flat is not out of the question in gale or storm-force conditions, especially if a vessel is overcanvassed and already heeling significantly prior to the impact of a breaking sea (see following section on capsize). This is especially true of wide, flatter-bottomed sailboats with shallow draft and a low ballast-to-displacement ratio (a ballast weight less than 35% of displacement).

Said another way, beam works in opposition to recovery from extreme angles of heel, contributing instead to negative or inverted stability. Recovery from a deep knockdown depends upon the pendu-

lum effect of the ballast and a small range of negative stability. A multihull is stable upside down because it has a very wide beam and its center of gravity is underwater when inverted. A narrower monohull, if watertight, is unstable upside down, especially if it has a high ballast-to-displacement ratio, a low center of gravity (when upright), and narrow or moderate beam at deck level. Its ballast and CG will be high when the boat is inverted, and the teetering or pendulum-like effect of seas rolling by the hull will cause it to rotate back upright. A look at a sailboat's GZ curve shows how hard or easy it will be to capsize the boat and how likely it is to remain inverted. The area under the positive RM curve is an indication of the work needed to capsize the vessel. The area under the negative curve (to the right of the LPS) is the work needed to right the vessel once it's capsized. If the ratio of these areas is 2:1 or 3:1 in favor of the positive portion of the curve, the vessel is much more likely to self-recover from a capsize.

A multihull relies on a huge beam-derived righting moment that comes into play at very low angles of heel. Anyone who has sailed perfectly upright on a cruising cat at 10 knots in brisk trade winds knows what a pleasure this degree of form stability can be. Multihull sailors know that the stability of their boat will decrease precipitously at higher angles of heel, but they also know that the boat is unlikely ever to experience those heel angles. The boat has little or no ballast and therefore next to no secondary righting moment, but under most conceivable conditions, none will be needed. And if the boat does capsize and remain inverted, it will at least float.

Conditions for Capsize

A knockdown and a capsize are two different degrees of an unpleasant experience. A knockdown is usually caused by wind and ranges from a deep heel all the way to a partial capsize at the boat's limit of positive stability (LPS). A capsize exceeds the LPS and is usually caused by a large breaking sea, though wind may also play an important contributing role.

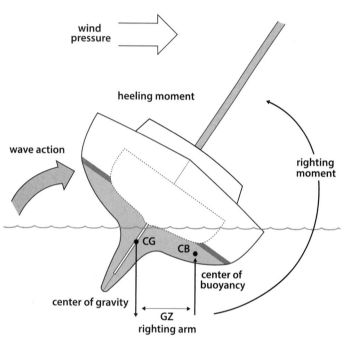

■ *Dynamic stability—stability in a seaway—is more complex than static stability, forcing us to consider wave action, roll mass moment of inertia, roll damping, and immersed surface areas, and, yes, luck. The lateral offset of the center of buoyancy (CB) from the center of gravity (CG) is the righting arm (GZ), and righting moment (RM) is the torque developed at specific angles of heel (the hull resists the heeling moment: RM = GZ × displacement). (Joe Comeau)*

STABILITY TERMS

Form stability: based on the shape of the hull;
Ballast stability: gravity's influence on ballast mass;
Initial stability: aproximately 0–60 degrees;
Ultimate stability: just shy of AVS;
Dynamic stability: underway flow over foils, wave-induced energy;
Static stability: no influence from preceding factors;
Transverse stability: term often used in the UK, for the ability to recover from a capsize.

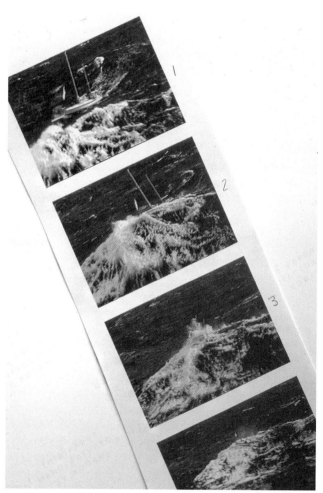

■ *Caught in a fall gale off Cape Hatteras, the crew of the Morgan Out Island 41* Malacte *await USCG rescue from the cutter* Alert. *The abandoned ketch weathered the storm. Note the impact of spreader-height seas, made even more dangerous by the effect of the Gulf Stream and the beam-to attitude of the boat. (Courtesy USCG)*

As we saw in Chapter 10, deep-water swells tend to be dominated by oscillatory energy (circular motion). In essence, this means that wave energy travels through the water column without moving the water itself in a net forward direction. As the wave passes, each molecule of water is taken on a circular journey—rising, moving forward, sinking, falling back—only to end up approximately where it began. The wave's kinetic energy passes onward without breaking the water surface or hurling it into motion. Large, rolling, long-period swells are mostly benign. Once the wave length shortens, swell becomes vertically unstable and gravity causes it to break. At this point, oscillatory energy is converted into energy of translation, and a cascading wave face turns into a violent torrent of moving water. The higher the crest, the greater the volume and momentum in the plunging cascade of white water. But the impact of the white water on the windward side of the boat is less damaging than the force encountered by the vessel being flung leeward into green water. Such un-aerated water cannot be compressed, and the slam of the leeward side of the vessel's hull and deck often results in the greatest damage.

Capsizes in violent encounters are fortunately rare, and they are especially rare in coastal passages though not unheard of. In 30 years of ocean crossings and coastal passages, I have encountered only five days of storm-force conditions at sea, including one smack in the middle of the Catalina Channel, 20

MORE KNOCKDOWNS?

Paul Miller, professor of naval architecture at the U.S. Naval Academy, worries that knockdowns are a growing danger, particularly for boats with a LPS less than 110 degrees (these tend to have more beam and less ballast). He believes that one key factor in such dynamic conditions is that the mast should hit the water well before the LPS is reached. Assuming some sail is still up, this will dampen the roll inertia, giving the boat a chance to right itself. But if the LPS is reached, the boat will simply continue to go over—a particular danger for a multihull or beamy monohull.

miles from Los Angeles. (Two were in the Tasman Sea and two off the coast of Africa.) Violent weather can occur anywhere. Those who spend significant time ocean sailing, and especially those who sail in and out of fickle ocean-facing river mouths, get to know the range of local conditions as well as their vessels' capabilities. Most bluewater veterans can recall a few mean episodes offshore when they were glad not to have been beneath a wave that broke just a few hundred yards away. Infrequently, a vessel caught under such a waterfall goes through three-dimensional contortions that test not only stability but construction quality and the crew's willingness to endure such an ordeal.

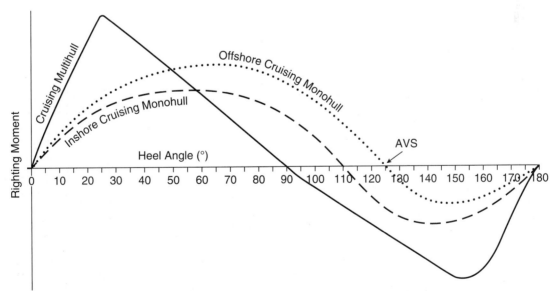

These three popular cruising sailboat types offer distinctly different stability profiles. The multihull, with a LPS of 90, relies upon its significantly larger initial or form stability but falls victim to an equally impressive willingness, once inverted, to remain that way (the large negative area of its curve after inversion at 90 degrees indicates this). The coastal cruiser's shedding of draft and ballast leads to fine gunkholing, but with a limit of positive stability (LPS) less than 110 degrees (the graph shows a 110 angle of vanishing stability), it is far from ideal as a long-distance voyager. The healthy ratio of positive to negative areas in the offshore voyager's GZ curve is an indication of its seaworthy stability. To gain its high righting moment and LPS (125), however, the voyager settles for less beam, more ballast, and/or deeper draft.

One controversial theory holds that when hit beam-on by a breaking sea, a vessel of modest beam, shallow draft, and high sides will heel a bit and skid to leeward. Paul Miller points out, however, that a response like this would require the wave jet to be mostly horizontal; a significant vertical component would cause rolling. And indeed, other heavy-weather veterans speak of the vertical movement on a wave face as an escalator or avalanche phenomenon capable of rolling just about any small craft.

What I encountered in my structurally modified Ericson 41 sloop *Wind Shadow* (discussed later in this chapter) during storm-force conditions leads me to believe that a true bluewater monohull must have as small a range of negative stability as sensible design allows. An LPS of 120 degrees is a reasonable minimum for an oceangoing sailboat of 40 to 60 feet, and the smaller and lighter the boat, the higher that number should be. In addition, features such as coachroof structures, pilothouses, and hull-deck joints need to be designed and built to survive a capsize (or a wave breaking on deck) and contribute to a quick recovery of positive stability. Those opting for a vessel with wide, flush decks should make sure the center of

gravity is low enough. In worst-case scenarios, wide, light-displacement, shoal-draft monohulls—overly reliant on beam for stability—have been known to remain inverted when capsized even after losing the rig.

Because most cruising vessels are not sailed like a sandbagger—with crewmembers and sacks of sand piled to windward to create a huge lever arm for sail-carrying ability—more moderate beam prevails. This does not necessarily mean that a beamy boat is unsuitable for offshore work, but it does mean that careful attention must be paid this boat's range of positive stability. Since LPS is very costly or even impossible to retrofit, the boat's range of positive stability needs to be understood before it is purchased.

Vertical Center of Gravity

The ideal stability meter, if one were ever to be invented, would graphically display the locations of a vessel's centers of gravity and buoyancy (relative to a level horizon) along with a digital readout of the righting moment in foot-pounds as the boat assumes varying degrees of heel. These are the key factors that forecast the potential for trouble under extreme conditions. At radical heel angles, features that normally enhance stability can detract from it instead. For example, with a spreader-dousing knockdown all those beefy crewmembers sitting on the windward rail—who a moment ago significantly contributed to the vessel's righting moment—now add their mass to the force instigating a capsize. This hypothetical crew, still clinging to the elevated rail, have moved to the negative side of an imaginary pivot point. In other words, the vertical center of gravity is now on the capsize-producing side of the center of buoyancy. (Henceforward we'll call the vertical center of gravity, or VCG, simply the center of gravity, or CG.) The term *metacentric height* (GM) helps define resistance to capsize and also helps clarify the important interactions between the center of gravity—which remains stationary as heel angle changes—and the center of buoyancy (CB), which shifts with heel angle (see illustration).

Imagine a vertical line through the CG as viewed in a hull cross section, and another vertical line through the CB. The horizontal separation between those two lines, as we have seen, is the righting arm (GZ). The length of the righting arm is like the distance from fulcrum to the heavier person in the see-saw analogy given above, and a longer righting arm provides a greater righting moment. When the CG and the CB are vertically aligned, the vessel is either perfectly upright (say, sitting out a calm at anchor) or teetering on the edge of capsize like a coin standing on end. In the latter case, the heel angle has become so extreme that the boat has reached its limit of positive

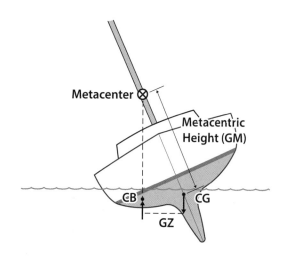

This means of comparing the location of the CB (which moves out and in with heel angle) with that of the CG (which remains fixed) gives a snapshot of a vessel's stability at any given angle of heel. A stiff boat will have a big righting arm (GZ) and thus a high GM (metacentric height, the distance between the center of gravity and transverse metacenter) at modest heel angles thanks primarily to a pronounced shift of the CB to leeward. At higher heel angles, however, the lateral distance between CB and CG begins to decrease again, and the boat depends more and more on ballast stability and displacement for its remaining righting moment and its ultimate stability (resistance to capsize). Bearing in mind that righting moment (RM) is the product of the righting arm and displacement, it is quite possible for a heavy boat to have a low GM but a high RM. (Joe Comeau)

🚩 *Cruising catamarans have popularity thanks to their roominess and negligible heel. A catamaran crew learns to keep a cruising cat sailing flat, and they're always ready to blow (release) the traveler or mainsheet if hit by an unexpected gust.*

stability, the point of capsize, known as the angle of vanishing stability (AVS), at which the GZ diminishes to zero, and the stability curve moves from positive to negative, perhaps causing the vessel to capsize. When GZ reaches zero, the outcome hangs in the balance, and a small force either way will either right the boat or capsize it. As stated above, a boat with a low LPS is inappropriate for offshore use, and a monohull with a deck that is wide and flat enough to make the boat stable in the inverted position is doubly so.

Ballast, machinery, batteries, hull materials, hardware, spars, rigging, and the galley sink all contribute to a vessel's mass and influence the location of its CG. The CG can move significantly upward, especially in high-sided, light-displacement craft, when hefty payloads of dinghies, scuba tanks, cases of beer, jerry cans of fuel, peanut butter, and so on are stashed well above the vessel's unloaded CG location. The resulting adverse effect on stability will become apparent when the seas get up.

As mentioned several times, the righting moment increases exponentially with vessel displacement—i.e., all things being equal, a larger vessel is far more resistant to capsize than a smaller vessel with the same LPS. Said another way, lighter boats accelerate in all directions—including roll-over—more

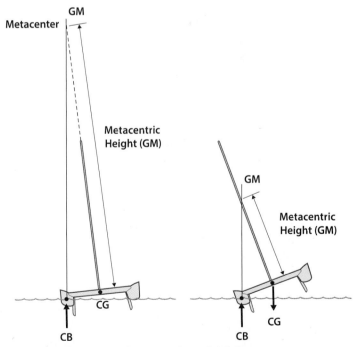

🚩 *Multihulls go through a major loss of righting moment with only a moderate heel angle. The multihull with both hulls on the water (left) has a large metacentric height (GM). When the multihull gets up on only one hull, as on the right, the metacentric height is greatly reduced. Capsize is close at hand. (Joe Comeau)*

EXPERTS SOUND OUT ON STABILITY

"Small boats (under 40 feet) can't have too much stability. Adding 40 pounds to the masthead may give you as much rotational inertia as adding 400 pounds to the bottom of the keel. I would always opt for the latter, however, because increasing the ballast at the foot of the keel lowers rather than raises the VCG [vessel center of gravity]."
—Chuck Paine (C.W. Paine Yacht Design, Inc.)

"For 100 percent of the world's cruising boats, crew ballast is out of the question. For 99.9 percent of the world's cruising boats, water ballast is usually out of the question. Ninety-nine percent of wave-impact recovery probably comes from a large reserve of positive stability. More than 99 percent of the time, the stability you care about is sail-carrying ability. Only rarely does ultimate stability [capsize avoidance and recovery] become an issue."
—Bill Lee (Santa Cruz Yachts)

"If the center of underwater area is really low, rotational wave motion and leeway will increase the roll moment. Keel area should be concentrated high for seaworthiness, but ballast volume should be low. Ways to achieve this include a flared keel of low aspect ratio, a highly tapered keel, or a keel/bulb combination."
—Dr. Paul Miller (Professor of Naval Architecture, USNA)

"Angles of downflooding need to be looked at in conjunction with the vanishing point of positive stability. A vessel with an offset companionway, outboard ventilators, large, poorly dogged hatches, and flimsy opening ports can jeopardize its stability by shipping a large volume of water."
—Alan Gilbert (Sparkman & Stephens)

"Tank testing large one-off designs can give some valuable insights into how small changes in VCG affect the overall stability of a vessel."
—King Yacht Design

quickly than heavier boats. Sailors taking smaller vessels offshore need to be very cognizant of their boats' LPS, stow gear carefully, and make hatches and ports as watertight as possible.

Most multihulls develop a greater maximum righting moment than a monohull of equivalent length, and a multihull develops that maximum righting moment as the windward hull is just clearing the water—in other words, at a much lower heel angle than the monohull's maximum righting moment. This is another way of saying what we've already said: a multihull has immense initial stability derived from its huge beam, but its limit of positive stability is much lower than a monohull's because it lacks the monohull's ballast keel and correspondingly low CG. Unballasted multihulls rely entirely on form stability, which disappears rapidly once one of the hulls lifts clear of the water. Further, due to the rig, most multihulls are even more stable upside down than right side up, as indicated by the area of the negative portion of a multihull's stability curve. Again, sailors taking multihulls offshore are willing to accept this because the immense initial righting moment makes capsize unlikely and because a capsized multihull will at least stay afloat.

Another school of thought stresses the capsize-abating role of rotational inertia. Recall that inertia refers to objects at rest tending to stay at rest unless acted upon by an outside force. Advocates contend that heavy spars and rigging with a high moment of transverse rotational inertia (also known as gyradius) tend to dampen or soak up energy imparted by breaking seas. They point out that enough time passes as the rig absorbs energy to allow some of the breaking wave to pass by the vessel before it heels too far to leeward and gets caught in a full capsize.

Dr. Paul Miller uses an analogy with the weighted pole of a tightrope walker to explain this. The more weight there is in the rig, the harder it is to rotate the boat, but once in motion it also tends to continue to roll. Dr. Miller also points out that since the roll axis is at the waterline, the weight at the other end—i.e., in the keel—is equally effective in absorbing the energy of a breaking sea and resisting roll, and weight in the keel has the added virtue of increasing stability. Thus, if you are going to add weight away from the roll axis, put it in a bulb rather than a mast! (A tall rig with sail set does, however, create a lot of air damping when the vessel rolls.)

Many stability debates focus solely on a vessel's LPS, a number that reflects the point at which the righting moment becomes zero and beyond which a vessel will move toward (and hopefully rotate through!) the inverted position. This point of no return (angle of vanishing stability, AVS) is important but should be viewed in context with the boat's righting moment at lesser angles of heel and its resistance to capsize throughout its range of positive stability.

Remember that all static stability numbers fail to reflect many dynamic factors linked to a seaway. Dynamic stability is complex. A prudent bottom line is that since small craft caught at sea in the worst weather are candidates for capsize, (continued page 364)

STABILITY MEASUREMENT SYSTEMS

To learn more about the stability characteristics of the boat you own or are considering buying, contact US Sailing and ask whether your boat has an International Measurement System (IMS) or Ameracap II certificate or whether it has been measured under the more recent Ocean Racing Rule (ORR). If so, important stability measurement data of a sister ship may be available. If not, consult with the builder or designer and ask for a stability diagram. If nothing is available, arrangements can be made to have a vessel measured by US Sailing, and for a reasonable fee, specific characteristics including the limit of positive stability and the *stability index* (STIX, see below) will be calculated.

The ORR measurement process determines the torque (heeling moment or weight × distance from the centerline) required to incline a vessel in light trim (i.e., with empty tanks and lockers) just a couple of degrees. The ORR stability algorithm compares the shape of a vessel, which is determined by a dimension-recording instrument during a haulout, with the inclining results to determine the vessel's LPS.

Perhaps the most useful piece of information derived from this process is the stability *(continued next page)*

🏴 *Modern beamy, canoe-body hull shapes afford good form stability, but it takes careful attention to the ballast and draft factors that control CG to deliver the secondary righting moment to recover from a knockdown.*

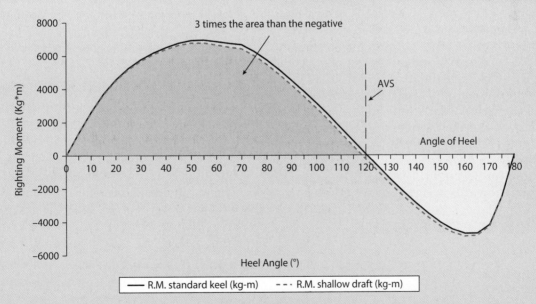

🏴 *With an LPS of 120 degrees, a nearly 3:1 ratio of the area of positive stability to the area of negative stability, and a righting moment of about 13,000 pounds at 80 degrees of heel, this vessel (a Hanse 400) will likely meet the criteria for an ISO Category A designation and is appropriate for a Bermuda or Hawaii race or an offshore passage. The two different curves show the slight difference in righting moment between the standard keel (solid line) and the shoal draft model (dashed line).*

STABILITY MEASUREMENT SYSTEMS, CONTINUED

index, a number that modifies the LPS based on the boat's length, beam, displacement, and sailing length. The stability index increases with length and displacement but is diminished by excess beam; it does not factor in the shape of the boat above the sheerline. In essence, the stability index starts with the LPS and adds or subtracts degrees based upon a logical set of parameters. The Newport Bermuda Race Committee has for years used a stability index rating (IMS rule) of 115 degrees as the entry minimum. At the heart of this numerical calculation is the assumption that longer boats and those with more ballast per given displacement are less likely to capsize. It can be argued

that cruisers need a higher stability index than racers, as racing boats usually rely on crew hiking over the rail to improve stability whereas cruisers rely solely on the boat's inherent capability.

Under the IMS measurement process, neither coachroof volume (an asset to positive stability) nor a large cockpit well (a detriment to positive stability) is considered. Even so, the numbers are indicative of the measured boat's transverse stability. Ian McCurdy, of the design firm McCurdy and Rhodes, likes the handicap rule's repeatability, especially in the realm of stability prediction. He feels it encourages designers to put weight where it belongs.

the real question becomes whether the structure is capable of enduring such trauma.

ISO Classifications and the Relationship to Stability Measures

As we've seen, the two key concerns in stability are the locations of the vessel's center of gravity (CG) and center of buoyancy (CB). The CG stays put, regardless of heel angle, as long as gear, cargo, or liquids in a partially filled tank do not move. Unfortunately, when poorly secured items move "downhill" due to heel, they exacerbate the vessel's angle of heel, and fuel or water in a partially filled tank has a similar effect. Keeping heavy masses in place is part of the designer's and builder's function, and a vessel survey should address how well this has been provided for.

As discussed, a vessel's static stability, calculated from its hull shape and the distribution of its enclosed volume and mass, is a valid measure of its resistance to capsize on a flat sea. Introduce breaking waves, however, and the calculations become much more dynamic and complex—a key reason why the ISO STability IndeX (STIX) takes much more than the static LPS into consideration. The STIX calculation is as much about how effectively a boat keeps water out

as it is about how effectively the boat resists heeling. Beginning around 1998 the ISO used these stability calculations as a means to categorize boats by their seaworthiness. STIX minimums were set for each certain category. (Higher STIX numbers correlate to a more seaworthy boat.)

The ISO classifications of small craft are as follows (also see the table below):

- ◆ 3.1.1 Category A (Ocean). Boats suitable to operate in seas with significant wave heights above 4 meters and wind speeds in excess of Beaufort Force 8, but excluding abnormal conditions, e.g., hurricanes. (STIX minimum 32.)

- ◆ 3.1.2 Category B (Offshore). Boats suitable to operate in seas with significant wave heights up to 4 meters and winds of Beaufort Force 8 or less. (STIX minimum 23.)

- ◆ 3.1.3 Category C (Inshore). Boats suitable to operate in seas with significant wave heights up to 2 meters and a typical steady wind force of Beaufort Force 6 or less. (STIX minimum 14.)

- ◆ 3.1.4 Category D (Sheltered Waters). Boats suitable to operate in waters with significant wave heights up to and including 0.3 meters with occasional waves of 0.5 meters height (e.g., from

MODIFIED ISO CATEGORIES

Design Category	A	B	C	D
Wave Height (up to)	4 meters and above	Up to 4 meters	Up to 2 meters	0.5 meter maximum
Beaufort Wind Force	Over 8	Up to 8	Up to 6	Up to 4

According to ISO Directive 2003/44/EC, amending the Recreational Craft Directive, "The definition of Boat Design Category A shall be replaced by the following: 'A. Ocean: Designed for extended voyages where conditions may exceed wind Force 8 (Beaufort scale) and significant wave heights of 4 meters and above, but excluding abnormal conditions, and vessels largely self-sufficient.' " (Significant wave height is the average of the highest one-third of waves, and over a 24-hour period you are likely to encounter a wave twice that height.)

Large sailboats score higher when stability indexes are calculated. The mass of a larger volume helps lessen the threat of capsize because of the acceleration that must take place prior to heel. This is why it's so important for a light-displacement, low-volume 35-footer to possess a 120-degree or higher LPS for offshore work, whereas this 120-footer does fine with a lower LPS. Note the size of the primary winch.

passing vessels) and a typical steady wind force of Beaufort Force 4 or less. (STIX minimum 5.)

This classification system represents a twelve-year effort to set standards for a very independent global industry. The U.S. response to the ISO standards has been lukewarm. The European approach is based on restrictive codes and strict governance, and product approval is gained by meeting detailed standards. U.S. boatbuilders face a challenge to meet these standards, but the effort certainly leads to better boats, and the appeal of a broader market is enticing. Yet the ISO standards are by no means the only way to improve boats.

Someone once said that when two or more people are together in a room you get politics, and when two or more sailboats are in sight of each other you get a race. But neither of these holds a candle to what happens when boatbuilders, naval architects, and arbiters of safety standards gather in a room to hammer out just how much strength and stability and how great a margin of safety should be required in the minimum standard. The knowledge that a given boat may be operated in conditions ranging from small lakes to large oceans adds more complexity. The Europeans were eager to generate specific use guidelines that would keep builders immune from liability when foolish people did foolish things with boats. If a sailor comes to grief off Greenland in a vessel with a Category C (Inshore) rating, for example, that ISO designation lessens the accountability of the boat's designer and builder.

On the other hand, a significant number of production cruising boatbuilders who know (off the record) that their vessels are far more appropriate as coastal cruisers have nevertheless bristled at being candidates for a B rather than an A rating. This led to a frontal assault to lower the stability and structural requirements. The British and Norwegians, in opposition to lowering the standard, introduced data showing that vessels with lower LPS have fared poorly when caught out in heavy weather, and a similar argument continued regarding structural factors. The outcome of both battles was a definition of a Category A (Ocean) boat that is less than optimal. One noted expert called the result "an empirical solution with unscientific underpinnings," while another called the ISO minimum LPS value for a Category A boat—100 degrees—an "absolute minimum," adding that "good designs should be expected to have an LPS about 20 degrees greater!"

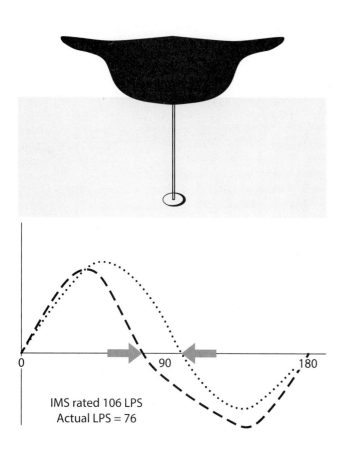

IMS rated 106 LPS
Actual LPS = 76

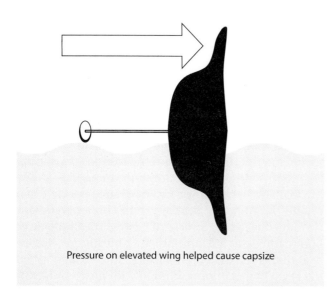

Pressure on elevated wing helped cause capsize

🔲 *Excessive topside flare, as shown in a cross section of a sailboat much like WingNuts, whose capsize is discussed in Chapter 10, is now penalized more heavily in the IMS Stability Index.*

In sum, the ISO 12217 working group charged with this process most certainly considered the key elements associated with stability and downflooding, but the final result seems based as much on politics as evidence. Yet the standards body did broaden the concept of stability to include the act of keeping water out of the interior of a vessel—which makes good sense given that staying afloat is every mariner's bottom line definition of survival.

The upper limits of wind and sea conditions ascribed to categories B, C, and D are similar to a "safe working load" approach to categorizing vessels. Initially, Category A included a similarly well-defined upper limit—Beaufort Force 10 and 7-meter seas—but this devolved through subsequent iterations into the fuzzier Category A definition given above. Each year, Cape Hatteras lows, New England's spring and fall nor'easters, and treacherous Gulf of Alaska lows spawn storms of greater ferocity than those original Category A limits, not to mention what hurricane season conjures up. All of these conditions exceed the scantlings and stability of a Category A vessel, and it's important not to forget that.

Most naval architects agree that the ISO STIX measurement is a sophisticated albeit convoluted approach to measuring seaworthiness, not just stability. The seven attributes encapsulated in the STIX calculation are quite clear:

- Righting force at the downflooding angle
- Ability to recover from inversion
- Ability to recover from a knockdown
- Effect of displacement and length
- Effect of topside flare on capsize vulnerability
- Potential for downflooding from wind-induced heel
- Potential for downflooding from a knockdown

Some deference is paid to the LPS in the ISO standards. The ratio of negative to positive areas on the stability curve is addressed, and even the impact that water in a sail plan—a breaking wave's effect on the heeling moment—has on a capsize recovery is factored into the mix. Heavier displacement gets credit, and excessive topside flare and beam are penalized. Downflooding angles and the influence of wind gusts are included as considerations. The final empirical result is influenced by weighting factors, and designers can treat the process like a handicap rule. For example, those designing boats with a low ballast ratio and shoal draft (factors that cost them points) may opt for a smaller rig, less sail area, and centerline hatches and no opening ports to still reach an Offshore (B) or Ocean (A) rating.

The negotiations required to get a consensus altered the weighting of the seven STIX attributes. The group never lost sight of the value of staying afloat, but they had differing opinions on how much to weight AVS versus issues such as the potential for downflooding. Some lobbied that not enough real-world capsize data were on hand, but the proprietary Wolfson study—carefully compiled research on actual capsizes and the AVS of the vessels involved—was reviewed and at least considered. Not surprisingly, the trend toward light, beamy, shoal-draft, low-ballast-ratio production boats was well represented, and advocates were determined to see their boats anointed with top category status regardless of how low the bar had to be dropped. The result was a very inclusive and watered-down lower limit for the Category A rating—namely, a STIX of 32 (originally it had been 38)—and a look at some of the vessels that comply is disconcerting. Still, the numerical stability index remains highly useful. You may be quite certain that an A-rated vessel with a STIX of 32 is not as seaworthy as an A-rated vessel with a STIX of 55.

A Less-Than-Perfect Rating System

Some boat designers rely on a large cabinhouse and its ability through buoyancy to add righting moment to boost the LPS. As discussed above, the problem with stability related to cabinhouse volume is that the vessel must be heeled significantly before the house is submerged to add such righting moment, at which point any open cabin windows and deck hatches create the potential for downflooding. At such deep angles of heel, crew may easily be pitched over the side, and gear below may threaten crew in the cabin.

Many naval architects feel that too little emphasis was given in the ISO standards to the LPS and too much placed on the prevention of downflooding. Others felt there was insufficient consideration to details such as the installation of fixed ports in topsides, cabinhouse structures, and reinforcement for large nonopening windows that seldom have effective cover plates. Vessels with a limited secondary righting moment, large nonopening windows, and low ballast ratios can qualify as Category A craft, the assumption being that the "structures" section—outlining construction standards—of the ISO directive has enough teeth to ensure that bulging cabin trunks and huge pilothouse windows can keep out the sea and induce the secondary righting moment not provided by ballast and draft. But such reasoning ignores the greater potential for crew-overboard incidents and crew injuries below that occur aboard A-rated vessels that are more likely to capsize.

Another concern was that builders of boats under 40 feet were allowed to do their own vessel evaluations.

Under ISO stability measurements, off-center hatches, dorade vents, and opening ports detract from a STIX score and can make a vessel with a high LPS and well-proportioned hull look equivalent to a less capsize-resistant vessel with no vents, no opening ports, and small centerline hatches. In short, the STIX rating is more inclusive of seaworthy characteristics—but many feel it undervalues the significance of a 120 or higher LPS for offshore-bound vessels.

My opinion is that the ISO effort ended up one category short of an absolute success. Missing is Category A+, defining the engineering standards for transoceanic high-latitude sailboats meant for expeditionary voyaging, high-stakes racing, and sailors who want ultimate reassurance of staying right side up come what may.

STRENGTH OF THE HULL, KEEL, RIG, AND CABIN/DECKS

The relentless battle between buoyancy, gravity, and the elements will fatigue the best of materials. Pressures from wind and sea create forces that are transferred throughout a boat's structure, and as builders have become more aware of these global forces, better engineering practices have evolved. Today, finite element analysis (FEA) provides computer-calculated values for the energy exerted throughout the structure, highlighting hotspots such as the garboard region, chainplates, mast step, and hull skin where the stresses of pounding into a seaway are most dramatic. Had someone given a piece of chalk to a gifted shipwright in 1850 and asked him to circle the areas of a schooner hull needing the most reinforcement, his chalk marks would probably coincide with the hotspots on an FEA screen today. One of the problems faced by early shipwrights was that the methods and materials available to them weren't appropriate for light-displacement craft. As a sailor friend once said, "If Nat Herreshoff were around today he would be buying lots of carbon fiber, and Eric Goetz would probably be his partner."

Feedback from sailors who have survived extreme sea conditions advances the art of seaworthiness and seamanship. Unfortunately, we don't get to hear from those lost at sea; we do, however, have access to more accurate data than ever before about the severity of storms at any given time and place, and we can accurately project the wind and sea conditions in which vessels and crews have succumbed. Designers of bluewater race boats and cruisers use such feedback, which has had a significant influence on design and scantlings.

The first concern of boat design and construction is staying afloat. Buoyancy must be maintained at all costs. The chances of being knocked down or capsized increase in heavy weather, so in addition to sufficient stability there's a need for enhanced structural strength to handle those loads. Once certain that the boat is strong enough to handle such energy transfers, a designer and builder's attention turns to attaching the appendages and keeping them there.

Keel

A rig or even a rudder malfunction is unlikely to be fatal for a boat, but the loss of a ballast keel very often is. The show is pretty much over if the keel parts company with the hull. Those who have survived such a calamity are both lucky and good sources of input as to how option-limiting the experience can be. Fellow Safety at Sea Seminar moderator Chuck Hawley was aboard a sloop headed to the U.S. mainland from Hawaii when the ballast keel tore free. The wind was light at the time, the hull was not breeched, and the responsive crew turned into the wind and got the sails down before the boat capsized. Fortunately, they had enough fuel and calm enough seas to motor back to Hawaii.

Round-the-world singlehander Tim Kent charged to a second-place finish in the Around Alone race in his powerful Open 50 *Everest Horizontal*. But in a later doublehanded return from Bermuda in 2003, both crew were caught in extremis when the lead ballast bulb let go and the sloop immediately capsized. Splashing to the surface with little more than a container of flares, the two sailors stared directly at a cruise ship lit up like a city passing close at hand. Their flares were immediately noticed by the attentive crew, and only minutes after disaster struck they were aboard the floating hotel and caught up in a drama that could have played out very differently had the ship not happened by.

A small but growing number of keel losses have claimed lives and gained the attention of the ISO and other regulatory bodies. (Note the concern of the International Sailing Federation [ISAF] over keel attachment scantlings in the accompanying sidebar.) When the super maxi *Rambler 100* lost her keel and flipped in the 2011 Fastnet race, twenty-one agile crew scrambled to safety: some climbed onto the overturned hull, while a few huddled together in the chilly water. Fast-thinking crew in the cockpit heaved sheet and halyard tails up and over the hull just as the big sloop rolled. These became a welcome handhold for those perched on the upturned hull.

Modern race boats tend to be canoe-body designs with a high-aspect fin keel (larger boat, on right) or fin/bulb keel (smaller boat, on left). These appendages attach to well-engineered support structures in the hull. The lever-like effect of these foils on the hull is considerable, and extra laminate and support structure are required in regions of highest stress.

Deck and Cabin Vulnerabilities

Because water so easily enters ports and hatches, downflooding is a key component in the ISO stability index, as described earlier. ISO regulations favor centerline hatches and penalize dorade vents and offset

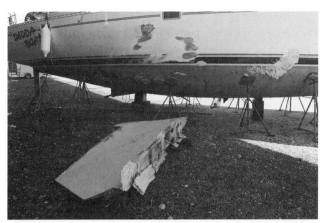
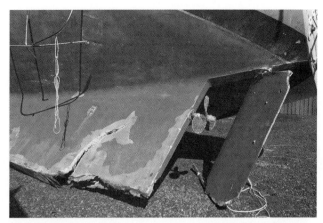

When a sailboat grounds hard on a rocky ledge, structure counts. The boat on the left lost its keel entirely. The keel shows no sign of ABS guideline adherence (see sidebar American Bureau of Shipping on Yacht Hull Strength, page 371)—the FRP skin is too thin at the hull-to-ballast junction; also there is no sign of transverse structure. The boat on the right lost the bottom portion of its keel and rudder, but would remain afloat. Even boats touted for their strength fare poorly when faced with rocks and a swell.

hatches. There is much misunderstanding about how water comes aboard in heavy weather, one result being the common tendency to put in only the lower companionway hatchboard when heavy weather brews up. Yes, this will help keep deck-sweeping water from rushing below when the vessel is upright, but in a knockdown it's the top portion of the hatch that is first exposed to downflooding, not the bottom, as shown in the illustration. A much wiser precaution is to keep the companionway completely closed and dogged when conditions are severe enough to threaten a knockdown.

Most production hulls are ruggedly built to withstand the stress and strain of a moderate seaway. The deck and especially the cabinhouse may be weaker, however, given their fewer plies of laminate and many sizable openings for hatches, windows, and ports. Unsurprisingly, damage sustained during violent weather is often seen above rather than below the rail.

When decks are submerged, there is a real chance of downflooding through a stove-in window or undogged hatch. A large expanse of window glass or plastic can be broken or detached from its mountings by the impact of a boarding wave or, perhaps more likely, by being slammed into the sea when the vessel is tossed to leeward by a large wave. The impact of water puts immense strain on the lens as well the surrounding support structure. Deep submersible research vessels have windows in their hulls that must withstand immense pressure, and one look at the small diameter, ultrathick conical window construction and immensely reinforced support structure explains how they do it. A bluewater cruiser may not need the viewport engineering of a deep sea research vessel, but its windows must be ready to do more than keep the rain and spray out.

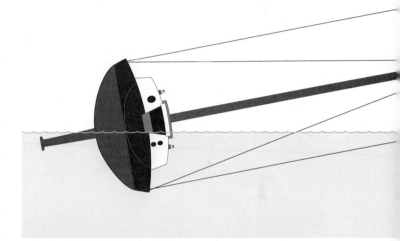

The bottom washboard does not stop downflooding in a knockdown because the angle of heel allows water to enter at the top of the companionway. Close all hatches and hatchboards securely before the seas kick up or before the squall is upon you. (Joe Comeau)

Keeping water out is critical because water sloshing freely around inside a vessel alters buoyancy. The water finds the lowest point in the inverted hull or cabin, greatly affecting stability. (In larger ships watertight bulkheads are designed into the vessels to minimize the movement of water throughout the hull in the event of a breach of the hull.) Though it makes a boat more likely to capsize, the free-surface effect, as this water sloshing is known as, also makes a capsized boat more likely to re-right itself—but then it makes the boat more likely to capsize a second time, and so on—not a scenario anyone wants to experience.

Anyone seeking a well-built passagemaker should

A recent trend in yacht design places large sculpted cabinhouse windows and ports in the hull skin. Those headed offshore should have a damage-control plan to respond to a window breach, or better yet, a strategy for doubling the strength of these surfaces to prevent breaching the hull or topsides in the first place.

The region along the centerline of a vessel adjacent to the keel bolts is another location where core material should not be used and additional fiber-reinforced plastic (FRP) layers should be added to strengthen and stiffen the structure. Boats built to the ABS offshore yacht-racing guidelines (see sidebar) will generally have sufficient reinforcements in critical areas.

ask the builder or broker how the area surrounding a hatch or port is reinforced. In many cases, this penetration of the deck structure ends up with no additional units of fiber-reinforced plastic (FRP) laminate, or perhaps worse, the raw edge of the core exposed by the cutout wasn't even rebedded and backfilled with epoxy putty. With a much more robust approach to hatch and port construction, the designer calculates the cumulative loss in structural strength created by multiple cutouts and adds longitudinal and transverse reinforcement to compensate. Quality boatbuilders mold in higher-density in-fills in the area surrounding large cutouts, resulting in a better engineered and manufactured deck.

Rig Loads

The standing rig and chainplates of a sailboat are in a constant tug-of-war, putting extra load on the mast step, coachroof (with a deck-stepped mast), and surrounding structures. More builders have settled upon a Euro-favored solution in which the chainplates are anchored to a hefty fore-and-aft member laminated to the inside of the hull or bonded to the

ISAF COMMENTS RELATING TO KEEL LOSS

Following are paraphrased comments from an ISAF memo.

The ISAF Offshore Committee has raised safety concerns relating to a growing number of keel failures. Careful design, build, and maintenance of keels and keel attachments are essential. The loss of a keel can be catastrophic and involve loss of life.

The ISAF Offshore Committee has appointed a working party to review the requirements for racing yacht design and boatbuilding and will recommend changes to the ISAF Offshore Special Regulations.

Under the existing regulations, yachts racing in Category 0, 1, and 2 should be constructed to one of the following three standards:

The EU Recreational Craft Directive (ISO) for Design Category A;

The ABS Guide for Offshore Yachts plan review for yachts under 24 meters, which was withdrawn, but their construction guidelines remain an important benchmark;

The newly approved International Standard for Yacht Structure, ISO 12215.

AMERICAN BUREAU OF SHIPPING ON YACHT HULL STRENGTH

During the 1980s the American Bureau of Shipping (ABS) lent some of its considerable technical ability to the challenge of engineering racing yacht hull structures. "The Guide for Building and Classing Offshore Racing Yachts" took on the challenge of defining the specifics of panel strength and structure. The first iteration fell a little short and keel failures caused a rethinking of hull-skin scantlings near where keel bolts penetrated the hull. Another scantling revamp took place after the 93–94 Whitbread fleet suffered delamination problems in the forward sections of those boats. The subsequent 1994 version of the guidelines remains valid today. It evolved as a minimum standard for keel bolt diameters, hull skin thickness, rudderstock dimensions, and laminate schedules. Despite the fact that the guidelines were prudently developed by well-trained engineers, ground-truthed and amended via ocean sailing feedback, the ABS guidelines have been labeled too stringent by many production boatbuilders. But in my opinion, they should remain an important reference for those building boats to cross oceans and for those planning to sail such voyages.

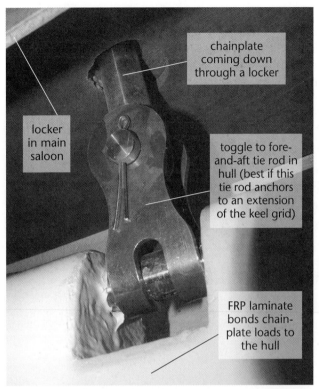

Many builders prefer an in-line shroud system and a single, all-eggs-in-one-basket chainplate arrangement that needs to be carefully engineered and fabricated. The molded FRP saddle that holds the toggle pin should afford easy inspection, and any welds in the multi-attachment chainplate should likewise be easy to inspect.

(Photo labels:) locker in main saloon · chainplate coming down through a locker · toggle to fore-and-aft tie rod in hull (best if this tie rod anchors to an extension of the keel grid) · FRP laminate bonds chainplate loads to the hull

grid that supports the mast step. A tie rod is used to secure the underdeck extension of a chainplate to this member. Some builders have made the mistake of attaching this support structure only to the inside skin of a sandwich hull, causing delamination problems and even catastrophic rig failure. It is preferable to remove the core and tie the chainplates to conjoined outer and inner skins of the laminate. An even better approach is to anchor the chainplate tie rod to an extension of a keel grid, forming an effective, load-spreading, partial ring frame.

Deck-stepped masts are popular because they eliminate the hole in the coachroof, the partners, and the nuisance leaks associated with a keel-stepped spar. But heavy compression loads are placed on the deck by a deck-stepped mast and must be dissipated through a compression post, bulkhead, ring frame, or other load-spreading structure. In addition, the mast must be significantly stiffer both fore-and-aft and transversely due to its reduced column support, which provides less resistance to buckling. The area of the vessel where mast and chainplate loads are focused should be carefully inspected on new as well as used boats. A disturbing trend is to place large opening ports and hatches in this area while adding little

or no additional reinforcement to compensate for the decrease in structural reliability. A deck-stepped spar makes sense as long as the mast heel fitting is substantial and the region of the compression loads is strong enough.

Rudder

The third member of the appendage triad is the rudder. Its loss may be less disastrous than loss of the rig or especially the keel, but losing a rudder brings an immediate halt to progress and may leave the crew with a hole in the boat. Jury-rigging an alternative rudder is high on the list of seamanship abilities (see Chuck Hawley's sidebar on this topic in Chapter 13), but even more important is departing on a voyage with a well-designed and well-maintained rudder. There is no perfect steering appendage, but it's important to understand the characteristics of common rudder designs.

Attached Rudders

An attached rudder pivoting on the trailing edge of a long keel is often thought of as the most bulletproof rudder design. To some extent this is true, but its biggest upside—its support from the keel—can also be a significant drawback. The bottom gudgeon supporting the rudderstock acts as a bushing, often handling both thrust and axial loads. The foot of the keel or deadwood area affords a stiff, solid attachment point, but in groundings many attached rudders are pounded too and the bottom gudgeon can be damaged and the rudderstock bent. The blade may not be torn from the hull, but the impact damage from

■ *Two ends of the spectrum of sailboat design, both built of FRP laminate but as different in rudder configuration as in all other aspects. The high-aspect spade rudder on the left makes fingertip steering a reality, but the long, narrow foil is far more vulnerable to debris than the barn-door rudder attached to the trailing edge of the keel on the heavy-displacement cutter at right.*

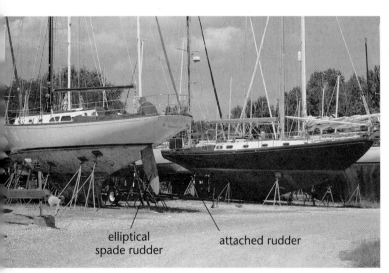

elliptical
spade rudder   attached rudder

■ *Two classic cruisers: an Ericson 41 (left) and a shoal-draft Hinckley Bermuda 40 (right). The custom elliptical spade rudder on the Ericson 41 is far enough from the foot of the keel to be protected in a grounding; in addition, the vessel rotates bow downward when aground and heeling. The Bermuda 40's attached rudder is less efficient and is supported by a heel gudgeon that's vulnerable at the trailing end of the long keel.*

a modest grounding can render it useless as a steering appendage. The best full-keel trailing-edge rudder designs keep the foot of the rudder blade and bottom gudgeon a bit above the low point of the keel, thereby lessening the chance of grounding damage.

An attached rudder is also less efficient for steering. Its lack of partial balance and its position well forward of the aftermost portion of the waterline make it a less responsive foil that steers more by water deflection than lift, and it also operates in a boundary layer of reduced flow. (It should be noted that transom-hung rudders likewise suffer a loss of efficiency, in this case due to pressure loss at the water surface.) Because directional stability is considered an asset in a long-keel long-distance cruiser, however, a barn-door rudder isn't the liability it would be on a race boat.

Spade Rudders

At the opposite end of the spectrum is the freestanding foil referred to as a spade rudder (see photo). Long the target of love, hate, and misinformation, this rudder has evolved into a highly engineered, efficient, and even reliable component able to endure the rigors of offshore use. It has been plagued by design and engineering shortfalls from its earliest days but has endured because it remains a most efficient steering appendage—providing strong direction-changing force with the least amount of surface area and drag, and this alone has endeared it to the racing community.

Cruisers with self-steering gear or an autopilot appreciate the two-finger pressure needed to achieve changes in rudder angle with a semibalanced spade rudder, and with better approaches to engineering and fabrication, these rudders are now earning higher grades for reliability. These structural improvements are linked to a better understanding of material science. Engineers have figured out what's required to transfer water-induced loads from the FRP skin of the rudder blade to an internal armature connected to the rudderstock and finally to the hull via support bearings. The most elegant solutions are the all-carbon rudders with a direct skin-to-stock bond, some of which are even engineered to allow the bottom third of the rudder to shear off if a bad grounding or allision threatens the appendage. Even less expensive foam-cored, stainless-steel-stock rudders now make better use of internal web reinforcement to ensure durability.

In short, a semibalanced (usually with 12% to 14% of the blade area forward of the stock) spade rudder delivers the best steering attributes, and because the tip of the blade is often much less deep than the maximum draft of the vessel, it is more out of harm's way in a grounding. A shoal-draft sailboat

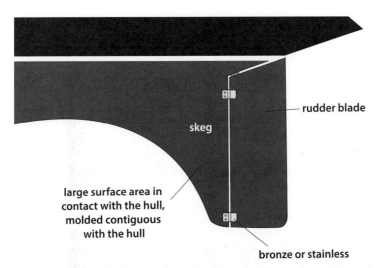

skeg

rudder blade

large surface area in contact with the hull, molded contiguous with the hull

bronze or stainless

When carefully designed and painstakingly fabricated, the skeg of a skeg-hung rudder has sufficient fore-and-aft length where it joins the hull—it is also internally reinforced with transverse structure, and its cavity is sealed from the vessel's interior. The appendage can be placed well aft, and as with the spade rudder, its increased distance from the center of lateral resistance improves the steering capability. (Joe Comeau)

with a rudder and keel of equal draft—or, worse yet, one in which the rudder descends deeper than the keel—needs to be particularly alert to the prospect of running aground.

Skeg-Hung Rudders

The skeg-hung rudder is a compromise that can be viewed as offering either the best or the worst of both worlds, depending on its design and construction. As with a keel-hung rudder, a skeg provides a bottom gudgeon to support the blade. But unlike a keel, a skeg is often a high-aspect projection with a short root (the fore-and-aft length of the skeg at the hull joint) that can be as vulnerable as or even more vulnerable than a spade rudder. In many cases, a cracked skeg has allowed water to enter the hull and the rudder to bind. This worst-of-both-worlds situation occurs when both the rudderstock and the skeg appendage are under-engineered. Skeg rudders also tend to be inefficient at high rudder angles due to the rudder blade being dragged through the water, acting more like a brake than a steering foil. A boat with a skeg rudder is likely to be slower to turn than a spade-rudder boat of similar size and shape. However a skeg-hung rudder will also add directional stability to a sailboat and this can be an asset to shorthanded cruisers.

SO WHAT KIND OF BOAT DO YOU WANT?

The first step in boat shopping consists of asking and answering three frank questions, the first being the most fundamental of all: What will you do with this boat? To answer this question honestly, base your answer less on future plans for grand adventures than on your likely sailing in the next five years.

The second question is the financial one: How much can you afford to spend, including a refit in addition to the purchase? A boat purchase is a major expense, and the size, age, structural quality, and level of fit and finish of the boat you choose all have a major impact on the purchase price. If you have a yachtsman's appetite for a first-rate finish and nautical elegance, be prepared to shoulder an annual maintenance expense that can exceed 10% of the vessel's purchase price—more if you buy a fixer-upper—and this number has nothing to do with refit costs, it's simply the expense of keeping a yacht in yacht-like condition. Those who roll up their sleeves and have the skill and time to do their own work will spend much less than the 10% on their maintenance of a modern fiberglass boat. In short, the purchase price gets you into the game, but the larger and more complex the boat, the more time and/or money you'll spend keeping it ready to go.

Next, pull together a reasonable array of sources to help in your quest for a boat. The Internet is brimming with websites that catalog powerboats and sailboats for sale locally and around the world. Despite such a rich resource, there's nothing like the one-on-one experience of looking at boats in local marinas and yards to get a feel for what's on the market and how the pricing is running. Weekend trips to marinas in adjacent states are enjoyable and potentially useful. Develop a short list of the boats that you're really interested in, and then visit a few brokers to hear their reaction to your target list. They will likely expand your initial set of alternatives with their own suggestions. Carefully scrutinize their ideas to see how they fit into your perspective. Yes, the broker is an expert at linking buyers with sellers, but you need to be happy with the vessel and its selling price. Don't get locked in too quickly to a single broker with promises of finding just the right boat for you. Beware of must-act-immediately deals.

In the early days of fiberglass boatbuilding, a few poorly designed and built boats gave the new material some bad press. Today, there's no excuse for problems such as hull or deck delamination—or the loss of a spar or rudder—arising from normal sailing or powering loads in protected inshore waters. (As naval architect Paul Miller put it, fewer plies built well are stronger than more plies built poorly.) In the 1960s and 1970s, FRP boatbuilding evolved through trial-and-error engineering that pitted less weight and more speed against market pressures and builders' margins. Many good boatbuilders went bankrupt due to poor business practices, and there were variations from one boat to the next in a specific make and model due to the financial health (or lack there-of) of the builder or simply quality control at an overseas builder's facility. The guidance of a competent marine surveyor will help you spot issues of inferior quality in the build. Even if you're buying a new boat, a prepurchase survey by a skilled marine surveyor is money well spent.

Cost is usually a major concern, and it is often the limiting variable that separates the boat in mind from the boat in hand. Avoid a boat that's just too much of a financial stretch. Contrary to the current spin, bigger is not necessarily better; better is better, and in many examples bigger is simply stretched-out mediocrity. A builder accustomed to the scantlings for a 35-footer may not have a good grasp on the panel loads and structural requirements for a 45-footer. Be cautious about becoming the owner of the largest boat ever hauled by your boatyard or the largest vessel built by a boatbuilder. Scaled-up mediocrity results in lower quality, inferior structural strength, and poor performance. As the irascible genius and race boat innovator Bill Lee once stated while looking over the "stretched" model of one popular production boatbuilder, "Now I see what you get with a big cheap boat—a lot of things to fix."

If the sailboat is to be your second home, and lengthy ocean passages or rough local waters are not likely, many seafaring shortfalls can be logged as unfortunate but acceptable. Features such as less ballast (lead), shallow draft, expansive beam, large windows, a short rig, and a big engine may become assets in an inshore or coastal context. In sum, the best way to stretch your boat-buying dollar is to carefully match the vessel's attributes to your intended sailing itinerary.

The third question: New or used sailboat? Whether to buy a new or used boat is complex un-

Long keel or short fin, plumb bow or sleek overhang—just visit a packed boatyard in the off-season to get a feel for the staggering range in sailboat design.

less your budget is very tight, in which case "used" wins hands down. New boats are getting more like new cars in the large depreciation that occurs in the first year. The first owner takes the biggest hit, the second owner may get the most cost-effective purchase, and the third owner may get a bargain but also find a lengthy list of potential maintenance issues, such as repowering, rerigging, refinishing . . . and refinancing your home to fix up the boat.

Look for boats with inherent value rather than simply hunting for a bargain. This may mean that the right choice is 30% more costly than a bargain version of the same boat. If the least expensive option needs a new engine, its systems are shot, the sails are blown out, and a blister repair job is needed, the cost of bringing it up to the standard of a well-maintained and fully functional sister ship may well exceed the asking price of the latter. A do-it-yourself survey is the best starting point.

Mainstream recreational boats encompass a diverse fleet, including cruisers and racers, light boats and heavyweights, monohulls and multihulls. Picking the right boat for your purposes is by no means easy. Luckily the search itself has its own rewards. To help your thinking, the following sections look at some broadly drawn types of sailboats.

COASTAL CRUISERS

Despite the fact that many builders seem reluctant to acknowledge its existence, the coastal cruiser is the mainstay of production sailboat building and the most popular and highly market-researched product in the industry. Builders apparently fear that the label "coastal cruiser" is a pejorative, inimical to the "go anywhere" image they seek to project. Still, potential buyers flocking to boat shows across the country looking for complex systems and big-boat interiors squeezed into short hulls will find plenty of options. And whether it's the second-home feel or an easy-to-operate sail plan that captures a buyer, one thing is certain—coastal cruisers sell.

Those who are serious about cruising the labyrinth of estuaries along the U.S. East and Gulf coasts or the intriguing cruising grounds of the Great Lakes will find a willing friend in the contemporary cruiser. A furling main and headsail with all sheets and halyards cockpit-led make setting, dousing, and reefing sails easier for a shorthanded crew. A reliable engine and drive train, plus a shoal draft, make skinny water exploration very feasible. The sounds, rivers, and bays from Maine to Key West and into the Gulf afford years of cruising opportunities.

Beneteau, Catalina, Hunter, Hanse, Bavaria, and

An in-water boat show mingles the recreational marine industry's latest creations, innovations, and examples of superior craftsmanship with the nautical counterparts of Fords and Chevys—cost-effective boats that target mainstream boaters. Within this wide-ranging array lie boats that fit the needs of daysailors, weekend voyagers, coastal cruisers, and ocean passagemakers.

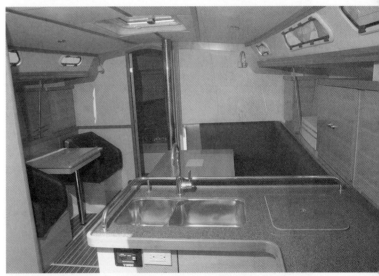

Even a performance-tuned cruiser/racer can pack plenty of amenities below. With a double-berth cabin forward, another one aft, a U-shaped galley, and a nav station, the only thing lacking aboard this 40-footer is a port-side sea berth, an available option in this case. Don't ignore seamanship when looking at a boat—put your perspective boat in a hypothetical strong breeze: what will happen at angles of heel—are there handholds in easy reach for all of the crew?

Jeaneau build the majority of production sailboats sold in the U.S. Their boats are a careful fusion of innovation, cost-effective boatbuilding, and modern competitive business practice. This isn't just a factor of happenstance but is a symbol of a mature industry in

The German-built Hanse production sailboats represent a return to the cruiser/racer concept. A good sailing boat optimized for weekend and vacation voyages, these boats have stirred up new interest in point-to-point club racing.

Production sailboat builders used to put cantankerous gasoline engines and obscure diesels in their boats, while Hinckley saw the value of a Westerbeke or Perkins diesel. Today's mainstream production boatbuilders use the same engines as Morris, Hinckley, and other high-end builders. The same goes for winches, deck hardware, and galley stoves, and this is a big plus for buyers.

which analysis, planning, and careful calculation have led to a long-term business model. The result has been good for builders and good for the mainstream boater. Long-distance voyagers are not mainstream boaters, however, and what the maturation of the production boatbuilder means for them is a little different.

Larger manufacturing operations can afford to better engineer their products, and engine installations, wiring, plumbing, and other systems reflect huge improvements in quality control over the last two or three decades. Builders recognize that eliminating problems that could burden boats just out the door is a builder's chief priority. Contemporary production builders also know where not to skimp—another example of a synthesis between good engineering and good marketing. Production boats that sell at half the price of custom sailboats of a similar size often have the same engine, the same fuel filters, the same hoses, and the same brand of wire. Don't get me wrong, however; I haven't lost sight of the significance of detail work, and in that category, the custom boatbuilder wins hands down. But the use of good-quality materials and engineering in lower-priced boats is a big step in improving life for all sailboat buyers.

At boat shows it's easy to find a good, modestly priced liveaboard coastal cruiser that's more of a motorsailer than the sailboats of a couple of decades ago. The endangered species is the modestly priced, simple, seagoing sailboat that's efficient under sail and capable of long-term ocean passages. Ironically, it's the racing sailor who understands what it takes to make a sailboat efficient offshore—and weight, windage, and wide, shoal draft lines are nowhere on the offshore racer's list of priorities.

Assuming that production builders have measured the inclinations of their clients and are providing what the consumer wants, rather than the other way around, what becomes clear is that for the vast majority of sailors, ocean sailing and long-range cruising is off the immediate radar screen. The owner of a vintage Cal 40 from the 1960s can take this antique racer/cruiser out on the bay and slip by most modern Hunters and Catalinas in the same size range—and could maintain that lead all the way to Hawaii if those coastal cruisers ever headed to sea. Since modern production builders don't see their clientele doing much clawing off a lee shore and open ocean sailing, they have little incentive to add sea berths and side deck space more appropriate for ocean sailing. It seems a bit ironic that in an age when modern materials and engineering can substantially improve sailboat structure and performance, there's less incentive to do so for a greater proportion of the fleet.

Most ocean voyagers begin with modest steps. They start sailing with an inshore commitment to daysailing, racing, or short-term cruising. And many find a lot of merit in a time-proven older boat. One of these oldies but goodies is the resilient Pearson 32. It's not the epitome of sailboat design but is representative of a great genre of older, bargain-priced sailboats that afford more than just bang for the buck. We'll examine the Pearson's strong seafaring and sea qualities as a point of comparison to many new production boats. In the end only you can decide what attributes matter.

Pearson 32

Designer Bill Shaw held sway at Pearson when he drew the lines of a modest cruiser/racer that can be a best buy for those who enjoy local sailing and are also looking for a simple-to-maintain boat seaworthy enough to cruise the coast from Maine to Florida.

The Bill Shaw–designed Pearson 32 was launched in 1979, twenty years after the first Alberg-designed Pearson Triton captured interest at the New York Boat Show, mainstreaming sailing as a middle-income activity. In the early sixties, the company's principals, Clint and Everett Pearson, designer Carl Alberg, and marketing strategist Tom Potter, developed a reputation for functional, well-built, cost-effective production sailboats that garnered mass appeal.

The Pearson 32 is wider and longer than other Alberg-era Pearsons. She sports fine forward sections and external lead ballast in a fin keel that provides better windward performance. She has a fairly high-aspect spade rudder that works in conjunction with the fin keel, guaranteeing turn-on-a-dime maneuverability and lift from the foil shapes, enhancing upwind performance. With a 10-foot, 7-inch beam and fairly flat sections, the boat's righting moment derives a big boost from form stability, and consequently she carries sail well and is less tender than earlier lean, full-keel models. Even with a 40% ballast ratio, the displacement of the boat is only 9,400 pounds, a weight that, with 474 sq. ft. of working sail area, adds up to decent light-air sailing ability. Bill Shaw had looked closely at what New England sailors and those on Long Island Sound and the Chesapeake

With a ratio of sail area to displacement tuned for light-air conditions (SA/D of 17) and a fin keel and spade rudder, the Pearson 32 is a delight to sail yet big enough to fulfill some summer cruising plans. This one is sailing with one reef in the main and a working jib.

▶ *Refitting a larger hatch over the main saloon gives this Pearson 32 better ventilation at anchor, making warm-weather cruising more palatable.*

▶ *With a linear-polyurethane paint job, diesel rebuild, and new canvas on deck and cushions below, this three-decade-old Pearson 32, a classic production cruiser/racer, has lots to offer.*

Bay were doing with their boats and designed the Pearson 32 as the cruiser/racer they were looking for.

Another Shaw design trait is the balance between accommodations and hull and deck configuration: the boat's side decks and cockpit work well underway and at anchor. Extremes were avoided, and the fin keel and spade rudder with canoe-body hull proved their value to performance. A hefty, well-reinforced keel stub provides a rugged garboard seam for the lead ballast keel and lessens worries about running aground.

Deck Layout. The Pearson 32's conventional cabin profile and narrow but adequate side decks lead to an aft cockpit protected by sizable coamings and a deep self-draining cockpit well. The sloop's user-friendly deck layout came standard with an Edson wheel and a mainsheet traveler set just aft of the companionway on the trailing edge of a short bridgedeck. This arrangement allows the mainsail trimmer to remain separated from the helmsman and jib trimmer when racing, but it also saddles a solo watchkeeper with jobs at either end of the cockpit. Because it's a relatively small cockpit, this separation of mainsheet and helm isn't as problematic as it would be aboard a larger vessel. But there is another concern with this mainsheet arrangement: the danger of an unintentional jibe. If it occurs just as a groggy crewmember makes his or her way up the companionway and into the cockpit, the mainsheet tackle sweeping across the cockpit can result in injury or even a crew-overboard incident.

Accommodations. A four-step stainless-tube-and-teak companionway ladder leads below to a cabin with 6-foot headroom that seems large for a 32-footer. Immediately to port and starboard are the nav station and galley, respectively. Pearson offered a quarter berth option on the port side aft of the nav station, which added a berth but eliminated the deep, spacious port-side cockpit locker. Many of the 113 built Pearson 32s came with a two-burner alcohol stove, but there's enough room in the in-line galley for a three-burner gimbaled stove with an oven, plus a sink on one side and an icebox on the other. Serious cruisers can easily convert the icebox into a refrigerator. This small but utilitarian galley is usable at anchor and underway, another good test of a functional sailboat.

Forward of the partial bulkhead that separates the galley and nav station from the main saloon are two settee berths and a table that folds up against the main bulkhead. The two settees are good sea berths and allow for comfortable seating during meal time. A small forepeak V-berth and compact head compartment are forward of the mast. The sloop's *(continued page 380)*

THE MULTIHULL ALTERNATIVE

Modern cruising multihulls feel like a house on the water and have a reaching performance that can be truly stellar. The crucial mandate is to keep the payload as light as possible, because the hulls gain wetted surface quickly when weighed down by unessential gear. A cruising cat, when overloaded, can be slower than a monohull on any point of sail, especially upwind. This makes a cruising multihull a prime candidate for a reliable watermaker and less voluminous water tanks. Whether or not these are optimum vessels for long-distance cruising is a subject for ongoing, passionate debate.

As mentioned earlier, the stability of a multihull derives from the immense overall beam with the span between its two or three hulls. Larger, heavier cruising catamarans combine wide beam with considerable displacement to create a righting moment that's quick to counter the sail plan's heeling moment, at least when the boat is appropriately reefed to match mainsail area with wind speed. The pressure on a sail increases exponentially with wind velocity, and reefing is the safety valve that keeps a multihull's heeling moment well shy of its maximum righting moment. The warning signs that precede a catamaran capsize are more subtle, however, than the signs aboard a monohull or, for that matter, a trimaran. Heeling of the latter involves lifting the windward ama, and as with a monohull's gradual tilt to leeward, you get a distinct warning of what's to come. In contrast, a large cat that lifts its windward hull toward the surface is already on the brink of capsize, and then even a modest puff can spell big problems. The rule of thumb is to remember at what wind velocity a reef needs to be taken, and follow the rule faithfully.

Larger rigs should be reefed sooner, and a savvy multihull crew keeps close track of sea state changes. This is because a multihull lacks secondary righting moment, and static stability numbers are based on a level sea surface. If a gust should hit when the leeward ama is canted downhill on a sloping wave face, the vessel's righting moment will be significantly diminished. A capsized multihull is very stable in the upside-down position—the Achilles' heel of an ocean-crossing multihull. And when a cat or tri is speeding down wave faces in extreme conditions, its low length-to-beam ratio and the modest volume in its bows can cause an ama or pontoon bow to bury in a wave trough, and that in turn could cause the boat to pitchpole, or cartwheel.

An interesting side note is that when Rich Wilson and Steve Pettengill were flipped over and dismasted while sailing Wilson's trimaran *Great American* around Cape Horn, the sea conditions were so rough that a large wave tossed the multihull right side up again—sans mast—just before the two men were rescued by a passing merchant ship.

On the other side of the coin, a cat or tri of modest length offers a huge outside deck that makes the enjoyment of warm tropical latitudes all that much better. Those who want to carry windsurfers and dive gear or just lounge about on deck will enjoy the vessel at anchor—it feels like living on a small island. At night, simply looking up at the stars from the hammock-like webbing makes an indelible *(continued next page)*

■ *One of the first decisions is whether a multihull (bottom) or a monohull (top) makes more sense. After considerable sea trialing of many of the options in both categories, I've come to the conclusion that this is as much an issue of personal taste as a question of naval architecture. Large multihulls offer room to spread out, and high-performance versions such as the Gunboat, shown here, get from here to there in a hurry as long as your destination isn't directly to windward.*

THE MULTIHULL ALTERNATIVE, CONTINUED

impression. Reaching in a warm trade wind breeze is about as good as it gets, but a snap roll can develop when the waves and breeze build, and the slapping of the sea on an excessively low athwartships bridgedeck can become disconcerting.

Sailing to weather in a multihull without dagger-boards is a lesson in patience, especially with a foul current. Pinching will nearly stop the boat in its tracks; you must find that sweet compromise between speed through the water and progress upwind. Big cats motor to windward quite well, and that offers another option, but a small fuel supply more often than not limits the range. Dead-downwind sailing is another question mark, and more performance-oriented crews prefer to heat up the boat speed by tacking downwind through a series of deep reaches rather than sailing a run—sailing a greater distance but perhaps getting there faster. Running downwind with a big mainsail can be tricky when the breeze gets up, and I know a capable multihull delivery skipper who solved his downwind sailing

blues by dropping the main altogether and running under a spinnaker with each clew sheeted to a block mounted on each stem. Control was simple, especially with a sock-type spinnaker snuffer, and in trade-wind conditions the catamaran runs before the breeze like Santa and his sled.

The windage of a multihull and its lighter weight make running before a significant storm a tenuous endeavor. If the vessel is well designed and the bows are full and buoyant enough not to bury in a wave trough, all is well. Even as wave faces must be negotiated, however, the wind and seas are making contact with the expansive topside surfaces, and when a storm-force gust works in conjunction with a steeply slanting wave face, things can get tricky fast. In addition, the sliding "patio doors" on most cats are very vulnerable when running before breaking seas, so lying to a sea anchor deployed from a bridle at the bow is a frequently preferred multihull storm tactic (see Chapter 11 for more on sea anchors).

SPECIFICATIONS FOR PEARSON 32

Length overall (LOA)	31.7'
Length at waterline (LWL)	25'
Hull speed	6.7 knots
Beam	10' 7"
Draft	5' 6"
Displacement	9,400 lbs.
Ballast	3,800 lbs.
Sail area	474 sq. ft.
Sail area (main)	208 sq. ft.
I dimension	40.9
J dimension	13.0
P dimension	35.4
E dimension	11.8
Sail area/displacement ratio	17
Ballast/displacement ratio	40
Displacement/length ratio	269
Mast height	44.6'
Fuel capacity	19 gal.
Water capacity	38 gal.
Auxiliary power	A4/D
Designer	Bill Shaw
Years built	1979–82
Number built	113
PHRF	165

relatively wide beam contributes to the spacious feel in the main cabin. The bunks are a little short, and crewmembers taller than 6 feet 3 inches will be unable to stretch out.

Performance. The Pearson 32 is absolutely fun to sail, small enough to singlehand easily yet large enough for a couple or young family to summer cruise. A 208 sq. ft. mainsail set up with a simple slab reefing system and a roller-furling 120% genoa covers the 8- to 20-knot wind range. Top off this two-sail inventory with a reaching asymmetrical spinnaker for light air and a small working jib to replace the furling genoa during breezy spring and fall conditions, and you're set to sail rather than motor from one harbor to the next. The advantage of cruising a boat with light-air efficiency lies in the enjoyment of making good progress even when the wind is 10 to 12 knots.

The 32's 5½-foot draft makes it just about right for coastal cruising and exploring estuaries along the East Coast, while its efficient foil shapes and external lead ballast provide enough lift and lateral plane to enhance sailing ability both on and off the wind. Add to the mix a respectable sail area–displacement ratio (SA/D) of 17, and it's clear that this Pearson is more than an oversize pocket cruiser. Envisioned originally as both a club racer and a family cruiser, the boat lives up to both expectations.

Pearson demonstrated better manufacturing controls than many of its competitors in the late 1970s thanks to Grumman's focus (continued page 382)

MOTORSAILERS

A well-known cruiser and boating writer once told me that he never made an ocean passage without keeping the engine running 24/7. He represents the growing segment of the cruising population who rely heavily on their engines. For a sailor not quite ready to give up sailing altogether and cross over to a trawler yacht, a motorsailer makes a lot of sense. A few subtle differences differentiate a real motorsailer from a sailing auxiliary with its small diesel and good-size sail plan. To start with, a true motorsailer carries a much more rugged drive train comprised of a large-diameter, slow-turning prop, a thicker shaft, and a heavy-duty strut as well as beefy engine beds and mounts. The engine preferably develops its torque and cruising RPM at lower revolutions than the typical lightweight sailboat auxiliary, which runs at or near automotive RPM levels. The motorsailer's slower-turning diesel tends to be a better shipmate and is certainly kinder to its drive train and the pumps and alternators, which don't have to endure such a wide range of engine operating RPMs.

Motorsailing uses more fuel, and this in turn means a hull shape change to accommodate the additional tank size and weight, not to mention the weight of the engine itself. These boats are usually quite beamy, with fuller sections forward and aft, and their increased ability under power often means less draft because a beat to windward is a thing of the past. A motorsailer can power directly into headwinds and head seas but can still forge along under sail when the breeze is aft of 45 degrees. The variation in motorsailers is wide, with close cousins to sailboats at one end and those that resemble motorboats in look and behavior at the other. Motorsailers with rudders that are large enough to provide efficient steering without prop wash usually sit at the 50/50 mark: 50% powerboat and 50% sailboat. Those with trawler-size horsepower, a vestigial keel, and a need to keep the engine running in order to steer lie more toward the 20/80 realm—20% sailboat and 80% powerboat. Flip that ratio to 80/20 and you're in the realm of a lot of cruising sailboats that are de facto motorsailers; a quick look at their engine-hour meter and logbook will show how much time is spent under power versus sailing.

These sailboat/motorboat blends heel less and provide more comfort. In contrast with most current production sailboats, they tend to be heavily constructed, with rugged rubstrakes, stout cleats and chocks, and the pervasive aura of a finely finished workboat rather than a frail yacht. A motorsailer's mechanical systems likewise are generally a cut above those of a limited-duty sailing auxiliary. Tell a mechanic about an engine problem you're having aboard your sailboat and you'll get a reluctant reply, but men-

A classic 50/50 motorsailer (unrigged) with a rudder large enough to provide steerage with the engine off, a retractable centerboard, and a long, protective, shallow-draft keel. Note the large propeller aperture—a sure sign of a good-size, reliable, slow-turning diesel.

Big diesel engines are mounted low in the bilge of most motorsailers. With the increased horsepower comes a significant need for fuel, and tanks must be placed where they have the least effect on trim as they cycle from full to empty.

tion that it's a motorsailer and he's likely to be much more interested. He knows he can expect a good-size engine room with real access to all sides of the engine. Components like pumps, fuel filters, and the stuffing box are anything but hidden. The overall scantlings are heavier duty, and the vessel's rugged demeanor hints of durability.

📕 *Well-proportioned side decks and cabinhouse, plus enough cockpit space for a dodger and bimini, make the Pearson 32 a cost-effective pocket cruiser with an able feel under sail.*

on quality engineering and manufacturing practices. Laminate materials were bench cut, premarked, and carefully overlapped inside the female mold. Crews wetting out the dry fiberglass used serrated rollers to remove air bubbles and better ensure interlayer bonding between the units of FRP composite material.

Access to the engine is easy thanks to its location immediately under the companionway ladder. Two wooden engine-bed stringers provide support for mount brackets, and the original Atomic 4 (gasoline) can be easily replaced with a small diesel. There's room for a water heater in the bottom of the cockpit locker to port (only models without a quarter berth), and a battery stowage box is located in the starboard locker. Even though the systems aboard this boat were intentionally kept simple, there is pressure water in the head and galley, and with the addition of a slightly larger alternator, a small evaporator-type sealed-compressor refrigeration system can easily be added, rounding out this boat's credentials as a capable summer cruiser. And best of all, in 2014 these boats sell for under $20,000—affording a bargain priced coastal cruising experience.

OCEAN-CAPABLE CRUISERS

When a dream of cruising farther afield takes hold, a different genre of sailboat enters the picture. A preference for a more seaworthy sailboat goes hand in hand with increases in the distance between all-weather harbor entrances. You think more about how well

your boat behaves at sea than seating at the saloon table. When passages are measured in days or weeks, not hours, being caught out in heavy weather becomes a big concern. It's true that many great voyages have been made in sailboats that are less than fit for sea, but how much risk do you really want to shoulder?

Many ocean-capable cruisers have come out of the mainstream market. These are not the more costly and esoteric custom and semicustom products of high-end builders. They are more accurately described as production boats for crews with a penchant for ocean sailing. They carry more ballast than coastal cruisers and more FRP laminate in the hull, and the focus has stayed on construction quality and seaworthy layout rather than glamorous décor.

Manufacturers bucking the advice of marketing consultants continue to build bluewater-optimized sailboats for ocean-bound sailors. Unfortunately, boatbuilders like Morris, Oyster, Kanter, and Hinckley have scared off mainstream buyers with sticker shock. Their prices make Halberg-Rassey, Hylas, Malo, Amel, Sabre, Tartan, and other builders elicit less sticker shock in comparison, but the truth of the matter is that building a sound, agile cruiser is more complex and costly than building an average coastal cruiser.

The price difference lies as much in what you don't see as what you do. An owner may never see how carefully layers of fiber reinforcement were laid up in the hull and where extra support was added to high-load areas, but when seas sweep the deck and the rig, rudder, and keel threaten to tear away from the hull, it's too late to do anything but hope that the engineering and fabrication created a sea-

🔖 *Bill Lapworth and Jensen Marine teamed up to produce cost-effective, fast, long-lived sailboats. The Cal 40 remains an icon of egalitarian yachting—a pleasure to cruise or race and a great choice as an oldie to refit.*

worthy boat. This hidden vault of survival attributes is handled differently by high-end fabricators who pay careful attention to detail and a hire a more skilled crew to laminate the hull and deck. In low-end production facilities, less-skilled workers fabricate the hulls under less supervision, resulting in greater variations in resin ratio and void content that can be hidden by pans and liners bonded to the inner hull. When the seas are up, the value you want most is in the hull laminate, the deck-core bond, and the quality of the hull-deck joint.

The escalation of fuel prices also has many implications for long-distance cruisers. At the time of this writing Mediterranean cruisers are paying $8 a gallon for diesel fuel—true "black gold." With such prices solar panels and wind generators are viable aids to add electrical power, curbing fuel consumption and resulting in less engine running time. Another approach to reducing engine dependence is to improve a boat's ability to sail in light air. Long-distance cruisers are looking more carefully at sail area–displacement ratios, windage, and light-air sail combinations to get increased performance in light air.

In the early days of fiberglass boatbuilding, racing was cruising's best friend. A one-size-fits-all mindset led to boats that were raced and cruised, and when a new model came out, many were soon being raced to Hawaii or Bermuda. Feedback from the racing fleet showed what was right and what was wrong with a specific design. For example, this near-instant feedback let Cal 40 owners and the builder know that the rudder design needed rethinking, as did the way the

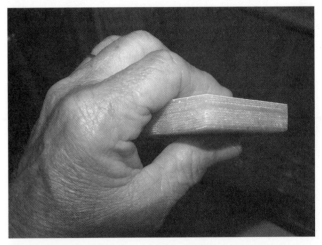

🔖 *The phrase "thick as a plank" describes the laminate cross section in many older, seat-of-the-pants, trial-and-error-engineered sailboats. Stiffness and strength were attained with layer after layer of FRP laminate, resulting in a bulletproof hull that was a lot heavier than it had to be (with the weight carried low in the hull the CG did not suffer much).*

joinerwork was tabbed into the forepeak. Hard racing and sailing honed a better flock of sailboats, and the cruisers who eventually took the helms of those same once-raced Swans, Cals, and Pearsons had a pretty good idea what to expect.

Classic Cruisers

The 40-something-footers in the following sections range from old models to new, each reflecting the

Pearson Yachts used the Bounty II molds it had purchased from Aero Marine to build their venerable Rhodes 41, a stoutly built full-keel, masthead sloop that lives on today. The Rhodes 41 shown here carries the large sail area effortlessly.

design theory of a builder and the appetite of an owner. Changes in both have steered the industry for nearly 50 years. Certainly an oceangoing sailboat can be less than 40 feet—boats such as the Cal 36, Pacific Seacraft 33, Bristol Channel Cutter, Cape Dory 36, Hinckley Pilot, and many others have demonstrated that over the years—and a better-built, better-equipped 36-footer may be acquired and outfitted on the same budget as a less strongly built and well-equipped 42-footer. Naval architect Paul Miller, for one, believes that many cruising couples are "overboated" in boats more than 40 feet long. Still, 40 to 44 feet is the mean size range for coastal and offshore cruising sailboats these days, and a wide choice of design approaches is available in this size. By focusing our attention here, we can compare capable cruising boats of similar size.

Pearson 41

With a lean beam, an LPS over 135 degrees, and relatively heavy displacement, the Pearson 41 boat would score an easy A (Ocean) rating under the ISO Small Craft Directive, described earlier in this chapter. The ISO stability index (STIX) calculations have never been done on older boats like this, but the number, if measured, would be impressive.

Introduced in the late 1950s and early 1960s, the Phil Rhodes–designed Bounty II/Pearson 41 was a true racer/cruiser in an era when gentlemen raced station wagons, not Ferraris. A relatively small sail plan (by modern racing standards) and a simple but utilitarian layout below gave this heavily built workhorse potential as both an ocean racer and a family cruiser. That these boats are still sought after by serious cruisers looking for a cost-effective DIY project speaks loudly to the longevity of their FRP construction. (As to the confusing names for this design: when the Bounty II molds migrated from California to Rhode Island, the boat was rebranded the Rhodes 41. Pearson made a few subtle but meaningful changes such as swapping lead ballast for iron and adding some Yankee trim to a mostly plastic interior. Eventually, the boat took on the Pearson 41 label.)

Just how successful these boats have been is demonstrated by owner Eric Crawford. After painstakingly restoring his three-decade-old Pearson 41 *Restless* to pristine condition and adding modern hardware, cordage, and winches plus a good suit of sails, Crawford and his able crew have tallied an impressive string of Chesapeake Bay race results. In 2000 he took *Restless* to sea, hoping for a respectable showing in a fleet of much newer, more race-refined sail-

The Pearson 41 remains a good choice for those looking for a well-made classic Rhodes design worthy of a refit. These boats aren't brimming with light air alacrity but do make capable ocean cruisers.

SPECIFICATIONS FOR PEARSON 41

LOA	40.83'
LWL	28'
Beam	10.25'
Draft (max.)	5.75'
Displacement	18,800 lbs.
Ballast	7,800 lbs.
Sail area	757 sq. ft.
Hull	fiberglass
Hull type	long keel
Rig	masthead sloop
Ballast	lead
Builder	Pearson Yachts (USA)
Designer	Phillip Rhodes
Years built	1961–67
Number built	50

Durable cast-bronze ports on a Pearson 41 have held up well and speak to the value of quality materials.

A new diesel engine in an old Pearson 41 is a tight squeeze, but careful measuring and the use of a mock-up will help you make the right engine choice during a refit.

boats. Crawford and crew did more than hold their own—they won the premier ocean race, the biannual Bermuda Race, taking home the coveted Lighthouse Trophy. Reaching conditions prevailed and an age allowance (for the boat) helped their rating, but as every Pearson 41 owner will attest, when the breeze fills in and the beat gives way to a reach, the thoroughbred in the classic Pearson 41 comes to life.

Another Chesapeake Bay sailor, George Dunigan, has restored his Pearson 41 *Lightfoot* for cruising, and the aesthetically appealing result underscores how modern coatings can give an older boat a facelift as well as making maintenance easier. With an Awlgrip-coated hull, an Interlux Perfection buff-colored deck, and Cetol-sealed woodwork, *Lightfoot* is an eye catcher and a great example of what can be done to rejuvenate a sound but cosmetically tired sailboat.

The Pearson 41 features a non-cored hull with encapsulated ballast held as tightly as an NFL fullback holds the ball when punching through the line. Hull stiffness is generated by extra units of alternating 24-ounce woven roving and 1.5-ounce mat. The high-quality polyester resin of the era and Pearson's hand lay-up methods delivered hulls with good void control and better-than-average blister resistance. On the boats where blistering has occurred, the thick laminate can be easily repaired without jeopardizing strength. Built before interior pans and liners dominated, these "stick built" accommodations were more time consuming to construct, but each bonded gusset and tabbed-in bulkhead provided additional support to the hull and deck. This approach also allowed access to more of the inner surface of the vessel, al-though some surveyors frown when they lift cutouts in the cabin sole and see tanks hiding much of the recess. The good news is that the encapsulated lead ballast has no keel bolts to inspect, and the tanks, at least in the earlier boats, were Monel, a nearly inert metal that's the material of choice for tanks, shafts, and heat exchangers. Unfortunately, the cost of Monel has skyrocketed, and it has all but disappeared from the waterfront.

Design. Structure and stability are strong points in the Pearson 41. Narrow beam and a healthy ballast/displacement ratio mean a better recovery from a deep capsize. The thick-as-a-plank glasswork perhaps made the boat heavier than necessary, but the resulting strength has lessened worry over fatigue cycle loading and issues such as flex in the garboard region leading to delamination and keel failure. These ruggedly built hulls will continue to deliver owner satisfaction for years to come.

Under Sail. There's no question that the Pearson 41 requires a breeze to get going. Its long keel is both thick at the foot and wide in the garboard region, adding more drag than one would find in a modern fin-keeler. The heavy displacement and substantial wetted surface makes sailing in light-wind conditions less than invigorating—but at sea the sloop has a kind motion with lots of directional stability. This is a big plus for shorthanded crews with an interest in energy-efficient self-steering. For decades, sailors simply added a mechanical steering vane to the transom and an anchor winch on the foredeck and headed for the Caribbean or South Pacific.

Every used-boat buyer confronts a key question: "When is a bargain really a bargain?" The answer—as stated repeatedly throughout this chapter—has as much to do with how well the boat in question fits your needs as it does with its condition and price tag. Those who enjoy sailing inshore and offshore and are looking for a cost-effective vessel that's as user-friendly underway as in the boatyard should take a close look at the old Pearson 41. A structurally sound but cosmetically neglected Pearson 41 is usually worth spending the time and money to repower, re-rig, and recoat with a linear-polyurethane makeover. You won't break the bank if you keep things simple. Savvy boat buyers may look for a boat that costs a little more but comes with a relatively new engine, sound rigging, and decent sails—in other words, a boat that has already benefited from the accumulated TLC of its previous owners.

Ericson 41

The Ericson 41 is another boat with a lean beam and an impressive LPS (140 degrees), one that would score an easy A (Ocean) rating under the ISO Small Craft Directive. As mentioned in Chapter 1, I've owned an Ericson 41 for the past three decades. This sloop represents the next step after the Pearson 41 on a performance-driven path that continues to evolve today. Designed by Bruce King and built between 1967 and 1971, the Ericson 41 is a little lighter than the Bounty II/Pearson 41 and offers a shorter run of keel and a more responsive underbody that sports a semibalanced spade rudder. She retains internal ballast, and the hull is built from alternating layers of 24-ounce woven roving and 1½-ounce chopped-strand mat, hand laid with isophthalic polyester resin. No core material is used

 Wind Shadow *(an Ericson 41) and the Naranjo crew reach before the Windward Island trade wind, easily attaining hull speed under a single reef and a high-cut double-headsail rig. The self-steering gear and the crew like the balance and modest heel that this cruiser-friendly sail combination offers. (Courtesy Madsen)*

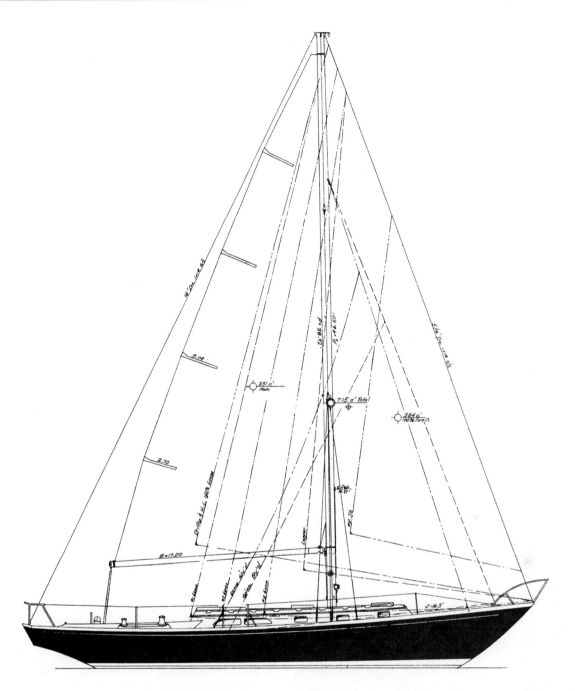

🚩 *The Ericson 41 has an easily driven, efficient hull shape and a versatile sail plan—big plusses for cruising sailors crossing oceans under sail.*

in the hull, but the decks are of sandwich construction incorporating balsa between FRP skins, a higher-maintenance structure. The added light-air performance and double-headsail rig make this sloop an efficient passagemaker for a shorthanded crew.

A graceful sheer, lean beam, and CCA (Cruising Club of America) race rule–inspired overhangs lead to a boat that's as easy to look at as she is to sail. Anyone visiting a sailboat show will have had a hard time missing the renaissance in lean, low-freeboard,

long-ended sailboats from some of the best builders in the country. It's nice to see that classic lines and utilitarian simplicity still have appeal.

The Ericson 41 is at her best under sail, and though slightly overshadowed by the legendary performance of the Cal 40, the Ericson 41 has done well enough on the race course to still be sought after as a classic cruiser capable of offshore as well as coastal challenges. The boat is a good size for a shorthanded crew, whether in light air or when a gale blows the

A 40-footer is large enough to make sailing to windward possible in a seaway, though perhaps not a preference. It's also small enough that a do-it-yourselfer can tackle most if not all of the work to be done. Such maintenance and refit experience pays off at sea. We did all of the work on our Ericson 41 Wind Shadow on our voyage around the world, shown here on the hard after a recent paint job.

Wind Shadow has a small U-shaped galley to port with deep sinks, a well-insulated refrigerator (seen to the left of the sink here), a gimbaled Shipmate stove, and locker and drawer storage nearby.

water sideways. The boat was built in an era that preceded reliable headsail and mainsail furlers, electric winches, and a host of other mechanical gear that today boosts a shorthanded crew's ability to cope with larger rigs. The boat's light-air efficiency and its ease of conversion to a double-headsail rig allow a shorthanded crew to do away with the heavy number one and two genoas and yet maintain upwind and off-wind performance. The double-headsail plan and moderate 715 sq. ft. of working canvas make foredeck work easy, and I've found that a big but easily handled lightweight 160% 2.2-ounce drifter/reacher can tune up light-air performance.

Thirty years after purchasing our Ericson 41, my wife Lenore and I still own and cruise the same boat. There's a roller furler on the headstay controlling a 120% genoa that's reefable to a working jib. The inner forestaysail can be quickly moved out of the foretriangle to expedite inshore sailing. Spectra has replaced wire for the running backstays and makes setting as well as tying off the backstays much simpler. I continue to favor a radial-clew drifter/reacher that now sets on a removable sprit and douses with an endless line furler. A spinnaker, storm jib, and storm trysail make up the remainder of the sail inventory. The boat is a cruiser for those who love to sail and are content with the trade-offs associated with simplicity and ease of handling.

The foil-shaped longish fin keel (see photo) is more streamlined than the keels of the Bermuda 40, Rhodes Reliant, and Pearson 41, all built during the same era. The hull uses extra FRP layers in lieu of a core to create stiffness, and the result is a tough structure that resists point loads and is topped with a solid inward turning deck flange. Thick by modern standards, the hull is further reinforced by a "stick-built" interior in which all joinerwork is tabbed to the inner hull surface, contributing to the boat's stiffness. The hull would have been lighter had a sandwich structure been used, but much of its toughness and longevity would have been sacrificed, and since most of the weight is below the vessel's center of gravity, there's not a lot to complain about.

I have always liked the layout of the Ericson 41, viewing its lean beam as an asset. To port of a user-friendly four-step companionway ladder lies a functional U-shaped galley, and to starboard is a chart table and quarter berth. A spacious dinette in the main saloon converts to a comfortable double berth, and a pilot berth is stacked above the port settee that extends out to make another berth. Forward of the mast is an enclosed head with hanging lockers to starboard and a comfortable V-berth in the pointy end of the boat. Adding a few opening ports and upgrading to modern hatches adds considerably to the comfort below.

The large cockpit and relatively wide side decks also underscore the Ericson 41's primary role as a sailboat, and although the early winches, tracks, and blocks were pretty stone-age, the deck plan lends itself to a modern gear makeover. The winch pedestals are heavily built and securely fastened, but if new blocks or tracks are to be added, it's important to carefully check into how the loads will be spread on the balsa-cored deck. The use of backing plates and core in-fills with G-10 or other stiffener material may be necessary.

The rudder of the early Ericsons failed many times, the problem stemming from a design change instituted by a subcontractor hired to build the rudders. Replacement was the best solution.

I've sailed my Ericson 41 around the world and have grown intimately familiar with her strengths as well as her quirks and idiosyncrasies. Over the years I've laid a teak cabin sole, replaced hatches, tackled rotten core in the overhead, installed a new headliner, re-rigged the boat, and rebuilt the engine. I converted the large cockpit by adding a raised hatch box just aft of the bridgedeck, adding room below for a child-size berth and extra storage. Epoxy and LPU do-it-yourself paintwork has rejuvenated the boat several times, which has stood the test of time. The hull and deck are sound, the original mast and engine block are in place, and the boat has amassed a track record as a capable daysailer, weekender, coastal cruiser, and oceangoing passagemaker, a fair test of any sailboat.

ERICSON 41 SPECIFICATIONS

LOA	41'4"
LWL	29' 2"
Beam	10' 8"
Draft	5' 11"
Displacement	17,800 lbs.
Ballast	8,200 lbs.
Sail area	715 sq. ft.
Sail area/displacement ratio	16.8
Ballast/displacement ratio	46
Displacement/length ratio	320
Mast height	54'
Fuel capacity	55 gal. (Wind Shadow 75 gal.)
Water capacity	85 gal. (Wind Shadow 120 gal.)
Holding tank	20 gal. (Wind Shadow 40 gal.)
Auxiliary power	Westerbeke 4-107
Headroom	6' 2"
Designer	Bruce King

Valiant 40/42: Venerable Voyagers

There's a lot to be said for looking closely at boats that have sailed to distant landfalls and continue to fare well at sea. The Valiant 40, first built in the mid-1970s, is one of these. It's one of the earliest production boats tailored to be a long-distance cruiser and over the decades has earned a been-there-done-that reputation as a proven passagemaker. It is high on many veteran passagemakers' lists of bluewater voyagers.

Two brothers, friends of mine, built the first Valiant 40, a one-off airex foam sandwich version before Uniflite purchased the building rights from Bob Perry. This boat, *Ruby*, and its molded FRP clones have a healthy combination of form and ballast stability along with the structural ruggedness to cope with heavy seaways. Perhaps the most dramatic Valiant 40 sea story belongs to a sister ship named *Windsong*. During a Roaring Forties transit from New Zealand to Cape Horn, a deep low-pressure system spawned in the Southern Ocean overtook the vessel, and in the midst of the tempest the boat capsized, rolling through 360 degrees, and was dismasted. Still structurally sound, with hull, deck, and cabinhouse intact, she remained afloat and provided refuge for the crew. An injured crewmember was transferred to a ship, but a couple of hardy souls remained aboard, jury-rigged a mast, and sailed back to Auckland, New Zealand, where the vessel was eventually refitted. The minimal

Tried and proven is the best description of the Valiant 40. Tamure *belongs to Scott and Kitty Kuhner, who with their two sons circumnavigated, retracing their adventures in an earlier voyage around the world. The seakindly proportions and user-friendly cutter rig make the Valiant 40 a perennial favorite among cruisers.*

Designer Bob Perry assembled the right traits in the Valiant 40, and Uniflite built these boats to rugged scantlings. Some blistering issues arose due to the use of fire-retardant resin, but it proved to be a repairable shortfall. The cutter's blend of stability, seakeeping, directional stability, and cabin comfort has endeared it to shorthanded sailors.

The Valiant concept of a safe, efficient, manageable vessel for a shorthanded crew is still a hit at boat shows (this is the newer Valiant 42) and especially appreciated by those voyaging far afield. Note the reliable servopendulum self-steering windvane, a topside finish–preserving rubstrake, and a deep protective cockpit—all cruiser-friendly amenities.

structural damage sustained in such an ordeal speaks volumes to how the boat was built.

The Valiant 40 molds have changed hands several times over the years. The deck has been modified, but the same proven hull is still available as the Valiant 42. Comparing the Valiant to most modern production 40-footers demonstrates how different today's mainstream sailboats are from proven blue-water performers. The Valiant carries more lead ballast, thicker laminate, a more rugged hull-deck joint,

and windows less prone to being destroyed by breaking seas.

Designer Bob Perry focused on the duality of stability and strength when he blended the attributes of the Valiant 40, and the builder, Uniflite, familiar with pounding loads on powerboats hulls and the heavy laminates used in workboat construction, built the vessel to last. Today the company is owned by Rich Worstell, and the Valiant 42 remains a high-quality cruiser fine-tuned for ocean voyaging.

Modern Cruisers

Hanse 400

Judel/Vrolijk & Company used cutting-edge two- and three-dimensional CAD programs in their boat-development projects. Modeling a new design in three dimensions keeps shop-floor surprises to a minimum—a big plus for the builder. Important details like locker door functionality, engine room space, and table heights end up with the clearances they need to function well.

At the heart of the Hanse 400 success is a canoe body shape with a lean entry, full beam, and flat sections aft making the boat look more like a racer than a cruiser, but when the modest keel appendage is attached, the draft adds up to either 6 feet 6 inches or 5 feet 5 inches (shoal-draft model) and the race boat aspect is greatly subdued. Much of the performance is retained—with 952 square feet of sail area, this modern iteration of the cruiser/racer plays well at both games. The accompanying polar diagram provides the expected boat speed with various sail combinations at various true wind speeds.

The logic behind an easy-to-sail performance cruiser has never been more sensible. Considering how much of the U.S. coastal zone sees predominantly light conditions during the summer sailing season, and the soaring price of diesel fuel, the advantage of a boat that can turn 6 to 8 knots of true wind into a fun sail is a distinct advantage.

The Hanse 400's wide beam carried aft delivers plenty of form stability, allowing the vessel to stand up to the heeling moment derived from its sizable sail plan. The ballast of the iron keel and lead bulb is 6,426 pounds, and the CG of the boat benefits from low ballast placement, giving the boat a good secondary righting moment. Those looking to maximize stability can opt for the 1,000-pound-lighter epoxy-resin-laminated hull and the deep-draft configuration. This combination provides a limit of positive stability of over 120 degrees. With ISO Ocean A categorization and certification that it is built to Germanischer Lloyd (GL) Yacht Plus standards, the Hanse 400 is a boat you can feel confident sailing offshore. (Note that, due to its wider beam and smaller ballast, this boat does not carry as high a Category A rating as the older boats covered in this section would.)

On Deck. The self-tacking 9/10 blade jib is easy to handle, and its single sheet means that there's no sheet swapping during a tack. The ability to set 952 square feet of sail without dealing with an overlapping genoa is a big plus for those who sail shorthanded.

The Hanse 400 is an example of the European trend toward performance cruisers for sailors who like to race and cruise. The modern canoe body and iron keel with lead bulb are more in keeping with current race boats than traditional cruisers, but multiple draft options allow an owner to select the performance level for expected conditions, dialing back as needed or appropriate.

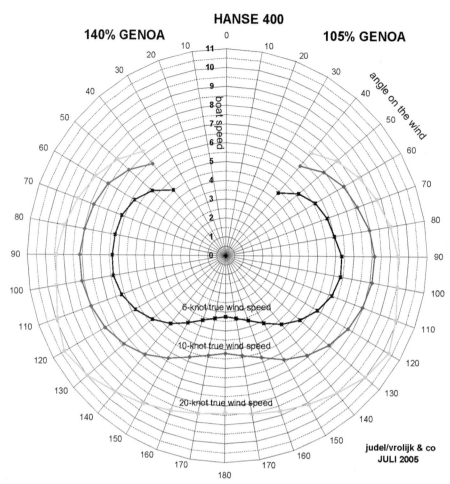

HANSE 400

140% GENOA   0   **105% GENOA**

angle on the wind

boat speed

6-knot true wind speed

10-knot true wind speed

20-knot true wind speed

judel/vrolijk & co
JULI 2005

◤ *A polar diagram provides a graphic representation of what boat speed targets a well-trimmed boat can achieve on all points of sail, in a variety of true wind speeds, and in this case with two different headsail options on the Hanse 400. Any cruiser will appreciate a boat that can achieve 8 knots in a 10-knot breeze over the beam. The left side of polar diagram (180°–360°) is for the 140% headsail; the right side of diagram (0°–180°) is for the 105% headsail. Look closely at the 6-knot (true wind speed) curves and you'll see that on the wind, the bigger sail delivers a .25 to .5 knot boost in boat speed. (Note that this is a big mainsail fractional rig so the boost from a larger headsail is less significant.)*

The 562 sq. ft. mainsail may seem daunting, but with lazyjacks—or, even better, a Dutchman sail-flaking system (see Chapter 7)—and appropriately run reefing lines, mainsail handling becomes user friendly.

Accommodations. Hanse offers several layout options, believing that one interior design doesn't fit all. By dividing the accommodations into forward, saloon, and aft cabin segments and offering mix-and-match alternatives for each, they add choices for the boat buyer. The forward owner's cabin can be altered by swapping extra locker space for a second head and moving the centerline double berth more to port. The main saloon can be set up with a dinette to starboard and a settee/sea berth to port, or an owner can eliminate the sea berth and opt for two built-in arm chairs and a small side table in the same location. The aft configuration allows for either two small cabins side by side or a single cabin and a storage area.

The Hanse 400 is not a long-term liveaboard sailboat, but it is a user-friendly cruiser for summer vacation sailing or yacht club point-to-point racing and cruising. The tight turn of bilge and open, airy layout leave less room for storage, and the two-burner stove and modest tankage also suggest this is a cruiser/racer that's kept light enough to remain agile and not bogged down by an accumulation of gear, supplies, and equipment. This doesn't mean that a run to Bermuda or a fast trip to Hawaii is out of the question; in fact, this is a boat that would take such summer passagemaking in stride and get the crew there in a hurry.

Performance. In contrast to mainstream production cruising boats, the Hanse 400 is an absolute performance standout, not only in its ability under sail but in its ease of operation.

The semibalanced spade rudder offers fingertip steering through a large wheel and the Jefa drag link

The U-shaped galley of the Hanse 400 is more than typical of a race boat but has less storage capacity than on hard-core cruisers. The stove, sink, and well-fiddled counters are quite functional.

The external ballast for the Hanse 400 comes in several draft configurations and is attached to the boat with stainless steel keel bolts.

steering system that nests just under the cockpit sole above what might be called the "weather deck."

Construction Detail. As expected from one of Europe's most technically competent countries (Germany), the Hanse 400 is a very well-made production boat. The hull comes in two styles of construction, the higher-tech option being an epoxy prepreg laminate cured under vacuum pressure. Epoxy is the gold standard of thermosetting resins, providing better adhesion and elasticity as well as more resistance to hydrolysis and other water-linked deterioration. Vacuum bonding core material is a big plus, and Hanse's epoxy-option hull uses the same approach to boatbuilding used by top-of-the-line custom builders.

The iron keel, lead bulb, and stainless steel keel bolts are a well-engineered choice of materials, and thanks to modern epoxy coatings, rust problems as-

HANSE 400 SPECIFICATIONS

LOA	39' 4"
LWL	35' 5"
Beam	13' 3"
Draft	6' 6" (shoal option 5' 5")
Displacement	18,519 lbs. (epoxy option 17,417 lbs.)
Ballast	5,919 lbs./6,426 lbs.
Sail area	952 sq. ft. (100%)
Sail area/displacement ratio	21.76
Ballast/displacement ratio	32
Displacement/length ratio	186
Fuel capacity	37 gal.
Water capacity	79 gal.
Auxiliary power	40 hp Yanmar
ISO/CE certification	A (Ocean)

The Yanmar saildrive diesel auxiliary on the Hanse 400 is tucked into a tight space beneath the companionway stairs, but side panels give access to key components. There's not much extra room for second alternators or other bolt-on components, which is probably part of the designer's intent to keep the boat as light as possible.

There's no perfect rudder or construction material, but some are better than others. An aluminum rudderstock like the one shown here (from a Hanse boat) is strong and can be lathe-cut to better fit the engineering requirements and the taper of the foil, but aluminum's propensity to corrode when submerged near more noble metals and in the presence of stray electrical currents makes it far from ideal. The current trend is toward rugged stainless steel stocks, but many naval architects have moved to carbon fiber or even more esoteric titanium. The material cost of a rudderstock is small relative to the importance of a fully functional rudder. Equally important are well-attached gussets or a framework that prevents the stock from rotating in the high-density foam blade.

sociated with the iron are greatly diminished. The rudder is a foam FRP blade, and the tapered aluminum stock has been well designed and constructed (see photo); aluminum is a galvanically active metal, however, and as with the corrosion-vulnerable alu-

minum saildrive, a wise owner will check zincs often and pay heed to potential problems such as stray dockside DC currents arising from other boats or the marina's wiring.

The J/46 versus the Island Packet 465

A few contemporary builders such as J/Boats (owned by the Johnstone family), C&C, and Beneteau (with their First series of boats) still cater to a market of sailors who enjoy club or one-design racing as well as cruising under sail. The J/46 is an example of a reincarnation and upgrade of the racer/cruiser, and such boats have gained a significant following.

In contrast, Island Packet owner and designer Bob Johnson (the United States representative in the development of the ISO stability standards) targets sailors who care little for racing performance. The Island Packet line consists of sturdy, full-bodied cruisers that place comfort afloat and seakindliness ahead of speed under sail. Johnson's target audience tends to be couples who have retired with a spirit of adventure and want a boat that's solidly built and forgiving and that features an easy-to-handle sail plan. A close look at the J/46 and Island Packet 465, two boats of a similar size, demonstrates the bookends that bracket production sailboat building. (The J/46 was first introduced in 1995 and stopped production in 2003; the Island Packet 465 was introduced in 2007.)

The Rod Johnstone–designed J/44/46 has a lean, efficient entry and an efficient waterline footprint, both good attributes for light-air sailing. The J's deep fin keel has a nicely sculpted lead bulb at its base, which, along with a carbon-fiber spar (J/46), lowers the center of gravity and gives the vessel a respectable static stability curve. The large mainsail is a powerhouse, and the nonoverlapping jib set on a 15/16 fractional rig provides a sail plan that serves a wide wind range. Sail-area reductions begin with mainsail reefing, and when it really starts to blow, the nonoverlapping jib is roller-reefed to a staysail-size headsail.

The Island Packet 465 is a horse for a different course, and its dissimilarity to the J/46 is exactly what makes it appeal to another class of cruisers. From stem to stern there's a different set of priorities at work. Instead of a clear, open foredeck for spinnaker handling, there are large cleats, a powerful electric anchor windlass, massive bow rollers on a short sprit, and a cabinhouse that dominates the deck. The sizeable cabinhouse provides more room below and a cabin sole that's high enough to make good use of the keel sump for tanks and storage.

The Island Packet's double-headsail rig is a roller-furling rendition of the tried-and-proven cutter rig,

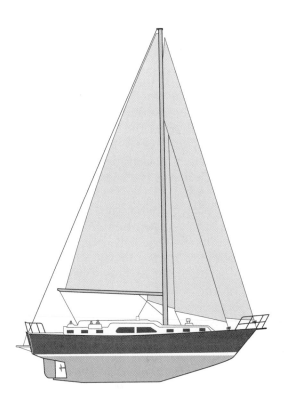
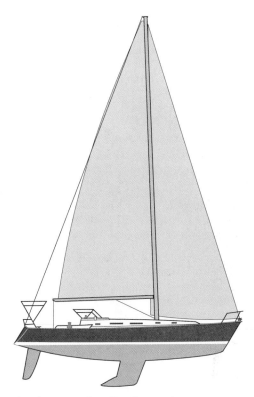

The Island Packet 465 (left) and the J/46 represent two ends of the cruiser/racer market. (Joe Comeau)

and each sail is small enough to be easily handled by a solo watchkeeper. The elevated center cockpit and dodger and bimini combination cause the boom to be about 11 feet above the water, and consequently, with the clearance of bridges such as on the ICW in mind, the mast is not overly tall and the mainsail is small, especially relative to the vessel's displacement. Light-air sailing is the Island Packet's Achilles' heel, and hence there is substantial diesel capacity. Motoring in light air is a reality for most sailboats with auxiliary engines, especially for those on a tight schedule. Increasing fuel prices may change this, but the direction of change is likely a reduction in RPM and a renewed interest in maximum range rather than maximum speed.

The J/46 and the Island Packet 465 are within a few inches of each other in overall length and only 8 inches different in beam, and both are called shoal-draft boats by their designers despite the fact that the Island Packet has 5 feet of draft and the J has 13 inches more than that. They both grew from earlier 44-footers, the J/46 a successful rethink of the popular J/44, and the Island Packet 440, 445, and 465 all having very similar hull shapes. However, J/Boats and Island Packets are as different as apples and oranges, and it's better to simply describe their flavors rather than decide which is a better choice.

The J/46 is a performance-oriented sailboat. Designer Rod Johnstone believes that a sailboat's primary role is sailing, and its component parts should

Gold Digger, one of the most competitive J/44s, sets practice sails with a crew of Safety at Sea participants in a sail-handling training session. The J/44 and J/46 are good examples of the crossover racer/cruiser—boats with performance under sail as well as amenities for hanging on an anchor in a quiet cove.

Bob Johnstone and Lenore Naranjo prepare to tack a new J/46. This well-behaved racer/cruiser goes upwind effectively even in its shoal draft iteration.

COMPARISON OF SPECIFICATIONS OF THE ISLAND PACKET 465 AND J/46

	IP 465	J/46
LOA	48' 9"	46'
LWL	38' 1"	40' 5"
Beam	14' 4"	13.8'
Draft	5' 0"	6.1' or 7.5'
Displacement	34,500 lbs.	24,400 lbs.
Ballast	12,800 lbs.	9,350 lbs.
Sail area (main and 100% jib)	904 sq. ft.	1,021 sq. ft.
Fuel capacity	160 gal.	80 gal.
Water capacity	260 gal.	120 gal.
Mast height	62' 0"	65'
Cabins/berths	3/7	3/7
Holding tank	55 gal	
Auxiliary power	75 hp	76 hp
Headroom	7' 3"	
Storage volume	460 cu. ft.	
STIX	53	
Sail area/displacement ratio	13.7	19.7
Ballast/displacement ratio	35	39.2
Displacement/length ratio	279	164
Builder	IP Yachts	Tillotson Pearson
Designer	Bob Johnson	Rod Johnstone

contribute to the mission. Bob Johnson's Island Packets boats elevate comfort and ease of sail handling, reducing the angle of heel and deemphasizing the competitor's obsession with sail trim. At 34,500 pounds displacement versus the J/46's 24,400 pounds, the Island Packet 465 has substantially more mass to push through the water, yet the Island Packet's mainsail, genoa, and staysail provide about the same sail area as the J/46's main and working jib. Consequently, the light-air capability of the Island Packet is considerably less than the J's.

It's logical to ask what causes such a big weight difference between two boats of nearly the same size. Most notable is the ballast differential, with the Packet carrying 12,800 pounds of lead encapsulated in a long, shallow full keel, while the J/46 has 9,350 pounds of lead bolted onto a deeper keel. Both boats get respectable secondary righting moments from a low center of gravity, and both boats have limits of positive stability (LPS) well above 125 degrees, but the J gets there with a smaller load of ballast on the end of a deeper keel. The Island Packet's foot less draft allows the boat to be more ICW- and Bahamas-friendly.

Keels are as much about providing lift and lateral plane as they are about housing the lead that helps keep a vessel upright, and for upwind sailing, deeper always trumps longer. The J/46 sails to weather much better than the Island Packet, not only because of keel design but also due to the J's finer sections forward and less drag above and below the water, plus a carbon spar that reduces weight aloft and provides a taller, higher-aspect rig. But structure also counts, and some J/44 and J/46 hulls have needed aftermarket keel-stub reinforcement—another factor to consider. The keel-hull connection is much more highly stressed and more easily damaged by grounding in a fin-keel boat than in its full-keel counterpart of similar size.

Both boats are built from FRP but are as different in how they are constructed as in how they look. The Island Packet hull is hand laid and incorporates lots of reinforcement into a shape that's effectively engineered to spread the modest rig and ballast loads. While other builders have sought ways to increase stiffness with lighter materials, Johnson and crew have remained committed to a tried-and-proven solid fiberglass hull, and they use a Polycore alternative to balsa- or foam-cored decks. Polycore is a resin-microballoon mixture that's heavier than other deck sandwiches but provides a superior bond between the inner and outer skins. The deck and cabinhouse are heavier with this approach, but core rot and water damage are all but eliminated, not only in the short term but for the second or third owner too.

High freeboard and heavy decks raise the Island Packet 465's center of gravity, another reason for the larger ballast requirement, and it's the combination of large surface area, lots of resin, and lots of lead that gives the Island Packet 25% more displacement than the J/46.

The J/46 is built with an eye on weight plus a composite-savvy engineer's approach to control of resin ratios in the FRP structure. Pearson Yachts built J/Boats using SCRIMP-molded hulls and decks, a proprietary resin-infusion approach to laminating. The process begins with all the fiber and core material in the sandwich structure placed in the mold dry; then a flexible plastic layer is placed over the last layer of the inside skin. Resin is sucked through a network of tubes into the dry laminate under vacuum pressure, and the result is a uniform primary bond. Excess resin is removed by the vacuum and by means of a special bleeder material used in conjunction with the plastic mold cover.

The J/46 hull and decks are balsa-cored, and the SCRIMP laminating process thoroughly fills the scores between squares of balsa, greatly reducing the chance of moisture migration in places where the core is penetrated by fasteners. In high-stress load points—such as the hull-keel joint and the rudder bearing mounts—the balsa core is replaced with solid FRP laminate or other high-density material.

Rudder Rhetoric. Both designs use semibalanced rudders, but the Island Packet supports the lower part of the rudder on a strut that trails aft from the keel. This strengthens the rudder installation, but it also places this vulnerable appendage closer to danger in a grounding. The J/46 supports its spade rudder with a heavy stock and internal armature and incorporates a sacrificial lower tip in the foam-filled FRP blade that can be damaged by impact yet still leave the upper portion of the rudder intact.

As noted earlier, today's better engineering practices have made spade rudders the preferred choice among performance sailors. They offer more lift and less drag, and in all but their most radical configurations they are strong enough to withstand the forces of sailing and encounters with flotsam. Care must be taken not to make a rudder so strong that it can act like a powerful lever capable of splitting open the stern of the boat.

Island Packet and J/Boats have engineered for sailing loads and added safety margins as each sees appropriate. The two boatbuilding philosophies differ, yet each is valid. The J/46 emphasizes agility under sail, while the Island Packet 465 delivers liveaboard amenities, smaller sail area, and a bow thruster. Which is the better boat depends on the mindset of the buyer.

(In 2013 Island Packet's Bob Johnson and naval architect Tim Jacket launched a 40-foot performance cruiser branded the Blue Jacket 40. Built in the IP factory, the sloop has performance written into the specs and comfort confirmed in the down-below accommodations.)

PURPOSE-BUILT SAILBOATS

Navy 44 MKII: Strength and Stability

The Navy 44 Mark II is arguably the strongest production sailboat built in the last two decades. Designed by David Pedrick in collaboration with Naval Academy staff and U.S. Navy engineering personnel, the vessel had a serious set of standards to meet. The resin-infused hull laminate sealed the kerfs in the core material, and extra reinforcement in the way of the keel sump combined with a massive grid structure provides a supersecure garboard for keel attachment. Everything from small ports to the ratio of positive to negative area in the stability curve hints of the vessel's role as a serious ocean passagemaker. The deep-dead-rise hull shuns the canoe-body trend in favor of kinder behavior in rough seas. Down below, each berth can be trimmed to compensate for the tack, and the galley and nav station are given premium space.

The Naval Academy's new sail-training sloop—known as Navy 44 MKII, completed in 2007—is meant to be cruised and raced for 20 years while enduring five or six times the wear and tear of an average production sailboat. Design priorities include handling offshore conditions and capability on all points of sail. The Navy's sloop is a utilitarian yacht that's workboat-tough and race boat–efficient.

■ *A crew of U.S. Naval Academy midshipmen spinnaker-reach down the Severn River, testing the Navy 44 MKII in gusty conditions. A large, semibalanced carbon-fiber rudder makes it easy to steer the boat under an oscillating spinnaker.*

The fleet of Navy 44 MKII sail-training craft are seaworthy thoroughbreds as well as workhorses capable of being ridden hard and put away wet. The development concept was to produce an ocean-going sailboat capable of 20 years of ocean racing and seamanship training.

More evolution than revolution, the Navy 44 MKII is by no means an example of a straightforward genesis. In fact, the pathway to design consensus was circuitous, at times seeming more like a coxswainless rowing shell crewed by bureaucrats. After years of collaboration and input from a wide range of stakeholders (Navy Sailing, Naval Academy midshipmen, the U.S. Naval Academy Naval Architecture Program, Naval Station Annapolis, the Fales Committee, Naval Sea Systems Command [NAVSEA], Combatant Craft Division, and others), a building contract was awarded to Pearson Yachts, and an improved sailing training vessel was eventually launched.

As mentioned, Pedrick designed the boat under highly specific criteria. The goal was to maintain what had worked well aboard the Mark I, modernize the hull shape, sail plan, and foils, and innovate where appropriate. The predecessor had been created by McCurdy and Rhodes in the mid-1980s, was built by Tillotson-Pearson, and had proven to be a durable, reliable, capable sailboat through 20 years of rigorous use. In fact, the Mark I had done such a commendable job of living up to its mission that there was talk of replicating the design instead of creating a new boat. But after years of mission statement development and design review, a Navy captain handed down the order: "We don't build the same destroyer over again, and we're not going to build the same sailboat either."

So Pedrick set out to design a "newish" sloop retaining many of the proven attributes of the original boat. He retained much of the deadrise forward, carried more beam aft, and flattened sections a little to increase sail-carrying ability. He modernized the foils

but kept the massive, heavily reinforced hull-keel joint. Some might call this overkill, but when you're designing a sailboat that sees triple the use of a charter boat and must be capable of two decades' worth of Bermuda racing without a major refit, the stakes are high. Add to this the need to endure jibes, groundings, knockdowns, and the press of well-meaning but overzealous and less experienced crews, and "margin of safety" takes on a whole new meaning.

Some will say, "Look at vessels like *Ticonderoga*, *Brilliant*, and *Stormy Weather*, and note how well they have stood the test of time." A closer look, however, reveals that all these memorable sailboats have been lovingly rebuilt from the keelson up, often more than once, and the cost of such rebuilds often exceeds their market value. This is why the Naval Academy prefers a rugged vessel that can deliver two decades of heavy-duty use without a major refit. Keeping the scantlings a significant cut above those of the prevailing recreational sailboat fleet is how the Navy 44 MKI delivered such strength, and the MKII approach was the same.

As the Vanderstar Chair at the Naval Academy at that time, I coordinated the initial phase of the MKII design. One of the toughest challenges was balancing the often-conflicting requirements of a sailboat that would act as a sail-training platform for all midshipmen but would also be the race boat for more experienced crews. The biggest concern was achieving the requisite strength, stability, and longevity while keeping weight from overwhelming performance. U.S. Naval Academy Naval Architecture Professor Paul Miller, a competitive sailor himself, enlisted two dozen students in applicable research projects. One midshipman's senior project delved into panel pressures, measuring the bending and impact load resistance associated with different laminate schedules. He tested a variety of resins, core materials, and fiber reinforcements using mechanical rams and impact devices, subjecting test coupons to a series of destructive loads. His research showed that layups of chopped-strand mat and polyester resin endured only a fraction of what high-fiber-content stitched and woven laminates could withstand. He also confirmed that well-executed sandwich structures with low void content provided excellent stiffness and strength, but in regions where high loads were focused—such as in the garboard region, chainplate area, and at the location of the lower rudder bearing—solid FRP laminate made the most sense.

The appendages on the new boat were changed considerably to achieve better steering characteristics and increased lift. The dual-purpose nature of the new boat made it more of a racetrack-friendly station wagon than a second home tied to the dock. They are

Professor Paul Miller and several First Class Midshipmen worked on naval architecture design projects related to the development of the Navy 44 MKII. One of the most significant was a stress analysis of laminate materials. They used an impact ram to test resistance to point loads in a solid fiber-and-resin coupon; another test revealed the fractured core material shown above. This destructive testing was coupled with finite element analysis to make a data-based decision on the materials used in the new sail training craft.

optimized for sailing with a full crew and designed to ensure that plenty of sail handling must be done. A look at the deck layout might lead one to believe that the Navy owns stock in a sailboat hardware company. There are six hefty two-speed 48 winches just aft of the spar, and the cockpit coamings are dominated by two powerful Lewmar 77s. Two more sizable secondary winches ride on the aft end of the house, and two 48s for mainsail trimming are located next to the traveler. The reason for this apparent winch overkill is twofold. First, it gives new sailing midshipmen a consistent lesson in handling a loaded line and eliminates the need to fumble with a rope clutch during an 0300 "all hands" response to a squall. Second, tasks such as reefing are expedited with dedicated winches and crewmembers to handle the sheet, halyard, and reefing line. The boat is usually sailed with a crew of ten, which means there are plenty of hands and tools to work with. The maintenance history of the MKI boats showed that oversizing the winches and other hardware improved reliability and longevity.

Instead of lofting lines on a shop floor, David Pedrick's digital design was sent to Donald L. Blount and Associates, where a space-age seven-axis cutter whizzed over a massive block of foam, sculpting a full-scale plug. A polyester resin was sprayed on the foam rough cut and a final finish cut made. The two plugs (one for the hull and one for the deck) were then shipped from Virginia to Pearson's plant in Warren, Rhode Island, for final fairness inspection and approval. The next step involved the application of a

Once the deck plug arrived at Pearson Yachts, the U.S. Naval Academy crew and David Pedrick placed the winches, tracks, and other key hardware on the deck and checked fairleads, mounting angles, and clearances.

waxy release agent and a sprayed layer of tooling gelcoat. The tool-making process included a heavy FRP layup, mold framing, and reinforcement, resulting in female hull and deck molds along with smaller parts such as the grid mold, cabin sole mold, etc.

Construction. The one-size-larger rule (see Chapter 1) prevailed in the construction of the Navy 44 MKII, as did adherence to standards such as those set by ABS (American Bureau of Shipping) in their guidelines for small craft. As noted earlier in the discussion of ISO standards, many U.S. builders of uninspected (non-USCG regulated) vessels ignore or only partially comply with standards set by ABYC, ABS, ISAF, and others. The build specification for the navy sloop called for mandatory compliance to these and other important guidelines.

NAVAL ACADEMY MKII SPECIFICATIONS

LOA	44.3'
Beam	12' 6"
Draft	7.5'
Displacement	28,000 lbs.
Sail area/displacement ratio	18.8
Ballast/displacement ratio	36
Displacement/length ratio	228
Fuel capacity	65 gal.
Water capacity	160 gal.
Holding tank	50 gal.
Auxiliary power	Yanmar 4JH4E 56 hp
Crew	10

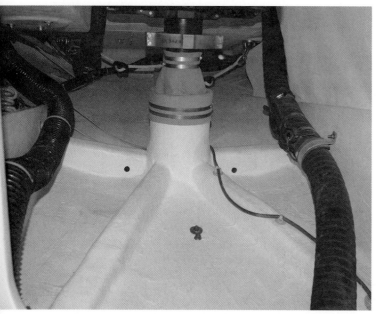

■ *The high-modulus carbon fiber rudderstock with a conventional cable and bronze quadrant steering system (top center) on the MKII is a calculated blend of old and new. The former was chosen for its strength, stiffness, and light weight, and the latter for its reliability and the ease with which it can be repaired.*

Hull and deck laminate schedules also followed this heavy-duty approach to boatbuilding. The layup thickened from the sheer to the garboard, and 1-inch-thick, 6-pound-density ATC core-cell foam was used in the sandwich structure portion of the boat. There were liberal cutbacks of the foam core in regions such as along the centerline of the vessel and in high-stress areas such as at or near the chainplates, rudderstock, winch-base attachments, and hull-deck joint. Chopped-strand mat was eliminated from the layup (except in the veil cloth), and alternating layers of woven roving and stitched E-glass were bonded using the SCRIMP infusion process previously described.

One of the interesting stipulations in the specifications was the elimination of pigment from the hull gelcoat, a requirement that allowed quality control inspectors to see any voids in the outer hull surface, which is laid up next to the mold and is the hardest area for resin to reach. Once complete and inspected, the topsides were sprayed with flag-blue Awlgrip. The importance of void elimination and strict control of resin-fiber ratios was spelled out in the contract and became a major goal in the construction process.

The hull-deck joint is a traditional inward-turning hull flange overlapped by the deck element itself. No core is present in either region, and the joint is made with 3M 5200 and mechanical fasteners. A heavy-duty extruded aluminum-alloy toe rail and a tough elastomer rubstrake are also part of the sheer, helping to protect the area from point-load impacts. The chainplates were one departure from the keep-it-simple specs. Their design calls for a flawless bond between a carbon fiber chainplate and a sizable section of hull and deck. The core in this area was removed, and the inner and outer skins are joined. The secondary bonding that attaches the carbon fiber chainplate to the hull and deck required careful execution.

Lightning strikes are an issue on the Chesapeake Bay, and over the years, several direct hits on Navy 44 MKI vessels have been recorded. The carbon fiber chainplates raised a conductivity question, and ABYC recommendations call for grounding the rig to the keel. In response, a special lug was designed to connect the ground system directly to the standing rigging.

Mechanical/Electrical. The Yanmar 4JH4E naturally aspirated diesel was designed to provide propulsion in a calm more than to deliver thrust to power into headwinds and steep seas. Its modest, smooth-running, 56-horsepower block sits in a secure box at the base of the companionway and provides all-around easy access to pumps and a dual alternator setup. Output from the 100-amp house alternator and the stand-alone 55-amp starting-battery alternator can be shared in case either fails. The banks of AGM batteries can be paralleled, and all of the vessel's electrical and electronic systems are energized via breakers on a control panel just outboard the nav station.

The Navy 44 MKII sloops, like the ships of the gray navy, are well equipped electronically. In addition to a full array of B&G electronics, Furuno radar, GPS, and NavNet digital chart system, there are Icom VHF and SSB radios. There's even room at the chart table for a laptop, and though a satellite communication system has not been built in, it's easy to add an Iridium or other portable satellite communications terminal as has been done aboard the Bermuda-bound Mark I boats for the past few years. The new Navy is all about technology, and gauge watching, for better or worse, has to some extent replaced the seaman's eye.

Accommodations. Spartan minimalism lies at the heart of this boat's interior design with only the essentials: a good berth, a functional galley, a head, and a very handy wet locker. One distinguished retired three-star admiral once said that the older

liner-less interior grants easy access to the underside of deck hardware

The Naval Station (the boatyard that maintains the 44 fleet) liaison for design development, Jim Mumper, was a key link between the technicians who would eventually maintain and repair the new boats and the building process. Note the utilitarian approach in the liner-less interior and rugged, well-reinforced gear such as the Bowmar main hatch. The ample galley includes a three-burner stove with a stout tubular rail in front of it and a deep double sink.

Large primary winches on the MKII are located on open clear coamings, with mainsheet and traveler lines situated well aft. The secondary winches for the spinnaker sheet and guy are on the coachroof, with all of the reefing lines and halyards clustered around winches at the base of the mast.

Mark I boats held "all the ambiance of an abandoned shack." The new boats are brighter and shinier but have not strayed far from a commitment to form and function.

To starboard of the companionway lies the galley, with a wet locker and nav station to port. The main saloon is occupied by upper and lower berths, and just forward of the mast is a head compartment with a hanging locker to port. The forepeak has four pipe berths that house sails more often than crewmembers. While underway, the crew "hot racks" using the four berths in the main saloon and a quarter berth aft. All berths have adjustable tackle and lee cloths and are designed for effective use on any tack.

The galley offers a gimbaled three-burner Force 10 LPG stove and oven along with a large, well-insulated icebox/refrigerator. There's ample counter and locker space along with a double sink and a stout stainless steel tubular rail that creates a U-shaped galley. Ample lighting, fans, and hatch placement add to the functionality of these sailboats, though the usable sea berths, six dorade vents, handholds galore, superb nonskid, and heavy-duty construction often go unnoticed. In fact, some of the most functional attributes of the boat would draw gasps rather than awe from brokers and many of their clients. For example, the liner-less overhead is studded with hundreds of big washers and acorn nuts capping machine screws. This is an honest testimony to how well the hardware is attached and how well the structure is reinforced, but there's been no effort to hide the fasteners. Leaks developing down the road will be easy to find and fix—not the case when all is hidden behind an overlay of vinyl, foam, and staples.

Performance. This sailboat is an ocean passagemaker with enough performance to make a good showing to Bermuda or in coastal competition. It is tough enough to handle a couple of decades' worth of offshore sailing and can cope with light-air and gale-force conditions. With a deep draft and full sections aft, the boat provides much more windward sailing capability than cruising boats of a similar size.

Designed as a masthead sloop with a removable inner forestay, the 44 MKII carries a basic sail inventory of a mainsail, genoas (ranging from a number one to a number four), spinnaker, storm jib, and storm trysail. Many wonder about the use of conventional piston-hanked headsails, and the answer is that with a full crew of agile midshipmen, it's good to have something to do. In addition, each sail is cut for a specific wind range, and the fail-safe nature and ease of repairing of piston-hanked sails are hard to beat. Head foils can easily be added, and race crews can use luff tape genoas if desired.

One of the first differences noticed while sailing the new boat is the fingertip-light feel of the spade rudder steering. The design of the new ruggedly built carbon fiber rudder has a much more efficient lifting surface than the MKI's rudder-skeg combination. When added to the boat's higher initial stability and reluctance to heel in puffs, handling characteristics went from good to excellent.

While beating in 20 knots we sailed with a single reef and a number three genoa, a sail combination that provided good balance and control. The mainsail trimmer worked just forward of the helm, while the genoa trimmers had plenty of room to crank the big Lewmars. The cabinhouse-mounted secondary winches separate those trimming the spinnaker, a sensible arrangement on a vessel designed with a priority for underway operation rather than at-anchor or in-port luxury.

Missing was the pounding of a modern race boat's ultraflat underbody, a feature that appeals less and less during an ocean passage. Neither lightweight nor rigged with a large fractional sail plan, the boat is a functional throwback to masthead-rig versatility. The removable inner forestay and running backstays offer an ideal means for setting a storm jib or adding a reaching staysail when desired. The symmetrical masthead spinnaker and full-hoist genoas make sense, especially with the Chesapeake Bay's light-air reputation. Like all sailboats, the Navy 44 MKII is a compromise of attributes, but when it came to the issues of seaworthiness and rugged construction, the line holds true. All it would take are a few creature-comfort modifications below and some sail-handling simplifications on deck to turn this sail-training workhorse into a performance cruiser's thoroughbred.

The Coast Guard's Leadership 44

The U.S. Coast Guard Academy's Leadership 44 is neither an all-out racer nor an ocean-crossing iceberg chaser. What the Coast Guard Academy wanted was a sailboat to teach leadership skills as well as small-boat seamanship. Like the Navy, the Coast Guard couldn't simply head to the Newport or Annapolis Boat Show and pick out their boat because nothing on these floating shelves quite met their needs. Both institutions realized they needed a vessel that could be driven hard, enduring year after year of intentional and unintentional encounters ranging from squalls to groundings. From their experience with the old Luders yawls, it was clear to the Coast Guard Academy that their demands were far more challenging than what individual owners or charter companies place upon mainstream production boats. The struc-

▰ *The U.S. Coast Guard's Leadership 44 balances efficiency under sail, rugged rubstrake fendering, and a seaworthy deck layout. Note the small dodger and open transom with life raft stowage beneath.*

tural requirements needed to be more rigid, and on the flip side, the interior luxury, fit, and finish of the trim could be more austere.

Once David Pedrick had a clear picture of what the Coast Guard desired, he took the lessons learned from the Naval Academy 44 MKII project and designed a lighter, fuller, canoe-body (the hull is fuller aft and flatter sections prevail) sloop with a fractionally rigged sail plan and a carbon spar.

Engineering. Taking weight out of a boat is easy if you're not concerned about strength and stability. But if you are, effective engineering is the only solution. Removing ballast cuts down on weight but also reduces the limit of positive stability (LPS), as described earlier. The primary mission of the Leadership 44 was coastal sailing, so reducing the weight of the NA 44 MKII to increase light-air sailing ability was justified. The decrease in ballast and LPS still delivered a boat that fulfilled the LPS threshold of 115 degrees for the Bermuda Race or similar race options.

The carbon mast also pared away pounds. On the hull, weight reduction with strength retention becomes more costly. Morris Yachts, the builder,

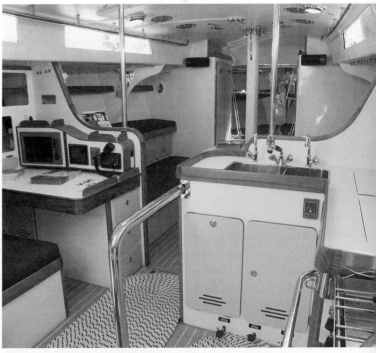

▰ *The Leadership 44 interior is a commitment to underway functionality, with nav station and galley given prime location. Four heel-angle adjustable bunks are situated just forward in the main saloon.*

The foredeck of the Leadership 44 sports a serious bow roller and hefty headsail roller-furling hardware.

LEADERSHIP 44 SPECIFICATIONS

LOA	44' 6"
LWL	38' 7"
Beam	12' 6"
Draft	7' 3"
Displacement	26,000 lbs.
Ballast	10,000 lbs.
Sail area	1,383 sq. ft.
Sail area/displacement ratio	25.2
Ballast/displacement ratio	38.5
Displacement/length ratio	200
Mast height	68'
Fuel capacity	50 gal.
Water capacity	130 gal.
Holding tank	50 gal.
Auxiliary power	Yanmar 4JH diesel 54 hp
Designer	Pedrick Yacht Designs

used the SP-High Modulus company to engineer the laminates for the hull and deck. Their B³ SmartPac system uses the designer's files and finite element analysis to create a layer plan for putting the right amount of reinforcement in every given area of the boat. Then SP uses computer-controlled nesting software and fabric cutters, similar to the way a sailmaker cuts panels. Cloth, mat, stitched fabric, and foam core are cut like parts of a tailored suit. Each piece or panel is marked and packed so that the mold can be loaded with perfectly cut material

that's been sequentially ordered. The process can be leveraged to favor light weight, low cost, or high strength—but not all of them at once. The upside is material standardization and less waste and clutter. The challenge lies in picking the right safety margin. Sailing loads are predictable, but wave impacts on decks or hitting a sharp edge of a large piece of flotsam may put loads where they weren't anticipated, so valuing toughness and point-load resistance to penetration is critical.

Some years ago I chatted with the late founder of Morris Yachts, Tom Morris, who shared a delightful monologue about his desire to spend more time building well-designed, able sailing boats with simple interiors and less complicated systems. I'm sure Tom would have looked at the Leadership 44 and given a vigorous nod of approval.

On Deck. Though not principally designed as a long-distance passagemaker, the boat has many offshore attributes. The low-profile cabinhouse, modest-size windows, and absence of ports in the hull speak of impact resistance and an ability to handle breaking waves. The functional rubstrake, a hard-won battle during the design of the Navy 44 MKII, made its way onto the Leadership 44 as well.

The rig and rigging of the Coast Guard boat reflect the modern trend of a large mainsail and smaller jib, and inboard shrouds without excess spreader length leaves open the option for a larger overlapping genoa. Whether roller-furler convenience will trump the value of time on the foredeck in the Leadership 44 is yet to be determined.

The vessel has deck priority: excellent ergonomics for getting around, especially underway. The Treadmaster nonskid is the epitome of a nonslip surface. Coachroof handrails are fabricated of stainless steel and through-bolted to stay in place. The 30-inch-high double lifelines, securely attached stanchions, and effective geometry of the bow and stern pulpits are in sync with the leads for jacklines and clipping points in the cockpit—all reflect the priority of crew safety.

Accommodations. Though far from getting a *Good Housekeeping* seal of approval, this Pedrick/Morris interior is an elegant vision of spartan utility. The open interior, well-ventilated via a quartet of large dorade vents, succeeds because of what it lacks as well as what has been installed. The accommodations work at varying angles of heel, so being underway is a pleasure rather than an ordeal. It's a retro look at the utility of going to sea. Four berths are given main saloon priority, a place where off-watch crew can sleep. Amidships, the motion is lessened and good ventilation is optimized. There's even a foursome of pipe berths in the forepeak that will be just fine for off-the-wind sailing or while at anchor. The no-nonsense interior has a spacious nav desk and a user-friendly L-shaped galley with a deep double (small/large) sink and a heavy-duty centerline restraining bar that keeps the cook from landing in the nav station when the boat is on a rough starboard tack. These accommodations work well in port and even better underway, and the plans for a civilian version of this boat should have much appeal. The crew at Morris Yachts trimmed things out with just enough wood to deliver a hint of their abiding joinerwork forte.

Farr 400

The Farr 400 is as divergent from the preceding 44 foot boats as could be chosen. Its mission as a race boat is as singular as that of a sport boat or one-design dinghy. The boat is included here first for purposes of comparison and second because it elevates the pure fun of going sailing to an epic level.

FARR 400 SPECIFICATIONS

LOA	38' 8"
LWL	36' 5"
Beam	11' 3"
Draft	9' 6"
Displacement	8,624 lbs.
Ballast	4,796 lbs.
Sail area/displacement ratio	40
Ballast/displacement ratio	60
Displacement/length ratio	84
Sail area	1,098 sq. ft (upwind); 2,530 sq. ft.
Fuel/water/waste (gal)	11/20/chemical toilet
Engine	Volvo D1-30 (27 HP) with saildrive
Electrical	50 Ah (engine); 80 Ah (house)
Designer	Farr Yacht Design
Builder	Premier Composite Technologies LLC, Dubai

▐ *Farr Yacht Design turned their talents to inshore racing with this all-carbon-fiber speedster. Bruce Farr calls the project a "refined one-design," a boat that sheds compromise to focus on the job at hand, by which he means, among other things, dramatic upwind sailing and heightened planing ability off the wind. The boat has a low-drag hull shape with a lean, flattened canoe body that's more surfboard than sailboat, and foils that are tuned to turn a quick-to-plane downwinder into an able upwind performer.*

A purpose-built race boat, the Farr 400 sheds extraneous weight and windage. Farr has intentionally created a Category B coastal racer, not an ocean-crossing Category A competitor, and thus didn't let concerns such as how to mitigate the effects of trough diving in 20-foot seas drive the equation. Nor did he face the need to fit a cruising boat interior into what's essentially a cabin-size sail bin. There are pipe berths triced up port and starboard, a stove, a small sink, a toilet, and room for a substantial cooler, but even spartan minimalists would underrate the 400's role as a comfy cruiser.

THE BOATS WE SAIL

There's a chasm-size rift between the Farr 400 and the Navy 44 MKII—wide enough to make today's political divides seem bridgeable. We profiled both boats to underscore a theme emphasized throughout this chapter: a vessel's mission should drive its design. The clearer, more realistic picture you have of how you will use your sailboat, the happier you will be with the outcome of your boat selection process. Just as every seasoned shipwright knows, there is a proper tool for every job.

13

STAYING SAFE AND COPING WITH THE UNEXPECTED

A bit of luck can mask a big mistake, allowing calamity to slip harmlessly astern. But instead of celebrating such good fortune, this is the time to examine what could have happened if a fickle variable had swung the other way. Even small mistakes can cascade into big problems, and part of every sailor's evolving seamanship is recognizing the difference between working your way out of danger and simply lucking out as a reef accidently passes a few feet to leeward. The former, in this case prudent navigation, is a skill to capitalize on, while pure luck should always be appreciated but never be counted on.

THE ROLE OF SEAMANSHIP

As noted in Chapter 1, safety at sea is built from three components, seamanship being the most important. Good seamanship keeps us out of trouble—and avoiding trouble is always better than overcoming it. The second component is the boats we sail in; a sound, seaworthy vessel, as detailed in Chapter 12, will make up for many (though not all) errors of omission or commission. And finally comes the safety gear we carry aboard. The present trend toward overreliance upon gear—and the misleading assumption that miracle equipment alone can atone for shortfalls in seamanship or an ill-suited or improperly prepared boat—is itself dangerous, especially when safety gear is merely stowed aboard and vital training is ignored. Still, when things really go bad, it's the safety gear that just might tip the scales in our favor.

Because seamanship is the longest leg of the safety triangle, it is also our primary focus throughout this book. When boats get into trouble, the trouble can usually be traced back through a chain of cause and effect to an original sin, which is usually an operator error. With this in mind, we can summarize the essential seamanship skills that lessen the likelihood of ever needing to tap the reserves in the third leg of the lopsided safety-at-sea triangle (see the sidebar on page 3, Seamanship Characteristics, in Chapter 1—that list could also be titled "The Safe Sailor"). Think of these traits and skills as risk mitigators.

This chapter examines the third leg of the safety triangle: preparing your boat for sea, outfitting it for safety, and dealing with emergencies. A review of several decades of USCG boating safety data makes it easy to see what spawned the federal government's mandatory safety equipment requirements. But the first big revelation from the data is how safe sailing really is. Sailors have a better safety record than motorboaters, who seem to have a higher per capita rate of accidents and fatalities. Some assume that speed is a factor, while others allude to training and a lack of understanding of the Rules of the Road as the gap between the two groups. Whatever the cause of the mishaps, research has shown that those wearing a life jacket—on a sail- or powerboat—are less likely to become a fatality. The accompanying table provides a look at recent fatal sailing accidents, many of which have been examined in this book.

A look at the few incidents involving ocean racing sailboats that have capsized reveals the downside of the elevated risk of racing with a shorthanded crew at double-digit speeds. Names such as Isabelle Autissier, Florence Arthaud, Tony Bullimore, Raphael Dinelli, Thierry Dubois, and Tim Kent come to mind as ocean racers who have survived having their vessels flipped or sunk. Their feedback adds data to the design files of naval architects and provides lessons for all sailors. Angus Primrose, Mike Plant, Gerry Roufs, Harry Mitchell, and other ocean racers have not been as fortunate.

Ocean voyaging may not up the ante as much as ocean racing, but those who venture out on large waters do raise the risks as well as the rewards of sailing. Thorough preparation helps even the odds. Long-distance passagemakers are less likely than ocean rac-

RECENT FATAL SAILING ACCIDENTS

Event	Summary
Chicago-Mackinac Race (Illinois), 2010	A violent squall line capsized the Kiwi 35 *WingNuts*, two lives lost
Farallones Race (California), 2011	The crew of a Sydney 38 cross over a shoal and are hit by a breaking wave, five sailors died
NARC Rally (North Atlantic), 2011	One crew swept overboard from an Island Packet 38 caught in heavy weather and lost at sea
Newport to Ensenada International Yacht Race (California), 2011	The crew of a Hunter 37 powered into the surf-swept cliffs of North Coronado island, four sailors died
San Clemente Race (California), 2013	Columbia 32 loses steering, drifts into surf zone, one crew drowns
America's Cup practice, San Francisco Bay (California), 2013	72-foot multihull flips and Olympic sailor Andrew Simpson drowns
Post Anitgua Race Week, Atlantic Ocean, 2014	Beneteau 40.7 begins taking on water, loses its keel, vessel overturns, all four crew lost at sea

Take a walk on the lee side before it becomes the wild side. Check the nonskid, the handholds, and where the deck camber and cabin sides send you. Designers of good sea boats take seriously the ergonomics of keeping crew on board. Inshore, in daylight and clement weather, this crewmember need not be clipped in with a harness for foredeck work, but at night he will enhance his safety significantly by wearing a PFD/harness and clipping his tether to a taught, inboard jackline.

ers to make the news if they come to grief, and when operating outside U.S. Coast Guard jurisdiction neither do they show up in Coast Guard statistics.

PREPARING YOUR SAILBOAT FOR SEA

The hazard of slipping on deck is well documented and does occasionally lead to sailors going overboard. The first line of defense lies in the quality of the nonskid surface and the shape of the deck itself. However, a look at a range of sailboats at any boat show reveals night-and-day difference in how builders perceive the importance of this vital characteristic. Significant design shortfalls such as omitting nonskid on some deck areas where crew regularly step are often seen. Some boats have side decks that are so narrow, thanks to their bulging cabins, that a crewmember needs to lean outboard to get around the shrouds and up to the foredeck. Other boats have stacked-up cabins that make them look like layer cakes; a stacked superstructure on a short waterline length exaggerates pitching, rolling, and yawing motion and in a choppy seaway can cause even a seasoned crew to become seasick. Another attractive nuisance seen all too often are cleats placed so far outboard that crewmembers must lean over the lifelines simply to make or release a cleat hitch.

Also check handholds lead to certain points on deck. Can they move a crewmember safely to the foredeck, or do they end prematurely, leaving a crew with nothing to hold onto other than the lifelines? Crewmembers often go forward on the leeward side deck using lifelines—the more dangerous route. While the lifeline wires may be capable of handling thousands of pounds of load, on some boats they terminate on a split bow pulpit or weak stern pulpit that

🚩 *Often all it takes is one failure of a shiny terminal to send a mast over the side. In this case a piece of rod rigging has failed near its cold-headed stemball terminal. Inspect your rigging regularly, and make sure each piece of standing rigging pulls in a straight line between the chainplate at its lower end and the mast tang or socket aloft. Cruisers are more likely to have wire than rod rigging, but either type can fatigue and fail after enough years or miles at sea. This is one reason why many ocean voyagers put stock in a cutter rig; with its redundant shrouds and running backstays, a cutter is much more likely to keep its rig intact when a wire parts.*

🚩 *It's hard to know how long you can wait to replace rigging before you've waited too long. It's like talking about two identical automobiles: one may have 150,000 miles on its odometer and the other only 35,000, but you also need to know how hard those miles were because the stress/strain fatigue curve is markedly affected by severity of use. As a rule of thumb, however, 10-year-old rigging is inappropriate for a lengthy ocean voyage.*

will crumple and cause the stanchions to fail at 15% of the breaking strength of the wire.

One 50-foot ocean-racing sailboat I was familiar with had such an unsafe cockpit that during a delivery a skilled professional sailor was tossed overboard and lost at sea. (The incident is described later in this chapter in a sidebar entitled A Quick-Stop Recovery Gone Wrong.) He wasn't on the foredeck making a difficult sail change—he was a few feet from the companionway hatch—but the beamy vessel lurched and pitched him out of the wide shallow cockpit and the lifelines didn't restrain his exit. Oceangoing cruising sailboats should have a deep cockpit well that affords protection from being launched by lateral accelerations. In heavy weather, a beamy, shallow, coaming-less cockpit can become as dangerous as a foredeck. On such a boat the crew needs to practice early harness attachment and develop a keen sense of when the next breaking wave is about to hit.

One well-meaning boat manufacturer installed swim-step seats with locker lids halfway down the transom on several models. Each locker had a flimsy clasp and a poor gasket, greatly increasing the chances for catastrophic downflooding. Anyone planning to sail offshore on a boat with transom-mounted locker hatches should have the openings permanently bonded shut. This will eliminate the potential for downflooding—but also render useless the handy storage locker. More difficult to remedy are problems associated with a rig, rudder, or keel attachment. Failure of any of these compo-

🚩 *Keeping water where it belongs is a major safety concern of naval architects and engineers. A vessel inspection before a voyage or race should reveal any material changes in parts of the hull that are often submerged. While ports in the hull have become more popular, they inevitably represent a decrease in structural integrity. Fasteners, flanges, sealant, and surrounding structure are as important as the lens itself. Engineers point out that an abrupt stiff spot in an otherwise flexible member will be a focus of stress when seas impact the structure, perhaps even causing a material failure. Such a junction is just what occurs in windows let into a hull. Carefully inspect these ports and carry cover plates.*

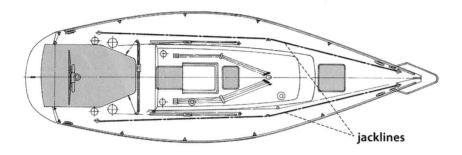

Jacklines should be rigged along port and starboard, ending about 6 feet short of the transom. Flat webbing has become the material of choice; regularly check all parts of the jackline for wear.

nents can lead to potentially life-threatening consequences (see Chapter 12).

Before heading offshore, double-check hatches and ports and make sure the chances of downflooding are minimized. It should be possible to pin companionway washboards in place, and all lazarette lids should be sealed and solidly latched. Heavy objects above and below deck should be lashed, dogged, bolted, or otherwise immobilized. Cabin sole boards, the galley stove, or a hefty toolbox can become lethal in a knockdown or capsize.

On deck, the crew needs pad eyes and jacklines to clip onto when conditions warrant wearing a harness tether. Jacklines should be taut and should be run inboard, along the cabinhouse, and end about 6 feet short of the stern. Flat webbing has become the material of choice for jacklines, and the lashed or shackled ends should be checked regularly.

The motion of a sailboat changes dramatically at sea, and keeping the crew and inanimate objects where they belong becomes more difficult but is always critical.

BOAT-RELATED EMERGENCIES

Another aspect of preparing before heading offshore involves understanding the kinds of emergencies that may occur at sea and having the right equipment—and the right knowledge—to avoid or respond to them, and thus to prevent potential disaster and the need for rescue. In the following section we explore many of these kinds of emergencies.

Dismasting and Jury Rigging

A dismasting is always unanticipated, and the first rule of order in such chaos is to check to make sure

none of the crew has been hurt. And just as quickly make sure that the mast heel has not jumped out of the step and is punching its way through the hull. This is much less likely if the mast heel has been pinned or otherwise locked to the step.

Next comes an "all hands on deck" response to release rigging and salvage parts of the mast, sails, and standing rigging that may be useful in your efforts to jury-rig a surrogate spar. Because in rough seas broken spars can damage the hull, it is critical to carry tools aboard for cutting rod or wire rigging. The rule of thumb is that the worse the weather, the less rigging and rig parts can be saved and the more must be cut away.

Once the boat and crew are safe and salvageable items have been saved, it's time to develop an engineering plan for the jury rig. Consider these questions: What will comprise the new spar? Is there a single piece long enough to do the job? How will new rigging be attached? Most sailors who have been through such episodes emphasize the importance of coming up with the sail plan you may want to use before starting to jury-rig. Very often the jury rig involves the storm jib and storm trysail, sometimes even setting the latter sideways. In any case, once you have an idea of the sails you will use, you can better estimate how high the hoist pulleys must be.

Modern high-modulus cordage makes jury-rigging much easier. Stays and shrouds can be directly lashed to the spar or knotted to fittings. The mast can be made up of a spinnaker pole telescoping from a broken mast stump or lashed to a standing part of the rig. A block and line can be set up on the forward and aft sides of the jury rig to act as jib and mainsail halyards. When stepping the replacement mast, raise the spar with the newly jury-rigged upper shrouds, backstay, and forestay in place, *(continued page 412)*

RESPONDING TO A STEERING FAILURE
Chuck Hawley

(Author note: For nearly two decades I've had the pleasure of working with fellow US Sailing Safety at Sea Seminar moderator Chuck Hawley, who has been responsible for carrying on a trend begun by the late Capt. John Bonds, U.S. Navy [ret.]—a pioneer in American sailboat safety training. Chuck recently spoke about a spate of steering failures, the most recent leading to the loss of life of a sailor in a Southern California offshore race, and he has kindly offered to share his insights in the following sidebar.)

A relatively rare but potentially debilitating failure of a sailboat's structure is the loss of steering, or more specifically, the loss of part or all of a rudder. Perhaps because rudders are such a fundamental part of a vessel's structure, many sailors set out to sea without having spent any time asking, "What would I do if my rudder [or quadrant, tiller, steering cables, or rudder bearings] were to fail?" Rudders and other aspects of steering systems do fail, and the sense of being entirely out of control when unable to steer has led many crews to abandon ship prematurely for lack of a solution.

There are several proactive things a sailor can do before setting off. First, if you have a production boat, research the history of rudder failures in your particular class. A popular 35-foot sailboat class launched in the late 1970s experienced a 100% rudder failure rate during a 1980 ocean race: each of the three boats of the class participating in the race lost steering. Other classes—even when the rudder is unprotected by a keel or skeg—experience few or no failures. Do your research.

Second, hire a naval architect, surveyor, or sailing expert to go over your existing steering system. This will require dropping the rudder, which you should do every few haulouts anyway. The expert will look for the many possible points of failure that can be remedied either with replacement items, by carrying spares, or by rebuilding. If you store your boat in freezing conditions over the winter, pay special attention to the ingress of water at the rudder shaft due to openings caused by the different rates of thermal expansion. Water ingress followed by freeze-thaw cycles tears a rudder apart from the inside out.

Third, based on the anticipated likelihood of rudder failure, your budget, and your boat's design, devise a reasonable emergency steering solution before you depart. Here too, a naval architect or boatbuilder can be enormously helpful. Your solution might use one of these approaches (in my order of preference):

- **Mounting a spare tiller-steered rudder.** On a boat with a near-vertical transom, attach a spare tiller-steered rudder blade by inserting its two strong pintles into premounted gudgeons on the transom. It will be very difficult to install the rudder with a sea running, and the tiller may collide with a backstay or pushpit.
- **Mounting a spare rudder on a track.** Mount a section of 1¼-inch T track vertically on the transom. There has to be enough vertical distance so the track has many fasteners holding it in place. Two Schaefer genoa cars sliding on the track then serve as gudgeons to receive the pintles in a spare rudder blade. The track is rugged and allows the rudder to be slid down the transom under a modicum of control.
- **Mounting a spare rudder with a "cassette" approach.** Mount a pivoting box on the transom into which the blade of your spare rudder will slide. This approach requires a lot of building in advance and some storage space, but many boats have sailed to Hawaii with a variation of this approach.
- **Using a "pole rudder."** Attach a flat board (for surface area) to the outboard end of a downwind pole of some sort, and create a pivot point using the pushpit or backstay chainplate. I know of people who have done this successfully, though I would strongly recommend a different solution.
- **Using a "pole rudder" with premounted fitting.** Mount a pole-end mast fitting on the transom, and use lines to hold the pole's far end down in the water and to control its side-to-side movement. This method has strong supporters, most of whom like the idea of a bare minimum amount of disruption and cost, since the likelihood of using the contraption is low.
- **Steering with drogues.** In desperation, some have had success with drogues, which allow you to steer the boat in approximately the right direction. This method is probably more effective downwind, ideally on a boat with a lot of provisions and a watermaker.
- **Search the web for some of the well-illustrated solutions from naval architect Jim Antrim.** Whatever else you do, survey your boat before you set off and contemplate your solutions before you need them.

Chuck Hawley has sailed approximately 43,000 miles on vessels ranging from ultralight sleds to singlehanded sailboats to the maxi-catamaran PlayStation. He has served on the boards of the American Boat and Yacht Council (ABYC) Technical Board, Transpacific Yacht Club, Santa Cruz Yacht Club, Singlehanded Sailing Society, and Pacific Cup Yacht Clubs. He worked for West Marine for 30 years and rose to the role of Vice President of Product Information. He lives in Santa Cruz with his wife Susan and five daughters and owns an Alerion Express 38 Yawl.

"WE'RE SINKING" —LESSONS LEARNED

Nothing has ever gotten me out of my berth faster than when a shipmate cried out, "We're sinking!" The incident happened decades ago but still seems recent. As mentioned earlier in the book, we were halfway to Hawaii when those words were uttered—and I bolted from my bunk onto the flooded cabin sole. The small cabin was cave dark, and a trade-wind swells caused the rising water to rush fore and aft. Pumping was a secondary concern; the leak had to be found and stopped. The electric system was submerged, and the lights and bilge pump didn't come on. I had an ingrained understanding of my little 26-foot sloop and knew where every through-hull resided. Getting to each in the dark was as familiar as finding the main halyard winch. Feeling around each likely location for a fitting failure, I discovered that a cockpit drain through-hull had been sheared away when a heavy, poorly secured tool box had fallen onto the fitting. A soft wood plug sealed the hole, stopped the leak, and kept us afloat but far from home free.

Water over the cabin sole rushing unimpeded from bow to stern instigated broaching on steeper wave faces. Keeping the centerline of the boat more or less perpendicular to the wave train lessened that threat and reduced the chance of downflooding. The two manual pumps on board were too small in capacity to handle the job. The medium-size electric pump would have been a big help, but the batteries were submerged, making the pump useless. What did work were three scared lads and a couple of big buckets. Rotating every 10 minutes through a routine of one person steering while two bailed, we spent an anxious hour driving the water level back into the sump. The slurry was actually a mélange of powdered bilge stores, freeze-dried rations, and oily residue. The lessons learned were meaningful:

1. Foremost is the need to stop a serious leak ASAP, recognizing the short window of time a crew has to respond.
2. Because of the unanticipated hazard of water reacting to roll, pitch, yaw, heave, sway, and surge, stability diminishes quickly, and with loss of buoyancy, these two factors conspire to make capsize much more likely.
3. Heavy gear must be secured with robust tie-downs, and an early warning bilge alarm should be installed to raise an alert as soon as possible.

In situations where leaks become gushers, seconds count, and manning manual pumps take a backseat to staunching the flow. Discerning the rate of water ingress drives your damage-control response.

ready to tension. Once roughly set in place, turn-buckles can be reused to tension the shrouds.

It pays to keep aboard a piece of 7×7 or 7×19 wire that can be cut and fixed with a Nicopress thimbled loop for a jury-rigged headstay. The wire stay tolerates the friction caused by sail luff hanks, which need to be used on jury-rigged sails. Otherwise, all of the other standing rigging can be done with high-modulus Spectra or Dyneema, or other low-stretch, high-strength rope.

Downflooding and Pumping Capacity

As mentioned in the accompanying sidebar ("We're Sinking"), water in the bilge belongs in a tank—otherwise it creates a double-edged problem that can jeopardize seaworthiness. Every gallon that accumulates on the wrong side of the hull skin decreases buoyancy and at the same time negatively impacts stability. The shortfall in righting moment is caused by the free-surface effect—a physical reality in which gravity coaxes a liquid toward the lowest point in any closed shape (see Chapter 12). By shifting the center of gravity to leeward, the weight of the water acts to further heel rather than right a vessel. Obviously, keeping unwanted water out of the hull is the first principle of staying afloat. And an important corollary is to install an effective dewatering system to rid your boat of water you haven't been able to keep out. Bilge pumps give crew on a leaking or downflooding vessel a fighting chance to staunch the flow and remain afloat.

Bilge Pumps

When it comes to leaks and pumps, flow volume is a big deal. The difference in effect between a dribble and a gusher is relative to the extraction rate of pumps in use. The rate of water ingress depends simply on the surface area of the hole and the water pressure related to the depth of the opening. A good rule of thumb is that a 1-inch diameter hole a couple feet below the surface is the most that the best of manual bilge pumps operated by fit, adrenaline-fired crew can contend with. Large centrifugal submersible DC pumps sling even more water, but they have a ravenous appetite for amperes, and continuous duty necessitates a reliable electrical supply.

Bilge pumps come in a wide array of shapes, sizes, and modes of operation. All have a capacity rating for extracting water from the bilge, but often these gallon-per-minute or gallon-per-hour ratings are too optimistic and fail to reflect real-world factors such as having to pump the water up 4 or 5 feet to the discharge, the circuitous route of a lengthy discharge hose, or other restrictions to flow created by the installation. For example, an electric centrifugal pump rated at 3,500 gallons per hour (gph) is likely to discharge only about 2,000 gph when the water must be lifted up 6 feet on its way out.

The ubiquitous lever-activated, diaphragm pump built by Edson has for decades served as a benchmark of bilge pumps. The original version of this cast-bronze, flap-valve pump was designed to lift wet cement as well as water. Today, the modern iteration of this titan is a 30-gpm pump that's worth its weight in silver if not gold. It's available in bronze or aluminum, and although the bronze version costs about $300 more, it's a worthwhile investment. Bronze prevents any oxidation around the stainless steel fasteners holding the flap valves. The 30-gpm rating is based on a pumping rate of 30 strokes per minute. A smaller, well-built 18-gpm Edson pump is also available.

Ideally, such a high-volume, long-lever pump is permanently mounted, securely plumbed, and always at the ready if the need arises. Those with less room in the bilge often rig the big Edson on a plywood board cut to fit in the cabin sole over the deepest part of the bilge. Hull design is a key factor, and vessels with an extreme canoe body design without a keel sump are hard to pump. In a seaway, water will rush fore and aft as well as athwartship as the boat is moved about. Keeping a bilge pump pickup in the right place can be challenging. In addition to the necessity of a moveable pickup hose for boats without a dedicated bilge sump, there's also the challenge of attaching a functional strum box to keep debris from clogging the check valves.

International Sailing Federation (ISAF) Offshore Special Regulations, which are quite specific in certain areas of safety, remain fairly sparse in bilge pump particulars. Section 3.23 states that a bilge pump discharge may not be plumbed into a cockpit drain or a hose simply led to the cockpit unless the water can run uninhibited to the sea. Even in the latter case, dumping oily bilge discharge into the cockpit can add more hazard for the crew trying to handle the vessel. The ISAF regulations also state that pumps and strum boxes must be accessible for easy maintenance and there should be one manual pump that can be operated in the cockpit with a lanyard to retain the pump handle. A couple of rugged 2.4-gallon buckets should also be at the ready.

Testing Your Pumps. Advertised pump capacity may be a starting point for comparing one product with another, but when it really comes down to knowing what you are depending on, nothing is better than a simple timed output test of each pump you have on

MEDICAL EMERGENCIES

Serious trauma and major injuries are difficult to manage at sea, and even physicians find conditions offshore far from conducive for patient treatment. Prevention of such incidents needs as much forethought as how a crew would respond to accidents and maladies. Start by addressing vessel safety and the general health of the crew, and be sure that those on board can handle the challenges that lie ahead. Anyone on board with a chronic health problem should have an ample supply of required medication along with a backup supply, as well as their doctor's permission to engage in the activities linked to racing or cruising a sailboat offshore.

While numerous first-aid kits are marketed in chandleries, it makes sense to look at the top of the line for a kit that contains effective wound dressings, splinting materials, and good-quality equipment such as scissors and tweezers. None of these kits come equipped with antibiotics and other prescription medications, so it is imperative to work with a physician when outfitting a medical kit.

First-aid training is paramount, and at least some of the crew should have taken a serious first-aid course that does more than tell a first responder to elevate the head and call 911. A crew member with some EMT training or a mountaineering remote area first-aid course can be very useful. The Red Cross and others train lay first-aid purveyors to address bleeding, breathing, and shock issues after calling for help. The same goes for those at sea, but when sailing, the slower help response time means that the first-aid provider will play a much larger role.

"Do no harm," is the concern in any active response to injury or illness, and by leveraging medical consultation through the use of electronic communications capabilities, shoreside expertise can be engaged. Commercial high seas medical consultation services are available as well as medical advice through Good Samaritan sources. In the most extreme cases of injury and illness, however, medical evacuation becomes essential. Those at sea are best served through the U.S. Coast Guard and other international emergency communications services, and the Cospas/Sarsat global distress system (see later in this chapter) also can be engaged when a life-threatening medical threat prevails.

Sailors do not become more proficient at first aid by engaging in more sailing. They must make a concerted effort to get additional training. Taking a CPR course and a comprehensive first-aid class is a good start. But just as it makes sense to have more than one person familiar with the vessel's communications equipment, it's important to have more than one person aboard able to handle basic first-aid challenges.

board. This evaluation includes the effect of friction caused by a lengthy run of hose and serpentine twists in the discharge plumbing, as well as the effect of gravity on lifting the water to the discharge point. Little things like hose barbs, connections through bulkheads, and check valves add more resistance to the flow and diminish output. So when you actually measure the discharge with a bucket and a timepiece, don't be surprised to find that the water being pumped out is considerably less than the pump's rating. This test also provides a good opportunity for crew to get a feel for the effects of a prolonged bout of manual pumping on shoulder and back muscles.

When testing your electrical bilge pump capacity, check the amp meter while running the pump and measuring volume and time. This will give you a good feel for the current cost in ampere-hours per gallon of water pumped. By measuring the time it takes to fill a bucket with a known volume, it's easy to calculate the total amount of water discharged in a minute or hour of continuous operation and the energy cost.

Nuisance leaks in timber boats were once simply a fact of life, and sailors became quite familiar with their bilge pumps. Each time the ship's bell coaxed the watch to man the pump, the number of strokes it took to clear the bilge was entered in the ship's log. Any increase or decrease was considered in the context of the sea state, the amount of sail area set, and how hard the vessel was being driven. Naturally, any sharp uptick in the stroke count caught everyone's attention.

Today's drier bilges plus electric automatic pumps and bilge alarms have caused many crews to abandon the practice of counting strokes of a manual pump at least once during each watch. Instead there are many elegantly simple approaches for an automated bilge alarm. For example, a simple mechanical float switch placed at a point in the bilge just above the low-volume automatic electric pump can do the job. If the smaller pump malfunctions or is overwhelmed by rising water, the high-water alarm float switch lifts and a car horn or other unmistakable sound signal catches everyone's attention. Then a high-capacity pump can be switched on or automatically toggle into action. With a rated capacity of 3,500 gph (as mentioned, about 2,000 gph with a 6-foot lift), these centrifugal pumps have a high capacity, but a 15-amp pump can quickly spike over 20 amps if debris starts to clog the intake. A carefully engineered installation involves both plumbing and electrical implications.

Bilge Pump Installation. Straight runs of a large-diameter hose and heavy-gauge wire are important for electric bilge pump efficiency. The plumbing should minimize restrictions and keep the pressure low and volume high. Restrictions in the discharge loop do just the opposite, causing pressure to increase and volume to drop. Bilge pump discharges near or below the waterline need a centerline high loop and an antisiphon break to prevent backflow that could flood the bilge when the pump is not operating. As a vessel moves through a seaway, its dynamic waterline changes. This can submerge bilge pump discharge through-hulls that otherwise sit well above the static waterline. Centerline gooseneck-like risers, antisiphon valves, and check valves have been used to lessen the chance of such back flooding, but each of these efforts adds more twists, turns, and restrictions to the discharge plumbing. Many sailors have set up their high-capacity electric pump with as straight as possible a discharge run and a large ball check valve at a discharge point well above the waterline. The valve is kept closed unless an emergency warrants the use of the pump, at which time the lever on the valve is thrown open before turning on the breaker for the pump. Why introduce unwanted complexity, inefficiency, and potential downflooding problems to a system that will spend over 99.9% of its time in a standby mode?

Properly wiring a high-volume bilge pump is as important as providing large-diameter, straight-run plumbing. The goal is to avoid voltage drop caused by excessive resistance. Watts are a measure of electrical power, used in this case to lift and propel water. It's a good example of a transfer of electrical to mechanical energy that accomplishes a measurable amount of flow. Regardless of whether the job is done with a bucket, hand pump, or electromagnetic energy running a bilge pump, the goal is to extricate the liquid as fast as possible. The more water to be moved through the discharge system, the more manual or electrical energy will be consumed. And that's why heavier gauge wire, like larger diameter hoses, or a manual pump operator with the muscles of a fullback, makes sense.

As the diameter of copper wire increases, its resistance to conducting electrical current decreases. This results in a higher voltage and more watts to be available at the pump. In short, instead of wasting energy heating up small gauge wire, more energy reaches the pump. Look carefully at the pump manufacturer's wire gauge recommendations, realizing that when a battery bank is 10 feet from the bilge pump, the wire run is actually 20 feet because the positive and negative legs must be added to the circuit. And don't be misled by a pump's wiring gauge. For example, a pump with 14-gauge leads does not signify that 14-gauge wiring is appropriate for the circuit. If it's a lengthy run, you're much better off with heavier

12- or 10-gauge wire. Make sure that all junctions use high-quality, marine-grade terminals and the crimping tool made a wide, even compression of the fitting. Shrink-tube sealing and other efforts to ensure watertight integrity are worth the effort. Corrosion at a wire-to-wire junction can be as inhibiting as a restriction in the plumbing. The corroded connection increases resistance and can cause a significant voltage drop even when the right wire gauge has been used. An underrated float switch wired in series with a heavy-duty pump can be another cause of poor performance; this is why many skippers use a high-quality manually operated single-pole, single-throw switch to engage a high-capacity pump.

Using the Engine to Pump Excess Water

For decades dockside wisdom has extolled the virtue of letting the auxiliary's raw-water pump save the day to rid the bilge of unwanted water. The idea is to swap the intake through-hull for a hose to the bilge using either a dedicated Y-valve or a jury-rigged hose attachment. If all goes well, a steady stream of clean water will both cool the engine and be extricated from the bilge. The problem is that the water sluicing around in the bilge when a sailboat has water rising above the cabin sole is seldom clean. The same debris that can clog a strum box and the valves inside a diaphragm pump can also choke off water essential for the engine's cooling system. Not only is the newly harnessed bilge pump lost, but also the engine is now overheated and out of action, as is the all-important alternator(s) that kept the batteries up and electrical pumps spinning. Further, the total volume of water moved by an engine-driven raw-water pump on a midsize sailboat auxiliary isn't as much as a big electrical pump can deliver. So think twice before turning

---

HULL PUNCTURE DAMAGE CONTROL KIT

In any well-stocked boson's locker reside damage control supplies that facilitate plugging holes and cracks of various sizes. When there's a need to stem the flow of water to save the boat, readily available supplies and tools play a key role. Following are worthwhile items to include in your damage control kit—they'll come in handy when and if a flooding situation arises.

Supplies
- Tapered soft wood plugs in sizes to fit all through-hulls
- Foam tapered plugs
- Closed-cell foam padding of varying thicknesses
- Cut plywood, 2 × 4 blocks, and wedges for shoring up patches
- External damage control patch with lines attached
- Hypalon or PVC scraps cut from old inflatable dinghy
- Two-part liquid foam
- 3M 5200
- Various epoxies (underwater cure, 5-minute, conventional laminating resin)
- Roll of 2-inch fiberglass tape
- Duct tape, short stuff

Tools and Fasteners
- Electric drill with carbide tip drill set
- Hacksaw and premium blades
- Carpenter's backsaw, coping saw
- Chisel set, sharp fixed blade knife
- Fasteners (self-tapping screws, Torx [star] driver, and machine screws plus threaded rods and nuts)
- C-clamps of various sizes
- Hammer and ring nails

A collision mat, softwood wedges, damage-control plugs, and shoring material are basic tools for those attempting to control water entering from a hole, through-hull, or crack in the hull.

the all-important engine raw-water pump into a tool for dewatering.

Other options include adding a dedicated engine-driven displacement pump with a mechanical or electric clutch as an emergency bilge pump. It can also be Y-valve-plumbed to do double duty as a fire hose pump with an unlimited water supply. Another option is a portable gasoline-powered high-volume centrifugal pump such as those made by Honda. These compact pumps hurl much more water than anything thus far mentioned, but they can be finicky to start and prime and must be carefully maintained. They are a smaller version of the emergency dewatering pumps used by the U.S. Coast Guard.

Fire

"Fire!" like the cry of "Crew overboard," is a shout no sailor wants to hear. The virtual disappearance of gas-oline auxiliary engines and pressurized alcohol galley stoves has minimized the risks of fire on a cruising boat. But at the same time, the addition of massive DC power systems, propane stoves, and fuel tankage equivalent to a motorboat has upped the ante when it comes to a galley flare-up or an electrical short–instigated fire getting out of control. A small fire can become an all-consuming conflagration in an alarmingly short period of time. One bit of data says it all: a fast-growing fire doubles in size every 30 seconds.

Every skipper needs to consider the prospect of fire breaking out on his or her vessel and how those on board should respond. The what-ifs that arise from such introspection should lead to a plan of action that needs to be shared with the crew. Statistics show that although fires occur infrequently on cruising sailboats, their effect can be devastating. The U.S. Coast Guard and ABYC wisely see the threat as very real and have put out regulations and recommendations for how certain systems should be installed and what firefighting equipment is mandatory.

Heat, fuel, and oxygen are the necessary components of the combustion triangle. A fire needs all three, and if any one of them is reduced below the threshold for combustion, the blaze is extinguished. Like many elegantly simple explanations, this one is often ignored until it's too late. For example, a small 2-pound dry-chemical fire extinguisher has only about 8–12 seconds of firefighting potential once the trigger lever is depressed. This will almost certainly be enough for an expert, but many untrained amateurs in the grip of the fight-fright-flight reflex expend the vaporized dust on the flames leaping high from the burning surface rather than at the base of the flames where it would have best results. The cor-

■ *Galley fires have decreased thanks in part to the disappearance of pressurized alcohol stoves. Modern propane stoves like the one shown here and following installation guidelines lessen the likelihood of mishap. Note Lenore Naranjo's safety harness, a restraint that keeps her from being launched into a hot stove when a tack puts the galley stove to leeward.*

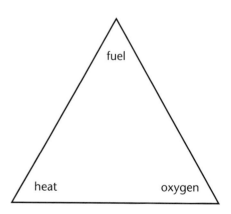

■ *The combustion triangle. Take these steps if you discover a fire aboard: stop the engine and heave-to; shut off the fuel valve; turn off the battery switches; close all hatches; and aim your fire extinguisher at the base of the flames, sweeping across the surface.*

rect approach smothers the fire by creating a barrier between the fuel and the oxygen.

Types of Fires and the Equipment to Fight Them

Fires are grouped into three classes based on their combustion profiles. Wood, paper, and other natural- and synthetic-fiber fires that leave an ash residue are typed as Class A fires and are best extinguished by lowering their temperature via flooding with water or aqueous foam. For Class A fires, consider installing a high-pressure, high-volume water system with a sink hose and sprayhead or a second in-cabin tap and hose linked to a powerful deck washdown pump. Even a few sturdy buckets may save the day after using a dry-chemical extinguisher.

Class B fires—those caused by flammable liquids such as gasoline, diesel, or alcohol fuel—are best tackled by smothering the flames with a fire blanket or oxygen-blocking extinguisher agent. Dry chemical, foam, CO_2, Halotron, and other nontoxic Halon replacements will do the job. (All dry-chemical extinguishers should be removed from their brackets and inverted every month or so in order to keep the contents from solidifying, and the pressure gauge should be checked regularly. Also worth a mention is the flimsiness of most mild steel brackets that come with extinguishers. Improving how these vital safety tools are housed is worth the expenditure of time or money.) An extinguisher should be kept near the galley stove, reachable even if the appliance is ablaze, and a second one in a cockpit locker and a third near the skipper's berth. Since flammable liquids are the greatest fire hazard on a boat, Class B extinguishers are mandated by the U.S. Coast Guard.

Class C blazes are caused by electrical components. Engine room fires are often of the Class C variety, and turning off the main battery bank switches is step one in combating this type of fire. If the current is not eliminated from the short circuit, the fire may continue despite the introduction of an extinguisher agent. With this need in mind, it's always a good idea to make sure that the main switches are not hidden away in the engine room or placed where they are likely to be quickly engulfed in flames. Not only does opening a door or hatch to the engine compartment raise the risk of being scorched by flames, it also provides more oxygen to a hungry fire. An automatic built-in fire suppression system on even a modest-size boat makes good sense. It also keeps the crew from having to fight an engine room fire with a Class B extinguisher, many of which are not very effective on Class C fires. (Further, if the powdery abrasive agent in a dry-chemical extinguisher is sucked into a running diesel engine, it's usually fatal to the

Small dry-chemical extinguishers function only a short time, but they can be kept handy for a prompt response to a flare-up. Regularly check the pressure gauge, and invert the extinguisher monthly to keep the powder from adhering to the bottom of the cylinder.

Small FE-241 heat-activated extinguishers can be placed in the engine room to quell fires. Many systems offer both manual and automatic activation options. The cage protects the nozzle and auto-on hardware that engages the extinguisher when high heat is detected.

engine.) So, shutting off the engine, if at all possible, is a priority.

Fire extinguishers are rated according to volume, the type of fire they are best suited for, and the material they contain. Automatic built-in systems such as those offered by Fireboy-Xintex can flood the engine room with an oxygen-blocking gas that can stop a blazing fuel fire in its tracks. But those who install such systems need to keep in mind that what kills a fire can also impact human respiration. Some years ago a friend of mine accidentally engaged a CO_2 fixed fire-suppression system while he was in the engine room of his boat. The gas quickly rendered him unconscious, and his wife, responding to his plight, suc-

▤ *Putting out a small pit fire with a dry-chemical extinguisher doesn't make one an experienced firefighter, but the experience of trying to do so teaches the difficulty of such a task. Prompt action is essential.*

cumbed to the same asphyxiation—both died in the mishap. The tragedy underscores the need to realize that limiting oxygen to quell a fire is tricky business. On the one hand, the rule of firefighting is to close hatches and ports in order to lessen the air inflow, but the crew also must recognize that oxygen depletion, acrid smoke, and toxic fumes in a closed boat can quickly create a lethal atmosphere. Compressed-liquid extinguishers that emit a gaseous cloud in a confined space such as an engine compartment vary in toxicity according to their suppression agent. Some systems use FE-241, which is meant for dispersal in an unoccupied space, while others use HFC-227ea, a gas that's safe if occupants are still in the cabin fighting a spreading fire.

The ideal is to prevent a fire in the first place, and secondly to have a quick-response plan ready to douse flames before they can spread. Many built-in fire-suppression systems have a heat-melting auto-discharge trigger, but it takes either direct proximity or a very hot fire—or the ambient temperature to rise to 179°F—for the system to deploy. By installing a manual-release cable, a crew can preempt the wait and choke off the flames before the fire builds.

Firefighting Procedures

Responding to a fire aboard a sailboat is like coping with a large hole punched in the hull. Both require immediate action, and neither forgives an ineffective response. At the same time that the crew confronts the all-consuming challenge of stopping the blaze

or a significant leak, they need to be prepared to cut their losses and instantly switch to an abandon-ship plan. Making that call is a tough decision but a reality shaped by the situation—waiting a little too long can be a big mistake.

A well-prepared crew understands the chaos that accompanies such disasters. They realize that their best chance for success is already in place, including the fire-suppression system they installed months or years ago and the extra extinguishers waiting in easily accessible locations. Even more important is the training that the skipper has done with the crew. The crew is prepared to aim the suppression agent on the base of the flames. If enough crew are on board, one may be assigned to communicate a Mayday, set off the EPIRB, and ready the abandon-ship gear and life raft. Others head the boat downwind to keep flames from engulfing the cockpit and hindering raft deployment if the need arises. Since a fire grows exponentially, there's only a short window of time to get it under control. It takes quick responses and gear at the ready to outwit the combustion triangle, and every second counts.

One of the best ways to determine the fire hazard your own boat poses is to analyze its combustible content. For starters, tally up the major materials that comprise the vessel. At first it may seem reassuring that glass fiber and lead won't burn, but the resin that comprises 50% of the FRP structure will self-ignite at about 880°F and burn to a crisp, creating a toxic cloud of harmful gasses. So will the core material and most of the wood and plastic liners in the interior of the vessel. Add flammable diesel fuel, combustible sails, dodger, and bimini, and you anxiously realize it's easier to list what won't burn than what will. Also note that just one candle produces a laminar diffusion flame that can reach 2,500°F—more than enough to instigate a roaring blaze.

Recognizing that there's plenty of fuel onboard ready to be ignited by a fast-growing fire is the first step in lessening the potential for such a calamity. The next step is to identify potential hot spots or regions where a fire is likely to start and where highly flammable liquids or solids are stored. The galley and the engine room are the two obvious concerns and why ABYC emphasizes electrical, fuel, and propane system specifications. By preventing fuel and LPG leaks and lessening the chance of an electrical short, you can drive the potential for a fire way down. The same consideration is needed for where flares and volatile chemicals like paint solvents and gas for the dinghy outboard are secured. Using a large propane locker as a combined storage area for gasoline and solvents is asking for trouble. Comingling explosive and flammable products may seem sensible, but with electrical wires leading to the propane solenoid, and given the salt-laden moist environment of most propane lockers, it's anything but a sensible seagoing hazmat container.

During spring commissioning, inventory what's on board and remove flammable substances that are not needed or haven't recently been used. Store solvents and other high-risk materials well away from the galley and engine areas, preferably isolating such materials in the forward portion of the vessel well away from where most fires on sailboats begin. With a bright flashlight trace all electrical conduits,

LENDING ASSISTANCE

Over the centuries, mariners have evolved a credo for aiding those in distress. This may be as minimal as offering a tow to a mooring when the wind quits and a boat's engine refuses to cooperate, or as spectacular as when a singlehanded sailor presses on through a gale to come to the rescue of a fellow competitor aboard a capsized vessel. Providing assistance at sea has become a codified mandate with rules set down by the IMO and the ISAF. Such regulations state that a vessel must come to the aid of another in distress and provide all possible assistance. However, an important caveat in the wording addresses the importance of not endangering one's vessel or crew when providing this assistance, and in very heavy weather this can become an issue.

Effective communication is at the heart of orchestrating a successful rescue. The skipper of the boat in distress needs to make it clear what problems have arisen and what support he or she requires. The responding vessel's captain needs to agree, recognizing the challenges for his or her own crew and vessel and considering whether their ability and capability are up to providing such support. There also needs to be a concerted effort among all vessels involved to inform the Coast Guard or other SAR agency about who's involved, what's happening, and whether the level of emergency rises to a Pan-Pan or Mayday distress status. The latter designates situations in which life is at risk and/or the survival of the vessel is in question. (See Chapter 14, Communications.)

In some situations, the right decision is for the crew attempting to render assistance to stand by, help to relay communications, and wait for an air or sea rescue by the Coast Guard. This is especially true in medical emergencies where a litter must be used to move a victim or where a helicopter ride to hospital is essential. In more remote locations or in situations where a vessel is foundering, the first vessel on the scene may have to execute a crew transfer. In most ocean conditions, directly transferring crew from one boat to the other is out of the question. Rig entanglement and hull damage can turn a one-vessel calamity into a double feature. In such a scenario it's best for rescuers to situate their boat to windward of the vessel in distress, then float or heave a line to the distressed vessel and transfer crew via a life raft deployed by the crew abandoning ship. It's vital to steer clear of rigging in a dismasting and stay to windward especially if fire is the reason for abandoning ship.

Once the life raft has been brought alongside and the crew has been transferred, check with the captain of the rescued vessel to make sure the entire team is now aboard your boat. Treat injuries and check for hypothermia. Make a call to the Coast Guard or other SAR agency and advise them of what has transpired and come to a mutual agreement on how the rescued crew will be transported. Communication throughout such incidents is crucial. Problems can arise when the captain of a boat requesting assistance has an unrealistic plan for what the responding vessel should and can deliver. This is often the case in heavy weather when seasick crewmembers want to abandon ship but the captain also wants his or her boat taken in tow. The three-dimensional gyrations caused by pitch, roll, yaw, heave, sway, and surge make lashing a sailboat of similar size to a towline seem like taking a squirrel-hunting Great Dane for a walk in the park. Rescuing a crew and simultaneously salvaging a boat during a gale is dangerous—often impossible—and most SAR pros avoid—i.e., refuse—such an effort.

Boat-to-boat communication sets the stage for what will happen in all forms of assistance. Note how Coast Guard pros handle such situations:

1. Gather details;
2. Get a firm understanding of the variables including wind, sea state, and visibility, and the rescue needed;
3. Formulate a plan and advise the boater what will happen in a detailed, step-by-step process.

It's not a negotiated agreement—it's a one-way delineated approach to solving the problem at hand.

When a sailor-to-sailor rescue is needed, the planning process is less one-sided. The captain of the vessel in distress has a vision of what he or she wants, while the skipper of the assisting boat may have a slightly or vastly different idea about what can or should be done. Following the Coast Guard's approach, the first step is to gather details about the vessel, home port, and number of crew on board. Next comes a succinct description of what's wrong and what's needed. If possible, before executing a rescue, both skippers need to agree on what's about to be done.

especially heavy-gauge, high-amperage leads to the starter, windlass, and bow thruster. Look for signs of chafe or potential contact with a ground. Give the same scrutiny to propane hoses. Many cruising sailors see their 12-volt DC electrical system as a benign energy source with no electrocution worries. The latter is true, at least until an inverter is wired into the system, but the assumption it's benign disregards the high current flows through low-voltage wiring that pose a potential for extreme heat generation if an unanticipated short circuit occurs.

Last, beware of the unexpected. A couple of years ago a transatlantic passagemaker explained how a sheeting snafu turned into a fire onboard. He had been motorsailing in a light breeze and had trimmed the mainsheet using an electric cockpit winch, and then went below to heat some water for tea. A malfunctioning solenoid switch, soaked by seawater, reengaged on its own, causing the self-tailing winch that held the mainsheet to haul away on the mainsail already on the centerline. The noise of the engine prevented the skipper from hearing the winch coming to a stop under full load. The motor winding in the nonrotating winch melted because the circuit breaker had also sustained water damage. A high-amperage fuse allowed more current than the wiring in the winch could safely carry, which turned into a red-hot copper filament that set the headliner on fire. The skipper responded effectively, switching off the current and dousing the flames with a fire extinguisher. He had never expected such an incident to occur, but he knew how to respond effectively to a Class C fire.

MANDATORY SAFETY GEAR

The list of mandatory safety gear for recreational craft is short compared with all the gear seen at your local chandlery. For a recreational boater to meet United States federal regulatory obligations, all that's required are an approved personal flotation device (PFD, or life jacket) for each person on board, fire extinguishers appropriate for the size of the vessel, and a visual and sound signaling kit. The exact number of and specifications for these items vary with the length of the vessel, and there are also stipulations covering navigation lights, antipollution regulations, and antiexplosion devices for gasoline engines. State laws also occasionally impose a few additional mandates to the short list of federal safety regulations. The fact that it's not illegal for a boater to head off without an anchor, bilge pump, VHF radio, compass, or chart may at first seem a glaring omission, but the U.S. Code of Federal Regulations is permissive rather than restrictive, so outfitting a boat for safety is left largely to the individual.

Without question, life jackets, fire extinguishers, and signaling devices help keep us safe out there. The Coast Guard didn't mandate this gear on a whim. Crew-overboard incidents rank near the top of fatal boating accidents. As mentioned, fires are less frequent but afford only a few minutes before any chance of control is lost. As Kip Louttit, a retired U.S. Coast Guard captain, said, "If you can stay afloat and signal us your location, a happy ending is the likely outcome." With minimal regulatory (continued page 422)

COAST GUARD EQUIPMENT REQUIREMENTS: QUICK REFERENCE CHART

Vessel Length (in feet)				Equipment	Requirement
<16	16<26	26<40	40<65		
X	X	X	X	Certificate of Number (State Registration)	All undocumented vessels equipped with propulsion machinery must be state registered. Certificate of Number must be on board when vessel is in use. Note: some states require all vessels to be registered.
X	X	X	X	State Numbering	(a) Plain block letters/numbers not less than 3 inches in height must be affixed on each side of the forward half of the vessel (contrasting color to boat exterior). (b) State validation sticker must be affixed within six inches of the registration number.
	X	X	X	Certificate of Documentation	Applies only to "Documented" vessels: (a) Original and current certificate must be on board. (b) Vessel name/hailing port marked on exterior part of hull—letters not less than 4 inches in height. (c) Official number permanently affixed on interior structure—numbers not less than 3 inches in height.
X	X	X	X	Life Jackets (PFDs)	(a) One Type I, II, III, or V wearable PFD for each person on board (must be USCG approved).
	X	X	X		(b) In addition to paragraph (a), must carry one Type IV (throwable) PFD.

COAST GUARD EQUIPMENT REQUIREMENTS: QUICK REFERENCE CHART (CONT.)

Vessel Length (in feet)				Equipment	Requirement
<16	16<26	26<40	40<65		
X				Visual Distress Signal (VDS)	(a) One electric distress light or three combination (day/night) red flares. Note: only required to be carried on board when operating between sunset and sunrise.
	X	X	X		(b) One orange distress flag or one electric distress light—or—three handheld or floating orange smoke signals and one electric distress light—or—three combination (day/night) red flares: handheld, meteor or parachute type.
X	X			Fire Extinguishers	(a) One B-I (when enclosed compartment)
		X			(b) One B-II or two B-I. Note: fixed system equals one B-I
			X		(c) One B-II and one B-I or three B-I. Note: fixed system equals one B-I or two B-II
X	X	X	X	Ventilation	(a) All vessels built after 25 April 1940 that use gasoline as their fuel with enclosed engine and/or fuel tank compartments must have natural ventilation (at least two ducts fitted with cowls). (b) In addition to paragraph (a), a vessel built after 31 July 1980 must have rated power exhaust blower.
X	X	X		Sound Producing Devices	(a) A vessel of less than 39.4 ft. must, at a minimum, have some means of making an efficient sound signal (i.e. handheld air horn, athletic whistle—human voice/sound not acceptable).
		X	X		(b) A vessel 39.4 ft. (12 meters) or greater, must have a sound signaling appliance capable of producing an efficient sound signal, audible for ½ mile with a 4 to 6 seconds duration. In addition, must carry a bell with a clapper (bell size not less than 7.9"—based on the diameter of the mouth).
	X	X	X	Backfire Flame Arrester	Required on gasoline engines installed after 25 April 1940, except outboard motors.
	X	X	X	Navigational Lights	Required to be displayed from sunset to sunrise and in or near areas of reduced visibility.
		X	X	Oil Pollution Placard	(a) Placard must be at least 5 by 8 inches, made of durable material. (b) Placard must be posted in the machinery space or at the bilge station.
		X	X	Garbage Placard	(a) Placard must be at least 4 by 9 inches, made of durable material. (b) Displayed in a conspicuous place notifying all on board the discharge restrictions.
	X	X	X	Marine Sanitation Device	If installed toilet: vessel must have an operable MSD Type I, II, or III.
		X	X	Navigation Rules (Inland Only)	The operator of a vessel 39.4 ft (12 meters) or greater must have on board a copy of these rules.

REQUIRED FIRE EXTINGUISHERS

Minimum number of hand-portable fire extinguishers on a boat with and without a fixed extinguishing system		
Length of Vessel	**No Fixed System in Machinery Space**	**Fixed System in Machinery Space**
Less than 26 ft.	1 B-I	none
26 ft. to under 40 ft.	2 B-Is or 1 B-II	1 B-I
40 ft. to 65 ft.	3 B-Is or 1 B-I and 1 B-II	2 B-Is or 1 B-II

CLASS B FIRE EXTINGUISHERS

Coast Guard Classification (type-size)	Underwriters Laboratories Listing	Aqueous Foam (gals.)	Carbon Dioxide (lbs.)	Dry Chemical (lbs.)	FE-241 (lbs.)
B-I	5B	1.25	4	2	5
B-II	10B	2.5	15	10	10

LIFE JACKET LOGIC

Certain life jackets are designed to keep your head above water and help you remain in a position for effective breathing.

To meet U.S. Coast Guard requirements, a boat must have a U.S. Coast Guard–approved Type I, II, III, or V life jacket for each person aboard. Boats 16 feet and over must have at least one Type IV throwable device as well.

All states have regulations regarding life jacket wear by children.

Adult sizes of life jackets will not work for children. Special life jackets are available. To work correctly, a life jacket must be worn, fit snugly, and not allow the child's chin or ears to slip through.

Life jackets should be tested for wear and buoyancy at least once each year. Waterlogged, faded, or leaky jackets should be discarded.

Life jackets must be easily accessible when properly stowed.

A life jacket—especially a snug-fitting flotation coat or deck-suit style—can help you survive in cold water.

Inflatables

- The most compact
- Sizes only for adults
- Only recommended for swimmers
- Wearable styles only
- Some with the best in-water performance

MINIMUM BUOYANCY

Wearable Size	Type	Inherent Buoyancy (Foam)
Adult	I	22 lbs.
	II and III	15.5 lbs.
	V	15.5 to 22 lbs.
Youth	II and III	11 lbs.
	V	11 to 15.5 lbs.
Child and Infant	II	7 lbs.
Throwable Cushion Ring Buoy	IV	20 lbs. 16.5 and 32 lbs.

MINIMUM BUOYANCY, INFLATABLE LIFEJACKETS

Wearable Size	Type	Inherent Buoyancy
Adult	I and II	34 lbs.
	III	22.5 lbs.
	V	22.5 to 34 lbs.

(Courtesy U.S. Coast Guard's Boating Safety Division)

mandates, it's essential that each skipper accept responsibility and act reasonably, equipping his or her boat with safety gear in keeping with how and where the vessel will be used. As you consider what safety gear and gadgets to carry, keep asking yourself how much each item contributes to the two needs you want most to satisfy when the chips are down: staying afloat and communicating your position and need for help.

Crew training should go hand-in-glove with safety gear. Not all crewmembers need to be able to handle all damage control and other emergency tasks, but you need more than one crewmember capable of each task unless you're a singlehander. The crew needs to develop a reflex-like ability to put safety gear into service. This applies to personal gear such as PFDs, harnesses, and signaling gear and to boat equipment such as fire extinguishers, anchors, life rafts, and crew-overboard recovery gear.

The types of gear referenced in this chapter are meant to either prevent emergencies afloat or help a crew respond to them. Everyone is familiar with the latter type of gear, such as the iconic life ring and the reassuring fire extinguisher. Items for mishap prevention are often less obvious. They typically lack the reassuring bright orange coating and may be as innocuous as an extra handhold near the companionway or strips of gray nonskid tape that can turn an ice rink–slick part of the coachroof into a safe foothold.

It bears repeating that preventing mishaps is always preferable to even the best rescue outcomes. Mariners of centuries past found their way across oceans aboard vessels lacking most of the safety gear we deem essential today. Their safety depended on a clear understanding of the perils they faced and an equally clear picture of how they could mitigate risk. No marine manufacturer sells a tight grip, a keen eye for trouble, and a well-braced stance gimbaled to the roll, pitch, and yaw of a vessel. These are developed through time underway.

Purchasing safety gear is only step one. Steps two and three involve practicing with the equipment and maintaining it in tip-top working order. Only then are crew and their equipment fully prepared for sea.

Personal Flotation Devices

Life jackets, or PFDs, lead the mandatory equipment list for a very important reason: drowning is the major cause of death in boating accidents. It's true that wearing a PFD doesn't guarantee survival, but it does greatly increase the wearer's chances. The specific product one chooses to enhance staying afloat has direct bearing upon survivability, and the Coast Guard's affinity for life jackets has led to classifi- *(continued page 424)*

PFDS AND LIFE JACKETS
Captain Kip Louttit,
USCG Retired and Auxiliary

The importance of having and wearing proper personal flotation devices, more commonly known as life jackets, cannot be overemphasized. Of those people who drowned in 2011, 84% percent were not wearing life jackets, and statistically, most would have survived if life jackets had been worn.

When to wear life jackets can be a personal decision or mandated by the skipper or racing rules. Considerations include whether it's day or night, inshore or offshore waters, wind and sea conditions, and number of people onboard. Good rules of thumb include wearing life jackets at night, when alone on deck, when reefed, when going forward, and during *any* emergency.

A victim wearing a life jacket in warm water can save strength by not having to swim or tread water, which increases the chance of a safe and successful outcome. In cold water, a victim wearing a life jacket extends the survival time because he or she can remain still, which delays the onset of hypothermia. (Swimming flushes away water that was warmed by the body and replaces it with cold water; remaining still retains water that is warmed by the body.) Wearing a life jacket also enables a swimmer to use the HELP (Heat-Escape Lessening Position—see illustration) and "Huddle" (multiple person) positions, both of which extend survival time.

A wide variety of life jackets are available in many colors, sizes, designs, and features. Life jackets need to be the right size in a comfortable design that you will wear. Everything else being equal, a Coast Guard–approved life jacket in a bright color such as red, orange, yellow, or lime green is best. However, there are wonderful, high-quality life jackets on the market that are not Coast Guard approved because they don't fit within the Coast Guard's narrow standards for approval. That should not be a showstopper. If the life jacket that is right for you is not Coast Guard approved, you can still use it as long as it is made by a reputable manufacturer; just carry a life jacket that *is* approved aboard your vessel, and show *that one* to the Coast Guard or other law enforcement authorities if you get boarded and inspected—the best of both worlds.

If something catastrophic happens to you and your vessel and you need to do some serious floating on the ocean, there is nothing better than an inherently buoyant Type I or II life jacket. This type will hold your head up and can't leak air as an inflatable can. The Type I floats the wearer higher than the Type II, which can be good in rough seas to avoid gulping water.

Most sailors wear Type IIIs or inflatables, which are fine as long as the wearer recognizes the limitations of these life jackets. Type IIIs don't hold the swimmer's face up, so a person hit by the boom and knocked overboard, unconscious, will be afloat, but if he or she lands in the water face down, he or she will remain in that position since the Type III will not turn the victim face-up. Inflatables are wonderfully wearable, and many Type I inflatables have greater buoyancy and will float the wearer face-up, but a small percentage of automatic inflation devices will malfunction and not work; they may also leak and can grow green crud inside the cover which can cause malfunction if not unpacked and washed out and dried after use in wet conditions. If the automatic inflation does not work, manually inflate the cartridge or blow into the inflation tube as shown when you watch airplane safety videos. More and more sailors agree that inflatables need crotch straps to benefit most from the buoyancy available in the neck area.

Captain Kip Louttit combines a U.S. Coast Guard career with a passion for sailboat racing and cruising, and now in retirement from active duty he focuses on communicating how recreational sailors can bolster their odds for staying safe. His bottom line: "Only through good preparation and practice is a crew ready to respond to offshore challenges." And it's often the little things that cascade into big problems. Kip is a regular contributor at Safety at Sea Seminars, and audiences leave with important lessons learned.

■ *If thrown overboard, conserve heat by staying in the HELP (Heat-Escape Lessening Position), as shown here. (Courtesy U.S. Coast Guard Office of Boating Safety)*

With cool early-spring weather and cold water, U.S. Naval Academy sailmaker John Jenkins (at the helm) wears a Type III PFD during sea trials of a new Navy 44 MKII sail-training sloop. (See review of this boat in Chapter 12.)

Midshipmen at the U.S. Naval Academy learn to both use and service personal safety equipment. This sailor is clipping a Type V PFD with a built-in harness with a snapshackle release. Checking stitching, bladders, inflatable PFD gas cylinders, and bobbins are all part of the routine.

cation based upon how well a victim is aided when immersed in salt or fresh water. (See the sidebar PFDs and Life Jackets.)

Inflatable PFDs

For over a century, PFDs were viewed as 100% reliable devices that were instantly ready for use and merely needed to be strapped on for the full effect that their inherent flotation provided. With the advent of inflatable PFDs, many sailors rallied to a type of life jacket that was much more comfortable and convenient to wear than any of the descendants of the early cork and kapok vests. At first regulatory bodies were skeptical, because in their noninflated state these PFDs offer no buoyancy at all. Regulators worried that boaters would assume that the gear would always work regardless of how much care and maintenance was provided.

In truth, these compact PFDs are highly reliable, and when reasonably maintained and regularly inspected, they can be counted on to work as advertised. At the heart of their operational design is a spring-loaded firing pin that penetrates the seal of a small CO_2 cylinder, causing the device to inflate. The specifications that come with an auto-inflatable PFD state that the unit is a "manually operated device with an automatic backup" to remind the user that pulling the tab to manually inflate the device is a faster and more reliable deployment. Most units on the market today use a dissolving bobbin to initiate the auto-inflate process, which may take up to 10 seconds in normal operating conditions. If moisture and age have caused the aspirin-like chemical in the bobbin to harden, the auto-inflate process can take even longer, and in some instances minutes can go by before the bobbin finally dissolves. To gain the most benefit from this type of auto-inflation system, an owner should annually change an unused bobbin, especially when the gear has been worn in wet weather and left to dry in humid confines aboard a sailboat. Regardless of how well an auto-inflatable is cared for and maintained, all crewmembers should recognize that pulling the manual tab is the surest way to achieve instant inflation. There are also hydrostatic inflation devices that are triggered by water pressure. As noted earlier, a user should view the auto function as a backup and be ready to pull the inflation cord as soon as possible.

During my tenure as the Vanderstar Chair at the U.S. Naval Academy, we did an end-of-season test of 20 randomly chosen inflatable PFDs used in the summer sail-training program. Three malfunctions occurred: one unit underinflated due to a leaking CO_2 cylinder seat and two failed to auto-inflate, one of which also failed to inflate (continued page 426)

The author's grandson Will Mitchell wears a child's life jacket that provides added head flotation via a buoyant collar and includes a crotch strap that keeps the PFD from riding up.

U.S. Naval Academy dinghy sailors combine dry suits, Type III life jackets, and neoprene wet suit gloves for comfort sailing early in the season.

U.S. Coast Guard crews make a functional fashion statement, wearing Type V combination jacket/PFD vests.

INFLATABLE PFD STANDARDS
Marty Jackson

The U.S. Coast Guard has noted various conditions of use for inflatable PFDs that are currently approved based on the type of inflation system and intended use. In general, inflatable PFDs are evaluated for use with the type of inflation system (automatic, manual, cylinder seal indication), ease of use, and configuration (yoke style or belt pack); also considered are whether it is part of a special-use package with a harness and whether it is intended for commercial users. All these factors set the conditions for use that typically are noted on the certificate of approval provided with a Type II, Type III, or special Type V PFD.

The approval standard for inflatable PFDs is UL1180, as indicated in 46 CFR 160.076. Because this standard does not require self-inflating PFDs, a variety of manual inflation systems are used.

An effort is currently in progress to provide a common PFD standard for the United States and Canada with the adoption of a more universal standard, ISO 12402, with some changes. This standard is currently used in Europe and could potentially provide for some additional levels of PFDs, including some of the lower-buoyancy inflatable PFD designs in use in Europe. While the adoption of the ISO 12402 standard is viewed positively, some details need to be ironed out. Therefore, a PFD with U.S. Coast Guard approval to this standard is not imminent.

Marty Jackson is Staff Engineer, U.S. Coast Guard (CG-ENG-4), Office of Design and Engineering Standards, Lifesaving and Fire Safety Division.

Even if an inflatable PFD is never used in a crew-overboard (COB) incident or during in-the-water training exercises, just wearing the device in wet marine conditions will eventually take its toll. Its life span may be extended with care and proper drying and storage, but a fixed replacement schedule is hard to determine. This is why it is so important to check for leaks via oral inflation and to carefully check the fabric and stitching.

Professional sail trainer Karen Prioleau stresses the value of equipment familiarization. Here she dons a Type V PFD, which, when inflated, offers as much as 34 pounds of buoyancy and keep the victim's head well above water. Note the backup oral inflation tube on the right of the wearer's face, and the whistle to the left.

manually even with a charged CO_2 cylinder. As a result, we replaced the 7- and 8-year-old inflatable PFDs that had been in regular summer use each year.

Thus, while inflatable PFDs are much more comfortable and convenient to wear, they are not as maintenance-free as a conventional life jacket. Every crewmember should take personal responsibility for the care and well-being of a device that may someday be called upon to save his or her life. Its serviceable life depends on how often it is used and how well it is cared for. You should air-dry the gear each time it gets wet, minimize its exposure to UV when not being worn, rinse it with fresh water after a cruise or race, and move the gear ashore during the off-season to provide dry, climate-controlled storage.

Each crewmember should at some point test the function of his or her inflatable PFD by jumping into a swimming pool or pond and allowing the unit to auto-inflate. However, doing this too often can weaken the bladder and some manufacturers offer specific advice about how often one may field test the auto-inflate system. It's valuable also to spend some time swimming with the PFD deployed. Thigh or crotch straps keep the buoyant bladder from riding up and are requirements in the Newport to Bermuda Race. See how well you float in windy, choppy conditions, and try using a rope ladder to climb into an inflatable dinghy. If hoisting gear is available (see below), have other crewmembers recover you from the water using a halyard and a winch. (Testing a PFD in fresh water makes the subsequent PFD cleanup and repacking a little easier. If you do the testing in salt water, follow up with a freshwater soak prior to drying the PFD, replacing the cylinder and bobbin, and repacking.)

A PFD that's comfortable to wear and provides plenty of flotation is more likely to be worn and more likely to save a life.

Inflatable PFD/Harness Combinations

Perhaps the best argument for inflatable PFDs is that many units have a combined safety harness to prevent crew-overboard incidents. These offer heavy-duty web straps and sewn-in stainless steel attachment rings to which the snapshackle at the end of a tether can be clipped. Usually straps or tie points are also provided for attaching a personal strobe and a whistle. All crewmembers should clearly mark their name on their own gear, which has been adjusted for a secure fit.

Inflatable life jacket/harness combinations have essentially cornered the safety market. Owners and users need to keep a few important facts in mind, however, beginning with the importance of a maintenance and inspection routine.

A built-in harness is only useful when it's connected to a through-bolted pad eye or jackline via a well-designed tether. These 6-foot lengths of webbing have stainless steel clips affixed at each end. The best combination seems to be a snapshackle on the end connected to the chest harness and a double-action hook on the end that clips to the pad eye or jackline. This combination allows the user to release from the tether under load if necessary simply by pulling the snapshackle tail. The double-action hook on the other end prevents an inadvertent release from the pad eye. Either clipping mechanism can be operated with one hand.

In a knockdown, a boat's deck becomes nearly perpendicular to the water surface, and a crew can fall the length of the tether (plus any slack in the jackline to which the tether is clipped). The increased force ex-

THE *WINGNUTS* TRAGEDY REVISITED

The tragic capsize of *WingNuts,* a Kiwi 35, in a thunderstorm-generated line squall in the 2011 Race to Mackinac is described in Chapter 10. Forensic accident reconstruction pinpointed severe weather and poor vessel stability as the primary causes, but safety gear issues also drew scrutiny. The loss of life caused safety experts to give serious attention to inflatable PFD and harness design.

Two sailors on *WingNuts* wearing fully functional inflatable PFD/harnesses and approved tethers drowned, while three others needed help from a shipmate to get free from the tethers that were trapping them under or against the rail of the inverted deck. Quick action from a couple of survivors likely kept the death toll from being higher.

Tethers need to be easily released under load via a snapshackle at the chest. A harness that must be cut with a knife (or other cutting tool) to be released endangers its wearer. All sailors should orally blow up their inflatable PFD and check to see how accessible the release clip becomes when the bladder is inflated.

Follow-up research shows that an auto-inflatable PFD—or for that matter any PFD—can make it harder to escape from beneath an overturned vessel. The effect of added buoyancy hinders a crew when it comes to diving under the cockpit well and lifelines. The advantage of an inflatable PFD is that it can be quickly deflated for escape and later orally reinflated.

Just as SCUBA divers are trained to don and doff their buoyancy compensator/tank combination, a sailor should go for a swim with an orally inflated PFD (with the CO_2 inflation deactivated) and get familiar with releasing the tether, deflating the bladder, reinflating, and climbing a boarding ladder or getting into a life raft.

I'm an advocate of the sensible use of safety equipment, but I also feel that good seamanship skills are the basis of safe, efficient voyaging. Here I'm wearing an inflatable Type V PFD and harness. During average daylight conditions the tether is draped around my neck instead of being clipped to a pad eye or jackline. (Note that the double-action clip is hooked to only one D-ring, but the quick-release snapshackle engages both D-rings.) I prefer a manual inflation system for my PFD when working on the foredeck because spray and breaking waves can cause an auto-inflate system to deploy. One must recognize the trade-off of foregoing automatic inflation, however, and the implications of going over the side semiconscious or worse. (Courtesy Steve D'Antonio)

Offshore, a crew finds the combination of an inflatable PFD and harness an easy-to-wear, utilitarian piece of safety gear.

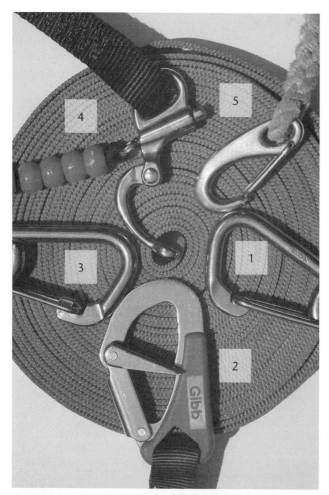

Most tether clips are single-action, double-action, or piston-type. Beware of the potential for a single-action clip to self-release if twisted the wrong way. Also recognize that a need might arise to release yourself from the tether while under load (perhaps underwater), which is why a snapshackle harness connection makes sense. Top, clockwise from top center: clips numbered 1, 3, and 5 are single-action clips—not the best choice for use on either end of a harness tether; clip 2 is a double-action device that provides a positive lock and is a good choice for the distal end of a tether. A snapshackle (4) allows a sailor to release a tether under load if trapped under a capsized vessel or tangled in rigging— it should be used at the chest end of the tether. Bottom: clipping onto a pad eye.

erted on the jackline by the momentum of falling can easily be two or three times the weight of the crewmember, and that same impact load must be absorbed by the crewmember reaching the end of the rope. To minimize such shock loads, it's wise to keep jacklines as taut as possible and never to use a harness tether longer than 6 feet. The 3 foot length option on a dual tether lessens shockloading even more, but one must be careful that the longer leg doesn't snag on some piece of hardware or get caught in a winch. Some crews on larger boats augment jacklines with sewn-in loops or fixed pad eyes that allow a foredeck crew to re-clip to a fixed point, thus avoiding the possibility of being knocked flat by a wave and suffering a bow-to-mast sluice run down the deck. In heavy weather, a harness and tether are as important to a sailor as to a mountain climber. Because mountain climbers need strong, lightweight hardware, high-strength aluminum clips prevail. However, on a sailboat, moist salt air and deluges of spray cause corrosion, and many aluminum alloy safety tether clips have been rendered unusable after a time in a cockpit locker. Stainless steel hardware remains the sailor's best bet.

The inflatable PFD with built-in harness is a big step forward in safety, but the U.S. Coast Guard specs have a couple caveats. First, nonswimmers and poor swimmers should not use an inflatable unless it's worn inflated, because they will need to manage staying afloat in the water until the PFD inflates. Also, the gear should not be used by those under 16 or weighing less than 80 pounds. Equally significant is the Coast Guard view that a Type V PFD provides the performance of a Type II or Type I PFD when inflated. Type I PFDs are the gold standard and are mandated on commercial vessels, where it's illegal to count an inflatable PFD as a life jacket. Type I PFDs tend to be handed out only in emergencies, when their bulk and movement-limiting design are not issues. The bottom line: an inflatable is not a PFD until it is filled with air, and maintenance shortfalls can lessen the chances of that happening.

DRESSING FOR SAFETY

"You are what you wear" may be a fashion maven's battle cry, but it's also common sense for those who spend time at sea. Humans are not as good at thermal regulation as most mammals, and the extent of clothing has always been the means by which we've handled climatic extremes.

Like skiers and mountaineers, sailors use layering to stay comfortable afloat, as touched upon in Chapter 11. A permeable and comfortable first layer wicks moisture away from the skin; add layers over

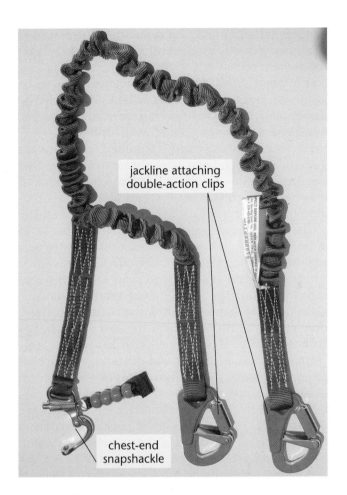

jackline attaching double-action clips

chest-end snapshackle

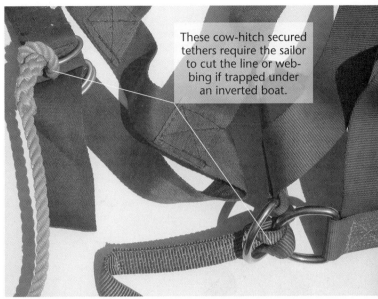

These cow-hitch secured tethers require the sailor to cut the line or webbing if trapped under an inverted boat.

Some sailors prefer a double-clip tether (left) that allows one to clip onto a secondary point prior to releasing the primary clip. Others find such a process limiting and continually get the extra appendage caught up where it doesn't belong. The biggest mistake is to attach the unused clip to both D-rings of the harness—this practice nullifies the function of the snapshackle and traps the user with a clip that's nearly impossible to release under load. Harnesses that have built-in tethers (top) that can't be released at the chest may endanger a crew forced by water or gravity to be 6 feet away from the attachment clip.

this to insulate according to temperature and wind chill. Multiple layers of fleece and other heat-retaining materials are more effective than a single heavy garment. The outer layer needs to be a waterproof barrier, preferably one that also allows one-way water vapor transfer. Such membranes block water from entering but allow water vapor to escape, and have revolutionized foul-weather gear. The waterproof exterior fabric is just as important as the inner layers. Stiff, heavy, restrictive jackets and pants hamper a sailor's agility and ability to function on deck, however, making every task a greater challenge. Much more energy is used during exercise, generating heat, causing spikes in the temperature of the air trapped under the clothing and producing perspiration. When the job is done and the crew heads back to the cockpit to sit in the cold and damp, the recently generated perspiration needs to be wicked away from the body and escape through a breathable fabric; otherwise, the cooling moisture trapped next to the skin becomes a serious concern.

Many sailors prefer two-part (jacket/pants) foul-weather gear because a jacket can easily be unzipped and removed after a downpour or when they duck under a spray dodger. Others swear by the warmth and flexibility of one-part suits. Whichever design

Cold weather can wear down a crew, and cold, wet weather is worse—in such conditions care must be taken to shorten watches and better insulate watchstanders.

Funny hats often do the job when the spray starts to fly. A towel around the neck, or in this case a jacket with a good neck seal that can be opened up between downpours, is a watchstander's best friend. Cinched wrist and ankle straps can keep out the rest of the deluge or flung spray.

A dry suit over a layered array of underclothing keeps water out and heat in. These lightweight waterproof suits are a little more awkward to wear than foul-weather gear but nowhere near as constricting as a survival suit. A sailor transiting high latitudes should consider carrying one in the sea bag.

you choose, be sure there is good reinforcement on the knees and in the crotch, and choose a suit of a very bright yellow or orange fabric, at least around the arms, shoulders, and hood. Finding a victim in the water is tough enough under any circumstances but even tougher when he or she is camouflaged in dark blue or black clothing.

A huge amount of heat radiates out from the body at the head, hands, and feet, and the seals on foul-weather gear need to be effective here. One look at a dry suit says it all. Since these garments must keep water out, tight (some would say annoying) gasket-like seals are used. In the worst of conditions, when the assault of breaking waves is like the spray from a fire hose, a dry suit is about all that will keep you dry. By the end of a 4-hour watch, crewmembers wearing dry suits are likely to be much warmer and drier than shipmates in conventional foul-weather gear, but they will use words like "imprisoned" to describe the feel of the attire. A good compromise can be found in higher-end offshore foul-weather gear with softer, adjustable wrist, neck, and ankle seals.

Boots, gloves, and hats play an integral role in heat retention. The head, hands, and feet are such good heat exchangers that, when poorly insulated, they can undo the benefit of the best foul-weather gear. Boots should be large enough to accommodate thick, well-insulated socks and still be easy to kick off in an emergency. Gloves can be layered with a thin underglove and a thicker, mitten-type overglove. Strip down to the undergloves for tasks requiring dexterity, but don the overgloves for steering or sheet trimming. Hats should have thermal insulating ability and block the wind. A wide range of styles is available from conventional watch caps (made with synthetic materials) to brimmed hats with drop-down ear covers. The colder the weather, the more serious the insulation becomes.

Layered, insulated clothing guards against hypothermia, a challenge faced by all humans in cold and even temperate climates. Hyperthermia is the opposite problem, arising when environmental conditions cause the human body to overheat. Peeling off layers of clothing, reducing activity, and drinking lots of fluids are the usual responses to overheating, but in sunny tropical latitudes there's danger in too much of a good thing, and protection from sunlight also becomes an issue. Big-brimmed floppy hats, sunglasses that stop ultraviolet A and B rays, and lightweight UV-blocking shirts augment sunscreen slathering, especially when cruisers are exposed to long durations of tropical sunlight. A bimini or awnings will also help, as does the commonsense action of staying below between 1000 and 1400.

Survival Suits

Hypothermia isn't the only threat posed by cold water. Canadian researchers have found that immersion in water below 52°F can cause laryngeal and upper-respiratory spasms that impede breathing and significantly raise the chances of drowning. This cold-water respiratory response, coupled with the potential hazard of hypothermia, explains why commercial fishermen, tugboat crews, and other professional mariners plying colder waters carry, carefully maintain, and practice using survival suits. These are well-insulated dry suits that afford entry via a waterproof zippered front and effectively seal in heat while keeping water out. They are quick and easy to don and offer enough protection from the elements to allow a crew to retain body heat and up the chances for rescue. Recreational boaters cruising or racing in cold waters should take a close look at the new technology that makes these suits easier to don, more watertight, and much more user-friendly than ever before.

Early survival suits were made from neoprene carefully stitched and glued to make all seams watertight. The design was a thicker version of a diver's wet suit, but the principle of operation was very different. Instead of functioning as a conventional wet suit, trapping and warming a thin layer of water between the wearer's skin and the neoprene, a survival suit keeps all the water out, and the suit itself, rather than

Distress signaling is covered in ISAF regulations—make sure you have updated flares and know how to use them.

a layer of body-warmed water, acts as the insulation. The loose fit of a survival suit is another difference between it and a conventional wet suit. This baggy fit makes it easier to put on, a critical feature in a crisis. If you do choose to carry a survival suit, study the options carefully, such as the differences between fixed and removeable gloves. Zipper maintenance is critical to ensure that the suit will seal efficiently in an emergency. As with all important gear, follow the manufacturer's recommendations for maintenance.

EMERGENCY GEAR FOR CREW-OVERBOARD SITUATIONS

The ISAF, of which US Sailing is a member, promulgates stringent safety standards for inshore and offshore sailboat racing. Their technical committee attempts to balance the need for vital emergency equipment with the reality that space on board and cost are also critical variables. The equipage mandate varies with the exposure category, which seems a logical approach.

Although the following sections focus on gear required for racing, all this equipment applies equally to inshore and offshore cruising as well. Anyone on a boat is at risk for ending up in the water, one way or another, and this emergency gear is needed to recover or rescue that unlucky crew.

Crew-Overboard Recovery Devices

The ISAF considers both safety gear for the vessel and personal safety gear. One of the most important subsets of boat safety gear is the equipment

The final tug of a survival suit zipper can be tough, but it's what closes the all-important face seal and keeps water out. Regularly waxing the teeth of the zipper helps keep it free from corrosion and ready for use.

for a crew-overboard (COB) rescue. Sailing is a safe sport, but when a crewmember falls overboard, those left onboard have much to do and need to be well practiced in recovery skills as well as how to use the equipment carried aboard. There are several variations in recovery maneuvers and numerous products to aid a rescue, but the key factor in all of them is crew understanding, familiarity, and practice.

Without appropriate COB gear, crew will not be able to physically mark a victim's location and provide additional flotation while simultaneously electronically marking the COB position—three import-

ant first steps in a COB situation. Lights and whistles attract attention, and throw lines can bridge the gap between the boat and the person in the water. This gear needs to be easily accessed and immediately deployable so that crew onboard can also keep the person in view at all times until rescued. If a rescue device is complicated to release, precious seconds will go by, separating the victim from the point where the gear finally hits the water. The greater the separation, the less likely it becomes that the victim can swim to the equipment. Even when the separation is wide, however, the deployed gear still helps by showing the crew where to return to for the victim.

UNCONSCIOUS OVERBOARD

Nothing is more difficult than the recovery of an unconscious COB victim. A successful recovery is much more likely if the lost crewmember was wearing a PFD. A water-activated light on the PFD can guide the boat back to the person in the water, but getting an unconscious crew back on board often requires a designated swimmer tethered to the boat to place the hoisting harness, Lifesling, or other lifting device onto the victim.

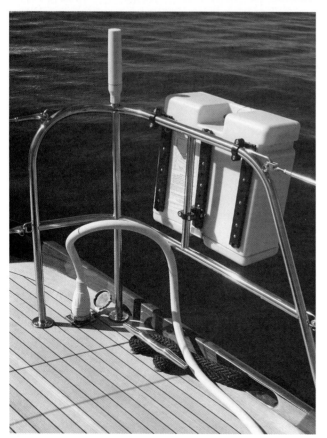

This Man Overboard Module (MOM) has been securely attached to a stern pulpit. The indentation in the top of the container houses the T-handle pull-to-deploy pin.

Inflatable Devices

One of the easiest—and fastest—pull-to-deploy options is the Switlik Man Overboard Module, or MOM. The downside is its reliance on an auto-inflation process. During a gear test in San Francisco sponsored by US Sailing, one of the two MOM deployed with a spar buoy had a kink in the line that led to the horseshoe float. The unit had been locally repacked the day before, and even an authorized service provider couldn't guarantee flawless operation. That said, the spar still floated a few feet above the surface with its light activated, another upside of such a device day or night.

All inflatable rescue devices require regular maintenance, and in some cases this must be carried out by the manufacturer or a designated service facility. Manufacturers do extensive testing, and recalls do occur, as was the case with the inflatable Lifesling, a product that was removed from the market. Keeping track of product recalls is important to owners, especially when it comes to safety equipment.

CREW OVERBOARD OR MAN OVERBOARD?

The long-used term "man overboard" (MOB) is slowly giving way (except for MOB buttons on most chartplotters) to the gender-neutral crew overboard (COB), which the U.S. Coast Guard has more recently side-stepped with the term "person in the water" (PIW) to better define (some would say further obscure) the situation. (Note, MOB is still used in international radio broadcasts, in formal training material such as the three-volume *International Aeronautical and Maritime Search and Rescue Manual* [IAMSAR], and in many ISAF, US Sailing, naval, and commercial training materials.) Whatever the victim is called, it's a chilling circumstance that tests to the utmost a crew's ability to respond.

RESCUE PROCEDURE CONTROVERSIES

One of the most controversial and contradictory bits of COB instruction is found in Appendix D of the ISAF rules (US Sailing version), which states that "Deployment of the (life buoy) pole, flag, dan buoy (MOM etc.) requires too much time. This gear should be saved to 'put on top' of the victim in case the initial maneuver is unsuccessful." This recommendation ignores data showing that a return to the victim is by no means guaranteed and that the first few seconds may represent the only opportunity to deploy COB equipment anywhere near the victim. Even if the victim is unable to reach the device, the presence of drogue-equipped flotation in the victim's vicinity makes him or her more visible and easier to find. This can become even more of a paramount issue during a nighttime COB recovery.

In 2010 the US Sailing Safety at Sea Committee reconsidered the Appendix D recommendation. Many committee members recognized the leap of faith inherent in the assumption that a vessel will be able to make an expedient return to a victim and that the victim will be wearing a PFD with a strobe or incandescent light. The language remains unaltered in the 2012/2013 edition of the ISAF rules, however. Hopefully it will change in the future. Several tragic recent incidents have shown how hard it is to return to an unmarked position, and delaying the deployment of a vital life buoy—and relying instead solely on an electronic MOB button push on a GPS receiver—runs counter to the practices taught by The Royal National Lifeboat Institution in England and other commercial marine training centers around the world. The following features are common to most COB recovery recommendations worldwide:

- Shout "Crew overboard" and begin COB recovery maneuver
- Assign crew to track the COB victim
- Deploy a life buoy with a pole or pylon, drogue, and light
- Press the MOB button on a GPS or chartplotter;
- Issue a VHF Mayday call
- Use an approach method that is appropriate for the conditions and the vessel
- Be aware of the victim's location and the danger posed by the boat
- Use a life ring on a tether or a Lifesling to make contact with the victim
- Hoist, lift, or use a ladder or swim step to bring the victim aboard

Rigid Devices

The rigid-pole dan buoy with attached horseshoe life ring, strobe, and mini-drogue has for decades been popular as a COB marker and recovery device. Its ready-to-float reliability is excellent, but its release mechanism is often too complex to ensure prompt deployment. Just as with inflatable devices, the closer to the victim the gear can be dropped, the more likely the victim will be able to reach it. This version of COB gear is usually supported independently on the stern of the vessel, with the horseshoe buoy attached to the stern rail and the pole either attached vertically to the backstay or housed horizontally in a dedicated stern tube. It must be well secured to prevent being plucked free by an ordinary boarding sea yet still be easy to deploy. These conflicting requirements are hard to reconcile, and many vessels encountering heavy weather at sea find themselves losing COB gear just when it may be needed most.

Lights

Darkness at sea is more complete than in most coastal waters, and a COB illuminated with a small incandescent light can often be distinguished from background darkness. In good visibility a helicopter pilot using night vision goggles can see a strobe light up to 50 miles distant. In nearshore waters, competing light from land sources can easily obscure low-lumen lights, causing the victim to blend in rather than stand out. This is the key reason why COB gear should include a bright strobe with plenty of battery power to lengthen its operational life.

A simple mercury-type switch allows an MOB position marking strobe to remain off when stowed in an inverted position but activates it when it's turned right side up, at which point the strobe immediately begins flashing. Even if unused, the battery should be replaced annually and the unit checked for rainwater intrusion. Over time, harmful UV rays can make the clear plastic dome brittle and cause it to craze and discolor. Covering or stowing the unit below when not underway will extend the life of the light.

Personal clip-on strobes and other lights come in many sizes and shapes and can be either water-activated or manually turned on. A water-activated unit incorporated in an auto-inflating PFD gives an unconscious victim some hope of being recovered. Small incandescent and strobe lights are clipped to or tucked into inflatable PFDs and can be easily accessed when the device is inflated. They can also be attached to any other type of standard PFD. Ideally these lights, especially the strobes, are not set up

Above: Waterproof flashlights and small dive lights are personal safety items and can be used when searching for a COB victim without destroying everyone's night vision. Right: Testing has shown that a COB victim with a high-intensity waterproof flashlight in his or her pocket has a much-improved chance of being recovered at night.

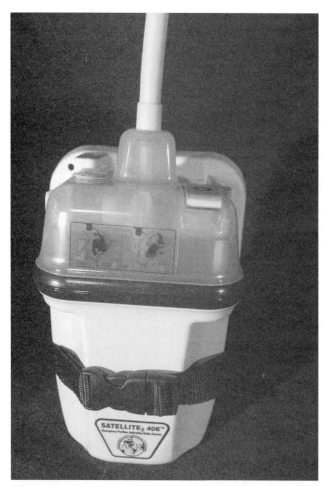

A 406 MHz EPIRB has proven a crew's best bet when and if it comes time to abandon ship. The unit floats, broadcasts continuously for a minimum of 48 hours, and acts as a good homing device for a helicopter crew with direction-finding gear. GPS-equipped EPIRBS (called GPIRBS) add a lat/lon fix to each signal transmitted.

directly in front of the victim's line of sight. Losing night vision is not a prerequisite for being seen. Place the lights on a lanyard that allows you to move it out of your line of sight.

Sound Devices—Whistles

Coaches everywhere have learned the value of the shrill call of the Acme Thunderer pea whistle. Police and NFL refs alike love the sound the little hands-free whistle makes, not to mention that it can be heard a mile away. Today there's a waterproof polycarbonate version of the revered Acme Thunderer, as well as a SOLAS-approved Acme Survival Whistle. These devices excel at making noise with minimum airway demand, and though a little more expensive than the bargain whistles that come with safety gear, their increased range can make a critical survival difference. Attach one to each life jacket.

Emergency Beacons and the Cospas/Sarsat Rescue Network

Calling for help is easier and more efficient today than ever before, and the number of EPIRB-driven rescue missions worldwide has topped 6,000 and continues to grow at a rate of over 600 per year. About 72% of those rescued are termed "maritime" incidents. Despite these bold, headline-grabbing rescues, however, some failed rescue attempts have resulted in lives lost, and these tragic incidents raise questions about the hardware and the process. As a firm believer in the old premise of never making the very good an enemy of the perfect, I tread carefully when it comes to raising such questions. But with another, equally valid premise in mind—that knowledge is power—I'll shed some light on how the International Maritime Organization's (IMO) well-organized worldwide safety network functions and what it takes for all parts of the rescue puzzle to fall into alignment.

First this: you should carry at least one 406 MHz EPIRB (emergency position-indicating radio beacon) whenever you head offshore. The EPIRB-based Cospas/Sarsat network is truly an impressive example of international cooperation and satellite-based signaling technology. (COSPAS is an acronym for the Russian words Cosmicheskaya Sistema Poiska Avariynyh Sudov or "Space System for the Search of Vessels in Distress." SARSAT is an acronym for Search And Rescue Satellite-Aided Tracking.) The system came into being in 1982, leveraging the 121.5/243 MHz beacons pioneered by the aviation community as emergency locator transmitters (ELTs). Morphing into the technology of choice for mariners, EPIRBs have streamlined search-and-rescue efforts. Improvements such as the switch from the 121.5/243 MHz to the 406 MHz system resulted in even more lives being saved. The current generation of beacons affords better position fixing and specific vessel identity information, linking each unit to a unique hexadecimal code. Many of the latest EPIRBs include a GPS chip. These GPIRBs broadcast latitude/longitude position data and allow for Doppler shift–based position finding. When the unit is switched on, a geostationary satellite receives the distress message and a GPS fix, while low-earth-orbit satellites resolve the fix via the Doppler effect. More effective signal handling and information gathering have shortened the response times of SAR missions. Many people are alive today thanks to a near seamless link connecting a beacon signal bouncing from a satellite to a local user terminal (LUT), which relays it to a mission control center (MCC), passing it along to a specific rescue coordination center (RCC) responsible for the SAR mission.

The other side of this success story is an ongoing saga of false alarms and infrequent but recurring instances of beacon failure. The stunning reality is that 96% of all EPIRB distress signals are false alarms. Of these, 85% are sorted out at the RCC level, where phone calls to those listed on the beacon's registration form usually nullify the distress situation. Often tough decisions must be made. With only 4% of the alerts being real distress situations, it's no surprise that a helicopter doesn't lift off or a cutter race out of the harbor the moment a distress message reaches

▲ EPIRB and PLB (personal locator beacon) signals are tracked around the world by geostationary and orbiting satellites, a part of the Cospas/Sarsat system. An ELT, PLB, or EPIRB broadcasts a distress message, satellites receive and forward it to LUT (a ground station), which routes the signal to a mission control center (MCC) which in turn engages the appropriate rescue coordination center (RCC). (The SAR community loves acronyms! See text for explanations.) (NOAA)

the RCC. Some significant lessons have been learned from past experiences.

For example, in a couple of situations where registration numbers were somehow incorrectly added to the United States 406 MHz Beacon Registration Database, deployment of a rescue mission was delayed due to the clerical misfiling. Concerns over additional miscues have prompted NOAA to encourage beacon owners to access their registration data online and double-check it for accuracy. To check your own beacon registration status, go to the website www.beaconregistration.noaa.gov and follow the step-by-step guidance.

Another far too frequent problem involves the malfunctioning of Category 1 automatically deploying float-free EPIRBs that are designed to be mounted on the stern rail or another deck location. These units are supposed to deploy automatically and switch on if the vessel founders, using a set of electrical contacts that turn on the device when immersed—but their hair-trigger water-sensing ability can lead to a false alarm when doused by a wave, soaked by freezing rain, or bumped and jarred. To prevent such unwanted beacon broadcasts, manufacturers install magnets in the case that cause a magnetic switch to open the circuit while the unit is in its protective housing. This technology has suffered from bracket problems and corroded magnets as well as installation errors, preventing the magnets from doing their job.

In cases such as the tragic disappearance of the 54-foot sloop *Flying Colours*, which vanished in a brutal storm off Cape Hatteras in 2007 (see Chapter 10 for the full story, parts of which are repeated here), the details of its beacon failure will never be known. In that particular instance, Coast Guard records show that an EPIRB signal was received from the Little Har-

bor 54 at 0330, but a position fix was not established until 0416. The EPIRB signals ended at 0700, and no sign of the vessel or its four-person crew was ever found.

In the same storm, the 44-foot Beneteau *Sean Seamour II* was capsized and dismasted. The sloop took on water, and the crew abandoned ship as the vessel sank. The EPIRB the owner had purchased overseas had been reregistered and inspected in the United States and did send a message that was received by a LUT and forwarded to a MCC and from there to an East Coast RCC. But when the RCC checked the database, the owner listed was a fisherman on the Gulf Coast who, when called, was awakened at home in bed. In consequence, the signal was apparently discounted. Fortunately, the skipper of *Sean Seamour II* had brought along the 406 MHz EPIRB that he had carried aboard his previous sailboat *Lou Pantai*, and it activated automatically upon being carried away by a breaking sea. A skilled Coast Guard helicopter rescue crew was vectored to the signal of the *Lou Pantai* beacon and saved the crew of *Sean Seamour II*, thus underscoring how valuable a second beacon can be.

Without question, a 406 MHz EPIRB should be the mainstay for distress signaling. It's a tried-and-proven system with worldwide coverage, and it has been in place long enough for most of the bugs to have been worked out. Despite a less than 100% rescue record, it is the mariner's first choice. The choice between an auto-deploying or a manually activated unit is tough, however. Notwithstanding the auto-deploying Category 1 unit's past problems with false triggers and being swept away by violent seas, it may still be the best bet in the chaos of a collision or capsize, though it probably would not help much in a fire. Many sailors prefer instead to keep a manual unit in an easily accessible ditch kit, but leaving the beacon behind when you climb into the life raft could have catastrophic consequences.

Whichever choice you make, check your unit regularly for signs of deterioration, noting the battery expiration date, and don't leave it on board during cold winter storage periods. You can test the unit's ability to transmit by following the manufacturer's step-by-step procedure while making sure the switch is pushed to the "test" position, not to "activate." Each test uses battery capacity, so keep the frequency and duration of such tests to the recommended minimum.

The 406 MHz beacon relies on low-earth-orbit and geosynchronous satellites, but a new technology slated to harness middle-earth-orbit satellites is scheduled to soon come on line and the existing 406 EPIRB program will overlap the implementation of the new system.

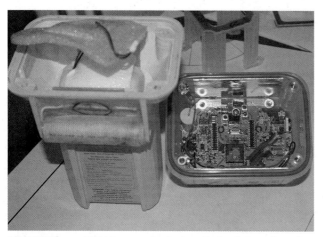

EPIRBs are 90% battery and a small circuit board, and it's essential to prevent water intrusion into the case. When it comes time to replace the battery, a manufacturer's service facility is the best bet.

Private Tracking Devices—SPOT

There has been a significant increase in the number of small, inexpensive, portable global tracking devices that can send friends and relatives, as well as ocean race organizers, a breadcrumb trail of the course you have been sailing. All this happens thanks to companies that link satellite data handling with online communication options and/or selected email targets. Products such as the popular SPOT communicator (about $150) are designed to transmit data including a GPS location to a low-earth-orbit satellite, which forwards it to a commercial communication center that interfaces it with email. A position report is sent to recipients on the owner's list. This cost-effective means of reporting in daily, hourly, or even more often is popular with sailors. The unit's portability allows it to be taken in a dinghy or ashore or into a life raft in an emergency. Its built-in functions include use as an emergency beacon, but that aspect needs to be understood.

There has been confusion as to whether these units function within the Cospas/Sarsat system. The simple answer is no—but they can still play a role in emergency situations offshore. Yet their role should be secondary to an EPIRB in a belt-and-suspenders approach to calling for help.

I sailed from Bermuda to New England with a handheld SPOT tracker on board, and it forwarded position updates without missing a beat. The weather was dominated by a deep trough producing heavy rain, a good test of the unit's moisture resistance and signal-acquisition capability. Several times a day I would manually send a position update simply by turning on the unit and pushing the OK button. It normally took 10–20 minutes to acquire a satellite and upload the GPS position. The unit worked well under the canvas dodger but, as expected, could not acquire satellite signals belowdecks. Each position report was automatically forwarded via email from the SPOT home base to the listed contacts. By noting the GPS lat/lon readouts on the sloop's Furuno NavNet DCS system and the GMT time, I was later able to compare SPOT position reports with actual GPS fixes. All paired fixes were nearly identical, with very slight (100 feet or less) discrepancies that were likely due to the sampling rate differences of the two GPS units.

On the other hand, when a SPOT beacon owner presses the SOS button (911 on older models), SPOT signal handlers, not a Cospas/Sarsat mission control center (MCC), receive the initial signal and relay the distress message on. The goal is to get it to the most appropriate rescue coordination center (RCC). And history has shown that although that usually is what happens, there have been instances where problems have arisen. Since SPOT beacons do not operate on

SPOT trackers and their sequels utilize low-earth-orbit satellite links and allow a few different prestored messages to be selected and forwarded via email to up to 100 recipients. In addition, there is a distress button that sends a "need help immediately" call to a private control center, which then must forward it to government SAR coordinators.

406 MHz, in addition, the new Coast Guard direction-finding equipment cannot help in the final approach as it can with an EPIRB by homing in on the 121.5 and/or 406 MHz frequency. Instead, the SPOT GPS alert relays a GPS position that is regularly updated via the private sector satellite system.

The U.S. Coast Guard prefers personal locator beacons (PLBs—see below) to SPOT trackers as a back-up for an EPIRB because PLBs do interface directly with the internationally approved Cospas/Sarsat/IMO system, are built to tightly controlled specs, and give users a compact distress beacon that affords both GPS position finding and final approach direction-finding capability on 121.5 and 406 MHz. PLBs do not function as tracking devices, however, and are not meant to notify those ashore of the whereabouts of their friends at sea.

When you're in serious trouble and lives are at risk, outside assistance may be your last hope for survival. In such situations having all your eggs in one communications basket is far from ideal. Further, search and rescue is a high-stakes process with contravening factors at play. On the one hand, false alarms eat up resources; on the other hand, a slow deployment can cost lives. The sooner a distress situation is verified, the sooner a SAR mission is put into effect. Having two means of satellite signaling for help is definitely better than one.

Investing a few hundred dollars in a secondary tracker or beacon can improve the probability of a successful rescue. So can a satellite phone call made directly to a Coast Guard rescue center. My first choice for an emergency satellite communications device to back up the EPIRB is a PLB. Its little-brother

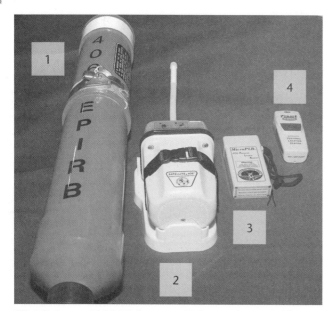

Miniature 406 MHz beacons, PLBs, can be carried by a crewmember and used to send a distress signal to the Coast Guard via Cospas/Sarsat and they also allow USCG helicopters to directly hone in with DF equipment. The units use the same international Cospas/Sarsat system as larger EPIRB units. Left to right: (1) An early 406 EPIRB; (2) an EPIRB of more recent vintage offering the same capability as (1); (3, 4) PLBs.

relationship to the EPIRB and its stand-alone autonomy are big pluses. Especially now that Coast Guard helicopters and Rescue 21 towers use direction finding on the 406 MHz signal, the advantages of a PLB make it the best backup. That said, there's nothing wrong with using a second, stand-alone system such as the SPOT for backup. Quite often there are delays in launching a search-and-rescue effort if no one answers the phone numbers listed on the beacon registration form. If a rescue coordination center (RCC) received both a 406 EPIRB signal and a call from the SPOT emergency network, both with the same GPS coordinates, a rescue mission would be far more likely to launch sooner than later.

Personal Locator Beacons (PLBs)

There's a good likelihood that the PLB, with its international linkage via MCCs and RCCs, will become as important a safety asset as its big brother the EPIRB. One important difference between PLBs and MOB alarms (see below) is that there's neither an onboard warning system nor an automatic immersion start function with a PLB. The unit's antenna must be deployed and a button pushed to initiate operation. It's a simple procedure but one that requires a conscious victim who is aware of what to do. The unit transmits a 406 MHz signal to geostationary and geosynchronous satellites, and these satellites forward the bea-

con registration number and position information to an MCC, which validates the signal and engages the RCC nearest the signal. Prior to launching a rescue mission, the RCC staff begin the identification and authentication process with one or more vital phone calls. The numbers they call are listed on the registration form, and the purpose is to gain confirmation from a family member, close friend, or business associate that the sailor is at sea. Then an MCC is given the situation report and a rescue mission starts.

Those who sail with a portable or fixed satellite phone should carry the phone numbers of RCCs. In the United States, these are Coast Guard stations, and by calling them via satphone in an emergency a COB victim with a PLB can be located via the RCC's lat/lon satellite fix. Keep in mind that if a crew loses sight of the victim the PLB or EPIRB does not signal the vessel and contacting a RCC is the only way to get a position fix of the victim. Such calls also confirm the emergency and can help to coordinate a rescue.

In or near U.S. waters, the rescue response to a person in the water may involve a Coast Guard vessel and/or an air asset (H-60, H-65, or C-130), and the time to the scene of the incident may be measured in hours or perhaps even minutes. Even such a rapid response may be too long, however, depending upon water temperature and the condition of the individ-

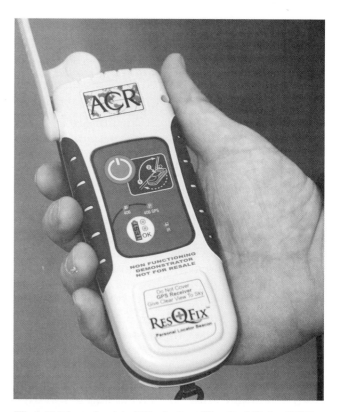

A PLB has about half the battery life of a full-size EPIRB but can be carried in a pocket.

ual in the water. For this reason a skilled crew and good boat handling remain the first line of defense.

Outside more highly developed parts of the world, the rescue mission instigated by a 406 MHz beacon may be assigned to a nation with few floating assets and no air rescue resources. The beacon still works, but the person in the water ends up in the Automated Mutual-Assistance Vessel Rescue (AMVER) System with a Cospas/Sarsat alert and a notification to ships in the region to keep a "sharp lookout" for the victim and lend assistance if in the area. The prospect of spotting the bobbing head of a person in the water is quite small. Obviously, both EPIRBs and PLBs are much more effective when the victim is close to well-established SAR facilities. Your chances of survival are better if you fall overboard in the coastal waters of the United States, Canada, Europe, New Zealand, Australia, or Japan, all of whose maritime agencies get high marks for SAR skills and equipment.

PLBs don't have as long a battery life as EPIRBs, but they still deliver 24 hours or more of continuous broadcasting. The trend among all these devices is toward even further miniaturization and reduction in power consumption, traits that make the technology more and more useful to offshore sailors. Note that some of the smaller PLBs do not float, lack a lanyard, and require a victim to maintain an iron grip on this electronic lifeline.

Other Crew-Overboard Alarm and Beacon Options

The primary purpose of small, light, clip-on COB alarm devices is to keep track of crewmembers when they are on deck. A radio-frequency reference signal on the boat keeps the alarm from sounding, but if the device no longer receives the signal, an alarm sounds on the boat to announce that the beacon wearer is beyond the very limited range of signal reception and therefore, in all likelihood, overboard. These devices do not broadcast a direction-finding signal, but the system can be linked to a digital charting system/GPS network to note a COB position where the crew went over the side.

Just as the U.S. Coast Guard uses direction-finding equipment in their final approach to a 406 MHz PLB or EPIRB, a boat with DF equipment can home in on a beacon signal. In fact, several manufacturers offer dedicated beacon and receiver units meant to be used autonomously aboard small boats. Some also provide an COB alarm and relay controls to shut off the engine, record the COB position, or disengage an autopilot.

The growing array of overboard alerts and radio direction-finding COB alarms and beacons can be a little bewildering. The units I've handled vary from

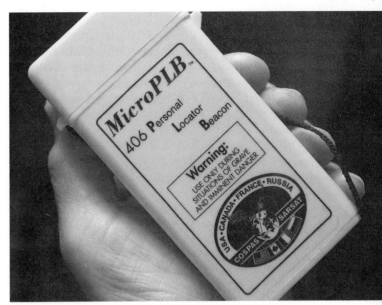

Smaller beacons with greater efficiency are now hitting the market, and some PLBs have full 48-hour battery ratings. By switching to lithium-ion batteries, many manufacturers also have developed small units that float.

quirky to reliable and Coast Guard–approved. One must weigh the value of a loud audible alarm that can alert the crew that someone has gone over the side against the virtues of a unit that lets the Coast Guard know you're in trouble. The best choice for you depends on your crew's size and composition and, above all, where you will be sailing. As of this writing, no one device answers all needs, and a prudent sailor may choose to use both types of devices. The dilemma may be resolved with a new breed of EPIRBs with signals that can also be displayed on an AIS (Automatic Identification System—see Chapters 8 and 14) screen. Existing AIS beacons can guide AIS-equipped vessels to a nearby person in the water. The small GPS-equipped transponder allows AIS-equipped vessels to pick up the short-range line-of-sight signal and hone in on the victim.

Analyzing COB Alarm and Beacon Choices

For now, though, the wide array of devices marketed as auxiliary lifesaving equipment includes alarms and beacons that differ in design as well as their approach to expediting a rescue. The following suggestions are based on what's available as of this writing.

In relatively warm coastal waters, such as between the Chesapeake Bay and Florida, a 406 MHz PLB is likely your best choice. In warm waters a COB's survival time will be long enough for a conventional 406 MHz PLB-initiated SAR mission to be executed if the crew fails in its recovery efforts.

In cold waters, however, such as from Auckland, New Zealand, to Punta Arenas, Chile, hypothermia is the worst enemy, and the crew must consider whether a device with direction-finding ability or AIS beacon would lead to a quicker and more likely successful rescue. A satellite-based system involving agencies thousands of miles away can only advise distant nations, often with limited SAR assets, to keep a lookout for the person in the water. Such SAR missions seldom lead to a quick rescue, and hypothermia sets in very quickly.

The vital question to consider is who is most likely to make a rescue. If self-reliance is the answer, the value of an immediate loud alarm and an AIS beacon increases the probability of a successful outcome. If the crew has practiced a recovery maneuver and can execute it with nearly reflexive precision, the chances of rescue are much greater.

But in many situations, it is a professional agency such as the U.S. Coast Guard, or a third party acting as a Good Samaritan, that accomplishes the rescue. In such cases, knowing the victim's real-time lat/lon coordinates is much better than knowing the coordinates where the crew went overboard, and a PLB in the hands of the victim ups the chances of rescue.

The future likely will see miniaturized PLBs that do three things simultaneously: send a GPS position via satellite to a mission coordination center, initiate an onboard alarm, and allow the crew to track an AIS signal from the unit. But until the technology catches up with this wish list, we must make do with the technology available today.

Radar Reflectors

For decades, passive radar reflectors have been used by sailors and powerboaters around the world. The technology is based upon microwave reflection by multisided metallic structures. The challenge lies in getting a powerful enough return signal from a small, lightweight, low-windage shape reflected to 360 degrees at all angles of heel. The common octahedral pattern used in many radar reflectors provides a barely adequate signal return. Engineers in testing laboratories note that these reflectors have intermittent high and low points (lobes) in their signal return. These peaks and valleys cause radar units on ships, yachts, and other commercial and recreational craft to display intermittent targets.

The higher in the rigging a radar reflector is hoisted, generally, the farther away the return signals can be seen. Nonetheless, the existing research shows most radar reflectors on the market today score a marginal C grade in their ability to provide a consistently strong return. ISAF Special Regulations call for reflectors with a 12-inch minimum diameter and a radar cross-section return equivalent to 10 square meters, while the US Sailing prescription has been watered

down to 6 square meters. The simple Davis Echomaster octahedral reflector, the much larger Firdell Blipper, the mast-mounted stepped-index Luneberg lens, and Tri-Lens reflectors consistently score better in independent testing. Although a passive reflector is a vast improvement over having none at all, these systems are not the only answer.

Active radar reflectors are another choice. They amplify microwave signals in the bounce-back reflection and show up as brighter, more consistent targets on radar screens. They are heavier and more expensive than passive reflectors, however, and they require a DC power supply. While some models have disappeared from the market, the SeaMe and Echomax Active XS models are popular. In addition to sending a stronger radar reflection, some models issue a sound signal to alert sailors, particularly singlehanders who may be resting, that they have been hit by a radar signal.

The widespread acceptance of AIS systems has shifted some sailors' approach to being seen in poor-visibility conditions, however, away from the importance of radar. Professional mariners scoff at such shortsightedness, and refer to the fact that vessels without AIS or with the units shut off are invisible to those with operational AIS units.

CREW-OVERBOARD RECOVERY METHODS

"Lost at sea" is a tragic epitaph. Without question, luck has a role in the handful of deadly sailboat accidents. Most serious accidents at sea begin as non-life-threatening incidents that evolve through a chain of contributory mistakes, mishaps, and failures to respond effectively. Their cumulative impact can transform a minor misfortune into a major calamity.

As discussed elsewhere in this chapter, chandlery shelves are packed with things to throw to a COB, tow the person within reach, and use to lift him or her from the water. As mentioned throughout this book, a COB victim is better off when wearing a PFD and has a light and whistle. The shock and disorientation associated with falling overboard is dramatic, and the buoyancy and psychological reassurance of a PFD can make a big difference in a victim's attitude. Even with an automatic inflation capability, wearers should pull the manual-inflate tab as soon as they hit the water. This provides immediate inflation and can save up to 10 seconds or more of waiting for the device to inflate.

The best response for a COB includes efficient boat handling and a well-choreographed, much-practiced deployment of the gear. Each crewmember

needs to be ready to fill any role, whether it be steering, trimming, spotting the victim, communicating, navigating, or preparing the recovery gear. With so many tasks involved, a shorthanded crew especially needs to have a plan in place.

US Sailing's COB recovery procedures train crews to recover victims under sail. The benefit of using the engine in a rescue versus the danger remains controversial to some, but from my perspective it is an option to keep at the ready. A sheet can get caught in the prop or the victim can be injured by the prop if the helmsperson is unpracticed, but just as one must become accustomed to docking and picking up a mooring under both power and sail, a crew should develop dual overboard recovery skills and be ready to put the engine to good use when and if the need arises. Having the engine running in neutral during a rescue approach at least provides the option of using it if necessary.

Testing COB Methods

In 2005, safety experts gathered on San Francisco Bay, California, to test crew-overboard rescue equipment and evaluate recovery methodology. Over 100 volunteers were on hand to help in the demonstrations and gain valuable training experience. One of the biggest questions on everyone's mind was whether a single recovery technique would really fit the bill. For years, US Sailing had endorsed the quick-stop maneuver for fully crewed vessels and a Lifesling recovery for shorthanded sailors and powerboaters. During three

A quick-stop COB maneuver begins with tacking into a heave-to position while a spotter is assigned, rescue gear is deployed, and the MOB button on the GPS is pushed. This adds up to a lot of unanticipated action at once. Note the deployed horseshoe buoy in the foreground (top photo) and how the crew reacts to the heel induced by the backed genoa, facing away from the victim—this is why the spotter (bottom photo) plays such an essential role.

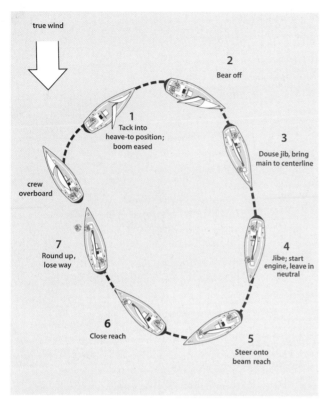

true wind

1
Tack into
heave-to position;
boom eased

2
Bear off

3
Douse jib, bring
main to centerline

crew
overboard

4
Jibe; start
engine, leave in
neutral

7
Round up,
lose way

6
Close reach

5
Steer onto
beam reach

US Sailing's preferred method of crew overboard recovery is the quick-stop maneuver, but the best maneuver has more to do with vessel design and the conditions at hand. The crews of larger boats with double-digit reaching speeds cringe at the thought of an abrupt tack into a heave-to position. They feel other methods—such as marking the spot, dousing sails, and returning under power—make more sense. (Joe Comeau)

days of evaluations in winds varying from calm to 25 knots, a variety of vessels were used to test gear and recovery techniques.

While the quick-stop maneuver seemed the preferable approach for those aboard agile, easy-to-steer, performance-oriented vessels, less maneuverable heavy-displacement cruisers and multihulls lacked the directional control to effectively use the maneuver, especially in lighter-air conditions. Once stopped, these boats were hard to accelerate, and they were much less responsive to the helm than their lighter, more agile cousins.

Following the San Francisco Bay rescue symposium, Dan Rugg, sailing master at the U.S. Naval Academy, contacted me about a project he was involved with to provide members of the Philadelphia Corinthian Sailing Club with both classroom and onboard COB training. Dan had worked with midshipmen for almost two decades, training them according to a blend of Navy standards and US Sailing's prescribed approaches. We agreed that factors ranging from crew skill and size to the vessel's behavior at differing speeds and in differing sea states affect the challenges involved in a rescue and determine the best maneuver to use. For example, the quick-stop maneuver, a logical method favored by many club racers, relies on having enough crew on deck to handle the multitude of tasks that arise at once. Just as the vessel is tacked and the headsail backwinded, flotation is deployed, a spotter is assigned, the position is marked on the

During the final approach of a figure-eight COB recovery, almost all boat speed is bled off. In this case the crew waited too long to furl the jib, and now to come alongside the victim on a close reach they will have to bear off and dip downwind, which will accelerate the boat and cause it to gather too much way. By keeping the main trimmed in tightly on the deep reach, boat speed will be reduced. The goal is to stop just as they make contact with the person in the water, as not dragging the victim through the water is essential. If possible, it is preferable to pick up the victim amidship on the leeside of the boat.

GPS, and preparations for headsail dousing or furling are made. In the midst of this well-orchestrated chaos, the crew jibes the boat, and, if all is timed correctly, a close reach leads back to the victim.

The final close-quarters maneuvering results—theoretically at least—in the vessel arriving alongside the victim with just enough speed to retain helm control. Someone has been assigned to toss a line or reach with a boathook to the person in the water. By taking a closer look Dan and I hoped to develop some insights into what works most effectively in any given situation and how to optimize a crew's chances for success. Our conclusions are summarized in the following sections and the sidebar Corinthians' and Midshipmen's Responses to Crew Overboard on page 447.

The COB rescue and recovery process can be best understood in three stages: (1) recognition of the incident and initial assumption of crew roles, (2) the return to the victim, and (3) bringing the victim back on board, as discussed in the following sections.

Crew Overboard: Phase One

Humans prefer a state of homeostasis with minimal threat and acceptable comfort level. A type A sailor is much more likely to push the envelope, while a type B mariner is less interested in wringing every last drop of performance from the boat. But regardless of which you are, a crew-overboard incident, by its very nature, will come as a complete surprise. It's hard to stay rational in those first few seconds, yet what happens in those minutes has much to do with the likelihood of a successful rescue. The scope of crew responses ranges from cool calculation to absolute chaos. The more practiced and familiar you are with crew recovery, the less chaotic your response will be. Practice can turn what initially seems like complex steps into a reflex action ready to deploy on a moment's notice.

Conditions can complicate things. Darkness and heavy weather can be the victim's and rescue crew's worst nightmare. Waking an off-watch with a shout of "Crew overboard!" can elicit a mixed bag of reactions. The biggest problem is that it is difficult to pre-assign specific rescue roles because you never know who or how many may go over the side. A general pecking order can be laid out, however, stacking the deck with key players in crucial slots. The watch on station at the time of the incident starts the process, but the most skilled helmsperson on board should take the helm. Naturally the person at the helm at the time of the incident must at least be able to carry out the initial steps in the maneuver.

Before the skipper or watch captain takes over, he or she must have a clear situational understand-

This victim's-eye view of a downwind quick-stop maneuver shows that it's neither as quick nor as straightforward as its on-the-wind counterpart. The spinnaker must be doused before a return can be made and the victim approached, and simply turning into the wind is only feasible in light air and flat seas. In a fresh or strong breeze, the boat will significantly separate from the victim before it can finally get turned back. This is why deploying COB gear and marking the spot electronically is so important.

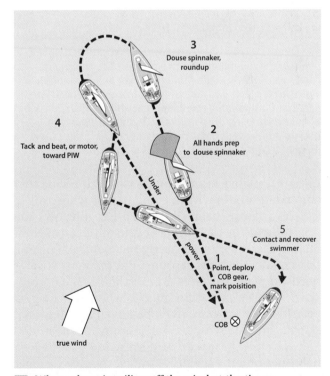

When a boat is sailing off the wind at the time a crewmember goes overboard, the remaining crew must deploy COB gear, electronically mark position, dump the spinnaker, disconnect the main-boom preventer, and get back to the victim with all possible haste. While all this is going on, one crewmember should be designated to track the PIW. (Joe Comeau)

The MOM gear is deployed by a simple pull of a pin (see photo of the rail-mounted unit on page 432), causing the canister's contents to drop into the water and auto-inflate. Quick deployment and careful tracking are key. The MOM here contains an inflatable spar buoy with an incandescent light at the top, an auto-inflatable horseshoe float with a backup oral blow-up tube, and an attached whistle, plus a drogue to keep the module from being blown away.

ing and a relative bearing to the victim. It is vital that command resides with the one person whose job it is to lead the rescue. If the skipper has gone over the side, it should be clear who's next in the chain of command. This may sound overly hierarchical, but in a crisis mode, the most capable—not the most vocal—needs to make the calls. In most major racing programs there's a clear delineation of who's in charge, especially when an owner is on board but a professional skipper and watch captains are running the boat.

Naturally, it makes most sense to have the best helmsperson on the wheel or tiller, the crewmember with 20 × 10 vision acting as the spotter, and a fit, agile former lifeguard ready to interact with the victim in or out of the water. But the situation seldom sets up so conveniently, and it makes sense to make the best use of opportunities at hand. For example, the person closest to the overboard gear should launch it, and

the person who first passes the GPS should hit the MOB button and shout to the crew that the position has been recorded. Scribbling a lat/lon position in the log or on the margin of a chart is also worthwhile.

Perhaps most important is the job of continually spotting the person in the water. That's why there's a universal consensus that if there are enough hands on board, the designated spotter does only that. Spotting can be assisted by night-vision equipment or with image-stabilized binoculars in daylight. An infrared imaging system such as FLIR (see photo on page 254) can also help by locating a warm spot on a cooler sea surface. Regardless of how much high-tech gear you have, such as position-finding beacons, the best fix of a person in the water remains a visual one—and a boat that stays closer to the victim has a much better chance of completing a successful recovery.

One of the most difficult things to simulate in training is the shock and disorientation that comes with an actual COB incident. The difference between a drill and the real thing is that a life is at stake, and surprise, fear, uncertainty, and confusion come to the forefront at the very worst moment. Crews tend to practice in flatwater inshore conditions, but in reality people fall overboard at sea, and their training experience is often very different from a real-world scenario that unfolds at 0300 with breaking seas sweeping the deck. A rough ocean creates a three-dimensional challenge, one that obscures the victim and makes each maneuver much more difficult. These are added reasons why a recovery maneuver needs to become as reflexive as possible, and crew training should include unannounced practice sessions at night and in daylight.

Crew Overboard: Phase Two

The second phase, after the crew have taken on their COB roles and the boat is turning, is to return to the victim to effect the rescue. The goal is to get back quickly and safely in a controlled manner, stopping next to the victim.

All too often, in the rush to quickly return to the victim, the boat speeds by at 3 knots or more, making rescue both dangerous and unlikely. The helmsperson and sail handlers should work in conjunction to bleed off way during the final close reach approach, arriving with a half-knot or less of boat speed. In an oceanic seaway, the pitching moment is like large-diameter disc brakes on a sports car, often killing forward motion prematurely. Conversely, in flat-water conditions the helmsperson must start the slow-down process much sooner. This is why practice should take place in all conditions in which the vessel will sail.

Several different methods may be used to return

to the person in the water. As mentioned earlier, the best method depends on the boat, the crew, and the present conditions. These methods are described later in the chapter.

Crew Overboard, Phase Three: Rescue Options

Ideally, a sailboat completes a COB maneuver by nudging alongside the person in the water. A line secures the person, who if conscious can scurry up a ladder or onto a swim step aft. More often than not, however, such precision and good luck falter, and a line, life ring, or boathook must be used to make contact. For an unconscious victim, using a Lifesling and a tethered crew member is usually the best option, described below.

Lifesling Recovery

The Lifesling-assisted rescue allows for less precise boat handling and can be used in both tack-only maneuvers and those incorporating a jibe. The instructions on the Lifesling container say "circle the victim until contact is made." Anyone who has water-skied understands the problem of getting a tow rope to a skier. While the boat circles the skier, the line tends to follow the wake of the circling vessel and never gets close enough to the skier in the middle of the circle. To move the line into the hands of the skier—or in this case, to get the rescue line attached to the Lifesling into the hands of the victim—a buttonhook approach is much better. Our testing revealed that during the final approach to the victim, the optimum Lifesling delivery always included a close passing of the victim before a sharp turn, rather than a turn that leaves the person in the center of a circle.

The Lifesling's floating polypropylene line should be stuffed, not coiled, into its bag. Beginning at the point farthest from the float, the line should be shoved to the bottom of the container. Properly packed and attached to a secure cleat or pad eye, the Lifesling is simply tossed astern, and the line will pay out as the vessel moves. If a snarl occurs, it can usually be coaxed out with a couple of tugs. If a tack-to-recover maneuver is used, the Lifesling is not deployed until the tack has been completed and the return to the victim begun.

If the Lifesling is deployed using a modified quick-stop maneuver, a jibe and modified circling procedure are involved. Centerline the mainsail early in the maneuver, and as the boat bears off, furl or

A QUICK-STOP RECOVERY GONE WRONG

A fast boat may be fun but it can make self-rescue efforts more difficult if someone goes over the side. A good friend of mine, a consummate sailor and well-trained yachtsman, experienced what we all hope to avoid.

He was at the helm of an offshore race boat in the predawn hours as the crew reached before a building November gale. The damaged mainsail had been struck, and only a number four jib was up. The most systems-knowledgeable person on board, the vessel's professional hand, had raced across the Atlantic and sailed for years with her owner and regular crew. The boat was being turned over to new owners, and the professional sailor had joined the delivery crew for a coastal passage from Long Island Sound to the Chesapeake Bay. At 0500 the pro had turned the watch over and, according to others aboard, went to the leeward side because the boom was lashed to starboard (leeward) and the crew was sitting on the windward deck. As he neared the companionway my friend asked if he was "hooked on" just as a gust and wave impact caused the boat to lurch. Apparently he had unhooked his harness prior to heading down the companionway but stopped to tighten a lashing on the boom. My friend immediately began to initiate the US Sailing preferred recovery procedure, known as the quick-stop maneuver, which begins with a tack into a heave-to position.

The jib-only sail plan had proved adequate for a beam reach in a growing northerly breeze, but several unanticipated problems arose when it came to implementing the quick-stop maneuver. First, the vessel refused to heave-to after tacking due to the absence of a mainsail. The light displacement 50-footer spun to leeward and charged downwind with the head of the jib on one side of the headstay and its foot on the other (known as a gullwing jibe). The victim was almost instantaneously passed close abeam, but the vessel had too much way on to affect a recovery and no crew-overboard gear was deployed.

By the time the headsail was struck the boat was close to a mile away from the victim, the lack of a masthead antenna hampered communications with the USCG, and when contact was finally made, and a helicopter crew sortied, the victim was found but hypothermia and drowning had taken their toll.

The aftermath was difficult for all involved, and a long list of Monday-morning-quarterbacking lessons learned were compiled. But lurking in the background was an important secondary issue that certainly helped to set the stage. The cold nor'easterly, building sea state, dropping temperature, and length of darkness all conspired to turn a familiar "milk run" into a survival situation, and I couldn't help but think of how fate had also played a cruel role in the outcome of this incident.

The final part of the recovery is extracting the victim from the water, and the physical condition of both rescuers and the rescued affects how difficult this will be. There is a risk of losing hold of the person, as can be seen in the photo at left, where the homemade sling is very high. If the victim reaches for the lift line, his arms could slip through the loop. A stern swim step can be helpful, but in a seaway the vessel's pitching motion can cause harm to the victim. Using a halyard to hoist the victim near the shrouds is a viable alternative. In the photo on the right a short section of line or sheet tail and a winch are used as an "elevator" boosting the victim out of the water. This technique needs practice and only works well for those familiar with the effect of a pitching and rolling boat in a seaway.

SINGLEHANDED AND DOUBLEHANDED COB METHODS

The worst-case scenario is faced by the single-hander whose COB nightmare is watching the vessel voyage on crewless. The solo sailor's last, long-shot hope may be a towline linked to a self-steering or autopilot disconnect or an electronic remote—and failing that, not much else. Rightly perceiving the threat, singlehanders must prevent an over-the-side incident. Staying clipped-in at all times is critical.

Nearly as challenging a situation is a double-hander suddenly becoming a singlehander. The challenge lies in steering the vessel while keeping the victim in sight, and at the same time coping with the sails, position recording, and other steps in the routine. All this is even more difficult with the wind up, and if the breeze is enough to drive the boat near hull speed, furling or dousing the headsail becomes vital. A Lifesling recovery helps to streamline the process.

drop the jib. This reduction in sail area is especially important in heavier winds, because once the victim has the line and slips on the horseshoe float, dragging him or her through the water can be very dangerous. Stopping the boat after contact is made can also be a challenge if only one person is left on board, but if the jib has already been furled or dropped, all it takes is a head-to-wind turn and release of the mainsail halyard to stop the boat in its tracks. Once the vessel is stopped, the line to the victim can be hauled or winched in and a ladder, swim step, or halyard used to bring the victim back aboard.

No extra points are given for rescuing a victim under sail. It's true that a spinning propeller is dangerous, but far more lethal is a vessel that never gets back to the person in the water. Starting the engine, keeping it in neutral, and using it as needed to help control the final approach (after checking for lines in the water) is prudent seamanship. In some short-handed scenarios, a Lifesling rescue under power may prove the best option. Naturally, the engine should be in neutral in the final approach to the victim, and as soon as contact is made, the engine should be shut off. *(continued page 448)*

CORINTHIANS' AND MIDSHIPMEN'S RESPONSES TO CREW OVERBOARD

The following observations relate to crew overboard recovery maneuvers practiced by two very different crews. Members of the Philadelphia Corinthian Sailing Club were representative of keelboat sailors across the nation in age, skill, and gender. The Navy midshipmen had a higher level of fitness and agility and also tended to push their boats more aggressively, mandating a need to be as reflexive with a rescue maneuver as they were with a spinnaker takedown. Looking closely at how each group performed COB drills sheds light on the challenges involved.

First of all, both groups demonstrated how problematic a new boat and new crew can be. The net effect of unfamiliarity was reduced response capabilities. One of the things most evident on the J/37 that the Corinthians used in their training sessions was the less-than-reflexive trimming and steering caused by an unfamiliar deck layout and steering response. Both the midshipmen and Corinthians proved how quickly teamwork and boat-handling skills improve with repetition of each technique. The need for cohesiveness and vessel awareness in a safety maneuver is the reason that US Sailing and race organizers around the world require racing crews to sign off on having practiced COB recoveries.

By the end of the training session, both groups demonstrated an ability to multitask and quickly cover the requisite shout-position fix-steer-throw aspects of the recovery drill. The biggest problem was developing the "three things at once" spatial awareness of vessel movement, true wind direction, and victim's location that is vital to the success of any recovery maneuver. The nemesis for many was not attending to the true wind and attempting to return to the victim with the breeze well aft, which made slowing down impossible. As noted for years among midshipmen at the Naval Academy and participants at the U.S. Merchant Marine Academy's Safety at Sea seminars, there's a direct correlation between time spent helming in race starts and exceling in COB maneuvers. It's also worth noting that those who regularly sail on and off a mooring, rather than keeping their boat in a slip, also have an easier time executing overboard recoveries. It takes a familiarity with close-quarters boat handling to place a boat where it belongs in COB maneuvers.

Another variable was the leadership displayed during each recovery attempt. The helmsperson who ran the drill and displayed the ability both to effectively steer and to lead rallied his or her crew into a more functional team. The most effective dialogue during the initial phase of a recovery included hastening COB gear deployment, assigning crew to specific tasks, and double-checking that the position had been recorded. The good communicator also informed the crew what would happen next and who would have a lead role in sail handling or in an aspect of victim recovery.

The Corinthians adjusted quickly to the helm characteristics of the J/37, yet its responsiveness surprised sailors accustomed to more traditional sailboats. Those familiar with long-keel, highly directionally stable cruising boats had a tendency to oversteer at first but quickly discovered that when maneuvering to the victim, a boat with a modern underbody and responsive helm was a big plus.

Dan Rugg stressed that practice conditions were optimum: daylight, flat seas, and fair weather. He also noted the drill awareness factor in play eliminated the shock of an actual incident. He stressed that these missing variables can greatly impact (continued next page)

▧ *Top: The J/37 used by the Philadelphia Corinthian Sailing Club in COB training. Above: Throwing a Lifesling to a person in the water.*

CORINTHIANS' AND MIDSHIPMEN'S RESPONSES, CONTINUED

■ *The agile crew aboard Navy 44 MKI sloops have no trouble adapting to the demands of the quick-stop maneuver. Note that they are wearing Type III life jackets during practice, a program prescription that's mandatory when the water temperature in the early spring is below 60°F.*

the response, and only by practicing with a regular crew can you improve the odds in favor of the victim.

The lesson learned by the Corinthians during this training session was that the quick-stop maneuver, though well suited to youthful midshipmen and appropriate for many round-the-buoys sailors, may not be the best bet for every crew. Similar findings were voiced during the 2005 San Francisco trials.

On the one hand, the quick-stop maneuver keeps a boat closer to the person in the water. But the abrupt stop can be complicated by a spinnaker and double-digit boat speed or by appendages such as running backstays or a preventer. Shorthanded crews are certainly better off with a Lifesling tow to the victim and the added value of having the person in the collar and ready to haul or hoist aboard as soon as he or she is brought alongside. Regardless of the recovery process chosen, it's vital that all crewmembers have spent time practicing it. Practice may not make the maneuver perfect, but it will make it a lot more likely to succeed.

Other Recovery Maneuvers: Figure Eight, Fast Return, and Deep-Reach Return

Recovery maneuvers carried out under sail can be separated into two categories: those using only tacking and those that also incorporate a jibe. The quick-stop maneuver endorsed by US Sailing is the most popular example of the latter. When a quick-stop maneuver is initiated during a beat, the first step is to tack, leaving the headsail backwinded, which stops the boat in its tracks. The next phase involves bearing off, getting rid of the headsail, and sailing deep enough prior to jibing to allow for a close-reach approach to the victim. This maneuver keeps the victim close at hand, but the initial tack and backwinding can be difficult in a heavy breeze, and the subsequent jibe becomes quite an undertaking.

The figure eight, fast return, and deep-reach return are all variations on a reach-away/tack/approach-the-victim maneuver that starts with the vessel intentionally sailing away from the person in the water. The idea is that the reach-away leg will last only a few boat lengths before tacking, but unless the crew has practiced well and is extremely disciplined, the actual distance sailed away from the victim will stretch well beyond the suggested two to five boat lengths—especially if a preventer is set or a spinnaker is flying. The upside is that there's neither a rail-burying backwinded tack nor a jibe to further complicate an already-chaotic scenario.

All of the figure-eight derivative maneuvers are like the quick-stop technique in that they involve a COB shout, flotation deployment, position marking, and role assignments. Yet there are key differences:

- ◆ Figure eight. The initial response is to reach off approximately five boat lengths, tack, drop or furl the jib, and return to the victim via a broad reach that rounds up into a close reach as the final approach is made.

- ◆ Fast return. This variation on the figure eight cuts the separation in half by defining the tack point as two to three boat lengths from the victim, and it leaves sails up and flogging during the pickup.

- ◆ Deep-reach return. In this variation—promoted by the California Sailing Academy—the leg away from the victim is a deeper reach. The tack is made after just two boat lengths of separation, and on the return close reach to the victim the sheets are cast free and the sails left to flog. The objective is to pick the victim up on the leeward side with the boom and headsail flailing away.

The latest modification to the figure eight has been developed by U.S. Naval Academy head coach Jahn Tihansky, who starts the maneuver by tacking into a heave-to position and getting control of the circumstance. The midshipmen then bear away and after just a few boat lengths tack over, heading onto a deep reach, dropping the jib, and when the angle is right for a close reach toward the victim the crews bring the boat onto a reach and can feather the main to add or decrease power.

Even though tack-only recoveries are easier to accomplish than a quick-stop maneuver, especially in heavier winds, several inherent pitfalls should be considered. The most significant is the initial necessity to sail away from the victim, another reason that USNA's added heave-to start to the figure eight makes sense. It's tough enough to minimize this dangerous separation during daylight drills with a flat sea, modest breeze, and a crew knowing what's about to happen. When the practice scenario is replaced by a 0300 real-world encounter in 20-knot-plus conditions, all bets about keeping the separation distance to just a few boat lengths are off. The shock of such an encounter can delay reactions, and when a vessel is reaching at 7 or 8 knots, a boat length flies by in 3–4 seconds. A 2-minute spinnaker takedown—which would be a creditable performance under the circumstances—can leave a victim a quarter-mile away. The "speed kills" slogan so apt on the highway applies equally to overboard recoveries.

One of the key benefits of all tack-only maneuvers occurs when the vessel is head to wind, midway through the tack, and the victim's location is noted. The reference used is an imaginary line perpendicular to the centerline of the vessel, and the objective is to note whether the victim is situated above or below that reference line. This tells the person at the helm how deep to steer prior to turning onto a close reach for the final approach.

The most common problem in any recovery is that the helmsperson fails to get far enough downwind and is thus forced to make the final approach on a beam reach. This makes it difficult to depower the boat, and the result is a victim "fly by" at a speed that makes recovery almost impossible.

Summary of Crew Overboard Options

The accompanying table summarizes and compares crew-overboard recovery maneuver options. In addition, different techniques work better in certain situations:

- ◆ Quick-stop. This requires a spontaneous reaction of the crew but keeps the victim close at hand. When sailing on the wind, the maneuver entails a jibe, and heavy weather can make this much more difficult. It's best suited to fully crewed vessels not moving at extreme speeds.
- ◆ Figure eight. This is a simple sail-away-and-tack-

CREW-OVERBOARD RECOVERY TECHNIQUES

Method	Proximity	Ease	Full Crew	Short-handed
Quick-stop	excellent	good	very good	fair
Figure eight	fair	excellent	very good	good
Fast return	very good	good	very good	fair
Deep-reach	good	very good	good	good
Lifesling	very good	good	good	excellent
Under power*	very good	very good	very good	excellent

*Prop hazard is an issue during rescues under power.

to-return maneuver that lessens the challenge of boat handling but introduces the risk of losing sight of the victim. This technique can be more feasible for less skilled, shorthanded crews, especially in heavy-air situations.

- ◆ Fast return. This technique hinges on making a tack within two to three boat lengths. This recovery's need for instant response and all-sails-flying agile boat handling makes it more suited to one-design daysailors in light to medium conditions.
- ◆ Deep-reach return. This calls for a tack at two boat lengths. Sheets are cast off, and the approach is made to keep the victim in the vessel's lee. Like the fast return, this all-sails-up recovery is most viable in daylight and round-the-buoys conditions when all hands are on deck and ready to respond.
- ◆ Lifesling. This combination of a life ring and waterski tow rope allows a shorthanded crew to turn a near miss into a snag-the-victim success story. The approach method varies depending on boat design and crew skill, but the concept of towing a lifeline to the victim remains the same.
- ◆ Under power. A surprising number of ocean racers and shorthanded cruisers have successfully recovered crew overboard using the auxiliary engine either for assistance or as the primary power for maneuvering. This is especially true when running before a strong breeze. In such cases, by the time the spinnaker is down, the victim is well to windward. Naturally it's essential to check for sheets over the side and recognize the danger of a spinning prop.

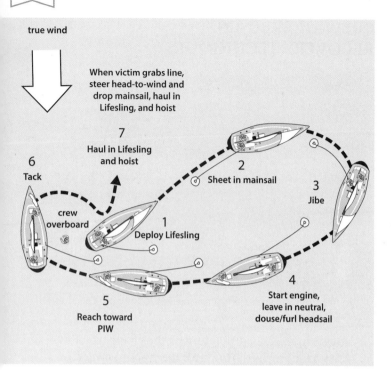

true wind

When victim grabs line, steer head-to-wind and drop mainsail, haul in Lifesling, and hoist

7
Haul in Lifesling and hoist

6
Tack

crew overboard

1
Deploy Lifesling

2
Sheet in mainsail

3
Jibe

4
Start engine, leave in neutral, douse/furl headsail

5
Reach toward PIW

 The Lifesling recovery under sail is akin to towing a waterski tow rope to a skier. 1. Deploy the Lifesling. 2. Sheet in mainsail. 3. Jibe. 4. Start engine but leave in neutral, douse or furl the headsail. 5. Reach toward the victim. 6. Tack. 7. When victim grabs line, steer head-to-wind, drop mainsail, shut off engine, haul in Lifesling, and hoist the victim aboard. In a strong breeze use the figure eight.

There is no perfect crew-overboard rescue technique. You need to test each alternative, and not just on a light-air Sunday afternoon but at sea in varying conditions and at night. A fender lashed to a milk crate with a tethered strobe can play the role of a COB victim. After your sea trials, settle on the technique that best fits the handling characteristics of your boat and the skills of your crew. Then practice regularly using a musical-chairs approach, giving differing responsibilities to all but the chosen victim, who is sent below to think about what it would be like in the water. Finally, recognize that preventing a crew-overboard incident is the only alternative that comes with a guarantee.

ABANDONING SHIP

How and when to abandon ship? This infrequent and unwelcome decision induces highly chaotic reactions steeped with anxiety, yet requires a multifaceted response. The first challenge is knowing when to curtail the damage control effort and switch gears into abandon-ship mode. More often than not, it's the intensity of a fire or the level of the water in the cabin that says it all.

 The Lifesling is an elegantly simple device that can be a great COB recovery asset for a shorthanded crew. Be sure that the Dacron tail is secured to a firmly attached part of the boat, add a water-activated light to the horseshoe, and stuff (don't coil) the floating polyester line into the bag. A person inside the horseshoe should rotate so that they are away from the direction of pull. Stopping the boat as soon as the victim is in the sling is essential.

A damage control effort carried on past the point of futility can jeopardize the abandon-ship process, especially when the crew is shorthanded. Commercial mariners refer to an abandon ship bill, a formal set of details that lay out what must be done. It is often prudent to make contact with rescue personnel when the damage control commences, to alert them to the situation. Once you have decided to abandon ship, a Mayday should be sent. There's usually a need to gather gear, ship's papers, an EPIRB, and perhaps a satellite telephone into a waterproof abandon-ship bag. Each crewmember should put on clothes that lessen the chance of hypothermia and don a dry suit, survival suit, or foul-weather gear. If time allows, gather up extra water and supplies. Launch the raft and secure it alongside as the crew and vital gear are transferred into the raft. The less time you have for this process, the more demanding it becomes and the more essential it is to have a good raft and a well-trained crew. (See the sidebar Step-by-Step Guide to Abandoning Ship.)

Most life rafts have a zipper to control the main opening(s), an aperture that, if not held closed, could become intolerable as well as unsafe in heavy weather and cold conditions (see later section on life rafts). Zippers vary in size, and some are simply much more rugged than others. If a zipper fails, it's important to have backup ties sewn in place. Many manufacturers sew in a series of simple loops or tabs along the perimeter of the zipper's arc that can be used to lash the openings closed with an emergency seal.

Once the raft has been launched and inflated, if rigging related to a dismasting is not an obstacle, it can be brought alongside a sinking vessel for the crew to transfer directly into the raft without jumping into the sea. A large opening is helpful for boarding but becomes a disadvantage once everyone is aboard. When a boat is abandoned due to a fire or rapid sinking, it may be necessary to enter the water before entering the raft, in which case the best method is to jump in close to where you can grab the painter and pull yourself to the life raft rather than attempting to swim to it. It may be possible to snap your harness tether to the raft's painter and remain attached all the way to the raft. Wet clothing, a survival suit, or even an inflated PFD can make climbing into a raft quite cumbersome. My son Eric, a professional mariner and ex-naval officer, ranks boarding aids as a raft's most important safety feature, saying, "A raft doesn't do you any good if you can't get in it."

Crews encumbered by the stress and strain of a survival situation are often near exhaustion when it comes time to get into a raft. Cold water further saps their strength. Research has shown that living through the first 10 minutes after abandoning ship greatly increases one's odds of survival, and getting into the life raft is a major focus of this effort.

The Bligh and Shackleton era of privation and self-rescue has given way to an attitude toward offshore survival that enlists modern technology and a floating shelter and relies on the ability to summon help. Phase one involves getting the raft launched and inflated and the crew transferred. Phase two is communications, both passive (raft color and reflec-

STEP-BY-STEP GUIDE TO ABANDONING SHIP

The abandon-ship process should go like this:

- Fire SOLAS flare(s), activate at least one EPIRB, and issue a Mayday call via VHF or SSB radio or satphone.
- Gather gear, satphone, PLBs, medications, passports, credit cards, cash, eye glasses into grab bag.
- Check that the raft painter is secure.
- Launch the raft.
- With the painter secured and on a short scope, yank to inflate the raft.
- Tie the raft alongside.
- Transfer crew directly from the boat to the raft if possible—and from the water to the raft only if necessary.
- Make sure the EPIRB(s), PLB(s), VHF, grab bag, and extra water have been transferred.
- Count crew and check once more for essentials: EPIRB, water, ditch kit (grab bag).
- Cut the painter and paddle clear of the sinking vessel.
- Deal with any medical issues and set a lookout.
- Reassure the crew and set up a command structure.
- Review raft instructions.
- Bail; keep watch; inventory gear; catch or make water.
- Establish a signaling plan.
- Build morale.

Tossing a life raft into the water means that the crew is about to abandon ship. A raft should never be launched prior to the decision to abandon ship, because its painter can be torn free or a dismasting can destroy the raft.

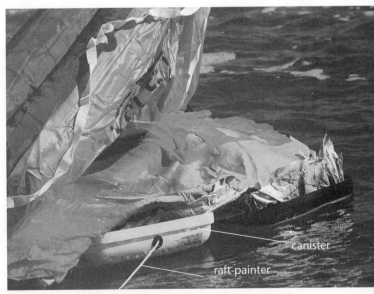

canister

raft painter

Once all the scope of the life raft's painter has been pulled from the canister, the rope jerks on the firing plunger that releases the gas into the raft buoyancy tubes and arch. The clamshell container separates and the vacuum bag splits.

tive tape) and active (signaling gear such as lights, mirrors, and flares). Hopefully, an abandon-ship bag arrives on the raft with the crew including a VHF radio, an EPIRB, and perhaps even a satellite phone. These items augment the call for help and justify the inflatable life raft's sit-and-wait design. Without the signaling gear, you're simply a tiny speck on a vast ocean, the very circumstance that forced many early mariners to sail their life boats to safety or perish. If you're voyaging in areas where immediate rescue is unlikely, a SOLAS-approved raft might be the right choice, along with a watermaker or two.

In all situations, keep in mind that your best chances for survival are still with your own boat, not your life raft. This was clearly demonstrated in the 1979 Fastnet Race, in which a serious storm crossed the Irish Sea just as the race fleet was most vulnerable to its effects. The tragic toll included fifteen deaths and twenty-three vessels sunk or abandoned. Some of the abandoned vessels were still afloat the morning after the storm, whereas some of the crew who had abandoned them were dead, having perished either while getting into a life raft or later. Unless water is lapping at the deck and a sinking is imminent,

stay with your boat. If your vessel's not on fire, you should wait until you have to step *up* into the life raft before crying out, "Abandon ship."

CHOOSING A LIFE RAFT

A good life raft not only prolongs your ability to survive after abandoning ship but also enhances your chances of being rescued. Despite the fact that some rafts can be trimmed up by collapsing water ballast bags and actually sailed downwind at a knot or two, the real hope for rescue is being found by others. This may mean a passing ship's crew seeing your yellow, orange, or red canopy, or a spotlight hitting the reflective tape at night. As mentioned, signaling mirrors, flares, water surface streamers, VHF radios (marine and aviation), an EPIRB and PLB, a search-and-rescue transponder (SART), AIS transponder, and cell and satellite phones can all play a role in getting yourself noticed by others.

Picking the right life raft starts with an evaluation of the risks and exposure you may encounter. In warm inshore and coastal waters, hypothermia and

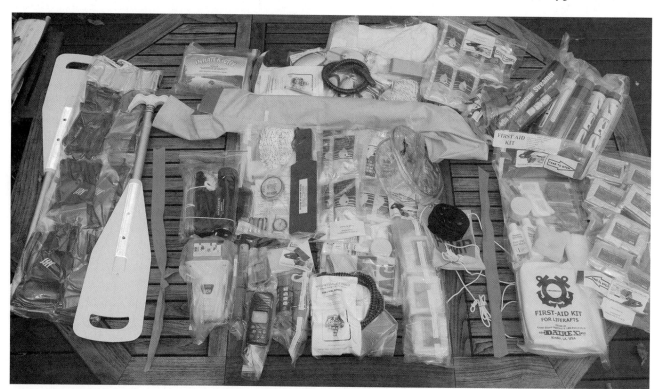

There are huge variations in what is packed in non-SOLAS-approved rafts. Some manufacturers offer extensive "load-outs" as an extra. Having an EPIRB, VHF radio, watermaker, and good first-aid kit added to the raft makes sense but adds weight and bulk. A grab bag can also be useful, but crews have been known to leave it behind. A full kit should include paddles, bailer, sea anchor, sponges, repair kit, repair plug set, repair clamps, relief valve stoppers, pump, raft ID tube (includes a document listing vessel name and primary contacts), heaving line, utility knife, first-aid kit, signal card, seasick pills, seasick bags, notebook, flashlights, extra batteries and bulbs, measuring cup, water bag, fishing kit, radar reflector, raft instructions/inventory, thermal blankets, water packs, rations, safety scissors, can openers, sunscreen, thermal gloves, compass, tools, flares (rocket, hand-held, and smoke), whistle, mirror, rescue streamer, and dye marker.

heavy gales are less likely, and assistance is closer at hand. Consequently, a lighter-duty, less expensive coastal-model life raft may suit your needs. If you're cruising offshore (20 miles or more from the coast) or transiting cold water, however, your life raft needs to

Ballast bags fill with water and help prevent a life raft from capsizing in heavy weather. If a capsize does occur, the nylon webbing handhold helps a crew to heel the overturned raft and turn it back over. The large + sign is made of SOLAS reflective tape. Note the large gas cylinder, another sign of a SOLAS-approved life raft.

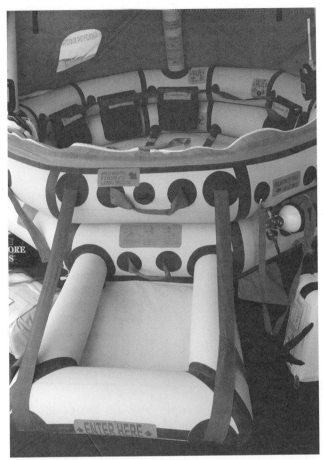

Getting into a life raft has proven a tough challenge for less agile crew, and manufacturers have responded with the addition of buoyant entry platforms and other boarding aids.

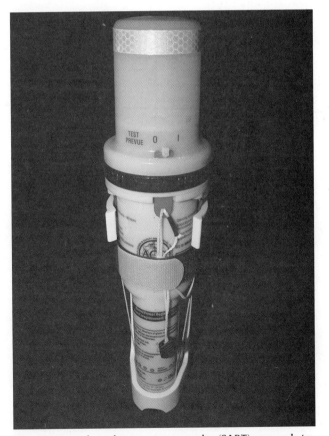

Life rafts for the recreational market are not as tightly controlled as are those for Coast Guard–inspected vessels, which must meet SOLAS standards. There are many differences among brands, and looking closely at what each offers is important. In this cluster of six-person life rafts, the one on the right is the only SOLAS raft; its tubes are of large diameter and its canopy is small.

This search-and-rescue transponder (SART) responds to radar signals by intensifying the return echo to make a nearly radar-invisible object like a life raft stand out clearly. SARTs are mandatory on commercial life rafts, and ship bridge crews as well as helicopter pilots attest to how well they enhance a target.

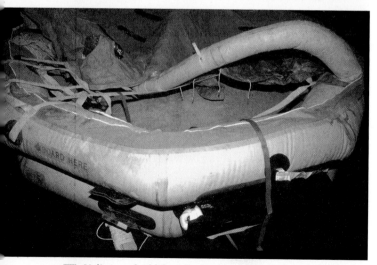

Valise-packed life rafts (top) are stored in a dry locker and can save the weight of a fiberglass canister, which by itself often weighs between 12 and 35 pounds. Rafts in either type of storage can be vacuum sealed (middle), better protecting the raft and its contained equipment from moisture intrusion. The life raft at bottom was not vacuum sealed, and water in its storage locker caused catastrophic damage, unnoticed until the raft was deployed at a safety training event.

be capable of coping with more significant seas and lower temperatures. When you abandon ship you put all your eggs in one basket, and you'll want that basket to be a good one.

Comparing different models of offshore life rafts is a little like grading graduate students at a good university: almost all of them are laudable, but each has a slightly different way of getting the job done. Typically there are more similarities than differences, but small nuances can become a big deal. Good components and simplicity often trump complexity and extra expense. Most rafts have two independent gas-inflated tube structures, water-ballast bags, and a canopy cover. Many rafts are sanctioned under at least one recognized marine life raft standard. The following discussion is meant to help you zero in on important criteria when it comes time to pick what's arguably your boat's most important piece of safety equipment.

Life Raft Standards

Commercial and military interests know the relationship between lifeboats or life rafts and survival at sea, and following the *Titanic* tragedy, more and more maritime agencies set standards for the structure and attributes of life rafts and other lifesaving devices. The IMO SOLAS convention set standards for commercial rafts, and these have become the benchmark by which all other rafts are measured.

Until recently, recreational life raft design and construction in the United States was a self-regulated industry in which manufacturers set their own design criteria, which might or might not comply with commercial, U.S. Coast Guard, SOLAS, and other raft regulatory bodies. But the recently completed European ISO Standard 9650 defines what a recreational life raft should be capable of enduring and how it should be built, and international raft companies and many domestic builders now manufacture their products to this standard. To complicate the issue, aviation life raft standards and the marine version of ISO standards differ, and compliance with one does not necessarily mean compliance with the other. The marine standards place higher importance on stronger, more durable material than the aviation version of the ISO standard.

The ISAF is another player in the regulatory game, and their life raft design parameters must be met by a competitor wanting to participate in a Category 0, 1, or 2 offshore race. ISAF mandates SOLAS rafts for Category 0 races (races held in the most extreme oceanic conditions) and also recognizes SOLAS rafts for all other events, a further endorsement of SOLAS as the gold standard of inflatable life rafts. Given the rea-

This large-canopy ISO raft is designed to meet the offshore recreational raft standards and still be compact and light.

Only a 2-foot by 2-foot space is allotted to each crew-member in a life raft, which is one reason why a four-person crew may want a six-person raft, as shown here. Another reason is that the six-person raft is more capsize-resistant due to its larger dimensions.

sonable prices of SOLAS rafts—in some cases less than recreational rafts—more would be seen aboard boats headed offshore were it not for the greater weight and bulk of the canisters plus the extra water and survival gear stowed aboard commercial rafts. When the chips are down, rafts meeting ISO Standard 9650 are very good, but SOLAS-approved rafts are even better.

Further guidance is found in ISO Standard #9650-1 (International Standard for Small Craft–Inflatable Liferafts): rafts built and maintained to ISO Type I standards should provide "a reasonably safe refuge for a shipwrecked person awaiting rescue" and should be "designed for extended voyages, where high winds and significant wave heights may be experienced, but excluding abnormal conditions such as hurricanes." Most notably, these rafts are not for "voyaging in extreme zones (e.g., Southern Oceans)." After investigating the Sydney-Hobart Race disaster of 1998, the Australian government mandated that racers in future events should carry SOLAS-grade life rafts. Put these findings together, and you start to get a feel for how the experts view the hierarchy of raft types. None comes with any guarantee of survival in all conditions; as one industry expert put it, "If the conditions are bad enough to cause your primary vessel to founder, how much can you expect from a 100-pound life raft?" The answer is—quite a bit.

Modern inflatable rafts are made of tough nylon fabrics that have been coated, or calendared, with natural or synthetic rubber to make them airtight. The tear strength of the material and seams is sufficient to withstand impact loads associated with breaking seas and abrasion from curious sea creatures.

How tough is tough enough is hard to answer, and the survivors of shipwrecks who tout one brand of raft or another are both fortunate and justifiably biased. Statistics regarding life raft failure are slim, and whether particular cases of fatalities are due to noninflation of a raft, its destruction by the elements, or failure to board a functioning raft remains for the most part unknown. Cruisers and racers in the cold, gale-swept high latitudes are without question better off with a SOLAS raft. If you have neither the room nor the ability to handle the larger canister and heavier weight, consider a valise ISO raft that features material of the same denier as a SOLAS raft.

Life Raft Weight and Stowage

The heaviest six-man rafts weigh about 60% more than the lightest, but the in-canister weight variation among six-person rafts is nearly 100%, the difference being due to other gear packed with the raft and the weight of the canister itself. In my testing, scrutiny of the heaviest raft revealed a 39-pound canister, 38 pounds of rations and safety equipment (including water, food rations, and SOLAS flares), and a larger gas bottle for faster inflation in colder weather. By comparison, the lightest raft (an ISO recreational raft, not a heavy duty SOLAS product) was housed in a high-tech laminate canister that weighed just over 12 pounds. The heavy SOLAS-A survival pack found in the first raft mentioned and its hefty canister are part of the SOLAS requirements. At the time this book is going to press the lightest six person ISO/ISAF raft weighs 74 pounds (valise) and the lightest

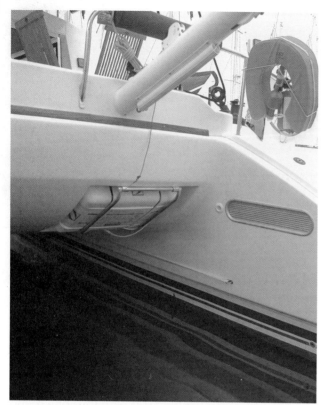

🚩 *A quick-to-deploy life raft is an asset aboard any offshore voyager as long as the locker or recess can prevent it from being torn free inadvertently. This bracketed canister-stowed raft is likely to stay put longer than will the strobe and horseshoe buoy.*

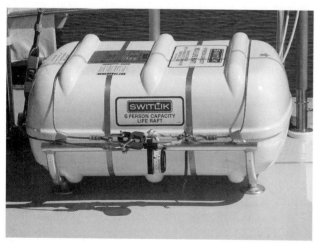

🚩 *This mulitihull carries a canister-stowed ISO-compliant raft; however, water pressure induced by fast reaching in a developed seaway will test the canister's seal.*

SOLAS six-person raft weighs 152 pounds (canister plus B pack).

Another issue is the float-free and self-release capability of a raft. Many manufacturers offer canister mounting brackets that are or can be equipped with a hydrostatic release mechanism for the automatic release of the raft should the vessel sink rapidly and the crew fail to manually deploy the raft in time. The

concept is simple: if the raft and vessel submerge, mounting water pressure causes the hydrostatic release to fire, unlatching the canister from its cradle. As the raft floats toward the surface, residual air in the canister and the deflated raft oppose the pull of the sinking vessel, creating enough tension in the painter to act as a surrogate tug on the inflation line. This uplift idea holds merit in theory, but having participated in the testing of many vacuum-packed rafts, I've seen the practical limitations: vacuum packing leaves so little residual air, and the resulting buoyancy creates so little up-thrust, that some hard-to-pull lanyards would not trigger inflation. A float-free capability is a great idea, but for these reasons, as well as rigging clutter, hydrostatic release malfunctions, and Murphy's Law, a manually deployed life raft is a much better bet.

Life raft stowage location is a challenge on a sailboat. A strong, fit person may be able to heft and drop over the lifelines a raft of about 100 pounds or so, but doing this in the dark on a deck that's awash or on fire and heaving violently significantly complicates the job. ISAF racing rules limit locker stowed rafts to 88 pounds (40 kg). Placing a raft where it will not be prematurely launched by a boarding sea yet can be slid over the side is the ideal, but such locations are hard to find. All too often the place of choice is high on the coachroof, and the brackets are bolted through a deck that was never intended to carry the load associated with a wave trying to shear the raft from its perch. The worst-case scenario is that the raft and mounting bracket rip away, resulting in a large hole in the cabintop and an anguished crew left with a sinking boat and a runaway raft. The value of a structurally sound mounting point that can handle the loads imposed by breaking seas is clear. I was disappointed recently to see one manufacturer show a life raft clamped to a stern pulpit, a structure not intended to take such loads and an invitation to lose the raft as well as the lifelines in conditions where both are needed most. It's sad to see how little attention naval architects give to raft storage and the life-or-death deployment process.

A life raft should be located in a spot that's accessible, secure, and unlikely to be trapped amidst the debris of a dismasting. The best solution is a dedicated raft housing designed into the stern of the vessel that allows access even if the boat has rolled over. Few yacht designers add such a location, so finding the next best alternative is a matter of weighing the options. Avoid attaching the mounting bracket to a vulnerable stern pulpit or bolting the canister support to a part of the coachroof that is not reinforced. Be sure also that there's a well-attached pad eye for attaching the pendant.

SAFETY AND SECURITY IN THE AGE OF MODERN PIRATES

The implication of piracy for cruisers headed to foreign lands is significant. Well over 90% of the world's countries and coastlines remain in the hands of friendly, law-abiding citizenry, but cruisers need to note other regions and steer clear of these troubled waters. Americans and other Western democracies have an inherent sense of freedom and the rule of law, but this precept does not have universal acceptance. In certain regions of Latin America, drug cartels have created a lawlessness that borders on near-anarchy, and this gang culture has spilled over to waterborne activities. Even worse are conditions along the northeast coast of Africa and in some parts of Indonesia. In these places the threat of terrorism is significant, and the ungoverned have formed brigades led by warlords. Perhaps worst of all is the near-coastal zone that runs from Somalia to Yemen, a region that's impacted by lawlessness, piracy, and a radical religious insurgency. One result is that the Red Sea route is no longer an alternative for small-craft voyagers making their way around the world. Yachts have been seized and lives lost in this most volatile part of the world. Just 20 years ago it was a preferred passage, when the biggest challenge was the strong northerlies that made progress up the Red Sea difficult.

Sadly, as the vast majority of the world's nations and their coastal waters have become more and more receptive to cruisers, a few egregious examples of a lack of rule of law taint the picture. The key security issue for every crew is to understand what's transpiring in the part of the world where you're headed. The U.S. government and others make it pretty clear where their citizens are welcome and where they are not. Defying common sense and voyaging into an unsettled region raises the risks of a security mishap. The chance of an unwelcome encounter should be enough to keep you away from those areas where bad things are happening.

The debate over whether long-distance cruisers should carry weapons in case of an assault from pirates or thieves has raged for decades, if not centuries. Many see weapons causing more problems than they are worth, often alluding to America's Cup–winning skipper Sir Peter Blake's confrontation with armed pirates in Amazonia. Blake's rifle jammed, and he was shot dead while his unarmed crew, some injured in the melee, survived.

The flip side of the argument is best illustrated by an incident often recounted by the late John Bonds. As mentioned previously, John was a safety advocate, avid ocean racer/cruiser, and retired U.S. Navy Captain who moderated Safety at Sea Seminars, and when his naval career ended, he signed on as the Executive Director of U.S. Sailing. During one of his sail-training cruises with a crew of ROTC midshipmen, he added a couple of M-16 assault rifles to the load-out list because he was headed to the Bahamas in the bad old days when government corruption and drug smugglers held sway. Occasionally cruisers encountered scenes that played out like the old "Miami Vice" TV show, and the chance of being in the wrong place at the wrong time was a valid concern.

During their transit across the Great Bahamas Banks, the ROTC crew were approached in the night by high-speed motorboats that did not respond to radio communication but continued to shadow the sailboat. John's solution was to set up a live-fire training drill off the port and starboard quarters, with the M-16s discharging a line of fire well away from the pursuing motorboats. The immediate reaction of the trailing vessels was to change course and disappear over the horizon. A few months later a commercial airline pilot was cruising aboard his sailboat in the same region near Andros Islands when his crew was confronted by armed attackers on high-powered motorboats. The pilot and his crew were also well armed, and several of the bad guys were killed. This resulted in enough international scrutiny and attention that the narco-terrorists that had taken over Norman's Cay were evicted, and payoffs by cartels to major public officials ceased. The tide turned, and by the mid-1980s, law and order had returned to the Bahamas.

To develop a balanced perspective on security, it's important to stay informed about developing situations in volatile regions and recognize the spillover effect it may have on parts of the world you may intend to visit. Carrying firearms may be appropriate for some, but when doing so one elevates the consequences associated with confrontation. Proponents of weapons on boats compare the absence of weapons to being in a fire without a fire extinguisher, while no-weapons advocates see a handgun-armed skipper confronting a boatload of pirates with AK-47s like being in a five-alarm fire with a tiny fire extinguisher. Both sides agree that steering clear of questionable locations is job number one.

THREE SIMPLE MISTAKES TO AVOID TO STAY OUT OF TROUBLE

Calling for help is a last-ditch effort to save your crew and your vessel. It escalates the situation by putting others at risk as well as placing your own well-

The U.S. Coast Guard has many missions, but their role in aiding those in distress at sea has been a long-standing tradition. A Coast Guard 47 MLB crew conduct a COB recovery drill, readying to make contact with the victim and haul him or her aboard.

being in the hands of others. Distress calls send the brave Coast Guard air and boat crews, Air National Guard, Navy, and other SAR resources into harm's way. They risk their own lives to aid others. In many of these cases, the sailboat or power cruiser should never have left port at that time to begin with. Every mariner should recognize that a call for help puts others at risk, and each skipper should work to avoid three simple mistakes.

First is a departure decision based on fair weather at the moment, ignoring mid- and long-range forecasts. Second is failing to track weather forecasts daily during a coastal or nearshore passage and to amend the voyage itinerary accordingly. And last is the habit of adhering to a calendar-based date for departure rather than one based upon forecasts. Informed decision making will reduce the need for SAR missions and put far fewer sailors, power cruisers, and SAR personnel in harm's way. Chapters 1, 2, and 10 more thoroughly discuss these issues.

14

COMMUNICATIONS

Until relatively recently, going to sea meant truly getting away from it all. Those without electronics were as remote from home and community as an astronaut on the far side of the moon. News of home might come, if at all, from a fortuitous gam with a passing ship, and aid in times of distress could come, if at all, only from a vessel that happened to be in sight. Today, ongoing contact with home, business, and emergency services is perfectly feasible, and how much connectivity you carry on board is a matter of preference and money. There are two quite different benefits of electronic communications: safety and vessel management, and the comfort and convenience of communicating with friends, relatives, and business associates.

Marine communications protocols and limitations are as much bureaucratic as technical. In this era of bandwidth reassignments and hardware innovations, it's hardly surprising that the Federal Communications Commission (FCC) in the United States and the International Maritime Organization (IMO) around the world are much involved. Our discussion here will steer clear of treaties and governing bodies to focus on gear and user information, but we do need to touch upon the internationally agreed communications zones and how they have been set up to make use of differing equipment.

When problems arise beyond a crew's ability to handle, an effective means of raising the Coast Guard or the search and rescue (SAR) assets of another nearby nation is worth its weight in gold. Some might reach into a pocket for a cell phone, but the best option in coastal waters is to switch the VHF to Channel 16 and hail the Coast Guard, or, in extremis, to push the distress button that initiates a digital selective calling (DSC) distress signal on Channel 70.

OCEAN ZONES AND COMMUNICATIONS EQUIPMENT

The IMO has divided the world's oceans into four zones. A1 is the coastal zone out to 30 miles offshore; A2 extends from 30 to 150 miles offshore; A3 covers the remaining vast oceanic realm outside the polar regions; and A4 is the polar regions. Different communications strategies are necessary in different zones.

Coastal (A1) Communications: VHF

In the nearshore region up to 30 miles from the coast, very high-frequency (VHF) radio remains the workhorse aboard recreational and commercial craft. Its latest incarnation moves it from analog to digital operation and incorporates what is known as digital selective calling (DSC), a key role in the Global Maritime Distress and Safety System (GMDSS), a mouthful of words for the international emergency communications system that standardizes equipment and communications procedures around the world. In U.S. waters, the new VHF-DSC technology links a vessel's VHF radio with a GPS receiver, providing the

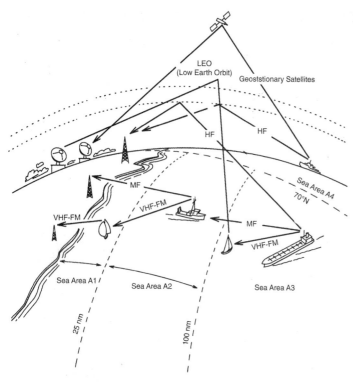

Radio wave propagation determines what communication system to use in a coastal or offshore region. IMO divisions A1 to A3 are based on distance offshore. VHF is useful 20–30 miles with a masthead antenna; MF stands for medium-frequency bands, found on marine single-sideband (SSB) radios (which also offer high-frequency [HF] operation); 100 miles is appropriate for MF transmission.

A remote-access microphone (RAM) allows a VHF radio at the nav station to be controlled from the cockpit, as just one example of an installation. It's a handy feature, but there are also good reasons for a stand-alone handheld instead.

Coast Guard with the vessel's position and an identifying Maritime Mobile Service Identity (MMSI) code unique to that vessel. The U.S. Coast Guard Rescue 21 program (see the Rescue 21 sidebar, page 463) is a VHF safety net that covers all inland waters and coastal regions out to 20 miles. In order to take advantage of the service, a boatowner must acquire a free MMSI nine-digit code, which can be done easily through the BoatU.S. (or US Power Squadrons) MMSI Program approved by the FCC and Coast Guard for recreational vessels navigating within territorial waters. Those voyaging beyond United States waters should instead apply for an FCC MMSI number which is registered with the international database (see sidebar). (Note, to be of most benefit, the VHF needs a GPS input—some newer units come with a built-in GPS but most are set up to be linked to a NMEA 0183/2000 cable from a GPS device.)

If a traditional marine VHF radio call is like a telephone conversation on an old-fashioned party line with eavesdroppers, a VHF-DSC radio call to another boat's MMSI is more like a direct-dialed phone call on a private line. Thus, a VHF-DSC radio is handy for daily communications as well as emergencies, but in an emergency the party-line nature of a Channel 16 call can raise help from other boaters in the local waters.

VHF communication relies on line-of-sight radio wave propagation, and in most conditions no bounce or refraction of radio waves takes place. Thus, VHF transmission distances are limited by the height and efficiency of the sending and receiving antennas. For example, two people with handheld VHF radios sitting in dinghies may have trouble contacting each other if separated by more than a mile or two, whereas the same two sitting in boson's chairs at the mastheads of their boats might be able to communicate over a distance of 10 miles or more. More efficient antennas connected *(continued on page 462)*

VHF ANTENNA INSTALLATION

Racers sometimes resist installing a masthead VHF antenna or use wire of the lightest gauge possible to lessen weight aloft. In emergency situations this has led to communication failures and loss of life. A good VHF installation includes a masthead antenna, RG-8U coaxial cable (or equivalent), and as few connector splices as possible. All too often an excellent VHF installation provides poor performance because the coax connector at the mast step lies drenched in a wet bilge. This is a critical junction point, and care must be taken to elevate the connection and keep it dry.

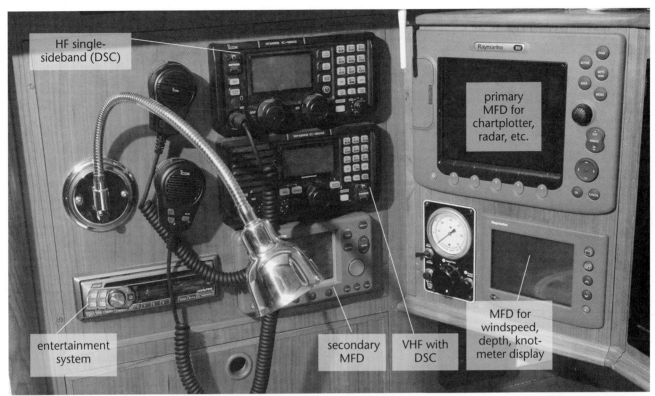

VHF radios are relatively inexpensive and are useful pieces of gear. Having two stand-alone units—one with a masthead antenna and one connected to a rail-mounted whip antenna—makes sense for redundancy and versatility. This installation includes a VHF-DSC radio and a DSC-capable high-frequency SSB transceiver. The latter is capable of broadband tuning, and those licensed to operate on HF amateur (ham radio) bands will appreciate its dual function.

USING YOUR VHF EFFECTIVELY

Maintaining a voluntary radio watch at all times on VHF Channels 16 and 13 (for commercial ships and bridge tenders) makes sense, especially when transiting congested waterways. Voice contact between commercial and recreational vessels can clear up ambiguities as to who's headed where and what maneuvering actions are about to be undertaken. The big challenge for a shorthanded crew engaged in watchkeeping, boat handling, navigation, and communications is allotting time for such communication.

Even in today's world of elevated communications capabilities and security concerns, commercial mariners are accustomed to finding most recreational mariners are a mute presence.

Owners of vessels under 65 feet, especially those of fiberglass construction, should realize that their boats paint a weak signature on radar and can be hard to spot visually. This dictates a proactive approach to collision avoidance, and the vigil should be ramped up when congestion increases and visibility decreases. When a large merchant vessel heaves into view on a course that hints of a close-quarters situation, try to raise the ship on Channel 13; if no response try Channel 16. When making the call, include your latitude/longitude position and a succinct description of your vessel. Give your course and speed and ask the ship's intentions. If you agree with the proposed maneuvers, repeat what will be done and stand by for further clarification. The entire dialogue may take place on Channel 16 on the open ocean, but in coastal regions, switching to another, mutually agreed working channel is mandatory. Channel 13 is often used inshore between ships, tugs, fishing boats, and other commercial interests constantly monitoring that frequency.

I once heard a New York–born radio operator complain that the accent of an Oxford-educated Brit was difficult to understand. The goal, of course, is clear communication—to be well understood when the bilge is filling or the boat's on fire. The key is to realize you must be clearly understood and may therefore need to consciously change how you speak. If you are from the Northeast, for example, slow down your rate of speech, enunciate each word, and be succinct. Effective communication is as much about the person holding the microphone as about how the gear was installed. As a rule, it's far better to speak too slowly than too fast, even in an emergency. A slow Mayday call that can be understood is far better than an unclear fast one.

EMERGENCY COMMUNICATION

All efforts should be made to carry out distress messaging on recognized Global Maritime Distress and Safety Systems (GMDSS) approved equipment and designated frequencies. As described in Chapter 13, the reason for this is the GMDSS link with rescue coordination centers and the assets they are able to quickly deploy. That said, when survival is at stake and preferred communication (comms) links are either not available or inoperative, you need to take advantage of every means at your disposal.

In extremis, frequency allocation and operational restrictions are eased. For example, those with an aviation VHF handheld transceiver in their ditch kit can make 121.5 MHz Mayday calls—this frequency is referred to as a "guard" channel and is internationally monitored by civilian and commercial aircraft (aircraft flying at 10,000' to 30,000' altitude are prime targets for this line-of-sight communication). The two-way communication capability these handhelds offer can, as with a marine VHF unit, be transferred to a life raft. The ever-growing number of aircraft aloft make it a sensible, albeit non-GMDSS, emergency backup. With an EPIRB, a marine VHF handheld, and an aviation VHF stowed in a ditch kit, the long-distance cruiser improves the chance of rescue if their vessel's built-in comms system shuts down or the need to abandon ship arises.

Amateur (ham) radio is another viable emergency communication tactic that has saved lives and proved its worth. With hundreds of thousands of listeners around the world, the chance of getting a Mayday message forwarded or crucial information relayed via ham radio is quite good. There are also valuable fringe benefits from the training one receives in radio theory and antenna function that will help you make better use of marine single-sideband and VHF communications.

Collision Avoidance

For collision avoidance, use your VHF on Channel 13 (the ship-to-ship channel) or Channel 16 (emergency channel). As described in Chapter 9, the Navigation Rules endorse bridge-to-bridge communications as a means of eliminating close-quarters maneuvering confusion. When communicating with a nearby vessel, confirm that the ship you are visually observing or tracking on radar is actually the one you are in radio contact with.

Distress Alerts

◆ **By voice on VHF Channel 16.** Mayday broadcast (see page 463).

◆ **Automated alert by VHF-DSC.** With a GPS signal and MMSI number entered, VHF units and SSB HF radios can automatically broadcast a Mayday with both vessel ID and position piggy-backing on the digital broadcast.

◆ **Visual, sound distress signals (whistle, lights, flares, etc.).** Timing is everything when it comes to preventing collision. All too often a mariner sees what may unfold well ahead of time, but due to an assumption that course or speed correction by the other vessel will alter the outcome, too much precious time goes by. When radio communication efforts to raise the crew on what you assume to be the give-way vessel fail, it's better to shift to whistle and/or flare up light signaling sooner rather than later. When all else fails a white flare can be fired to warn of the potential for collision.

(Note: Changes in frequency coverage—at the time of publication, the USCG has ended monitoring 2182 kHz, but the Canadian Coast Guard and Bermuda Radio continue to do so, and have indicated that they will do so into the near future.)

to more powerful 25-watt fixed VHF radios can extend the range to about 25 miles in optimum conditions. Infrequently, a phenomenon called atmospheric ducting bends VHF transmissions over the horizon in a manner like an SSB ionosphere skip, and VHF communications may take place at distances well over 100 miles. This is rare and unpredictable, however.

As mentioned, coastal VHF communication in the United States has taken a big stride forward with the introduction of DSC and the construction of the Rescue 21 tower and station network. This approach to line-of-sight communications on VHF frequencies adds automated digital emergency calling with position and ID reporting. As also discussed, to acquire

the full array of DSC features, a boatowner must register the radio and acquire an MMSI number. This is the same ID needed for AIS and SSB usage; details about acquiring an MMSI can be found on the Coast Guard website (www.navcen.uscg.gov/mmsi). DSC radios can also be programmed with the MMSI numbers of the stations/vessels you wish to call.

Voice radio traffic should be succinct and descriptive, and operators must recognize that Channel 16 is for hailing and emergencies only. A call initiated on 16 should be brief, such as this:

"Pompano, Pompano, Pompano, this is *Wind Shadow,* Channel 16 (one–six), over."

"Wind Shadow, this is *Pompano,* switching

71 (seven–one)" [a working channel on which to carry out the conversation].

Following are some standard uses of other VHF channels:

- Commercial ship contacts and bridge tenders—use Channel 13
- Conduct radio checks—use Channel 9
- Working frequencies—use Channels 67, 68, 69, 71, 72, and 78a

In safety situations Channel 16 still plays an important role. Three levels of alert are internationally recognized. Sécurité is the lowest threat and is generally used for accident prevention such as when a vessel is underway in fog or crossing a traffic separation zone. A Pan-Pan call is linked to a serious problem on board such as a leak or crew issue that has not yet become an imminent risk to life or threat to the vessel.

Mayday is the call used when imminent threat is present (life at risk or the vessel sinking, on fire, etc.) and there's need for immediate aid from others. The term is repeated three times followed by a brief but clear indication of vessel name, location, problem, and crew on board. Once contact is made with a SAR (search and rescue) shore station, vessel, or aircraft, other details will be requested. But during the initial communication the key information is the Mayday

RESCUE 21

Rescue 21 may sound like a new reality TV show, but it's more than a catchy new name for the United States' Coast Guard's upgraded coastal emergency radio system. The former National Distress Response System utilized voice broadcasts on VHF Channel 16 for emergency traffic, which was often besieged by bogus Mayday calls and extraneous traffic and further hindered by antiquated equipment at coastal stations. The several factors that drove the Rescue 21 revamp included the IMO regulations for A1/A2/A3/A4 marine communication zones and the Coast Guard's commitment to DSC.

As mentioned earlier, each vessel with DSC communications has an MMSI (but these must registered), a unique nine-digit number that identifies the boat. With a VHF-DSC radio connected to a GPS receiver all it takes is a push of a button to send out a digital distress message that includes the vessel's identity and location. This digital signal is received at Coast Guard stations as well as on all DSC radios in the area.

The Rescue 21 is also an effort to curtail hoax calls—which is a very good thing in view of the large number of such calls the Coast Guard receives—but there have been unanticipated downsides as well. One is the fevered reaction among vessels in the vicinity who receive the DSC distress signal and then try to establish voice contact with the vessel in trouble. These calls can overfill Channel 16 and flood Coast Guard communications centers. Another issue is that users are not consistently following up their digital distress messages with voice communications. And there is also some unintended channel switching with DSC radios. There are bound to be growing pains as the new DSC emergency communications system is implemented, and these bugs are being worked out. What does get A+ grades are the position-finding capability of the system and the tower-to-tower coverage out to 20 miles or so.

There's been some question about the impact of the Coast Guard's role within the larger Department of Homeland Security—which has precipitated an increased interest in "maritime domain awareness"—and how use of DSC and the Automatic Identification System (AIS) that tracks vessel movements will affect the Coast Guard's emergency response. Rescue 21 and AIS use the same MMSI numbers, and whether the ongoing escalation of DSC signals and the vastly increased numbers of vessels tracked via the AIS will aid or hamper emergency response is yet to be determined. Already, AIS B signals are being crowded off the screen in high traffic density areas—as AIS signal concentration grows even denser, the effect of the clutter factor may raise unintended issues. (And as AIS becomes more intertwined with search and rescue it's likely to fall under the GMDSS umbrella.)

VHF Channel 16 was originally to have been phased out as the emergency frequency that all commercial ships must monitor in U.S. waters by 2005, but that phase-out was postponed indefinitely. A voice distress call on Channel 16 is still a recognized emergency procedure worldwide.

As of this writing, your best bet is to do an online search for "Rescue 21" to see if the system is fully running in your home waters and in the regions you plan to cruise. It makes sense to upgrade to a VHF-DSC radio connected to GPS, and register it to acquire your MMSI number. If you plan to visit foreign waters, get an FCC (international) MMSI number (see sidebar A Note from BoatU.S. on MMSI Numbers). Study the radio's manual and carefully review the emergency procedures. (In one case report, a crewmember pushed the button marked emergency to activate the system but had not read the manual and did not notice the boldly lettered instruction: "Hold the button down for 5 seconds.") Knowing how to use safety equipment is as important as having purchased it in the first place. Learn what Rescue 21 has to offer, and keep in mind that Channel 16 is still part of the VHF safety network and can be accessed also with a VHF-DSC radio.

status, vessel, location, and nature of the threat. Make sure that those responding to the Mayday read back the lat/lon coordinates.

Cell phones help save lives ashore, and the same is true afloat. The U.S. Coast Guard does not endorse their use as an alternative to marine VHF radios, but cell phones do have a recognized value as a secondary means of communication. Some cellular plans even provide links to the Coast Guard. Cell phones

---

A NOTE FROM BOATU.S. ON MMSI NUMBERS

BoatU.S. MMSI numbers (and those provided by US Power Squadrons) are coded for recreational vessels cruising in U.S. waters only not otherwise required to be licensed; the registrations are downloaded into the U.S. Coast Guard Search & Rescue Database only. FCC-assigned MMSI numbers are coded for international waters and go into the International Search and Rescue Database (ITU). To be accepted into the ITU database, any FCC-assigned MMSI must end in zero. This is why the BoatU.S. MMSI number (or Power Squadrons-issued number) cannot be reused when later applying for an FCC license for international cruising.

---

have performed well in many emergency situations because owners understand how they work. Ideally, a similar level of familiarity should pertain to the VHF radio and other communications equipment on board your boat.

Offshore (A2, A3, and A4) Communications

Beyond the range of VHF ship-to-shore contact, VHF radios still play a key role in bridge-to-bridge communications between vessels that are crossing or nearby. Beyond the coastal zone, however, the lion's share of communication is accomplished by marine single-sideband radios, a technology that has been the offshore mainstay for decades, and new satellite telephone options.

Marine Single-Sideband (SSB) Radio

Just as single-sideband (SSB) radio seemed to be teetering toward retirement along with SatNav, radio-directional finders, and double-sideband AM transceivers, it gained a second wind thanks to its cost-effectiveness and its implementation in the IMO's new plan for worldwide marine communications. Marine single-sideband and amateur (ham) radio frequencies sit side by side in adjacent spectrum bands between 2

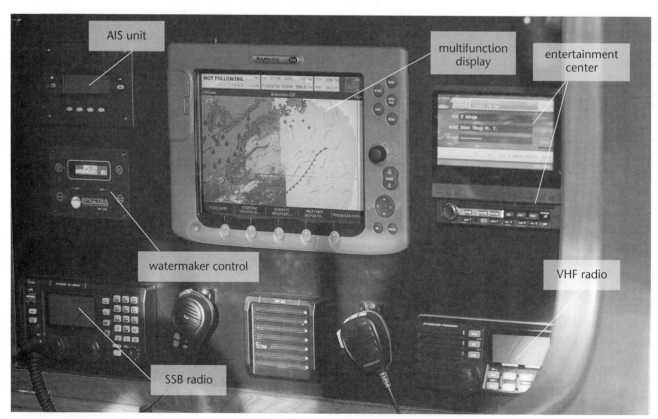

A vessel equipped with VHF, SSB, and satellite telephones covers all three communications bases and stands the best chance of staying in touch worldwide.

and 30 MHz, and some manufacturers offer equipment that functions on both marine and amateur frequencies. The big advantage of SSB radio (which includes both marine and ham radios) is also its biggest drawback: "skip," a feature of radio wave propagation in which the radio frequency (RF) energy bounces back and forth between the ionosphere and the surface of the earth, creating the potential for long-distance communications. In essence it's the opposite of line-of-sight VHF radio wave behavior. Skip-enabled long-range communications is the good news, but the bad news is the finicky behavior of the ionosphere and its ability to close the door on long-range communications. Vertical movement of this layered region of charged particles just above our atmosphere is influenced by the sun's radiation, and everything from the sun's declination and the time of day to the prevailing intensity of sunspot activity can affect SSB propagation. These daily, monthly, and annual changes influence SSB signals and affect long-distance communications. For example, contacting a specific location may be possible only early in the morning and late in the afternoon, or it may require a midday call on another band. Those who assume that a SSB radio is like a telephone with a funny handset and that all it takes is to push a button to call

The modest cost, versatility as a platform for digital text communication, weather forecast reception capacity, and all-stations broadcast reach give SSB radio a compelling value for boaters. The number on the plaque above the unit shown here is the vessel's radio call sign, which is provided by the FCC. Those sailing internationally need an FCC license (there is no test) and an international MMSI number.

home are initially very disappointed. One of the first lessons a new SSB user needs to learn is what band to use and when transmission conditions will be best.

The Coast Guard and other rescue coordination bodies have recognized the value of party-line communications. Having multiple listeners on the same

USING SSB FOR WEATHER INFORMATION

SSB transceivers also unlock NOAA's treasure chest of marine weather information (via the Ocean Prediction Center) available in voice, facsimile, and web download formats. Other nations' broadcasts of fax and voice weather information is also available on marine SSB frequencies.

An easy way to update an offshore forecast is to listen to the National Weather Service's high seas voice SSB broadcast from one of several radio stations maintained by the U.S. Coast Guard. (NMN in the table below is the call sign of the station.)

Broadcasts are made from stations on the U.S.

East Coast, West Coast, and Hawaii and Alaska. Since broadcast schedules and frequencies occasionally change, it's best to download the latest schedule from the U.S. Coast Guard website (http://www.nws.noaa.gov/om/marine/hfvoice.htm) before departure. A small digital recorder may come in handy for recording lat/lon coordinates of fronts and lows. You can plot the location of weather systems on a small-scale chart and update it daily. A way to snag even more data with less labor is to tune in to weather fax broadcasts and attach a laptop with weather fax software.

SAMPLE BROADCAST SCHEDULE, CHESAPEAKE

Chesapeake (NMN) HF Voice Broadcast Schedule (24-hour Clock)					
4426, 6501, 8764 kHz (USB)	0 0330Z[1]	0 0515Z[2]	0 0930Z[1]		
6501, 8764, 13089 kHz (USB)			1 1115Z[2]	1 1530Z[1]	2 2130Z[1]	2 2315Z[2]
8764, 13089, 17314 kHz (USB)			1 1715Z[2]		

[1] Offshore forecasts, hurricane information.
[2] High seas forecast, hurricane information. (Broadcast of hurricane and other weather broadcasts from this station may on occasion be preempted, as the frequencies are shared with other USCG stations.)

VHF VERSUS SSB

From a user's perspective, voice SSB operation has a lot in common with VHF. In both cases, the ubiquitous term "over" is used to separate bouts of transmitting and receiving. Speaking a little more slowly with intentional awareness of good diction pays off. The emergency parlance of Sécurité, Pan-Pan, and Mayday is the same in each. And SSB, like VHF-DSC, has a digital emergency button to broadcast location and the vessel's ID, identified with the same MMSI number.

SSB operation is more complex than VHF, however. There are more options with regard to frequencies, and choosing the right one involves a whole new realm. As mentioned in the text, an operator must learn how to cope with diurnal and periodic changes in the ionosphere, distance to station, time of day, and frequencies. By no means is SSB communication as reliable or convenient as communication with a VHF or satellite telephone. However, those who spend time learning about signal propagation will derive useful benefit from SSB communication. VHF radio is like an automatic transmission and SSB more akin to a stick shift: like learning good clutch work, it takes a little time to learn antenna tuning, frequency selection, and other facets of SSB technology.

frequency can pay off in emergency situations. Another big plus is the price of SSB communications, which includes a moderate cost for hardware and installation but little or no cost for the ongoing service.

Another key reason for the resurgence of SSB among cruisers is SailMail, a relay network that allows sailors to interface their laptops with a global email service via SSB radio. Thanks to this innovation by some gifted West Coast sailor/engineers, both voice and digital communications can now be conducted with SSB radio. A ham operator with an SSB radio enabled for marine as well as amateur bands or a sailor with a marine-only SSB can connect their transceiver to a modem and laptop computer and sign up for SailMail or one of the similar nonprofit marine SSB services that have sprung up. The baud rate is slow, but the price is right, and those wanting email capability from an SSB radio—which is an IMO-approved A2/A3/A4 communications tool—are in luck.

The SailMail annual fee as of this writing is $250, and the purchase of a Pactor modem (about $900) sets you up with remote email to communicate your adventures to friends around the world. With an email address, you can even order parts to be sent to the yacht club in Fiji. The SailMail network offers

good coverage but is contingent upon SSB propagation, and in some countries, operation of SSB requires a special license and may be regulated. Services like SailMail lack sufficient bandwidth and speed to handle graphics, however, or to browse the web.

Marine SSB radios (as stated above, 3–30 MHz radios are SSB, and many allow the operator to work both marine and amateur/ham bands if appropriately licensed) provide free airtime (unlike the fees associated with satellite phones, discussed below), and the international fraternity of ham operators thrives on making long-distance friends, especially when navigating their own radio stations across an ocean. The licensing process has been streamlined, and the information you study is directly applicable to maritime mobile operation. Some long-term and long-distance cruisers on a tight budget see ham radio as the best bang for the buck when it comes to staying in touch.

Several decades ago, while cruising the South Pacific, I used my ham radio and an essential phone patch to connect with a forecaster in the Navy's weather office in Hawaii. His satellite data update helped me avoid an encounter with Cyclone Robert, a storm packing 100-knot-plus winds. The most recent radio warning I had heard had the storm's track moving away from our projected course. The only long-range voice weather warning available in those days was the once-an-hour WWV storm warning broadcast on the time signal frequencies 5, 10, 15, and 20 MHz. These warnings consisted of a storm's lat/lon position and the direction and speed of its movement. But the "real time" satellite images seen by the forecaster showed that the storm's heading had switched from southwest to southeast. His warning gave us time to alter course and avoid all but the outermost wind bands and a very large swell. Both forecasting and communications technologies have improved since then, and in-depth voice and data weather forecasts are accessible via SSB and satellite.

The National Institute of Standards and Technology (NIST) broadcasts on SSB a time and frequency service from stations WWV in Fort Collins, Colorado, and WWVH in Kekaha, Hawaii, commonly known to mariners as "time ticks." Included in these are hourly voice broadcasts of storm warnings for the Atlantic, Pacific, and Gulf of Mexico provided by the National Weather Service.

A lot of commercial, military, and recreational vessels navigate just beyond the A1 coastal zone and out of VHF range of shore stations. The U.S. Coast Guard is revamping its 2- to 3-megahertz SSB equipment to handle traffic in this region. They terminated medium-frequency (MF) band services on 2182/2187.5/2670 kHz including weather broadcasts in August 2013. Many other nations continue to use these and other lower SSB frequencies in the MF band; this part of the communications spectrum is handled by marine SSB transceivers that also operate in the high-frequency (HF) spectrum (4 to 30 MHz) and thus fill the bill for A2, A3, and A4 compliance.

SSB Installation

One more key SSB issue is the importance of the installation itself. Three critical factors must be in place for optimum performance. The first is the recognition that voltage drop is a big enemy. Although it may only take 0.5 amp to run the unit in receive mode, the talk mode draws 15–20 amps. You therefore need #8 heavy-gauge wire to deliver 12-volt DC current to the radio to minimize voltage drop and improve the SSB signal.

Next comes the antenna. For most sailboats, an insulated backstay and an antenna tuner provide the best compromise. A key aspect of SSB radio wave propagation is the need to have an antenna cut to exactly the right length for each frequency on which you wish to operate. To achieve resonance, early ham maritime mobile operators manually adjusted their antenna lengths to within an eighth of an inch using the magic formula (0.25 × wave length = antenna length) for each frequency they worked. Today matching antenna length to frequency is done automatically with an electronic antenna tuner. While not perfect, these devices make switching bands and frequencies a simple turn of the dial or push-button experience rather than a lesson in inductance and impedance.

The third essential ingredient in a successful SSB installation is the creation of a counterpoise, or ground plane, which involves wiring the radio, tuner, and antenna coax cable to a common connection with grounded and bonded metal surfaces, such as ballast, engine block, lifelines, and through-hull fittings. Some builders bond copper foil or screen to the hull's inner skin for this very purpose (see photo). The closer this collection of ground plane metal is to the base of the antenna, the better.

Satellite Phones

The satellite era of communications has revolutionized line-of-sight radio wave propagation. By targeting an orbiting satellite—whether in a geosynchronous location 23,000 miles above the earth or a low-earth-orbit (LEO) satellite a few hundred miles up—a line-of-sight signal can now be bounced or relayed to a destination well beyond the horizon, so the curvature of the earth is no longer an impediment. The big downside is the cost of placing enough

Some builders go to the extra effort of tabbing copper foil to the inner skin of the hull to enhance the SSB ground plane effect. Radio frequency electric current travels on the surface of conductors, and these thin, wide bands of copper foil close to the antenna base act like a radial counterpoise, increasing antenna efficiency. Quite often when technicians measure the standing wave ratio (SWR), a measure of antenna efficiency, it's an inferior ground plane that causes poor readings.

satellites in orbit to provide nearly worldwide coverage, and the resulting cost per minute of "sat time." As with GPS, military and commercial needs have driven the technology, and recreational boaters have benefited.

The various satellite phone systems differ in their quality of voice communications, speed and ability to handle digital data, and type of antenna required. The large dome-shaped antennas used by the Inmarsat A and B systems and the other big-boat installations seen on megayachts and commercial ships house a gimbaled dish that stays locked on a chosen satellite. Such systems provide the best voice quality and data speeds available. Under the thin protective dome lies a gyroscope-stabilized parabolic dish antenna that is fed the azimuth and angle of the satellite and tracks that point in the sky as the vessel yaws, pitches, and rolls. The large dish has better sensitivity and selectivity than smaller versions of the same technology, but the antenna's size and the unit's cost make such systems inappropriate for mainstream cruising boats. Scaled-down systems pioneered by KVH and others have made such fixed installations more practical in boats under 65 feet.

Inmarsat's Mini-M phone provided an answer for those looking for a little sibling of the big-league satellite systems for voice, fax, and data services. Its 10-inch (25 cm) dome fits nicely on an aft pedestal, the current drain is small, and it provides the ability to call home anytime. Small-dome units like the KVH TracPhone and Cobham SeaTel handle data more slowly than large-antenna FleetBroadband systems. It takes a larger-diameter, heavier, much more expensive dish antenna to handle lots of data. Large-diameter FleetBroadband antennas and competing products are seen aboard megayachts and commercial and military craft. Still, KVH offers miniaturized equipment that's attractive to midsize and larger cruising sailboats. Equipment and installation costs of $20,000 may seem steep, but operational costs (minute time) are less than handheld units because of faster baud rates and deeply discounted minute packages. There's also the can't-be-dropped-over-the-side value of having a fixed station at a known location. Compression software allows data and email traffic to be handled reliably.

Handheld satellite phones from Iridium, Globalstar, and Inmarsat utilize low-earth-orbit satellites with an omnidirectional built-in or remote antenna. Handhelds have slower data rates and are not as effective in rough offshore conditions due to the lack of a gyrostabilized dish antenna. These units provide good voice quality and a slow to moderate data-handling capability. All of them offer chargers/docking devices and other options that allow them to be tucked into semipermanent positions near the nav station. Their portability is an added value in an emergency, and their true worth may be discovered when they become part of the abandon-ship bag.

Inmarsat C is another option for a long-distance cruiser, but this system is only for data and does not provide voice communication. Its advantages include its small, conical, omnidirectional antenna, which is easy to mount on deck, and its proven record as an IMO-approved digital communicator, a tracker feature, and an emergency beacon function. The system has gone around the world with racers and cruisers, and despite its notoriously slow baud rate, its reliability is excellent.

An interesting incident in 1998 illustrates the importance of understanding the characteristics of the satellite communication system you're using. Dr. Dan Carlin (World Clinic), an emergency room physician who consults with people facing serious medical issues in remote locations, guided Around Alone sailor Viktor Yasykov through a do-it-yourself surgical procedure on an abscessed elbow that likely saved Yasykov's life. The episode stretched Yasykov's physical limits but also the limits of the Inmarsat's satellite email service he was using. Dr. Carlin was advising Yasykov about a fast-developing medical problem, but the system's store and forward design incorporates a time lag between transmission and reception which can become a number of hours. That may be fine for chitchat but is potentially disastrous in an emergency.

In addition to two-way satellite communications options, even a satellite TV can be taken aboard. Perched on the stern arch of this coastal cruiser are two GPS antennas, a radar dome, a stabilized TV dish, and a low-earth-orbit (LEO) tracker/sat phone remote antenna.

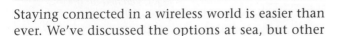 *The portable satellite phone has come of age, and many are now waterproof, energy efficient, and useful gear to take in a life raft. Sat phones like the Imarsat shown here aren't an alternative to an EPIRB, but they provide a backup capability. The Isatphone, Iridium, and Globalstar handhelds all use LEO satellite technology.*

Iridium handheld sat phones have become popular among cruisers and Bermuda racers wanting to harness satellite connectivity without a huge dollar commitment. Its coverage is nearly global, and the number of units in operation exceeds all competitors.

As satellite phone technology continues to evolve, new devices with new features come on the market frequently. Data transmission rates are improving, and some devices now include a button to automatically send a Mayday with your location. Real-time vessel position reporting is included in some systems. With satellite capability one can send engine readings directly to a mechanic or regularly download custom weather forecasts from a private provider such as Commander Weather. Connectivity from foreign ports or high seas locations has never been better.

Sat phone technology is changing rapidly, and the future may involve sat phones connecting with smart phones and navigation apps. Keep in mind that the most advantageous solutions for offshore emergency communications need to fit GMDSS protocols to ensure the highest chances of functionality in an emergency. With a satellite telephone, as well, make sure you have key phone numbers to contact search and rescue centers on a 24/7 basis—not just the number for their daytime main desk.

WI-FI AND THE NETWORKED BOAT

Staying connected in a wireless world is easier than ever. We've discussed the options at sea, but other possibilities open up when you make landfall. Specifically, wi-fi can provide a valuable link for coastal cruisers who spend weeks, months, or years cruising from one hotspot to the next. Much as ham radio caught the interest of serious long-term cruisers several decades ago, wi-fi has become a preferred link to email and the world online.

Wi-fi (wireless fidelity) uses line-of-sight microwave-band radio. The system is used throughout the world.

Wi-fi hotspots, a physical space depending on signal range, vary from the size of a room to a square mile or more. Because wi-fi operation involves both sending and receiving, the signal's transmit power is only half of the equation for operational range; the ability to receive and decode weak signals is the other half. To receive a wi-fi signal on a boat, the antenna may not have to be at the masthead but will perform better if it's well above the deck. Signal-to-noise ratio (SNR) is another vital factor. Competing with wi-fi on or near the 2.4 GHz band are cordless phones, baby monitors, microwave ovens, security cameras, and ham radios, among other things. Ham operators, incidentally, are the FCC-licensed primary operators on this band; wi-fi users are considered unlicensed users and are granted no right to complain about transmissions up to 100 watts by ham operators that can disrupt local wi-fi operation. Interference is not a huge problem, but it does sometimes explain why a setup

NAVTEX

There's something elemental and reassuring about a gadget that automatically turns on, whirs, and sends out a paper ribbon of text weather information, notice-to-mariner updates, and special warnings. The term NAVTEX refers to the overall system of broadcasting and receiving these text-only messages in English, but is often used also to refer to the receiver hardware. The tiny receiver/printer unit is part of the IMO mandate for equipment aboard commercial ships, but it has considerable value also for leisure craft plying foreign and domestic waters. While the system was first designed to provide printouts, some newer NAVTEX receivers have LCD screens or can relay the messages to a smartphone or computer.

As with many sources of information, it takes a little culling to sort the useful NAVTEX information from the extraneous. If allowed to run constantly, NAVTEX will scroll a litany of trivia such as future light changes and missing daymarks even well away from your area. But by considering broadcast segments and times, you can turn on the unit just to receive weather forecast information. That the information is provided in English is a big plus when cruising in areas where the local VHF forecast is in another language.

▨ *NAVTEX is an easy-to-use text message about weather and notices to mariners specific to the region you are sailing. The cryptic weather summary on the NAVTEX printout gives enough detail to reassure mariners of fair weather or alert them to take a closer look at synoptic charts. Broadcasts can be printed on paper scrolls (as shown here) or displayed on a laptop or a multifunction display.*

works well at one time and in one place and not in another.

The simplest approach to wi-fi afloat unfortunately affords the least range. Most laptops and desktop computers sold today, as well as smartphones and tablets, have a built-in wi-fi transceiver to connect the computer wirelessly with a nearby access point or router. The computer's built-in antenna has little gain, however, and unless the hotspot is close by or very powerful, the computer will be unable to connect. Sometimes you can carry your laptop up on deck for improved performance, though this seldom makes a difference.

A stronger add-on antenna and more powerful signal booster can increase the range of wi-fi reception on a boat, however. Some wi-fi users can even use remote boosters inside the cabin. These devices are small enough to sit on a shelf while increasing the effective size of the antenna and the power of the signal. Boosters can be purchased for under $100 and often answer the needs of marina liveaboards who are not too far from the marina's router. Note that alternator RF noise, inverter ripple, radar, and other sources of onboard interference can cause problems, but it's easy to eliminate the interference by shutting off whatever equipment is found to cause the interference.

Another option that's especially appealing to those with a PCMCIA or USB slot in their computer but no built-in wi-fi is the purchase of a wi-fi card or USB device, which may include an antenna or a plug-in point for an external antenna. Online retailers such as RadioLabs offer a wide range of such solutions for wi-fi signal boosting. One effective solution is to mount an external antenna hard-wired with an appropriate cable to the computer. Hardwiring usually affords a more reliable, higher-quality signal than adding a wireless LAN (local-area-network) to the boat because of RF interference trouble. If you're willing to spend upwards of $500 for a top-of-the-line setup and antenna, you may be able to connect to a hotspot 2–5 miles away. Be sure the exterior elements of the system you choose are fully waterproof and corrosion resistant. Dedicated marine units provided by Syrens Onboard Wifi, Port Networks, and RadioLabs are well-designed systems that can, under optimum conditions, reach hotspots 5 or more miles away.

The good news is that wi-fi is a worldwide protocol, and the hardware has been designed with international use in mind. In the U.S., wi-fi users have access to channels 1–11, but five adjacent channels are used in operation, which leaves just three actual channel alternatives (1, 6, and 11). European wi-fi works on channels 1–13, and operation requires four adjacent channels, so European wi-fi equipment picks up an extra operational cluster (channels 1, 5, 9, and

13). Italy requires wi-fi users to register with a government agency, but most nations allow unlicensed access free of operational restrictions. Travelers can find free and fee-based hotspots in most developed coastal areas around the world. Most marinas have moved from hardwired Internet access to wi-fi. Cruisers in the Mediterranean, Mexico, and even Tahiti will find anchorages where a node is accessible and the Internet is at your fingertips.

Questions have been raised about how much microwave energy you want flying around your cabin. Health disclaimers and articles about the effects of RF propagation on health are becoming more common, and researchers in Germany have become outspoken about the need to lessen RF contact. This also argues for a hard-wired computer configuration rather than an onboard LAN, the former providing both better wi-fi signal quality and lower exposure to RF energy.

Smartphones and tablets with cellular connectivity offer sailors an option to remain connected when sailing beyond the range of wi-fi hotspots, as long as there is a cell signal. (Stand-alone devices with cellular connectivity, such as FreedomPop, are also available to create your own local wi-fi hotspot for use with laptops or other devices.) Such devices may increase the power of apps requiring connectivity, such as weather graphics, GRIB files, and route planning options. Electronic equipment manufacturers are also developing equipment to network smartphones and tablets and turn a smart device into a wireless display or a remote control for a networked navigation system. While such inshore access to cellular connectivity can provide valuable data, one needs to make sure that their navigation and communications regime is prepared to remain operational after the small window of cell tower connectivity closes down.

AUTOMATIC IDENTIFICATION SYSTEM (AIS)

The Automatic Identification System (AIS) is an interactive electronic vessel-tracking technology implemented internationally. The system merges a vessel's GPS position with VHF broadcast capability to give other AIS-equipped vessels and shore stations key information about the vessel and its position, speed, and heading.

AIS hardware and usage by sailors is discussed in detail in Chapter 8, and we'll not repeat that information again here in the communications chapter. Nonetheless, it is important to realize that AIS is a form of communication as much as it is a navigational tool. The system automatically communicates information about other vessels in range, and can

similarly broadcast information to others about your own vessel—it's your choice whether and how to use it. Consider some of the implications of AIS for sailors:

- It provides additional data to a crew that can help with collision-avoidance efforts.
- You cannot assume it shows the position of all boats, as many small vessels lack the gear, so it does not replace visual watchkeeping or using radar in reduced visibility.
- In a crowded waterway, the AIS screen can be easily overwhelmed when too many targets occupy too small a space.
- Since commercial vessels may filter out Class B signals, even if you're transmitting your AIS signal, it may not be seen by all ships in the area.
- In dangerous areas such as those experiencing piracy, AIS should be turned off to avoid broadcasting your presence to everyone in range.

As mentioned in Chapter 13, a new type of small, portable AIS beacon has recently been approved by the FCC for a different use: crew-overboard recovery. These units can be attached to a PFD, and a wearer who falls overboard can turn it on to transmit his or her COB location on the vessel's AIS display. On the horizon is yet another new AIS add-on feature that will be able to plot a 406 MHz EPIRB signal if one is transmitting in the vicinity; similarly, the capability to track a COB victim carrying a PLB would be a big plus. This, like the AIS beacon, and radar SART will be a line-of-sight feature that would help SAR crews make their final approach to a vessel, life raft, or person in the water. Sailors would gain the ability to see a PLB-wearing victim on their vessel's multifunction display.

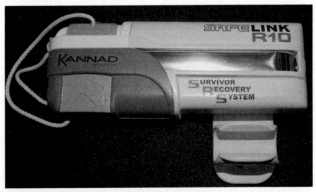

Waterproof, manually operated, personal AIS beacons can aid in crew-overboard recovery. The victim shows up on the vessel's AIS and other AIS units in range. The signal provides a "steer-to-dot" means of navigating back to the person in the water.

SUMMARY OF COMMUNICATION CHOICES

The most important thing to keep in mind when considering communication gear is your own priorities, but don't lose sight of the emergency side of the equation. Cell phones and satellite phones let you access the Coast Guard if you have the right number, but you won't be able to talk with nearby ships or a helicopter crew coming to save your life. VHF radio therefore is still the cornerstone of marine communications, and a handheld unit as well as a fixed installation make absolute sense.

To reiterate, communication is critical in any emergency. In a situation like rising bilge water you might think the top priorities are damage control and dewatering efforts, but communicating the in-extremis plight of the crew and the location of the vessel is just as important. In Mayday situations an automated DSC distress message should be implemented if you are within VHF range (approximately 30 miles or less from shore). If there's no response to the digital distress call implement a voice Mayday call on Channel 16. In many parts of the world DSC-equipped shore stations are rare, and a voice distress message on Channel 16 remains the best means to obtain assistance.

Satellite phone technology has become very valuable in search and rescue. In the past, a radio distress message was sent out as a vessel foundered, and the crew then shuttled into their life raft, leaving the communications system to sink with the vessel. The 406 EPIRB added a one-way communications capability that could be brought along in the life raft, and now portable satellite phones are a two-way backup carried as well. Sat phones are a complement to an EPIRB, however—not a replacement. A 406 EPIRB still needs to be at the top of the emergency communications list, but it is always nice to have a backup option, especially when your life may depend on it.

Another form of backup involves the newer tracking systems using low-earth-orbit satellites to regularly forward position-report from a vessel, such as the SPOT handheld unit described in Chapter 13. Other units have fixed mounts and connect to the vessel's electrical system. These units work well to keep friends and relatives apprised of progress and provide a remote record of your track but are not linked to the Cospas-Sarsat 406 EPIRB program.

SELF-RELIANCE IN THE WIRED WORLD

Like it or not, two of the most favored tools of modern Western society are the cell phone and the credit card. Some of us see a threat to self-reliance in these, but dependence on others is not always a bad thing. In many ways there's nothing wrong with a "call for help" culture—at least as long as the call goes through. Therein lies the conundrum for sailors: just how much off-the-boat reliance should we count on?

Communications technology—and sufficient funds—give us new ways to solve problems. For example, with engine sensors and a sat phone, our mechanic can know the engine's vital signs. Our voyage consultant can study our digital breadcrumb trail. Our concierge meteorologist is on call, our remote health care provider is at the ready, and even our indispensable banker is de facto along for the ride. All this is fine as long as we view these gadgets the way we view the beloved freezer on the boat. Both are great assets we would hate to lose, but we still know how to live without them when Murphy's Law steps in and pulls the plug. As John Martino, the owner of the Annapolis School of Seamanship, is fond of saying, "All electronics fail—it's just a matter of when."

Don't get me wrong—I am a big advocate of technology and embrace new equipment. However, I also see the elegance of simplicity and marvel at the usefulness of a Windex, magnetic compass, and self-steering windvane. Every sailor can choose whatever level of complexity they favor, but those going to sea will face an enemy of automation and need a good backup plan to cope with contingencies.

A SAILOR'S LIBRARY

Note, not all of the books listed here are still in print, but they are worth seeking at your favorite used-book purveyor.

HOW-TO/TECHNICAL

Bascom, Willard. *Waves and Beaches: The Dynamics of the Ocean Surface.* Anchor

Bowditch, Nathaniel. *The American Practical Navigator.* Defense Mapping Agency

Bruce, Peter, and K. Adlard Coles. *Adlard Coles' Heavy Weather Sailing, Sixth Edition.* International Marine/McGraw-Hill Education

Calder, Nigel. *How to Read a Nautical Chart, Second Edition.* International Marine/McGraw-Hill Education

Chapelle, Howard I., *Boatbuilding: A Complete Handbook of Wooden Boat Construction.* W.W. Norton & Co.

Chesneau, Lee S. and Mike Ma-Li Chen. *Heavy Weather Avoidance.* Paradise Cay Pub.

Cutler, Thomas, with Dunlap, G. P. and H. H. Shufeldt, *Dutton's Nautical Navigation, 15th Edition.* Naval Institute Press

ISAF. *Guide to Offshore Personal Safety for Racing and Cruising*

Karl, John. *Celestial Navigation in the GPS Age.* Paradise Cay/Celestaire

Lewis, David. *We, the Navigators: The Ancient Art of Landfinding in the Pacific.* The University Press of Hawaii

Naranjo, Ralph. *Boatyards & Marinas.* International Marine

Nicolson, Ian. *Surveying Small Craft.* International Marine

Roth, Hal and Margaret Roth. *How to Sail Around the World.* International Marine/McGraw-Hill Education

Skene, Norman L. *Skene's Elements of Yacht Design.* Dodd, Mead & Co.

Street, Don. *The Ocean Sailing Yacht.* W.W. Norton & Co.

Williams, Jack. *The AMS Weather Book: Ultimate Guide to America's Weather.* University of Chicago Press

Wing, Charlie. *One-Minute Guide to the Rules of the Road.* International Marine/McGraw-Hill Education

US Sailing. *Passagemaking*

NARRATIVES/ NON-FICTION

Chichester, Sir Francis. *Gipsy Moth Circles the World.* International Marine/McGraw-Hill Education

Hiscock, Eric C. *Beyond the West Horizon.* Adlard Coles Nautical

Hiscock, Eric. *Cruising Under Sail.* International Marine

Huntford, Roland. *Shackleton.* Fawcett Columbine

Moitessier, Bernard. *The First Voyage of the Joshua.* (Also sometimes titled *Cape Horn: The Logical Route.*) William Morrow & Co

Moitessier, Bernard. *The Long Way.* Sheridan House

Naranjo, Ralph. *Wind Shadow West.* Hearst Marine Books

Robertson, Dougal. *Survive the Savage Sea.* Sheridan House

Rousmaniere, John. *Fastnet, Force 10.* W.W. Norton & Co.

Smeeton, Miles. *Once is Enough.* International Marine/McGraw-Hill Education

NAVIGATION PUBLICATIONS

World Pilot Charts
Coast Pilot
Sailing Directions
Eldridge Tide and Pilot Book
Reed's Nautical Almanac
ChartKits
Local Cruising Guides

GLOSSARY OF SELECT TERMS AND ACRONYMS

(Note, we have chosen to define only less-common terms and acronyms used in *The Art of Seamanship*.)

ABS The American Bureau of Shipping is a classification society that develops engineering and construction guidelines for shipbuilding. Their 1994 guidelines for racing yacht construction remains one of the most useful references defining scantling minimums for essential structures such as keel-to-hull attachment.

CCA Rule The Cruising Club of America rule (a.k.a. The Bermuda Race Rule) was a type-defining rating rule passed in 1937. It reigned supreme in the United States until the 1960s when another type favoring rule, the International Offshore Rule (IOR), moved into the limelight. The CCA Rule's stereotypical sailboat was a beamy centerboard yawl (the mizzen sail area was un-penalized) with a good-sized two-blade fixed propeller that could be hidden in an aperture behind the deadwood.

Carlin a fore-and-aft running timber that stiffens and adds strength to the cabinhouse and the deck.

Finite Element Analysis (FEA)—a computer software program that provides graphic representations of how forces travel through a structure causing hotspots known as stress risers. The graphic display uses warm tone colors to indicate higher stress concentrations, regions where more structure should be incorporated in the hull in order to handle the increased loads.

FRP the catchall term for fiber-reinforced polymer (plastic), a composite material that is comprised of a resin matrix and a multi- or unidirectional fiber grid. The higher the fiber-to-resin ratio, the higher the strength-to-weight ratio becomes. Glass, aramid, and carbon fiber are the most often-used reinforcing fibers. Most sailboats built today have FRP hulls and decks.

Garboard originally the name of the plank closest to the keel, the word has become synonymous with the surface area on of a sailboat where the hull joins the keel. It is an area of immense stress and strain and whether it's a wooden, FRP, or metal hull, the structural reinforcement in this region is the strongest found anywhere on the sailboat.

GFS the Global Forecast System is a National Weather Service atmospheric model that plays a major role in weather forecast development. Its numerical outputs are transformed into gridded binary files known as GRIBS, and these graphics can be broadcast or Internet-shared allowing sailors to access in-depth information depicting near term and longer range weather conditions.

Header a shift in the true wind direction that causes the apparent wind to move forward, the opposite effect of a "lift" were the apparent wind moves aft. By tacking, a crew can turn a header into a lift.

ORR Rule the Ocean Racing Rule is a handicapping system administered by US Sailing that's an outgrowth of the AMERICAP II rule. Meant to be a non-type-defining handicapping system, it allocates time allowances based upon size, design type, and age of a boat. The goal was to develop a rule that allowed a wide range of suitable vessels to be competitive in offshore racing regardless of their inherent speed potential.

Rudderstock often incorrectly referred to as a rudderpost, it is the tube or shaft-like appendage that is bonded to the core, or otherwise fastened to the rudder blade. Spade rudderstocks transfer all of the loads imposed on the blade to the support bearings affixed to the hull, while skeg-hung and attached rudderstocks are supported at both ends of the blade.

Scantling originally used as cross-section references defining rib dimensions or plank thickness, the term has taken on a more generic reference today, and is often used as a reference to the overall strength of a sailboat's hull and deck. Normally, offshore cruisers are built to higher scantlings than sailboats designed for coastal or inshore sailing.

Scarf a timber joint that's made by cutting plank ends on a diagonal so that the interfacing surfaces are elongated and afford a larger gluing surface. The angled cut may be a straight line or incorporate an interlocking zig-zag that adds an additional locking effect. The key to a top quality scarf joint involves evenly mated surfaces, carefully mixed epoxy, and a uniformly clamped, but not overly tightened joint.

SCRIMP the acronym for Seemann Composites Resin Infusion Molding Process, a closed-mold approach to FRP laminating that utilizes a vacuum to draw resin into dry laminate carefully draped inside a sealed female mold. Low void content, high fiber resin ratios, and low VOC emissions are valuable attributes of this process.

Split Rig a sailboat with sails set on more than one mast. Ketches, yawls, and schooners are the modern iterations of multi-mast sailboats. The advantages include smaller sails that are easier to handle, a more versatile sail plan, and lower masthead height for those desiring to navigate the ICW (65-foot fixed bridge clearances). The downside includes less efficiency per given amount of sail area, extra weight aloft, and more complex rigging.

ACKNOWLEDGMENTS

Every author, whether they've written a thin pamphlet or a thick book, has two key milestones in common. There's the day the writing begins and the day the work is published—but it's in between these benchmarks that the process becomes a team effort.

It was eight years ago that Jon Eaton and I began a preliminary "what if" discussion about a book that would tackle the theory as well as application of good seamanship. Neither of us imagined the course that lay ahead. Jon's portion of the passage was instrumental and even his retirement didn't completely sideline him from involvement in the project. But with the watch turnover at International Marine, and Molly Mulhern's taking the helm, a loosely linked fleet of chapters was finally shaped into *The Art of Seamanship*. Her firm grasp on the literary tiller resulted in a steady course.

Our collaboration has been a productive two-way street, and with good editing instincts and a fair dose of down east industriousness, she tamed a meandering manuscript—trimmed the arcane technical talk and deep-sixed a few underwhelming sea stories—making this a much better book. Molly likes sailboats, owns one herself, and favors spending time on board. She recruited writer/sailor Tom Lochhaas to fact-check and help refine the content, and Joe Comeau who took my very rough sketches and turned them into informative line art. The clean layout and smooth flow of the text was steered along by Shannon Swanson of Olive Juice Design, without whose patience and professionalism we would surely have run aground.

I also appreciate the inputs from five good friends, my seafaring wife, and my son-in-law/windsurfing buddy. Their collective effort has worked to liven up things by injecting personal accounts of important seamanship and lessons learned. Sheila McCurdy, Chuck Hawley, Paul Miller, Lee Chesneau, Kip Louttit, Lenore Naranjo, and Scott Mitchell have brought both expertise and impartiality to the work, giving readers another valuable perspective.

The research behind the material in these chapters spans over four decades and includes some mimicry of the old salts, plus more than a few lessons learned the hard way. In New Zealand I paid heed to where Eric and Susan Hiscock chose to anchor. During night watches, Rod Stephens taught me how to inspect a rig, and during boat-show–sea trials Chuck Paine made a good case for why spade rudders made sense aboard performance cruisers. In short, inputs from mariners, yacht designers, and gear experts have helped to shape my slant on seamanship, and throughout this book I make an effort to pass along that collective knowledge.

INDEX

C

Q

R